41: *Afro-American Poets Since 1955,* edited by Trudier Harris and Thadious M. Davis (1985)

42: *American Writers for Children Before 1900,* edited by Glenn E. Estes (1985

43: *American Newspaper Journalists, 1690-1872,* edited by Perry J. Ashley (198

44: *American Screenwriters,* Second Series, edited by Randall Clark, Robert E
phen O. Lesser (1986)

45: *American Poets, 1880-1945,* First Series, edited by Peter Quartermain (19

46: *American Literary Publishing Houses, 1900-1980: Trade and Paperback,* edited by Peter Dzwonkoski (1986)

47: *American Historians, 1866-1912,* edited by Clyde N. Wilson (1986)

48: *American Poets, 1880-1945,* Second Series, edited by Peter Quartermain (1986)

49: *American Literary Publishing Houses, 1638-1899,* 2 parts, edited by Peter Dzwonkoski (1986)

50: *Afro-American Writers Before the Harlem Renaissance,* edited by Trudier Harris (1986)

51: *Afro-American Writers from the Harlem Renaissance to 1940,* edited by Trudier Harris (1987)

52: *American Writers for Children Since 1960: Fiction,* edited by Glenn E. Estes (1986)

53: *Canadian Writers Since 1960,* First Series, edited by W. H. New (1986)

54: *American Poets, 1880-1945,* Third Series, 2 parts, edited by Peter Quartermain (1987)

55: *Victorian Prose Writers Before 1867,* edited by William B. Thesing (1987)

56: *German Fiction Writers, 1914-1945,* edited by James Hardin (1987)

57: *Victorian Prose Writers After 1867,* edited by William B. Thesing (1987)

58: *Jacobean and Caroline Dramatists,* edited by Fredson Bowers (1987)

59: *American Literary Critics and Scholars, 1800-1850,* edited by John W. Rathbun and Monica M. Grecu (1987)

60: *Canadian Writers Since 1960,* Second Series, edited by W. H. New (1987)

61: *American Writers for Children Since 1960: Poets, Illustrators, and Nonfiction Authors,* edited by Glenn E. Estes (1987)

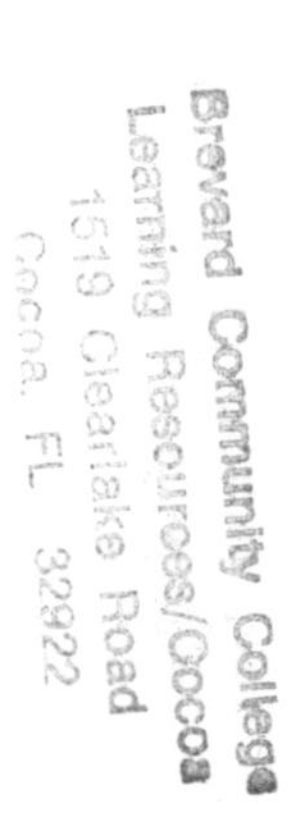


62: *Elizabethan Dramatists,* edited by Fredson Bowers (1987)

63: *Modern American Critics, 1920-1955,* edited by Gregory S. Jay (1988)

64: *American Literary Critics and Scholars, 1850-1880,* edited by John W. Rathbun and Monica M. Grecu (1988)

65: *French Novelists, 1900-1930,* edited by Catharine Savage Brosman (1988)

66: *German Fiction Writers, 1885-1913,* 2 parts, edited by James Hardin (1988)

67: *Modern American Critics Since 1955,* edited by Gregory S. Jay (1988)

68: *Canadian Writers, 1920-1959,* First Series, edited by W. H. New (1988)

69: *Contemporary German Fiction Writers,* First Series, edited by Wolfgang D. Elfe and James Hardin (1988)

70: *British Mystery Writers, 1860-1919,* edited by Bernard Benstock and Thomas F. Staley (1988)

71: *American Literary Critics and Scholars, 1880-1900,* edited by John W. Rathbun and Monica M. Grecu (1988)

72: *French Novelists, 1930-1960,* edited by Catharine Savage Brosman (1988)

73: *American Magazine Journalists, 1741-1850,* edited by Sam G. Riley (1988)

74: *American Short-Story Writers Before 1880,* edited by Bobby Ellen Kimbel, with the assistance of William E. Grant (1988)

75: *Contemporary German Fiction Writers,* Second Series, edited by Wolfgang D. Elfe and James Hardin (1988)

76: *Afro-American Writers, 1940-1955,* edited by Trudier Harris (1988)

77: *British Mystery Writers, 1920-1939,* edited by Bernard Benstock and Thomas F. Staley (1988)

78: *American Short-Story Writers, 1880-1910,* edited by Bobby Ellen Kimbel, with the assistance of William E. Grant (1988)

79: *American Magazine Journalists, 1850-1900,* edited by Sam G. Riley (1988)

**(Continued on back endsheets)**

Dictionary of Literary Biography • Volume One Hundred Ten

# British Romantic Prose Writers, 1789-1832

## Second Series

Dictionary of Literary Biography • Volume One Hundred Ten

# British Romantic Prose Writers, 1789-1832

## Second Series

Edited by
John R. Greenfield
*McKendree College*



A Bruccoli Clark Layman Book
Gale Research Inc.
Detroit, London

Matthew J. Bruccoli and Richard Layman, *Editorial Directors*
C. E. Frazer Clark, Jr., *Managing Editor*

Printed in the United States of America

Published simultaneously in the United Kingdom
by Gale Research International Limited
(An affiliated company of Gale Research Inc.)


Gale Research Inc.
835 Penobscot Bldg.
Detroit, MI 48226-4094

ISBN 0-8103-4590-0
91-27535 CIP

*For Judy*

# Contents

# Plan of the Series

*... Almost the most prodigious asset of a country, and perhaps its most precious possession, is its native literary product–when that product is fine and noble and enduring.*

Mark Twain*

The advisory board, the editors, and the publisher of the *Dictionary of Literary Biography* are joined in endorsing Mark Twain's declaration. The literature of a nation provides an inexhaustible resource of permanent worth. We intend to make literature and its creators better understood and more accessible to students and the reading public, while satisfying the standards of teachers and scholars.

To meet these requirements, *literary biography* has been construed in terms of the author's achievement. The most important thing about a writer is his writing. Accordingly, the entries in *DLB* are career biographies, tracing the development of the author's canon and the evolution of his reputation.

The purpose of *DLB* is not only to provide reliable information in a convenient format but also to place the figures in the larger perspective of literary history and to offer appraisals of their accomplishments by qualified scholars.

The publication plan for *DLB* resulted from two years of preparation. The project was proposed to Bruccoli Clark by Frederick G. Ruffner, president of the Gale Research Company, in November 1975. After specimen entries were prepared and typeset, an advisory board was formed to refine the entry format and develop the series rationale. In meetings held during 1976, the publisher, series editors, and advisory board approved the scheme for a comprehensive biographical dictionary of persons who contributed to North American literature. Editorial work on the first volume began in January 1977, and it was published in 1978. In order to make *DLB* more than a reference tool and to compile volumes that individually have claim to status as literary history, it was decided to organize volumes by topic, period, or genre. Each of these freestanding volumes provides a biographical-bibliographical guide and overview for a particular area of literature. We are convinced that this organization–as opposed to a single alphabet method–constitutes a valuable innovation in the presentation of reference material. The volume plan necessarily requires many decisions for the placement and treatment of authors who might properly be included in two or three volumes. In some instances a major figure will be included in separate volumes, but with different entries emphasizing the aspect of his career appropriate to each volume. Ernest Hemingway, for example, is represented in *American Writers in Paris, 1920-1939* by an entry focusing on his expatriate apprenticeship; he is also in *American Novelists, 1910-1945* with an entry surveying his entire career. Each volume includes a cumulative index of subject authors and articles. Comprehensive indexes to the entire series are planned.

With volume ten in 1982 it was decided to enlarge the scope of *DLB*. By the end of 1986 twenty-one volumes treating British literature had been published, and volumes for Commonwealth and Modern European literature were in progress. The series has been further augmented by the *DLB Yearbooks* (since 1981) which update published entries and add new entries to keep the *DLB* current with contemporary activity. There have also been *DLB Documentary Series* volumes which provide biographical and critical source materials for figures whose work is judged to have particular interest for students. One of these companion volumes is entirely devoted to Tennessee Williams.

We define literature as the *intellectual commerce of a nation:* not merely as belles lettres but as that ample and complex process by which ideas are generated, shaped, and transmitted. *DLB* entries are not limited to "creative writers" but extend to other figures who in their time and in their way influenced the mind of a people. Thus the series encompasses historians, journalists, publishers, and screenwriters. By this means readers of *DLB* may be aided to perceive litera-

*From an unpublished section of Mark Twain's autobiography, copyright © by the Mark Twain Company.

ture not as cult scripture in the keeping of intellectual high priests but firmly positioned at the center of a nation's life.

*DLB* includes the major writers appropriate to each volume and those standing in the ranks immediately behind them. Scholarly and critical counsel has been sought in deciding which minor figures to include and how full their entries should be. Wherever possible, useful references are made to figures who do not warrant separate entries.

Each *DLB* volume has a volume editor responsible for planning the volume, selecting the figures for inclusion, and assigning the entries. Volume editors are also responsible for preparing, where appropriate, appendices surveying the major periodicals and literary and intellectual movements for their volumes, as well as lists of further readings. Work on the series as a whole is coordinated at the Bruccoli Clark Layman editorial center in Columbia, South Carolina, where the editorial staff is responsible for accuracy of the published volumes.

One feature that distinguishes *DLB* is the illustration policy–its concern with the iconography of literature. Just as an author is influenced by his surroundings, so is the reader's understanding of the author enhanced by a knowledge of his environment. Therefore *DLB* volumes include not only drawings, paintings, and photographs of authors, often depicting them at various stages in their careers, but also illustrations of their families and places where they lived. Title pages are regularly reproduced in facsimile along with dust jackets for modern authors. The dust jackets are a special feature of *DLB* because they often document better than anything else the way in which an author's work was perceived in its own time. Specimens of the writers' manuscripts are included when feasible.

Samuel Johnson rightly decreed that "The chief glory of every people arises from its authors." The purpose of the *Dictionary of Literary Biography* is to compile literary history in the surest way available to us–by accurate and comprehensive treatment of the lives and work of those who contributed to it.

The *DLB* Advisory Board

# Foreword

*Dictionary of Literary Biography*, volume 110: *British Romantic Prose Writers, 1789-1832: Second Series* is a companion volume to *DLB* 107: *British Romantic Prose Writers, 1789-1832: First Series*, which deals with British Romantic prose writers who were born in 1775 or earlier. The writers treated in the *Second Series* were all born after 1775 and wrote most of their important prose works between 1810 and 1845, years of war, reaction, reform, and general political and social change.

A movement as pervasive and complex as British Romanticism can be traced to many sources and influences, philosophical, historical, social, and literary. The ideas and ideals, the promises and disappointments associated with the French Revolution, the Napoleonic period, and its aftermath are so much a part of the Romantic movement in England that most of the writers recognized their importance either for themselves or for society. The writers included in this volume had a profound effect upon both society and literature, shaping literary tastes, moral questions, and political ideology.

The philosophical origins of British Romanticism may be found in the empiricism of John Locke, the skepticism of David Hume, the associational psychology of David Hartley, and the political radicalism of William Godwin and Mary Wollstonecraft, among others. These various writers helped to create an atmosphere in which received beliefs about human nature, (especially the model of the mind), the natural world, the structure of society, and the place of tradition could be called into question. The writers included in this volume may be grouped into six general categories with some obvious overlapping: (1) There are the great literary prose essayists, exemplified by Thomas De Quincey and William Hazlitt. (2) Many of the writers included in this volume were journalists who wrote articles on political and social issues as well as literary reviews of their contemporaries. For example, John Wilson Croker, Leigh Hunt, John Gibson Lockhart, William Maginn, and John Wilson were first and foremost journalists who helped shape the popular reception of contemporary writers. (3) Some writers, such as Henry Peter Brougham, Richard Carlile, and William Hone, as well as some of the journalists mentioned above, wrote highly polemical prose and became directly involved in political issues. (4) Some writers best known for their contributions in other genres, such as poetry or fiction, nevertheless produced significant works in prose which helped to shape the literary milieu of the time: George Gordon, Lord Byron; Percy Bysshe Shelley; Mary Wollstonecraft Shelley; and John Keats. (5) A small group of writers are known primarily for their associations with their well-known contemporaries: for example, Benjamin Robert Haydon (friend of William Wordsworth, Keats, and Charles Lamb) and Edward John Trelawny (friend of Byron and Shelley). (6) There are also writers who are now considered minor, even though they produced significant bodies of writings and were popular in their own day: Charles Bucke, William and Mary Howitt, and Mary Russell Mitford.

Many of these writers challenged established beliefs, customs, and traditions, helping to shape the questions that would be debated during the rest of the nineteenth century. In addition to addressing the uncertainties of political change, even upheaval, and the challenges of new philosophies, the second generation of British Romantic prose writers was conscious of building upon their immediate predecessors' efforts in the development of a new aesthetic of poetry; they produced seminal prose works to explain and defend their innovations in the practice of poetry. For example, William Hazlitt characterizes the cult of personality and the spirit of individualism in *The Spirit of the Age* (1825), his collection of essays on his contemporaries. Lord Byron's letters and journals, Shelley's letters, prefaces, and essays, especially *A Defence of Poetry* (written in 1821), and Keats's letters are essential not only for understanding each writer's poetry but also in understanding the ideals and aesthetic of the Romantic movement in England. The informal literary essay, the biographical and autobiographical essay, and the familiar essay—marked by imaginative vision, reverie, and playful ideas, flourished as a genre in the capable hands of writers such as Charles Lamb, Samuel Taylor Coleridge, Walter Savage Landor, Henry Crabb Robinson, and—in the second generation of writers—of course, Thomas De Quincey and William Hazlitt.

If the British Romantic movement may in one way be viewed as a reaction against the Augustan Age, with its neoclassical aesthetic premises of imitation, balance, and order, it must also be viewed as a continuation and outgrowth of literary developments that were already under way in the eighteenth century. The literary origins of the Romantic movement may be found in Jean-Jacques Rousseau, especially in *Julie; ou La Nouvelle Héloïse* (1761) and *The Confessions* (written 1765-1770); in the young Johann Wolfgang von Goethe, as the author of *The Sorrows of Young Werther* (1774); in so-called pre-Romantic English poets such as James Thomson and William Collins, who began to cultivate an interest in nature and in the feelings; in the cult of sensibility, of which Henry Mackenzie's *Man of Feeling* (1771) is the prime example; in the ballad revival, which was accompanied by an interest in things medieval and primitive in general; and in the popularity of Gothic literature, exemplified by Horace Walpole's *The Castle of Otranto* (1765) and M. G. Lewis's *The Monk* (1795), both of which fostered an interest in the supernatural.

Many of the writers included in this volume wrote reviews (often anonymously) for the various periodicals. Though literary magazines undertook to be arbiters of taste, they were also often politically biased and used the review as a means of attacking an author's political stance, or they simply gave writers with opposing political stances bad reviews. The Romantic writers' contemporary critics saw the various poets of both the first and second generations not as a monolithic movement all agreeing upon the basic premises of Romanticism, but as belonging to various schools with different orientations concerning taste, religion, and politics. The literary establishment of the time was generally conservative and highly conscious politically, often condemning writers ostensibly for matters of taste but really for matters of politics. The reviewers created various schools of poetry including the following: Joseph Johnson's radical circle in the 1790s, which included William Blake, William Godwin, and Mary Wollstonecraft; the Lake Poets, who included Wordsworth, Coleridge, and Robert Southey and derive their name from the beautiful Lake District in northwest England; the "Cockney School," which included Keats and Leigh Hunt and refers to certain colloquialisms of style that may be found in their poetry; and the "Satanic School" of Shelley and Byron, so-called for Byron's reputation for immorality and Shelley's reputation for atheism and radicalism. An appendix to this volume includes essays on literary reviewing in several of the most important periodicals of the time in order to give a sense of the rich and interrelated milieu in which these writers worked. In addition to providing an overview of the great diversity in literary taste and political ideology of the Romantic period, these fifteen articles on magazines focus on the reviewers' treatment of the major poets: Wordsworth, Coleridge, Byron, Shelley, and Keats.

Of the twenty writers covered in *British Romantic Prose Writers, 1789-1832: Second Series*, two writers—De Quincey and Hazlitt—receive extended treatment. Reading the essays on the rest of the writers in this volume will suggest a rich interplay of personalities, influences, and relationships, evoking an active literary life within a dynamic social context.

In addition to the appendix on literary magazines of the Romantic period, there is at the end of this volume a selected bibliography that focuses on the most important studies of the historical, social, cultural, aesthetic, psychological, linguistic, and literary dimensions of the British Romantic movement.

The contributors to this volume, some of whom are friends or acquaintances of mine and many others whom I have never met, deserve special gratitude for their promptness in meeting deadlines, their conscientiousness in compiling bibliographies and in checking facts, their efficiency in making revisions, their helpfulness in making suggestions for illustrations, and perhaps most of all, for their cooperation and patience. Three secretaries at McKendree, Nancy Ferguson, Ella Doty, and Naomia Severs, deserve thanks for the help they gave me in handling the correspondence associated with this volume. I would especially like to thank Karen Rood and the staff at Bruccoli Clark Layman for their tireless attention to accuracy and detail and their insistence upon high standards. Finally, I would like to thank Judy Durick Greenfield for her patience and understanding during all the time that I spent in editing this project.

*—John R. Greenfield*

# Acknowledgments

This book was produced by Bruccoli Clark Layman, Inc. Karen L. Rood, senior editor for the *Dictionary of Literary Biography* series, was the in-house editor.

Production coordinator is James W. Hipp. Projects manager is Charles D. Brower. Photography editors are Edward Scott and Timothy C. Lundy. Permissions editor is Jean W. Ross. Layout and graphics supervisor is Penney L. Haughton. Copyediting supervisor is Bill Adams. Typesetting supervisor is Kathleen M. Flanagan. Systems manager is George F. Dodge. Charles Lee Egleston is editorial associate. The production staff includes Rowena Betts, Teresa Chaney, Patricia Coate, Gail Crouch, Margaret McGinty Cureton, Sarah A. Estes, Robert Fowler, Mary L. Goodwin, Cynthia Hallman, Ellen McCracken, Kathy Lawler Merlette, Catherine A. Murray, John Myrick, Pamela D. Norton, Cathy J. Reese, Laurrè Sinckler-Reeder, Maxine K. Smalls, Teri C. Sperry, and Betsy L. Weinberg.

Walter W. Ross, Timothy D. Tebalt, and Henry Cunningham did library research. They were assisted by the following librarians at the Thomas Cooper Library of the University of South Carolina: Jens Holley and the interlibrary-loan staff; reference librarians Gwen Baxter, Daniel Boice, Faye Chadwell, Jo Cottingham, Cathy Eckman, Rhonda Felder, Gary Geer, Jackie Kinder, Laurie Preston, Jean Rhyne, Carol Tobin, Virginia Weathers, and Connie Widney; circulation-department head Thomas Marcil; and acquisitions-searching supervisor David Haggard.

Sara Hodson and Kathy Schneberger at the Henry E. Huntington Library provided valuable assistance in illustrating this volume.

Some of the research for Linda Mills Woolsey's entry on Thomas De Quincey was funded by the Mellon Foundation through a James Still Fellowship at the University of Kentucky.

Dictionary of Literary Biography • Volume One Hundred Ten

# British Romantic Prose Writers, 1789-1832

## Second Series

# Dictionary of Literary Biography

## Henry Peter Brougham, Baron Brougham and Vaux

*(19 September 1778 - 7 May 1868)*

Robert Stewart

SELECTED BOOKS: *An Inquiry into the Colonial Policy of the European Powers*, 2 volumes (Edinburgh: Printed by D. Willison for E. Balfour, Manners & Miller, 1803);

*A Concise Statement of the Question Regarding the Abolition of the Slave Trade* (London: Printed for J. Hatchard and T. N. Longman & O. Rees by M. & S. Brooke, 1804);

*An Inquiry into the State of the Nation, at the Commencement of the Present Administration* (London: Printed for Longman, Hurst, Rees & Orme and J. Ridgeway, 1806);

*Inaugural Discourse on Being Installed Lord Rector of the University of Glasgow, Wednesday, April 6, 1825* (Glasgow: J. Smith, 1825);

*Practical Observations on the Education of the People* (London: Printed by Richard Taylor & sold by Longman, Hurst, Rees, Orme, Brown & Green, 1825); republished as *Practical Observations on Popular Education* (Boston: Office of the *Massachusetts Journal*, 1826);

*A Discourse of Natural Theology* (London: Charles Knight, 1835; Philadelphia: Carey, Lea & Blanchard, 1835);

*Thoughts upon the Aristocracy of England. By Isaac Tomkins, Gent.* (London: H. Hooper, 1835);

*"We can't afford it!" Being Thoughts upon the Aristocracy of England, Part the Second. By Isaac Tomkins, Gent.* (London: H. Hooper, 1835);

*Speeches of Henry Lord Brougham upon Questions Relating to Public Rights, Duties, and Interests* (4 volumes, Edinburgh: A. & C. Black, 1838; 2 volumes, Philadelphia: Lea & Blanchard, 1841);

*Dissertations on Subjects of Science Connected with Natural Theology*, 2 volumes (London: Charles Knight, 1839);

*Historical Sketches of Statesmen who Flourished in the Time of George III*, first series, 2 volumes (London: Charles Knight, 1839; Philadelphia: Lea & Blanchard, 1839); second series, 2 volumes (London: Charles Knight, 1839; Philadelphia: Lea & Blanchard, 1839); third series, 1 volume (London: Charles Knight, 1843; Philadelphia: Lea & Blanchard, 1844);

*The Oration of Demosthenes upon the Crown*, translated, with notes, by Brougham (London: Charles Knight, 1840);

*The Critical and Miscellaneous Writings of Henry Lord Brougham*, 2 volumes (Philadelphia: Lea & Blanchard, 1841);

*Political Philosophy*, 3 volumes (London: Society for the Diffusion of Useful Knowledge, 1842-1843);

*British Constitution* (London: Charles Knight, 1844);

*Lives of Men of Letters and Science who Flourished in the Time of George III*, first and second series (London: Charles Knight, 1845, 1846; Philadelphia: Carey & Hart, 1845, 1846);

*Portrait by James Lonsdale (National Portrait Gallery, London)*

*History of England and France under the House of Lancaster* (London: J. Murray, 1852);

*Analytical View of Sir Isaac Newton's Principia*, by Brougham and E. J. Routh (London: Longman, Brown, Green & Longmans, 1855);

*Works of Henry, Lord Brougham*, 11 volumes (London & Glasgow: R. Griffin, 1855-1861);

*Contributions to the Edinburgh Review*, 3 volumes (London & Glasgow: R. Griffin, 1856);

*Lord Brougham's Acts and Bills, from 1811 to the Present Time*, edited by Sir John E. Eardley-Wilmot, Bart. (London: Longman, Brown, Green, Longman & Roberts, 1857);

*Addresses on Popular Literature, and on the Monument to Sir Isaac Newton* (London: E. Law, 1858);

*Tracts, Mathematical and Physical* (London & Glasgow: R. Griffin, 1860);

*The Life and Times of Henry, Lord Brougham*, 3 volumes (Edinburgh & London: William Blackwood, 1871; New York: Harper, 1871-1872);

*Albert Lunel; or, The Château of Languedoc* (3 volumes, London: Charles Knight, 1872; 1 volume, New York: Harper, 1872).

Francis Horner, a friend of Brougham from early childhood and a colleague on the Whig benches at Westminster, predicted in 1804, when Brougham was setting out on his legal and political careers, that if he failed in those ventures he might bury himself in retirement for the remainder of his life and occupy himself in "some vast scheme of literary ambition." As it turned out, Brougham combined the forensic, the parliamentary, and the literary. Indeed the reviewer of his *Historical Sketches of Statesmen . . . in the Time of George III* for the *Gentleman's Magazine* (March 1840) described him as "one, who being one of the leading and most active statesmen of his day, has learned to soften the rugged path of politics with the elegance of literature." That judgment is, however, somewhat misleading. Brougham, indeed, published his first work, a paper on Sir Isaac Newton's optics, in *Philosophical Transactions of the Royal Society* (1796). His first separately published work, the massive *Inquiry into the Colonial Policy of the European Powers*, made its appearance in 1803; and for the rest of his life his pen was rarely idle. Yet down to 1834, when his political career as the Whigs' leading front-bencher (he first entered Parliament in 1810 and left the House of Commons in 1830) and his ministerial career as lord chancellor came to their end, all his writing was highly polemical, intended to prosper either political objects or his own pet educational projects, the Mechanics' Institutes and the Society for the Diffusion of Useful Knowledge. It was only after 1834, when he was no longer what Henry Crabb Robinson called him, "the busiest man living," that the astonishing series of publications ranging over nearly every branch of literature—history, science, political philosophy, theology, and fiction—flowed from his pen.

The son of Henry and Eleanor Syme Brougham, Henry Peter Brougham was born at no. 21 St. Andrew's Square, Edinburgh, on 19 September 1778, the eldest of three sons. The two major familial influences on young Henry were his mother's uncle, the well-known historian Dr. William Robertson, and his grandmother, Robertson's sister. They inspired Henry with boundless enthusiasm for knowledge, with bursting confidence and ambition, and with a humanitarian sense of liberty and justice. A precocious child, Henry was sent to the high school at Edinburgh when he was barely seven years old, and, when he left at thirteen in 1791, he was the top student. In October 1792 he entered the University of Edinburgh, where he excelled in mathematics and science. After completing the four-year course of philosophy and humanities, in 1795, he began to study law.

By June of 1800 he was practicing law in Scotland. He was called to the English bar in 1808 and rapidly made a name for himself by his eloquence and the driving power of his arguments. For the next twenty-two years his fame on the northern circuit was rivaled only by that of Sir Francis Scarlett. Yet he was to make his real mark as one of the leading liberal Whig politicians of the first third of the nineteenth century and as an inspired orator, advocating the liberal side of major political controversies, including the questions of slavery and slave trade, Catholic emancipation, universal education, a free press, and other social causes. His liberal temperament and advocacy of reform led him naturally to be one of the founding members, along with Sydney Smith, Francis Horner, and Francis Jeffrey, of the liberal *Edinburgh Review* in 1802. Through the years he wrote articles attacking Tory positions and was in turn a target of attacks by the *Edinburgh Review*'s adversary, the Tory *Quarterly Review*.

G. T. Garratt, in a life of Brougham published in 1935, wrote that Brougham "just failed to earn his niche in the temple of literature," then added, somewhat contradictorily, that "most of his eleven volumes [in the collected edition] should never have left his study drawer." Brougham's contemporaries held the latter view. *An Inquiry into the Colonial Policy of the European Powers*, a rambling, verbose essay in neo-Smithian political economy whose chief purpose was to advance the antislavery cause, was impressive for one so young and brought Brougham's name to the attention of the political world. Sir James Mackintosh, the author of *Vindiciae Gallicae* (1791), the Whig answer to Edmund Burke's *Reflections on the Revolution in France* (1790), praised Brougham's work as the best book on political economy since Adam Smith's *Wealth of Nations* (1776). One or two small pamphlets, especially *Practical Observations on the Education of the People* (1825), had commercial success. The wit and point of his brief lives, notably *Historical Sketches of Statesmen who Flourished in the Time of George III* (1839-1843), were justly admired. The rest of Brougham's publications met with critical scorn and public indifference.

Brougham's lasting contribution to English letters lies in the unstinting service which he gave to the *Edinburgh Review*, the first of the great quarterly reviews which so enlivened and deepened the intellectual and political life of the nineteenth century. For thirty-five years he wrote for nearly every issue, sometimes three or four long articles, despite the heavy burdens which the northern circuit and a parliamentary career placed on his time. Jeffrey, the first editor of the *Edinburgh Review*, suffered from Brougham's native imperiousness, but nevertheless praised him as "the surest and most voluminous of men." Brougham wrote on every subject under the sun and took special responsibility for political, scientific, and mathematical subjects. His want of restraint landed the *Edinburgh Review* in some scrapes, none more embarrassing than that caused by his misguided and

*Brougham's attempts to educate the common man were ridiculed by George Cruikshank, who satirized Brougham's role in the 1825 founding of the Univeristy of London, and C. J. Grant, whose mock frontispiece (circa October 1832) to the* Penny Magazine, *a publication of the Society for the Diffusion of Useful Knowledge, depicts Brougham as "The Penny Trumpeter" and shows workmen so busy reading the magazine that they neglect their work.*

simply foolish dismissal of Thomas Young's theory of the undulation of light (January 1803). Two essays of 1808 had unexpected consequences. The intemperate review of George Gordon, Lord Byron's juvenilia (January) called forth *English Bards, and Scotch Reviewers* (1809), in which Byron announced his powers of satire; and the bold assertion of the claims of democracy in the review of Don Pedro Cevallos's book on the Spanish war provoked Walter Scott and other conservatives to establish the Tory *Quarterly Review* as a counterweight to the Whig *Edinburgh.* Although Brougham claimed the "Don Cevallos" article and included it in a collection of his *Edinburgh* essays (1856), much of it was written by Jeffrey. In his *Journal* entry for 6 April 1852 Henry Cockburn recorded that Jeffrey was put out at Brougham's theft of authorship, since most of the pages, except for a few paragraphs at the beginning, were not his. Cockburn, neither friend nor admirer of Brougham, did "not wonder that Brougham should claim them, for he never wrote or spoke anything approaching to them in energy or eloquence." Other evidence, however, suggests that the essay was more equally a joint affair.

In February 1811 Brougham strengthened his reputation as a champion for liberal causes with his successful defense of John and Leigh Hunt in their trial for seditious libel after they published an article critical of military flogging in their liberal *Examiner.* He was less successful in December 1812, when both Hunts were brought to trial again, this time for defaming the Prince of Wales, and were sentenced to two years in prison. More because of common political and social goals than similarities in temperament, Brougham was a member of the exclusive circle of Benthamites from 1812 on, and was in close contact with James Mill.

Brougham married Mary Ann Eden Spalding, a widow with two children, in the spring of 1819. He and his wife had two daughters, the first of whom died shortly after childbirth.

In 1820 Brougham found himself, partly by his own doing, embroiled in one of the biggest political scandals of the Regency period. George III died in January 1820 leaving the path to the throne open to his son George, the Prince of Wales, who had been Prince Regent since 1811. Beginning in that year Brougham had became an adviser to the Prince Regent's wife, Caroline of Brunswick. The feud between the royal couple, who had been separated since 1796—with gossip and accusations by the Prince Regent that his wife, who was abroad, was having adulturous affairs—was taken up by the opposing political parties, the Whigs supporting Caroline's cause and the Tories siding with the prince. In 1820, acting for George IV and the government, the prime minister, Robert Banks Jenkinson, Lord Liverpool, made an offer through Brougham to pay off Caroline if she would agree not to come to England and try to participate in the coronation. Brougham, however, from uncertain motives, withheld the information from Caroline until she had already returned to England amid tumultuous support from the crowds in London. In the queen's trial for adultery, Brougham gave a masterful defense, exposing the weakness of the opposition's evidence, which included bribed testimony gathered by the so-called Milan Commission and contained in an infamous "green bag." The government was made to look foolish, and the liberals were triumphant. Percy Bysshe Shelley satirized George IV and the government ministers in his burlesque *Oedipus Tyrannus; or, Swellfoot the Tyrant* (1820). Brougham's triumph was met with enthusiastic support from the populace for himself and Queen Caroline. Many pubs were named "Brougham's Head," and Brougham's continued popularity helped the liberal Whigs gain the long-term support that would eventually lead to the Reform Bill of 1832. In November 1830 Brougham was made lord chancellor and elevated to the peerage with the title of baron Brougham and Vaux.

The 1820s were also years in which Brougham devoted much time to the education of the people. In 1825, the year that he became rector of Glasgow University, Brougham and the poet Thomas Campbell founded the University of London, and the following year Brougham started the Society for the Diffusion of Useful Knowledge (SDUK).

In 1838 Brougham told Jeffrey that his "chief ambition as to literary character" had always been "the rank and station of an historian." He brought to historical writing, he said, "some little knack of narrative, the most difficult by far of all styles" and "as much oratory and science ... as most of my predecessors." His only full-scale historical work, *History of England and France under the House of Lancaster* (published anonymously in 1852; republished under his name in 1861), was undistinguished and went largely unnoticed; its manner exemplifies Brougham's quarrel with Thomas Babington Macaulay's "anecdotal school" of history writing. *Political Philosophy* of 1842-1843 is more historical than analytical or speculative in its discussion of the monarchies of Europe and the East. It failed to sell out its first printing and was "trunked" (that is, used to line the insides of travelers' trunks). "It is needless," Walter Bagehot wrote (*National Review*, July 1857), "to point out how completely an excitable, ungenial nature, such as we have so much spoken of, incapacitates Lord Brougham for abstract philosophy. His works on that subject are sufficiently numerous, but we are not aware that even his most ardent admirers have considered them as works of really the first class. . . . The error was in writing them; he who runs may *read*, but it does not seem likely he will think. The brooding disposition, and the still, investigating intellect, are necessary for consecutive reasonings on delicate philosophy."

Brougham published two series of brief lives. *Historical Sketches of Statesmen who Flourished in the Time of George III* (1839-1843) was followed by *Lives of Men of Letters and Science who Flourished in the Time of George III* (1845, 1846). These two series, especially the former, constitute Brougham's chief literary claim on posterity. John, Lord Campbell wrote, after reading Brougham's novel, *Albert Lunel* (1872), that he doubted whether Brougham possessed "the tact of presenting an individual personality before the readers of a book ... making them take a sympathetic interest in his progress and adventures." It is a just criticism of the novel (after it was printed in 1844 Brougham was wise to suppress its publication in his lifetime), but the outstanding virtue of the sketches, especially those of men whom Brougham had known and observed, is the sprightliness with which the subjects' features are drawn. The sketches do not, perhaps, fulfill his high intent, announced in the introduction to *Historical Sketches of Statesmen*, of instructing readers in the errors and wisdom, and vices and virtues, of their predecessors "by only stating the facts with careful accuracy and drawing the inferences with undeviating candour," for Brougham wrote too hastily for accuracy and his

and most of them as individuals
my hearty pity – if not contempt –
My principles will require the
one – & justice towards myself – the
other course –

What any thing short of the
absolute necessity of the case
could ever have made me
enter the same cabinet with
them – you must, then plainly see
to have been impossible –

I don't envy them what
Ld H. calls their "triumphant
"return" – to ~~house~~ office – (home
they will have none) – but they will
as soon as they are strong
enough to stand alone

*Pages from an 1835 letter to John Allen in which Brougham comments on his omission from the cabinet formed that year by William Lamb, Viscount Melbourne (from Robert Stewart,* Henry Brougham, 1778-1868. His Public Career, *1986)*

have some questions to answer
respecting me – & if I don't put
them, others will – No man
can be expected so far to forget
what he owes to himself as
to be quiet a moment longer
than the necessity of repelling
the common enemy requires –
They (the ministers) are now
too weak to make any shake
a safe thing – I hope they will
soon be strong enough to bear it,
and then we shall ascertain
how far all parties – & the country
indeed – are to be made playthings
to amuse Lord Grey's children –
Yours ever truly H. B.

*Brougham at eighty-five, dressed in the robes of the chancellor of the University of Edinburgh (portrait by Sir Daniel Macnee, P.R.S.A.; Parliament House, Edinburgh)*

candor was distinctly Whiggish. Yet they are masterpieces of what would now be called "higher journalism," and they deserve to be reprinted. The prose is delightful, for one thing because Brougham practiced what he preached, namely the virtue of employing a "chaste style" marked by the most sparing use of metaphor and ornament. Bagehot was not alone in finding the lives of the philosophers "poor and meagre," but he considered *Historical Sketches of Statesmen* to contain "the best sketches of the political men of his generation, one with another, which the world has, or is likely to have."

*Albert Lunel; or, The Château of Languedoc* was published in three volumes in 1872. Brougham, who ranked Voltaire alongside Sir Isaac Newton as the greatest representatives of the Enlightenment, called it a "philosophical romance," but it has neither the irony nor the urgency of argument which Voltaire brought to *Zadig* (1747) and *Candide* (1759). Written in the early 1840s to distract him from grief at the death of his daughter (on whom the novel's heroine is modeled), *Albert Lunel* is a clumsy mixture of the picaresque and the Gothic and should not have been exposed to the public.

Of Brougham's remaining literary works, there is little to remark beyond the extraordinary versatility of mind which they display. All his life Brougham took pleasure in what he called mathematical *divertissements*, and in 1855 he published, with the Cambridge don E. J. Routh, *Analytical View of Sir Isaac Newton's Principia*. It was followed in 1860 by his *Tracts, Mathematical and Physical*, a collection of thirteen essays—ranging over geometry, astronomy, optics, and morphology—written between his days as an undergraduate and his installation as chancellor of Edinburgh University in May 1860, for which occasion they were published and presented to the university. Brougham's forays into the ancient classics and theology were embarrassing disasters. *The Oration of Demosthenes upon the Crown* (1840), Brougham's translation, with notes, of Demosthenes' *De Corona*, demonstrates that Brougham, despite his deep reading of ancient orators, was not fitted to be a translator. His schoolboy Greek, savagely exposed by Joseph Blakesley of Cambridge in the longest review ever printed in the *Times* (spread over four issues from 21 March to 4 April 1840 and running close to thirty-five thousand words), was not up to the task. *A Discourse of Natural Theology* (1835), published as an introductory volume to an edition of William Paley's *Natural Theology*, became the butt of Benjamin Disraeli's sarcasm. Informed that Brougham was preparing a German translation of the work, Disraeli wrote in *The Letters of Runnymede* (1836) that "the translation of a work on a subject of which you know little, into a tongue of which you know nothing, seems the climax of those fantastic freaks of ambitious superficiality which our lively neighbours describe by a finer term than quackery."

Brougham's career in politics spanned half a century, and he continued to be active in social-science associations and in educational concerns into his seventies. After his younger daughter's death in 1839, Brougham began to divide his time between Brougham Hall and the house he built at Cannes, which he called the Chateau Eleanor Louise in memory of his daughter. Brougham died at Cannes on 7 May 1868.

Superficial Brougham often was, and he was ambitious. But both the ambition and the superficiality had their ennobling side. The ambition was to educate the nation, especially that part of it whom Oxbridge had always excluded, in order to help bring a people on the brink of democracy into their inheritance. The classical scholars who denounced his writings did so partly because they trembled at his ambitions for the nation. Yet by the end of his life even the Tory *Quarterly Review* ( January 1869) had learned to estimate his true measure: "What Brougham did for literature and science must be taken in the block, and not judged individually or by the pieces. His multifarious writings were the wheels and cogs of the machinery by which he upheaved prejudice and bigotry, the slings and arrows with which he assailed ignorance, the aqueducts and sluices by which he diffused knowledge. The real aim of the essay or article was attained by the enquiry it stimulated or the example it set."

**Letters:**

*Letters from Lord Brougham to William Forsyth*, edited by William Forsyth (London: Printed by Bradbury, Evans, 1872);

*Brougham and his Early Friends. Letters to James Loch, 1795-1809*, 3 volumes, edited by R. H. M. Buddle Atkinson and G. A. Jackson (London: Privately printed, 1908).

**Biographies:**

John, Baron Campbell, *Lives of Lord Lyndhurst and Lord Brougham* (London: J. Murray, 1869);

G. T. Garratt, *Lord Brougham* (London: Macmillan, 1935);

Frances Hawes, *Henry Brougham* (London: Cape, 1957);

Chester W. New, *The Life of Henry Brougham to 1830* (Oxford: Clarendon Press, 1961);

Robert Stewart, *Henry Brougham, 1778-1868. His Public Career* (London: Bodley Head, 1986).

**References:**

Arthur Aspinall, *Lord Brougham and the Whig Party* (Manchester: Manchester University Press / London & New York: Longmans, Green, 1927);

John Clive, *Scotch Reviewers: The Edinburgh Review, 1802-1815* (Cambridge, Mass.: Harvard University Press, 1957; London: Faber & Faber, 1957).

**Papers:**

Brougham manuscripts are held by the University of London. The British Library has important collections, among them the Brouham/Allen manuscripts and the Brougham/Grenville manuscripts.

# Charles Bucke

*(16 April 1781 - 31 July 1846)*

Thomas L. Cooksey
*Armstrong State College*

BOOKS: *The Philosophy of Nature; or, the Influence of Scenery on the Mind and Heart,* 2 volumes (London: John Murray, 1813); expanded as *On the Beauties, Harmonies and Sublimities of Nature: with Occasional Remarks on the Laws, Customs, Manners and Opinions of Various Nations* (4 volumes, London: G. & W. B. Whittaker, 1821; revised and expanded again, 3 volumes, London: Printed for Thomas Tegg & Son, 1837);

*Amusements in Retirement; or, The Influence of Science, Literature, and the Literal Arts, on the Manners and Happiness of Private Life* (London: Printed for Henry Colburn, 1816);

*The Fall of the Leaf and Other Poems* (London: G. & W. B. Whittaker, 1819);

*The Italians: or, The Fatal Accusation: A Tragedy* (London: Printed for G. & W. B. Whittaker, 1819);

*A Classical Grammar of the English Language with a Short History of its Origin and Formation* (London: Baldwin & Cradock, 1829);

*Julio Romano: or, The Force of the Passions: An Epic Drama in Six Books* (London: J. Rodwell, 1830);

*On the Life, Writings, and Genius of Akenside: with some Account of his Friends* (London: J. Cochrane, 1832);

*The Book of Human Character,* 2 volumes (London: C. Knight, 1837);

*The Life of John, duke of Marlborough* (London: Printed for Thomas Tegg, 1839);

*Ruins of Ancient Cities; with General and Particular Accounts of their Rise, Fall, and Present Condition,* 2 volumes (London: Thomas Tegg, 1840; New York: 1841).

**Edition:** *On the Beauties, Harmonies, and Sublimities of Nature,* selected and revised by Reverend William P. Page (New York: Harper, 1841).

PLAY PRODUCTION: *The Italians: or, The Fatal Accusation: A Tragedy,* London, Theatre Royal, Drury Lane, 3 April 1819.

Charles Bucke, who stood at the periphery of Romantic literary circles, is remembered chiefly as a hack writer in the employment of publisher John Murray, among others. In a 21 April 1813 letter to Murray, George Gordon, Lord Byron, observed, "I see the Examiner threatens some observations upon you next week. . . . I presume all your Scribblers will be drawn up in battle array in defence of the modern Tonson—Mr. Bucke for instance." Bucke's attempts at fame and literary success, especially his play *The Italians* (1819), are noteworthy for their failure. Yet *On the Beauties, Harmonies and Sublimities of Nature* (1821), his most enduring work, is a lucid and thorough exposition of the Romantic search for the sublime and the beautiful in nature. In this work, he provides a natural and philosophical context that shows the coherence and continuity between Edmund Burke's treatment in *A Philosophical Enquiry into the Origin of Our Ideas of the Sublime and Beautiful* (1757) and Thomas Carlyle's in the doctrine of "natural supernaturalism."

Charles Bucke was born at Worlington, Suffolk, on 16 April 1781. Little information is available on his background or early education. His own disclaimer in the preface of his biography of poet and physician Mark Akenside is applicable to himself: "The reader will not expect me to give more than it was possible to obtain. I hope, he will rather thank me for what little I have been able to collect of this eminent person." Nevertheless, some facts about Bucke's life may be inferred. While Bucke's origins were modest, he received a thorough classical education. For Bucke education and intellectual merit were justifiable substitutes for the advantages and prestige of family background. In his biography of Akenside he took Byron to task for the snobbish dismissal of another poet, Bucke's friend Robert Bloomfield: "Lord Byron was, doubtless, a captivating poet; but his critical qualifications were slight. To be so good a man as Robert Bloomfield were a distinction almost enough for any. . . . Lord Byron might have learnt many noble lessons of conduct

THE

PHILOSOPHY OF NATURE;

OR,

THE INFLUENCE OF SCENERY

ON

The Mind and Heart.

———The sounding Cataract
Haunted me like a passion; the tall Rock,
The Mountain, and the deep and gloomy Wood,
Their colours and their forms, have been to me
An appetite.

*Wordsworth.*

Rura mihi placeant, riguique in vallibus amnes,
Flumina amem sylvasque,

*Georg.* ii. l. 485.

VOL. I.

*LONDON:*
PRINTED FOR JOHN MURRAY,
NO. 50 ALBEMARLE-STREET.

1813.

THE following pages are the result of hours, stolen from an application to higher interests, and from the severity of graver subjects.—They were written in the privacy of retirement, among scenes, worthy the pen of Virgil and the pencil of Lorrain:—Scenes, which afford perpetual subjects for meditation to all those, who take a melancholy pleasure in contrasting the dignified simplicity of nature, with the vanity, ignorance, and presumption of man.

" There is no one," says one of the

ii

best and soundest moralists of our age, " there is no one, however limited his powers, who ought not to be actuated by a desire of leaving something behind him, which should operate, as an evidence, that he once existed."—During those hours of peaceful enjoyment, in which these pages were composed, such was the ambition, by which the writer was animated. Upon revising what he has written, however, and comparing it with those ideas of excellence, which, in no very courteous language, whisper a knowledge of what abler pens, than his, would have written, on a subject, so well selected for eliciting all the best energies of genius, he is awed from any expectation of an honourable distinction; and nothing supplies the place of

iii

those golden dreams, which once delighted him, but the satisfaction of having passed, happily and innocently, hours, which would otherwise have been useless, listless, and unnumbered.

*Title page and preface for Bucke's first attempt to examine the sublime and beautiful in nature* from the poet, he presumed to despise." In a telling remark Bucke added, "Bloomfield was of mean parentage; and so was Akenside. The lower the rank, the greater the merit."

Bucke's first published work, *The Philosophy of Nature,* which appeared anonymously in 1813, began as a compilation of interesting anecdotes and information about nature, much in the spirit of popular works such as Isaac D'Israeli's *Curiosities of Literature* (1791). Bucke's *Philosophy of Nature* might be compared with Pliny's *Natural History.* In creating a source book of literary, natural, and historical allusions to illustrate the sublime and the beautiful in nature, Bucke drew on a wide assortment of materials from natural science, literature, history, travel, and geography culled from his wide reading at the British Museum. The book is organized into articles describing the sublime and beautiful of various natural phenomena such as oceans, stars, seasons, and "the intellectual universe." The article on oceans is exemplary of his approach. He begins by discussing the role of the sea in the sublime. He then presents various descriptions of it, followed by a series of testimonials drawn from world culture, including passages from works by Robert Burns and Italian dramatist Vittorio Alfieri, as well as from the lore of the Chewyan Indians in North America. Bucke then examines the role of the ocean in mythology, comparing various "marine Deities," and concludes his discussion by looking at various associations in literature, history, and elsewhere.

The topic caught Bucke's imagination, and, throughout much of his life, he revised and expanded his book, retitling it *On the Beauties, Harmonies and Sublimities of Nature* for the second edition, published under his name in 1821. Thereafter, he was identified as its author. At the time of his death, he had accumulated twelve manuscript volumes. As the book grew, its conception was altered. While *The Philosophy of Nature* was essentially a collection of miscellaneous information, *On the Beauties, Harmonies and Sublimities of Nature* speculated more fully on the significance of the sublime in nature. Bucke's conception of the sublime is conventional, glancing back to Edmund Burke's formulation in *A Philosophical Enquiry.* Nevertheless, Bucke's later articles point to a preoccupation with natural theology. Observing an apparent order or design in the world, he asks, "who teaches the swallow, the wood cock, and the nightingale, to traverse the atmosphere from one climate to another, and different seasons of the year?" The answer, he suggests, is "the same Power, the same Intelligence which teaches the worm to weave its silken net, and the spider to waft itself through the lower regions of air!" In "The Great—the Little," Bucke is more explicit, declaring, "Natural Theology is the most elevated and sublime, therefore the most delightful of all human studies; for it embraces all that can be seen, felt, imagined, and reasoned upon, its empire being the universe both of matter and mind." In this belief Bucke looks back to the natural theology of William Paley (1743-1805) and other philosophers who tried to argue the existence of God by means of the idea that the existence of order, purpose, or design in the world logically posits the existence of a designer. Paley had innovated this teleological proof by appealing to examples of design or purpose in biology. Bucke augmented Paley's approach by ranging over more material and examples. Sir James Mackintosh described *On the Beauties, Harmonies and Sublimities of Nature* as "one of the most beautiful works he had ever read, and that it must stand at the head of its class in modern times."

*On the Beauties, Harmonies and Sublimities of Nature* offers few original insights into the nature of the sublime. Its importance rests in showing the link between the Romantic conception of nature and the natural theology of the eighteenth century. It also suggests how that conception looks forward to the "natural supernaturalism" of Carlyle, or the *Cosmos* (1845-1862) of Alexander von Humboldt, a Prussian naturalist and explorer. Underlying such thinking was the desire to work an intellectual compromise that allowed both the existence of God and the validity of science. While Enlightenment materialists had argued that miracles were impossible because they violated natural law, Bucke and later Carlyle argued that the order of nature and natural law were themselves the miraculous manifestation of the divine. For Bucke, the study of nature was ultimately a profound and intense moral and religious experience. Echoing Blaise Pascal, he observed, "I have ever felt an intense delight in the cultivation of astronomical science; but I am ready to confess that, after venturing into the ocean of infinity, I desisted for some time out of pure cowardice."

After the modest success of *The Philosophy of Nature* in 1813, Bucke produced *Amusements in Retirement; or, The Influence of Science, Literature, and the Literal Arts, on the Manners and Happiness of Private Life* in 1816. This book proved less successful, receiving little notice. With the need to support his wife and children, and finding himself on the edge of poverty, Bucke turned his interest in poetry to the theater in the hope of achieving fame with a successful play. His verse tragedy, *The Italians: or The Fatal Accusation,* was submitted to the committee of the Drury Lane theater. To Bucke's gratification, they accepted it quickly, promising him "the freedom of their house," and "the whole strength of the Theatre." His initial gratification was quickly tempered by a series of delays and frustration.

First, the theater closed for several weeks because of the death of Princess Charlotte in November 1817. Upon the reopening of the theaters, Bucke's play was put aside to make way for a production of William Dimond's *Bride of Abydos* (inspired by Byron's poem). It was then thought appropriate to follow that tragedy with a comedy, so *The Italians* was again delayed. At this point, Edmund Kean, who was in charge of the production and who was to play the main character, expressed a desire to revive Christopher Marlowe's *Jew of Malta.* As recompense for yet another delay, Bucke was invited to write a prologue. He declined this offer, finding Marlowe's play "barbarous, and so entirely unfitted for the present age." At this time Kean began to express doubts about *The Italians,* suggesting that his part did not adequately display his talents. Further delays led to an escalating exchange of letters, first in private and then in the press, and finally in prefaces to successive editions of the play itself. In February 1819 a crisis occurred when Kean gave what was described as a "discreditable" performance in Jane Porter's tragedy *Switzerland.* Fearing that Kean might similarly maul his play, Bucke withdrew *The Italians* from the Drury Lane theater.

Controversy raged on, Kean was compelled to apologize, and *The Italians* finally appeared at Drury Lane on Saturday evening, 3 April 1819, with Kean in the main role. This, however, was not the end of the controversy. The audience was divided between Bucke's friends and supporters, and those of Kean, each group ready to be avenged for the humiliations and recriminations that had surrounded the play. The reviewer from the *Herald* noted that "there were ample proofs of the presence of a large and well organized party, perfectly versed in the science of mockery, and sufficiently vulgar to give the loud laugh, the ironical yell, and the affected scream their fullest effect." After several more performances, the curtain came permanently down on *The Italians.* Ironically, though the play had little success on the stage, the surrounding controversy had made it a cause célèbre, with the result that it went through some eight editions in 1819.

Bucke had high aspirations for his play. He had an elevated conception of the genre of tragedy: "A good TRAGEDY, in all enlightened ages," he noted in the preface, "has been esteemed, next to EPIC, the most difficult of all mental operations." He labored, therefore, for balance in his characters, making them neither entirely good nor evil. This complexity proved to be a point of contention with Kean, who preferred a role that allowed for more bombast. Glancing toward Kean, Bucke complained in his preface that "some ACTORS regard nothing but the opportunity of displaying their own peculiar talent; and having only a knowledge of stage effect, they are weak enough to suppose, that stage effect necessarily embraces plot, character, and sentiment."

*The Italians* has limited merits as a great tragedy. Set on a battlefield before Renaissance Naples, it has all the features of a Romantic melodrama marked by overwrought set pieces. A monologue by the character Albanio (Kean's role) on a moonlit crag in front of Mount Vesuvius is indicative:

> How glorious!—Lo—Vesuvius appears!—
> Itself a planet.—Towering o'er the vale,
> It gives new grandeur to sublimity.—
> Magnificent!—Oh Nature!—How thy works
> Dissolve my soul in holiest admiration!—
> Roll on, ye heralds of omnipotence;—
> Roll to the utmost limit of the spheres.

While these lines point to Bucke's preoccupation with the sublime in nature, his imagery and diction are suggestive of Byron in *Childe Harold's Pilgrimage* (1812-1818) or *Manfred* (1817). Ironically the value of *The Italians* rests not in the play itself, but in Bucke's preface and the exchange of letters with Kean and the Drury Lane committee, which give such insight in the workings of the theater at the time.

While the controversy over *The Italians* raged, Bucke managed to publish *The Fall of the Leaf and Other Poems* in 1819. His poetry dwells on the same themes found in *On the Beauties, Harmonies and Sublimities of Nature,* the divinity found in the workings of nature.

Throughout his career, Bucke and his family suffered great poverty. He found it necessary

ON THE

LIFE, WRITINGS, AND GENIUS

OF

AKENSIDE:

WITH

SOME ACCOUNT OF HIS FRIENDS.

BY CHARLES BUCKE,

AUTHOR OF THE BEAUTIES, HARMONIES, AND SUBLIMITIES OF NATURE.

——————— "The spacious west,
And all the teeming regions of the south,
Held not a quarry to the curious flight
Of knowledge, half so tempting and so fair
As MAN to MAN."

*Pleasures of Imagination.*

LONDON:
JAMES COCHRANE AND CO., WATERLOO-PLACE.
1832

*Title page and preface for the first book-length biography of the author of* The Pleasures of the Imagination *(1744), a poem Bucke describes as "rich in materials and brilliant in imagery and versification"*

---

HAVING always esteemed the PLEASURES OF IMAGINATION the finest didactic Poem in our language, it was with no small pleasure, that I accidentally discovered, some time since, a few MS. notes of AKENSIDE at the British Museum.

These notes are not very important; but they led me to regret,—as, indeed, I had often done before,—that all the accounts, we have, of this great poet, should be so meagre and deficient:—and having formerly known two gentlemen, who had been intimately acquainted with him, I combined what I had heard them say of him with what was already known; and taking his works for a general guide—(and few speak more in their works than Akenside does)—I have, I hope, been enabled to give a correct and, perhaps, not altogether an uninteresting outline of a virtuous and high-minded man, gifted with very considerable poetical powers.

The Reader will not expect me to give more than it was possible to obtain. I hope, he will rather thank me for what little I have been able to collect of this eminent person; though I cannot but feel, that he must greatly regret, that the subject did not fall into abler hands.

*London.*
*January,* 1832.

ERRATA.

Page 186, 6 lines from bottom, *dele* Bowles.
192, 4 lines from bottom, *for* Edward, *read* Edmund.

to obtain grants on several occasions from the Literary Fund. He also found it necessary to produce volumes such as *A Classical Grammar of the English Language* (1829) and *The Life of John, duke of Marlborough* (1839), as well as further compilations such as *The Book of Human Character* (1837) and *Ruins of Ancient Cities* (1840), to survive. While these volumes have some merit, they lack the interest or inspiration of *On the Beauties, Harmonies and Sublimities.* Bucke eventually received economic relief when a monthly endowment was provided by the statesman Thomas Grenville, son of George Grenville, and a noted bibliophile who occasionally helped needy writers.

In 1830 Bucke turned to play writing again, publishing *Julio Romano,* an epic drama in six books. As with *The Fall of the Leaf,* Bucke's efforts received little attention. Aside from *On the Beauties, Harmonies and Sublimities,* Bucke's most enduring work was *On the Life, Writings, and Genius of Akenside,* published in 1832, the first extended study of the life and works of Mark Akenside (1721-1770), author of *The Pleasures of the Imagination* (1744). The germ for Bucke's book was his discovery of several manuscript notes by Akenside in the British Museum. Bucke's treatment is balanced. He is aware of Akenside's weaknesses as well as his strengths. "As a lyric poet, Akenside yields, on the whole, to Gray and Collins," Bucke admits, "He is defective in pathos; his images occasionally want warmth, and his verse melody; but his lyrical productions, nevertheless, exhibit a fine glow of sentiments, an ardent admiration of the great and good . . . and a fine sensibility to all the best and noblest feelings of the heart." Bucke's estimates of Akenside remain the starting point for work on the poet.

Bucke died at Pulteney Terrace, Islington, on 31 July 1846, at the age of sixty-five. He was survived by his wife, two daughters, and two sons. He had lived a quiet life devoted to literature, and his efforts yielded neither the fame nor the success that he had desired. They now give some insight into the Romantic conception of nature and the sublime. His merits are perhaps best summarized by William Page, the American editor of *On the Beauties, Harmonies and Sublimities of Nature:* "The author's manner of writing is not a little peculiar, being discursive, abrupt, and irregular: at the same time, he abounds in interesting facts, in striking sentiments, and in beautiful imagery; in rich classical allusions, and in illustrations at once novel, and in a high degree impressive."

**References:**

"Charles Bucke," *Gentleman's Magazine,* 27 (May 1847): 558;

Harold N. Hillebrand, *Edmund Kean* (New York: Columbia University Press, 1933), pp. 182-184.

# George Gordon, Lord Byron

*(22 January 1788 - 19 April 1824)*

John Spalding Gatton
*Bellarmine College*

See also the Byron entry in *DLB 96: British Romantic Poets, 1789-1832: Second Series.*

BOOKS: *Fugitive Pieces* (Newark: Privately printed by S. & J. Ridge, 1806); revised as *Poems on Various Occasions* (Newark: Privately printed by S. & J. Ridge, 1807); revised again, with differing contents, and publicly printed as *Hours of Idleness, A Series of Poems, Original and Translated* (Newark: Printed & sold by S. & J. Ridge, 1807); second edition, revised, published as *Poems Original and Translated* (Newark: Printed & sold by S. & J. Ridge, 1808); republished as *Hours of Idleness: A Series of Poems, Original and Translated* (London: Printed for W. T. Sherwin, 1820);

*English Bards, and Scotch Reviewers. A Satire* (London: Printed for James Cawthorn, 1809; second edition, revised and enlarged, London: Printed for James Cawthorn, 1809; Charleston, S.C.: Published by E. Morford, Willinton & Co.; J. Maxwell, printer, Philadelphia, 1811);

*Childe Harold's Pilgrimage. A Romaunt* [Cantos I and II] (London: Printed for John Murray, William Blackwood, Edinburgh, and John Cumming, Dublin, by Thomas Davison, 1812; Philadelphia: Published by Moses Thomas, printed by William Fry, 1812; second edition, enlarged, London: Printed for John Murray, 1812; seventh edition, enlarged, London: Printed by Thomas Davison for John Murray, 1814);

*The Curse of Minerva* (London: Privately printed by T. Davison, 1812; Philadelphia: Printed for De-Silver & Co., 1815);

*Waltz: An Apostrophic Hymn,* as Horace Hornem, Esq. (London: Printed by S. Gosnell for Sherwood, Neely & Jones, 1813);

*The Giaour, A Fragment of a Turkish Tale* (London: Privately printed by T. Davison for John Murray, 1813; first published edition, London: Printed by T. Davison for John Murray, 1813; Philadelphia: M. Thomas, 1813; second, third, fourth, fifth, and seventh editions, enlarged, London: Printed by T. Davison for John Murray, 1813; second American edition, from the fifth London edition, Philadelphia: M. Thomas, 1813);

*The Bride of Abydos. A Turkish Tale* (London: Printed by T. Davison for John Murray, 1813; third and fourth editions, slightly enlarged, London: Printed by T. Davison for John Murray, 1813; Boston: Printed & published by N. G. House, 1814; Philadelphia: Published by Moses Thomas, printed by William Fry, 1814);

*The Corsair, A Tale* (London: Printed by Thomas Davison for John Murray, 1814; second edition, enlarged, 1814; Baltimore: Printed & published by B. Edes, 1814; Boston: Published by West & Blake, 1814; New York: Eastburn, Kirk & Co., 1814; Philadelphia: Published by Moses Thomas, printed by J. Maxwell, 1814);

*Ode to Napoleon Buonaparte* (London: Printed for John Murray by W. Bulmer, 1814; Boston: Munroe, 1814; New York: Printed by J. Low, 1814; Newburyport: W. B. Allen, 1814; Philadelphia: Published by Edward Earle, 1814);

*Lara. A Tale* [by Byron]. *Jacqueline. A Tale* [by Samuel Rogers] (London: Printed for J. Murray by T. Davison, 1814; Boston: Wells & Lilly, 1814; New York: Eastburn & Kirk, 1814);

*A Selection of Hebrew Melodies Ancient and Modern . . .,* poetry by Byron with musical arrangements by Isaac Nathan and John Braham (London: I. Nathan, 1815); Byron's verses republished as *Hebrew Melodies* (London: Printed for John Murray, 1815; Philadelphia: Published by James P. Parke, Wm. Fry, printer, 1815; Boston: Published by John Eliot, 1815; New York: Printed and sold by T. & J. Swords, 1815);

*The Siege of Corinth. A Poem. Parisina. A Poem* (London: Printed for John Murray, 1816; New York: Van Winkle & Wiley, 1816);

*George Gordon, Lord Byron (engraving by H. Meyer, after an 1815 drawing by G. H. Harlow)*

*Poems* (London: Printed for John Murray by W. Bulmer, 1816; New York: Published by Thomas Kirk & Thomas R. Mercein; Moses Thomas, M. Carey & Son, Philadelphia; Wells & Lilly, Boston; Coale & Maxwell, Baltimore; printed by T. & W. Mercein, 1817);

*Childe Harold's Pilgrimage. Canto the Third* (London: Printed for John Murray, 1816; Boston: Published by Munroe & Francis, 1817);

*The Prisoner of Chillon, and Other Poems* (London: Printed for John Murray, 1816; Boston: Munroe & Francis, 1817);

*Monody on the Death of the Right Honourable R. B. Sheridan* (London: Printed for John Murray, 1816);

*Manfred, A Dramatic Poem* (London: John Murray, 1817; New York: Published by D. Longworth, 1817; New York: Van Winkle & Wiley, 1817; Philadelphia: Published by M. Thomas, printed by J. Maxwell, 1817);

*The Lament of Tasso* (London: John Murray, 1817; New York: Van Winkle & Wiley, 1817);

*Beppo, A Venetian Story* (London: John Murray, 1818; Boston: Munroe & Francis, 1818; New York: A. T. Goodrich, 1818; fourth edition, enlarged, London: John Murray, 1818);

*Childe Harold's Pilgrimage. Canto the Fourth* (London: John Murray, 1818; New York: Published by James Eastburn & Co., printed by Clayton & Eastland, 1818; New York: A. T. Goodrich, 1818; New York: Kirk & Mercein, 1818; Philadelphia: Printed by J. Maxwell for M. Thomas, 1818);

*Mazeppa, A Poem* (London: John Murray, 1819; Boston: Wells & Lilly, 1819; Philadelphia: Published by M. Thomas and J. Haly & C. Thomas, New York, 1819);

*Don Juan* [Cantos I and II] (London: Printed by Thomas Davison, 1819; New York: W. B. Gilley, 1820);

*Childe Harold's Pilgrimage, A Romaunt, in Four Cantos,* 2 volumes (London: John Murray, 1819;

*Byron and his mother, Catherine Gordon Byron (portrait by an anonymous artist; location of original unknown; from Frederic Raphael,* Byron, *1982)*

Nuremberg & New York: Frederick Campe & Co., 1831);

*Letter to **** ****** on the Rev. W. L. Bowles' Strictures on the Life and Writings of Pope* (London: John Murray, 1821);

*Marino Faliero, Doge of Venice. An Historical Tragedy, in Five Acts. With Notes. The Prophecy of Dante, A Poem* (London: John Murray, 1821; Philadelphia: M. Carey & Sons, 1821);

*Don Juan, Cantos III, IV, and V.* (London: Printed by Thomas Davison, 1821; New York: William B. Gilley, printed by J. Seymour, 1821);

*Sardanapalus, A Tragedy. The Two Foscari, A Tragedy. Cain, A Mystery* (London: John Murray, 1821; Boston: Wells & Lilly and Munroe & Francis, 1822; New York: S. Campbell, 1822; New York: W. B. Gilley, 1822);

*The Age of Bronze; or, Carmen Seculare et Annus Haud Mirabilis* (London: Printed for John Hunt, 1823; Cincinnati: Printed for the publishers, 1823; New York: Published by S. Campbell & Son, W. B. Gilley, Collins & Co., Collins & Hannay, E. Bliss & E. White, printed by J. & J. Harper, 1823; New York: Published by R. Norris Henry and E. Littell, Philadelphia, 1823);

*The Island, or Christian and His Comrades* (London: Printed for John Hunt, 1823; New York: E. Duyckinck, 1823; Philadelphia: H. C. Carey & I. Lea, 1823);

*Don Juan. Cantos VI.—VII.—and VIII.* (London: Printed for John Hunt, 1823; Philadelphia: H. C. Carey & I. Lea, 1823);

*Don Juan. Cantos IX.—X.—and XI.* (London: Printed for John Hunt, 1823; Albany,

N. Y.: Printed by E. & E. Hosford, 1823; Philadelphia: J. Mortimer, 1823);

*Don Juan. Cantos XII.—XIII.—and XIV.* (London: Printed for John Hunt, 1823; New York: Charles Wiley, 1824);

*Werner, A Tragedy* (London: John Murray, 1823; Philadelphia: H. C. Carey & I. Lea, 1823);

*The Deformed Transformed; A Drama* (London: Printed for J. and H. L. Hunt, 1824; Philadelphia: H. C. Carey & I. Lea, 1824);

*Don Juan. Cantos XV. and XVI.* (London: Printed for John and H. L. Hunt, 1824; New York: W. B. Gilley, 1824; Philadelphia: H. C. Carey & I. Lea, 1824);

*The Parliamentary Speeches of Lord Byron* (London: Printed for Rodwell & Martin, 1824);

*Letters and Journals of Lord Byron With Notices of His Life, by Thomas Moore,* 2 volumes (London: John Murray, 1830; New York: Printed & published by J. & J. Harper, 1830);

*The Works of Lord Byron: Letters and Journals,* 6 volumes, edited by Rowland E. Prothero (London: John Murray, 1898-1901; New York: Scribners, 1898-1901);

*Byron's Letters and Journals,* 12 volumes, edited by Leslie A. Marchand (London: John Murray, 1973-1982; Cambridge, Mass.: Harvard University Press, 1973-1982).

**Editions:** *The Works of Lord Byron: Poetry,* 7 volumes, edited by Ernest Hartley Coleridge (London: John Murray, 1898-1904);

*The Complete Poetical Works of Lord Byron,* edited by Paul Elmer More (Boston & New York: Houghton Mifflin, 1905); revised by Robert F. Gleckner (Boston: Houghton Mifflin, 1975);

*Byron's* Don Juan: *A Variorum Edition,* edited by Truman Guy Steffan and Willis W. Pratt (Austin: University of Texas Press, 1957);

*Lord Byron's* Cain: *Twelve Essays and a Text with Variants and Annotations,* edited by Steffan (Austin & London: University of Texas Press, 1968);

*Byron's* Hebrew Melodies, edited by Thomas L. Ashton (Austin: University of Texas Press, 1972; London: Routledge & Kegan Paul, 1972);

*Lord Byron: The Complete Poetical Works,* edited by Jerome J. McGann (volumes 1-5, Oxford: Clarendon Press / New York: Oxford University Press, 1980-1986; volume 6-, forthcoming 1991- ).

PLAY PRODUCTION: *Marino Faliero,* London, Theatre Royal, Drury Lane, 25 April 1821.

George Gordon, Lord Byron—by his own reckoning renowned as a poet from that day in March 1812 when he awoke to find himself famous as the author of *Childe Harold's Pilgrimage,* Cantos I and II—likewise merits recognition as a master of prose expression. On occasion he claimed to prefer prose to poetry. In 1813 he wished he could have made a name for himself not as a writer of poetry but as a writer of prose, but the public insisted that he continue writing poems. Even in 1824, in a 23 February letter to his half sister, Augusta Leigh, he noted that his daughter Ada's "preference of *prose* (strange as it may now seem) *was* and indeed *is* mine—(for I hate *reading* verse—and always did)." Although much of Byron's poetry is autobiographical, of necessity he obscured the more personal details. "In rhyme," he wrote on 17 November 1813, "I can keep more away from facts; but the thought always runs through, through ... yes, yes, through." To apprehend the true man one must turn to his prose performances: to his trio of speeches in the House of Lords; to his critical essays addressed to William Lisle Bowles on the poetry of Alexander Pope, his replies to reviewers, and his other published occasional pieces; to several brief, often unfinished, fictions; to his conversations; to prefaces and notes accompanying many poems and verse dramas; and, especially, to his correspondence and journals. In approximately twenty-nine hundred letters dating from 8 November 1798 (his first) to 9 April 1824 (his last) and in his five surviving diaries, Byron blazes to life. In the absence of his memoirs (burned in his publisher's parlor in May 1824 by zealous friends anxious to protect his reputation), these records of quotidian activities, sketches of contemporaries in literature, politics, and society, reminiscences, meditations, business dealings, libertarian ideals, libertinism, and confidences to intimates project Byron's protean nature, variously and vigorously witty, introspective, ironic, sincere, passionate, literate, Rabelaisian, forceful, inquisitive, playful, generous, and loving. Everywhere his prose is stamped with his candor and humanity. Less frequently in the letters is he the moody or tortured soul; that spirit found fuller expression in his weltschmerz poetry, notably in *Childe Harold's Pilgrimage* (1812-1818) and *Manfred* (1817). The letters and journals, augmented by the poems, help bring

*Byron at Harrow, 1801 (sketch by I. W.; location of original unknown; from Frederic Raphael,* Byron, *1982)*

the whole Byron into focus.

George Gordon Noel Byron was born in London on 22 January 1788, the son of Catherine Gordon of Gight, an impoverished Scots heiress, and Captain John ("Mad Jack") Byron, a profligate widower with a daughter, Augusta; he died in France three years later, an exile from English creditors. With the death in 1798 of his great-uncle, the "wicked" fifth Lord Byron, George became the sixth baron Byron of Rochdale. After Harrow (1801-1805), he attended Trinity College, Cambridge, where he received an M.A. degree in 1808.

In the summer of 1813, he began an affair with his twenty-nine-year-old married half sister, Augusta Leigh. On 15 April 1814, Augusta gave birth to a girl, Elizabeth Medora, who believed herself to be Byron's daughter, although he never acknowledged the paternity, as he did for his other illegitimate offspring. There is no extant proof on either side of the question.

On 2 January 1815, Byron married Anne Isabella (Annabella) Milbanke, a bluestocking widely read in literature and philosophy and with a talent for mathematics. That December, their daughter Augusta Ada was born (the first name was later dropped). Byron's rages and irrational behavior, brought on by financial worries and heavy drinking, as well as Lady Byron's suspicion of incest between her husband and his half sister, resulted in the couple's legal separation on 21 April 1816; four days later, Byron departed for the Continent, never to return to England alive.

During the separation crisis, he had a casual liaison with Claire (Jane) Clairmont; Byron named their daughter, born on 12 January 1817, Clara Allegra and called her by her second name.

*Byron circa 1804 (miniature by an anonymous artist; private collection; from Frederic Raphael,* Byron, *1982)*

After a sojourn in Switzerland and almost seven years' residence in Italy, where he formed his "last attachment" with the Countess Teresa Guiccioli, Byron sailed for Greece in July 1823, to assist that country in its war for independence from the Turks. Having been soaked by a heavy rain while out riding in early April 1824, Byron fell ill and died on the nineteenth in Missolonghi, Greece. He was thirty-six years old.

John Keats, in distinguishing his style from Byron's, declared, "He describes what he sees—I describe what I imagine." Byron's descriptions of exotic locales and striking vistas enrich works from *Childe Harold* through the Oriental tales and *Manfred* to *Don Juan* (1819-1824). In his letters, however, he tended to shun picturesque passages or to treat facetiously those he included. Writing to Francis Hodgson during his tour of the Mediterranean and Near East (1809-1811), he interrupted his comments on Seville and the Sierra Morena, exclaiming, "but damn description, it is always disgusting" (6 August 1809). Yet colorful word pictures of a sunset, native costumes, architecture, and individuals animate the lengthy account (addressed to his mother on 12 November 1809) of his visit to Ali Pasha in his palace at Tepelenë. Vivid also are his early letters from Venice, "the greenest island of my imagination" (17 November 1816). And his publisher John Murray received an arresting eyewitness report of the guillotining of three robbers in Rome: "the first head was cut off close to the ears—the other two were taken off more cleanly" (30 May 1817).

Byron's poetic philosophy found forceful presentation in his letters and journals. The lack of absolute consistency in his statements may be laid to competing strains in his writing: his desire, on the one hand, to emulate the neoclassical balance, wit, and satire of Alexander Pope; and, on the other, his predilection for Romantic self-revelation. While this latter inclination informed most of his poetry, including some of his finest, "in his deepest being," writes Leslie A. Marchand, Byron's modern biographer and the editor of his unexpurgated letters and journals, "he did not completely approve of it. Hence his deprecation of Romantic poetry, his own and others." To his future wife, Annabella Milbanke, Byron wrote on 29 November 1813, "I by no means rank poetry or poets high in the scale of intellect—this may look like Affectation—but it is my real opinion—it is the lava of the imagination whose eruption prevents an earth-quake. . . ."

In his prose, as in his poetry, Byron's pen portraits of contemporary literary figures limn their subjects, if not always objectively, certainly candidly, sharply, and memorably. He particularly belittled Robert Southey, William Wordsworth, and John Keats (though after Keats's death Byron regretted his harsh judgments); besides his master Alexander Pope, he had praise for Samuel Taylor Coleridge, Thomas Moore, Walter Scott, and Percy Bysshe Shelley, among others.

Byron composed his letters the same way that he said he thought—"rapidly" (journal entry, 17 December 1823). As he explained to Leigh Hunt on 30 October 1815, "I write in great haste— . . . you have it hot & hot—just as it comes—. . . ." To Mary Shelley he maintained, "I am not a cautious letter-writer and generally say what comes uppermost at the moment" (14 November 1822). If that spontaneity gave his letters immediacy and vitality, his keen, even theatrical, awareness of his audience infused them with individuality, for he suited his precisely, felicitously phrased correspondence to the recipients' interests and temperaments. As John Clubbe observes, "The letters often read like dramatic monologues. Although they are remarkably free of pose, Byron assumes with each correspondent a slightly different persona or mask." (Marguerite, Countess of Blessington, recorded Byron's admission that, "Now, if I know myself, I should say, that I have no character at all. . . . But, joking apart, what I think of myself is, that I am so changeable, being everything by turns and nothing long.") Byron's versatile nature illustrates his remarks on "mobility" in *Don Juan* (Canto XVI). In a note to stanza 97, he defined this "quality" as "an excessive susceptibility of immediate impressions—at the same time without *losing* the past." Like "actors" and "romancers," among others, Byron seemed "strongly acted on by what is nearest" (stanzas 97-98). In writing to Augusta Leigh, he is the brother-lover, confiding, entreating, playful, caring: "*A thousand loves* to *you* from *me*—which is very generous for I only ask *one* in return" (15 October 1816). To his Cambridge friends John Cam Hobhouse, Douglas Kinnaird, and Scrope Berdmore Davies, he is the bantering bachelor and sophisticate given to ribaldry. To Thomas Moore, he is the convivial man of letters: "I am not quite sure that I shall allow the Miss Byrons (legitimate or illegitimate) to read Lalla Rookh— . . . that they mayn't discover that there was a better poet than papa" (22 June 1821). To Annabella Milbanke, he is the candid suitor, then, the pleading, bitter spouse and former husband. To John Murray, he is the man-of-the-world and the exasperated author: "—When I write to you as a friend you will of course take your own time and leisure to reply, but when I address you—as a publisher—I expect an answer" (16 May 1822). To Teresa Guiccioli, with whom he usually corresponded in Italian, he is the ecstatic and tender "*amante in eterno*." To the assorted seekers after advice, assistance, and favor, he is the patient, courteous, helpful gentleman.

Many of Byron's most dazzling letters are addressed to Elizabeth, Lady Melbourne (an aunt of Annabella Milbanke and mother-in-law of Lady Caroline Lamb, with whom he had had a brief affair). Testifying to Byron's abiding enthusiasm for the theater ("I could not resist the *first* night of any thing," 23 April 1815) is a sequence of letters rich in sparkling dialogue, ironic scenes, and farcical intrigues in which he fairly dramatizes as a Restoration or eighteenth-century comedy his unconsummated affair with the twenty-year-old Lady Frances Wedderburn Webster in the autumn of 1813. As in plays by George Farquhar, Oliver Goldsmith, Arthur Murphy, and David Garrick—to whose works, among others, Byron alludes—authentic speech and action in these vivacious letters treat of adultery, jealousy, cuckoldry, billets-doux, and compromising situations, all drawn from what Byron cheerfully termed "a perfect comedy."

During a rendezvous in "a billiard room," where Byron "made love" to Lady Frances with words "(for there we have hitherto stopped)" and "with pen & paper—in tender & tolerably turned *prose* periods (no *poetry* even when in earnest)," the couple was surprised by the unexpected entrance of her husband, who, for all his jealousy, conceit, and philandering, suspected neither of them of impropriety (8 October). This part of the correspondence assumes the immediacy of a theatrical performance for, in the midst of writing these very events to Lady Melbourne, Byron is again interrupted by the "*Marito*" (8 October). When Lady Frances put herself "entirely" at Byron's "*mercy*," he "spared" her—"I know not whether I can regret it—she seems so very thankful for my forbearance" (17 October). "*Platonism*," once "in some peril," was not lost.

4

8. St. James's Street
March 5th 1812

My dear Hodgson,

We are not answerable for reports of speeches in the papers, they are always given incorrectly, & on this occasion more so than usual from the Debate in the Com^s on the same night. — The M. Post should have said 18 years. — However you will find the speech as spoken in the Parlia=
=mentary Register, when it comes out. —
Lds Holland & Grenville, particularly the latter paid some high compts in the course of their speeches as you may have seen in the papers, & Lds Eldon & Harrowby answered me. — — I have had many

*On this and the next two pages: letter to Francis Hodgson in which Byron reports praise for one of his speeches in the House of Lords and announces the imminent publication of* Childe Harold's Pilgrimage, *Cantos I and II (HM 24053; Henry E. Huntington Library and Art Gallery)*

marvellous eulogies repeated to me since
in person & by proxy from divers persons
ministerial—yea ministerial! as well as
oppositionists, of them I shall only mention
Sir F. Burdetts.— He says it is the
best speech by a Lord since the "Lord
knows when" probably from a fellow fee-
=ling in ye sentiments.— Ld H. tells me
I shall beat them all if I persevere &
Ld G. remarked that the construction of some of my periods
are very like Burke's!!— And so much
for vanity.—— I spoke very violent
sentences with a sort of modest impudence,
abused every thing & every body, & put the
Ld Chancellor very much out of humour,
& if I may believe what I hear, have not

lost any character by the experiment.— As
to my delivery, loud & fluent enough, perhaps
a little theatrical.— — I could not recognize
myself or any one else in the Newspapers.— —
I hire myself unto +Griffiths, & my poesy
comes out on Saturday.— Hobhouse is
here, I shall tell him to write.—
My Stone is gone for the present, but
I fear is part of my habit.— — —
We all talk of a visit to Cambridge.

yrs ever
B

+NB.— Hhouse requested Moore to leave out this
name — JCH —

On 14 November 1813 Byron began his first journal. In its initial entry he recorded, "This afternoon I have burnt the scenes of my commenced comedy"; his reason appears three days later: "the scene ran into *reality.*" While he could create amusing incidents and dialogue in correspondence (see, too, his comic accounts to Murray of Venetian liaisons with Angelina, a noble's daughter, and with Margarita Cogni, "La Fornarina," 18 May and 1 August 1819) as well as in such poems as *Beppo* (1818) and *Don Juan,* Byron refused to write comedies for the stage, persuaded as he was that the genre was "the most difficult of compositions, more so than tragedy" (journal entry for 10 December 1813). In light of the affair with Lady Frances Webster, which soon ran its course, Byron could with honesty claim that "there is no comedy after all like real life" (14 October 1813).

In July 1818, Byron, resident in Venice, began his comic masterpiece *Don Juan* (its evolution, like that of other of his works, can be traced in the letters). Thereafter, his correspondence pales in brilliance, though rarely declines into dullness. By 1820 "dreadful" was "the exertion of letter writing" (31 January). In August of that year he told Augusta Leigh, "Pray excuse my rare epistles.—I have almost given up letter-writing except on absolute business"; many of his later letters chronicle publishing concerns, financial matters, and Italian political unrest, in which he was involved. He devoted his creative energies to his epic ("As to 'Don Juan,'" he goaded Douglas Kinnaird on 26 October 1819, "—confess—confess—you dog—and be candid—that it is the sublime of *that there* sort of writing—it may be bawdy—but is it not good English?—it may be profligate—but is it not *life,* is it not *the thing?*").

From Pisa in the spring and summer of 1822 he wrote movingly of the death and funeral arrangements of five-year-old Allegra, his illegitimate daughter by Claire Clairmont ("The blow was stunning and unexpected"; 23 April), as well as of the drowning of Percy Bysshe Shelley and the cremation of his remains on the seashore ("All of Shelley was consumed, except his *heart,* which would not take the flame, and is now preserved in spirits of wine," he wrote to Thomas Moore on 27 August).

The letters Byron wrote between April 1823 and April 1824, primarily from Greece, introduce a new group of correspondents, a new purpose, and a new tone. Dedicated to the cause for Greek independence, he communicated with Edward Blaquiere and John Bowring, founders of the London Greek Committee; with rival political parties among the insurgents; and with Samuel Barff and Charles Hancock, his business agents in the Greek islands, and Charles F. Barry, a banker friend in Genoa. All received confidential accounts of personal and Greek activities. To Teresa Guiccioli he wrote brief English postscripts to longer letters from her brother Pietro, who had accompanied him to Greece. Cast in somber phrases, with wit rarely flashing forth, Byron's Greek letters and dispatches demonstrate his command of strategy, his understanding of human motivation, and his enduring love of liberty. On 9 April he wrote Barff and Barry his last known letters. Ten days later he was dead.

Byron kept five distinct journals during the last eleven years of his life. With only himself as audience (except in the "Alpine Journal," destined for Augusta Leigh), he recorded in their pages—with probably more honesty than in his letters—religious speculations, private reflections on his past life, and objective analyses of his emotional state, along with daily happenings, personal concerns, and his constant fascination with people. The diaries contain details that enlarge the reader's knowledge of the inner man.

He opened his first journal on 14 November 1813 by remarking, "If this had been begun ten years ago, and faithfully kept!!!—heigho! there are too many things I wish never to have remembered, as it is." In a brief but searching self-examination he judged much of his life a waste: "At five-and-twenty, when the better part of life is over, one should be *something;*—and what am I? nothing but five-and-twenty—and the odd months." He added entries rather faithfully until 18 December, when he broke off for a month. Resuming the diary on 16 January 1814, he continued it intermittently until 19 April. He found the journal "a relief. When I am tired—as I generally am—out comes this, and down goes every thing. But I can't read it over;—and God knows what contradictions it may contain. If I am sincere with myself (but I fear one lies more to one's self than to any one else), every page should confute, refute, and utterly abjure its predecessor" (6 December).

The journal of 1813-1814 captures something of the multifaceted Byron: the literary lion who risks becoming a "solitary hobgoblin"; the man of letters who spars with John "Gentleman" Jackson, "the Emperor of Pugilism"; the lover of

*Etching by George Cruikshank published shortly before Byron left England forever on 24 April 1816, three days after he and his wife, who stands on the shore holding their child, signed final separation papers. Byron recites lines from "Fare Thee Well!" written on 18 March, the day after the couple agreed to separate, and published in early April.*

"only one woman—at a time" who claims to have "no very high opinion of the sex."

Whatever his personality of the moment, his intellectual curiosity remains intense. Near the end of the first section of the journal, on 17, 18 December 1813, he comments, "How I do delight in observing life as it really is!—and myself, after all, the worst of any." Lionized by Whig society, the author of *Childe Harold* set down in his diary the news, views, and gossip of this titled circle; yet he preferred the "unequalled" conversation of such figures as the dramatist and politician Richard Brinsley Sheridan. On 20 March 1814 he confided to his journal, "I always begin the day with a bias towards going to parties; but, as the evening advances, my stimulus fails, and I hardly ever go out—and, when I do, always regret it." "I would give the world," he wrote Lady Melbourne in October 1813, "to pass a month with Sheridan or any lady or gentleman of the old school—& hear them talk every day & all day of themselves & acquaintances—& all they have heard & seen in their lives."

He felt that if he "could always read," he "should never feel the want of society" (27 February 1814). From his journal emerge his diverse literary tastes, born of voracious reading from an early age. Embedded in the entries are quotations from such authors as Juvenal, Virgil, Horace, Laurence Sterne, Alexander Pope, and, especially, William Shakespeare (who, Byron wrote Murray on 14 July 1821, was "the *worst* of models" for dramatists, "though the most extraordinary of writers"). In his entry for 24 November 1813, illustrated with a "triangular 'Gradus ad Parnassum,' " Byron ranked contemporary poets. Walter Scott ruled as "the Monarch of Parnassus, and the most *English* of bards." Next in "the living list" came Samuel Rogers. Thomas Moore and Thomas Campbell were "both *third.*" Robert Southey, William Wordsworth, and Samuel Taylor Coleridge occupied the step below. At the base of the triangle figured "THE MANY," dismissed in the text as " ὁι πολλοι " (hoi polloi). After reading "a quantity" of Robert Burns's "unpublished and never-to-be-published, Letters," which were "full of oaths and obscene songs," Byron concluded, perhaps with an eye toward his own complex character, "What an antithetical mind!—tenderness, roughness—delicacy, coarsen ess—sentiment, sensuality—soaring and grovelling, dirt and deity—all mixed up in that one compound of inspired clay!" (13 December). Regarding personal literary efforts, Byron wished he had "a talent for the drama; I would write a tragedy *now.* But no,—it is gone.... To write so as to bring home to the heart, the heart must have been tried,—but, perhaps, ceased to be so. While you are under the influence of passions, you only feel, but cannot describe them.... When all is over,—all, all, and irrevocable,—trust to memory—she is then but too faithful" (20 February 1814).

His political interests are expressed in the journal with customary directness and insight. "I have simplified my politics into an utter detestation of all existing governments.... The fact is, riches are power, and poverty is slavery over the earth, and one sort of establishment is no better, nor *worse,* for a *people* than another" (16 January 1814).

Byron's religious speculations, here and elsewhere, often center on immortality and the afterlife. He sees "no such horror in a 'dreamless sleep,' " nor does he have a "conception of any existence which duration would not render tiresome" (27 November 1813).

In the closing grim entry, dated 19 April 1814—ten years to the day before his death—Byron cites *Macbeth:* " 'And all our *yesterdays* have lighted fools / The way to dusty death,' " then adds, "I will keep no further journal of that same hesternal torch-light; and, to prevent me from returning, like a dog, to the vomit of memory, I tear out the remaining leaves of this volume...."

In June 1816, Byron, then legally separated from his wife, moved into the Villa Diodati near Geneva. On 8 September he wrote Augusta Leigh that he was in good health but that the separation had "broken my heart...." In this humor he kept an "Alpine Journal," with entries dated from 17 to 29 [28] September 1816, during his tour of the Bernese Alps with John Cam Hobhouse. As he noted on the eighteenth, he wrote up "each day's progress" for Augusta. Having a specific audience gives this journal a focus and singleness of purpose lacking in Byron's other diaries. These pages, which he termed a "record of what I have seen & felt" (28 September), contain certain playful incidents—his pelting of Hobhouse with a snowball then later getting "bemired all over" in a morass ("laughed & rode on") (23 September)—but the entries especially, significantly, preserve the descriptions of nature's awesome grandeur and force as well as the poet's melancholy state, which would inform his drama *Manfred* (1817), begun that month but not mentioned until 15 February 1817, in a letter to Murray. In a passage remarkable for its revelation of intense personal anguish, Byron wrote on 23 September 1816 that he passed "*whole woods of withered pines—all withered*—trunks stripped & barkless—branches lifeless—done by a single winter—their appearance reminded me of me & my family.—"

He closed this short diary with a wrenching, heartfelt confession: "the recollections of bitterness—& more especially of recent & more home desolation—which must accompany me through life—have preyed upon me here—and neither the music of the Shepherd—the crashing of the Avalanche—nor the torrent—the mountain—the Glacier—the Forest—nor the Cloud—have for one moment—lightened the weight upon my heart—nor enabled me to lose my own wretched identity in the majesty & the power and the Glory—around—above—& beneath me.—I am past reproaches—...."

On 4 January 1821, while living in Ravenna, Byron wrote, " 'A sudden thought strikes me.' Let me begin a Journal once more." He continued to record his daily life until 27 February. Commanding less space than might be expected are his meetings with the Countess Teresa Guiccioli, whose *cavalier servente* he had become in 1820. Instead, he notes his eclectic reading, his writing, his involvement with the Carbonari (one of the secret revolutionary societies seeking to overthrow Austrian despotism in Italy), and his ruminations and introspections while awaiting the insurrection.

Early in the journal, on 6 January, he wondered why he had been, all his lifetime, "more or less *ennuyé*? ... I do not know how to answer this, but presume that it is constitutional...." The "happiest, perhaps, days" of his life, Byron re-

*Byron in traveling costume (drawing by an anonymous artist; private collection; from Frederic Raphael,* Byron, *1982)*

called on the twelfth, were spent at Cambridge with Edward Noel Long, who drowned in 1809. "*His* friendship, and a violent, though *pure,* love and passion [for John Edleston, a Cambridge chorister]—which held me at the same period—were the then romance of the most romantic period of my life."

He opened his birthday entry on 22 January with a mock epitaph for "the Thirty-Third Year / of an ill-spent Youth"—another statement of regret for "having lived so long, and to so little purpose." Pervading succeeding entries are a sober tone not found in letters of this time and a return to religious musings. "Scrawled this additional page of life's log-book. . . . It has been said that the immortality of the soul is a 'grand peut-être'—but still it is a *grand* one. Every body clings to it—the stupidest, and dullest, and wickedest of human bipeds is still persuaded that he is immortal." On the twenty-eighth, continuing to reflect on "what is to come," he concluded, "It is all a mystery. I feel most things, but I know nothing, except [here, Thomas Moore noted in his edition, the page was marked 'with impatient strokes of the pen']."

Toward the end of the Ravenna journal, Byron wrote at some length on the shifting fortunes of the Italian revolutionary movement. He proclaimed the country's liberation "a grand object—the very *poetry* of politics. Only think—a free Italy!!! Why, there has been nothing like it since the days of Augustus" (18 February). Then, when Neapolitan resistance to Austrian forces faltered, he lamented, "Thus the world goes; and thus the Italians are always lost for lack of union among themselves." He remained undaunted: "Whatever I can do by money, means, or person, I will venture freely for their freedom" (24 February).

*Byron in 1822 (portrait by William West; National Galleries of Scotland)*

At the outset of his next diary (1 May 1821), Byron recalled that he had "carried . . . on" the Ravenna journal until he had filled "one paper-book (thinnish) and two sheets or so of another"; he had "left off partly" because he thought there were military and political matters to attend to, "& partly because I had filled my paper-book.—But the Neapolitans have betrayed themselves & all the World—& those who would have given their blood for Italy can now only give her their tears.—"

Byron's fourth journal, one of his most fascinating, is a compilation of diverse thoughts and memories which he began in Ravenna on 1 May 1821, under the title "My Dictionary." He abandoned it after completing only a reflective introduction and two entries—on "Augustus," the Roman emperor, and on the Scots city of his "earliest childhood," "Aberdeen—Old and New or the Auldtoun & Newtoun." He was doubtless interrupted in this project to write "Anything that comes uppermost" by the banishment, in early July, of Teresa Guiccioli's father and brother, the Counts Ruggero and Pietro Gamba, active in the cause for Italian liberty. Byron resumed the journal, as "Detached Thoughts," on 15 October 1821, making numbered entries until 6 November (he had arrived in Pisa five days earlier to join the Gambas and Teresa). He added only one subsequent paragraph, ending with item number 120 on 18 May 1822.

Here are mingled lively recollections of school days and classmates at Harrow and Cambridge, unvarnished pictures of people and events, and warm anecdotes about women, gamblers, men about town, politicians, actors, and others of his acquaintance. Here, too, are tantalizing hints about incidents too intimate even for inclusion in a private journal. "If I could explain at length the *real* causes which have contributed to increase this perhaps *natural* temperament of mine—this Melancholy which hath made me a bye-word—nobody would wonder——but this is impossible without doing much mischief.—— . . . I cannot conceive anything more strange than some of the earlier parts of [my life]——I have written my memoirs—but omitted *all* the really *consequential & important* parts—from deference to the dead—to the living—and to those who must be both.—" (number 74); "I sometimes think that I should have written the *whole*—as a *lesson*——but it might have proved a lesson to be *learnt*—rather than *avoided*—for passion is a whirlpool, which is not to be viewed nearly without attraction from it's [*sic*] Vortex.——" (number 75); "I must not go on with these reflections—or I shall be letting out some secret or other—to paralyze posterity.—" (number 76).

In other "Detached Thoughts," Byron again speculated on the immortality of the soul—"(as surely the *Mind* or whatever you call it—*is*)"—of which he had "little doubt" (numbers 96, 97, 98). "I am always most religious upon a sunshiny day," he claimed without apparent sarcasm, for he continued, "The Night is also a religious concern—and even more so—when I viewed the Moon and Stars through Herschell's telescope—and saw that they were worlds.—" (numbers 99, 100).

After his arrival in Greece, Byron composed his final journal, his fifth, primarily in the Cephalonian village of Metaxata; there, he awaited a favorable opportunity to join the mainland Greeks, not yet united against the Turks. Beneath some poetic lines dated 19 June 1823, he began the diary on 28 September with a summary of his experiences since sailing from Genoa in mid July. He also recorded his frustrations with the divided Greeks: "I did not come here to join a faction but a nation"; then, more positively, he added, "After all—one should not despair— . . . they may be mended by and bye.—" He "discontinued" the journal "abruptly" on 30 September after receiving news from Augusta Leigh that his daughter Ada was ill. Although he learned early in November of her recovery, he resumed the diary only on 17 December, when the beauty of the village and its natural surroundings "quieted [him] enough to be able to write," an undertaking he claimed was always "a task and a painful one." He closed the entry with an accounting of his financial and personal means to create and "keep on foot a respectable clan or Sept or tribe or horde" of Suliotes, "the best and bravest of the present combatants." His sole motive was "the well-wishing to Greece." Twelve days later he sailed for Missolonghi, arriving on 3 January 1824. There, he took up his journal a last time on 17 February to record that two days earlier, for about ten minutes, he had been seized by a violent convulsion which rendered him "speechless with the features much distorted—but *not* foaming at the mouth."

In 1830, six years after Byron's death in Missolonghi, Murray published Thomas Moore's two-volume edition of *Letters and Journals of Lord Byron With Notices of His Life,* which gave Byron's private prose a wider public. In nearly half of the 561 letters included, Moore made numerous omissions (generally indicated by asterisks); most of the original manuscripts have since disappeared. (Leslie A. Marchand, modern editor of the correspondence and journals, reprints some 2900 letters, "complete and unexpurgated" whenever possible.) Moore likewise bowdlerized the journal of 1813-1814 and the Ravenna journal, whose manuscripts are now lost.

Major critics and writers have lauded Byron's prose. John Gibson Lockhart, reviewing Moore's biography in the *Quarterly Review* ( January 1831), felt confident that "had his life been prolonged," Byron "would have taken his place in the very first rank of our prose literature"; Lockhart was also of the opinion that Byron would "henceforth hold a place in the very first ranks of English letter-writers." In *Praeterita* (1885-1889) John Ruskin analyzed Byron's defense of Sheridan against his detractors (letter to Moore, 1 June 1818); he judged the passage to be "noble. . . . But it is more than noble, it is *perfect,* because the quantity [of thoughts] it holds is not artificially or intricately concentrated, but with the serene swiftness of a smith's hammer-strokes on hot iron; and with choice of terms which, each in its place, will convey far more than they mean in the dictionary." Ruskin also cherished Byron's "measured and living *truth.*" In this century G. Wilson Knight has said of Byron, "I do not know where we shall look for his master in prose."

Lord Byron, pilgrim in life as well as "of Eternity" (as Shelley said in *Adonais,* 1821), penetrated unblinkingly and unblinkered into the world and into himself. As he wrote Lady Melbourne, "anything that confirms or extends one's observations on life & character delights me . . ." (1 October 1813). His letters and journals preserve his diligent investigations and clear-sighted

Missolonghi. Western Greece.
March 4th. 1824.

My dear Moore / Your reproach is unfounded. I have received two letters from you and answered both previous to leaving Cephalonia.— I have not been "quiet" in an Ionian Island but much occupied with business— as the Greek Deputies (if arrived) can tell you.— Neither have I continued "Don Juan" nor any other poem— you go as usual— I presume by some newspaper report or other.

When the proper moment to be of some use— arrived— I came here— and am told that my arrival (with some other circumstances—) has been of at least temporary advantage to the Cause. I had a narrow escape from the Turks— and another from shipwreck on my passage.— On the 15th. (or 16th.) Feby. I had an attack of Apoplexy or Epilepsy— the physicians have not exactly decided which— but the Alternative is agreeable.— — — My Constitution therefore remains between the two opinions— like Mahomet's Sarcophagus between the Magnets.— — All that I can say is— that they nearly bled me to death— by placing the leeches too near the temporal Artery— so that the blood could with difficulty be stopped even with Caustic.— I am supposed to be getting better, slowly however— but my homilies will, I presume, for the future— be like the Archbishop of Granada's— in this case "I order "you a hundred ducats from my treasurer "and wish you a little more taste."— For public matters I refer you to Col. Stanhope's and Capt. Parry's reports— and to all other reports whatsoever.— — There is plenty to do— war without— and tumult within— they "kill a man a week" like Bob Acres in the country.— Parry's Artificers have gone away in alarm— on account of

*Letter to Thomas Moore in which Byron responds to Moore's report of rumors that "instead of pursuing heroic and warlike adventures" in Greece Byron was staying in a comfortable villa and writing a continuation of* Don Juan *(HM 12375; Henry E. Huntington Library and Art Gallery)*

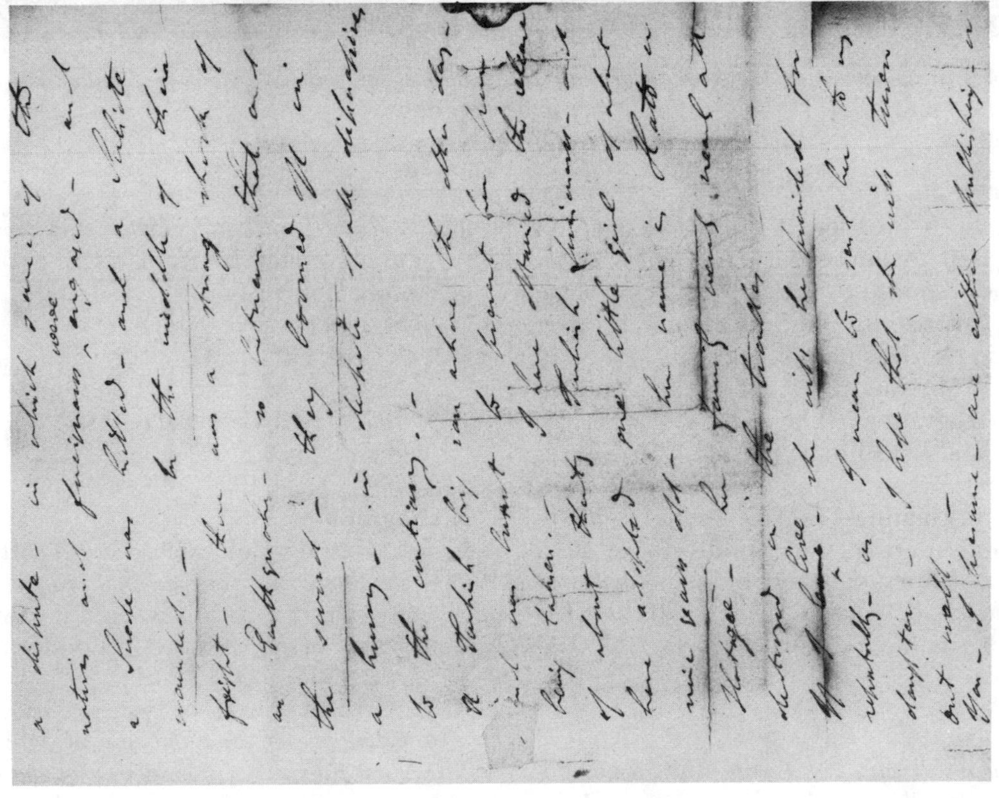

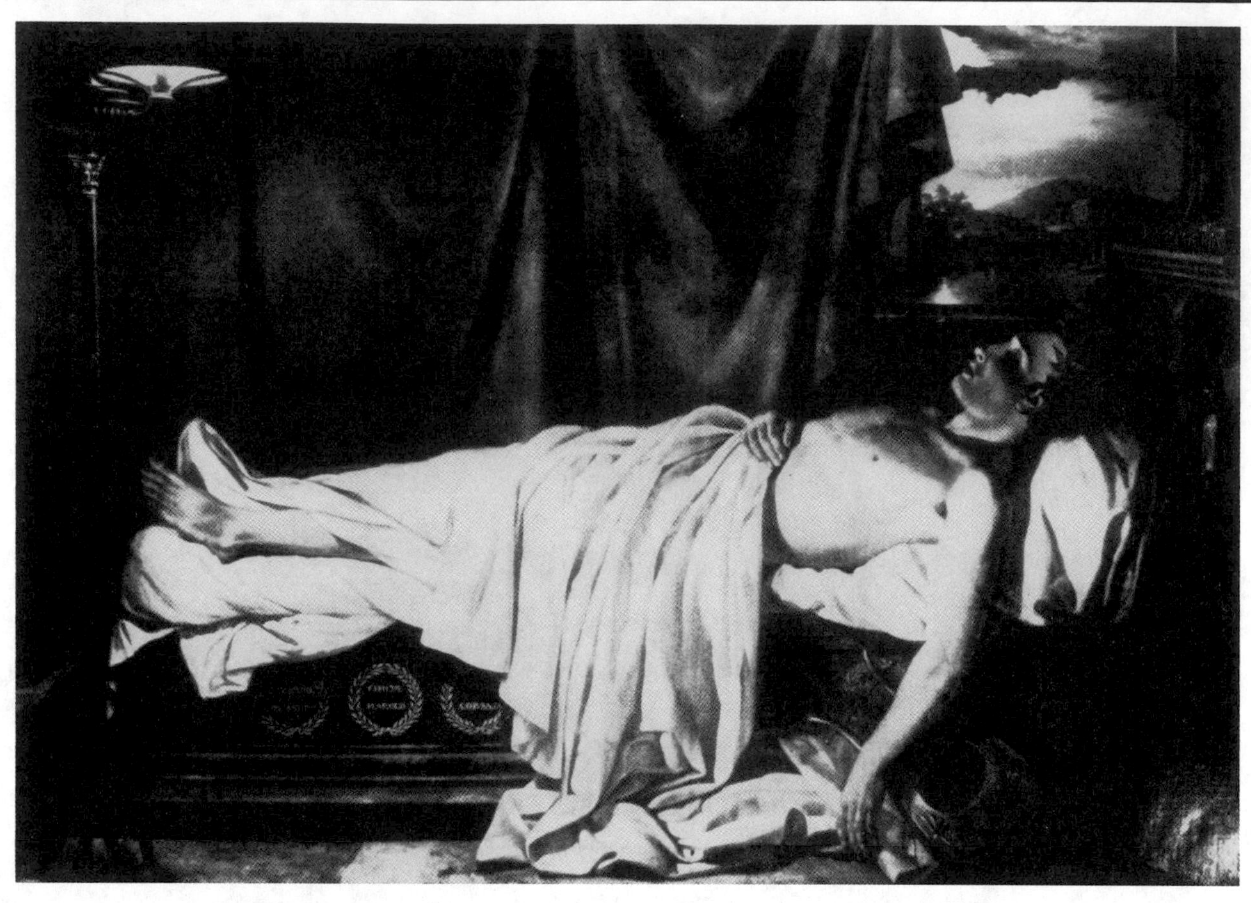

The Death of Byron, *painted by Joseph Odevaere circa 1826, portrays the poet with a crown of laurel and a silenced lyre (Musée Gronginge, Bruges).*

discoveries, which broadened his knowledge and revealed himself to himself, as well as to his intimates. They continue to educate, challenge, amuse, and surprise the modern reader by their honesty, lucidity, vivacity, and mobility. As Mary Shelley wrote Murray in January 1830 concerning Moore's biography: "The great charm of the work to me, and it will have the same for you, is that the Lord Byron I find there is our Lord Byron—the fascinating—faulty—childish—philosophical being—daring the world—docile to a private circle—impetuous and indolent—gloomy and yet more gay than any other. . . . His own letters and journals mirror himself as he was, and are invaluable—."

**Letters:**

*Letters and Journals of Lord Byron With Notices of His Life, by Thomas Moore,* 2 volumes (London: John Murray, 1830; New York: Printed & published by J. & J. Harper, 1830);

*The Works of Lord Byron: Letters and Journals,* 6 volumes, edited by Rowland E. Prothero (London: John Murray, 1898-1901; New York: Scribners, 1898-1901);

*Byron's Letters & Journals,* 12 volumes, edited by Leslie A. Marchand (London: John Murray, 1973-1982; Cambridge, Mass.: Harvard University Press, 1973-1982).

**Bibliographies:**

Ernest Hartley Coleridge, ed., *A Bibliography of the Successive Editions and Translations of Lord Byron's Poetical Works,* in *The Works of Lord Byron: Poetry,* volume 7 (London: John Murray, 1904), pp. 89-348;

R. H. Griffith and H. M. Jones, eds., *A Descriptive Catalogue of an Exhibition of Manuscripts and First Editions of Lord Byron at the University of Texas* (Austin: University of Texas, 1924);

Samuel C. Chew, *Byron in England: His Fame and After-Fame* (London: John Murray, 1924; New York: Scribners, 1924);

Elkin Mathews, *Byron and Byroniana: A Catalogue of Books* (London: Elkin Mathews, 1930);

T. J. Wise, *A Bibliography of the Writings in Verse and Prose of George Gordon Noel, Baron Byron,* 2 volumes (London: Privately printed, 1932, 1933);

Willis W. Pratt, *Lord Byron and His Circle: A Calendar of Manuscripts in the University of Texas Library* (Austin: University of Texas Press, 1947);

Robert Escarpit, *Lord Byron: Un tempérament littéraire,* 2 volumes (Paris: Le Cercle du Livre, 1957), II: 269-324;

David Bonnell Green and Edwin Graves Wilson, eds., *Keats, Shelley, Byron, Hunt and Their Circles. A Bibliography, July 1st, 1950-June 30, 1962* (Lincoln: University of Nebraska Press, 1964);

John Jump, "Byron," in *English Poetry: Select Bibliographical Guides,* edited by A. E. Dyson (London: Oxford University Press, 1971);

Samuel C. Chew and Ernest J. Lovell, Jr., "Byron," in *The English Romantic Poets: A Review of Research and Criticism,* third edition, revised, edited by Frank Jordan (New York: Modern Language Association of America, 1972);

A. C. Elkins, Jr., and L. J. Forstner, *The Romantic Movement Bibliography, 1936-1970,* 7 volumes (Ann Arbor, Mich.: Pierian Press, 1973);

Oscar José Santucho, *George Gordon, Lord Byron: A Comprehensive Bibliography of Secondary Materials in English, 1807-1974,* with "A Critical Review of Research," by Clement Tyson Goode, Jr. (Metuchen, N.J.: Scarecrow Press, 1977);

Robert A. Hartley, David Bonnell Green, and others, *Keats, Shelley, Byron, Hunt and Their Circles. A Bibliography, July 1st, 1962-December 31, 1974* (Lincoln: University of Nebraska Press, 1978);

Francis Lewis Randolph, *Studies for a Byron Bibliography* (Lititz, Pa.: Sutter House, 1979);

John Clubbe, "George Gordon, Lord Byron," in *The English Romantic Poets: A Review of Research and Criticism,* fourth edition, edited by Frank Jordan (New York: Modern Language Association of America, 1985).

**Biographies:**

R. C. Dallas, *Recollections of the Life of Lord Byron, from the Year 1808 to the End of 1814 . . .* (London: Printed for Charles Knight, 1824);

John Galt, *The Life of Lord Byron* (London: Colburn & Bentley, 1830);

Edward John Trelawny, *Recollections of the Last Days of Shelley and Byron* (Boston: Ticknor & Fields, 1858); revised and enlarged as *Records of Shelley, Byron and the Author,* 2 volumes (London: B. M. Pickering, 1878);

Ralph Milbanke, Earl of Lovelace, *Astarte* (London: Chiswick Press, 1905); revised and enlarged edition, edited by Mary, Countess of Lovelace (London: Christophers, 1921);

Ethel Colburn Mayne, *Byron* (2 volumes, London: Methuen, 1912; New York: Scribners, 1912; second edition, revised, 1 volume, London: Methuen, 1924; New York: Scribners, 1924);

Peter Quennell, *Byron: The Years of Fame* (New York: Viking, 1935);

Quennell, *Byron in Italy* (London: Collins, 1941; New York: Viking, 1941);

Willis W. Pratt, *Byron at Southwell: The Making of a Poet* (Austin: University of Texas Press, 1948);

Iris Origo, *The Last Attachment: The Story of Byron and Teresa Guiccioli* (London: Cape, 1949; New York: Scribners, 1949);

Leslie A. Marchand, *Byron: A Biography,* 3 volumes (New York: Knopf, 1957); revised and abridged as *Byron: A Portrait,* 1 volume (New York: Knopf, 1970);

Doris Langley Moore, *The Late Lord Byron: Posthumous Dramas* (London: John Murray, 1961; Philadelphia: Lippincott, 1961; revised edition, London: John Murray, 1976);

Moore, *Lord Byron: Accounts Rendered* (London: John Murray, 1974; New York: Harper & Row, 1974).

**References:**

Bernard Blackstone, *Byron: A Survey* (London: Longmans, 1975);

Samuel C. Chew, *Byron in England: His Fame and After-Fame* (London: John Murray, 1924; New York: Scribners, 1924);

John Clubbe, "Byron as Autobiographer," *South Atlantic Quarterly,* 82 (Summer 1983): 314-320;

Clubbe, "Byron in His Letters," *South Atlantic Quarterly,* 74 (Autumn 1975): 507-515;

Clubbe, *Byron in the Alps: The Journal of John Cam Hobhouse, 17-29 September 1816,* in *Byron et la Suisse: Deux Etudes* (Genève: Librairie Droz, 1982): pp. 7-59;

Clubbe, "Byron's Letters: The Poet as Prosaist," *South Atlantic Quarterly*, 77 (Spring 1978): 242-250;

Peter W. Graham, ed., *Byron's Bulldog: The Letters of John Cam Hobhouse to Lord Byron* (Columbus: Ohio State University Press, 1984);

Peter Gunn, Introduction to *Lord Byron: Selected Prose*, edited by Gunn (Harmondsworth, U.K.: Penguin, 1972);

G. Wilson Knight, *Lord Byron: Christian Virtues* (London: Routledge & Paul, 1952; New York: Oxford University Press, 1953);

Ernest J. Lovell, Jr., ed., *His Very Self and Voice: Collected Conversations of Lord Byron* (New York: Macmillan, 1954);

Lovell, ed., *Lady Blessington's* Conversations of Lord Byron (Princeton, N.J.: Princeton University Press, 1969);

Lovell, ed., *Medwin's* Conversations of Lord Byron (Princeton, N.J.: Princeton University Press, 1966);

Alan Lang Strout, ed., *John Bull's Letter to Lord Byron* (Norman: University of Oklahoma Press, 1947);

Paul G. Trueblood, *Lord Byron*, revised edition (New York: Twayne, 1977).

**Papers:**

Rich holdings of Byron papers are housed in the archives of John Murray, London, Byron's publisher; in the Roe-Byron Collection at Newstead Abbey, the poet's ancestral home outside Nottingham; and in the Library of the University of Texas. Other major institutions with notable Byron collections include Yale, Harvard, the Pierpont Morgan Library, the Carl H. Pforzheimer Library, the New York Public Library, the University of Pennsylvania, the Henry E. Huntington Library, and the Keats-Shelley Memorial House, Rome. Especially useful is the section devoted to Byron in *The Index of English Literary Manuscripts*, volume 4: 1800-1900, part 1, A-G, compiled by Barbara Rosenbaum and Pamela White (Bronx, N.Y.: Mansell, 1982).

# Richard Carlile

*(8 December 1790 - 10 February 1843)*

Richard D. Fulton
*Clark College*

SELECTED BOOKS: *The Order for the Administration of the Loaves and Fishes; or, The Communion of Corruptions Host* (London: R. Carlile, 1817);

*A Letter to the Society for the Suppression of Vice, on Their Malignant Efforts to Prevent a Free Enquiry After Truth and Reason* (London: R. Carlile, 1819);

*The Life of Thomas Paine, Written purposely to Bind with His Writings* (London: Printed & published by R. Carlile, 1821);

*An Address to Men of Science; Calling upon Them to Stand Forward and Vindicate the Truth from the Foul Grasp and Persecution of Superstition* (London: R. Carlile, 1821);

*An Effort to Set at Rest Some Little Disputes and Misunderstandings between the Reformers of Leeds* (London: R. Carlile, 1821);

*To the Reformers of Great Britain* (London: R. Carlile, 1821);

*Observations on "Letters to a Friend on the Evidences, Doctrines, and Duties of the Christian Religion, by Olinthus Gregory, LL.D."* (London: R. Carlile, 1821);

*Every Man's Book; or, What Is God?* (London: R. Carlile, 1826);

*Every Woman's Book; or, What Is Love?* (London: R. Carlile, 1826; revised, 1828);

*Richard Carlile's First Sermon upon the Mount. A Sermon upon the Subject of Deity, Preached on Sunday, Sept. 9* (London: R. Carlile, 1827);

*The Gospel According to Richard Carlile, Shewing the True Parentage, Birth, and Life of Our Allegorical Lord and Saviour, Jesus Christ* (London: R. Carlile, 1827);

*An Exposure of Freemasonry, or, A Mason's Printed Manual* (London: R. Carlile, 1831);

*A New View of Insanity; in which is set forth the present mismanagement of public and private madhouses* (London: R. Carlile, 1831);

*Church Reform: The Only Means to that End, Stated in a Letter to Sir Robert Peel* (London: R. Carlile, 1835);

*A Dictionary of Some of the Names of the Sacred Scriptures Translated into the English Language, Showing that They Are Names of Offices, Principles, and Attributes of Deity* (Manchester: T. P. Carlile, 1837);

*A View and Review of Robert Owen's Projects: or, The Manspel, According to Robert Owen, Criticised by the Gospel, According to Richard Carlile* (London: Printed by Alfred Carlile, 1838);

*An Address to That Portion of the People of Great Britain and Ireland Calling Themselves Reformers* (Manchester: Published by T. Paine Carlile, 1839);

*Unitarian, or Socian and Social Catechism* (New York: G. Vale, 1846).

PERIODICALS: *Sherwin's Weekly Political Register,* 1-5, edited by William T. Sherwin, published by Carlile (London, 5 April 1817 - 21 August 1819);

*Gracchus,* no. 1 [no more published], edited by John Whitehead, published by Carlile (London, 1818);

*Gorgon,* nos. 1-8, edited by John Wade, Francis Place, and John Gast, published by Carlile (London, 1818);

*Republican,* 1-14, edited by Carlile (London, 27 August 1819 - 29 December 1826);

*Deist,* edited by Carlile (London, 1819 1820; 1826);

*Moralist,* nos. 1-16, edited by Carlile (London, 1823);

*Newgate Monthly Magazine,* 1-2, edited by Carlile and other radicals in Newgate Gaol (London, September 1824 - August 1826);

*Lion,* 1-4, edited by Carlile (London, 4 January 1828 - 25 December 1829);

*Prompter,* nos. 1-53, edited by Carlile (London, 13 November 1830 - 12 November 1831);

*Union,* nos. 1-10, edited by Carlile (London, 26 November 1831 - 28 January 1832);

*Devil's Pulpit* [weekly], edited by Carlile (London, March-April 1831);

*Richard Carlile (artist unknown; from Theophila Carlile Campbell,* The Battle of the Press, as Told in the Story of the Life of Richard Carlile, *1899)*

*Isis,* 1, formally edited by Eliza Sharples; many issues edited by Carlile (London, 11 February - 15 December 1832);

*Gauntlet,* nos. 1-60, edited by Carlile (London, 9 February 1833 - 29 or 30 March 1834);

*Political Soldier,* nos. 1-5, edited by Carlile (London, December 1833 - April 1834);

*London Star,* nos. 1-2, edited by Carlile (London, April 1834);

*Scourge for the Littleness of "Great" Men,* nos. 1-16, edited by Carlile (London, 4 October 1834 - 21 February 1835);

*Phoenix,* 1, nos. 1-4, edited by Carlile (London, 5-26 February 1837);

*Church* [weekly], nos. 1-8, edited by Carlile (London, April-May 1838);

*Carlile's Railroad to Heaven* (London, 1838);

*Carlile's Political Register* [weekly], nos. 1-9 (London, October-December [?] 1839);

*Christian Warrior,* 1, nos. 1-4, edited by Carlile (London, 7-28 January 1843).

Richard Carlile is a paradoxical figure. He was a radical journalist who split with most of the radicals of his day. He was a freethinker, a self-professed infidel, who embraced a mystical, personal form of Christianity and even published a short-lived periodical titled *Carlile's Railroad to Heaven* (1838). He was a moral reformer who left his wife and proclaimed a "moral marriage" to Eliza Sharples. He was an indifferent orator who spoke to crowds numbering in the thousands. In life, he had hundreds of loyal followers who supported him morally and monetarily while he served numerous prison sentences for attacking the government. At his funeral his mourners could be counted on the fingers of one hand. He was, however, at the very center of the battle for press and religious freedom in the early nineteenth century, and even his detractors admit that his actions and his example advanced those causes immeasurably.

CARLILE
AND
PAINE'S
Age of Reason

BRITISH FORUM
Removed to the
CROWN AND ANCHOR TAVERN,
STRAND.
*Friday, June 25th,* 1819.

QUESTION

*Ought the Conduct of Mr. CARLILE, the Bookseller, in continuing to publish PAINE'S AGE OF REASON, and other Deistical Works, notwithstanding the numerous Prosecutions instituted against him, to be censured as a serious Aggravation of his Offence, and an obstinate Defiance of the established Religion of his Country; or approved as a striking Instance of the rectitude of his Intentions, and of his bold and manly Perseverance in the Cause of Reason and Truth?*

The approaching Trial of Mr. Carlile for the Publication of Paine's Age of Reason, &c. has attracted the Attention of the Religious, and Political World, and excited a more than ordinary Interest among the Friends and Advocates of Rational and Free Inquiry,

The Subject is of momentous Importance, inasmuch as it involves not only Great and Essential Points of our Established Faith, but also that Liberty of Conscience, which has ever been considered as the Constitutional Privilege of every Briton, and which can only be exercised through the Medium of Free and Rational Discussion.

In compliance with the Wishes of several respectable and enlightened Friends of this Institution, the above most Elegant and Spacious Room has been engaged by the Managers, hoping that the Attendance of that Evening will sufficiently compensate them for the Increased Expense and Trouble which they have Incurred upon this Occasion.

N. B. Tickets of Admission, Price One Shilling each, to be had at Mr. Carlile's, 55, Fleet Street.

Doors open at half past Seven.—Chair taken at half past Eight precisely.

ADMITTANCE ONE SHILLING.

*Announcement for a meeting called by Carlile after he was charged with blasphemous libel for publishing and selling an edition of Thomas Paine's* Age of Reason

He was born on 8 December 1790 in Ashburton, Devon, to Richard and Elizabeth Brookings Carlile. His father was a workingman, self-taught, whose great achievement was to publish a now-forgotten book of mathematics. Shortly after the birth of Mary-Anne, Richard's younger sister, Richard Carlile, Sr., deserted his family. Carlile later claimed that his father had been a hopeless alcoholic; he himself rarely touched liquor, possibly because of the example his father had set. His mother was a pious Church of England woman whose insistence on devotions and church duties had the effect of turning Carlile toward free thought as he grew older. His education was typical of that experienced by most working-class children: some church schooling, some free schooling, some home schooling. He was for all intents and purposes self-taught; because of that, he maintained a high regard for learning throughout his life and never stopped trying to improve his own range of knowledge.

After Carlile left home, in 1803 he took up the rather parlous trade of tinplate working, a craft whose usefulness was fast being replaced by the products of the Industrial Revolution. The precariousness of his employment, the brutal conditions for all workingmen, the resentments that he felt from a young lifetime of taking orders, and his dawning recognition of his own brilliance all contributed to his dissatisfaction with his lot. In addition, he had the pressures of being a family man, having married Jane Carlile, whom he had gotten pregnant, in 1813.

His dissatisfaction led him to radical politics in 1816-1817. He gave up his tinplate job and began hawking the *Black Dwarf, Political Register,* and other radical newspapers and pamphlets in the London streets. In the spring of 1817, he took on the politically dangerous job of being named publisher of *Sherwin's Weekly Political Register,* dangerous because government prosecutors trained their attention on publishers when carrying out their increasingly numerous reprisals against the radical press. Carlile's publishing activities, especially his pamphlet publishing, piqued the interest of prosecutors in the Home Office. They watched him, spied on him, and eventually charged him with blasphemous libel in 1817, after he had published three parodies by William Hone (without Hone's permission and after Hone had agreed to withdraw the publications because *he* had been threatened with prosecution). Because of Carlile's unauthorized printing, Hone was charged with the same crime. He gained wide publicity by skillfully defending himself, and he emerged from the trials a hero of the radical movement. Carlile, who had hoped for similar adulation, was quietly released after serving four months, when the case against Hone was dropped. Carlile never lost his resentment against the mainstream radical reformers who celebrated Hone's release while totally ignoring him.

Despite this slight, Carlile's prison time established his credentials in the movement. While in prison, he carried out perhaps his most important publishing project, the reprinting of Thomas Paine's essays in the *Weekly Political Register.* After he was released, he began republishing the essays in cheap bound volumes, thus making available to the masses the important works of the chief anti-Christian republican of the day. That simple act may have been his most important contribution to the culture and politics of the early nineteenth century, more than his battles for press freedom, more than his battles for political reform. Paine's works provided guidance and ideas to two generations of radicals struggling against what they perceived as a repressive political, social, and religious system. Carlile not only published Paine, but he also read the works avidly and became a convert especially to the radical free-thought doctrines that guided his development over the next twenty-five years. And it was because of Paine that he suffered his second prosecution.

One of the most effective semiofficial tools of the Home Office prosecutors was the Society for the Suppression of Vice and the Encouragement of Religion and Virtue. Its original purpose was to combat drinking, gambling, whoring, and the other pastimes that its middle-class membership saw as staples of the working class, but by 1819 it had turned its attention chiefly to infidel literature, the kind of radical and free-thought publications on which Carlile was making a modest fortune. In January 1819 the society swore out an indictment against Carlile for the publication and sale of Paine's *Age of Reason.* Although he spent some time in Newgate Gaol in February, he did not come to trial until late in the year, after the Peterloo Massacre, in Manchester on 16 August, which he witnessed. Eleven died and more than four hundred were injured during a cavalry charge intended to disband a mass meeting in St. Peter's Field of demonstrators for parliamentary reform. The Peterloo Massacre permanently established Carlile's reputation. His articles attacking the government over the incident in the last issue of the *Weekly Political Register* (21 August) and in early issues of the *Republican* (which he began after the demise of the *Register*) resulted in charges of seditious libel being added to the earlier charges of blasphemy and set the stage for the prosecutions that made him a symbol for radical resistance.

Carlile's blasphemy trial began on 13 October in front of a large crowd which included the radical reformers Hone, Thomas J. Wooler, and Henry ("Orator") Hunt. In the tradition of Hone and Wooler, he defended himself. Unlike Hone and Wooler, he lost, either because of the ineptness of his defense (as his biographer Joel H. Wiener claims) or because of the corruptness of the judicial system (as another biographer, Guy Aldred, would claim). He was equally unsuccessful in his second trial; the final sentence was for three years in Dorchester Gaol, and a fine of fifteen hundred pounds.

Life at Dorchester was not overly difficult for Carlile. While radical booksellers and journalists waged the so-called War of the Shopmen against the government, he lived in private rooms, and spent two or three pounds a week on food to avoid the terrible meals suffered by the common prisoners. He was allowed to continue his writing and his learning. He edited the *Republi-*

# The Republican.

No. 2. Vol. I.] LONDON, FRIDAY, SEPT. 3, 1819. [PRICE 2D.

A LETTER TO HIS ROYAL HIGHNESS THE PRINCE REGENT,

*On his thanking the Magisterial and Yeomanry Assassins of Manchester for* MURDERS COMMITTED *by them on the 16th of August last.*

*London, August* 30, 1819.

SIR,

THE general indignation and disgust excited in the public mind, in consequence of the *atrocious Murders* committed by the Yeomanry Cavalry, at the instigation of the Magistrates of Manchester, on the bodies of the inhabitants of that town, assembled in a legal and peaceable meeting, for the purpose of discussing the best means to obtain a redress of their grievances, and a radical reform of the representative system, could have been exceeded by nothing but the Chief Magistrate of the Country sanctioning, and actually returning thanks to the *murderers!!!*—This, Sir, it appears you have done, through the medium of your Secretary of State for the Home Department, the ever-memorable SIDMOUTH; and as the document cannot be too generally read, or too much known, I shall here insert it, and make such observations upon it, as to me seem necessary.

*First page of Carlile's third article on the Peterloo Massacre*

*can* until his release, and continued his political agitation throughout the early 1820s from prison—paradoxically, a position of relative safety. Meanwhile, his wife, Jane, continued the work of composing the *Republican* in the London offices, a position of decided peril during the War of the Shopmen. She was charged with seditious libel in 1820. Carlile insisted on writing her defense, because, according to Wiener, he believed that "lawyers were parasites who belonged to an oppressive political faction." She was convicted in January 1821 and joined him at Dorchester. In spring of that year his sister Mary-Anne was charged with seditious libel for publishing one of his tracts and a piece on Thomas Paine. He wrote her defense. Mary-Anne joined Jane and Richard at Dorchester in July. One by one his shopmen were charged; he defended them; they joined him and his immediate family. Clearly, he was using the trials to make political statements; just as clearly, the statements were not yet having any practical effect, at least as far as Carlile's immediate associates were concerned.

But the longer he and his tribe stayed in jail, the more famous he became. His words in the *Republican* and in his various pamphlets rang with the note of authority. As a matter of principle he refused to pay his fine, and his sentence was extended, again and again. Finally, the government relented, and he was released after stretching a three-year sentence to six years, but in part because of his intransigence the government curbed its almost reactionary prosecutions of radical journalists. To the freethinkers, republicans, anarchists, and all the radical underground, Carlile had won, and his sacrifice had been worthwhile.

After the *Republican* folded in 1825, Carlile began to turn his attention away from the radical political movements and to focus on free thought, "infidelity," and anti-Christian agitation. In the 1830s he quarreled with most of the political agitators of any importance, insisting that only through religious reform could anything meaningful in political and social reform be accomplished. He opposed two of the fundamental programs of the political reformers of his day: cooperatives and universal suffrage. In 1830 he established a forum for his ideas by leasing a large building-cum-meeting-hall on Blackfriars Road, which he called the Rotunda. He and his new philosophical partner, the Reverend Robert Taylor, used the Rotunda to promote infidel programs. Perhaps more important, Carlile rented space at the Rotunda to other radical groups—even those whose positions he opposed, like the Owenites' cooperative societies—and thus turned the Rotunda into a center for radical politics and working-class teachings. Thus, he reestablished himself as a central figure in the radical movement, even though it was more as landlord than as philosophical leader (or martyr).

In January 1831 Carlile was once again in the courts, this time answering a charge of seditious libel. The charge was a result of a rather modest article in the *Prompter,* a political newspaper he established in late 1830. In the article, he merely showed sympathy for agricultural rioters—the so-called Swing Rioters—and urged them to continue their resistance until they met success. Although the prosecution was totally unexpected, Carlile welcomed it as another opportunity to battle with the government for freedom of expression. Again he defended himself. Again he was convicted, and he was sentenced this time to two years in prison and a two-hundred-pound fine, which he again refused to pay. Within a few months he was joined by Taylor, who was convicted for blasphemous libel. Clearly, the government considered Carlile and his Rotunda to be a serious, continuing menace to public order; in fact, it is revealing that Carlile the radical journalist was convicted of sedition, while William Cobbett, the radical politician who was arrested at about the same time on similar charges, was acquitted. On the other hand, Cobbett did not have Carlile directing his defense, and Carlile did. In any case, Carlile's refusal once again to pay his fine stretched the two-year sentence to thirty months.

In 1832, while still in prison, he announced that he was taking young Elizabeth Sharples, the Rotunda manager in his absence, as a "moral mistress." The devoted Eliza launched a new periodical, the *Isis,* for which Carlile wrote extensively (whether or not he edited it, coedited it, or merely wrote for it is a matter of debate among literary historians). Through the pages of the *Isis,* and the *Gauntlet* (which he also edited while in prison), he developed his new religious philosophy, a creed that went beyond the simple anti-Christianity that he had preached at the Rotunda and embraced Christ as the embodiment of human reason. For years he had claimed that the Bible and other religious documents were allegories; now, with time to convert his attitudes into a coherent philosophy, he created a new Christian religion and, in the pages of the *Isis,* declared himself its first convert.

In early 1833 he announced his "moral divorce" from Jane and his "moral marriage" to Eliza. After his release from prison in August 1833, he devoted himself to spreading his gospel across England. For the next seven years he traveled widely, virtually abandoning Eliza and his three new children, obtaining living expenses for himself through the generosity of a few old-time supporters and subscriptions. His audiences varied from a handful in Cumberland to crowds of two thousand in Lancaster. However, his support dwindled in the 1840s as he became more mystical and less disposed to support the bread-and-butter issues of the working class: chartism, anti-Corn Law agitation, universal suffrage, cooperatives and so on. His later newspapers were little more than periodical tracts concerned with the establishment of a pure church that would sweep away bad government and bad law and bad social conditions. He died on 10 February 1843; at his funeral, several members of his family left when an Anglican priest insisted on conducting services. Only some old friends and a few curious associates observed his interment. His brain, which he left to science, was dissected at St. Thomas's Hospital.

Carlile's political beliefs changed radically over his fifty-two years. As a young man, under the influence of Wooler, Hunt, and others, he espoused a radical republicanism that included thinly veiled calls for revolution. It should be remembered, though, that he lived during a time when many English fully expected a French-style revolution in Great Britain, and the language of reform tended toward the language of revolution. In these early days, when he considered religion at all it was only to attack it as a portion of the oppressive system which unfairly condemned the majority of the people of England to a life of

*Eliza Sharples Carlile (artist unknown; from Theophila Carlile Campbell,* The Battle of the Press, as Told in the Story of the Life of Richard Carlile, *1899)*

misery. Slowly he moved toward a belief that religious reform was a necessary prerequisite for any political or social reform; only when the people could clearly see that their salvation lay in his (Carlile's) Jesus Christ could they be truly free.

He began to see his mission to be the apostle of a unified Christian religion which he called the new Catholicism. In 1832 he outlined his basic beliefs in the *Isis:* "The kingdom of heaven is to be the reign of reason and honesty . . . Who is christ? It is the personification of the principle of reason, that cometh from man and man only, and thus is figuratively termed the Son of Man" (12 April 1832). Later, he said "I DECLARE MYSELF A CONVERT TO THE TRUTH AS IT IS IN THE GOSPEL OF JESUS CHRIST. I DECLARE MYSELF A BELIEVER IN THE TRUTH OF THE CHRISTIAN RELIGION." "This now only remains to be done," he said. "All the disputes between the Christian sects must be brought to the one question of *letter or spirit, allegory or history, personification or principle of the Godhead.* I declare for the *spirit,* the *allegory, and the principle*" (5 May 1832). He immersed himself so thoroughly in the allegorical truth of Scripture that he became monomaniacal and at times sounded unbalanced: in the *Political Register* in 1839 he insisted that the queen should appoint a group to examine scriptural interpretations and thus prove that he, Carlile, was a prophet. After that, his teachings would transform mankind and the queen would be "crowned on Zion" and "triumph over the Philistines" (23 November 1839).

Carlile's attitude toward science and literature closely approximates the general attitude of nineteenth-century reformers. Even at his most mystical, when he began signing himself Reverend Richard Carlile, he insisted on adding MBAAS (Member British Association for the Advancement of Science). Like many radicals in later years, he saw science as mankind's salvation. He became fascinated with pseudosciences such

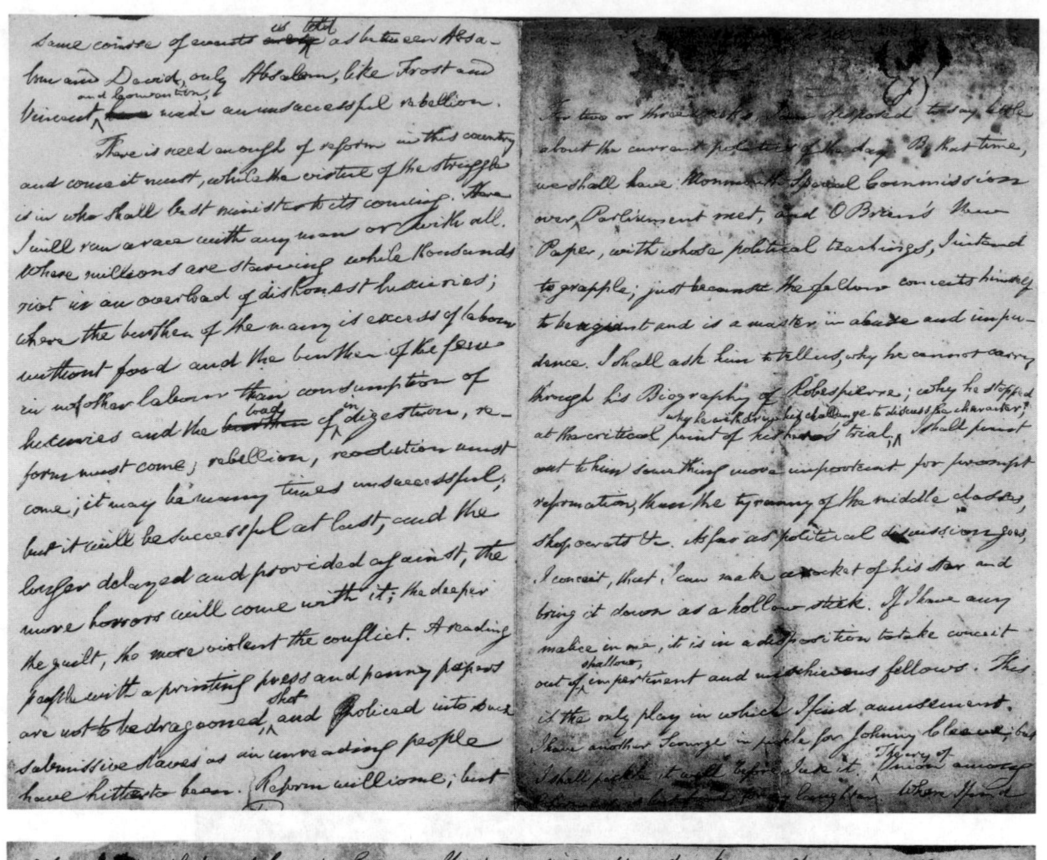

same course of events as that as between Absalom and David, only Absalom, like Frost and Vincent, and Convention, made an unsuccessful rebellion.

There is need enough of reform in this country and come it must, while the virtue of the struggle is in who shall best minister to its coming. Here I will run a race with any man or with all. Where millions are starving while thousands riot in an overload of dishonest luxuries; where the burthen of the many is excess of labour without food and the burthen of the few in no other labour than consumption of luxuries and the load of indigestion, reform must come; rebellion, revolution must come; it may be many times unsuccessful; but it will be successful at last, and the longer delayed and provided against, the more horrors will come with it; the deeper the guilt, the more violent the conflict. A reading people with a printing press and penny papers are not to be dragooned, shot and policed into such submissive slaves as an unreading people have hitherto been. Reform will come; but

(7)

For two or three weeks, I am disposed to say little about the current politics of the day. By that time, we shall have Monmouth Special Commissions over, Parliament met, and O'Brien's New Paper, with whose political teachings, I intend to grapple; just because the fellow conceits himself to be a giant and is a master in abuse and impudence. I shall ask him to tell us, why he cannot carry through his Biography of Robespierre; why he stopped at the critical point of his hero's trial, why he withdrew his challenge to discuss his character; I shall point out to him something more important for prompt reformation, than the tyranny of the middle classes, shopocrats &c. As far as political discussion goes, I conceit, that I can make a rocket of his star and bring it down as a hollow stick. If I have any malice in me, it is in a disposition to take conceit out of shallow, impertinent and mischievous fellows. This is the only play in which I find amusement. I have another Scourge in pickle for Johnny Cleave, but I shall pickle it well before I use it. Theory of Union among [illegible] laughter. When I find

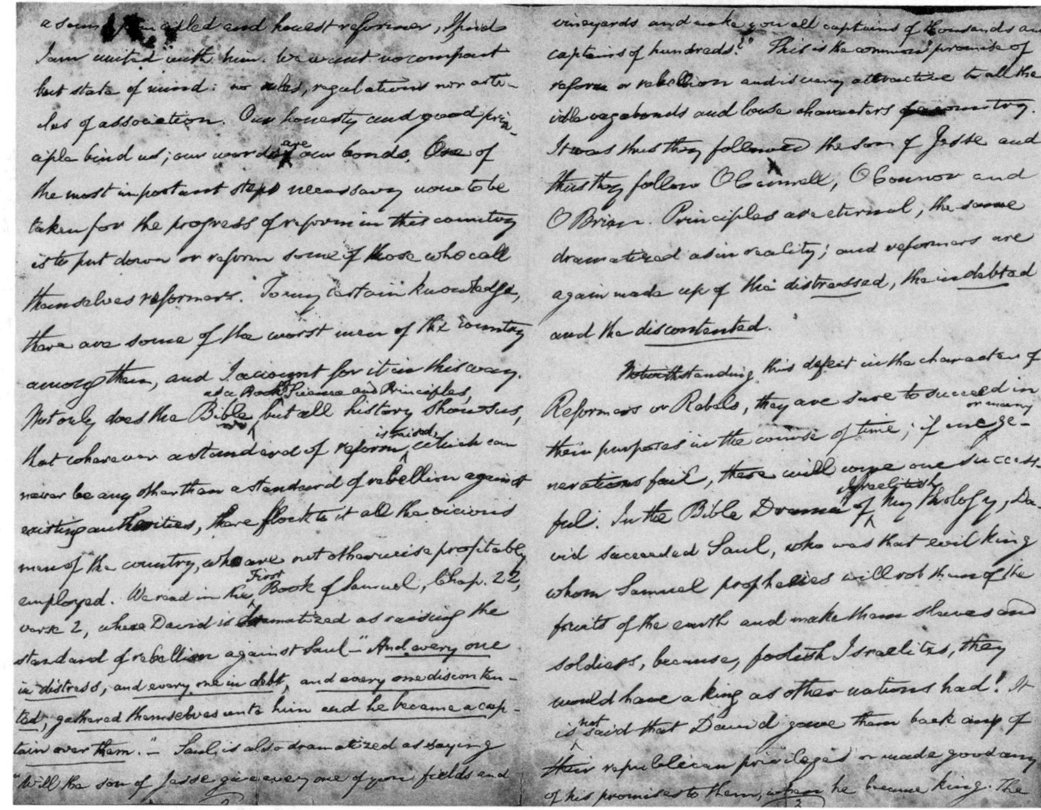

a sound [illegible]cipled and honest reformer, I find I am united with him. We want no compact but state of mind: no rules, regulations nor articles of association. Our honesty and good principle bind us; our words are our bonds. One of the most important steps necessary now to be taken for the progress of reform in this country is to put down or reform some of those who call themselves reformers. To my certain knowledge, there are some of the worst men of the country amongst them, and I account for it in this way. Not only does the Bible as a Book of Science and Principles, but all history shows us, that wherever a standard of reform is raised, which can never be any other than a standard of rebellion against existing authorities, there flock to it all the vicious men of the country, who are not otherwise profitably employed. We read in the First Book of Samuel, Chap. 22, verse 2, where David is dramatized as raising the standard of rebellion against Saul – "And every one in distress, and every one in debt, and every one discontented, gathered themselves unto him and he became a captain over them." – Saul is also dramatized as saying "Will the son of Jesse give every one of you fields and

vineyards and make you all captains of thousands and captains of hundreds?" This is the common promise of reform or rebellion and is very attractive to all the idle vagabonds and loose characters [illegible]. It was thus they followed the son of Jesse and thus they follow O'Connell, O'Connor and O'Brien. Principles are eternal, the same dramatized as in reality; and reformers are again made up of the distressed, the indebted and the discontented.

Notwithstanding this defect in the character of Reformers or Rebels, they are sure to succeed in their purposes in the course of time; if one or many generations fail, there will come one successful. In the Bible Drama of [illegible] theology, David succeeded Saul, who was that evil king whom Samuel prophesied will rob them of the fruits of the earth and make them slaves and soldiers, because, foolish Israelites, they would have a king as other nations had! It is not said that David gave them back any of their republican privileges or made good any of his promises to them, when he became king. The

*Pages from an 1839 speech in which Carlile criticized young radical leaders such as Bronterre O'Brien, Feargus O'Connor, and Daniel O'Connell for being too egalitarian (RC 340; Henry E. Huntington Library and Art Gallery)*

Your petitioner therefore most humbly but most earnestly and religiously prays, that this question, so simple as to its authorities and means of enquiry, yet of so great an immediate interest to all the nations of the earth, as a correction of religious and political errors, one of greater import than was ever before presented to a legislature, may be referred to a Special Committee of the Spiritual or other Peers of your Right Honourable House and receive that thorough and honest investigation the which so grave and important a question is entitled to as having upon the present and future welfare of the whole human race; but more especially upon the present moral, political and religious conditions of the people and Church of this country.

Your humble petitioner is fortified with an abundance of religious, political and moral reasons for the step he is now taking; but above them all in the necessary retention of a well endowed Church Establishment, that shall contain morally and religiously retain and educate the whole people of this country and so remove its present painful and dangerous divisions about the all important subject of religion.

So prays your Lordships' humble servant Richard Carlile

Enfield Highway
March 2 - 1840

To the Right Honourable, the Lords Spiritual and Temporal, in Parliament assembled.

1840 (C)

The Petition of Richard Carlile, of the Parish of Enfield, in the County of Middlesex, most humbly showeth: (C)

That your petitioner is most zealous and anxious for the extension among the whole people and for the means of preserving a Church Established by Law, as a necessary and indispensable moral power in the State.

That the idea of Dissent from the Church Established by Law has always been painful to your humble petitioner, when considered as consisting of the initiation of civil and political strife.

That the Church now Established by Law, is, in its articles, constitutions and canons, a popular institution corrective of whatever may from time to time admit of being improved in its doctrine and discipline, and therefore affords no just ground of separation and dissent.

That, as the Church, now established, is alleged to have had its origin in Jewish History, your most humble petitioner has devoted a large portion of the last twenty years of his life to the search of causes, grounds and reasons of dissent, schism and heresy in ecclesiastical history, and humbly opines, that he has reached the root of religious error and dissension in the discovery of a mistake made in Jewish History, and that he has found correct data which warrant him to say, that neither Jews, nor Israelites

as [illegible] existed as an independent political nation in any known or recorded part of the earth, before the time of Herod the Great, who was made King of a small territory in Palestine of Syria then first called Judea, by the Roman Emperor Augustus, about the third year of his reign, Herod himself not being a Jew, nor the choice of the Jews, the office being despotic and in burlesque of the theocracy and religion of the Jews.

That the Jews retained this nominal political distinction tributary to the Roman Empire, just one hundred and six years after the Romans appointment of Herod to the office and title of King of Judea, and that during that hundred and six years, the name of the Lord and Saviour Jesus Christ, as of a man then born and passing the course of life, was not known or of record among them, other than in the Prophecies of their Sacred Scriptures, as a Spirit or Messiah to come for the salvation of the human race, which was to come out of the Spiritual Judea; but not out of the Herodian Territory, just then beginning to bear that name, a coming that is yet wanted and waited for. All these points are to be verified in and by the Epistles of the New Testament.

That in all the Books of Profane History, from those of Herodotus to the Commentaries of Julius Caesar, there is no recognition of the Jews in any political character or station, though from Berosus to Diodorus Siculus, they are recognized as a philosophical or theocratical sect in Asia and Africa, and were found as such at

2

the place, then and now improperly called Jerusalem, by Pompey the Roman General.

That the inference which your petitioner most humbly draws is, that the Bible, from the Book of Genesis to Saint John's Gospel inclusive, is not a book of political or of human corporeal history, nor of geography, nor of time as a chronology; but is a Spiritual Mystery or a collection of the Ancient Mysteries of general human physiology in relation to mind, and prophetic of the conditions of human salvation, of a much more sublime and important character, than making it as a piece of political history can lead the human mind to understand, being the perfection of moral science made dependent on the study of physical science: that the Spirit of the Book has been misconceived, mistranslated and lost in being read after the manner of profane history confined to time, people and place; and your humble petitioner, understanding it as a general sacred history, in mystery, of the creation and generation, bondage, exode, law, promised land, captivity through idolatry and final restoration of human souls, not of bodies, can raise no further objection to it and renounces all of that kind he has hitherto erroneously published, now knowingly allowing it to have been written by divine inspiration among holy men of old, which was as unnecessary as inapplicable to political history of human action in time and place.

3

*Petition to Parliament in which Carlile asks for the formation of a special committee to study the historical justification for the establishment of the Anglican church as the Church of England (RC 341; Henry E. Huntington Library and Art Gallery)* as mesmerism and phrenology. Eventually, he tried to merge science and his Christianity (with no great success).

As for literature, Carlile had no use for it. His first broadsides were fired in 1824 in the *Republican,* and he continued his attacks in the *Lion* (1828), *Isis* (1832), and the *Gauntlet* (1833) as well. "The stuff that is called literature, in the present day, is nothing more than the mad working of the human brain in poetry or prose, in romance or fiction," he said in *Isis.* "Nothing composed of letters is worth notice, but that which is now calculated to make a change in the manners and circumstances of society; so as to lay the foundation of justice and wisdom, and to conquer a peace upon such honourable treaties as may last for ever" (15 September 1832). To Carlile as to other reformers (James Mill comes to mind) imagination unalloyed to usefulness is at best useless, and at worst mischievous. He compared literature to opium and religion, and asked "what is a pretty stringing together of words, when the only use that can be made of them are imaginary and relate to nothing of this earth?" (*Isis,* 15 September 1832).

Assessing Carlile's place in literature is a difficult task. Reading Carlile is interesting, if not particularly profitable. His prose is somewhat turgid, and his political essays resound with the bombast so common among nineteenth-century radicals. His political positions are not extraordinary. His theology is extraordinary, but verges many times on silliness. Yet he continues to be read, in part because he is representative of a whole class of journalists and essayists, and in part because he was a martyr for press freedom. Perhaps his martyrdom interests us most; we like reading the words that doomed a man. Whatever it is, he still stirs passions more than a century later. Of two of his twentieth-century biographers, Guy Aldred worshiped him, and Joel H. Wiener grew to dislike him intensely. His casual readers react in much the same way, but few come away neutral.

**Biographies:**

G. J. Holyoake, *The Life and Character of Richard Carlile* (London: J. Watson, 1870);

Theophila Carlile Campbell, *The Battle of the Press, as Told in the Story of the Life of Richard Carlile* (London: A & H. B. Bonner, 1899);

Guy Aldred, *Richard Carlile, Agitator* (Glasgow: Strickland Press, 1941);

G. D. H. Cole, *Richard Carlile, 1790-1843* (London: Gollancz, 1943);

Joel H. Wiener, *Radicalism and Freethought in Nineteenth-Century Britain: The Life of Richard Carlile* (Westport, Conn. & London: Greenwood Press, 1983).

**References:**

Alexander Andrews, *The History of British Journalism from the Foundation of the Newspaper Press in England, to the Repeal of the Stamp Act in 1855, with Sketches of Press Celebrities,* 2 volumes (London: Hutchinson, 1903);

Richard D. Fulton, "An *Ubermensch* with Feet of Clay," *Papers on Language and Literature,* 20 (Spring 1984): 233-238;

James Grant, *The Newspaper Press: Its Origin, Progress and Present Position,* 2 volumes (London: Tinsley, 1871);

Patricia Hollis, *The Pauper Press* (London: Oxford University Press, 1970);

Paul Thomas Murphy, "Imagination Flaps its Sportive Wings: Views of Fiction in British Working-Class Periodicals, 1816-1858," *Victorian Studies,* 32 (Spring 1989): 339-364;

J. Holland Rose, "The Unstamped Press, 1815-1836," *English Historical Review,* 12 (1897): 711-726;

Edward Royle, *Radical Politics 1790-1900: Religion and Unbelief* (London: Longmans, 1971);

Trygve Tholfsen, *Working Class Radicalism in Mid-Victorian England* (New York: Columbia University Press, 1977);

William Thomas, *The Philosophic Radicals* (Oxford: Clarendon Press, 1979);

Joel H. Wiener, *The War of the Unstamped: The Movement to Repeal the British Newspaper Tax, 1830-1836* (Ithaca, N.Y.: Cornell University Press, 1969).

**Papers:**

The Carlile Collection at the Henry E. Huntington Library has manuscripts and letters.

# John Wilson Croker

*(20 December 1780 - 10 August 1857)*

Thomas L. Cooksey
*Armstrong State College*

BOOKS: *The Opinion of an Impartial Observer Concerning the Late Transactions in Ireland* (Dublin: John Parry, 1803);

*Familiar Epistles to Frederick J —— s, Esq. on the Present State of the Irish Stage* (Dublin: J. Barlow, 1804; facsimile, New York & London: Garland, 1979); republished as *Familiar Epistles to Frederick Jones, Esq. on the Present State of the Irish Stage* (Dublin: M. N. Mahon, 1805);

*An Intercepted Letter from J -- T -- Esq., Writer at Canton, to his Friend in Dublin, Ireland* (Dublin: M. N. Mahon, 1804);

*The History of Cutchacutchoo* (Dublin: M. N. Mahon, 1805);

*The Amazoniad; or, Figure and Fashion: A Scuffle in High Life: With Notes Critical and Historical, interspersed with Choice Anecdotes of Bon Ton* (Dublin: Printed by John King, 1806; facsimile, New York & London: Garland, 1979);

*Histrionic Epistles* (Dublin: John Barlow, 1807; facsimile, New York & London: Garland, 1978);

*A Sketch of the State of Ireland, Past and Present* (Dublin: M. N. Mahon, 1808; London: J. Carpenter, 1808; revised edition, London: John Murray, 1822);

*The Battles of Talavera: A Poem* (London: John Murray, 1809; facsimile of second edition [1809], New York & London: Garland, 1979; enlarged edition, London: John Murray, 1810; Philadelphia: J & A. Y. Humphreys, 1811); enlarged as *Talaverea, 9th ed. To which are added others poems* (London: Printed for John Murray, William Blackwood, Edinburgh, and M. N. Mahon & J. Cumming, Dublin, by Harding & Wright, 1812);

*A Key to the Orders in Council* (London: Printed for John Murray, 1812);

*The Letters on the Subject of the Naval War with America, which Appeared in the Courier, under the Signature of "Nereus"* (London: Printed by B. M. Swyny, sold by J. Stockdale, 1813);

*Stories Selected from the History of England, from the Conquest to the Revolution: for Children* (London: John Murray, 1817; Hartford, Conn.: H. Huntington, Jr., 1825);

*A Letter from the King* (London: W. Turner, 1820);

*The Reply of the People to the Letter from the King* (London: F. C. & J. Rivington, 1821);

*Two Letters on Scottish Affairs from E. Bradwardine Waverly Esq. to Malachi Malagrowther Esq.* (London: John Murray, 1826);

*Elements Geography for Children. By the Author of "Stories for Children"* (London: John Murray, 1829);

*The Speech of the Right Honourable John Wilson Croker, on the Reform Question, on Friday, March 4, 1831* (London: John Murray, 1831);

*The Speech of the Right Honourable John Wilson Croker, on the Reform Question that "the Reform Bill do Pass," Tuesday, 22nd. September, 1831* (London: John Murray, 1831);

*Resolutions Moved by Mr. Croker on the Report of the Reform-Bill. March 14, 1832* (London: John Murray, 1832);

*The Croker Papers: The Correspondence and Diaries of the Late Right Honourable John Wilson Croker*, edited by Louis J. Jennings (3 volumes, London: John Murray, 1884; 2 volumes, New York: Scribners, 1884; revised edition, 3 volumes, London: John Murray, 1885); revised and abridged as *The Croker Papers: 1808-1857: New and Abridged Edition*, edited by Bernard Pool (London: Batsford, 1967; New York: Barnes & Noble, 1967).

OTHER: François de Bassompierre, *Memoirs of the Embassy of the Marshal de Bassompierre to the Count of England in 1626*, translated, with notes, by Croker (London: John Murray, 1819);

Mary Hervey, *Letters of Mary Lepel, Lady Hervey. With a Memoir and Illustrative Notes*, edited by Croker (London: John Murray, 1821);

*John Wilson Croker (etching after a portrait by William Owen, R.A.)*

Henrietta Howard, Countess of Suffolk, *Letters to and from Henrietta, Countess of Suffolk, and her second Husband, the Hon. George Berkeley; from 1712 to 1767. With Historical, Bibliographical, and Explanatory Notes,* edited by Croker (London: John Murray, 1824);

Horace Walpole, *Letters from the Honble. Horace Walpole, to the Earl of Hertford, during his Lordship's Embassy in Paris. To which are added Mr. Walpole's Letters to the Rev. Henry Zouch,* edited by Croker (London: Charles Knight, 1825);

James Boswell, *The Life of Samuel Johnson, LL.D., including a Journal of a Tour of the Hebrides: with Numerous Additions and Notes by John Wilson Croker,* edited by Croker (5 volumes, London: John Murray, 1831; 2 volumes, Boston: Carter, Hendee, 1832); revised, with two supplementary volumes of Johnsoniana compiled and edited by Croker (7 volumes, London: John Murray, 1835); supplementary volumes republished as *Johnsoniana, by Hawkins, Piozzi, Murphy and Others,* edited by Croker (London: John Murray, 1839; Philadelphia: Cary and Hart, 1842); revised edition (London: John Murray, 1848);

John Hervey, *Memoirs of the Reign of George the Second from His Accession to the Death of Queen Caroline,* 2 volumes, edited by Croker (London: John Murray, 1848; Philadelphia: Lea & Blanchard, 1848);

Alexander Pope, *The Works of Alexander Pope: New Edition, Including several hundred unpublished letters and other new materials. Collected in part by the late Rt. Hon. John Wilson Croker,* 10 volumes (London: John Murray, 1871-1889).

Today John Wilson Croker is remembered as the man who "murdered" John Keats—at least if we are to trust Percy Bysshe Shelley, who claimed that Croker's savage review of Keats's *Endymion* (*Quarterly Review,* May 1818) "produced the most violent effect on [Keats's] susceptible mind; the agitation thus originated ended in the rupture of a blood-vessel in the lungs . . ." (preface to *Adonais,* 1821). While Keats's letters reveal that he took the criticism of the *Quarterly Review* with greater equanimity than is suggested by Shelley's account, the myth surrounding Croker's assault remains. In fact, Croker earned the enmity of many liberal and revolutionary figures of his day, from William Hazlitt, who called him a "*talking potatoe*" (*The Plain Speaker,* 1826) to Thomas Babington Macaulay. William Makepeace Thackeray caricatured him as Mr. Wenham in *Vanity Fair* (1847-1848). Sydney, Lady Morgan, used him as the model for Conway Crawley in her novel *Florence Macarthy* (1818). He was pilloried by Benjamin Disraeli in the character of Mr. Rigby, the unscrupulous politico in Disraeli's roman à clef *Coningsby* (1844). A protégé of Arthur Wellesley, Duke of Wellington, Croker enjoyed a long career both as a politician and a man of letters. He was an active member of Parliament, noted for his effective command of details. He was a vigorous opponent of the first Reform Bill in his later years. In addition to his elective office, he held the appointed post of first secretary of the Admiralty for more than twenty years. In the midst of this political life, Croker was an equally active scholar, editing books, including an edition of Boswell's *Life of Johnson,* and compiling additional volumes of Johnsoniana. He was also a regular and prolific contributor to the *Quarterly Review,* publishing many articles and reviews and earning himself the reputation as a leading authority on the French Revolution. At his death, he was working on an edition of the works of Alexander Pope.

John Wilson Croker was born in Galway, Ireland, 20 December 1780. His father, John Croker, of Scottish descent, was the surveyor-general of custom and excise. The first years of young Croker's life were spent in Newport, county Mayo. Because of a stutter, his early education was at an "Academy of Elocution" run by James Knowles (first cousin of the playwright Richard Brinsley Sheridan). From there he attended a school run by French émigrés who had fled the revolution in France. The effect of this experience was to provide Croker with both a fluency in French and an abiding hatred of the French Revolution. After a classical education in Mr. Willis's school at Portarlington, Croker entered Trinity College, Dublin, in November 1796. Thomas Moore, later a friend, was a student there, graduating a year before Croker, who took his B.A. in 1800. He subsequently entered Lincoln's Inn, London, to read law and prepare for admission to the Irish bar. Croker seems to have enjoyed this stay in London, where he soon earned a reputation as both a ready wit and as an effective arguer. During this period he published his first work, a bit of Swiftian satire in the form of a letter to the London *Times* (6 April 1801), reputedly describing the visit of Jean Lambert Tallien, one of the regicides of the Ninth Thermidor, to the Holland House Whigs. Completing his legal education in 1802, Croker returned to Dublin when he was called to the Irish bar.

Croker enjoyed an active legal practice in Dublin, including many revenue cases that he received through the influence of his father. He also enjoyed a reputation as a local wit, publishing satirical poetry on various topics. Among the first was the *Familiar Epistles to Frederick J —— s, Esq. on the Present State of the Irish Stage* (1804). Croker directed his attack against the unscrupulous practices of Frederick Jones, the manager of the important Crow Street Theater:

> Nor let your native sense and taste
> By others' follies be disgraced,
> Catch timid merit as it springs,
> Give to your liberal soul full wings,
> The stages golden age restore
> And censure shall return no more.

Another work that appeared at this time was *The Amazoniad* (1806), a mock-heroic epic about a battle between two society ladies over the possession of a theater box. While the bite of his satires revealed some literary skills, his aesthetic vision was limited, looking back to the age of Alexander Pope.

The year 1806 marked a series of transformations in Croker's life, both personal and professional. He married Rosamond Pennell, the start of a long and happy relationship. He also entered Parliament, the start of a long and busy public and political career. Originally he had gone to Downpatrick to help the Tory candidate. When the man withdrew from the race, Croker obtained the seat by petition. The following year he was successfully returned to Parliament in a

*Croker circa 1830 (engraving by S. Cousins, after a portrait by Sir Thomas Lawrence, P.R.A.)*

general election, holding various protected seats until his retirement from public life in 1832. Several of these were controlled by the powerful, if dissolute, Francis Charles Seymour-Conway, third Marquis of Hertford (satirized as marquis of Steyne in Thackeray's *Vanity Fair* and Lord Monmouth in Disraeli's *Coningsby*), who became Croker's patron. At about this time, Croker also came to the attention of Sir Arthur Wellesley, (later duke of Wellington), then the chief secretary for Ireland. In 1808, following his appointment to command the British forces in the Peninsular War against Napoleon, Wellesley entrusted his business to Croker on the recommendation of Spenser Perceval. The following year Croker commemorated Wellesley's military success in his *Battles of Talavera,* a narrative poem of about 750 lines in the manner of Walter Scott's *Marmion* (1808). Both Scott and Robert Southey praised the work; Wellesley was amused by it. In a letter to Croker, he quipped, "I did not think a battle could be turned into anything so entertaining."

Croker's friendship with Wellesley resulted in his elevation in Tory political circles. In 1809 he was appointed first secretary of the Admiralty, a position he held some twenty-one years. As the political and administrative liaison between Parliament and the first lords of the Admiralty, Croker was active in the modernization of the British navy and bore much of the brunt of parliamentary criticism over British defeats in the American War of 1812. In his "Croker" (*Dry Sticks,* 1858) Walter Savage Landor quipped, "Disposer of our fleet is Croker, / He should have been at most a stoker." Early in his career, Croker established a reputation for honesty and controversy, when he challenged the appropriation of funds by the paymaster of Marines.

In February 1809, the publisher John Murray, Sr., joined with Walter Scott, George Ellis, William Gifford, and others to establish the *Quarterly Review,* a Tory periodical to compete with the

*Portrait by Daniel Maclise in the* Fraser's Magazine *"Gallery of Illustrious Literary Characters" (1830-1838)*

Whig *Edinburgh Review.* Croker, also among the founding members, initially played a minor role, contributing short poems, political squibs, and occasional reviews. His first contribution was a review of Maria Edgeworth's *Tales of Fashionable Life* in the August 1809 issue. In his *Spirit of the Age* (1825) Hazlitt offered an ironic portrait of the *Quarterly Review* circle, which included Croker, George Canning, Isaac D'Israeli, William Jacob, and Robert Southey as well as the editor, William Gifford: "The poetical department is almost a sinecure, consisting of mere summary decisions and a list of quotations. Mr. Croker is understood to contribute the St. Helena articles and the liberality, Mr. Canning the practical good sense, Mr. D'Israeli the good-nature, Mr. Jacob the modesty, Mr. Southey the consistency, and the Editor himself the chivalrous spirit and the attacks on Lady Morgan." When Croker retired from the Admiralty after the collapse of the stormy Wellington administration in 1831, he became a regular contributor, receiving an income of about six hundred pounds a year, about twice the usual rate for an average of two articles an issue.

It is for his contributions to the *Quarterly Review* that Croker is now chiefly remembered. In his association with the periodical from 1809 to 1854, Croker published some 269 articles and reviews, ranging over history, politics, current events, and literary matters. In the course of his writing, he established himself as a vigorous spokesman of Toryism, introducing the term *conservative* into the political vocabulary in the January 1830 issue of the *Quarterly* to characterize his brand of ultra-Toryism. His writings were a vehicle not only for conservative politics, but for a conservative view of art and literature. Among the many reviews that he produced for *Quarterly* were negative notices of Leigh Hunt's *Rimini* (January 1816) and *Foliage* (January 1818), Mary Shelley's *Frankenstein* (January 1818), Keats's *Endymion* (April 1818), and the young Alfred Tennyson's *Poems* (April 1833).

Croker's conception of poetry looked back to the aesthetics of Pope and the critical standards of Samuel Johnson, both of whom he deeply revered. In a 28 November 1816 letter to the Reverend George Croly, he observed, "I read more Pope and Dryden than I do of even Scott and Byron." Elaborating on this point, Croker gives some insight into his aesthetic principles: "Mr. Scott and Lord Byron have adopted subjects to which their peculiar styles are appropriate." For him, poetry should not be merely a mode of expression but a vehicle for ideas. The language of the poet should be appropriate to the subject. With the sharp eye of a practiced lawyer, he interrogated the language of his poets for inconsistencies or contradictions. Thus, while he could not resist mentioning that Leigh Hunt had been briefly imprisoned for treason, it was the incoherence and incongruity of Hunt's poetic language that damned his poetry. Similarly, recognizing Keats's affiliation with the "school" of Hunt, Croker complained that *Endymion* was governed by its sounds rather than its sense: "He seems to us to write a line at random, and then he follows not the thought excited by this line, but that suggested by the *rhyme* with which it concludes." He added, "There is hardly a complete couplet inclosing a complete idea in the whole book. He wanders from one subject to another, from the association, not of ideas but of sounds. . . ." Analogous charges were later leveled at the poems of Tennyson, who, Croker astutely recognized, had an affinity with Keats. With heavy sarcasm, he observed, "we gladly seize this opportunity of repairing an unintentional neglect, and of introducing to the admiration of our more sequestered readers a new prodigy of genius—another and a brighter star of that galaxy or *milky way* of poetry which the lamented Keats was the harbinger." He proceeded then to lay out the incongruities in Tennyson's thought.

Much of Croker's writing in the *Quarterly* focused on politics and history. In part because of his lifelong antipathy to the French Revolution and his long tenure at the Admiralty, Croker had collected a large body of letters, periodicals, broadsides, tracts, and other primary sources about the French Revolution, recognizing the historical values of "contemporary ephemeral publications." He eventually sold these to the British Museum in three batches (1817, 1831, and 1856), the final catalogue of the entire collection comprises some fifty thousand items, filling four thousand volumes. From this wealth of primary material, Croker established himself as one of the leading authorities on the French Revolution in his day. From that position he evaluated the authority of books on the Revolution and the Napoleonic era. Questioning the authenticity of several volumes proporting to be the memoirs of Robespierre and his sister, Croker went so far as to suggest that Robespierre had in some sense been made the "scape-goat of the Revolution" to protect the interests of many who still held power. From his position as an authority on the Revolution, Croker also watched with increasing alarm the state of politics in England.

As a member of the government as well as the Tory party, Croker was deeply concerned by the move toward parliamentary reform that emerged in the early 1830s. He saw in the breakdown of the status quo a release of restraints on ambition and political factionalism that would sweep away the British constitution and its institutions. Comparing the Cromwellian Revolution of 1640 and the French Revolution as guides to the future of reform, he declared, "the consequence is that a revolution in England would now exhibit, not the austere and so far salutary fanaticism of Harrison or Cromwell, but rather, we fear, the bloody and impious profligacy of *Egalité* and Clootz." Perceiving himself as the protector of the British Constitution, Croker became a leading opponent of the first Reform Bill, debating it in Parliament—in which he bested Thomas Babington Macaulay—and publishing many articles attacking it. When the Reform Bill passed in June 1832, Croker withdrew from public life. Haunted by visions of a Napoleon, he despaired in a memorandum dated 15 March 1833, "my opinion is that a democracy, once set a-going, must sooner or later work out till it ends in anarchy, and that some kind of despotism must then come to restore society."

No longer in public office, Croker turned full attention to his contributions to the *Quarterly*, focusing primarily on political and historical matters. He also continued his scholarly pursuits. Spurred on by a love of the eighteenth century, Croker had edited and published collections of letters, including those of Mary, Lady Hervey, a friend of Pope, John Gay, and Voltaire (1821), those of Henrietta, Countess of Suffolk, and George Berkeley (1824), and those of Horace Walpole to Francis Seymour Conway, Earl of Hertford (1825). At the time of the struggle over the Reform Bill, he began a project of special love, a new edition of James Boswell's *Life of Samuel Johnson, LL.D.* He had first broached the project to John Murray in 1829. With Murray's approval, Croker threw himself into collecting materials and searching out survivors of Johnson's circles, including his executor, Lord Stowell, and Hester Thrale's daughter. The result of these efforts was a new edition of Boswell's life into which Croker inserted additional anecdotes, supplemented with two additional volumes of John-

"I said the great article of Christianity is the Revelation of immortality! Johnson admitted it was!"

[This is loosely expressed. The ancients believed in immortality, and even a state of retribution. Warburton argues that Moses was not ignorant of, and the Mahomedans acknowledge, a future state. On so vital a question it is not safe to rest on Mr. Boswell's colloquial phrases, which have some importance when they appear to be sanctioned by the concurrence of Dr. Johnson. Immortality is indeed assured, and a thousand social benefits & blessings are vouchsafed to us by the Christian revelation; but "the great article of Christianity" is surely the atonement! Ed.]

*Note by Croker for his edition of James Boswell's* Life of Samuel Johnson, LL.D. *(LR 67; Henry E. Huntington Library and Art Gallery)* soniana. Macaulay, perhaps recalling his parliamentary debate with Croker, denounced the work as full of errors and a distortion of Boswell's work. While most of Macaulay's criticisms involve trivial matters, his judgment that Croker's insertions distort Boswell are valid. The later standard critical edition has removed these emendations. Nevertheless, Croker rendered a significant service in his accumulation of Johnsoniana, much of which would otherwise have been lost.

The last part of Croker's life was spent in literary and political circles. Croker was always an active clubman, having been among the founding members of the Athenæum Club in 1824. In declining health, Croker withdrew as an active contributor to the *Quarterly Review* in 1854. Among his last literary projects was an edition of his beloved Alexander Pope. Although he did not live to complete the project, his efforts became the foundation on which a critical edition would eventually be produced. Croker died on 10 August 1857 at the age of seventy-six.

While little of John Wilson Croker's work is read today, he was a prominent and prolific voice in the political and literary circles from the Romantic era through the high noon of the Victorian era. A conservative spokesman in an age of revolutions and reform, Croker earned the praise or enmity of many men and women, and left none indifferent.

**References:**

Hedva Ben-Israel, *English Historians on the French Revolution* (Cambridge: Cambridge University Press, 1968);

Myron F. Brightfield, *John Wilson Croker* (Berkeley: University of California Press, 1940);

Audrey C. Broadhurst, "The French Revolution Collections in the British Library," *British Library Journal,* 2 (Autumn 1976): 138-158;

E. S. De Beer, "Macaulay and Croker: The Review of Croker's Boswell," *Review of English Studies,* new series 10 (November 1959): 387-388;

Peter F. Morgan, "Croker as Literary Critic in the *Quarterly Review,*" *Wordsworth Circle,* 8 (Winter 1977): 62-68;

John Riley, "John Wilson Croker and Keats' Endymion," *Studies in the Humanities,* 5, no. 2 (1976): 32-37.

**Papers:**

There are collections of Croker's correspondence in the William L. Clements Library, University of Michigan, and in the British Library.

# Thomas De Quincey

*(15 August 1785 - 8 December 1859)*

Linda Mills Woolsey
*King College*

BOOKS: *Close Comments Upon a Straggling Speech* (Kendal: Printed by Airey & Bellingham, 1818);

*Confessions of an English Opium Eater* (London: Printed for Taylor & Hessey, 1822; Philadelphia: E. Littell / New York: R. Norris Henry, 1823);

*The Stranger's Grave*, possibly by De Quincey (London: Longman, Hurst, Rees, Orme, Brown & Green, 1823);

*Klosterheim; or the Masque* (Edinburgh: William Blackwood / London: T. Cadell, 1832);

*The Logic of Political Economy* (Edinburgh & London: William Blackwood & Sons, 1844);

*De Quincey's Writings*, 22 volumes, edited by J. T. Fields (Boston: Ticknor, Reed & Fields, 1851-1859);

*Selections Grave and Gay from Writings, Published and Unpublished, of Thomas De Quincey, Revised and Arranged by Himself*, 14 volumes (Edinburgh: Hogg, 1853-1860);

*China. A Revised Reprint of Articles from Titan, with Prefaces and Additions* (Edinburgh: Hogg / London: Groombridge & Sons, 1857);

*The Collected Writings of Thomas De Quincey*, 14 volumes, edited by David Masson (Edinburgh: Adam & Charles Black, 1889-1890);

*The Uncollected Writings of Thomas De Quincey*, 2 volumes, edited by James Hogg (London: Printed by S. Sonneschein for James Hogg, 1890; New York: Scribner & Welford, 1890);

*The Posthumous Works of Thomas De Quincey*, 2 volumes, edited by Alexander H. Japp (London: Heinemann, 1891, 1893);

*A Diary of Thomas De Quincey, 1803*, edited by Horace A. Eaton (London: Noel Douglas, 1927; New York: Payson & Clarke, 1927);

*New Essays by De Quincey: His Contributions to the Edinburgh Saturday Post and the Edinburgh Evening Post, 1827-8*, edited by Stuart M. Tave (Princeton, N.J.: Princeton University Press, 1966).

**Editions:** *Recollections of the Lake Poets*, edited by Edward Sackville-West (London: John Lehmann, 1948);

*Confessions of an English Opium-Eater in Both the Revised and the Original Texts with its Sequels, Suspiria De Profundis and the English Mail Coach*, edited by Malcolm Elwin (London: MacDonald, 1956);

*Reminiscences of the English Lake Poets 1834-1840*, edited by John E. Jordan (London: Dent, 1961; New York: Dutton, 1961).

OTHER: *Walladmor: 'Freely Translated into the German from the English of Sir Walter Scott' and now freely translated from the German of G. W. Haering into English*, 2 volumes (London: Taylor & Hessey, 1825);

*Niels Klim: Being an Incomplete Translation by Thomas De Quincey from the Danish of Ludvig Holberg*, edited by Sydney Musgrove (Auckland, New Zealand: Auckland University College, 1953).

In her 1926 essay on "Impassioned Prose," Virginia Woolf declared that Thomas De Quincey was "an exception and a solitary." Subsequent readers have often agreed that he defies categorization. From the beginning of his writing career, De Quincey enchanted and infuriated readers with his paradoxical combinations of reticence and revelation, elegance and slapstick. He was, by his own confession, a hack writer for the periodical press, and yet, even as he chafed against magazine deadlines, he produced a haunting and eloquent prose. His work is in many ways the scholar's nightmare and the writer's dream. Moving from room to room, piling up papers, and revising incessantly, he created a bibliographic labyrinth with sketchy and tantalizing clues. Digressing from his subjects and reworking ideas from various sources, he has evaded scholarly attempts to pin him down neatly and defied Romantic ideas of originality central to his own aesthetic. But readers such as Jorge Luis Borges

*Thomas De Quincey circa 1845 (portrait by Sir John Watson Gordon; National Portrait Gallery, London)*

and D. H. Lawrence have found themselves addicted to the rhythmic, labyrinthine prose that strings together books, personal experience, and dreams to produce powerful narratives. The complexities of De Quincey's work tend to call into question simplistic ideas about Romanticism; and his career, stretching from the 1820s to the 1850s, reminds us that scholarly divisions between Romantic and Victorian are often arbitrary. While De Quincey does provide twentieth-century readers with insights into the characters of other first-generation Romantic writers, the world of nineteenth-century journalism, and the anxieties and concerns of the nineteenth-century reading public, he is most important for his mastery of prose style. The Opium-Eater came late to professional writing life, publishing his first major work when he was thirty-six, but his writing paved the way for other experimenters and pioneers as it tested the limits of prose.

Thomas De Quincey was born in Manchester in the summer of 1785, the fourth of eight children born to the prosperous Quinceys. Shortly after Thomas's birth, the family moved outside the city boundaries to The Farm, Moss Side. There, De Quincey's mother, Elizabeth Penson Quincey, a woman of strong evangelical principles and an associate of Hannah More, sought to instill moral principles and religious fervor in her growing family. Her husband, Thomas Quincey, was a successful textile merchant, whose ill health and prolonged absences from the household made him a shadowy figure in his son's early childhood. Since his older brother, William (born 1781 or 1782), had been sent away to school, Thomas spent his early years primarily in the company of his sisters: Elizabeth (born 1783), Mary (born 1784), and Jane (born 1786). Half a century later, De Quincey described them as gentle devotees of their frail brother, and, as a child, he sometimes playfully imagined himself one of them, signing his notes to them "Tabitha." When Jane, who was one year younger than Thomas, died in 1790, the sorrow of the surviving chil-

*Thomas Quincey, Elizabeth Penson Quincey, and their two-and-a-half-year-old son Thomas (left: The Bodley Head; center and right: Collection of Rosemary Blok van Cronesteyn)*

dren was soon overshadowed by the bustle of the move to a larger house the family called Greenhay. There, the children played on the lawn and read in the well-stocked family library. Then, in 1792, Elizabeth died, and, for her brother, paradise was lost forever. Creeping to the room where her body lay prepared for burial, De Quincey understood mortality as terrible separation and caught what he was later to remember as a glimpse of the infinite. Fifty years later, the death of this intelligent, sympathetic sharer of his boyhood feelings and imaginings still colored his dreams and the prose he built on them.

In 1793 Mr. Quincey, who was suffering from tuberculosis, came home to die. In his later autobiographical sketches, De Quincey labeled the ensuing epoch his entrance into "the world of strife." He soon came to resent the control of his mother and the other guardians appointed by his father's will, and he longed for the liberty to prove his imaginative and intellectual powers. Sometime after his father's death, Thomas and his mother began to sign their last name "De Quincey," an aristocratic touch in keeping with De Quincey's own ideal of the gentleman's life. William came home, and he and Thomas were tutored by the Reverend Samuel Hall from 1793 until 1796, confronting jeering factory boys as they walked to and from their lessons. At home William's imaginary kingdom of Tigrosylvania vanquished his brother's Gombroon, much to young Thomas's mortification. In 1796 Mrs. Quincey moved to Bath, taking with her Mary, a second daughter named Jane (born sometime after 1790), and the youngest child, Henry (born in 1793, after the death of his father). William had been sent to study art in London and died there of typhus in November 1797. Thomas and his younger brother Richard (born 1789), known to the family as "Pink," remained in Manchester for three months, boarding with a family named Kensall and studying with Samuel Hall. In November Mrs. Quincey brought them to Bath and sent Thomas to the Bath Grammar School, run by Dr. Morgan. Here Thomas had his first taste of the praise his mother felt duty-bound to deny her children, and excelled in Greek and Latin studies. Here too, sometime in 1799, Thomas probably read poems by William Wordsworth for the first time.

In the same year, Thomas was taken out of school at Bath and sent to study at Winkfield in Wiltshire. Then, in the summer of 1800, he traveled to Ireland with Howe Peter Browne, Lord Westport, the son of John Denis Browne, Lord Altamont, an Irish peer. In autumn he enjoyed a prolonged visit at the home of Lady Susan Carbery at Laxton, Northamptonshire. After these months of travel and of conversation with adults impressed by his abilities, De Quincey chafed at a return to the schoolboy role, but his mother and guardians were adamant.

In November 1800 De Quincey entered Manchester Grammar School, where he was increasingly unhappy. Toward the end of his stay there De Quincey probably read the 1800 edition of *Lyri-*

5

Everton — Saturday morning, August 22, 1806.

Concerning happiness — this ~~further specul.~~ addition to my specul.ns at Coniston occurred to me.

Nature provides ~~specially~~ to all men a sufficient supply of happiness during that time when they have not sufficient intellect to apprehend and ascertain ... or foresight to secure to themselves ye sources of voluntary happiness, in ~~an exuberance of~~ involuntary happiness proceeding from an exuberance of animal joy and spirits:- this she withdraws in regular progression with the advancement of ye intellect and through the instrumentality of that very intellect:- on the decay of these self-supporting spirits, commences the incumbency (which rests on every man) to provide for himself a source of permanent stimulus; and at this crisis it is that wisdom most fails the rout of men; for at this period most men ~~become~~ begin to ~~set~~ & resort to liquors and the turbulent bustle of the world to give a feverish warmth to their else shivering spirits:- this is obviously every way a low and ruinous stimulus; but, as some source of excitement is necessary, it ~~is eminently~~ remains to inquire what:- and ~~the~~ this I answer that I am firmly persuaded yt there is none but a deep interest in ~~and that~~ ye exhaustless and most lofty subjects of human life and human nature: ~~the this are~~ to . . .

*Page from manuscript for "Constituents of Happiness," written by De Quincey a few days after his twenty-first birthday (offered for sale by Burgess Browning, catalogue three, 1991) cal Ballads*. The world opened up to him by his acquaintance with contemporary poetry pointed up his dissatisfaction with the commercial world of Manchester, where, as he wrote to his mother in the spring of 1802, "trade is the religion, and money is the god." In the same letter he complained that the commercial world intruded upon his imaginative life: "I cannot stir out of doors but I am nosed by a factory, a cotton bag, a cotton dealer, or something else allied to that most detestable commerce. Such an object dissipates the whole train of romantic visions I had conjured up, and frequently gives the colouring to all my associations of ideas during the remainder of the day." His mother had warned him (4 March 1802) that imagination needed to be "restrained and brought under religious government" and that his reading was of the sort to "weaken [his] mental optics."

In July 1802 De Quincey fled Manchester, at first intending to make a pilgrimage to visit Wordsworth at Grasmere. Lacking the courage to face the poet, he instead confronted his mother, who agreed to let Thomas undertake a walking tour of Wales underwritten by a modest allowance. When the weather turned cold and his money ran short, De Quincey feared that his guardians would insist on his return to school. Once again, he fled, this time to London where he hoped to borrow money against his inheritance. De Quincey failed in his negotiations with the moneylenders, but his experience of the privation and community of London street life became the foundation for his best-known work.

De Quincey was reconciled with his guardians in March 1803, staying at Everton, where he read voraciously, especially popular Gothic fiction, and kept a diary which included plans for poetry of a melancholy and melodramatic sort. This notebook, oddly enough, contains no references to the suffering of the months in London he would dramatize so successfully nearly twenty years later. Instead, De Quincey's thoughts were set on literature, and in May of 1803 he finally summoned up the courage to open a correspondence with William Wordsworth. It took him two weeks to write the first letter, carefully drafting and revising his self-introduction to his literary hero. In August he returned to his mother's current residence in Chester, having finally received the long-awaited reply from Wordsworth.

In December of 1803 De Quincey went up to Worcester College, Oxford, where he remained as a student until May 1808. The Oxford years were important for De Quincey not so much for the prescribed course of study, but for the reading he pursued on his own and the people he met. He read Immanuel Kant and, on a visit to London in 1804, took opium for the first time. The next two years were, by his own account, dark years for De Quincey, as he suffered from a lingering pulmonary illness that made him fear consumption and from yet another personal loss when his brother Richard ran away to sea. On 6 April 1806 De Quincey wrote to Wordsworth that the last two years had been a complete "blank in the account of happiness." But even the somber letters addressed to Grasmere signaled an important change for De Quincey as he discovered in relationships with contemporary writers the intellectual society he had dreamed of as a boy. He met Charles Lamb sometime in 1804 or 1805 and Samuel Taylor Coleridge in July 1807. Having spent his earlier Oxford vacations at Everton, Bath, and London, at last, in November 1807, he made his pilgrimage to the Lake District and finally met William Wordsworth face-to-face. Here, too, he was introduced to a circle that included William's sister, Dorothy, and Robert Southey.

De Quincey had come into his inheritance in 1806, a circumstance that gave him a new sense of freedom and the chance to manage his own affairs, something he was to do very badly for the rest of his life. In November 1807 he made an anonymous gift of three hundred pounds to Coleridge, a generosity he could ill afford. Then, in 1808 De Quincey left Oxford without taking a degree. According to contemporary accounts, De Quincey distinguished himself in the written Latin examination, but fled before the oral examinations in Greek. He went to the Lake District, where he lived with the Wordsworths at Allan Bank, in Grasmere, from November 1808 until February 1809. There he played with the children, talked philosophy and literature, and met John Wilson, who was to play an important role in De Quincey's Edinburgh years. The continued close association with the Wordsworth-Coleridge circle was a formative experience for the brilliant and impressionable young man. His talks with Wordsworth, especially, were to provide him with ideas he could reshape for his own ends in narratives and essays. In turn, he was a part of the intellectual cross-pollination of those years as he read and responded to his friends' works in progress, including manuscripts for the autobiographical poem that was to be-

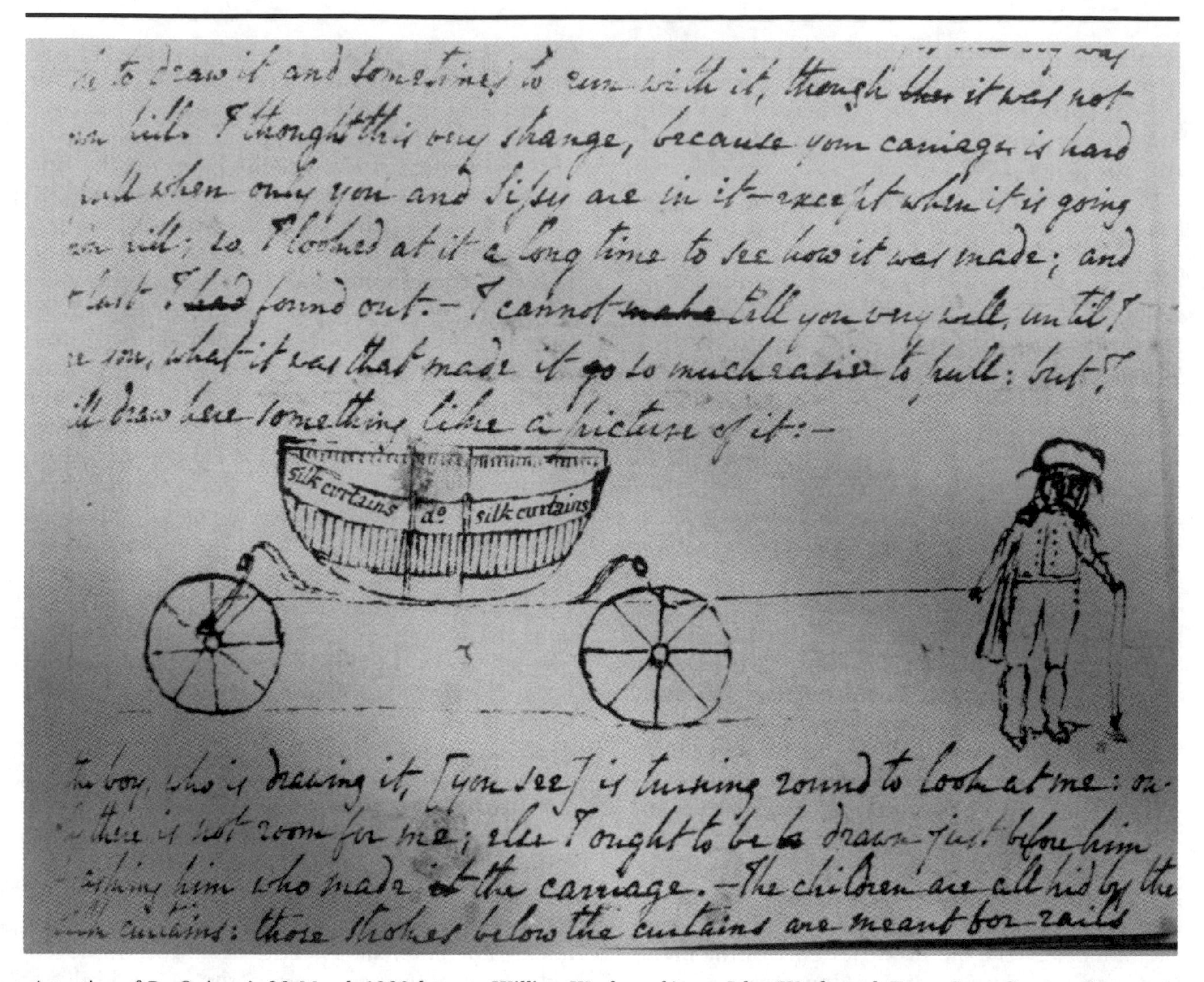

to draw it and sometimes to run with it, though it was not
hill. I thought this very strange, because your carriage is hard
pull when only you and Sissy are in it—except when it is going
hill; so I looked at it a long time to see how it was made; and
last I found out.—I cannot tell you very well, until I
you, what it was that made it go so much easier to pull: but I
ill draw here something like a picture of it:—



the boy, who is drawing it, [you see] is turning round to look at me: on
there is not room for me; else I ought to be drawn just before him
him who made the carriage.—The children are all hid by the
curtains: those strokes below the curtains are meant for rails

*A portion of De Quincey's 28 March 1809 letter to William Wordsworth's son John (Wordsworth Trust, Dove Cottage, Grasmere)*

come Wordsworth's *Prelude* (posthumously published in 1850) and the ongoing numbers of Coleridge's periodical *The Friend* (1809-1810, enlarged 1818).

He went down to London in February 1809 to see Wordsworth's pamphlet *The Convention of Cintra* through the presses. Wordsworth sent drafts and corrections from Grasmere, while De Quincey labored over the punctuation of the galley sheets and studied Peninsular affairs, composing substantial notes and addenda to the pamphlet. The Wordsworths sent him off with high hopes but soon became disillusioned by the slow progress of the pamphlet at the press. The Wordsworths blamed De Quincey; De Quincey blamed the printer; and still the pamphlet was delayed. Although the tensions over the production of *The Convention of Cintra* strained his relationship with William, De Quincey returned to Grasmere in October and stayed with the Wordworths for more than a month until he moved into Dove Cottage, where the Wordsworths had lived before moving to Allan Bank. There he piled up books, which the Wordsworths and Coleridge borrowed, took increasing doses of laudanum, a liquid tincture of opium, and—much to the dismay of Dorothy Wordsworth—made changes in the garden she had so carefully tended.

By 1812 he was making a desultory effort at studying law, keeping terms in the Middle Temple. He was in London when little Catherine Wordsworth died in June 1812, and his letters to Grasmere are filled with the narrative of his grief over the death of this child. He spent much of 1813 shut up in Dove Cottage with his opium bottle, and his relationships with the Wordsworths were strained. His financial resources dwindled while he dreamed of being a renowned polyhistor, a creator of systems, and a writer. Brilliant and well-read as he was, De Quincey had as yet no sure vocation and no paying work.

In the years 1814-1816 he moved about, staying at Wrington, Somerset, and London, as well as at Grasmere. He spent the winters of 1814 and 1815 in Edinburgh with Professor John Wilson, still reading, talking, and taking opium. He enjoyed the intellectual climate of early-nineteenth-century Edinburgh and impressed people with his talk, playing to perfection the role of the gentleman scholar. In 1816 De Quincey's inheritance ran out and his debts began to mount. At the same time, he courted Margaret Simpson, a Grasmere farmer's daughter. In November 1816 she bore him a son, christened William Penson, and on 15 February 1817, Thomas and Margaret were married. The Wordsworths did not approve. The De Quinceys led a solitary and precarious existence at Dove Cottage, in a state of cold war with the Wordsworths and desperately in need of money to support a growing family.

Still De Quincey cherished a dream of his own genius and an ideal of life as a scholar-gentleman, writing to his mother in 1818 that he believed himself in possession of "*original* knowledge not derived from books" and hence "indisposed to sell my knowledge for money, and to commence trading author." Yet, in the same year, he was willing to commence trading editor. Westmorland politics produced an opportunity for a temporary thaw in the relationship with the Wordsworths, and William Wordsworth did not block De Quincey's bid for the editorship of the *Westmorland Gazette* in the late spring of 1818. Finding a point of renewed contact with the Wordsworths in his support of Sir William Lowther, Lord Lonsdale, Wordsworth's patron and the Tory candidate, De Quincey wrote a substantial letter for the *Kendal Chronicle* in February, signing it "Philadelphus." In April he published a pamphlet, *Close Comments upon a Straggling Speech*, based in part on Dorothy Wordsworth's notes on one of Henry Brougham's speeches. This pamphlet, with its staunch Tory horror of Jacobinism and its scorn for the authority of the mob, is in many ways typical of De Quincey, whose writings were to reflect a lifelong concern with current affairs and a consistent horrified fascination with the power of magistrates and mobs. Several other lifelong preoccupations emerged during De Quincey's editorship of the *Westmorland Gazette*, which had been established in May 1818 to rival the *Kendal Chronicle*. Under his direction, which began in July, local politics soon gave way to sensational accounts of murder trials and articles on metaphysics, political economy, and language. The proprietors of the paper grew increasingly dissatisfied with De Quincey's work, and he soon tired of editing a paper in Kendall while living at Grasmere. Thus, in November 1819 De Quincey left the *Gazette* and returned to opium. Listless and despairing, he read David Ricardo's *Principles of Political Economy* (1817), which inspired a burst of intellectual energy and a renewed sense of possibility. With Margaret as amanuensis, he began to make notes on a prologomena to the science of political economy. Concerned for his growing family and plagued by mounting debts, however, De Quincey soon abandoned his plan. By early 1820 he was in Edinburgh, making an abortive attempt to write for *Blackwood's Edinburgh Magazine*. His correspondence with the editors shows a pattern he repeated throughout his career as a magazine writer. John Wilson had recommended De Quincey highly, and the editors were eager to have his manuscripts. De Quincey sent proposals and promises, failed to finish the projected articles, then sent substantial letters explaining the delays, writing at length about not writing.

After the Edinburgh plan fell through, De Quincey went to London, still looking for work. Reducing his doses of opium, he began to write in earnest, turning to opium itself and to his youthful experiences in London as the subjects of his narrative. The *London Magazine* published the resulting *Confessions of an English Opium Eater* in two parts, in the September and October 1821 issues. In this work, tincture of opium, a housewife's remedy, becomes the hero of the narrative as De Quincey describes the pleasures and pains of his addiction with an air of frankness. In his opening address, "To the Reader," De Quincey adopts the cultivated, respectable voice of the scholar-gentleman that predominates in his writing, and he presents the ensuing tale as a record of self-conquest, provided as a service to his readers. The Opium-Eater thus came before his public as a moralist of sorts, but the tale that follows is at odds with simple moralism. At the heart of the narrative are the privations and the community of suffering of his 1802-1803 sojourn in London, the mythic power of opium, and the haunting world of dreams. A decade earlier, in *The Friend*, Coleridge had expressed a desire to devote a whole work to the powerful communications of dreams;

I

My studies have now been long interrupted. I cannot read to myself with any pleasure, hardly with a moment's endurance. Yet I read aloud sometimes for the pleasure of others; because reading is an accomplishment of mine, and, in the slang use of the word accomplishment as a superficial and ornamental attainment, almost the only one I possess: and formerly if I had any vanity at all connected with any endowment or attainment of mine, it was with this; for I had observed that no accomplishment was so rare: players are the worst readers of all: — reads vilely: and Mr —, who is so celebrated, can read nothing well but dramatic compositions: Milton she cannot read sufferably. — People in general read poetry either without any passion at all, or else overstep the modesty of nature and read not like scholars. — Of late, if I have felt moved by anything in books, it has been by the grand lamentations of Samson Agonistes or the great harmonies of the Satanic speeches in Paradise Regained when read aloud by myself. A young lady sometimes comes and drinks tea with us: at her request and M's I now and then read W—'s Poems to them (W. by the bye is the only Poet I ever met who could read his own verses: Blank verse he reads admirably.)

This then has been the extent of my reading for upwards of 16 months. It frets me to enter those rooms of my cottage in which the books stand. In one of them, to which my little boy has access, he has found out a use for some of them: somebody has given him a bow and arrows; God knows who: certainly not I: for I have not energy or ingenuity to invent a walking-stick. Thus equipped for action, he rears up the largest of the Folios that he can lift, places them on a tottering base; and then shoots until he brings down the enemy. He often presses me to join him: and

*Page from a draft fragment for* Confessions of an English Opium Eater *(Henry W. and Albert A. Berg Collection of English and American Literature, New York Public Library)*

with *Confessions of an English Opium Eater*, De Quincey took up Coleridge's hint, transforming it into the first of a series of haunting works that expand the boundaries of lyrical prose. The "Preliminary Confessions" recount De Quincey's introduction to opium and his life among the pariahs of outcast London, including a young prostitute named Ann, ending with their separation and his fruitless searches for her. Part 2 opens with a recapitulation of the theme of premature suffering in the hostile world of Oxford Street and a picture of the rebirth of suffering in the forms of addiction and of separation from his ministering wife. "The Pleasures of Opium" follows, with a celebration of the "Paradise of Opium" and the peace and equipoise it brings as it expands his pleasure in music and in the company of the city's laboring poor. In "The Pains of Opium" and the introduction to it, the tone shifts as De Quincey recounts the visit of a Malay and the powers of opium. Under the "Circean spells of opium" the dream world and his accounts of it become disjointed as the moralist is swept away by the sheer force of his visions of seventeenth-century courtiers, endless architecture, lakes, vast oceans, and crowds of human faces. The work concludes with a series of dream narratives involving Eastern religion and repellent beasts, a transfigured Ann, and swelling music accompanied by anguished parting from loved female forms. At the close, the promised moral is displaced by the power of opium and the experience of getting out from under it.

The Confessions were well received as the public speculated about the identity of the Opium-Eater and the veracity of his tale. *Confessions of an English Opium Eater* appeared in book form in 1822, and early reviewers praised its powerful combination of fact and fantasy. A few grumbled about the lack of humility evidenced in the Opium-Eater's intellectual display, and some were scornful of or troubled by his picture of opium as a key to inspiration. Throughout the nineteenth century, De Quincey's *Confessions* had many admirers, though some of them were uneasily conscious of the dubious moral quality of the work, particularly as the Victorian period wore on. In 1860, on the other hand, Charles Baudelaire, writing in *Les Paradis artificiels*, protested De Quincey's capitulation to "British hypocrisy" in ending the work with his seeming escape from addiction.

Twentieth-century critics have approached *Confessions of an English Opium Eater* from several different angles, valuing it as a work of psychological insight into the addictive personality, an example of Romantic visionary prose, and a masterful tour de force of prose style and structure. The work has often been compared with Wordsworth's *Prelude*, usually to the deprecation of De Quincey's achievement. Both works do connect youthful experience with adult vision and imaginative power, but De Quincey's narrative is more mixed in tone and form, playfully manipulating the limits of prose conventions with calculated shifts of tone, diction, and cadence. As he spins out his tale, De Quincey at once exploits and caricatures the vantage points of moralist, scientist, scholar, deviant, and victim. The loss of Ann, which forms a narrative, emotive, and thematic center for the tale, has drawn much critical comment. Even in the nineteenth century, readers wondered if she were a real or fictional figure. Twentieth-century scholars, tending to acknowledge the riddle as unsolvable, have concentrated on her value as a symbolic figure, recognizing the thread of loss that links Elizabeth, Ann, and Catherine Wordsworth to create the lost female and the dream encounters with her that De Quincey repeats, with variations, throughout his writing.

With the success of the *Confessions* De Quincey had established a basis for selling his work to a public eager to hear more from the Opium-Eater. For the rest of his life, despite his inability to meet deadlines, his peripatetic habits, and his voluminous footnotes, addenda, and digressions, De Quincey generally found a ready market for his work. Publishers found him difficult to work with, but often worth the trouble—a masterful showman who wrote about a variety of popular and scholarly topics in a daring, mobile, and often incantatory prose. In the decades that followed the publication of *Confessions of an English Opium Eater*, De Quincey moved from periodical to periodical, often writing for several at one time, sometimes signing his articles, but often writing anonymously or as the Opium-Eater and X.Y.Z.

Thus, in the early 1820s De Quincey began his prolific career as reviewer, autobiographer, essayist, and storyteller. His early contributions to the *London Magazine* were characteristically varied, including translations and adaptations from German works, as well as meditations on political economy, politics, language, and literature. He was equally at home pontificating on Kant and adapting a popular German tale of revenge and the supernatural. From the beginning of his magazine career, De Quincey exploited the personae of polyhistor and deviant. In the guise of the polyhistor, De Quincey convinced many of his contemporaries that his scholarship was not only vast but profound, though later critics have modified or denied De Quincey's claims to originality as a philosopher, economist, and critic. He was, for the most part, a brilliant popularizer who derived many of his ideas from other men's work, but who transformed those ideas in the mint of his shaping prose.

Two of De Quincey's 1823 contributions to the *London Magazine* develop ideas that influenced later prose works and contributed to De Quincey's reputation as a literary critic and theorist. In "On the Knocking at the Gate in *Macbeth*" (October), De Quincey dramatized the narrative effect of an "awful parenthesis" between the heightened tension of the murder and the return to the everyday world of detection and consequence. In his five "Letters to a Young Man whose Education has been Neglected" (January-March, May and July) De Quincey introduced his well-known distinction between the provisional and didactic "literature of knowledge" and the "unalterable" and moving "literature of power." Drawing on his conversations with Wordsworth and his own experience of writing, De Quincey frequently returned to the problems of knowledge and power in later essays.

By late 1823 De Quincey was overtaken by power of another sort, as his opium addiction worsened. While the original confessions had suggested the perspective of a reformed addict, the "Appendix" to the 1822 version made it clear that the links of opium had not been unwound. Moving between rooms in London and his growing household at Grasmere, De Quincey piled up papers and debts at an astounding rate. There is some evidence to suggest that he may have published anonymously a novel of sexual guilt and revenge, *The Stranger's Grave*, in 1823. Edward Stanley, the hero of the tale, shares with De Quincey the experiences of convalescence, leaving Oxford without a degree, debts, and having a pregnant sweetheart. This novel's handling of the themes of guilty love and a hostile, persecuting world—if the novel is indeed De Quincey's—looks forward to his narratives of the next two decades.

Despite his struggles with opium, in 1824 De Quincey continued to publish miscellaneous essays, including "The Dialogues of Three Templars on Political Economy" (*London Magazine*, April and May 1824) which combines a tribute to David Ricardo and an exposition of his ideas, with a curious portrait of the scholar-gentleman X.Y.Z. as an intellectual gladiator. As he had suggested in *Confessions of an English Opium Eater*, De Quincey saw in David Ricardo an example of intellectual power, a scholar capable of deducing a priori laws which contained and displaced the uncomfortable welter of facts and problems of the commercial and material world. Yet, even as he celebrates Ricardo's power over the word, De Quincey's tongue-in-cheek treatment of X.Y.Z. and his intellectually impotent opponents tends to reduce the world of political economy to a metaphorical fistfight among gentleman waiting for their dinner. While De Quincey was to remain fascinated by political economy throughout his life, even through years when editors refused articles on the subject, his impulse toward humor approached self-satire in creating X.Y.Z. as an intellectual hero.

In October 1824, De Quincey stumbled onto another project that grew out of his dependence on magazine work and his enjoyment of literary puzzles and hoaxes. Earlier in that year, Wilhelm Häring, a German hoping to capitalize on Sir Walter Scott's popularity, had published a novel that he claimed was a translation of a new Waverley romance. Although De Quincey's review, "Walladmor, Sir W. Scott's German Novel" (*London Magazine*, October 1824), playing on the slang use of "German" for "a cheap substitute," had humorously disparaged the tale, it had also created a market for it in England. When Taylor and Hessey approached De Quincey about doing the translation, he consented, planning to toss off the work in about three weeks. As he actually read the novel, De Quincey discovered that it was ponderous and dull. Unwilling to have his magazine account of it shown up as false, De Quincey went to work, pruning "forests of rubbish," polishing the prose, and turning a sinister outlaw into a sympathetic hero. He even changed the central catastrophe and created a tragic ending. The result was essentially a new novel, slimmer and more readable than its German counterpart. When his version of *Walladmor* came out in 1825, De Quincey reveled in his share of this literary hoax.

Despite the income from *Walladmor*, De Quincey was once again in financial difficulty and the new editor at the *London Magazine* was not interested in more notes from the Opium-Eater's pocketbook. Having exhausted his London resources, De Quincey turned to Edinburgh,

*Page from the manuscript for "William Wordsworth and Robert Southey," the installment of De Quincey's "Lake Reminiscences" that appeared in the July 1839 issue of* Tait's Edinburgh Magazine *(MA 903; Pierpont Morgan Library)* still writing miscellaneous articles, this time for *Blackwood's*, from 1826-1833. The most significant of the early works for *Blackwood's* was the essay "On Murder Considered as One of the Fine Arts" published in February 1827. Here, De Quincey's odd sense of humor—based on incongruous juxtapositions, satirical inversions, wordplay, and slapstick—serves as the framework for the essay. This paper begins with an introductory letter, written from the perspective of a virtuous X.Y.Z., who wishes to expose a society of murder fanciers. At this point the editors inserted a note drawing attention to the Swiftian quality of the piece, lest their readers misread the ensuing narrative. This is followed by a supposed lecture to a society of men who meet to discuss the artistic qualities of murder, justifying themselves by appealing to the "two handles" for taking hold of everything—the moral and the aesthetic. The lecturer is another of De Quincey's polyhistor protagonists, citing authorities, sketching portraits of murder in various ages, discoursing on being murdered as the mark of a true philosopher, and commenting on the principles of amateur and professional murder in the early nineteenth century. His account closes with the juxtaposition of his claim that murder, like any other art, is humanizing with an account of his "patriotic" murder of a tomcat. This essay was popular with many nineteenth-century readers for its playful manipulation of the line between the horrible and the ordinary and its send-up of scholarly and critical pretensions. From 1827 through 1829 De Quincey wrote political articles and reviews of the quarterlies for the *Edinburgh Saturday Post*, the *Edinburgh Evening Post*, and the *Edinburgh Literary Gazette*, spending much of his time in Edinburgh, though his family remained at Grasmere. His financial affairs were, as usual, in disarray, despite a fairly steady income from his writing. The family held leases on more than one cottage in Grasmere and De Quincey owed money to more than one landlord in Edinburgh. In 1830 Margaret and the seven De Quincey children joined him in the city. De Quincey's known work dwindled to a trickle during the next two years, though he may have begun work on his Gothic novel, *Klosterheim* (1832), and was probably doing more newspaper work and some anonymous political articles for *Blackwood's*.

In February 1832 the last of De Quincey's children, Emily, was born, and in the summer his wife's sister, Ann, came to live with the family. In the same year De Quincey's world was shaken by the passage of the Reform Bill, his own imprisonment as a debtor, and the death of his three-year-old son, Julius. More than ever, the world of the nineteenth century seemed threatening to De Quincey's Tory sense of order and his belief in the sanctity of private life. Reform, for De Quincey, was synonymous with revolution that sweeps away the distinctions and harmonies of private and social life. And he feared a concurrent revolution of intellectual life, for reform, he believed, "brutalizes by keeping the mind under the pressure of the material—the Tangible—the definite" and "all the business of the furnace and the dissecting room" rather than expanding it to take in a spiritual knowledge that might elevate and refine human feelings. His essays of 1832 and 1833 contain reflections on power and revolution as he considered Charlemagne, the Caesars, and world politics.

The year 1832 also saw the Edinburgh publication of De Quincey's *Klosterheim; or the Masque*. A generally stiff and labored echo of De Quincey's youthful Gothic reading, his conventional tale of secret passageways, omens, and revenge, set in the midst of the Thirty Years' War, was not well received. The novel has had few admirers, though some critics have looked at it for keys to the development of De Quincey's prose persona and heightened style. Maximillian, the hero of the tale, is a legitimate prince, fighting incognito as the "masque" who terrorizes the usurping Landgrave and his supporters. Some passages in the novel do suggest De Quincey's developing facility with a prose that captures the mood of nightmare. The denouement—in which Maximillian's identity is revealed at a masked ball and the Landgrave, meaning to kill Maximillian's beloved Countess Paulina, instead murders his own daughter—is typical not only of the fictional conventions of the period but of De Quincey's consistent love for reversals and his persistent fascination with the female as sacrifice.

The following year saw the complete wreck of De Quincey's household economy as he declared bankruptcy and fled to sanctuary at Holyrood, where he would spent most of his time until 1839. There, shut off from his books and sometimes from his family, De Quincey began to write for *Tait's* in 1834. While he continued to produce miscellaneous essays, De Quincey turned to his experiences with the Lake Poets for much of his material during these years, writing anecdotal reminiscences that focused on physical descriptions, personalities, and relationships rather than on textual criticism. His candor was not always flattering. The Wordsworth and Coleridge families felt that De Quincey had violated the trust of friendship, and some of De Quincey's contemporaries felt that he had overstepped the boundaries of biographical discretion. But scholars in subsequent generations have continued to find a lively and sometimes telling human record of the first generation of Romantic writers in De Quincey's accounts.

In exile in Holyrood, De Quincey continued to write, evading creditors while worrying about money and Margaret's deepening depression. In 1835, his promising eldest son, William, died at the age of eighteen. De Quincey's lingering sorrow over this loss was compounded by the death of his wife two years later. Distraught, De Quincey turned more and more to memories for relief. Though they had often been separated for months at a time, Margaret had been for her husband a sort of emotional mainstay, always remaining for him a child-woman to come home to. At her death, their oldest daughter, also named Margaret, took charge of the younger children, the household, and, increasingly, De Quincey's finances.

In the same year, De Quincey began a series of contributions to the *Encyclopædia Britannica* on German and British writers and published his "Revolt of the Tartars" in *Blackwood's* (July 1837). The contribution to *Blackwood's* is one of the most readable of De Quincey's historical narratives. It is also typical of De Quincey's method of writing history. He pieces together material from several sources, using a relatively minor historical event to create a narrative with mythic resonance. In De Quincey's account the Kalmuck Tartars, slighted by the Russian empress and harboring a traitor within, make their exodus eastward through an arduous wilderness. The narrative climaxes in a bloody battle on the margin of a lake and ends with the reception of the surviving remnant by a benevolent Chinese emperor who offers them a new home in a pastoral paradise. As he tells the story, De Quincey's narrative power coincides with some of the insistent themes of his historical essays, including the providential nature of betrayal, conflict, and power as loss paves the way for progress. Here, as in his discussions of the two-party political system and the struggles between Christianity and paganism, conflict moves the world forward, and individual losses are made up in corporate gains.

Two tales contributed to *Blackwood's* in 1838 take up this theme in another key, as social class and sexual double standards move the plots of "The Household Wreck" (January) and "The Avenger" (August). Scholars have generally considered the first of these De Quincey's own, while suspecting that "The Avenger" is adapted from a German source. In "The Household Wreck," an ineffectual gentleman learns that his wife, Agnes, has been accused of theft by an unscrupulous shopkeeper after she has refused to yield to his advances. Her husband is unable to save her, and her subsequent imprisonment, escape, and death form the center of a narrative that broods on vengeance, which the gentleman takes only in the telling of the tale. Maximillian, the "avenger" of the second tale, is more forceful, destroying the tradesman-magistrates who dishonored his mother and sisters by creating his own "bloody system" of disguise and murder. Yet his creation engulfs those he loves, destroying his Margaret and their infant son and ending in his suicide. In both tales De Quincey's uneasiness about the stability of the post-Reform Bill world and his personal sense of guilt, sorrow, and outrage over the deaths of his wife and sons work with his melodramatic narrative style to create apocalypses of public and private lives.

When De Quincey once again returned to his theme of "Murder Considered as One of the Fine Arts" in the November 1839 issue of *Blackwood's*, that sense of apocalypse fueled an anarchic humor that has fewer admirers than the satire of the first paper. In the second paper, the society of murder fanciers reconvenes, but this time, after parrying the slanders of detractors among the reading public, the lecturer's account of the deterioration of murder since the French Revolution is gradually drowned out by the drunken choruses of his club mates, delighted with the very idea of unmaking even a fellow member, by declaring him "Non inventus."

In 1839 and 1840 De Quincey rounded out his recollections of the literary figures of his day with sketches of Southey and minor literary figures and an account of his gradual estrangement from Wordsworth. He was still pursuing many pet themes in his miscellaneous essays, ranging over history from the the sect of the Essenes to the contemporary Chinese opium question. In 1840 he settled with his three daughters and two of his sons at Mavis Bush, Lasswade, near Edinburgh. De Quincey's working habits were as erratic as ever and his daughters, visitors, and De

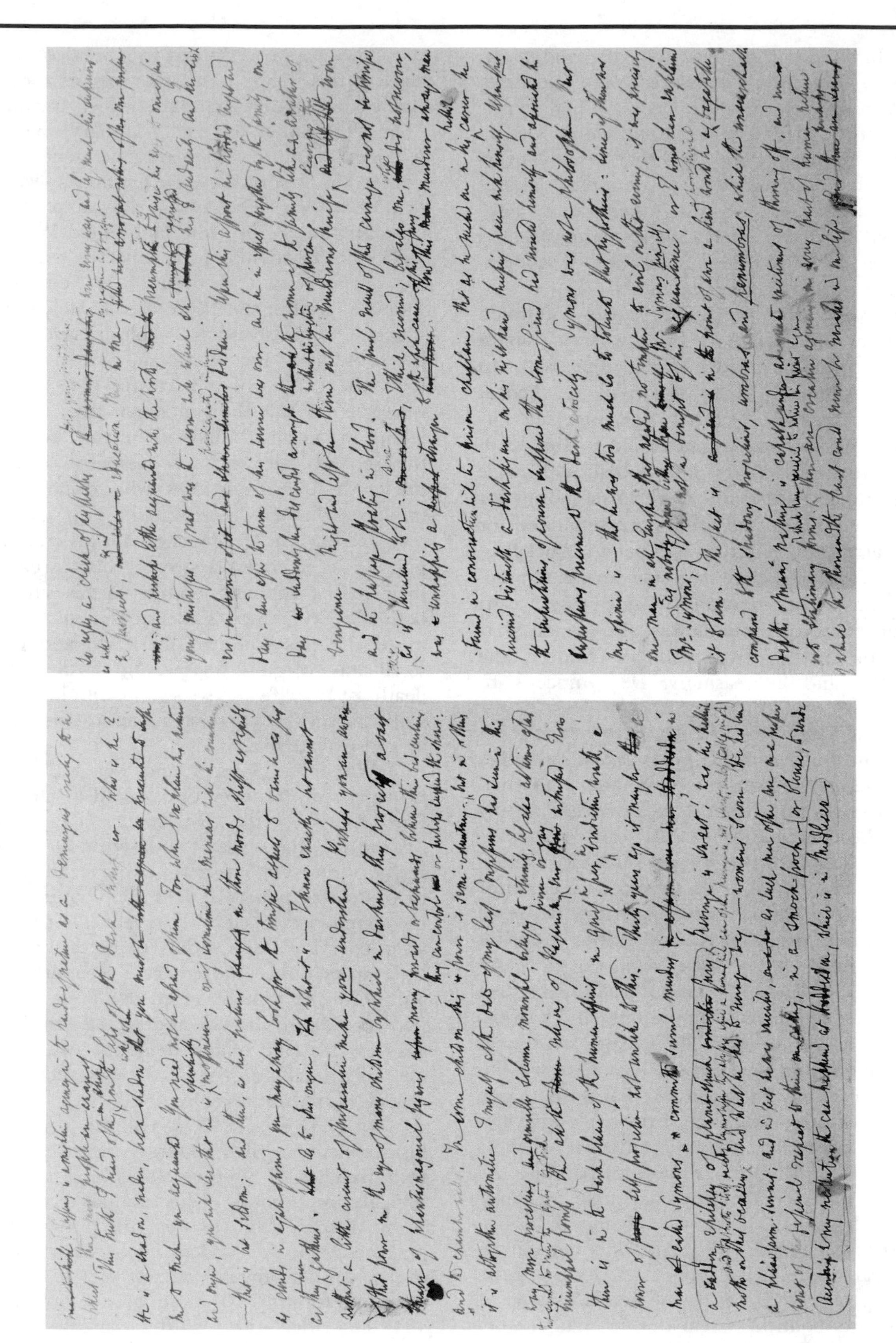

*Manuscript for "The Dark Interpreter," collected by Alexander H. Japp in volume one of* The Posthumous Works of Thomas De Quincey *(1891) but written circa 1845 as part of De Quincey's* Suspiria de Profundis *(Special Collections, Thomas Cooper Library, University of South Carolina)*

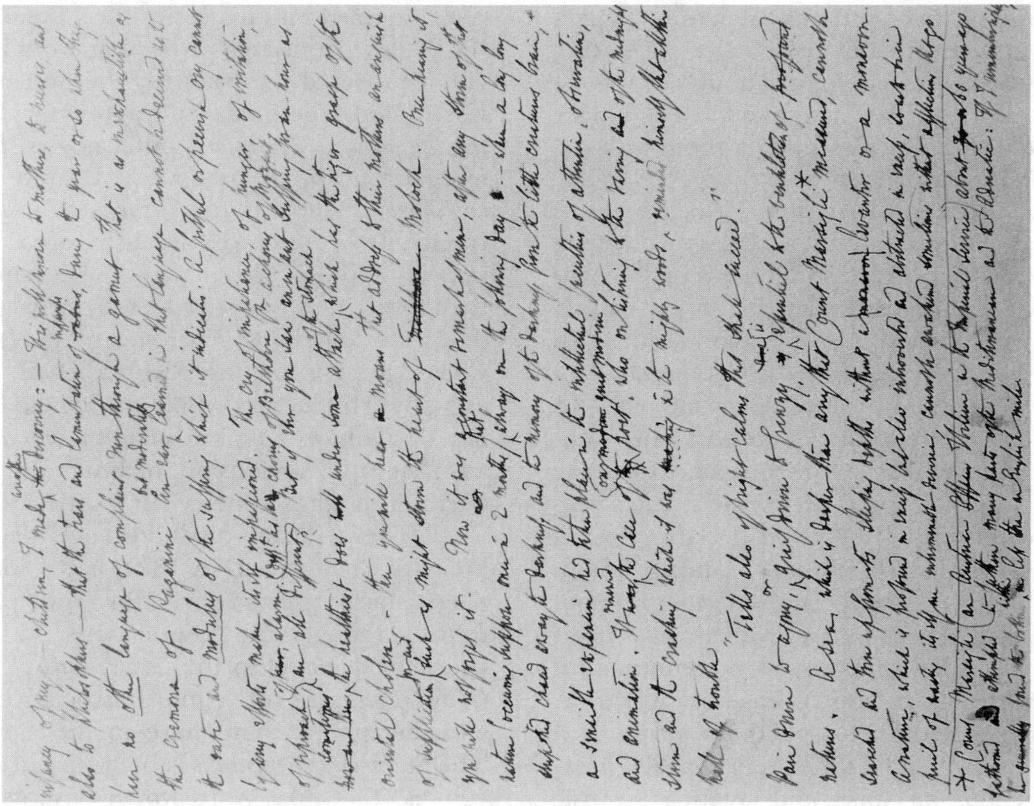

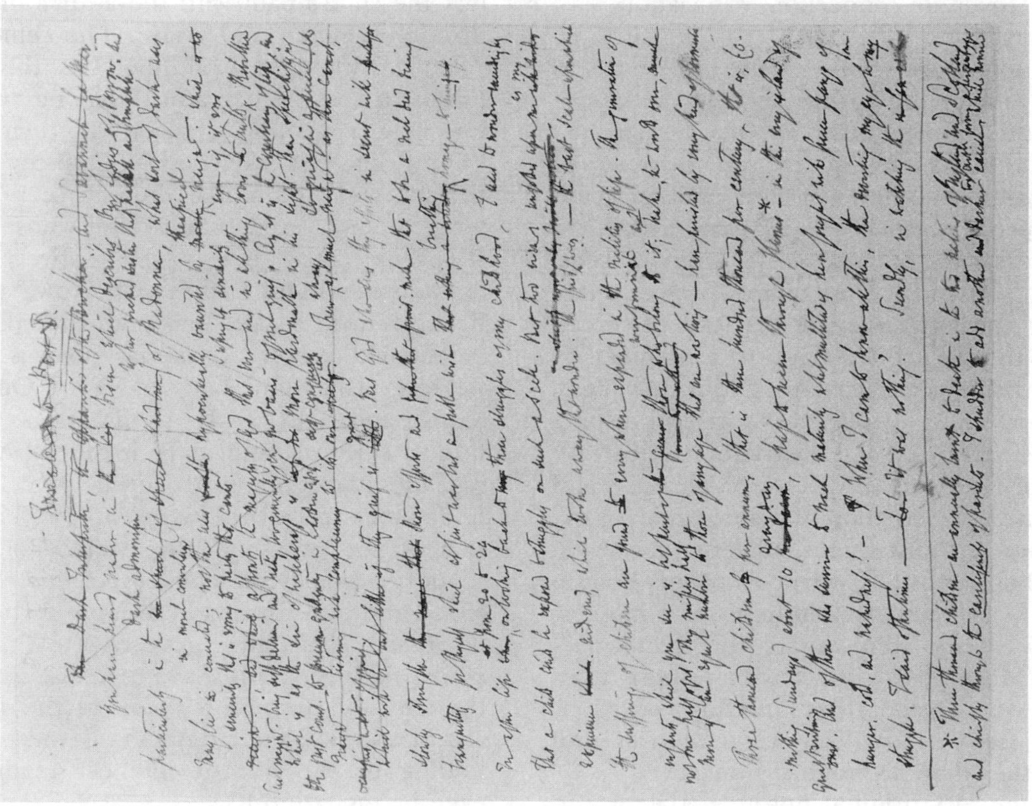

Quincey himself give accounts of piles of papers which he was continually in danger of setting afire as he wrote by candlelight. Though he was ostensibly living with his daughters, De Quincey often wrote in Edinburgh, filling a room with papers and then moving on.

From March 1841 to June 1843, De Quincey lived in various houses in Glasgow, staying for some time with Professor John Pringle Nichol, dodging creditors and engaging in journalistic work. In 1842, when his son Horace died in China, De Quincey responded by contracting to pay his son's debts in a series of installments. In the midst of the personal trials of the early 1840s, De Quincey turned once again to literary theory, writing on "Style" (*Blackwood's*, July, September, and October 1840) and declaring, in an essay on Herodutus (*Blackwood's*, January 1842), that prose had its own laws of composition. While in earlier works he had sometimes echoed contemporary views of prose as a medium connected inextricably to the commercial world, in these essays De Quincey argued for prose as a high art in its own right, a medium capable of expanding the human spirit and creating a music of its own through connection, association, and conflict.

Once more, De Quincey's use of opium was escalating, and in the spring of 1844 he experienced a serious opium crisis. By June he had succeeded in reducing his dosage. In the wake of this crisis came another work on political economy. In *The Logic of Political Economy* (1844), De Quincey depicted that science as stagnant since the death of David Ricardo, failing through a laxity of logic and language. De Quincey attempted to restore the Ricardian vigor to economics by means of a patient explication of Ricardo's ideas, especially on value. De Quincey's careful distinctions between the used and the useful implicitly reminded the reader of the roles of pleasure and imagination in the creation of value, while his extravagant use of illustrations suggested a tension between the ostensible purpose of explication and De Quincey's persistent indulgence in intellectual display. While John Stuart Mill treated elements of De Quincey's work with respect, most readers have agreed that in this work, as elsewhere, De Quincey was a popularizer and teacher, rather than an original thinker.

De Quincey's original power was at play in several significant works that followed *The Logic of Political Economy*, for the scholarly economist was also a dreamer, whose waking and sleeping visions, coupled with his desire for a flexible, powerful, highly connected prose that would incarnate vision provided the basis for the best of his later work. One of these was the fragmentary but haunting *Suspiria de Profundis*, published in *Blackwood's* in March through July 1845. Despite De Quincey's lists of subjects for *Suspiria de Profundis*, the fragments of other visions discovered among his papers, and his laments over the papers for it that perished in a sort of literary brushfire on his desk, the *Suspiria de Profundis* of the 1840s, like Coleridge's fragmentary "Kubla Khan," functions as a powerful literary whole. It does so by exploiting De Quincey's typical imaginative merging of autobiography and vision, ordinary narrative and heightened "prose-poetry" in a series of sketches.

"The Affliction of Childhood," like the "Preliminary Confessions" of 1821, lays a sort of autobiographical groundwork for the pieces that follow, though the connections in this self-proclaimed sequel to the *Confessions of an English Opium Eater* are often more associative, indirect, and metaphoric than those in the earlier work. The *Suspiria de Profundis* is built up out of the "involutes" that, like Wordsworth's "spots of time," link the child's pain with the adult's illumination through memory and vision. The centerpiece of "The Affliction of Childhood" is the death of Elizabeth and the narrator's ensuing vision of an infinitely retreating chariot of divine power. "The Palimpsest" sketches De Quincey's vision of private and communal human experience in terms of a layered manuscript whose messages are overwritten but never entirely lost. In "Levanna and Our Ladies of Sorrow," the female figure returns to De Quincey's dreamscape with heightened power. Levanna governs a mythic world in which Our Lady of Tears, Our Lady of Sighs, and Our Lady of Darkness incarnate human suffering and make it redemptive, plaguing the narrator's heart until they have "unfolded the capacities of his spirit." In "The Apparition of the Brocken," the narrator's magnified shadow becomes an emblem of his spirit, projected and transformed in dreams as the Dark Interpreter. This figure governs the finale of the piece, the vision of "Savannah-la-Mar," leading the narrator through a vision of the submerged city that stresses the judgment of God and the unfolding of the human intellect made possible even by the painful sacrifice of suffering infants. The second part of the *Suspiria de Profundis* consists of a "Vision of Life," a narrative which views suffering from a more private, individual view-

38 THE SPANISH MILITARY NUN.

so that the two principals had to tie white handkerchiefs round their elbows, in order to descry each other. In the confusion they wounded each other mortally. Upon that, according to a usage not peculiar to Spaniards, but extending (as doubtless the reader knows) for a century longer to our own countrymen, the two seconds were obliged in honour to do something towards avenging their principals. Kate had her usual fatal luck. Her sword passed sheer through the body of her opponent: this unknown opponent falling dead, had just breath left to cry out, "Ah, villain, you have killed me!" in a voice of horrific reproach; and the voice was the voice of her brother!

The monks of the monastery, under whose silent shadows this murderous duel had taken place, roused by the clashing of swords and the angry shouts of combatants, issued out with torches to find one only of the four officers surviving. Every convent and altar had a right of asylum for a short period. According to the custom, the monks carried Kate, insensible with anguish of mind, to the sanctuary of their chapel. There for some days they detained her; but then, having furnished her with a horse and some provisions, they turned her adrift. Which way should the unhappy fugitive turn? In blindness of heart she turned towards the sea. It was the sea that had brought her to Peru; it was the sea that would perhaps carry her away. It was the sea that had first showed her this land and its golden hopes; it was the sea that ought to hide from her its fearful remembrances. The sea it was that had twice spared her life in extremities; the sea it was that might now, if it chose, take back the bauble that it had spared in vain.

THE SPANISH MILITARY NUN. 39

16.—*Kate's Ascent of the Andes.*

Three days our poor heroine followed the coast. Her horse was then almost unable to move; and on *his* account she turned inland to a thicket, for grass and shelter. As she drew near to it, a voice challenged, "*Who goes there?*"—Kate answered, "*Spain.*"—"*What people?*"—"*A friend.*" It was two soldiers, deserters, and almost starving. Kate shared her provisions with these men: and, on hearing their plan, which was to go over the Cordilleras, she agreed to join the party. *Their* object was the wild one of seeking the river *Dorado*, whose waters rolled along golden sands, and whose pebbles were emeralds. *Hers* was to throw herself upon a line the least liable to pursuit, and the readiest for a new chapter of life, in which oblivion might be found for the past. After a few days of incessant climbing and fatigue, they found themselves in the regions of perpetual snow. Summer would come as vainly to this kingdom of frost as to the grave of her brother. No fire, but the fire of human blood in youthful veins, could ever be kept burning in these aerial solitudes. Fuel was rarely to be found, and kindling a fire was a secret hardly known except to Indians. However, our Kate can do everything; and she's the girl, if ever girl *did* such a thing, that I back at any odds for crossing the Cordilleras. I would bet you something now, reader, if I thought you would deposit your stakes by return of post (as they play at chess through the post-office), that Kate does the trick; that she gets down to the other side; that the soldiers do *not;* and that the horse, if preserved at all, is preserved in a way that will leave him very little to boast of.

The party had gathered wild berries and esculent roots at the foot of the mountains, and the horse was of very great use in carrying them. But this larder was soon

64 THE SPANISH MILITARY NUN.

words that are destined to remain untranslated in their original Spanish. The good senora, though she could boast only of forty-two years' experience, by supposing was not altogether to be "*had*" in that fashion—she was as learned as if she had been fifty, and she brought matters to a speedy crisis. "You are a Spaniard," she said, "a gentleman, therefore; *remember* that you are a gentleman. This very night, if your intentions are not serious, quit my house. Go to Tucuman; you shall command my horses and servants; but stay no longer to increase the sorrow that already you will have left behind you. My daughter loves you. That is sorrow enough, if you are trifling with us. But, if not, and you also love *her*, and can be happy in our solitary mode of life, stay with us—stay for ever. Marry Juana with my free consent. I ask not for wealth. Mine is sufficient for you both." The cornet protested that the honour was one never contemplated by *him*—that it was too great—that——. But, of course, reader, you know that "gammon" flourishes in Peru, amongst the silver mines, as well as in some more boreal lands that produce little better than copper and tin. "Tin," however, has its uses. The delighted senora overruled all objections, great and small; and she confirmed Juana's notion that the business of two worlds could be transacted in an hour, by settling her daughter's future happiness in exactly twenty minutes. The poor, weak Catalina, not acting now in any spirit of recklessness, grieving sincerely for the gulf that was opening before her, and yet shrinking effeminately from the momentary shock that would be inflicted by a firm adherence to her duty, clinging to the anodyne of a short delay, allowed herself to be installed as the lover of Juana. Considerations of convenience, however, postponed the marriage. It was requisite to make

THE SPANISH MILITARY NUN. 65

various purchases; and for this, it was requisite to visit Tucuman, where also the marriage ceremony could be performed with more circumstantial splendour. To Tucuman, therefore, after some weeks' interval, the whole party repaired. And at Tucuman it was that the tragical events arose, which, whilst interrupting such a mockery for ever, left the poor Juana still happily deceived, and never believing for a moment that hers was a rejected or a deluded heart.

One reporter of Mr De Ferrer's narrative forgets his usual generosity, when he says, that the senora's gift of her daughter to the Alferez was not quite so disinterested as it seemed to be. Certainly it was not so disinterested as European ignorance might fancy it: but it was quite as much so as it ought to have been, in balancing the interests of a child. Very true it is—that, being a genuine Spaniard, who was still a rare creature in so vast a world as Peru, being a Spartan amongst Helots, a Spanish Alferez would in those days, and in that point, have been a natural noble. His alliance created honour for his wife and for his descendants. Something, therefore, the cornet would add to the family consideration. But, instead of selfishness, it argued just regard for her daughter's interest to build upon this, as some sort of equipoise to the wealth which her daughter would bring.

Spaniard, however, as she was, our Alférez, on reaching Tucuman, found no Spaniards to mix with, but instead, twelve Portuguese.

21.—*Kate once more in Storms.*

Catalina remembered the Spanish proverb, "Subtract from a Spaniard all his good qualities, and the remainder makes a pretty fair Portuguese;" but, as there was nobody

*De Quincey's corrected proofs for pages from volume three (1854) of* Selections Grave and Gay *(HM 31019; Henry E. Huntington Library and Art Gallery)*

point as the narrator recounts the history of a family of women whose lives are wasted and destroyed by masculine betrayal. In the end of the narrative, a female child plays in a garden, oblivious to the sorrows of her family's past and the pain that lies in her future. The narrator, looking on, concludes that birth, which brings us into this life of sorrows, is more terrible to contemplate than death. The *Suspiria de Profundis* had many nineteenth-century admirers, who found its prose-poetry haunting, mysterious and unearthly. Some readers, however, objected to the very idea of prose-poetry as a bastard form and saw the work as fragmentary and formless evidence of great power wasted.

From the beginning, there were tensions with *Blackwood's* over the publication of the *Suspiria de Profundis* as the editors tried to keep De Quincey's installments within the normal sixteen-page limit. Disgruntled by the delays in getting the installments before the public, De Quincey worked feverishly on revisions, despite an attack of pleurisy and his disputes with the editors. *Blackwood's* suspended publication of the *Suspiria de Profundis* in July and, despite a reconciliation of sorts in November, with De Quincey promising to provide more *Suspiria* material, De Quincey turned to *Tait's Edinburgh Magazine*. Though Margaret was slowly untangling De Quincey's finances, he was still in debt and pursued by creditors, a circumstance that spurred him to write more articles than *Tait's* could print.

In September of 1845, *Tait's* published his essay "On Wordsworth's Poetry" which demonstrated that although his relationship with Wordsworth had failed, his admiration of Wordsworth's poetry remained unchanged. De Quincey applauded the poet laureate's observations of nature, his delineation of moods and motives, and his insight into human feelings. In the months that followed, De Quincey wrote assorted articles and worked at recovering his health, walking at least six miles a day, often going round and round the garden at Lasswade.

In January of 1846, De Quincey's mother died, leaving her property to his unmarried sister Jane and a small income from her capital to Thomas. In December, after *Tait's* was bought by the *North British Daily Mail*, he moved to Glasgow again in order to write for both periodicals. Without Margaret to care for him, De Quincey's clothing soon reached such a shabby state that one friend's landlady turned him away, mistaking him for a tramp. By 1847 De Quincey's financial state was relatively stable, thanks to Margaret; he continued to rent more than one lodging in both Glasgow and Edinburgh. In April of that year he returned to Lasswade to visit his son Francis and daughters Margaret, Florence, and Emily. By this time another son, Paul Fred, was serving with the army in India. Back in Glasgow in September, De Quincey fell ill of a fever he believed he had picked up during his talks with homeless Irish immigrants camped by the river. By mid October he had recovered and was writing again.

Among his writings for 1846 and 1847 were "Joan of Arc" and "The Nautico-Military Nun of Spain" (later retitled "The Spanish Military Nun"), two very different accounts of the woman warrior from the perspectives of the historian and the raconteur. De Quincey's "Joan of Arc" (March and August 1847) celebrates both the redemptive martyrdom of the girl-woman and the power of the historian to vindicate her memory. The essay is typical of De Quincey's approach to history, playing fast and loose with sources in order to create an evocative, symbolic picture. For De Quincey, the "angel of research" was ever superseded by the "angel of meditation," whose imaginative vision cleansed the lying documentary record and brought it back to life in a new form. De Quincey's tale of the military nun, published by *Tait's* in three installments in May, June, and July of 1847, makes a different use of source materials, turning accounts based on the historical Caterina De Erauso's memoirs into a picaresque narrative with tragicomic overtones. De Quincey's narrator is always in the foreground of the tale, managing the show as "his" Kate escapes from the convent, dons trousers, and pursues a series of adventures in the New World, gambling, soldiering, and eluding infatuated women. This narrative has never received much attention from De Quincey scholars, most of whom tend to dismiss it as uneven. Some early readers appreciated the sometimes rollicking quality of Kate's adventures, but twentieth-century critics often find it difficult to square with the prevailing picture of De Quincey as a Romantic practitioner of the prose of vision.

In 1847 and 1848 De Quincey continued to indulge in his fascination with the mysterious and oracular in his accounts of secret societies and in his picture of "Protestantism" (February 1848). For him, the Bible was itself an oracle, not in specific words or formulas but by its inner consistency, the deep core of meaning that survived successive interpretations of its textual surface.

De Quincey had never become the evangelical thinker of whom his mother would have approved, but for him Christianity and a Christian ethic of charity were central to a vision of the world as providential, even in its tragedy. Some of De Quincey's contemporaries saw him as a defender of the faith, broadly defined, and as a deeply spiritual writer.

By 1848, by dint of walking, dosing himself with various concoctions, and keeping somewhat more regular hours, De Quincey had reached a truce with opium that would last to the end of his life. His contributions to the *North British Review* on Goldsmith (May), Pope (August), and Lamb (November) show his hard-earned awareness of the commercial side of literature as he reflects on the literary market and economic necessities that helped to shape writers' careers. Although he had turned hack writer from necessity, reluctantly giving up his gentlemanly amateur status, he had remade his role as he worked, retailoring the world of the working professional to suit his purposes. This was perhaps nowhere more evident than in the work that began to appear in October of the following year as De Quincey returned to *Blackwood's* with the first part of his series of essays built around his experience of riding on the mail coaches in his Oxford days.

In "The English Mail-Coach, or the Glory of Motion," De Quincey celebrated the vanished splendors of animal velocity, replaced by the mechanical forces of the railroad age. De Quincey made the mail coach, thundering along the highways with its cargo of political news and young men from Oxford, an emblem of power. But the news of victory is also the news of death, and the masculine powers associated with the mail coach carry the narrator to the brink of nightmare as he recounts his flirtation with the coachman's granddaughter Fanny and his subsequent dreams of that grandfather as an avenging crocodile. This narrative was followed in December by "The Vision of Sudden Death" and the "Dream-Fugue on the above theme of Sudden Death." In "The Vision of Sudden Death" De Quincey moved from a meditation on Roman and Christian responses to the link between sudden death and moral responsibility to an account of an accident on the Bath road. The narrator of the tale is riding the mail and enjoying his opium reveries when the coachman falls asleep and the coach strays into the path of a fragile gig in which two lovers are whispering in one another's ears. Powerless to avert disaster, the narrator manages to shout a warning and glimpse the woman's agony of terror; then the coach rolls away into darkness. The "Dream-Fugue" recounts a series of visions taking up the themes of power, endangered females, and the bursting of "sepulchral bonds," building from a vision of an encounter between an "English three-decker" and a "fairy pinnace" to a sonorous finale in which the mail coach sweeps through a cathedral with its news of the Waterloo victory. As it publishes victory, the coach destroys a female child who is then resurrected in womanly form, the sacrifice that saves England and Christendom, proving God's endless love. This work of impassioned prose has fascinated De Quincey's readers from the start. Though Leslie Stephen objected to its "exaggerated patriotism" (*Fortnightly Review*, 1 March 1871), many readers have been moved by its powerful linkage of public symbol and private emotion. This work has received careful attention from critics interested in the psychological and sexual dimensions of De Quincey's images of masculine power, feminine frailty, and anxious guilt.

De Quincey next took his miscellaneous articles on topics such as "Presence of Mind" and "The Theban Sphinx" to *Hogg's Instructor*, where he was a steady contributor in the early 1850s. There, in his 1851 essay "On the Present State of the English Language," De Quincey argued once more for the importance of the laborers of the mint, those writers who carried the seminal ideas of more original thinkers to the public in a powerful and living prose. In three decades of writing for the magazines, he had attempted to create a prose medium of singular power, the equal of the poetry so highly prized by Romantic theory and literary tradition. He had also tested the limits of commercial writing with its restrictions on length, subject, and language. In 1852 his manipulation of those limitations reached a characteristic extreme in the essay entitled "Sir William Hamilton." There, in three installments that continually promised but never quite delivered information on the stated subject, De Quincey played with the writer-reader contract in a spiraling series of digressions and some tongue-in-cheek meditations on the infinity of writing and the finitude of the magazines.

In 1851 James T. Fields began the publication of De Quincey's collected works in the United States. Although there was no international copyright agreement, Fields visited De Quincey and paid him a share of the profits. As

*Pages from a draft for "My Brother Pink," first published in the March 1838 issue of* Tait's Edinburgh Magazine *and revised by De Quincey for volume one (1853) of* Selections Grave and Gay *(HM 36040; Henry E. Huntington Library and Art Gallery)*

he was consigned to the care of a gentleman who won from him by kindness what he had refused to importunities or menaces. An express was thereupon forwarded from Liverpool to our nearest male relative — a military man, then by accident on leave of absence from a remote colony. He came over, took my brother back [looking upon the whole as a boyish frolic of no permanent importance], made some stipulations in his behalf as to indemnity from punishment, and immediately returned home. Left to himself the grim tyrant of the school easily evaded the stipulation, and repeated his brutalities more fiercely than before — now acting in the double spirit of tyranny and revenge. 3

In a few hours my brother was again on the road to Liverpool. But not on this occasion did he resort to any inn, or visit any treacherous haunts of the picturesque. He offered himself to no temptation now nor to any risk. He went right on wards to the docks, addressed himself to a grave elder master of a trading vessel bound upon a distant voyage, and instantly procured an engagement. The skipper was a good and sensible man, and (as it turned out) as a sailor accomplished in all parts of his profession. The ship which he commanded was a South Sea whaler belonging to Lord Grenville; whether lying at Liverpool or in the Thames at that moment I am not sure: however they soon afterwards sailed.

For completed more than two years my brother continued under the care of this good man, who was won by his appearance and by some resemblance which he fancied in his features to a son whom he had lost. Fortunate indeed for the poor boy was this interval of fatherly superintendance: for under him he was not only preserved from the perils which afterwards beleigred him until his years had made him more capable of confronting them; but also he had then an opportunity which he improved to the utmost of making himself acquainted with the two separate branches of his profession — navigation, and seamanship, qualifications which are not only often united.

After the death of this captain, my brother ran through many and wild adventures until at length after a severe action fought off the coast of Peru the armed merchantman in which he then served was captured by Pirates. most of the crew were massacred: my brother, on account of the important services he could render, was spared: and with these Pirates, cruising under a black flag, and perpetrating unnumbered atrocities, he was obliged to sail for the next two years and a half: nor could he in all that period find any opportunity for effecting his escape.

4

Fields patiently gathered material from numerous periodicals, De Quincey became convinced that a collection of his works could be done. Working with James Hogg, editor of *Hogg's Instructor*, De Quincey began to gather, arrange and revise his writings, using the American edition as a starting point. As he worked on the collection, he was still projecting large multivolume scholarly ventures. De Quincey saw the collected edition itself as an opportunity for extensive reworking of earlier materials.

He began with the autobiographical sketches he had done for *Tait's* in the 1830s, *Blackwood's* in the 1840s, and *Hogg's* in the 1850s, carefully reworking the texts and piecing them together into a unified framework. The result, in 1853, was the first volume of *Selections Grave and Gay*, the author's own collected edition. The *Autobiographic Sketches* sparked renewed interest in De Quincey as an autobiographer. His recounting of childhood memories and the crises of growing to manhood is unusual in its heightened treatment of small incidents and in its interweaving of personal experience with material from De Quincey's reading. While some readers have disliked the lack of proportion evidenced in the juxtaposition of the death of a kitten and the death of a sister, De Quincey's work exemplifies Romantic beliefs about the importance of childhood experience and the role of subjective response in creating poetry and prose. In the same year, Margaret, who was then thirty-five years old, married Robert Craig, the son of a Lasswade neighbor, and went with her husband to live in Ireland. Twenty-six-year-old Florence then took charge of the De Quincey household. The volumes of the collected edition sold well, and De Quincey received a share of the profits. For the rest of his life the collected edition of his writings was to be his main work.

The most significant additions of the following year were a second volume completing the autobiographical work and an addition to De Quincey's murder essays in the form of a "Postscript," written for those who took pleasure in the earlier murder papers. It begins with De Quincey's assertion that a central difference between his own work and Jonathan Swift's is that Swift's was based on a totally fantastic idea while De Quincey's essays are rooted in a real human propensity to find pleasure in horrors they cannot change or prevent, such as murders already committed. De Quincey follows this with accounts of murders committed by Williams and by the M'Keans. De Quincey's murder narratives are skillfully told, concentrating on the murder itself, although they include summaries of the detection. As the tale unfolds, De Quincey manipulates the reader's sympathy, depicting murder as a conflict between murderer and victim and emphasizing the motif of the locked door that stands between ordinary life and the brutal business of murder. In this narrative, too, the female victim reappears, but this time, while older women are killed, the young girl escapes through the efforts of the journeyman lodger. Diverging from the satire and slapstick of the first two murder essays, the "Postscript" takes up the aesthetic challenge of creating a murder narrative. In doing so, De Quincey both demonstrates power and studies it, as he skillfully builds tension and dramatizes scenes of violence and suspense.

In 1855 Florence married Colonel Baird Smith and went with him to India, leaving only Emily at home. By this time, however, De Quincey was spending most of his time in Edinburgh, working amid his perpetual pile of papers at 42 Lothian Street. No volume of the collected edition appeared in 1855, probably because De Quincey was hard at work on a massive revision of the *Confessions of an English Opium Eater*. He added substantial portions to the autobiographical section, writing for the first time publicly about his conflict with his mother. Where he made textual changes they tended to move in the direction of the more elaborate prose he had developed in the *Suspiria de Profundis* and "The English Mail-Coach." Finally, he added "The Daughter of Lebanon," originally intended for the *Suspiria de Profundis*, as a sort of finale. This dream vision of a repentant prostitute and the powerful evangelist who oversees her conversion and death, bears curious resemblances to nineteenth-century religious tracts. Most readers have preferred the 1821/1822 *Confessions of an English Opium Eater*, seeing the 1856 version as less visionary and more cumbersome. Those who have commented on "The Daughter of Lebanon" fault De Quincey's decision to include it, seeing it as anticlimactic and as weakening the structure of the work. Still, "The Daughter of Lebanon" brings full circle the motif of the lost sister begun in the "Preliminary Confessions," and its version of impassioned prose overwrites the boundary between dream vision and structured narrative.

*De Quincey with his daughters Emily and Margaret and his granddaughter Eva, 1855 (pastel by James Archer; Collection of Rosemary Blok van Cronesteyn)*

The summer of 1857 was a time of tension and change for De Quincey. In June, England learned of the Indian Mutiny and De Quincey feared for the safety of Florence and her baby. After erroneous news of a massacre at Delhi, De Quincey was plagued by nightmares. In July, Emily and Paul Fred persuaded De Quincey to go with them to Ireland to visit Margaret and her children. For all his intellectual and professional wanderings, it had been a long time since De Quincey had journeyed so far from home. His children, however, were outdistancing him. Paul Fred, who had left the army, was soon to immigrate to New Zealand. Having learned that Florence and her family had survived the Mutiny, De Quincey turned the energies of his personal nightmares to public advantage, writing on India and the Mutiny for the *Titan* in the fall of 1857.

By late 1858, De Quincey's health was failing and he worked intermittently, still recording his dreams and laboring over revisions of his work. The thirteenth volume of the collected edition came out in May of 1859. In the months that followed, illness gradually overtook him, and his landladies cared for him as if he were a child. He slept more and more as the weeks wore on, and Emily returned from a prolonged visit to Ireland to nurse him. On 2 December she sent for Margaret to come from Ireland. As De Quincey lay dying, he murmured about childhood days, talking of his father, his mother, and his sister Elizabeth. He died quietly on the morning of 8 December 1859 and was buried beside his wife in St. Cuthbert's churchyard.

The obituaries and posthumous assessments of his career were mixed. There were few who did not regard him as a genius, but many saw in him an emblem of wasted potential. Before the publication of the collected editions in the 1850s, De Quincey had primarily been known as the "Opium-Eater" and, by the readers of the quarterlies, as a scholar. Increasingly, from the 1850s on, critics focused on De Quincey's impassioned prose, recognizing him as a prose stylist in the grand manner and a weaver of mystery and vision. In the last half of the nineteenth century personal reminiscences of the eccentric man with his odd clothes and kindly but impractical ways endeared him to the reading public, even as charges of moral bankruptcy leveled by anonymous reviewers and well-known figures such as Harriet Martineau made him suspect. At the turn of the twentieth century, there was still a high degree of interest in De Quincey as a man, followed in the early twentieth century by more detached attention to his style. After World War I, several book-length biographies of De Quincey were published, and scholars began serious disputes over De Quincey's literary and intellectual influence and the originality of his contributions to philosophy, political economy, and literary theory. After World War II, critics tended to turn back to biographical and psychological issues, looking at De Quincey's relationships with other writers, the effect of opium on his work, and the tensions within his work.

De Quincey's place in the history of prose writing is still disputed. He was a prolific writer, and his work is so voluminous and various that it defies easy categorization. Some literary historians have sided with Leslie Stephen's view of De Quincey as representative of a "particular side-current in English thought" (*Fortnightly Review*, 1 March 1871). Idiosyncratic and digressive, De Quincey strikes many readers as too labyrinthine and eccentric to be considered a major writer. Then too, his bold shifts of tone and voice strike many readers as clumsy. Yet for all this, there are few in the twentieth century who would deny that De Quincey is a master in the management of prose style as he balances his control of word and cadence with his revolt against convention and prescription. While late-nineteenth-century readers were sometimes bothered by the "bastard" quality of a style that mixed the imagery and rhythms of poetry with the syntactic and structural qualities of prose, this is the aspect of De Quincey most likely to please an appreciative twentieth-century reader. A bicentenary collection of essays on De Quincey edited by Robert L. Snyder suggests the range and richness of late-twentieth-century response to De Quincey's work, as scholars investigate his manipulation of the magazine context, his reworking of Gothic motifs, and his intellectual context. Recent book-length studies by Vincent De Luca, David Devlin, and John C. Whale have called attention to De Quincey as a conscious artist, struggling to retailor his Romantic visions to suit the commercial press for which he wrote. Their work makes possible a new appreciation of De Quincey as a masterful artist in prose, defying the categories of major and minor to create, as Virginia Woolf said, "a class for himself."

**Letters:**

H. A. Page (A. H. Japp), *Thomas De Quincey: His Life and Writings. With Unpublished Correspondence* (2 volumes, London: J. Hogg, 1877; New York: Scribner, Armstrong, 1877; revised and enlarged edition, 1 volume, London: J. Hogg, 1890);

*De Quincey Memorials: Being Letters and Other Records*, 2 volumes, edited by A. H. Japp (London: Heinemann, 1891; New York: United States Book Company, 1891);

*De Quincey at Work: As Seen in One Hundred and Thirty New and Newly Edited Letters*, edited by W. H. Bonner (Buffalo, N.Y.: Airport Publications, Inc., 1936);

*Unpublished Letters of Thomas De Quincey and Elizabeth Barrett Browning*, edited by Sydney Musgrove (Auckland, N.Z.: Auckland University College, 1954);

John E. Jordan, *De Quincey to Wordsworth: A Biography of a Relationship, With the Letters of Thomas De Quincey to the Wordsworth Family* (Berkeley & Los Angeles: University of California Press, 1962).

**Bibliographies:**

David Masson, "Appendix Chronological and Bibliographical" in volume 14 of *The Collected Writings of Thomas De Quincey* (Edinburgh: Adam & Charles Black, 1890);

J. A. Green, *Thomas De Quincey: A Bibliography Based upon the De Quincey Collection in the Moss Side Library* (Manchester: Free Reference Library/Moss Side Library, 1908);

W. E. A. Axon, "The Canon of De Quincey's Writings, with References to some of His Unidentified Articles," in *Transactions of the Royal Society of Literature*, second series 32 (1914): 1-46.

John E. Jordan, "Thomas De Quincey," in *The English Romantic Poets & Essayists: A Review of Criticism and Research*, revised edition, edited by Carolyn Washburn Houtchens and Lawrence Huston Houtchens (New York: Published for the Modern Language Association of America by New York University Press, 1966), pp. 289-331;

Harold O. Dendurant, *Thomas De Quincey: A Reference Guide* (Boston: G. K. Hall, 1978).

**Biographies:**

H. A. Page (A. H. Japp), *Thomas De Quincey: His Life and Writings. With Unpublished Correspondence* (2 volumes, London, J. Hogg, 1877; New York: Scribner, Armstrong, 1877; revised and enlarged edition, 1 volume, London: J. Hogg, 1890);

David Masson, *De Quincey* (London: Macmillan, 1880; New York: Harper, 1901);

J. R. Findlay, *Personal Recollections of Thomas De Quincey* (Edinburgh: Adam & Charles Black, 1886);

James Hogg, ed., *De Quincey and His Friends: Personal Recollections, Souvenirs and Anecdotes* (London: Sampson, Low, Marston, 1895);

Malcolm Elwin, *De Quincey* (London: Duckworth, 1935);

Horace A. Eaton, *Thomas De Quincey: A Biography* (London & New York: Oxford University Press, 1936);

Edward Sackville-West, *A Flame in Sunlight: The Life and Work of Thomas De Quincey* (London & Toronto: Cassell, 1936); also published as *Thomas De Quincey: His Life and Work* (New Haven, Conn.: Yale University Press, 1936);

John Calvin Metcalf, *De Quincey: A Portrait* (Cambridge, Mass.: Harvard University Press, 1940);

John E. Jordan, *De Quincey to Wordsworth: A Biography of a Relationship, With the Letters of Thomas De Quincey to the Wordsworth Family* (Berkeley & Los Angeles: University of California Press, 1962);

Grevel Lindop, *The Opium-Eater: A Life of Thomas De Quincey* (London: Dent, 1981; New York: Taplinger, 1981).

**References:**

M. H. Abrams, *The Milk of Paradise: The Effect of Opium Visions on the Works of De Quincey, Crabbe, Francis Thompson and Coleridge* (Cambridge, Mass.: Harvard University Press, 1934);

Elizabeth Bruss, *Autobiographical Acts: The Changing Situation of a Literary Genre* (Baltimore: Johns Hopkins University, 1977);

Hugh Sykes Davies, *Thomas De Quincey* (London: Longmans, Green, 1964);

Vincent A. De Luca, *Thomas De Quincey: The Prose of Vision* (Toronto: University of Toronto Press, 1980);

David D. Devlin, *De Quincey, Wordsworth, and the Art of Prose* (New York: St. Martin's Press, 1983; London: Macmillan, 1983);

Albert Goldman, *The Mine and the Mint: Sources for the Writings of Thomas De Quincey* (Carbondale & Edwardsville: Southern Illinois University Press, 1965);

Michael Haltresht, "The Meaning of De Quincey's 'Dream Fugue on . . . Sudden Death,' " *Literature and Psychology* 26, no. 1 (1976): 31-36;

Ian Jack, "De Quincey Revises His *Confessions*," *PMLA*, 72 (March 1957):122-146;

Mary Jacobus, "The Art of Managing Books: Romantic Prose and the Writing of the Past," in *Romanticism and Language*, edited by Arden Reed (Ithaca, N.Y.: Cornell University, 1984), pp. 215-246;

F. Samuel Janzow, "De Quincey Enters Journalism: His Contributions to the *Westmorland Gazette*, 1818-1819," Ph.D. dissertation, University of Chicago, 1968;

John E. Jordan, *Thomas De Quincey, Literary Critic: His Method and Achievement* (Berkeley: University of California Press, 1952);

Karen M. Lever, "De Quincey as Gothic Hero: A Perspective on *Confessions of an English Opium Eater* and *Suspiria de Profundis*," *Texas Studies in Literature and Language*, 21 (Fall 1979): 332-346;

Judson S. Lyon, *Thomas De Quincey* (New York: Twayne, 1969);

Robert M. Maniquis, " 'Lonely Empires': Personal and Public Visions of Thomas De Quincey," in *Mid-Nineteenth Century Writers: Eliot, De Quincey, Emerson*, volume 8 of *Literary Monographs*, edited by Eric Rothstein and Joseph Anthony Wittreich, Jr. (Madison: University of Wisconsin Press, 1976), pp. 49-127;

J. Hillis Miller, *The Disappearance of God: Five Nineteenth Century Writers* (Cambridge, Mass.: Harvard University Press, 1975);

Mario Praz, *The Hero in Eclipse in Victorian Fiction*, translated by Angus Davidson (London: Oxford University Press, 1956);

Sigmund K. Proctor, *Thomas De Quincey's Theory of Literature* (Ann Arbor: University of Michigan Press, 1943);

Robert L. Snyder, ed., *Thomas De Quincey: Bicentenary Studies* (Norman: University of Oklahoma Press, 1985);

David Sundelson, "Evading the Crocodile: De Quincey's 'The English Mail Coach,'" *Psychocultural Review: Interpretations in the Psychology of Art, Literature, and Society*, 1 (1977): 9-20;

René Wellek, "De Quincey's Status in the History of Ideas," *Philological Quarterly*, 23 (July 1944): 248-272;

John C. Whale, *Thomas De Quincey's Reluctant Autobiography*. (London: Croom Helm, 1984; Totowa, N.J.: Barnes & Noble, 1984);

Virginia Woolf, "De Quincey's Autobiography," in her *The Common Reader, Second Series* (London: Hogarth Press, 1932).

**Papers:**

De Quincey's papers are literally scattered around the world. The most complete existing copies of the major works are in the form of corrected proofs, and many of the manuscripts are fragmentary or divided among several collections. The Wordsworth Trust owns one of the extant fragments of the manuscript for the 1821-1822 *Confessions* at Dove Cottage, Grasmere. The most extensive collections of De Quincey's letters are in the Berg Collection of the New York Public Library, the Gluck Collection of the Buffalo and Erie County Library, the Huntington Library, the National Library of Scotland, and the Wordsworth Library at Dove Cottage. Important collections of De Quincey's corrected proofs—as well as manuscript fragments—are held by the British Library, the Gluck Collection, and the Huntington Library. De Quincey's journal, notes, and draft letters from 1803 are in the Liverpool County Libraries Record Office.

Other collections which include De Quincey manuscripts and corrected proofs are: the Berg Collection, New York Public Library; Boston Public Library; Brown University Library; the University of Chicago; the University of Edinburgh; the Folger Shakespeare Library; the Grey Collection, Auckland Public Library, New Zealand; Houghton Library, Harvard University; the Historian's Papers, 1779-1942, Duke University Library; King's School, Canterbury; Magill University; the Montague Collection, New York Public Library Manuscript Division; the National Library of Scotland; Pierpont Morgan Library; the Robert J. Taylor Collection, Princeton University; Worcester College, Oxford; the Wordsworth Collection, Cornell University; and Yale University. Collections including manuscript fragments or small holdings of letters are at the Bodleian Library; Boston University; Georgetown University; Samuel Carter Hall and Anna Maria (Fielding) Hall Collection, Knox College Archives; Tracy William McGregor Collection, University of Virginia; the University of California at Berkeley; Manchester Central Library; Carl H. Pforzheimer Library; and Thomas Cooper Library, University of South Carolina. A more detailed description of specific works held by many of these collections is included in the article on De Quincey in *Index of English Literary Manuscripts, Volume IV, 1800-1900, Part I: Arnold to Gissing*, compiled by Barbara Rosenbaum and Pamela White (London & New York: Mansell, 1982), pp. 681-693.

# Benjamin Robert Haydon

*(25 January 1786 - 22 June 1846)*

Howard M. Wach
*Clarkson University*

SELECTED BOOKS: *The Judgment of Connoisseurs upon works of art compared with that of Professional Men; in reference more particularly to the Elgin Marbles* (London: G. Schulze & J. Dean, 1816);

*New Churches considered with respect to the opportunities they afford for the encouragement of Painting* (London: Printed by C. H. Reynell & published by J. Carpenter, 1818);

*Comparaison entre la Tête d'un des Chêvaux de Venise, qui étoient sur l'arc triomphale des Thuilleries, et qu'on dit être de Lysippe, et la Tête de Cheval d'Elgin du Parthenon* (London: Printed by W. Bulmer, 1818);

*Erreur de Visconti relative à l'action de la Statue de l'Illisus dans la collection d'Elgin, au Muséum Britannique* (London, 1819);

*Description of Mr. Haydon's picture of Christ's triumphant entry into Jerusalem, now exhibiting* (London: C. H. Reynell, 1820; Edinburgh: J. Ruthven, 1820);

*A Descriptive Catalogue of Mr. Haydon's great picture of the raising of Lazarus, now exhibiting at the Egyptian Hall* (London, 1823);

*Explanation of the picture of Chairing the members, a scene in the mock election, which took place at the King's Bench Prison, July, 1827* (London: Printed for the proprietor, 1828);

*Some Enquiry into the causes which have obstructed the advance of historical Painting for the last seventy years in England* (London: Published by Ridgeway & at B. R. Haydon's Exhibition Room, 1829);

*Painting, and the Fine Arts: being the articles under these heads contributed to the seventh edition of the Encyclopædia Britannica, by Benjamin Robert Haydon and William Hazlitt* (Edinburgh: A. & C. Black, 1838);

*Thoughts on the relative value of Fresco and Oil Painting, as applied to the Architectural decorations of the Houses of Parliament* (London: Hooper, 1842);

*Lectures on Painting and Design,* 2 volumes (London: Longman, Brown, Green & Longmans, 1844, 1846);

*Life of Benjamin Robert Haydon, Historical Painter, from his Autobiography and Journals,* edited and compiled by Tom Taylor (3 volumes, London: Longman, Brown, Green & Longmans, 1853; 2 volumes, New York: Harper, 1853); republished as *The Autobiography and Memoirs of Benjamin Robert Haydon,* 2 volumes, introduction by Aldous Huxley (London: P. Davies, 1926; New York: Harcourt, Brace, 1926);

*Benjamin Robert Haydon: Correspondence and Table-Talk. With a Memoir by His Son, Frederic Wordsworth Haydon,* 2 volumes (London: Chatto & Windus, 1876; Boston: Estes & Lauriat, 1876).

**Editions:** *The Autobiography and Memoirs of Benjamin Robert Haydon, 1786-1846 Compiled from his "Autobiography and Journals" and "Correspondence and Table-Talk,"* edited by Alexander P. D. Penrose (London: G. Bell, 1927; New York: M. Balch, 1929);

*Autobiography of Benjamin Robert Haydon,* introduction and epilogue by Edmund Blunden (London: Oxford University Press, 1927);

*Autobiography and Journals of Benjamin Robert Haydon,* edited, with an introduction, by Malcolm Elwin (London: Macdonald, 1950; New York: Coward-McCann, 1950);

*The Diary of Benjamin Robert Haydon,* 5 volumes, edited by Willard Bissell Pope (Cambridge, Mass.: Harvard University Press, 1960-1963).

Benjamin Robert Haydon would doubtless be flattered, though a bit surprised, by his inclusion in a volume on Romantic prose writers. His fame rests first, as he would have wanted, on his reputation as a historical painter and figure of controversy in the art world of Regency London, and second on his friendships with John Keats, William Wordsworth, and other notable British

*Benjamin Robert Haydon, 1815 (portrait by David Wilkie; Ashmolean Museum, Oxford)*

Romantic writers. Apart from descriptions of his paintings, scattered polemics aimed against the Royal Academy and other perceived enemies, an article on painting written for the *Encyclopædia Britannica,* and a series of lectures on painting and design he gave toward the end of his life, Haydon published no major literary work in his lifetime. But shortly after his death in 1846, his wife and his publisher commissioned Tom Taylor, a dramatist and professor of English literature at London University, to edit and bring out an autobiographical fragment Haydon had worked on until 1843 and the journals and diaries he had kept since his youth. The result was the three-volume *Life of Benjamin Robert Haydon* (1853), which revealed an archetypally romantic artistic existence expressed with a literary skill conspicuous enough to produce republication of the book, in various forms and under varying titles, seven times.

Haydon was born to Benjamin Robert Haydon, a Plymouth printer and bookseller, and Sarah Cobley Haydon, the daughter of a Devonshire rector. His interest in drawing originated in early childhood. After a brief and unhappy apprenticeship to his father, the eighteen-year-old aspiring artist gained permission to break the indenture and move to London in 1804, where he enrolled in the Royal Academy school. "I hated day books, ledgers, bill books and cash books," he recalled, and his father's pleas to stay and inherit the family business went unanswered. "I could not help it. Why? Because my whole frame convulsed when I thought of being a great painter." He credited Sir Joshua Reynolds's *Discourses on Art* (1769-1791) with his earliest inspiration. On reading them, he said later, "I felt my des-

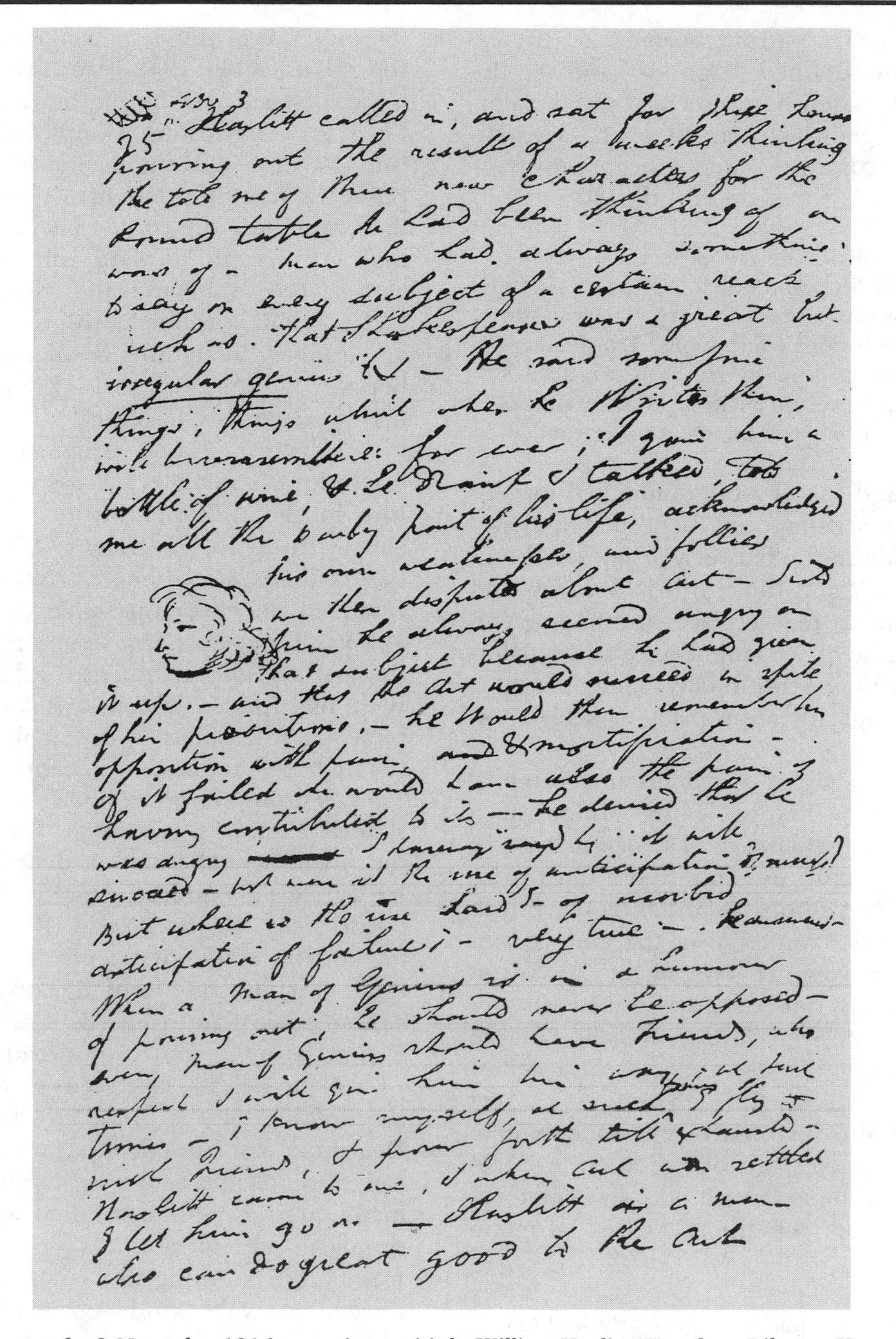

*Haydon's diary entry for 3 November 1816, reporting a visit by William Hazlitt (Houghton Library, Harvard University)*

tiny fixed. The spark which had for years lain struggling to blaze, now burst out forever." In the *Autobiography,* he recast the apprenticeship and his father's resistance into the first of a long series of struggles: "now began that species of misery I have never been without since,—ceaseless opposition."

His descriptions of discovering the artist's calling contained the tone and themes which dominate his writing. His mission (and he saw it in those terms) was to revive the tradition of grand historical painting. He modeled himself after Raphael and Michelangelo, the Renaissance masters of what Haydon called "high art." The phrase carried multiple meanings: a mixture of patriotism, religious piety, artisanal skill, and mastery of emotional expression. Above all, he differentiated it from portraiture, still lifes, and the small-scale domestic paintings of the Dutch school, which Haydon dismissed as "carrot paintings" and which, to his endless dismay, patrons seemed to prefer. His early writing defined "high art" and the degraded taste of those who preferred "carrot paintings" in language which carries a characteristically romanticized and exalted conception of vocation and self. He wrote on 23 July 1808:

> can Painters really excite pity or terror or love or benevolence or lift your soul above this world by sublime, heavenly fancies, or carry your mind to Hell by grand furious conceptions? Can Painters really stimulate a Man to Heroism, or urge a Man to Repentance, or excite a Man to virtue? No, certainly, not in such minds, it never can.

Haydon's life and career were dominated by conflict, much of it self-imposed: between "high art" and "carrot paintings," between an elevated and stubborn idealism and the shifting demands and aesthetics of the art marketplace, and between an exaggerated sense of self-importance and a painting establishment he continually antagonized. It all came to a tragically appropriate conclusion in 1846.

The young artist received his first commission from Henry Phipps, Lord Mulgrave, a highly placed Tory politician. *The Assassination of Dentatus* (1808) won a one-hundred-guinea prize for best historical painting awarded by the British Institution for the Promotion of the Fine Arts in 1810. A dispute over the hanging of *Dentatus* in the Royal Academy was the first in a long series of antagonisms between Haydon and the London art establishment. His good friend and fellow student David Wilkie, through whom he met Mulgrave, had also suffered from Academy politicking, and Haydon's account of their troubles typically credited himself with both greater fortitude and a kind of impetuous emotional intensity:

> the first blow Wilkie got, his sagacity showed him the power of his rivals, and he sank down in submission, while my blood rose like a fountain. I returned with all my might, blow for blow, and heated a furnace for my foe so hot that I singed myself, reckless of consequences.

The success of *Dentatus* led to a commission for a scene from *Macbeth*. Dispute over the painting's size consumed nearly a year. In private and public writing, Haydon accused the Academy of poisoning the minds of patrons. The painting was eventually purchased, but the conflict led Haydon to another lifelong obsession: "high art" as the province of public patronage. His diary entry for 21 December 1812 records a dream of clothing the "spacious & ample sides" of the House of Lords with "illustrious examples of Virtue & Heroism." Vacillation in the face of his own noble purposes left him despondent: "These are the prejudices and these the rooted habits a Student in the high Art has to contend with in this Country, with a People uncultivated, a Nobility tastless, and a Prince unskilled, with a government cold, an Academy intriguing, & an Institution without honour. . . ." As early as 1812, his legions of enemies were already in place.

Haydon's early years in London were marked with notable successes, despite the picture in the *Autobiography* of constant suffering and betrayal. *The Judgment of Solomon* (1814) and *Christ's Entry into Jerusalem* (1820) were each executed on an enormous scale (*Solomon* measures 154 x 130 inches, *Christ's Entry* 228 x 192 inches), successfully and lucratively exhibited, and sold for a high price. Of course, taking years to complete gigantic canvases, the single-minded pursuit of "high art" at any cost, meant high debt as well. *Solomon* brought him six hundred guineas and substantial exhibition proceeds, which reduced but did not nearly eliminate a debt which had swollen to eleven hundred pounds. When he began *Christ's Entry into Jerusalem* in 1815, Haydon was living on the credit of friends and moneylenders, small teaching fees, and the occasional sum advanced against future work. The pattern of quite real suffering to come was already set.

Nonetheless, his treatment of this period in the *Autobiography* is fond, affecting, and elegiac. Descriptions of student days, entry into London society, friendships, and even the beginnings of his many quarrels, are all recalled with characteristic simplicity and humor. "Happy period!," he remembered, "painting and living in one room, as independent as the wind—no servants—no responsibilities—reputation in the bud—hopes endless—ambition beginning—friends untried, believed to be as ardent, as sincere as ourselves—dwelling on the empty chairs after breaking up, as if the strings of one's affections were torn out, and such meetings would be no more." He also remembered the great city itself as the setting for equally great dreams and ambitions:

> So far from the smoke of London being offensive to me, it has always been to my imagination the sublime canopy that shrouds the City of the World. Drifted by the wind, or hanging in

Christ's Entry into Jerusalem, *in which Haydon included portraits of William Wordsworth (standing third from right with bowed head), John Keats (directly above Wordsworth's head), and William Hazlitt (above Christ's left thumb). In his diary Haydon called the public exhibition of this painting (25 March - 4 November 1820) "one of the most glorious triumphs of my life" (The Athenaeum of Ohio, Saint Gregory Seminary, Cincinnati).*

gloomy grandeur over the vastness of our Babylon, the sight of it always filled my mind with feelings of energy, such as no other spectacle could inspire.

Advocacy for Britain's acquisition of the Elgin Marbles helped to establish Haydon's contemporary reputation. In the work of Periclean sculptors, Haydon discovered the elements of his conception of "high art": mastery of form based on knowledge of nature synthesized with an elevated artifice inspiring deep emotion. He engaged Richard Payne Knight, the director of the British Gallery who denied the authenticity and artistic merit of the statuary, in a bitter public feud. Haydon's pamphlet *The Judgment of Connoisseurs upon works of art compared with that of Professional Men* (1816) excoriated Knight and Lord Elgin's detractors and brought the painter his first taste of true notoriety. Despite further damage to his reputation and patronage prospects, Haydon never regretted championing Elgin's cause. In his eyes the marbles represented "the most heroic style of art, combined with all the essential details of actual life," as well as illustrating the earliest and best example of public patronage. His *Autobiography* records days consumed sketching and studying them in a "dream of abstracted enthusiasm; secluded from the world, regardless of its feelings . . . a being of elevated passions. . . ." They inspired him to master anatomy as well as inducing characteristic reveries of immediate, impassioned creativity and the suffering of the visionary. In a December 1809 diary entry he wrote of the horse's head in the marbles:

> I never look at that horse's head but I fancy I see the Artist in a fury fix his chisel at a point, and with a blow rip round with the rapidity of lightning—and stop—he then changed his direc-

> tion and with another blow ran along on the verge of incorrectness, with perfect security—again checked his fire—where he ought. In an instant that furious eye started from the stone—the next moment the nostril, the mouth, the jaw, and every muscle that ought to move trembled on the marble. The artist, overpowered by his feeling, would then rest exhausted and contemplate in agitation—These are the moments of rapture every Man of Genius sees as the reward, at the end of his disappointments and labour—till this delightful stupendous power is acquired, what miseries, what anxieties, what checks, what struggles must he not undergo—

Parliament voted to purchase the Elgin Marbles in June 1816. Thomas Bruce, Earl of Elgin, had submitted Haydon's name as a "friendly" witness, but at a critical moment in the debate Haydon was not called to testify, another grievance he never forgave. A year later the Russian Imperial Academy of Arts commissioned Haydon to execute casts of the marbles and voted him honorary membership. His reputation was at its height, and the painter moved in exalted company. Wordsworth and Keats were regular visitors to his studio. Both appear in *Christ's Entry into Jerusalem* and dedicated sonnets to the painter. Haydon's record of their friendship transmits a deep sense of companionship rooted in shared aesthetic purpose. Haydon idolized Wordsworth, whom he portrayed alongside Voltaire and Isaac Newton, and his critical view of the poet's work isolated a capacity for the communication of emotional truth he deeply admired. As he wrote on 13 June 1815:

> Wordsworth is original surely on this principle—he has one part (& perhaps the finest) of the genius of the great but he has not all. He has not the lucidus ordo [clearness of order]; he does not curb, direct his inspirations for a positive moral, but leaves them to be felt only by those who have a capacity to feel with equal intensity. The moral is not obvious, only the feeling; but he that can feel the feeling will feel the moral too.

Haydon's aesthetics drew deeply from literature. Shakespeare, Milton, Dante, and Homer were constant companions and frequently entered his language. He aspired after their sweeping humanity, their ability to move either "the uncultivated or the refined fancy" and to "melt with pity or love or inflame by terror or sublimity" (20 April 1813). In Shakespeare particularly the painter found a richness of observed detail and an exact mastery of the familiar, the indispensable prerequisites to the emotional communion produced by "high art." The visual analogue to this literary skill was "a perfect Knowledge of Nature as she is" (28 September 1811), which empowers the artist to "give vent to your feelings with furious certainty." Only then, he thought, can the creative act rise from the mere communication of human feelings, or "pathos," to the mastery of "sublimity," where the expressive power of art channels emotion to its own higher purpose. Haydon found such qualities in Rembrandt, as in this description of a day studying his work at an "Old Masters" exhibition in 1815:

> How did I enter into Rembrandt, how drink his excellence, how did I profit by his beauties! How did I recognise effects of shadow on arms, gradations of colour, softness, & tones which I have seen in Nature often, and which "lie in my mind like substances." . . .
>
> What a wonderful creation is the World! how beautiful in ornament, how intensely deep in principle, how simple in arrangement. How singularly delightful that the elements requisite to our physical being should afford materials for the exercise of our intellectual faculties. (22 June 1815)

Appropriately, the painter found his response to Rembrandt's mastery reflected in the language of Wordsworth's *Excursion* (1814): "Deep feelings had impressed / So vividly great objects that they lay / Upon his mind like substances."

Unlike Wordsworth, whom he saw as a figure of paternal wisdom, Haydon felt a brotherly affection for Keats, who was nine years his junior. He judged Keats "really and truly a man after my own heart"; other than Wordsworth, Keats was "the only man I ever met with who is conscious of a high call and is resolved to sacrifice his life or attain it" (7 April 1817). Haydon published a laudatory anonymous review of Keats's 1817 *Poems,* which included two sonnets dedicated to Haydon (*Champion*, 9 March 1817). The artist was immensely proud of these friendships, which both inspired him and confirmed his sense of vocation. His record of their association, in the *Autobiography* and diaries, is filled with evocative portraits of High Romantic London, such as this description of a dinner with Wordsworth, Keats, and Charles Lamb, in his studio on 28 December 1817:

> There was something interesting in seeing Wordsworth sitting, & Keats & Lamb, and my Picture

*Self-portrait by Haydon (National Portrait Gallery, London)*

of Christ's entry towering up behind them, occasionally brightened by the gleams of flame that sparked from the fire, & hearing the voice of Wordsworth repeating Milton with an intonation like the funeral bell of St. Paul's & the music of Handel mingled, & then Lamb's wit came sparkling in between, & Keats's rich fancy of Satyrs & Fauns & doves & white clouds, wound up the stream of conversation.

The completion of *Christ's Entry into Jerusalem* marked Haydon's last great public success. Some thirty thousand people paid to view the painting in Edinburgh and in London's Egyptian Hall. London receipts alone amounted to nearly thirteen hundred pounds. On 10 October 1821 he married the recently widowed Mary Cawrse Hyman, whom he had met several years previously and with whom he fell passionately in love. Mary brought two young children to the marriage, and a third was born fourteen months later. Haydon continued to borrow as he worked on a new painting, *The Raising of Lazarus*. Commercial creditors and moneylenders had long had him in their grasp; now that he had a family to support, he began to reap the consequences. The first of innumerable arrests, this for a sixty-six-pound printer's debt, occurred in November 1821. The first of several imprisonments occurred in May 1823, just as *Lazarus* went on exhibition. The exhibition was immediately closed, his property seized, and *Lazarus* sold to his upholsterer as settlement of a thirty-pound debt. His legal adviser laid down a new regime for Haydon in 1824. He advanced the painter regular sums against future income, instructed him to seek and complete portrait commissions, and prohibited work on canvases over a certain size. For the acolyte of high art, whose studio had been crowded not only with genius but with "rank, beauty, and fashion," it was hard, humiliating, teeth-grinding work; in effect, a surrender to "carrot painting." When he began *Christ's Entry into Jerusalem* ten years before, he had asked, he says in the *Autobiography,* "Shall I paint for money, or by borrowing, . . . keep my mind in its high key, and go on watching, exciting, and regulating the public mind?" His self-estimation may have been delusional, but his sense of vocation had not changed, even if his circumstances had. "In portrait," he reflected, "I lose that divine feeling of inspiration I always have in history. I feel as a common man; think as a common man; execute as the very commonest."

The next few years saw Haydon in and out of prison, attempting to keep his family housed and fed. Three more children were born; of six altogether, only two survived to adulthood. He painted portraits of varying quality; not surprisingly, his 1842 portrait of Wordsworth is among his best work. He also executed smaller pictures of contemporary life (including the *Mock Election,* a scene drawn from his time in the King's Bench Prison), some of which show great humor and power. He struggled and survived, though barely, his sense of mission hardly reduced by his troubles. He sent torrents of paper to government ministries petitioning for state patronage of historical painting. In the mid 1830s he took up the cause of state support for training textile designers, the issue which, in 1835, finally gave him his chance to be heard in Parliament.

Late in the same year, Haydon began a new career as a public lecturer. He traveled the country, speaking to provincial art societies and mechanics' institutes. Haydon's natural extroversion and enthusiasm, coupled with long years of experience, made for entertaining, knowledgeable, and well-received lectures. Collected and published in 1844, the lectures are imaginative, technically sophisticated, opinionated, and clearly based on a lifetime of practical experience. In addition to detailed treatments of anatomy, color, and composition, he repeated his favorite themes: the pernicious effect of the Reformation on English art, the malevolence of academies, historically illustrated arguments for state sponsorship of the arts, the ineffable mysteries of genius, the sad neglect of historical painting. At times, a hard-won knowledge appears in his judgments. Criticizing an article in the *Westminster Review* for July 1830, which asserted that poverty and suffering are a spur to genius, he replied that "All the nonsense about the poverty of genius is cant. Poverty never helped any man's powers, painter or poet."

Haydon never escaped that poverty. The diaries, which in earlier years record a beguiling, quixotic, if discomfortingly self-serving version of the Romantic odyssey, trail off to a bitter and tragic conclusion. In 1843 his entry in a cartoon competition for prospective decoration of the new Houses of Parliament was unceremoniously passed over, reviving for him "all the old horrors of Execution & arrest & debt" (30 June 1843). Early in 1846, impoverished and virtually forgotten by the art world, he attempted once more to mount an exhibition. He had conceived the paintings, *The Banishment of Aristides* and *The Burning of Rome by Nero,* on a visit to Parliament in 1812, recalling in the *Autobiography* how a series of designs adorning the House of Lords could evoke "the horrors of anarchy—then the injustice of democracy—then the cruelty of despotism—the infamies of revolution—then the beauty of justice—and to conclude with limited monarchy and its blessings." The exhibition floundered. While his paintings went unnoticed, P. T. Barnum drew enormous crowds to the neighboring large room in the Egyptian Hall, site of Haydon's greatest triumphs, to see General Tom Thumb. This final rejection broke Haydon's will. Burdened with debt, failure, and humiliation, he lost all hope. "Their eyes are open," he said of the crowds streaming to view Barnum's midget curiosity, "but their sense is shut. It is an insanity, a Rabies, a madness, a Furor, a dream. I would not have believed it of the English people" (13 April 1846). He sank into a deep depression. One month after the exhibition closed, he put his affairs in the best order he could, wrote out a will, retreated to his studio, and shot himself. Nineteen years earlier, perhaps in a moment of similar despair, Haydon had composed an epitaph, calling himself one who "fell a victim to his ardor & enthusiasm." To it he appended a sadly appropriate line from Samuel Johnson: "What various ills the Painter's life assail; Pride, envy, want, the *Patron,* and Gaol" (10 October 1827).

**Letters:**

*Benjamin Robert Haydon: Correspondence and Table-Talk. With a memoir by his son, Frederic Words-*

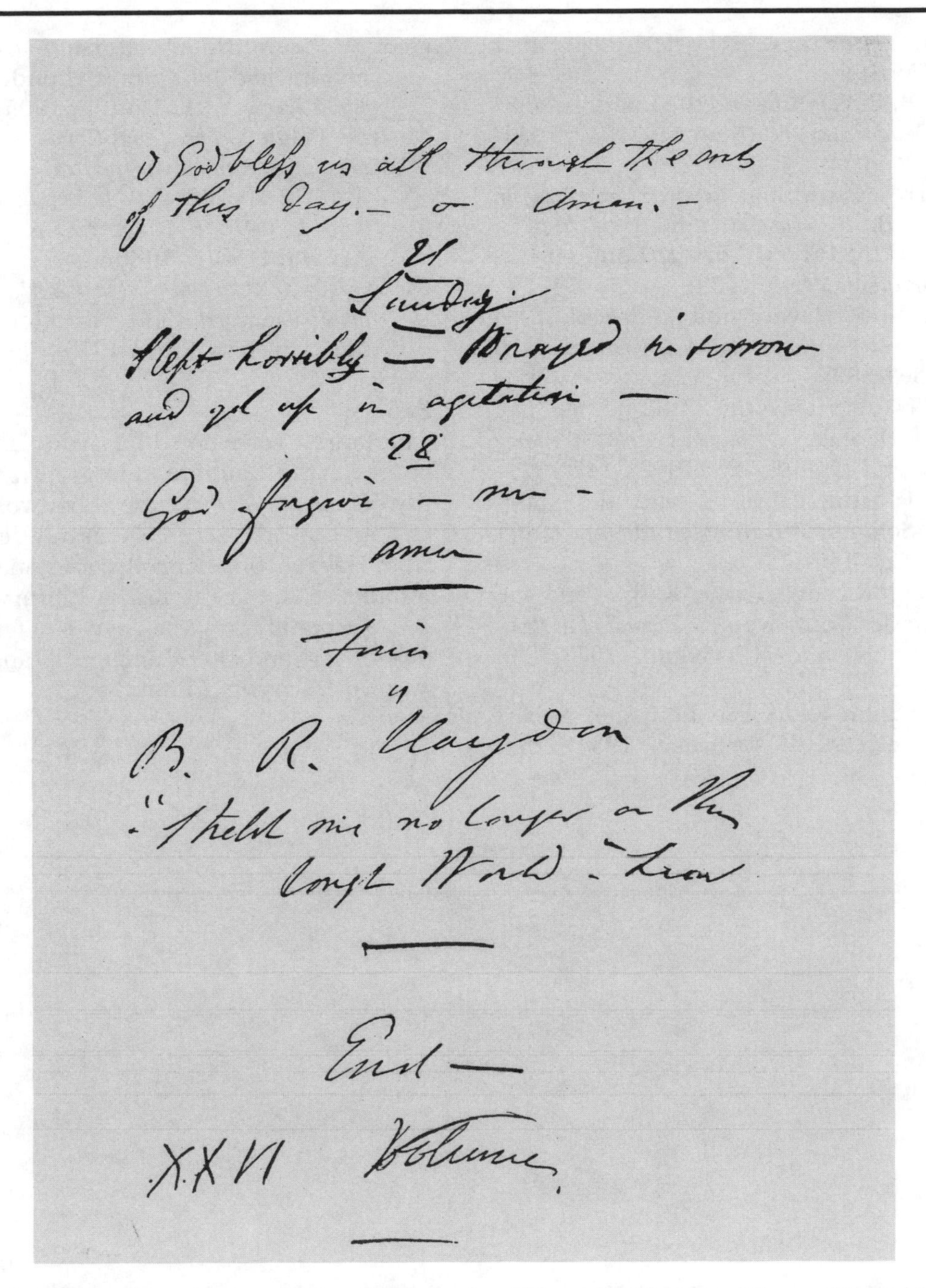
O God bless us all through the evils of this day. — Amen. —

21

Sunday

Slept horribly — Prayed in sorrow and got up in agitation —

22

God forgive — me —

Amen

Finis

of

B. R. Haydon

"Stretch me no longer on this rough World" — Lear

End —

XXVI Volume.

*Haydon's final diary entry, written on 22 June 1846, the day of his suicide (Houghton Library, Harvard University)*

*worth Haydon. With facsimile illustrations from his journals,* 2 volumes (London: Chatto & Windus, 1876; Boston: Estes & Lauriat, 1877);

*Invisible Friends: The Correspondence of Elizabeth Barrett Browning and Benjamin Robert Haydon, 1842-1845,* edited by Willard Bissell Pope (Cambridge, Mass.: Harvard University Press, 1972).

**Biographies:**

Eric George, *The Life and Death of Benjamin Robert Haydon, 1786-1846* (London & New York: Oxford University Press, 1948); second edition, revised and enlarged by Dorothy George (Oxford: Clarendon Press, 1967);

Clarke Olney, *Benjamin Robert Haydon, Historical Painter* (Athens: University of Georgia Press, 1952);

Robert Peters, *Haydon: An Artist's Life* (Greensboro, N.C.: Unicorn Press, 1989).

**References:**

A. Ballantyne, "Knight, Haydon, and the Elgin

Marbles," *Apollo,* new series 128 (September 1988): 155-159;

P. J. Barlow, "B. R. Haydon and the Radicals," *Burlington Magazine,* 99 (Summer 1957): 311-312;

Elizabeth Barrett Browning, *Letters from Elizabeth Barrett to B. R. Haydon,* edited by Martha Hale Shackford (New York & London: Oxford University Press, 1939);

F. Cummings, "B. R. Haydon and his School," *Journal of the Warburg and Courtauld Institutes,* 26 (1963): 367-380;

Cummings, "Nature and the Antique in 'The Death of Dentatus,'" *Journal of the Warburg and Courtauld Institutes,* 25 (1962): 147-157;

Cummings, "Poussin, Haydon, and the Judgment of Solomon," *Burlington Magazine,* 104 (April 1962): 146-152;

F. J. Messman, "Richard Payne Knight and the Elgin Marbles Controversy," *Journal of Aesthetics and Art Criticism,* 13 (Winter 1973): 70-79;

Clarke Olney, "John Keats and Benjamin Robert Haydon," *PMLA,* 49 (February 1934): 258-275;

George Paston (Emily Morse Symonds), *B. R. Haydon and his Friends* (London: J. Nisbet, 1905; New York: Dutton, 1905);

Michael Pidgley, *The Tragi-Comic History of B. R. Haydon's Marcus Curtius leaping into the Gulf: A Bi-Centenary Tribute to Benjamin Robert Haydon, 1786-1846* (Exeter: Exeter College of Art and Design, 1986);

David Allan Robertson, *Sir Charles Eastlake and the Victorian Art World* (Princeton, N.J.: Princeton University Press, 1978).

**Papers:**

The largest collection of Haydon manuscripts is housed at the Houghton Library, Harvard University. These papers include thirty volumes of diaries and nearly seven thousand letters to and from Haydon. Smaller collections, mainly of correspondence, are at the British Library, the University of Iowa Library, the Getty Center for the History of Art and the Humanities, and the Northwestern University Library.

# William Hazlitt

*(10 April 1778 - 18 September 1830)*

Patricia L. Skarda
*Smith College*

BOOKS: *An Essay on the Principles of Human Action: being an Argument in favour of the Natural Disinterestedness of the Human Mind. To which are added, some remarks on the systems of Hartley and Helvetius* (London: Printed for J. Johnson, 1805);

*Free Thoughts on Public Affairs: or Advice to a Patriot; in a letter addressed to a member of the old opposition* (London: Printed by R. Taylor & sold by J. Budd, 1806);

*An Abridgment of the Light of Nature Pursued, by Abraham Tucker, Esq. Originally published, in seven volumes, under the name of Edward Search, Esq.*, abridged by Hazlitt (London: Printed for J. Johnson by T. Bensley, 1807);

*A Reply to the Essay on Population, by the Rev. T. R. Malthus. In a Series of Letters. To which are added, Extracts from the Essay; with Notes* (London: Printed for Longman, Hurst, Rees & Orme, 1807);

*A New and Improved Grammar of the English Tongne* [sic]: *for the use of schools* (London: Printed by M. J. Godwin, at the Juvenile Library, 1810);

*Memoirs of the Late Thomas Holcroft, Written by Himself, and continued to the Time of his Death, from his Diary, Notes, and other Papers*, 3 volumes, continuation by Hazlitt (London: Printed for Longman, Hurst, Rees, Orme & Brown, 1816);

*The Round Table: A Collection of Essays on Literature, Men, and Manners*, by Hazlitt, with twelve essays by Leigh Hunt, 2 volumes (Edinburgh: Printed for Archibald Constable and Longman, Hurst, Rees, Orme & Brown, London, 1817);

*Characters of Shakespear's Plays* (London: Printed by C. H. Reynell for R. Hunter and C. & J. Ollier, 1817; Boston: Published by Wells & Lilly, 1818);

*A View of the English Stage; or, a Series of Dramatic Criticisms* (London: Printed for Robert Stodart, Anderson & Chase, and Bell & Bradfute, Edinburgh, 1818);

William Hazlitt, 1808 (miniature by John Hazlitt; Maidstone Museum and Art Gallery)

*Lectures on the English Poets. Delivered at the Surrey Institution* (London: Printed for Taylor & Hessey, 1818; Philadelphia: Published by Thomas Dobson & Son, printed by William Fry, 1818);

*A Letter to William Gifford, Esq. from William Hazlitt, Esq.* (London: Printed for John Miller, 1819);

*Lectures on the English Comic Writers. Delivered at the Surrey Institution* (London: Printed for Taylor & Hessey, 1819; Philadelphia: Published by M. Carey & Son, printed by T. H. Palmer, 1819);

*Political Essays, with Sketches of Public Characters* (London: Printed for W. Hone, 1819);

*Lectures chiefly on the Dramatic Literature of the Age of Elizabeth. Delivered at the Surrey Institution* (London: Stodart & Steuart, and Bell & Bradfute, Edinburgh, 1820);

*Table-Talk; or, Original Essays,* 2 volumes: volume 1 (London: John Warren, 1821); volume 2 (London: Printed for Henry Colburn, 1822); republished with differing contents, 2 volumes (Paris: Published by A. & W. Galignani, 1825);

*An Essay on the Spirit of Monarchy* (Falmouth: Printed at the Minerva Press, by J. Philp, 1822?);

*Liber Amoris; Or, The New Pygmalion* (London: Printed for John Hunt by C. H. Reynell, 1823);

*Characteristics: In the Manner of Rochefoucault's Maxims* (London: Printed for W. Simpkin & R. Marshall, 1823);

*Sketches of the Principal Picture-Galleries in England. With a Criticism on "Marriage a-la-Mode"* (London: Printed for Taylor & Hessey, 1824);

*The Spirit of the Age: or Contemporary Portraits* (1 volume, London: Printed for Henry Colburn, 1825; revised and enlarged edition, 2 volumes, Paris: A. & W. Galignani, 1825; second British edition, revised and enlarged, 1 volume, London: Henry Colburn, 1825);

*The Plain Speaker: Opinions on Books, Men, and Things,* 2 volumes (London: Henry Colburn, 1826);

*Notes of a Journey through France and Italy* (London: Printed for Hunt & Clarke, 1826);

*The Life of Napoleon Buonaparte,* 4 volumes: volumes 1 and 2 (London: Printed for Hunt & Clarke, 1828); republished with volumes 3 and 4 (London: Published by Effingham Wilson and Chapman & Hall, 1830);

*Conversations of James Northcote, Esq., R.A.* (London: Henry Colburn & Richard Bentley, 1830);

*Literary Remains of the Late William Hazlitt. With a Notice of his Life, by his Son, and Thoughts on his Genius and Writings, by E. L. Bulwer, Esq., M.P. and Mr. Sergeant Talfourd, M.P.,* 2 volumes (London: Saunders & Otley, 1836);

*Painting, and the Fine Arts: being the articles under those heads contributed to the seventh edition of the Encyclopædia Britannica, by B. R. Haydon, Esq. and William Hazlitt, Esq.* (Edinburgh: Adam & Charles Black, 1838);

*Sketches and Essays. By William Hazlitt. Now first collected by his son* (London: John Templeman, 1839);

*Criticisms on Art: and Sketches of the Picture Galleries of England,* first series, edited by William Hazlitt, Jr. (London: J. Templeman, 1843);

*Criticisms on Art,* second series, edited by William Hazlitt, Jr. (London: C. Templeman, 1844);

*Winterslow: Essays and Characters Written There,* edited by William Hazlitt, Jr. (London: D. Bogue, 1850);

*A Reply to Z,* edited by Charles Whibley (London: First Edition Club, 1923);

*New Writings,* first and second series, edited by P. P. Howe (London: Secker, 1925, 1927; New York: MacVeagh, 1925, 1927).

**Edition:** *The Complete Works of William Hazlitt,* Centenary Edition, 21 volumes, edited by Howe (London & Toronto: Dent, 1930-1934).

OTHER: *The Eloquence of the British Senate; or, Select Specimens of the Most Distinguished Parliamentary Speakers, from the beginning of the reign of Charles I. to the present time. With Notes Biographical, Critical, and Explanatory,* 2 volumes, edited, with an advertisement and notes, by Hazlitt (London: Printed for Thomas Ostell, 1807; Brooklyn: Printed by T. Kirk, 1809);

William Oxberry, ed., *The New English Drama,* 20 volumes, volumes 1-12 include introductions by Hazlitt to eighteen plays (London: Published for the Proprietors by W. Simpkin & R. Marshall and C. Chapple, 1818-1825);

*Select British Poets, or New Elegant Extracts from Chaucer to the Present Time, with Critical Remarks,* edited, with a preface and remarks, by Hazlitt (London: Published by Wm. C. Hall, 1824); abridged as *Select Poets of Great Britain* (London: Printed by Thomas Davison for Thomas Tegg; R. Griffin, Glasgow; R. Milliken, Dublin; M. Baudry, Paris, 1825).

Among the notable themes in William Hazlitt's essays are the disappointments in his life. He failed in love and in social life; yet he recognized his intellectual superiority and exercised it in essays, reviews, and books throughout his fifty-two years. His reputed last words, "Well, I've had a happy life"—whether actually said or invented by a biographer—express relish for life even in the passing moments of his existence.

*Grace Loftus Hazlitt and Reverend William Hazlitt (miniatures by John Hazlitt; from P. P. Howe, ed.,* The Complete Works of William Hazlitt, *volume one, 1930)*

William Hazlitt, third son and fourth child of the Reverend William Hazlitt, was born in Maidstone, Kent, on 10 April 1778. His father, a Unitarian minister, identified as a Dissenter for opposing the articles of the Church of England, cultivated in his son the capacity for provoking controversy. His handsome mother, Grace Loftus Hazlitt, the daughter of an ironmonger, moved willingly with her controversial husband from church to church, even country to country. In 1778 Reverend Hazlitt had been preaching for eight years at the chapel in Maidstone, but in March of 1780 the Hazlitts were forced to move to Ireland because of what the essayist's grandson, W. Carew Hazlitt, called "some disagreeable rupture among the congregation." In 1784 they went to America, where Reverend Hazlitt found work as a substitute minister, sowing seeds of Unitarianism up and down the East Coast; in Boston he is still regarded as a founding father of the first Unitarian church there. In 1786 Reverend Hazlitt returned to England, and the family followed in 1787. Soon Reverend Hazlitt became minster to a small Presbyterian congregation at Wem in Shropshire, from which he continued to write in support of the Unitarian cause. He hoped that his precocious youngest son, William, would follow in his footsteps.

Hazlitt wrote about his father often, recalling in *Table-Talk* (1821-1822), "A shrewd man said of my father that he would not send a son of his to school to him on any account, for that by teaching him to speak the truth, he would disqualify him from getting his living in the world" ("On the Disadvantages of Intellectual Superiority"). Speaking the truth as he knew it kept Hazlitt always on the verge of indigence, but his spirit was ever free. Part of the truth their strict father inculcated in his children was the practice and study of arts, which were allowed under the gentle and cheerful Unitarian doctrines. In another *Table-Talk* essay William fondly remembered his father "in a green old age, with strong-marked features and scarred with the small-pox," reading with the help of spectacles Shaftesbury's *Characteristics* (1711), as he sat patiently for William to draw his portrait ("On the Pleasure of Painting," first published in *London Magazine,* December 1820). The children's imaginations were encouraged by painting and sketching, reading novels, and going to the theater. William's older brother John grew up to be a professional miniaturist, and, for a time, William painted portraits for a living because the arts cultivated excellence, not merely entertainment. Early in life William affected an air of superiority. As he later wrote in

*Hazlitt circa 1785 (miniature by John Hazlitt; Maidstone Museum and Art Gallery)*

"On the Conduct of Life" (first published in the 1825 edition of *Table-Talk*), "It was my misfortune (perhaps) to be bred up among Dissenters, who look with too jaundiced an eye at others, and set too high a value on their own peculiar pretensions." With the wisdom of hindsight, however, he went on to caution schoolboys: "Do not begin to quarrel with the world too soon. . . . If railing would have made it better, it would have been reformed long ago: but as this is not to be hoped for at present, the best way is to slide through it as contentedly and innocently as we may." He came to this conclusion, however, after years of hard railing and serious hard work.

His sister Margaret recorded in her journal that, after the disappointed Reverend Hazlitt had left Boston to return to England, John taught his brother William Latin grammar. When the family joined Reverend Hazlitt at Wem, William was enrolled in the village school, where he applied himself with vigor. He soon began spending much of his free time in his room, where he could read and think alone. He flaunted his achievements before his admiring, if austere, father. With the fall of the Bastille in 1789 he shared his father's enthusiasm for the "dawn of a new era" when "the sun of Liberty rose upon the sun of Life in the same day, and both were proud to run their race together" ("On the Feeling of Immortality in Youth," *Monthly Magazine*, March 1827). What amazed the young Hazlitt about the French Revolution was the powerful expression of the people's will, a sense that remained with him throughout his life and was recorded at its end in his four-volume *Life of Napoleon Buonaparte* (1828, 1830).

In 1793, aided by a fund for needy preachers' sons, William Hazlitt was sent to the Unitarian New College at Hackney to study for the ministry. Learning from eminent Dissenters—among them Joseph Priestley, whom Hazlitt had defended in a 1791 letter to the *Shrewsbury Chronicle*—Hazlitt proved to himself and to his father that the pulpit was unsuitable for him. At Hackney he was trained to discover for himself ideas and ideals that he could espouse rather than accepting wholesale those tenets of faith others had espoused before and for him. While his father, at Wem, pored over the Bible and perused biblical commentators, dreaming "of infinity and eternity, of death, the resurrection, and a judgment to come" ("My First Acquaintance with Poets," *Liberal,* April 1823), Hazlitt, on the northern outskirts of London, read William Godwin's *Enquiry concerning Political Justice* (1793), Thomas Paine's *Rights of Man* (1791-1792), David Hartley's *Observations on Man, his Frame, his Duty, and his Expectations* (1749), and Jean-Jacques Rousseau's *Émile* (1762), *Julie ou la Nouvelle Héloïse* (1761), and *Confessions* (1781, 1788). Godwin's demands for a personal revolution of consciousness and an independent life of reason, free from what Hazlitt was to call "the gross and narrow ties of sense, custom, authority, private and local attachment" ("William Godwin" in *The Spirit of the Age,* 1825), became for a time Hazlitt's own. Godwin rescued him from a paternally appointed destiny and set him on his own wavering path. On 17 September 1794 Hazlitt met with Godwin for the first of many times, and within a year of this meeting Hazlitt left the college at Hackney in despair. The college itself closed in 1796.

Hazlitt's first encounter with Godwin was at tea in the home of John Hazlitt and his wife. The families were intimately connected by more than political sympathies because Reverend Hazlitt had succeeded Godwin's father as minister at Wisbeach, Cambridgeshire, where he had courted and married his wife. In 1799, when Hazlitt was in London, he saw Godwin about a dozen times, and as Godwin's diary testifies, he continued to see him off and on throughout his life. In 1807 Godwin helped Hazlitt publish his abridgment of Abraham Tucker's *Light of Nature,* and in 1810 Godwin himself published Hazlitt's *New and Improved Grammar of the English Tongue.* He saw to it that Hazlitt was given the commission to piece together a biography from the memoirs of Thomas Holcroft, a playwright and friend of liberty who had been arrested for high treason but released in 1794. Godwin volunteered to edit Hazlitt's work on Holcroft, whom Hazlitt had met in 1795 or 1796, because Holcroft's diary exposed more of Mary Wollstonecraft Godwin's private life with her first lover, Gilbert Imlay, than Godwin wanted known. He never actually edited the whole work, but it is clear from the finished product of 1816 that passages were omitted, probably to placate Godwin as well as Holcroft's widow and her friends. Godwin voiced his approval of Hazlitt's *Political Essays* (1819) but ignored his later works, while Hazlitt critically but sincerely reviewed Godwin's novel, *Cloudesley,* along with his other works, for the *Edinburgh Review* in April 1830, and ended his *Conversations of James Northcote* (1830) with an elaborate conversation with Godwin. In his review of *Cloudesley* Hazlitt presented Godwin as an example of a literary man unable to adapt himself to life: "Enclosed in the shell of self, he sees a little way beyond himself, and feels what concerns others still more slowly." Godwin hurt Hazlitt deeply by failing to respond to his *Reply to the Essay on Population* (1807)—an answer to Thomas Robert Malthus's attack on the Godwinian belief that man could achieve utopia if left free to exercise his reason and natural benevolence—until too late for it to be of any use in promoting Hazlitt's book, but Hazlitt remained loyal to Godwin's aims to the end while exposing the weakness of his system. Godwin's ultimate failure, according to Hazlitt, derived from his fundamental but erroneous assumption that men act from purely rational motives. Although Hazlitt came to know better, in his youth he drew from Godwin's idealism the hope that reason could and would result in progressive reform of society. But Godwin, according to the mature Hazlitt writing in *The Spirit of the Age,* "conceived too nobly of his fellows . . . [,] raised the standard morality above the reach of humanity. . . . The author of *Political Justice* took abstract reason for the rule of conduct, and abstract good for its end." Where Godwin failed, Hazlitt hoped to conquer but would not.

But try he did. The cataclysmic turn of the revolution in France followed by the treason trials in 1794 anticipated Hazlitt's own intellectual ferment. As he turned from learning to thinking, he focused his energies first on modern philosophy and political theory. At Hackney he had begun "A Project for a New Theory of Civil and Criminal Legislation," submitting a draft of it to his tutor in place of assigned themes. His first task when he left Hackney was to complete this essay, for which he had to read and think more. In fact, the essay was not finished until sometime in 1828; it was published posthumously in his *Liter-*

*The parsonage at Wem, Shropshire, where the Hazlitts settled after they returned to England from the United States in 1787*

*ary Remains* (1836). "A Project for a New Theory of Civil and Criminal Legislation" expresses Hazlitt's fundamental belief that each man has the right and duty to assert his "personal identity." Civil legislation "is the emanation of the aggregate will," and no government can legislate morals because they "have to do with the will and affections." Building on a series of examples of the will of one against the will of another, Hazlitt would limit the role of government to the protection of the independence of its members and establish "perfect toleration in matters of religion." The argument of this essay directly opposes what Hazlitt here calls the "scaly finger" of Thomas Hobbes's Leviathan, Edmund Burke's "cloudy sophistry," Jeremy Bentham's "wide waste of utility," and William Godwin's "omnipotence of reason"—all philosophies in which Hazlitt had an early interest. The way to this clear and precise statement of Hazlitt's sensible idealism about the way things ought to be (without muddling the discussion with insoluble questions of administration and finance) required a lifetime of discovering how others thought and imagined—and how he himself thought and imagined in relation to others and, most important, to himself.

It is interesting to speculate on how different a philosopher and critic Hazlitt might have been if he had been given a classical education at Oxford or Cambridge, but admission was restricted to those who subscribed to Anglican articles of faith and attended Anglican worship services. In short, English universities were open only to Anglicans or those willing to pose as Anglicans. Hackney was less a school than a society of Dissenters. Hazlitt had much to learn on his own with little system or guidance. Back at Wem, where his father's disappointment in his refusal to become a clergyman was alienating, he set off in several directions at once. In 1798 he bought John Milton's *Paradise Lost* (1667) and Burke's *Reflections on the Revolution in France* (1790), both of which he read avidly. Burke's prose became the model for Hazlitt's own, but he rejected Burke's ideas. As W. P. Albrecht puts it, "Burke and

Hazlitt are alike in accepting the imagination as a moral guide and in distrusting any political scheme based on a selfish calculation of consequences." Unlike Burke, however, Hazlitt regarded the powerful British aristocracy as an obstacle to the free inquiry necessary for the full development of individual citizens. Much later, in *The Spirit of the Age,* Hazlitt remarked on "the influence exercised by men of genius and imaginative power over those who have nothing to oppose to their unforeseen flashes of thought and invention, but the dry, cold, formal, deductions of the understanding."

On 14 January 1798 he felt firsthand the force of genius when he heard Samuel Taylor Coleridge preach a sermon at Shrewsbury, ten cold miles from Wem, on the text "And he went up into the mountain to pray, HIMSELF, ALONE." Far from reconciling Hazlitt to his father's aspirations for him, the sermon confirmed for him the possibility for a new combination of sensibilities: "Poetry and Philosophy had met together. Truth and Genius had embraced, under the eye and with the sanction of Religion." The sermon ranged widely, as Coleridge's conversations typically did, touching "upon peace and war; upon church and state—not their alliance, but their separation—on the spirit of the world and the spirit of Christianity, not as the same, but as opposed to one another." Coleridge included "a poetical and pastoral excursion" to show the effects of war. As Hazlitt wrote later, "I could not have been more delighted if I had heard the music of the spheres." When Coleridge came to call on Reverend Hazlitt the Tuesday following, William met him. His often-anthologized record of this visit and subsequent ones in "My First Acquaintance with Poets" (*Liberal,* April 1823) is remarkable for the contrast it makes between Reverend Hazlitt and Coleridge, preacher and poet, age and youth, nondescript and extraordinary even in appearance. The young Hazlitt registered his "great opinion of Burke," adding that "speaking of him with contempt might be made the test of a vulgar democratical mind." Coleridge complimented the young man on his observation, pressing Hazlitt further as to his opinions of Godwin, Mary Wollstonecraft, and Holcroft and instructing him to define his terms clearly before proceeding. Holcroft's definition of common terms seemed then to Coleridge to be "barricadoing the road to truth," but Coleridge's insistence on definitions made a forceful impression: Hazlitt remembered and recorded the demand some twenty-five years later, and on 27 November 1811 when dining at Charles and Mary Lamb's with Coleridge, he even asked Coleridge to define poetry distinctly. Many of Hazlitt's best essays are elaborate definitions of terms such as *gusto, egotism,* and *imitation,* but he was a long way from such precision in 1798.

The next morning Coleridge announced that he had accepted a £150 annuity from Thomas Wedgewood and that he would devote himself entirely to the study of poetry and philosophy. The pain of this news to Hazlitt, who was expecting a series of sermons from Coleridge, was ameliorated by Coleridge's invitation to the young Hazlitt to visit Nether Stowey. Excited at the prospect, Hazlitt walked six miles with Coleridge, spellbound by his opinions of David Hume, Bishop George Berkeley, Thomas Paine, and Bishop Joseph Butler. Since Coleridge expressed himself with a decided air of certainty, Hazlitt attempted to explain his own discovery on the natural disinterestedness of the human mind. Hazlitt failed to make himself understood then, but the attempt inspired him to try again to write what he meant while awaiting his appointed visit to Nether Stowey, a visit that lasted three glorious weeks in June.

One memorable comment Hazlitt heard Coleridge make that June came in response to a fisherman's account of a boy who had drowned the day before, despite the fishermen's risk of their lives to save him. The fisherman said, "He did not know how it was that they ventured, but, Sir, we have a *nature* towards one another." Coleridge said to Hazlitt that the fisherman's expression "was a fine illustration of the theory of disinterestedness" Hazlitt and Butler had adopted. Hazlitt recalled this exchange when he finally wrote his first book, *An Essay on the Principles of Human Action* (1805), on the moral force of the imagination, a topic with which he had struggled since his days at Hackney. In this essay Hazlitt put himself in the place of the fisherman and enlarged the bounty: "Suppose it were my own case—that it were in my power to save twenty other persons by voluntarily consenting to suffer for them: why should I not do a generous thing, and never trouble myself about what might be the consequence to myself the Lord knows when?" In answering his own question Hazlitt refuted the claims of all who participated in the long debate on self-interest and benevolence throughout the eighteenth century, among them Thomas Hobbes; Adam Smith; John Locke; David Hart-

*Margaret and John Hazlitt (paintings by John Hazlitt; Maidstone Museum and Art Gallery)*

ley; Joseph Priestley; Paul Thiry, Baron d'Holbach; Claude-Adrien Helvétius; Bernard de Mandeville; Abraham Tucker; François, Duc de La Rochefoucauld; William Godwin; and others. Hazlitt's example, with its strikingly Christian overtones, shows that he was still battling with Christian sentiments while unwilling to commit himself to faith in Christianity, a conflict he recognized in Rousseau, where he found that only by imagination does a man go out of himself into the feelings of others. As Hazlitt wrote in *A Letter to William Gifford, Esq.* (1819), which includes a later exposition of his essential argument, imagination "carries us out of ourselves as well as beyond the present moment"; it "pictures the thoughts, passions and feelings of others to us, and interests us in them"; it "breathes into all other forms the breath of life, and endows our sympathies with vital warmth, and diffuses the soul of morality through all the relations and sentiments of our social being." In writing *An Essay on the Principles of Human Action* Hazlitt realized that he would choose to save twenty others so that in times to come he would not regret having failed to do so: "I saw plainly that the consciousness of my own feelings which is made the foundation of my continued interest in them could not extend to what had never been, and might never be, that my identity with myself must be confined to the connection between my past and present being. . . ." Immortality of the soul is not so much at issue as is continued self-interest. By imagining the future self, the self today acts not in the interest of others but out of concern for that future self. The concept of disinterested benevolence, shaped and encouraged by Coleridge, became the cornerstone of Hazlitt's whole theory of metaphysics, ethics, and aesthetics. He was to recommend his *Essay on the Principles of Human Action* in lectures, later essays, and in his *Letter to William Gifford, Esq.*, where he restates its entire argument and rates his first book as the best of his works.

During his June 1798 visit to Coleridge Hazlitt had the pleasure of seeing at Alfoxden, the nearby home of William and Dorothy Wordsworth, manuscripts for poems published later that year in *Lyrical Ballads.* Hazlitt himself is mentioned in "Expostulation and Reply" as the "good friend Matthew," who preferred books to nature. Since Hazlitt was at the time busy with his *Essay on the Principles of Human Action* and since he admitted in "My First Acquaintance with Poets" that he "got into a metaphysical argument with Wordsworth," the identification of Matthew as Hazlitt, confirmed by Wordsworth's early editor Thomas Hutchinson, seems certain. Years later, when enmity replaced the friendship with both Wordsworth and Coleridge, Wordsworth recalled Hazlitt's "extraordinary acuteness, but perverse as Lord Byron himself" (letter to William Rowan Hamilton, 26 September 1830). What Wordsworth saw as perversity, Stanley Jones describes as contumacy. Even in 1798 Hazlitt was committed to holding fast to his own opinions, while carefully depositing in his memory Coleridge's friendly support of his ideas on benevolence. The marked difference that Hazlitt saw in 1798 between Wordsworth's steady watchfulness and Coleridge's quick darting and drifting, between Wordsworth's composition while "walking up and down a straight gravel-walk" and Coleridge's composition "in walking over uneven ground, or breaking through the straggling branches of a copse-wood," grew more dramatic in later meetings with the poets.

Coleridge became an enormous disappointment to Hazlitt. At the 1811 dinner at the Lambs mentioned above, Hazlitt directly accused Coleridge of not being competent to lecture on Shakespeare, and he further indicted his one-time mentor for the laziness that was to become something of a trademark for the poet. Hazlitt grew markedly impatient when Coleridge turned Tory, especially with his *Lay Sermon on the Distresses of the Country* (1816), which Hazlitt reviewed for the *Examiner* without reading, saying "Let him talk on for ever in this world and the next; and both worlds will be the better for it. But let him not write, or pretend to write, nonsense" (8 September 1816). Reviewing Coleridge's *Statesman's Manual* (1816) for the *Examiner* (29 December 1816) Hazlitt says, "Here Mr. Coleridge is off again on the wings of fear as he was before on those of fancy." In his portrait of Coleridge in *The Spirit of the Age,* Hazlitt draws an elaborate contrast between Godwin and Coleridge, his first and most promising mentors. He applauds Godwin, who "with less natural capacity, and with fewer acquired advantages, by concentrating his mind on some given object, and doing what he had to do with all his might, has accomplished much. . . ." He scorns Coleridge for "dallying with every subject by turns," for talking when he should have been writing, and for doing "little or nothing to justify to the world or to posterity, the high opinion which all who have ever heard him converse, or known him intimately, with one accord entertain of him." Brutally reviewing Coleridge's *Christabel; Kubla Khan, a Vision; The Pains of Sleep* (1816) for the *Examiner* (2 June 1816), Hazlitt lobs such barbs as: "The fault of Mr. Coleridge is, that he comes to no conclusion. He is a man of that universality of genius, that his mind hangs suspended between poetry and prose, truth and falsehood, and an infinity of other things, and from an excess of capacity, he does little or nothing"; "The sorceress seems to act without power—Christabel to yield without resistance"; "*Kubla Khan,* we think, only shews that Mr. Coleridge can write better *nonsense* verses than any man in England." Such venom carries some truth, of course, but it stands in stark contrast to an extraordinary comment by Coleridge on Hazlitt to which Stanley Jones draws attention: In January 1817 Coleridge not only wrote "that he had been a brother to Hazlitt" but added "that Hazlitt was *the only one who knew him.*" Their early enthusiasm for one another was apparently mutual, and the rupture of friendship was apparently painful to both. The rapport they enjoyed at Nether Stowey was never to be repeated.

Although Hazlitt desired most to become a philosopher, after his 1798 visit to Nether Stowey he set out to become a portrait painter like his brother John. While never quite putting aside his love for politics, philosophy, and literature, he went to see the works of Titian, Raphael, Guido Reni, Domenichino, and Caracci at a Pall Mall gallery in late 1798 or early 1799, when Italian masters from the collection of the duc d'Orleans were exhibited. He was "staggered" and looked at them "with wondering and with longing eyes." He extends his rhapsody in biblical terms: "A mist passed away from my sight: the scales fell off. A new sense came upon me, a new heaven and a new earth stood before me. . . . From that time I lived in a world of pictures" ("On the Pleasure of Painting"). He ensconced himself for a time at Rathbone Place in London with his brother John and made pilgrimages into the provinces to see private collections and to find commissions for portraits. He worked as hard at his painting as he did at his studies of modern philosophy, later crediting his painting (and his acquaintance with the author of *The Ancient Mariner*) for his ability to write and speak ("On Public Opinion," *London Weekly Review,* 19 January 1828). He made a little money and enough of a

*Hazlitt circa 1800 (portrait by John Hazlitt; Maidstone Museum and Art Gallery)*

reputation to get a commission in 1802 from Joseph Railton of Liverpool, a manufacturer whose daughter Hazlitt may have courted, to go to Paris and copy some of the old masters at the Louvre. In his *Life of Napoleon Buonaparte* (1828-1830), Hazlitt praised Napoleon for amassing the paintings in the Louvre, "collected, heaped, massed together to a gorgeous height. . . . Instead of robbery and sacrilege, it was the crowning and consecration of art." He went to the Louvre, he said in his lecture "On the Works of Hogarth" (in *Lectures on the English Comic Writers,* 1819), as a votary, to worship "as in a temple" the "triumphs of human genius." The art of the great painters approximated for him what nature was to Wordsworth: "the stay, the guide, and anchor of our purest thoughts." Visiting galleries became something of a religion to him, and he was rightly proud of his ability to gain admission to the most inaccessible galleries. "Neither the surliness of porters, nor the impertinence of footmen could keep me back," he wrote in "Of Thought and Action" in *Table-Talk;* "my liking to the end conquered my scruples or aversion to the means." His persistence proved invaluable for his *Sketches of the Principal Picture-Galleries in England* (1824), and his devotion to painting gave him an excuse to return to the Lake Country in the summer of 1803.

Hazlitt was welcomed to a larger community, for Wordsworth had married and was established at Grasmere with his wife, Mary, and an infant son as well as Dorothy, and Coleridge, at Keswick, had two sons, Hartley and Derwent, and an infant daughter, Sara. Hazlitt had been commissioned by Sir George Beaumont to paint portraits of Coleridge and his son Hartley, and by 23 July Hazlitt had completed portraits of Wordsworth and Coleridge. Both portraits are lost, but, according to Robert Southey, the portrait of Coleridge made him look as if he were on trial "and certainly had stolen the horse; but then you did it cleverly" (letter to Coleridge, 11 June 1804) while Wordsworth's portrait seemed to show the subject "At the gallows—deeply affected by his deserved fate—yet determined to die like a man" (letter to Richard Duppa, 14 December 1803).

Having had little success as a painter of the Lake Poets, Hazlitt had even less success with a country hoyden, whom he allegedly whipped when she refused to yield to his wishes. The populace was incensed, according to Henry Crabb Robinson, who recorded the story in his diary on 15 June 1815 after hearing it from Wordsworth who also told it to Lamb and Benjamin Robert Haydon as revenge for Hazlitt's "Observation on Mr. Wordsworth's Poem the Excursion," published in the *Examiner* for August-October 1814 (it was later collected in *The Round Table,* 1817). Robinson's secondhand account, of events recalled by Wordsworth a dozen years later, ought not to be taken as fully factual. Robinson said that Hazlitt "escaped to Wordsworth, who took him into his house at midnight, gave him clothes and money (from three to five pounds)." Coleridge elaborated on the story in 1817, after Hazlitt's review of the *Statesman's Manual,* adding that he gave Hazlitt all the money he had in the world and even "the very Shoes off my feet to enable him to escape over the mountains" (letter to Francis Wrangham, 5 June 1817). After Hazlitt left the Lake District, Coleridge arranged for Hazlitt's clothes, painting box, and canvases to be sent after him to London (letter to Sara Coleridge early January 1804). More easily than Wordsworth, Coleridge could understand Hazlitt's sexual nature, which made him restless and unhappy all his life, and finally humiliated him in middle age, when he had an affair with Sarah Walker, the coquettish daughter of his landlady, and poignantly recounted it in *Liber Amoris* (1823). Thomas De Quincey later declared that Hazlitt had made an offer to Dorothy Wordsworth, but no corroboration can be found for that claim. As a meager attempt to balance the attacks and counterattacks on Hazlitt's sexual adventures, Coleridge gracefully though tardily praised the originality and ability of the author of *An Essay on the Principles of Human Action* in chapter 24 of his *Biographia Literaria* (1817), remembering his own enthusiasm for the mind if not the person of William Hazlitt.

One of the greatest gifts given to Hazlitt by Coleridge and Wordsworth was his lasting friendship with Charles and Mary Lamb, whom he met at one of Godwin's evening parties, on 22 March 1803, when the guests also included Coleridge and Holcroft. The only surviving portrait by Hazlitt is the one he painted in 1804 of Charles Lamb in the dress of a Venetian senator; the style is reminiscent of Titian, whose work Hazlitt loved. Hazlitt and the Lambs together enjoyed art, books, the theater, and many conversations at tea and dinner, where Charles Lamb, with his keen sense of humor, "always made the best pun, and the best remark in the course of the evening. His serious conversation, like his serious writing, is his best" ("On the Conversation of Authors," in *The Plain Speaker,* 1826). Despite Mary Lamb's bouts with madness, which had led her to murder her mother in 1796, she was the best of the "Good Women" Hazlitt names in his conversational essay "Of Persons One Would Wish to Have Seen" (*New Monthly Magazine,* January 1826), a subject suggested to Hazlitt by Charles Lamb. The Lambs' evening parties inspired many of Hazlitt's liveliest essays, and Charles Lamb's standards as a writer and thinker raised Hazlitt's own. On 21 December 1816 Coleridge told Robinson that Hazlitt had pilfered from Lamb all the good things in his journalism, and in his later years Coleridge made the charge again. Hazlitt acknowledged his debt by dedicating his *Characters of Shakespear's Plays* (1817) to Charles Lamb "as a mark of old friendship and lasting esteem" and as a subtle acknowledgment of Charles and Mary Lamb's *Tales from Shakespear* (1807) for children.

It is perhaps no coincidence that Hazlitt met the Lambs at the beginning of his career as a writer. Their friendship enabled Hazlitt to break his writer's block and finish the essays he had begun at Hackney. Hazlitt's first pieces were, however, "still-born from the press" ("On Public Opinion"). After his *Essay on the Principles of Human Action* (1805), Hazlitt published two pamphlets that applied his ideas on benevolence and disinterestedness to the political situation of his day: *Free Thoughts on Public Affairs* (1806), attacking the Tories and urging peace with France, and *A Reply to the Essay on Population, by the Rev. T. R. Malthus* (1807), an angry, extensive response to Malthus's attempt "to increase [the] indifference and apathy" toward the poor. The Lambs must have

*Self-portrait by Hazlitt, 1802 (Maidstone Museum and Art Gallery)*

cared little for these works, being profoundly apolitical, but they sympathized with the failure of any of them to gain much public notice. Needing money, Hazlitt published two books for more popular consumption: *An Abridgment of the Light of Nature Pursued, by Abraham Tucker, Esq.* (1807), important for its belief in intuition or instinct rather than reason, and an anthology of speeches, *The Eloquence of the British Senate* (1807), intended "to revive what was forgotten, and embody what was permanent." Neither sold well. Having begun to notice style and improve his own from analyzing the speeches and prose of others, Hazlitt was forced to reconsider his options for making a living.

In 1806 or 1807 the Lambs introduced Hazlitt to their friend Sarah Stoddart, an unconventional but sociable woman three years older than Hazlitt; she had just returned from Malta and was unquestionably shopping for a husband. Her friendship with Mary Lamb recommended her to Hazlitt, though he probably did not realize that Mary often scolded Sarah into something approaching the dignity that would make her worthy of Hazlitt or any other man sitting down to the Lambs' table. Mary Lamb enjoyed being a matchmaker and encouraged the relationship as best she could. Among Sarah Stoddart's principal charms were a home at Winterslow, near Salisbury, and a modest legacy of eighty pounds a year that promised to grow to a third more on her mother's death. Her brother, John, well advanced toward becoming a Tory, had also to be courted, and, after considerable delay, he agreed reluctantly to the match. During the months of waiting, Charles Lamb, opposed to the match, sent a friend a joking report of Hazlitt's suicide, allegedly from lovesickness (letters to Joseph Hume, 29 December 1807, 12 January 1808). The couple was married on 1 May 1808 at St. Andrews Church, Holborn. The wedding was witnessed by Charles and Mary Lamb, the former laughing, the latter triumphantly serious.

Winterslow became Hazlitt's home, a country retreat where he could indulge himself in thought amid silence broken only by birds. In less than three months, it became clear to him that "grand scenes of Nature are more adapted for occasional visits than for constant residence" ("Common Places," *Literary Examiner,* 6 September - 13 December 1823). He went often to London, and the Lambs visited Winterslow to share with him "the Claude Lorraine skies" ("A Farewell to Essay-Writing," *London Weekly Review,* 29 March 1828) though not domestic tranquility. His home life was not without travail almost from the first. Sarah Hazlitt, though almost constantly pregnant for the first eight years of their marriage, bore but one child, William, who lived to maturity. Their first son, born 15 January 1809, died 5 July of that same year. Two miscarriages on 6 March and 6 September 1810 intervened before William's birth on 26 September 1811. Another miscarriage occurred on 15 October 1813, after the Hazlitts had returned to London, and the last child, John, born 28 November 1815, died of measles on 19 June 1816. Amid this turmoil, Hazlitt tried to paint and write, preparing in 1809 a prospectus for a critical history of English philosophy. He did complete *A New and Improved Grammar of the English Tongue* (1810), which required many visits with Godwin, who published it and who, against Hazlitt's wishes, added his own "New Guide to the English Tongue," under the pseudonym Edward Baldwin. At Winterslow Hazlitt also began his long work on the *Memoirs of the Late Thomas Holcroft,* not published until 1816. Neither his writing nor the painting of several commissioned portraits could save him from penury, and his visits to Godwin and the Lambs, where he sometimes saw Coleridge, could not prevent his unhappiness.

His next scheme was to present a series of lectures on modern philosophy for the Russell Institution. In doing so, he was imitating Coleridge, whose fifteen lectures on William Shakespeare and John Milton had begun on 18 November 1811. Hazlitt solicited subscribers with the help of Robinson, had his proposal approved, and led off with a dry disquisition on Thomas Hobbes and Sir Francis Bacon on 14 January 1812. Hazlitt had far more material than he needed for an hour's performance and from nervousness read too rapidly and monotonously to be understood. His brother-in-law, John Stoddart, wrote a condescending letter of advice, much of which Hazlitt followed, and the rest of the series went well, ending in late April. Hazlitt's views on modern philosophy are ably summarized in his 1809 prospectus, published in *Literary Remains* along with some of the lectures or, more probably, some version of the lectures. In his prospectus, he stated: "According to this philosophy, as I understand it, the mind itself is nothing, and external impressions everything. All thought is to be resolved into *sensation,* all morality into the *love of pleasure,* and all action into *mechanical* impulse." Instead, he said, "The mind has laws, powers, and principles of its own, and is not the mere puppet of matter" that Hobbes, "the father of the modern philosophy," would have it be. John Locke, according to Hazlitt, merely popularized Hobbes's system, while Hartley and others applied it. Hazlitt's 1812 lectures "On the Writings of Hobbes," "On Locke's 'Essay on the Human Understanding,' " "On Abstract Ideas," "On Self-Love," "On Liberty and Necessity," and "On Tooke's 'Diversions of Purley,' " state and restate his central notion, one often repeated in later essays: "The business of the mind is twofold—to receive impressions and to perceive their relations; without which there can be no ideas" ("Madam de Staël's Account of German Philosophy and Literature," *Morning Chronicle,* 3 February 1814). Having expressed his misgivings, if not his anxieties, about the influence of eighteenth-century philosophers, Hazlitt had cleared the way for his own march of intellect.

Through Charles Lamb's influence, Hazlitt landed a position as parliamentary reporter for the *Morning Chronicle* in October 1812 and began his six-year career as a journalist. The editor, James Perry, had begun as a parliamentary reporter himself and made his paper the leading Whig organ of political coverage. Hazlitt's work did not sufficiently challenge him, but it provided material for a distinguished essay, "On the Difference between Writing and Speaking" *(London Magazine,* July 1820), in which he describes his long observations in Parliament as being "in a go-cart of prejudices, in a regularly constructed machine of pretexts and precedents; you are not only to wear the livery of other men's thoughts, but there is a House-of-Commons jargon which must be used for every thing." The "formality and mummery" of Parliament did not, however, deafen him to style or truth. As if compensating for the drivel he was subjected to as a reporter, in August of 1813 Hazlitt submitted to Perry several of his own essays for consideration. Perry published three: "On the Love of Life" (4 September 1813), "On Classical Education" (25 September 1813), and "On Patriotism—A Fragment" (5 January 1814); others would reach readers of the *Examiner*. These brief essays reveal Hazlitt's views on parliamentary reporting in lines such as: "There can be no true elegance without taste in style" ("On Classical Education"), and "The Great are life's fools—dupes of the splendid shadows that surround them, and wedded to the very mockeries of opinion" ("On the Love of Life"). More important, however, the essays demonstrate that Hazlitt had found his métier as an essayist of inspired common sense, shrewd insight, and remembered, impassioned enjoyment. Dining at the Lambs', visiting painter James Northcote, one of the last survivors of Samuel Johnson's circle, and making the acquaintance of such men as painter Benjamin Robert Haydon, a friend to John Keats and an articulate defender of the Elgin Marbles, Hazlitt was clearly becoming a man of letters. Haydon immortalized him by including his face along with Wordsworth's and Keats's in his huge painting, *Christ's Entry into Jerusalem,* first exhibited on 25 March 1820. Hazlitt deserves his place for the force and brilliance of his writing, but his truculence and prejudices kept him from receiving the admiration he should have had in his own day.

In 1813, when Southey accepted the post of poet laureate and Wordsworth his sinecure as Distributor of Stamps in Westmorland, Hazlitt launched the first of many attacks on these poetic apostates in the *Chronicle,* the *Courier,* and most important in the *Times*. Speaking of Southey, Hazlitt wrote in a public letter to Perry, "The literary sycophants of the day, Sir, are greatly enamoured (from some cause or other) with hereditary imbecility and native want of talent" ("Dottrel-Catching," *Morning Chronicle,* 27 January 1814). Controversy invigorated Hazlitt and pleased Perry, who could sell more papers because of it. On the political plane Hazlitt replied vigorously (19 November 1813 - 5 January 1814) to the *Times* editorials of "Vetus," a pseudonym for Edward Sterling, whose "exclusive patriotism" and anti-Gallican position enraged Hazlitt, ever the libertarian who wanted peace with France and praise for his hero Napoleon. But he more certainly advanced his own career by responding to William Mudford's essay in the *Chronicle* (17 September 1813) on the decay of modern comedy with two letters (4 and 15 October 1813) that led to his promotion to drama critic for the paper. One of his first tasks was to evaluate Catherine Stephens's debut in *The Beggar's Opera* (23 October 1813). He recalled the review with enthusiasm in "On Patronage and Puffing" (in *Table-Talk*): "I was not a little proud of it by anticipation. I had just then begun to stammer out my sentiments on paper, and was in a kind of honeymoon of authorship." The honeymoon was not to last, in part because Hazlitt became enamored of Miss Stephens and in part because Hazlitt would not qualify the truth as he saw it.

Almost everything Hazlitt wrote designated him as the prevailing spirit of his age, an age not quite ready to accept new standards. His enthusiastic review of Edmund Kean's London debut as Shylock in *The Merchant of Venice* (26 January 1814) was noticed by other drama critics, who could not relinquish John Philip Kemble's classical dignity for Kean's romantic but inspired inelegance. In the political arena, Hazlitt's attack on Vetus was complicated by the fact that his brother-in-law John Stoddart was then writing leaders for the *Times,* and when Stoddart endorsed the position of Vetus, Hazlitt's retorts grew increasingly vituperative. The public exchange of rhetoric had its effect at home. Unwavering in his idolatry of Napoleon, Hazlitt angered his wife and friends by his political wrangling, earning Lamb's disfavor and Robinson's curt judgment: "He mixes passion and ill-humour and personal feelings in his judgments on public events and characters more than any man I know. . . . He always vindicates Buonaparte, not because he is insensible to his enormous crimes, but out of spite to the Tories of this country and the war of 1792" (16 December 1813). As the political situation in France worsened, Southey celebrated the successes of the Allies and the prospect of the restoration of a monarchy in France in his first offering as poet laureate, *Carmen Triumphale,* which Hazlitt duly reviewed as "romantic without interest, and tame without elegance. . . . we wish to see Mr. Southey, like Virgil, in his Georgics, 'scatter his dung with a grace' " (8 January 1814). He reviewed Mme de Staël's *De l'Allemagne,* banned in France, with a philosopher's eloquence (13 November 1813), and he answered the question of why the arts are not progressive by making a crucial distinction: "Nothing is more contrary to the fact than the supposition that in what we understand by the *fine arts,* as painting and poetry, relative perfection is only

THE

ROUND TABLE:

A COLLECTION OF

ESSAYS

ON

LITERATURE, MEN, AND MANNERS,

By WILLIAM HAZLITT.

VOL. I.

EDINBURGH:

PRINTED FOR ARCHIBALD CONSTABLE AND CO.
AND LONGMAN, HURST, REES, ORME, AND BROWN, LONDON.

1817.

*Title page for the book that collects essays Hazlitt wrote for Leigh Hunt's* Examiner *between May 1814 and January 1817*

the result of repeated efforts, and that what has been once well done constantly leads to something better. What is mechanical, reducible to rule, or capable of demonstration, is progressive, and admits of gradual improvement: what is not mechanical or definite but depends on genius, taste and feeling, very soon becomes stationary or retrograde, and loses more than it gains by transfusion ("Fragments on Art," 11 and 15 January 1814). Supporting the primacy of the creative over the mechanical, he then reviewed the annual exhibition of the British Institution at the British Gallery, Pall Mall (5 and 10 February 1814), asking for "a Prometheus to give life to the cumbrous mass" of correct but uninspired reflections of the English character. Haydon, disappointed in not being mentioned as a candidate for Hazlitt's Prometheus, was somewhat soothed by his 4 and 5 May review of Haydon's *Judgment of Solomon*, but he took Hazlitt's reservations seriously and was hurt. A few months later, when covering the Royal Academy Exhibition, Hazlitt described Sir Thomas Lawrence's portrait of Robert Stewart, Lord Castlereagh, as having "a smug, smart, upstart, haberdasher look" (3 May 1814), and he had gone too far. Accurate though his criticism was, Hazlitt had insulted the work of the very man who was then painting his editor's portrait, and, worse, he had done so with clearly political overtones. Hazlitt was summarily dismissed by Perry, who did not know, as Mary Russell Mitford put it, "that he had a man of genius in his pay." His dazzling apprenticeship behind him, Hazlitt moved on to free-lance work, with short stints at the *Champion,* at John and Leigh Hunt's *Examiner,* at the *Times,* and at the prestigious *Edinburgh Review* in the next four years.

While Hazlitt was earning his reputation as a journalist, his wife and child moved to London in late 1812 to take up residence with him in an old, shabby Westminster house, number 19 York Street where Milton once lived, a fact of abiding interest to Hazlitt but never to Sarah. The house was owned by Jeremy Bentham, who lived next door, and its previous inhabitants were James Mill and his family. The house was never made gracious by Sarah Hazlitt, whose domestic concerns moved toward comfort and convenience rather than any measure of elegance. Their housekeeper, Mrs. Tomlinson, and her two daughters cared little for decorum and ruled the household as it pleased themselves. Hazlitt, a doting father, said nothing, but Sarah's country manners began to annoy him, and her indifference to their son, William, pained the fond father. As husband and wife grew increasingly distant, Hazlitt looked for tenderness and love outside the home. Even at Winterslow in the first years of his marriage he had dallied with a Sally Shepherd, named by Sarah Hazlitt in her divorce journal of 1822, and in London he was "familiar" with street women: "I admire the Clementinas and Clarissas at a distance: the Pamelas and Fannys of Richardson and Fielding make my blood tingle. . . . What is worse, I have an utter aversion to *blue-stockings*. I do not care a fig for any woman that knows even what *an author* means. . . . I would have her read my soul: she should understand the language of the heart; she should know what I am, as if she were another self!" ("On Great and Little Things," in *Table-Talk*). His dalliances ranged from Miss Stephens to nameless ladies of the night to Sarah Walker, whose attentions precipitated personal disaster. His marriage, always far from ideal, ended in separation in 1819 and in divorce in 1822.

Tension at home may have added to Hazlitt's growing feistiness in his essays. From the careful polemic of his essay on capital punishment for the Society for the Diffusion of Knowledge on the Punishment of Death (written in 1812 but not published until January 1831, in *Fraser's Magazine*), to "On Hogarth's Marriage-a-la-Mode" (*Examiner,* 5 June 1814), "The Elgin Marbles" (*Examiner,* 16 June 1816), and "On Mr. Kean's Iago" (*Examiner,* 24 July 1814) was a large leap. In art and drama Hazlitt asked for nothing less than a change in public taste. Wordsworth was so outraged at Hazlitt's politics that he misread Hazlitt's qualified praise of *The Excursion* as brutal criticism. In his extended review for the *Examiner* (21 and 28 August, 2 October 1814), however, Hazlitt recognized in Wordsworth's poetry "a depth, an originality, a truth, a beauty, and grandeur, both of conception and expression, which place him decidedly at the head of the poets of the present day, or rather which place him in a totally distinct class of excellence," despite his "intense intellectual egotism." While acknowledging that Wordsworth's "powers of feeling are of the highest order," Hazlitt deeply wounded Wordsworth by saying that he "is certainly deficient in fanciful invention." Hazlitt's comments were ill-timed, for Wordsworth was then rearranging his poems for a collected edition with headings such as "Poems of Fancy," "Poems of the Imagination," "Poems Founded on the Affections." In his lecture on the living poets (delivered on 3 March 1818), Hazlitt summarized Wordsworth's reaction by saying: "His egotism is in some respects a madness; for he scorns even the admiration of himself, thinking it a presumption in any one to suppose that he has taste or sense enough to understand him." But Hazlitt was not prepared to bear the brunt of Wordsworth's tactless bruiting about of Hazlitt's 1803 misadventure with the country girl at Keswick. During a visit to London in May and June 1815, Wordsworth engaged in a campaign to discredit Hazlitt with his friends, though he was unsuccessful with Lamb.

When news of Napoleon's defeat at Waterloo on 18 June 1815 hit London, Hazlitt went into a serious decline complete with drunkenness and dissipation. Forever after, he refused hard liquor, but his spirits were slow to recover, and his bitter disappointment resolved itself only by hard work. The next two years were his most productive; in 1817 alone he produced nearly one hundred essays. Having met John and Leigh Hunt in 1813, while they were serving two-year prison sentences for seditious libel, Hazlitt was impressed by their ardor for reform. For their *Examiner* he wrote twenty-two short, tight pieces in the manner of Joseph Addison including "On Manner" (27 August 1815), "On the Tendency of Sects" (10 September 1815), "On the Causes of Methodism" (22 October 1815), "On Beauty" (4 February 1816), "On Imitation" (18 February 1816), and "On Gusto" (26 May 1816), an essay defining power and passion as the source and test of all great art, a definition John Keats embraced wholeheartedly. Genially and gracefully, Hazlitt teaches what he knows, what he believes, and what he imagines. Little of political value escaped his notice, and he exposed unmercilessly the sins of Toryism. Hazlitt turned out major pieces not only for the *Examiner,* but also for the *Edinburgh Review,* Archibald Constable's *Edinburgh Magazine,* and two essays on art for the *Encyclopædia Brittanica.* These and a few others were brought together in his first book of essays, *The Round Table* (1817), the title under which his *Examiner* essays had appeared. Like Montaigne, who "had the courage to say as an author what he felt as a man" ("On the Periodical Essayists," in *Lectures on the English Comic Writers,* 1819), Hazlitt wrote the truth as he saw it, and he sometimes revealed it where it was least expected. In his essay on *Comus* in the 11 June 1815 issue of the *Examiner,* for example, he alludes to Wordsworth and Southey, saying that Milton "was not appointed Poet-Laureat to a Court which he had reviled and insulted; he accepted neither place nor pension; nor did he write paltry sonnets upon the 'Royal fortitude' of the House of Stuart," as Wordsworth did in his sonnet "November 1813," where the words "regal fortitude" appear. In "On Poetical Versatility" (*Examiner,* 22 December 1816) he strikes again, saying that poets "do not like to be shut out when laurels are to be given away at Court—or places under Government to be disposed of, in romantic situations in the country. They are happy to be reconciled on the first opportunity to prince and people, and to exchange their principles for a pension." Hazlitt occasionally misquoted, but, as Stanley Jones points out, it is no accident that Hazlitt quoted Wordsworth more often than any other contemporary poet. Though he detested Wordsworth's politics, Hazlitt admired his poetry and knew it would endure.

Hazlitt was most pleased to be asked to contribute to the *Edinburgh Review.* He had been recommended by Catherine Stuart, Lady Mackintosh, the wife of Sir James Mackintosh, lawyer and politician and member of the Holland House circle. Yet Lady Mackintosh's recommendation alone could not keep Hazlitt in the good graces of Francis Jeffrey, editor of the *Edinburgh Review,* who shared Hazlitt's strong opinions. No doubt he recognized something of the sharpness he cultivated in his own reviews in the work Hazlitt submitted to him. In his first contribution (February 1815), a review of Fanny Burney's *Wanderer* (1814), Hazlitt took the opportunity to provide a broad sweep of novels, beginning with *Don Quixote* (1605) and proceeding through Tobias Smollett, Henry Fielding, Samuel Richardson, and Ann Radcliffe to Fanny Burney. The scope gave him the opportunity to praise the "*instinct of imagination*" as the "intuitive perception of the hidden analogies of things" revealed in Cervantes and Shakespeare but missing in Radcliffe and Burney. At the heart of Burney's failure to arouse our passions and to exercise her own imagination is her sex, Hazlitt charges: women "have less muscular power,—less power of continued voluntary attention,—of reason—passion and imagination: but they are more easily impressed with whatever appeals to their senses of habitual prejudices. The intuitive perception of their minds is less disturbed by any general reasoning on causes or consequences." Hazlitt's judgment contributes much to current feminist arguments as to the effects of gender on genre ("The whole is a question of form, whether that form is adhered to, or violated"), decorum and passion, imagination and observation. Women, he says, do not want "talent" so much as the passion that men have long had and long exercised. Hazlitt excuses the offensive female effusions he finds in contemporary novels by recalling the tumult of the times, saying "our prose has run mad, and our poetry grown childish."

Jeffrey liked the review of Burney's novel far better than did her brother, Captain James Burney, a one-time friend of Hazlitt, but keeping a friend was of less importance to Hazlitt than expressing his judgment. Novels of home life and decorous manners could not please a critic passionate about the tough ideals of the revolutionary age. Hazlitt preferred reviews that allowed him more philosophical considerations, such as his second for the *Edinburgh Review,* on Jean Charles Léonard Simonde de Sismondi's *De la Littérature du Midi de l'Europe* (June 1815), or his third, on August Wilhelm von Schlegel's *Lectures on Dramatic Literature* (February 1816), where he defines his role as a critic: "no man can be a true critic or connoisseur, who does not possess a universality of mind,—who does not possess that flexibility which, throwing aside all personal predilections and blind habits, enables him to transport himself into the peculiarities of other ages and nations,—to feel them as it were from their proper and central point,—and to recognize and respect whatever is beautiful and grand under those external circumstances which are necessary to their existence, and which sometimes even seem to disguise them." In this way, he likens himself to Shakespeare, going out of self into others,

Dear Sir,

I fear this will hardly do. The two passages I am apprehensive of most are p. 10-12 "This was the reason" to "farthing about", & p. 64-66 "Of these pragmatical personages" to "liberty & Humanity." They are easily left out. In case of the worst, may I request you to let me have it again, as I can make use of the first dozen pages for an Essay. I hope to make something better of Salvator which I will send you by the end of the week, & remain Dear Sir your

most oblig'd humble servt

W. Hazlitt.

Sunday evening, 25th April [1824]

Melrose

*Letter to Francis Jeffrey suggesting cuts in Hazlitt's review of Walter Savage Landor's* Imaginary Conversations *(1824), published in the March 1824 issue of the* Edinburgh Review *(which often appeared late), and promising a review of* Salvator Rosa, *by Sydney Owenson, Lady Morgan, which appeared in the July issue (Cambridge University Library)* recreating in his mind the time and place and circumstances of dramatist, novelist, or poet. In all his work Hazlitt made crucial distinctions between ancient and modern poetry, between mere observation and suggestive association, form and effect, mere excellence and true superiority: "By an art like that of the ventriloquist, he [Shakespeare] throws his imagination out of himself and makes every word appear to proceed from the mouth of the person in whose name it is spoken. His plays alone are expressions of the passions, not descriptions of them."

During this period, Hazlitt was also drafting his *Characters of Shakespear's Plays* (1817), a natural extension of his work on Schlegel as well as a public rejoinder to Coleridge's lectures on Shakespeare and a natural continuation of his interest in drama. As its title indicates, Hazlitt's concern was the characters rather than the language of Shakespeare, and his comments are more subjective than objective, focused more on passion aroused in the reader than the impression created word by word or scene by scene. In reading *Lear,* he says, we learn "That the greatest strength of genius is shewn in describing the strongest passions: for the power of imagination, in works of invention, must be in proportion to the force of the natural impressions, which are the subject of them." As Hazlitt explained in his 20 January 1818 lecture "On Shakespeare and Milton," passion is the energy of human conflict and the dynamism of circumstance, a force generated by sympathies and antagonisms, by the motives of individuals as they exist only in combination with each other and in response to some extraordinary challenge to the generic resources of the human soul. Hazlitt's belief in the primacy of passion is everywhere obvious in *Characters of Shakespear's Plays.* In *Othello* "the doubtful conflict between contrary passions, though dreadful, continues only for a short time, and the chief interest is excited by the alternate ascendancy of different passions, by the entire and unforeseen change from the fondest love and most unbounded confidence to the tortures of jealousy and the madness of hatred." Describing Romeo as "Hamlet in love," Hazlitt adds, "There is the same rich exuberance of passion and sentiment in the one, that there is of thought and sentiment in the other." And of *Antony and Cleopatra,* Hazlitt says, Shakespeare "brings living men and women on the scene, who speak and act from real feelings, according to the ebbs and flows of passion, without the least tincture of pendantry of logic or rhetoric." Shakespeare projects passion without Wordsworth's egotism: "Shakespear does not stand reasoning on what his characters would do or say, but once *becomes* them, and speaks and acts for them." Crediting Hazlitt, his favorite critic, Keats built on this central perception, extending it and shaping it into his concept of "negative capability." He also enlarged Hazlitt's vision of tragedy as purgatorial rebirth into all human suffering that is potentially part of the process of "soul-making." Despite the fact that Hazlitt's Shakespeare criticism did not supplant Coleridge's, his *Characters of Shakespear's Plays* received the praise of Francis Jeffrey in the *Edinburgh Review* (August 1817), a notice Hazlitt solicited to extend his reputation; he was now considered a man of letters worth reading and hearing.

Responsible critics heard him, praised him, and supported him. Francis Jeffrey became a kind of mentor for Hazlitt, as Godwin and Coleridge had before him. His notice of Hazlitt on Shakespeare was but one of many kindnesses from a man not given to compassion, especially not to an author. Jeffrey's generous payment of twenty-five pounds for Hazlitt's first contribution to the *Edinburgh Review* prevented financial hardship when Hazlitt stopped writing for the *Champion,* where a vicious but subtle attack on his personal life by John Scott, the editor, had appeared on 19 March 1815. Always a tough critic, Jeffrey rejected Hazlitt's review of Thomas Reid's *Inquiry into the Human Mind* in 1818 as too florid and heavily corrected another because it included too many paradoxes. For these reproofs Hazlitt was apparently grateful, though he believed that Jeffrey's editing would make him "dull," as he put it in his only poem, "The Damned Author's Address to his Reviewers":

The rock I'm told on which I split
Is bad economy of wit—
An affectation to be thought
That which I am and yet am not,
Deep, brilliant, new, and all the rest:
. . . . . . . . . . . . . . . . . . . . . . . . . . . . .
From Mackintosh I'll nature learn,
With Sidney Smith false glitter spurn;
Lend me, oh! Brougham, thy modesty,
Thou, Thomas Moore, simplicity;
Mill, scorn of juggling politics;
Thy soul of candour, Chenevix;
And last, to make my measure full,
Teach me, great J———y, to be dull!

Characters

OF

SHAKESPEAR'S PLAYS.

BY WILLIAM HAZLITT.

LONDON:

*Printed by C. H. Reynell, 21, Piccadilly,*

FOR R. HUNTER, SUCCESSOR TO MR. JOHNSON,

IN ST. PAUL'S CHURCH-YARD;

AND C. AND J. OLLIER,

WELBECK-STREET, CAVENDISH-SQUARE.

1817.

*Title page for the book that Francis Jeffrey called a work "of very considerable originality and genius" and that Leigh Hunt praised as a corrective to "the dogmatical and half-informed criticisms of Johnson"*

Jeffrey, Hazlitt wrote in *The Spirit of the Age*, "can censure a friend or a stranger, and serve him effectually at the same time," and "in his disposition there is nothing but simplicity and kindness" despite the power of his pen and position. Under Jeffrey the *Edinburgh Review* became the preeminent organ of the age precisely because opinions therein were given with force and spirit. When an author's work is reviewed, "nothing is ever adverted to but his literary merits," and "where a vein of sarcasm or irony is resorted to, the ridicule is not barbed by some allusion (false or true) to private history." When Hazlitt asked for money and advice during the difficult preparations for his divorce in 1822, Jeffrey came to his aid, and he did so again when Hazlitt was on his deathbed, sending fifty pounds, five times as much as Hazlitt asked for, enough so that he could die without debts. Hazlitt wrote regularly for the *Edinburgh Review* until 1824 and sporadically to the end of his life. His essays include the condemnatory reviews of Coleridge's *Lay Sermon* (December 1816) and *Biographia Literaria* (August 1817), as well as essays on Horace Walpole's letters (December 1818), Joseph Spence's anecdotes on Alexander Pope (May 1820), Joseph Farington's life of Sir Joshua Reynolds (August 1820), "The Periodical Press" (May 1823), Walter Savage Landor's *Imaginary Conversations* (March 1824), Shelley's *Posthumous Poems* (July 1824), Lady Morgan's *Life and Times of Salvator Rosa* (July 1824), William Channing's sermons (October 1829), John Flaxman's lectures on sculpture (October 1829), Walter Wilson's memoirs of Daniel Defoe (January 1830), Godwin's *Cloudesley* (April 1830), and perhaps a review of Thomas Moore's *Loves of the Angels* and Lord Byron's *Heaven and Earth* in the February 1823 issue. This last review shows signs of Jeffrey's firm hand but the marks of Hazlitt's critical trope: "The poetry of Moore is essentially that of *Fancy;* the poetry of Byron that of *Passion.*" In each of these extraordinarily wide-ranging review-essays, Hazlitt reached a standard he probably thought to be beyond his grasp. Writing for Jeffrey gave Hazlitt an audience he could count on for fairness and the highest principles of criticism. Meeting the challenge was formative to his development.

Hazlitt's extraordinary efforts as a journalist exhausted him, and he drew his full-time journalistic career to a close, collecting almost all his essays written between 1812 and 1819 in book form: *The Round Table* (1817), *A View of the English Stage* (1818), and *Political Essays* (1819). The political pieces were published a few days before the Peterloo massacre (16 August 1819) and dedicated to John Hunt,

> *The tried, steady, zealous, and conscientious advocate of the liberty of his country, and the rights of mankind;—*
>
> *One of those few persons who are what they would be thought to be; sincere without offence, firm but temperate; uniting private worth to public principle; a friend in need, a patriot without an eye to himself; who never betrayed an individual or a cause he pretended to serve—in short, that rare character, a man of common sense and common honesty.*

John Hunt and his brother Leigh supported Hazlitt's decision to excuse himself from the constant journalistic writing that had added to the prestige of their *Examiner.* In 1818 Hazlitt had collaborated briefly with John Hunt on the *Yellow Dwarf,* a short-lived weekly that published some of Hazlitt's best political essays such as "On Court-Influence" (3 and 10 January 1818), "On the Clerical Character" (24 and 31 January, 7 February 1818), "What Is the People?" (7 and 14 March 1818), and "On the Regal Character" (16 May 1818). Hazlitt shared the Hunts' liberal political stand, but he kept himself carefully out of the center of the political melee, explaining in the preface to *Political Essays:* "I am no politician, and still less can I be said to be a party-man: but I have a hatred of tyranny, and a contempt for its tools; and this feeling I have expressed as often and as strongly as I could. I cannot sit quietly down under the claims of barefaced power, and I have tried to expose the little arts of sophistry by which they are defended."

The Hunts, on the other hand, espoused radical politics and controversial opinions, among them Percy Bysshe Shelley's. Hazlitt angered Leigh Hunt with his comments against Shelley in volume one of *Table-Talk* (1821), where he said the author of *Prometheus Unbound* "has a fire in his eye, a fever in his blood, a maggot in his brain, a hectic flutter in his speech, which mark out the philosophic fanatic.... He strives to overturn all established creeds and systems . . ." ("On Paradox and Common-Place"). Leigh Hunt saw himself as one of reformers, "the excessive egotists" mentioned in the same essay and in another *Table-Talk* essay, "On People With One Idea," and he responded curtly by letter (20 April 1821). Thus provoked, Hazlitt replied on 21 April with one of his longest and most interesting letters. The letter clearly distinguished John Hunt, who "never played me any tricks," from Leigh Hunt, who was "one of the pleasantest and cleverest people I ever knew," but whose methods were not Hazlitt's own. Never one to sacrifice a theory for a friend, Hazlitt concluded pathetically, "I want to know why everybody has such a dislike to me." Leigh Hunt obliged by presenting Hazlitt a list of his faults (23 April); Hazlitt saw truth in it, but refused to change his ways. And his ways were strange. He was introverted, unsociable, and careless in dress. His passion for truth did not include social climbing or political posturing for attention or favors. He spoke his mind, and he wrote what he thought with little regard for the friends or acquaintances who might be injured. He summarized his refusal to do as others do in "A Farewell to Essay-Writing" (*London Weekly Review,* 29 March 1828), where he addresses many items on Hunt's list of offenses:

> He is puzzled to reconcile the shyness of my pretensions with the inveteracy and sturdiness of my principles.... My standing upright, speaking loud, entering a room gracefully, proves nothing; therefore I neglect these ordinary means of recommending myself to the good graces and admiration of strangers, (and, as it appears even of philosophers and friends)....
>
> ... I am neither a buffoon, a fop, nor a Frenchman, which Mr. Hunt would have me to be. He finds it odd that I am a close reasoner and a loose dresser....

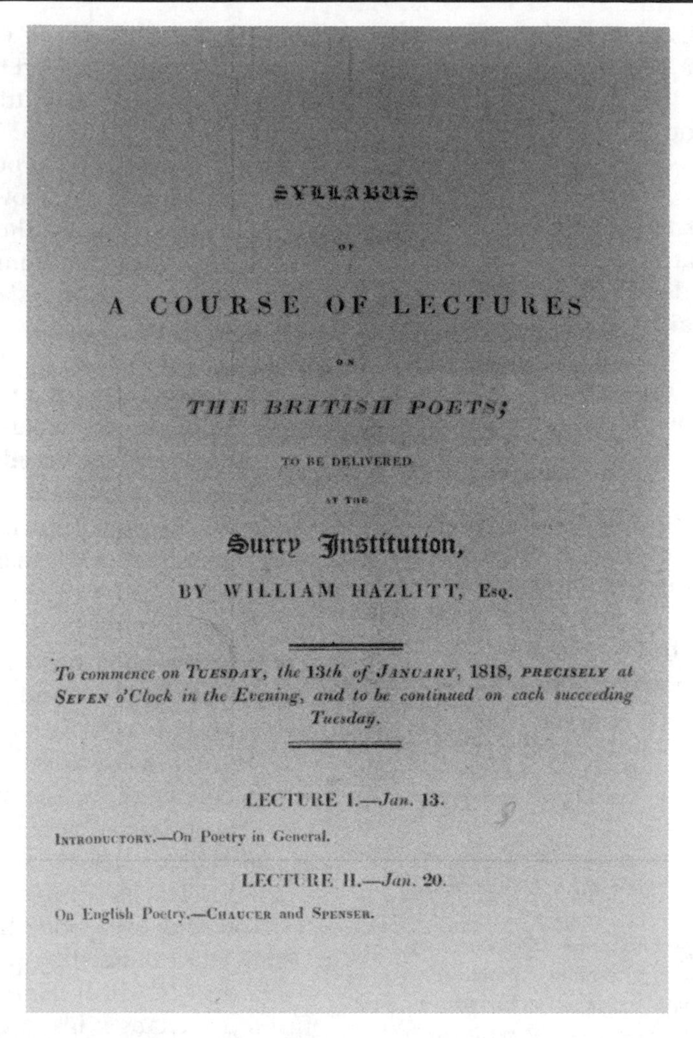

SYLLABUS

OF

A COURSE OF LECTURES

ON

*THE BRITISH POETS;*

TO BE DELIVERED

AT THE

**Surry Institution,**

BY WILLIAM HAZLITT, Esq.

*To commence on* TUESDAY, *the* 13*th of* JANUARY, 1818, PRECISELY *at* SEVEN *o'Clock in the Evening, and to be continued on each succeeding Tuesday.*

LECTURE I.—*Jan.* 13.

INTRODUCTORY.—On Poetry in General.

LECTURE II.—*Jan.* 20.

On English Poetry.—CHAUCER and SPENSER.

*First page of the syllabus for Hazlitt's second lecture series (unique copy; from Geoffrey Keynes,* Bibliography of William Hazlitt, *second edition, revised, 1981)*

> I am charged with using strange gestures and contortions of features in argument, in order to 'look energetic.' One would rather suppose that the heat of the argument produced the extravagance of the gestures, as I am said to be calm at other times. It is like saying that a man in a passion clenches his teeth, not because he is, but in order to seem, angry.

Hazlitt's real friends learned to tolerate his idiosyncrasies and admire his forceful opinions, and, in return, Hazlitt relished his friends' genius even when he could not accept their positions.

In autumn 1816 Hazlitt had met John Keats. Although Keats came to perceive Leigh Hunt's limitations as "self delusions" (letter to Haydon, 11 May 1817) and Haydon's perceptions as "worn out discourses" (letter to Georgiana Keats, 13-28 January 1820), he always admired Hazlitt, quoting him frequently and molding his opinions into his own carefully sculpted poetry. Keats's attraction to Hazlitt's ideas let him disregard Hazlitt's personality, though Keats worried about Hazlitt's lack of reputation, writing to John Hamilton Reynolds, "How is Hazlitt? We were reading his Table [*The Round Table*] last night—I know he thinks himself not estimated by ten People in the world—I wishe he knew he is" (21 September 1817). Reading Hazlitt and hearing some of his lectures on the English poets at the Surrey Institution early in 1818 moved Keats well beyond Hunt and Haydon, teaching him to admire Shakespeare and Milton and to aspire to go beyond Wordsworth. After reading Hazlitt on Shakespeare, Keats wrote to Haydon, "I am very near Agreeing with Hazlit that Shakespeare is enough for us" (11 May 1817). Hazlitt's arguments against egotism and for ventriloquism or going out of self into others served Keats well; so did the belief Hazlitt expressed in one of the essays he collected in *The Round Table:* that works of genius come not from love of fame but "naturally from the mind of the author, without consciousness or effort" ("On Posthumous Fame," *Examiner,* 22 May 1814); Keats echoed the sentiment in his 27 February 1818 letter to John Taylor: "if Poetry comes not as naturally as the Leaves to a tree it had better not come at all." Keats enjoyed Hazlitt's strong opinions: "Hazlitt has damned the bigotted and the blue-stockined how durst the Man?! he is your own good damner and if ever I am damn'd—‹damn me if›I shoul'nt like him to damn me" (letter to Haydon, 21 March 1818). In his 27 April 1818 letter to Reynolds, Keats announced his plan "to ask Hazlitt in about a years time the best metaphysical road I can take." Valuing Hazlitt's speculations, what Keats called "surmises," Keats read Hazlitt's *Essay on the Principles of Human Action,* and kept it close at hand until he left for Italy in 1820.

Keats so admired Hazlitt's *Letter to William Gifford, Esq.* (1819) that he copied out five pages of it for his brother George. This letter, addressed to the editor of the *Quarterly Review,* was Hazlitt's defense of himself in an ongoing war with the periodical press. Hazlitt thought the *Quarterly Review* killed the sales of the second edition of *Characters of Shakespear's Plays* with the review published in its January 1818 issue, and its review damning Hazlitt's *Lectures on the English Poets* (July 1818) added insult to an old injury from its April 1817 review ridiculing *The Round Table.* After Hazlitt wrote "On the Ignorance of the Learned" (July 1818) for Archibald Constable's *Edinburgh Magazine, Blackwood's Magazine* entered the fray by publishing a venomous essay, "Hazlitt Cross-questioned" (August 1818), signed "An Old Friend with a New Face," and written by John Gibson Lockhart and John Wilson, who intended to destroy Hazlitt's reputation, ruin his always perilous credit, and guarantee the ascendance of *Blackwood's* over the *Edinburgh Magazine.* Hazlitt sent Constable a powerful invective, *A Reply to Z,* which remained unpublished until 1923, and then built himself up to full-scale triumph in the response to Gifford, provoking high praise from Keats: "The Manner in which this is managed: the force and innate power with which it yeasts and works up itself—the feeling for the costume of society; is in a style of genius—He hath a demon as he himself says of Lord Byron" (letter to George and Georgiana Keats, 4 February - 3 May 1819). It is the style as much as the subject of *A Letter to William Gifford, Esq.* that Keats admired and later emulated in the vital phases of his poetry. The quotation about Byron is from Hazlitt's lecture "On the Living Poets," where Hazlitt adds, "and that is the next thing to being full of the God." Hazlitt's *Letter to William Gifford* exposed to public opprobrium the slanderers of the "Cockney School" of poets, whom Lockhart and Wilson had been attacking since October 1817, when the magazine published Lockhart's review panning Leigh Hunt's *Story of Rimini* (1816). Keats, who regarded Hazlitt's stand as disinterested valor, did not realize that Wilson and Lockhart had heard of Hazlitt's Keswick indiscretions and referred to them in "Hazlitt-Cross-questioned." Hazlitt threatened to sue for libel and received one hundred pounds in damages from *Blackwood's Magazine.*

Keats learned mental courage from Hazlitt, courage he would need to withstand attacks on his own work. On 18 January 1818, a few days after Hazlitt's first lecture on English poets, Keats, who had not attended the lecture, dined with Hazlitt and Haydon, recording the effects of his evening in his 23-24 January letter to his brother George: "I think a little change has taken place in my intellect lately—I cannot bear to be uninterested or unemployed, I, who for so long a time, have been addicted to passiveness—Nothing is finer for the purposes of great productions, than a very gradual ripening of the intellectual powers—As an instance of this—observe—I sat down yesterday to read King Lear once again the thing appeared to demand the prologue of a Sonnet, I wrote it. . . ." He then copied out his sonnet "On Sitting Down to *King Lear* Once Again" as a testament to his growing powers of seeing into the life of literature as Hazlitt's example taught him.

Keats's pattern of hearing or reading Hazlitt and writing poetry continued into the series of lectures Hazlitt gave on the English comic writers at the Surrey Institution in the fall of 1818. Keats did not hear them, but he read at least one in manuscript, which he obtained from Hazlitt in December. In his 16 December - 4 January 1819 letter to George and Georgiana Keats, following a transcription of his "Ever let the Fancy roam," Keats quoted a substantial section of Hazlitt's sixth lecture, a passage on Godwin's *St. Leon* (1799), as "a specimen of his [Hazlitt's] usual abrupt manner, and fiery laconiscism," appending his own "Bards of Passion and Mirth." Here, as David Bromwich points out, Keats interleaves

*Hazlitt in 1824 (portrait by William Bewick; National Portrait Gallery, London)*

Hazlitt's eloquence with his own "as a single continuous act of expression."

For his part, Hazlitt deferred to Keats by revising a comment on Thomas Chatterton in his *Lectures on the English Poets* that had offended the young Keats, and later in "The Periodical Press" (*Edinburgh Review,* May 1823), he charged that Keats was victimized by Gifford's *Quarterly Review* because he had been praised in the *Examiner:* Keats's "fine fancy and powerful invention were too obvious to be treated with mere neglect; and as he had not been ushered into the world with the court-stamp upon him, he was to be crushed as a warning to genius how it keeps company with honesty. . . ." Hazlitt repeated his charges against Gifford in *The Spirit of the Age,* where he praises "the rich beauties and the dim obscurities" of "The Eve of St. Agnes," and in an essay collected in *The Plain Speaker* he says that reading Keats's poem "made me regret that I was not young again" ("On Reading Old Books," *London Magazine,* February 1821). In his *Table-Talk* essay "On Effeminacy of Character," Hazlitt uses Keats as the final example of the individual in whom there is a "prevalence of the sensibility over the will": "I cannot help thinking that the fault in Mr. Keats's poems was a deficiency in masculine energy of style. . . . He painted his own thoughts and character; and did not transport himself into the fabulous and heroic ages. There is a want of action, of character, and so far, of imagination, but there is exquisite fancy. . . . His mind was redolent of spring. He had not the fierceness of summer, nor the richness of autumn, and winter he seemed not to have known, till he felt the icy hand of death!" Hazlitt was the first to anthologize Keats's work, including in his *Select British Poets* (1824) three passages from *Endymion,* one from *Hyperion,* the "Ode to a Nightingale," "Fancy," and "Robin Hood." There he wrote his summary of Keats's achievement:

> Mr. Keats is also dead. He gave the greatest promise of genius of any poet of his day. He displayed extreme tenderness, beauty, originality, and delicacy of fancy: all he wanted was manly strength and fortitude to reject the temptations of singularity in sentiment and expression. Some of his shorter and later pieces are, however, as free from faults as they are full of beauties.

As David Bromwich puts it, "No other encounter between poet and critic has been so fortunate in literature." Hazlitt's pace, gusto, disinterestedness, and even his aphorisms became a model and an inspiration for Keats's poetry and for the prose in his remarkable letters.

After the success of Hazlitt's delivery and publication of his *Lectures on the English Poets* and *Lectures on the English Comic Writers,* complimentarily reviewed and elaborately excerpted in the Hunts' *Examiner,* Constable's *Edinburgh Magazine,* and Perry's *Morning Chronicle,* Hazlitt began preparing at once his last series, *Lectures chiefly on the Dramatic Literature of the Age of Elizabeth,* delivered at the Surrey Institution in late 1819 and published in 1820. What Keats calls "Hazlitt's depth of Taste" (in his 10 January 1818 letter to Haydon) applies as much to these lectures as to Hazlitt's earlier pronouncements on literature. Hazlitt describes what he senses and ranges widely: "The sweetness of Deckar, the thought of Marston, the gravity of Chapman, the grace of Fletcher and his young-eyed wit, Jonson's learned sock, the flowing vein of Middleton, Heywood's ease, the pathos of Webster, and Marlow's deep designs, add a double lustre to the sweetness, thought, gravity, grace, wit, artless nature, copiousness, ease, pathos, and sublime conceptions of Shakespear's Muse." Like Thomas Heywood, Hazlitt produced a prodigious number of pages, "for the more a man writes, the more he can write." He wrote at Winterslow alone, entertained by simple pleasures, undistracted by enemies or friends. But even in that period and place of calm, he sensed imminent disaster, concluding his last lecture with unusual poignance: "A cloud is upon our onward path, and we fancy that all is sunshine beyond it. . . . We stagger on the few remaining paces to the end of our journey; make perhaps one final effort; and are glad when our task is done!"

The task was not to be done for a decade, but sunshine was rare in the years to come. Threatened with eviction from the York Street house in London, Hazlitt asked Jeffrey for a loan of £100, which he expected to repay from the £150 he would receive for lecturing on the Elizabethan dramatists (25 September 1819). The money was not enough to keep Bentham from calling in the bailiffs. At the end of 1819, he lost his home and with it his wife and son, William—Sarah Hazlitt having decided that they live apart from the improvident husband and father. At forty-one with fifteen books to his credit, Hazlitt saw himself as a total failure as author and painter, husband and father, friend and reformer. He took rooms at number 9 Southampton Buildings in the home of a tailor named Micaiah Walker, a Dissenter whose wife, Martha, was determined to make shrewd matches for her six children. The oldest daughter had married a tenant, Robert Roscoe, a solicitor, and the wily mother had designs on Hazlitt for her second daughter, Sarah, who was half Hazlitt's age. While Hazlitt was writing *Table-Talk* essays for John Scott's new *London Magazine,* he was also dallying with Sarah in his lodgings. The very weaknesses that made Hazlitt difficult as a man, bringing disaster and anguish, become in *Table-Talk* his strength as an essayist. He reveals himself in "On the Pleasure of Painting" (December 1820), as well as in "On Living to One's-Self" and "On the Aristocracy of Letters" (both first published in the 1821-1822 collected edition) with remarkable honesty and felicity, combining graceful reminiscence and hopeful delight in all he observed. Between June 1820 and December 1821 he wrote thirteen *Table-Talk* essays in addition to various other articles and reviews, and moving to the *New Monthly* in 1822 he wrote eleven more *Table-Talk* essays in the next two years. When the *Table-Talk* collection was published in 1821 and 1822, only five of the thirty-three were reprints from the magazines. In one of the new Table-Talk essays he calls his style "familiar," consciously rejecting "not only all unmeaning pomp, but all low, cant phrases, and loose, unconnected, *slipshod* allusions" ("On Familiar Style"). Love for Sarah Walker focused his mental energies though his heart was out of control.

In 1822 the affair ended, Hazlitt won a Scottish divorce from his wife, and he wrote *Liber Amoris* (1823) in which he told more about his relationship with Sarah Walker than most readers want to know. "I am not mad," he wrote, "but my heart is so; and raves within me, fierce and untameable, like a panther in its den, and tries to

10

bestows a *turn* for any thing on the individual, she implants a corresponding taste for it in others. We have only to "throw our bread upon the waters, & after many days we shall find it again." Let us do our best, & we need not be ashamed of the smallness of our talent, or afraid of the stupified calumnies & contempt of envious maligners. When Goldsmith was talking one day to Sir Joshua of writing a fable in which little fishes were to be introduced, Dr. Johnson rolled about uneasily in his seat & began to laugh, on which Goldsmith said rather angrily—"Why do you laugh? If you were to write a fable for little fishes, you would make them speak like great whales!" The reproof was just. Johnson was in truth conscious of Goldsmith's superior inventiveness & of the lighter graces of his pen, but he wished to reduce every thing to his own pompous & oracular style. There are not only *books for children*, but books for all ages & for both sexes. After we grow up to years of discretion, we do not

*Manuscript fragment for "On Egotism," an essay written in 1824 and first published in the Paris edition (1825) of* Table-Talk *(from P. P. Howe, ed.,* The Complete Works of William Hazlitt, *volume twenty-one, 1934)*

get loose to its lost mate, and fawn on her hand, and bend lowly at her feet." The pain of her eventual rejection of him and her alliance to another lodger, one John Tomkins, a solicitor, left Hazlitt disconsolate: "no flower will ever bloom on earth to glad my heart again!" There is no doubt that *Liber Amoris* memorializes, exorcizes, and perhaps even consummates his passion for Sarah Walker, but by fictionalizing the affair Hazlitt also consciously objectifies it, as did Lamb in his Elia essays and Thomas De Quincey in his *Confessions of an English Opium Eater,* both of which were appearing in magazines in 1821 and 1822, and as Jean-Jacques Rousseau and Johann Wolfgang von Goethe had done years before in the *Confessions* (1781, 1788) and *The Sorrows of Young Werther* (1774). The personal, though exaggerated account does, however, reveal more about Hazlitt than his essays. Marilyn Butler argues convincingly that long before the affair concluded Hazlitt intended to make a novel of it, and that intention excuses more than a few of the book's excesses without keeping it from remaining an unusual and underrated Romantic autobiography. Hazlitt published the book anonymously, and he attempted to disguise its autobiographical nature by including in it an advertisement claiming that the book is based on a manuscript written by a now deceased "native of North Britain, who left his own country early in life, in consequence of political animosities and an ill-advised connection in marriage," but reviewers saw through the ruse and exposed more of Hazlitt's affair than he wanted known. One of his own love letters was even published in the *John Bull* (22 June 1823), probably by the same John Wilson Croker who had lambasted Keats's *Endymion* (1818); the *Literary Register* announced his name and Sarah Walker's name without apology (3 August 1823); and *Blackwood's* renewed its attacks (June 1823).

As usual, Hazlitt was in debt, but he never became hardened at being desperate for money. It is curious that despite his anxiety, he continued to meet his own high standards in his essays. He turned to a series on important art collections, which he published in the *New Monthly Magazine* (April 1822) and the *London Magazine* (December 1822 - March 1823; June, July, October, and November 1823) and collected as *Sketches of the Principal Picture-Galleries in England.* And he wrote for the Hunts' new *Liberal,* producing early in 1823 "On the Scotch Character" (January) and "On the Spirit of Monarchy" (January), and "My First Acquaintance with Poets" (April), now perhaps his best-known essay of all. Also for the *Liberal* he exposed theological pretension in "Pulpit Oratory—Dr. Chalmers and Mr. Irving" (July 1823) and wrote a splendid lament on political apostasy in "Arguing in a Circle" (July 1823). There is perhaps a considerable falling off of powers in his "Common Places" (September-December 1823), reworked considerably and published anonymously in his *Characteristics: In The Manner of Rochefoucault's Maxims* (1823). Without large theory to link maxims and paragraphs, Hazlitt concentrates on making his style "sententious and epigrammatic, with a certain pointedness and involution of expression." He reveals in many cases a dour bitterness as in "Some persons can do nothing but ridicule others"; in the 434 apothegms man's follies, especially in love, dominate. His misfortunes in love resolve themselves in truths that he would come to live by during the last of his disappointed life: "It is better to desire than to enjoy—to love than to be loved"; "We revenge in haste and passion: we repent at leisure and from reflection"; "Women are not philosophers or poets, patriots, moralists, or politicians—they are simply women." The rhythm of his thoughts, like the rhythm of his prose, has clear and memorable cadence.

Family had become increasingly important to him after the death of his father on 16 July 1820. Throughout his affair with Sarah Walker and the prolonged proceedings for his divorce from Sarah Stoddart Hazlitt, he frequently visited his mother, sister, and brother. He also reestablished connections with an Irish cousin, Kilner Hazlitt, and kept up regular visits with his son, William. He began looking for another wife, one who could finance a pilgrimage for him to Italy. He found one in a Scotswoman, Isabella Shaw Bridgwater, who had been a widow since 1820; they married in April of 1824, and late in August they set out for France and Italy as planned, returning to London in October 1825. *The Spirit of the Age,* published early in 1825, guaranteed Hazlitt's lasting reputation as an observer of men of his time; his second marriage confirmed his inability to keep a wife happy. Just before leaving, Hazlitt paid his old friend William Godwin a visit, and there saw Mary Shelley, who somewhat later described him at this critical juncture of his life in a 10 October 1824 letter to Marianne Hunt, wife of Leigh Hunt:

> Hazlitt is abroad—he will be in Italy in the winter. He wrote an article in the E.R. on the Vol of

On a Sun-Dial.

Horas non numero nisi serenas.

This is the motto of a sun-dial near Venice. There is a softness &
a beauty in the words & in the thought unparalleled. Of all conceits it
is surely the most classical. "I count only the hours which are serene."
What a bland & care-dispelling feeling! How the shadows seem to fade
on the dial-plate as the sky lowers, & time presents only a blank unless
as its progress is marked by what is joyous, & all that is not happy sinks
into oblivion! What a fine lesson it conveys to the mind — to take no
note of time but by its benefits, to watch only for the smiles & neglect
the frowns of fate, to compose our lives of bright & gentle moments, turning always to the sunny side of things, & letting the rest slip from our
imaginations, unheeded or forgotten! How different from the common art
of self-tormenting! For myself, as I rode along the Brenta, & the sun shone
hot upon its sluggish, slimy waves, my sensations were far from comfortable, but the reading this inscription on a glaring wall in an instant
restored me to myself, & still whenever I think of or repeat it, it has the power of waft-
ing me into the region of pure & blissful abstraction. I cannot help fan-
cying it is a legend of Popish superstition. Some monk of the dark ages
must have invented & bequeathed it to us, who loitering in trim gardens
& watching the silent march of time, as his fruits ripened in the sun or
his flowers scented the balmy air, felt a mild languor steal over his sen[ses,]
& having little to do or to care for, determined (in imitation of his sun-
dial) to efface that little from his thoughts, making of his life one long
dream of quiet! Horas non numero nisi serenas — he might repeat,
when the heavens were overcast & the gathering storm scattered the falling
leaves, & turn to his books & wrap himself in his golden studies! Out
of some such mood of mind, indolent, elegant, thoughtful, this exquisite
device (speaking volumes) must have originated. —

Of the different modes of counting time, that by the sun-dial is perhaps the
most apposite & striking, if not the most convenient. It "morals on the
time." It is slow, silent, imperceptible, chequered with light & shade.
If our hours were all serene, we might probably take almost as little note
of them, as the dial does of those that are clouded. It
is the shadow thrown across, that gives us warning of its flight. Otherwise, all our impressions would take the same undistinguishable hue;
we should scarce be conscious of our existence. Those who have had none of the
cares of this life to agitate & disturb them, have been obliged to have recourse
to the hopes & fears of the next to enliven the prospect before them.

*Page from the manuscript for an essay first published in the October 1827 issue of the* New Monthly Magazine *(HM 12220; Henry E. Huntington Library and Art Gallery)*

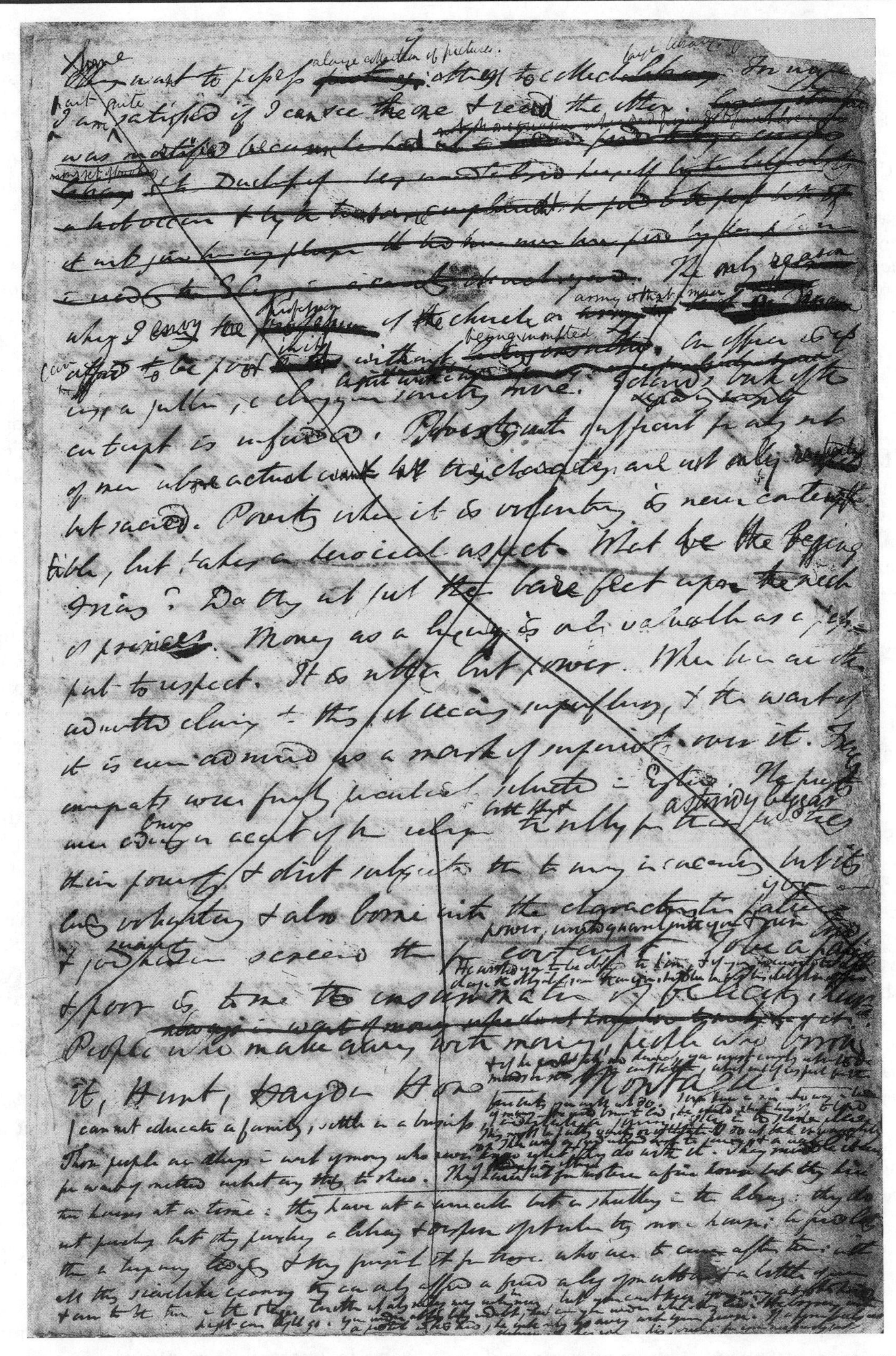

*Fragment of draft for an early version of "On the Want of Money," written on the last page of the manuscript for "On a Sun-Dial" (HM 12220; Henry E. Huntington Library and Art Gallery). The final version of "On the Want of Money" was first published in the January 1827 issue of the* Monthly Magazine.

> Poems which I published [Percy Bysshe Shelley's *Posthumous Poems* which Hazlitt reviewed for *Edinburgh Review,* July 1824]—I do not know whether he meant it to be favourable or not—I did not like it at all—but when I saw him I could not be angry—I never was so shocked in my life, gau[nt] & thin, his hair scattered, his cheek bones projecting—but for his voice & smile I shd not have known him—his smile brought tears into my eyes, it was like a sun-beam illuminating the most melancholy of ruins—lightning that assured you in a dark night of the identity of a friend's ruined & deserted abode.

Perhaps seeing Mary Shelley, whose first work was a journal of a tour with Percy Shelley, inspired Hazlitt to make copious notes for his *Notes of a Journey through France and Italy* (1826), but certainly the visit must have reminded him of his early enthusiasm for William Godwin's schemes and ideals. At any rate, he left England with a promise from the *Morning Chronicle* for serial publication of his travel letters.

The trip was not an unqualified success. Isabella kept far better account of expenses than Hazlitt ever had, and she apparently cared little about Hazlitt's complicated negotiations with A. & W. Galignani for publication in 1825 of Paris editions of *Table-Talk* and *The Spirit of the Age,* both with contents differing somewhat from the British edition. Hazlitt met Stendahl and, of course, returned to his beloved Louvre. In February of 1825, he and Isabella arrived in Florence where he called on Walter Savage Landor and saw Leigh Hunt again after nearly four years. Rome disappointed him by contrast, but in Switzerland he recalled his joy and hope when first he had read of Julie and Saint-Preux in Rousseau's *Julie ou la Nouvelle Héloïse* (1761) thirty years before. For all the beauty of his surroundings Hazlitt regretfully realized that "imagination is entirely a *thing imaginary* and has nothing to do with matter of fact, history, or the senses."

In Switzerland he found Jeffrey's patronizing notice of *The Spirit of the Age* in the *Edinburgh Review* (April 1825), and he was disheartened. *The Spirit of the Age,* with its depth and breadth, testifies to his taste and critical judgment. His portraits of his major contemporaries are tied to the notion that the greats of the generation had failed to fulfill their promise. Taken as a whole, the book explores what Herschel Baker calls "the reciprocal relations of convention and revolt, of freedom and restraint." Beneath the facts and lists of publications, *The Spirit of the Age* reveals the growth and progress of Hazlitt's own mind as it acted and reacted to writers, politicians, and influential editors: Coleridge; Sir Walter Scott; Byron; Southey; Wordsworth; Thomas Campbell; George Crabbe; Thomas Moore; Leigh Hunt; Lamb; Washington Irving; Horne Tooke; Mackintosh; Henry Peter Brougham; William Cobbett; Sir Francis Burdett; John Scott, Lord Eldon; William Wilberforce; George Canning; Bentham; Godwin; Thomas Robert Malthus; Jeffrey; Gifford; and Edward Irving. The resonance of his prose gives Hazlitt's inevitable signature to the work. With quick strokes and meaningful details Hazlitt brings alive an age he knew intimately, loved passionately, and understood as perhaps no one else of the time. Even Sir Walter Scott, a Tory with whom he would soon compete with a biography of Napoleon, he could salute as "undoubtedly the most popular writer of the age" because he thought of his subjects rather than himself when writing. Although none of his figures receives only his praise, each sketch bears the stamp of his genius and cautious judgments.

Learning of Scott's projected work on Napoleon, Hazlitt wasted little time in beginning his own. He and Isabella returned to France in July 1826, shortly before Haydon read the first of Hazlitt's "Conversations" with James Northcote in the August issue of *New Monthly.* Haydon blamed Isabella for the "malice" he read into Hazlitt's comments on art and artists and spread malicious scandal about Hazlitt's "not quite respectable" marriage. (Hazlitt had married Isabella in Scotland because his Scottish divorce was not recognized in England.) Hazlitt met Scott and even James Fenimore Cooper in Galignani's reading room, but, plagued by lack of funds, he found it difficult to keep up his periodical writings and accomplish what he wanted to do with his *Life of Napoleon Buonaparte* (1828-1830). By the autumn of 1827 his marriage had come to an end, certainly due in part to a lack of money. Perhaps another cause was the arrival in Paris of William Hazlitt, now fifteen or sixteen, at the end of the 1826 summer term. The father's artistic ambitions for the son outweighed the attractions of his wife. The unhappy threesome went to Florence and Venice together, traveling under cramped conditions and staying in unseemly but affordable housing. On their return to Paris, Isabella demanded that Hazlitt return his son to London. Hazlitt obliged

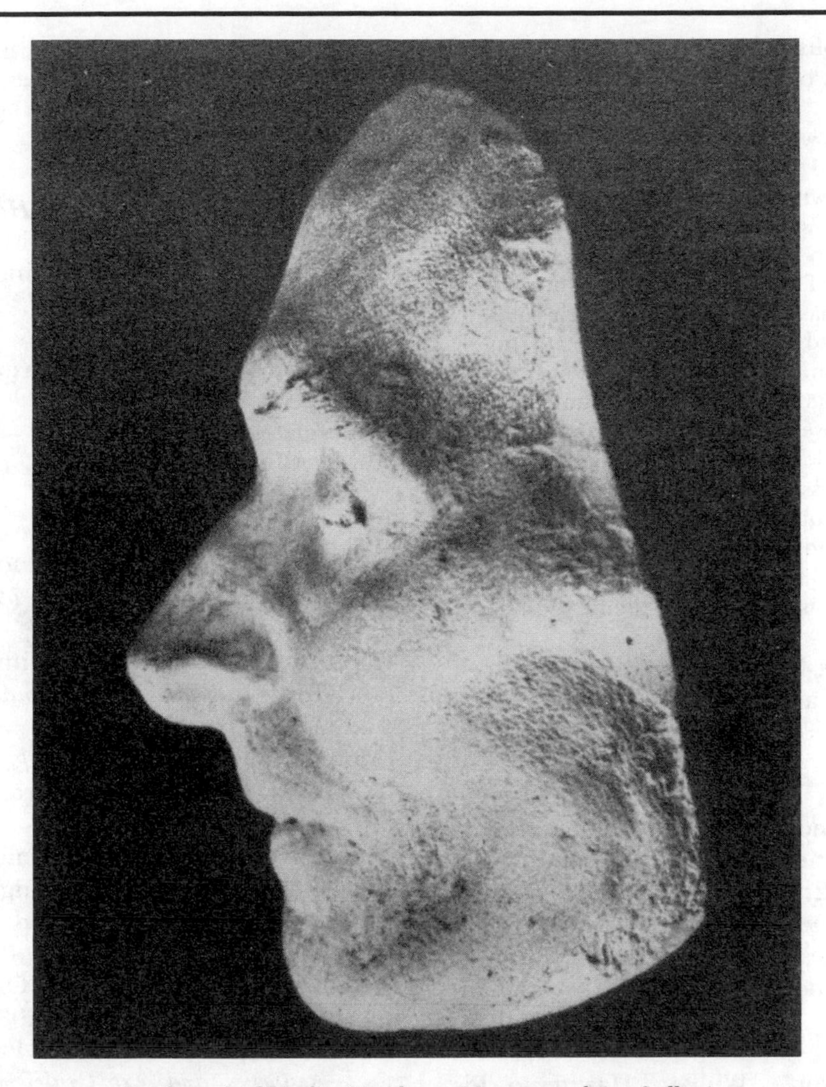

*Death mask of Hazlitt (Maidstone Museum and Art Gallery)*

in late August or early September of 1827 but Isabella refused to follow. Announcing that their separation was permanent, she joined her sister in Switzerland. She outlived her husband, dying in Haddingtonshire in 1869.

Hazlitt's last years were as active as ever. He wrote frequently for the *London Weekly Review,* the *Atlas,* the *New Monthly,* and the *Edinburgh Review,* but no record remains of his personal life in the journals and letters of his friends, Lamb, Robinson, Haydon, Peter George Patmore, and Godwin, from which most of the information about Hazlitt's activities can be gleaned. Always a poor letter writer, Hazlitt was almost silent during his last years, save for notes to publishers and odd jottings about occasional dinners or teas. The first two volumes of his biography of Napoleon were published in late January 1828, and in June of that year he may have gone to Paris for two or three months. At life's end, he remembered his beginnings more and more, recalling Godwin in the last of his *Conversations of James Northcote* (1830) and in his last work for the *Edinburgh Review,* a review of Godwin's *Cloudesley* (April 1830), and recalling always his hope for the French Revolution and the promise of Napoleon in his four-volume biography, the last two volumes of which came out not long before he died. It is no small consolation that he lived to see the Bourbons deposed in the July Revolution of 1830, but he did not live to write of it. He died of stomach cancer on 18 September with his son beside him to hear him say, "Well, I've had a happy life." The only friends who attended his funeral in St. Anne's Churchyard in Soho were Lamb and Patmore.

Hazlitt commented on what constitutes a "happy life" at the end of "Mind and Matter," a two-part essay published in the 26 February and 9 April 1815 issues of the *Examiner:*

> Happy are they who live in the dream of their own existence, and see all things in the light of their own minds; who walk by faith and hope; to whom the guiding star of their youth still shines from afar, and into whom the spirit of the world has not entered! They have not been 'hurt by the archers,' nor has the iron entered their souls. They live in the midst of arrows and of death, unconscious of harm. The evil things come not nigh them. The shafts of ridicule pass unheeded by, and malice loses its sting. The example of vice does not rankle in their breasts, like the poisoned shirt of Nessus. Evil impressions fall off from them like drops of water. The yoke of life is to them light and supportable. The world has no hold on them. They are in it, not of it; and a dream and a glory is ever around them!

The "happy life" as Hazlitt defined it was indeed his own. In his pleasures and in his difficulties, William Hazlitt embodies the spirit of his age.

**Letters:**

Stanley Jones, "Some New Hazlitt Letters," *Notes and Queries,* new series 24 (July-August 1977): 336-342;

*The Letters of William Hazlitt,* edited by Herschel Moreland Sikes, Willard Hallam Bonner, and Gerald Lahey (New York: New York University Press, 1978; London: Macmillan, 1979);

Charles E. Robinson, "William Hazlitt to his Publishers, Friends, and Creditors: Twenty-seven New Holograph Letters," *Keats-Shelley Review,* no. 2 (1987): 1-47.

**Bibliographies:**

Geoffrey Keynes, *Bibliography of William Hazlitt* (London: Printed for the Nonesuch Press, 1931);

James A. Houck, ed., *William Hazlitt: A Reference Guide* (Boston: G. K. Hall, 1977).

**Biographies:**

William Hazlitt, Jr., "Biographical Sketch," in *Literary Remains of the Late William Hazlitt. With a Notice of his Life, by his Son, and Thoughts on his Genius and Writings, by E. L. Bulwer, Esq., M.P. and Mr. Sergeant Talfourd, M.P.,* 2 volumes (London: Saunders & Otley, 1836), I: i-lxxiii;

W. Carew Hazlitt, *Four Generations of a Literary Family: The Hazlitts in England, Ireland, and America, Their Friends and Their Fortunes, 1725-1896,* 2 volumes (London & New York: George Redway, 1897);

P. P. Howe, *The Life of William Hazlitt* (New York: Doran, 1922);

Herschel Baker, *William Hazlitt* (Cambridge, Mass.: Harvard University Press, 1962);

Ralph M. Wardle, *Hazlitt* (Lincoln: University of Nebraska Press, 1971);

Stanley Jones, *Hazlitt: A Life from Winterslow to Frith Street* (Oxford: Clarendon Press, 1989).

**References:**

W. P. Albrecht, *Hazlitt and the Creative Imagination* (Lawrence: University of Kansas Press, 1965);

Albrecht, "Hazlitt, Passion, and *King Lear,*" *Studies in English Literature, 1500-1900,* 18 (Autumn 1978): 611-624;

Albrecht, "The Tragic Sublime of Hazlitt and Keats," *Studies in Romanticism,* 20 (Summer 1981): 185-201;

Albrecht, *William Hazlitt and the Malthusian Controversy* (Albuquerque: University of New Mexico Press, 1950);

David Bromwich, "The Genealogy of Disinterestedness," *Raritan,* 1 (Spring 1982): 62-92;

Bromwich, *Hazlitt, The Mind of a Critic* (New York: Oxford University Press, 1984);

Bromwich, "The Originality Of Hazlitt's Essays," *Yale Review,* 72 (Spring 1983): 366-384;

Norman Bryson, "Hazlitt on Painting," *Journal of Aesthetics and Art Criticism,* 37 (Fall 1978): 37-45;

John M. Bullitt, "Hazlitt and the Romantic Conception of the Imagination," *Philological Quarterly,* 24 (October 1945): 343-361;

Marilyn Butler, "Satire and the Images of Self in the Romantic Period: The Long Tradition of Hazlitt's *Liber Amoris,*" in *English Satire and the Satiric Tradition,* edited by Claude Rawson, with the assistance of Jenny Mezciems (Oxford: Blackwell, 1984), pp. 209-225;

Stanley P. Chase, "Hazlitt as a Critic of Art," *PMLA,* 39 (March 1924): 179-202;

John Kinnaird, "Hazlitt, Keats, and the Poetics of Intersubjectivity," *Criticism,* 19 (Winter 1977): 1-16;

Kinnaird, *William Hazlitt, Critic of Power* (New York: Columbia University Press, 1978);

Edith J. Morley, ed., *Henry Crabb Robinson on Books and Their Writers,* 3 volumes (London: Dent, 1938);

J. D. O'Hara, "Hazlitt and the Functions of the Imagination," *PMLA,* 81 (December 1966): 552-562;

Charles I. Patterson, Jr., "Hazlitt's Criticism in Retrospect," *Studies in English Literature,* 21, no. 4 (1981): 647-663;

Patterson, "William Hazlitt as a Critic of Prose Fiction," *PMLA,* 68 (December 1953): 1001-1016;

Bill Ruddick, "Recollecting Coleridge: The Internalization of Radical Energies in Hazlitt's Political Prose," *Yearbook of English Studies,* 19 (1989): 243-255;

Elisabeth Schneider, *The Aesthetics of William Hazlitt* (Philadelphia: University of Pennsylvania Press, 1933);

Patrick Story, "Emblems of Infirmity: Contemporary Portraits in Hazlitt's *The Spirit of the Age,*" *Wordsworth Circle,* 10 (Winter 1979): 81-90;

Clarence Thorpe, "Keats and Hazlitt: A Record of Personal Relationship and Critical Estimate," *PMLA,* 62 ( June 1947): 487-502;

Robert W. Uphaus, *William Hazlitt* (Boston: Twayne, 1985);

Richard Verdi, "Hazlitt and Poussin," *Keats-Shelley Memorial Bulletin,* no. 32 (1981): 1-18;

R. M. Wardle, "Outwitting Hazlitt," *Modern Language Notes,* 57 ( June 1942): 459-462;

*Wordsworth Circle,* special Hazlitt issue, 6 (Spring 1975).

**Papers:**

Many of Hazlitt's manuscripts are at the Lockwood Memorial Library, State University of New York at Buffalo; in the Alexander Ireland Collection at the Manchester Central Library; and at the British Library. Apart from the portrait of Lamb in the National Portrait Gallery, all of Hazlitt's extant pictures are in the Maidstone Museum and Art Gallery.

# William Hone

*(3 June 1780 - 6 November 1842)*

Jonathan E. Hill
*St. Olaf College*

SELECTED BOOKS: *Buonaparte-phobia, or Cursing made Easy to the Meanest Capacity:—A Dialogue Between the Editor of "The Times,"—Doctor Slop, My Uncle Toby, & My Father* [broadside] (London: Printed for W. Hone, 1815);

*Hone's Weekly Commentary; or, Political & Social Miscellany,* nos. 1 and 2 (London: Printed for W. Hone, 18 and 25 January 1817); retitled *Hone's Reformists' Register and Weekly Commentary,* volumes 1-2 (London: Printed by & for William Hone, 1 February - 25 October 1817);

*The Sinecurist's Creed, or Belief; as the Same Can or May be Sung or Said Throughout the Kingdom. By Authority. From Hone's Weekly Commentary, No. 2* (London: Printed for one of the Candidates for the Office of Printer to the King's Most Excellent Majesty and sold by William Hone, 1817);

*The Bullet Te Deum; with the Canticle of the Stone* (London: Printed for one of the Candidates for the Office of Printer to the King's Most Excellent Majesty and sold by William Hone, 1817);

*The Political Litany, Diligently Revised; to be Said or Sung, Until the Appointed Change Come, Throughout The Dominion of England and Wales, and the Town of Berwick upon Tweed. By Special Command* (London: Printed for one of the Candidates for the Office of Printer to the King's Most Excellent Majesty & sold by William Hone, 1817);

*A Political Catechism, Dedicated, Without Permission, to His Most Serene Highness Omar, Bashaw, Dey, and Governor, of the Warlike City and Kingdom of Algiers; The Earl of Liverpool; Lord Castlereagh, and Co. By an Englishman* (London: Printed for one of the Candidates for the Office of Printer to the King's Most Excellent Majesty & sold by William Hone, 1817);

*The Late John Wilkes's Catechism of a Ministerial Member; Taken from an Original Manuscript in Mr. Wilkes's Handwriting, never before printed, and adapted to the present Occasion. With Permission* (London: Printed for one of the Candidates for the Office of Printer to the King's Most Excellent Majesty & sold by William Hone, 1817);

*The First Trial of William Hone, on an Ex-Officio Information. At Guildhall, London, December 17* [sic], *1817, Before Mr. Justice Abbott and a Special Jury, for Publishing the Late John Wilkes's Catechism of a Ministerial Member* (London: Printed by & for William Hone, 1817);

*The Second Trial of William Hone, on an ex-Officio Information. At Guildhall, London, December 19, 1817, Before Lord Ellenborough and a Special Jury, for Publishing a Parody, with an Alleged Intent to Ridicule The Litany, and Libel the Prince Regent, the House of Lords, and the House of Commons* (London: Printed by & for William Hone, 1817);

*Great Gobble Gobble Gobble, and Twit Twittle Twit, or Law Versus Common Sense, Being a Twitting Report of Successive Attacks on a Tom Tit, His Stout Defences & Final Victory. A New Song, with Original Music by Lay Logic Esq.re Student in the Law of Libel* [broadside] (London: Published by William Hone, 1817);

*The Third Trial of William Hone, on an ex-Officio Information. At Guildhall, London, December 20, 1817, Before Lord Ellenborough and a Special Jury, for Publishing a Parody, on the Athanasian Creed, Entitled "The Sinecurist's Creed"* (London: Printed by & for William Hone, 1818);

*The Three Trials of William Hone for Publishing Three Parodies; viz. The Late John Wilkes's Catechism, The Political Litany, and The Sinecurist's Creed; on Three Ex-Officio Informations, at Guildhall, London, During Three Successive Days, Dec 18, 19, & 20, 1817; Before Three Special Juries, and Mr. Justice Abbot, on the First Day, and Lord Chief Justice Ellenborough, on the Last Two Days* (London: Printed by & for William Hone, 1818);

*The Bank Restriction Barometer; or, Scale of Effects on Society of the Bank Note System, and Pay-*

William Hone

*ments in Gold. By Abraham Franklin . . . with the "Bank Restriction Note"* [single sheet, folded] (London: Published by William Hone, 1819);

*The Political House that Jack Built* (London: Printed by & for William Hone, 1819);

*The Man in the Moon* (London: Printed by & for William Hone, 1820);

*The Queen's Matrimonial Ladder, A National Toy, with Fourteen Step Scenes; and Illustrated in Verse, with eighteen other Cuts* (London: Printed by & for William Hone, 1820);

*"Non Mi Ricordo!" &c. &c. &c.* (London: Printed by & for William Hone, 1820);

*The Right Divine of Kings to Govern Wrong! Dedicated to the Holy Alliance. By the Author of The Political House that Jack Built* (London: Printed for William Hone, 1821);

*The Political Showman—At Home! Exhibiting his Cabinet of Curiosities and Creatures—All Alive! By the Author of the Political House that Jack Built* (London: Printed for William Hone, 1821);

*A Slap at Slop and the Bridge-Street Gang* [single sheet, folded] (London: William Hone, 1821);

*Aspersions Answered: An Explanatory Statement, Addressed to the Public at Large, and to Every Reader of The Quarterly Review in Particular* (London: Printed for William Hone, 1824);

*The Every-Day Book, or, Everlasting Calendar of Popular Amusement* (London, published weekly, January 1825 - December 1826; republished

*Illustration by George Cruikshank for* Great Gobble Gobble Gobble, and Twit Twittle Twit, *a comic song written by Hone to celebrate his December 1817 acquittal on three charges of blasphemous libel. Hone is depicted as Little Tom Tit, while Lord Chief Justice Ellenborough, who presided at the second and third trials, is portrayed as a turkey, and Justice Charles Abbott, the judge for the first trial, is shown as a fleeing owl.*

in 2 volumes, London: Published for William Hone, by Hunt & Clarke, 1827);

*Facetiae and Miscellanies* (London: Published for William Hone by Hunt & Clarke, 1827);

*The Table Book* (London, published weekly, January 1827 - January 1828; republished in 2 volumes, London: Published for William Hone, by Hunt & Clarke, 1827-1828);

*The Year Book of Daily Recreation and Information* (London, published weekly, January-December 1831; republished in 1 volume, London: William Tegg, 1832).

OTHER: *The Apocryphal New Testament, Being all the Gospels, Epistles and Other Pieces now Extant, Attributed in the First Four Centuries to Jesus Christ, His Apostles, and their Companions and not Included in the New Testament by its Compilers. Translated from the Original Tongues, and now First Collected into One Volume*, edited by Hone (London: Printed for William Hone, 1820);

*Ancient Mysteries Described, Especially the English Miracle Plays, Founded on Apocryphal New Testament Story, Extant Among the Unpublished Manuscripts in the British Museum; Including Notices of Ecclesiastical Shows, The Festivals of Fools and Asses—The English Boy-Bishop—The Descent into Hell—The Lord Mayor's Show—The Guildhall Giants—Christmas Carols, &c.*, edited by Hone (London: Printed for W. Hone, 1823);

Joseph Strutt, *Sports and Pastimes of the People of England*, edited by Hone (London: William Reeves, 1830);

William Hone, Sr., *The Early Life and Conversion of William Hone . . . A Narrative written by Himself. Edited by his son, William Hone* (London: T. Ward, 1841).

William Hone was one of the radical publishers, writers, and journalists—among them William Cobbett, Thomas Wooler, and Richard Carlile—who vigorously attacked the Tory government and its supporters during the Regency period. He achieved particular fame in 1817, when he successfully defended himself against government prosecution for blasphemous libel. He went on to publish a series of enormously popular satiric pamphlets illustrated by George Cruikshank. Later he became widely read as the compiler of a series of miscellanies based upon his extensive antiquarian knowledge. For all his fame as a political activist, however, Hone's private life was difficult and distressing. He was persistently insolvent, and throughout his life he suffered a protracted inner struggle with the evangelical faith in which he had been raised.

Hone was born on 3 June 1780 in Bath. His mother was Frances Maria Stawell. His father, William Hone, Sr., was a clerk and a devout nonconformist who had undergone a conversion experience as a young man. He became a follower of the Calvinistic Methodist William Huntington, and soon after his son's birth Hone, Sr., moved his family to London, where Huntington had set up a chapel. The father's influence upon his son was deep. He maintained in his household an atmosphere of austere and anxious faith, though he was also in his way kind and compassionate. Intermittently young Hone attended several schools, but he was mainly taught at home by his father, a rigorous and narrow regimen of Bible study. His father's piety began to have quite the opposite effect of what was intended. One one occasion, when given yet another set of biblical verses to learn by heart, the young Hone threw his Bible down the stairs and vowed, "When I am my own master, I will never open you."

Between the ages of twelve and twenty Hone held a variety of clerical jobs and began to live away from home. Though his father removed him from each job when he sensed his son was lapsing from virtue and right thinking, he could not check his son's intellectual and imaginative development. Hone pursued his love of early printed books and engraved prints. He discovered poetry with a passion, worked up an insatiable desire for novels and romances, and became, in his own words, "play-house mad." Even more significant, at the age of sixteen, under the influence of Thomas Paine and William Godwin, he joined the London Corresponding Society, the leading radical association of the day, and in the spirit of a freethinker more or less abandoned his religious faith.

On 19 July 1800 Hone married Sarah Johnson, the daughter of his landlady in Lambeth. They were eventually to have a large family (accounts range from ten to thirteen children). They took up residence with his mother-in-law in Lambeth Walk, and with one hundred pounds borrowed from her Hone opened his first business, a circulating library. For the next fifteen years Hone's life was a varied and confused one of business initiatives followed by repeated financial failures. There were too few customers in Lambeth to support the circulating library, so he moved his business and family to St. Martin's Lane. Several mishaps necessitated a move back to Lambeth. In 1803 he became bookkeeper to a hop factor in Southwark; shortly thereafter the business went bankrupt. The following year he became secretary to a business founded by John Bone, former secretary to the London Corresponding Society. Innovative and well-intentioned, it combined a savings bank, insurance office, and employment agency, and they named it "Tranquillity" (clearly more attractive than "Hone and Bone"). It failed, and Hone went back to Lambeth. In 1808 he and Bone took over a booksellers' business in the Strand, and here Hone had his first taste of supporting radical causes. That business also went bankrupt. He became clerk and cataloguer to a book auctioneer, who failed, and again he went back to Lambeth. Hone opened another shop, this time in Bloomsbury, and then in 1811 he was chosen by his fellow booksellers to become a trade auctioneer, and this occupation seemed to provide more security.

Even as he was riding out one crisis after another and trying to support his expanding family, Hone was increasing his expertise in the book trade and widening his circle of professional and political acquaintances. There are scattered references to writing and editing in these years, but it was in 1815 that he began to publish under his own name and establish his reputation. Between 1815 and his death twenty-seven years later, Hone published some 220 titles, in addition to writing, editing, or compiling many of them. The majority of these, about 200, appeared between 1815 and 1821. The succession of imprint addresses he used became well known: 55 Fleet Street, 67 Old Bailey, and 45 Ludgate Hill. Most of his publications were swiftly produced, inexpensive, quick-selling reactions to passing events and current affairs. In format they range from complete books to pamphlets, portraits, broadsides, and caricatures. The issues and subjects they address represent the full range of late-Regency social and political concerns as seen through the

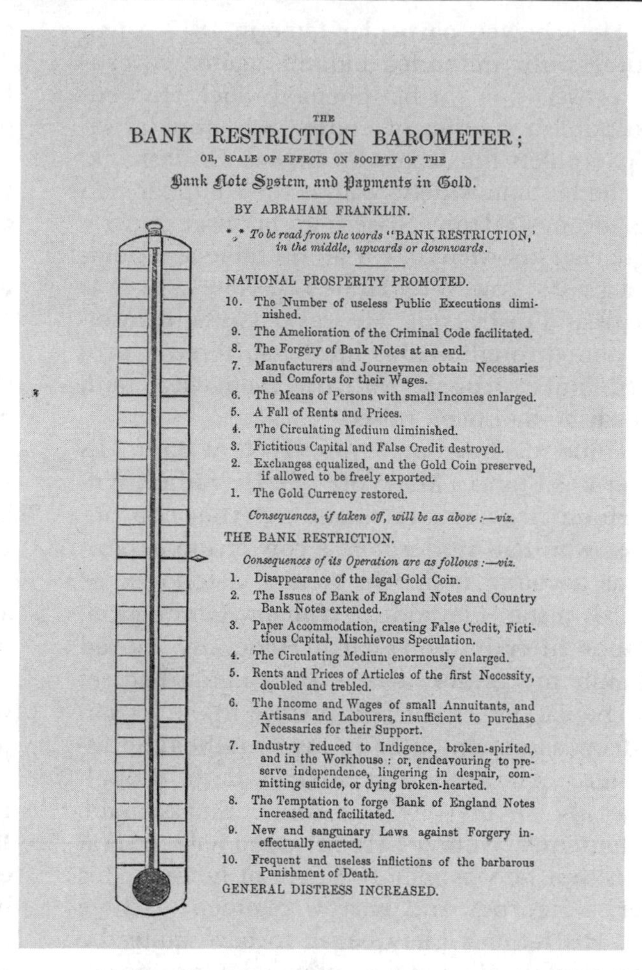

THE
BANK RESTRICTION BAROMETER;
OR, SCALE OF EFFECTS ON SOCIETY OF THE
Bank Note System, and Payments in Gold.

BY ABRAHAM FRANKLIN.

*** *To be read from the words "BANK RESTRICTION," in the middle, upwards or downwards.*

NATIONAL PROSPERITY PROMOTED.

10. The Number of useless Public Executions diminished.
9. The Amelioration of the Criminal Code facilitated.
8. The Forgery of Bank Notes at an end.
7. Manufacturers and Journeymen obtain Necessaries and Comforts for their Wages.
6. The Means of Persons with small Incomes enlarged.
5. A Fall of Rents and Prices.
4. The Circulating Medium diminished.
3. Fictitious Capital and False Credit destroyed.
2. Exchanges equalized, and the Gold Coin preserved, if allowed to be freely exported.
1. The Gold Currency restored.

*Consequences, if taken off, will be as above :—viz.*

THE BANK RESTRICTION.

*Consequences of its Operation are as follows :—viz.*

1. Disappearance of the legal Gold Coin.
2. The Issues of Bank of England Notes and Country Bank Notes extended.
3. Paper Accommodation, creating False Credit, Fictitious Capital, Mischievous Speculation.
4. The Circulating Medium enormously enlarged.
5. Rents and Prices of Articles of the first Necessity, doubled and trebled.
6. The Income and Wages of small Annuitants, and Artisans and Labourers, insufficient to purchase Necessaries for their Support.
7. Industry reduced to Indigence, broken-spirited, and in the Workhouse : or, endeavouring to preserve independence, lingering in despair, committing suicide, or dying broken-hearted.
8. The Temptation to forge Bank of England Notes increased and facilitated.
9. New and sanguinary Laws against Forgery ineffectually enacted.
10. Frequent and useless inflictions of the barbarous Punishment of Death.

GENERAL DISTRESS INCREASED.

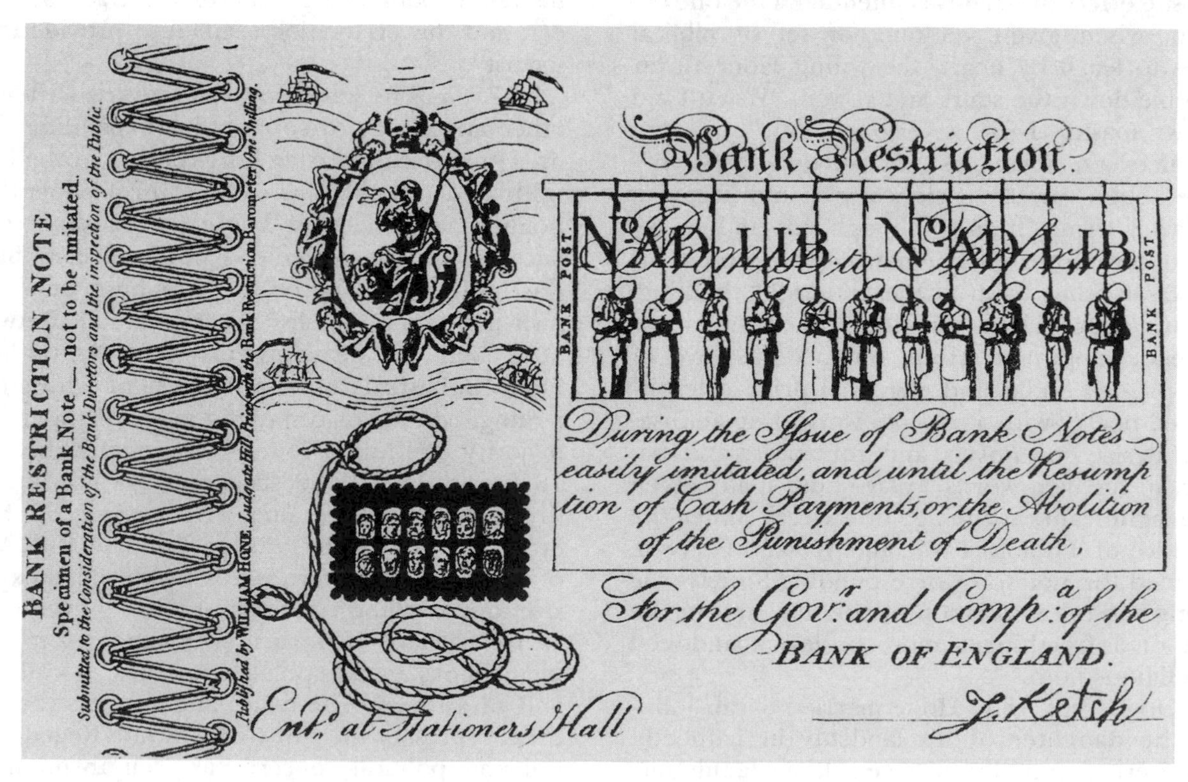


*Hone's protest against the Bank Restriction Act and George Cruikshank's imitation bank note, published together in 1819 to call attention to the problems caused by the easily forged paper currency issued by the Bank of England*

eyes of a radical reformer and opportunistic publisher: Napoleon and the aftermath of the wars with France; the treatment of the insane; murder and political trials; speeches and sermons; legal reform; riots and demonstrations; property and income tax; the wedding—and later the death—of Princess Charlotte; the extravagances and lifestyle of the Prince Regent; the Queen Caroline affair; the behavior of government ministers and supporters; and, above all, parliamentary reform and freedom of the press. In addition to ephemera, Hone published work by William Hazlitt (*Political Essays, with Sketches of Public Characters*, 1819) and Jeremy Bentham (*On the Liberty of the Press and Public Discourse*, 1821). Like most subsistence publishers of his day, he also published pirated works, taken from Walter Scott (an edition of *Guy Mannering* in 1816) and George Gordon, Lord Byron (*Poems on his Domestic Circumstances* in 1816). In all this extensive output and in the works he wrote and designed himself, where Hone excelled was in his use of illustrated satiric parody.

An early example of his satiric ingenuity is *Buonaparte-phobia, or Cursing made Easy to the Meanest Capacity* (1815). Long an admirer of Napoleon, Hone took on one of the emperor's most vituperative English adversaries, John Stoddart, who, as leader writer for the *Times*, had become notorious for the intemperance of his attacks upon Napoleon (they eventually became so virulent that he was dropped by the *Times* in 1816—and he started up his own newspaper, the *New Times*). *Buonaparte-phobia* is printed as a single newspaper sheet in partial imitation of the *Times*. Hone assumes the persona of Laurence Sterne's Tristram Shandy and records a conversation between his father, Uncle Toby, and Dr. Slop. The core of the piece is Slop's outpouring of abuse against Napoleon—every one of the phrases is taken from Stoddart's pieces for the *Times*. The name "Slop" stuck with Stoddart from that moment on.

By 1817 Hone was sufficiently sure of himself as a writer and political commentator to start his own weekly newspaper. Its first two numbers appeared as *Hone's Weekly Commentary; or, Political & Social Miscellany* (18 and 25 January 1817); it continued, with a drop in price from six pence to two pence a number, as *Hone's Reformists' Register and Weekly Commentary* (1 February - 25 October 1817). Its main purpose was to promote reformist politics of the kind represented in the House of Commons by Sir Francis Burdett. It achieved a wide circulation, but it was quite overshadowed by the results of five, brief pamphlets Hone had published in January and February of the same year. Each of these, to the end of satire on the government and the Regent, parodied liturgical and religious texts. *The Sinecurist's Creed* was based on the creed of St. Athanasius (still a part of the Anglican liturgy in Hone's day); *The Bullet Te Deum; with the Canticle of the Stone* parodied the Church of England morning prayer; *The Political Litany* was a comic version of the litany or general supplication; *A Political Catechism* used a catechismal format of questions and answers to outline the need for parliamentary reform; and *The Late John Wilkes's Catechism of a Ministerial Member* blended elements from the Anglican catechism, the Apostles' Creed, the Ten Commandments, and the Lord's Prayer. Hone disavowed writing *The Political Litany*, and he claimed that *The Late John Wilkes's Catechism of a Ministerial Member* was indeed the composition of John Wilkes, the late-eighteenth-century politician. Whatever the precise details of authorship, all five share common features: they take revered texts at the very heart of the cultural establishment and with hilarious comic technique turn them against the very powers they were meant to support. The familiar stylistic ingredients of biblical and ecclesiastical language—solemn repetition, chantlike refrain, singsong meter, and elevated imagery—are transformed by the skillful alteration of key words and names into impudent and mocking burlesque. In the following extract from *The Sinecurist's Creed*, Hone ridicules the trinity of Lord Eldon (John Scott Eldon), the lord chancellor; Lord Castlereagh (Robert Stewart), the foreign secretary; and Lord Sidmouth (Henry Addington), the home secretary, referring to each by their contemporary nicknames: "Old Bags," "Derry Down Triangle," and the "Doctor," respectively:

> But the Ministry of Old Bags, of Derry Down Triangle, and of the Doctor, is all one: the folly equal, the profusion coeternal.
>
> Such as Old Bags is, such is Derry Down Triangle: and such is the Doctor.
>
> Old Bags a Mountebank, Derry Down Triangle a Mountebank: the Doctor a Mountebank.
>
> Old Bags incomprehensible, Derry Down Triangle incomprehensible: the Doctor incomprehensible.
>
> Old Bags a Humbug, Derry Down Triangle a Humbug: and the Doctor a Humbug.
>
> And yet they are not three Humbugs: but one Humbug.

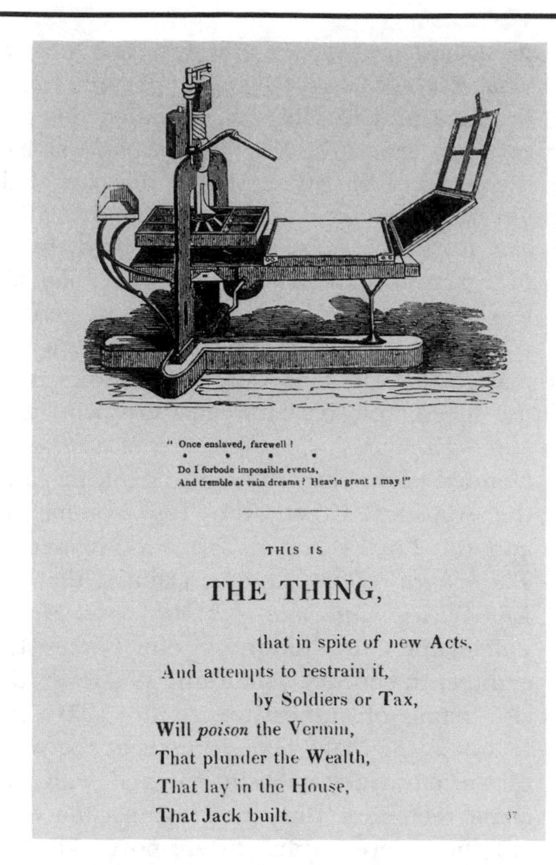

"Once enslaved, farewell!
* * * *
Do I forbode impossible events,
And tremble at vain dreams? Heav'n grant I may!"

THIS IS

THE THING,

that in spite of new Acts,
And attempts to restrain it,
by Soldiers or Tax,
Will *poison* the Vermin,
That plunder the Wealth,
That lay in the House,
That Jack built.

37

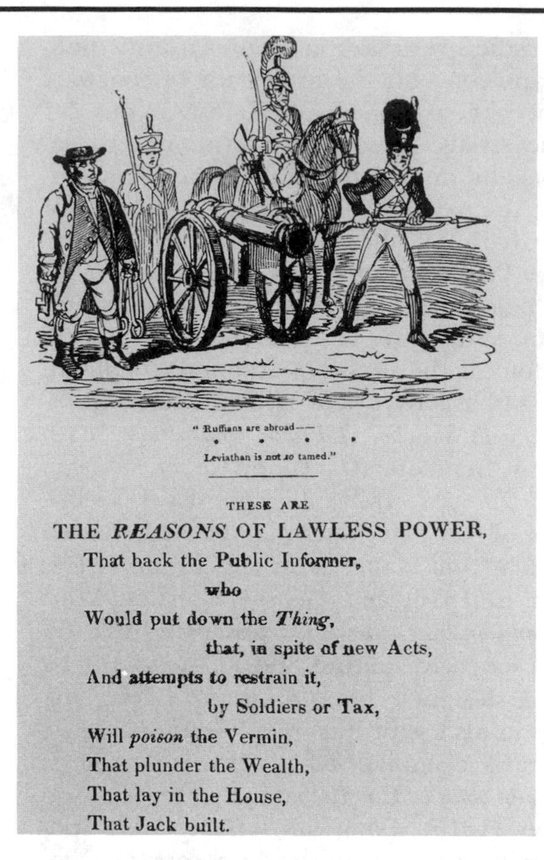

"Ruffians are abroad——
* * * *
Leviathan is not *so* tamed."

THESE ARE

THE *REASONS* OF LAWLESS POWER,
That back the Public Informer,
who
Would put down the *Thing*,
that, in spite of new Acts,
And attempts to restrain it,
by Soldiers or Tax,
Will *poison* the Vermin,
That plunder the Wealth,
That lay in the House,
That Jack built.

——"Great offices will have
Great talents."

This is THE MAN—all shaven and shorn,
All cover'd with Orders—and all forlorn;

38

THESE ARE

THE PEOPLE

all tatter'd and torn,
Who curse the day
wherein they were born,
On account of Taxation
too great to be borne,
And pray for relief,
from night to morn:
Who, in vain, Petition
in every form,

*Pages, with illustrations by Cruikshank, from Hone's* Political House that Jack Built

> And also they are not three incomprehensibles, nor three Mountebanks: but one Mountebank, and one incomprehensible.

The parodies sold swiftly, but—alarmed by news of government displeasure—Hone withdrew them from sale soon after publication. Nevertheless, he was arrested on 3 May and charged with publishing blasphemous libels. Unable to raise bail or afford a copy of the charges against him (offenders had to purchase their own) and unwilling to plead without such a copy, Hone remained in prison until 2 July. He continued to write the *Reformists' Register* from there, but four months later problems with sales and the wish to get back to publishing compelled him to bring the journal to a close.

There was an assumption after his release that the government would not go forward with the prosecution, but it did. On three successive days, 18-20 December, Hone was tried at Guildhall for publishing the three of the pamphlets that the government considered most offensive: *The Late John Wilkes's Catechism*, *The Political Litany*, and *The Sinecurist's Creed*. Hone defended himself. His main line of argument was that the parodic use of sacred texts as social or political satire had a long history (indeed, as he pointed out, George Canning, a leading member of the government, had once written one himself), and the texts themselves suffered no disrespect in being used in this manner. The attorney general, Sir Samuel Shepherd, prosecuted; each day a new jury was impaneled; and on the second and third days—determined to get a guilty verdict out of the jury—the lord chief justice himself, Edward Law, Lord Ellenborough, presided. But Hone was acquitted on all three charges. The case vindicated honest juries, strengthened freedom of the press, humiliated the government, and made Hone into a national celebrity. Friends and members of the public raised a substantial subscription for him. Caricaturists celebrated the outcome with glee; Hone himself published one of the finest, a comic song illustrated by George Cruikshank and titled *Great Gobble Gobble Gobble, and Twit Twittle Twit, or Law Versus Common Sense, Being a Twitting Report of Successive Attacks on a Tom Tit, His Stout Defences & Final Victory* (1817). Hone published accounts of the trials, separately and together, and began to advertise a substantial work, "The History of Parody." It was to be based on the extensive research he had carried out in preparation for his trials, but though he continued to labor on it and advertise it for several years it never appeared.

It was not until 1819 that he again published a work of note, *The Bank Restriction Barometer . . . with the "Bank Restriction Note."* By the 1797 Bank Restriction Act, Parliament had permitted the Bank of England to issue paper currency in lieu of cash payments. Paper currency became associated not only with rising prices and economic depression, but with the spread of forgery and a concomitant rise in public executions (forgery being a capital crime). By 1819 the annual debate over whether the act should be prolonged, or at least whether the Bank of England should introduce paper money that was more difficult to forge, had become bitterly intense. In this atmosphere, Hone published *The Bank Restriction Barometer*, using the pseudonym Abraham Franklin. It was printed as a single half sheet, on which were listed, alongside a barometric scale, the contrasting effects of continuing or dropping the provisions of the act. The sheet was folded to form an envelope, in which was placed an imitation bank note. Drawn and etched by Cruikshank, this note was a macabre and parodic facsimile of the real thing. The elements of its design included eleven corpses swinging from the gallows, manacles, and a hangman's rope; it was signed with the traditional name of the hangman, Jack Ketch. It caused a sensation.

Hone's imagination was not only verbal but visual, and Cruikshank was able to realize his graphic ideas for him. At the end of 1819 they produced their most celebrated collaboration. It was innovative in format—an inexpensive pamphlet illustrated throughout with woodcuts—and it put an old satiric technique to fresh use, the parody of a well-known nursery rhyme. *The Political House that Jack Built* uses the infantile style and incremental repetitions of the genre to mock the repressiveness and venality of the Regent and his government, and to defend the freedom of the press and the rights of the common people. It reputedly sold one hundred thousand copies and ran to more than fifty editions (or printings). Cruikshank's simple and vigorous woodcuts distilled years of caricaturing the Prince Regent while complementing the sardonic naiveté of Hone's text:

> This is THE MAN—all shaven and shorn,
> All cover'd with Orders—and all forlorn;
> THE DANDY OF SIXTY,
> who bows with a grace,

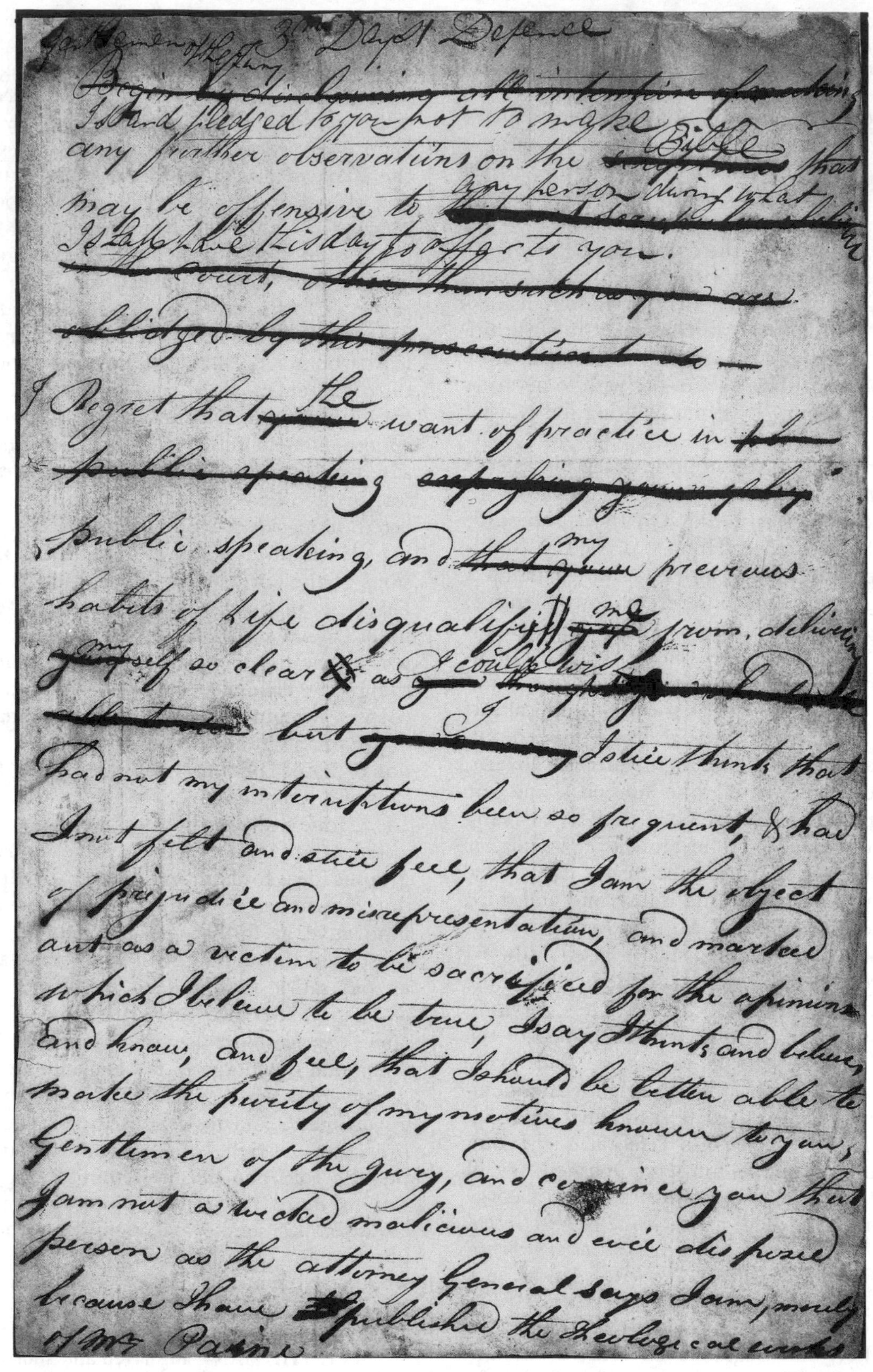
Gentlemen of the Jury 3rd Dayst Defence

I have pledged to you not to make
any further observations on the Bible that
may be offensive to any person during what
I shall have this day to offer to you.

I Regret that the want of practice in
public speaking, and that my previous
habits of life disqualify me from delivering
myself so clearly as I could wish
but I still think that
had not my interruptions been so frequent, & had
I not felt and still feel, that I am the object
of prejudice and misrepresentation, and marked
out as a victim to be sacrificed for the opinions
which I believe to be true, I say I think and believe
and know, and feel, that I should be better able to
make the purity of my motives known to you,
Gentlemen of the Jury, and convince you that
I am not a wicked malicious and evil disposed
person as the attorney General says I am, merely
because I have published the theological works
of Mr Paine

*Pages from a defense Hone wrote for Richard Carlile when Carlile was tried for blasphemous libel in October 1819 (RC 544; Henry E. Huntington Library and Art Gallery)*

2

But though I cannot express myself with the eloquen[ce]
I desire, and though I deeply deplore that the
command of words is no more in my power than
the command to believe, which the attorney General
~~the~~ insists I ought to do — though I say I can no more
speak as I desire than think as he desires, yet I hope
I have convinced you of the sincerity of my heart,
and if I have done that, I have done all that I am
now solicitous about, for I shall have done my
duty and it will become you you Gentlemen of
the Jury to do yours But before you do this,
before you proceed to deliberate upon what you
have heard Remember the solemnity of the sub-
=ect you have to investigate — remember that all
the advantages that ever have been obtained for mankind
in all ages, and in all nations, have been gained by
Men of honest and sincere dispositions from the
clutches of power and the grasp of the oppressor —
Remember that Jesus himself was called a disturber
of the people — that the Public ~~[illegible]~~ Accuser the
Attorney General of that day, prosecuted him
for Blasphemy and there being no trial by Jury he
got a Judge to condemn him

And has *taste* in wigs, collars,
cuirasses and lace.

The pamphlet was immediately and extensively imitated, but none rivaled the original.

Hone and Cruikshank repeated the format of the illustrated pamphlet in a series of highly successful publications over the following two years. *The Man in the Moon*, an attack on the Regent, appeared in January 1820. Later that year they produced two pieces during the Queen Caroline affair, George IV's efforts to divorce his wife and prevent her becoming queen by putting her on trial for adultery. *The Queen's Matrimonial Ladder* tells Caroline's version of the royal couple's relationship over the preceding twenty-five years, and each step is accompanied by a woodcut. The pamphlet was published with a child's cardboard toy ladder; on each rung is drawn in miniature the successive stages of the king's moral rise and fall. Even more hilarious is "*Non Mi Ricordo!*," in which Hone parodied one of the government's chief prosecution witnesses, an Italian named Teodor Majocchi called to give evidence about the queen's behavior overseas. Majocchi's most frequent reply under cross-examination was "Non mi ricordo," which instantly became a catchphrase. In Hone's pamphlet it is the king (the Regent succeeded to the throne in 1820) who is being cross-examined about his own, well-known adulteries, and it is he who replies, time and again, "Non mi ricordo." Cruikshank supplied only three illustrations, but the first brilliantly sets the tone for the pamphlet—it shows the king dressed as a bloated, bewhiskered, and debauched dandy.

The year 1821 saw *The Right Divine of Kings to Govern Wrong!*, an adaptation of Daniel Defoe's *Jure Divino* (1706); *The Political Showman—At Home!*, a sixteen-page pamphlet with twenty-four illustrations, in which the government is presented as a menagerie of animals, introduced and described by the showman, a printing press; and *A Slap at Slop*, another attack on Stoddart, this time in the shape of a parody of his *New Times*, a single sheet folded into four pages and carrying twenty-seven small woodcuts by Cruikshank.

After 1821 Hone published no further political satire. In part this was a reflection of changing political conditions: economic prosperity had begun to ease unrest and social tensions. In part it is due to changes in Hone himself. The stresses of political activism and the force of the attacks upon him in the Tory press led him to pursue his other, less contentious interest, antiquarian research. A foretaste had appeared in 1820, *The Apocryphal New Testament*, which presented twenty-three apocryphal books in eighteenth-century translations. It was vigorously criticized by Tory journals since Hone seemed to be passing off the translations as his own. He countered their charges four years later with *Aspersions Answered* (1824). In 1823 he came out with *Ancient Mysteries Described*, a compilation of miracle plays and religious-festival performances taken mainly from manuscript sources. This book was well received. There followed the three works upon which his later and, during the nineteenth century, his most lasting reputation was based, *The Every-Day Book* (1825-1826), *The Table Book* (1827-1828), and *The Year Book* (1831). All three volumes were published serially in inexpensive weekly numbers and illustrated with woodcuts. *The Every-Day Book* and *The Year Book* were organized as almanacs, celebrating anniversaries and calendar dates of note. All three offered rich, intriguing, and informative miscellanies of literary, historical, and folklore material. The works reflected Hone's wide and recondite reading, as well as the contributions of friends and the general public. They were constantly reprinted throughout the nineteenth and into the twentieth century.

"Those *Every-Day* and *Table* Books will be a treasure a hundred years hence, but they have failed to make Hone's fortune," wrote Charles Lamb to Robert Southey (10 May 1830). Notwithstanding the success of the miscellanies, which were written but not published by him, Hone's financial affairs during the 1820s and 1830s were as precarious as ever. In April 1826 he was arrested for debt and spent the next two-and-a-half years in the King's Bench Prison, Southwark. Conditions were such that he was able to continue working, and it was there that he finished *The Every-Day Book* and wrote *The Table Book*. In 1827 he was forced to sell off the library he had built up toward writing his history of parody, and in an effort to reap a further yield from earlier successes, he republished twelve of his satiric pamphlets as the volume *Facetiae and Miscellanies* (1827).

Three years later a group of friends (Hone never lacked them), including Charles Lamb, raised a subscription to set him up as the proprieter of a coffeehouse, the Grasshopper Hotel in Gracechurch Street. It was managed by his

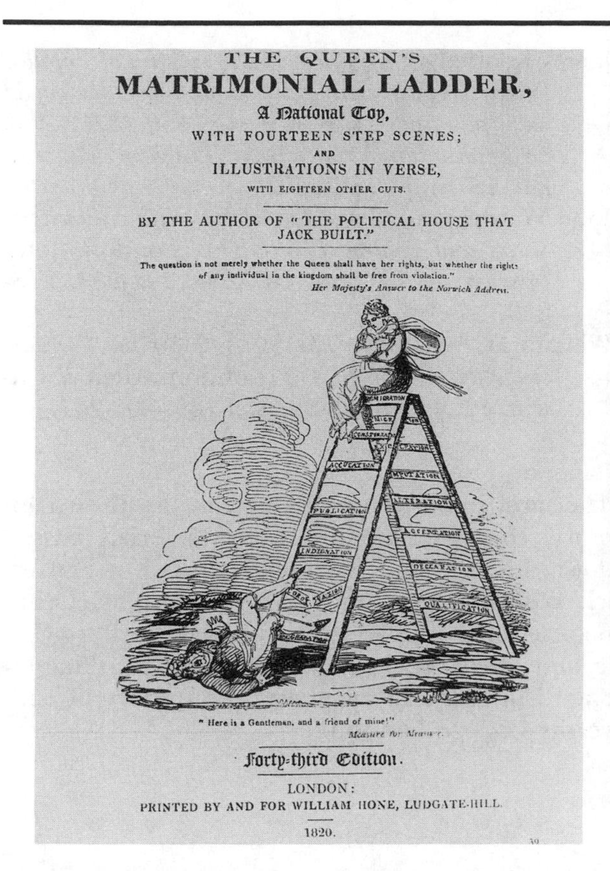

THE QUEEN'S
MATRIMONIAL LADDER,
A National Toy,
WITH FOURTEEN STEP SCENES;
AND
ILLUSTRATIONS IN VERSE,
WITH EIGHTEEN OTHER CUTS.

BY THE AUTHOR OF "THE POLITICAL HOUSE THAT JACK BUILT."

"The question is not merely whether the Queen shall have her rights, but whether the rights of any individual in the kingdom shall be free from violation."
*Her Majesty's Answer to the Norwich Address.*

"Here is a Gentleman, and a friend of mine!"
*Measure for Measure.*

Forty-third Edition.

LONDON:
PRINTED BY AND FOR WILLIAM HONE, LUDGATE-HILL.
1820.

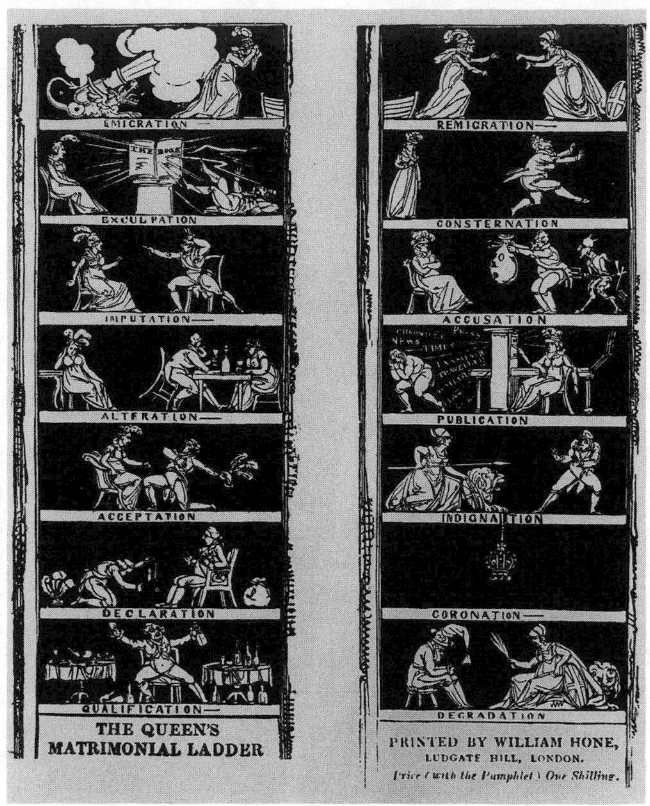



*Title page and "ladder" from one of the many editions of Hone and Cruikshank's popular protest against the adultery trial of Queen Caroline*

wife and daughters. They kept the business going for two years before it failed. While there, Hone produced another notable antiquarian work, a new edition of Joseph Strutt's *Sports and Pastimes of the People of England* (1830; first published in 1801). He also underwent a religious rebirth. He happened to attend a service conducted by the noted Congregational minister Thomas Binney at the Weigh House Chapel, Eastcheap, on New Year's Day, 1832, and he experienced a spiritual revelation. Despite his childhood rebellion, adolescent freethinking, and adult irreverence, Hone had always counted himself a Christian, but now he regained something like his father's fervor. His remaining years were dominated by this event. In subsequent letters and statements, and in an unfinished autobiography (published in Frederick William Hackwood's biography), he talked of most of his earlier life as being that of a deluded sinner.

The family moved several times after leaving the Grasshopper. The last regular employment Hone had was from 1835 to 1840, as subeditor of the *Patriot*, a mouthpiece for evangelical nonconformity. Declining health forced him to resign. His final work was to edit his father's autobiographical fragment, *The Early Life and Conversion of William Hone* (1841), and to try to finish his own. He died before he could do so, on 6 November 1842. In a letter to C. C. Felton (2 March 1843), Charles Dickens gave a vivid account of Hone's funeral.

A wealthy London banker told the story of how one day in the City he was waiting in his doorway holding his hat in his hand. A shortsighted stranger, thinking he was begging, benevolently placed a coin in the hat as he passed. It was Hone, characteristically giving away money he could not afford to someone who had no need of it. Hone's contemporaries were struck by the disparity between the person—ingenuous, compassionate, generous—and the reputation—radical, subversive, heinous. Hone was equally surprised by his own notoriety. Only someone whose piety was as ambivalent as it was deep could have used religion so subversively and yet been so taken aback at the reaction of the authorities. He spent his last years repenting his early wit, unable to reconcile himself to his achievements.

**Biographies:**

[Frances Rolleston], *Some Account of the Conversion of the Late William Hone* (London: F. J. Rivington; W. Kent & Co. / Keswick: James Ivison, 1853);

Frederick William Hackwood, *William Hone: His Life and Times* (London: Unwin, 1912).

**References:**

Ann Bowden, "William Hone's Political Journalism, 1815-1821," Ph.D. dissertation, University of Texas at Austin, 1975;

Arthur Calder-Marshall, *Lewd, Blasphemous & Obscene* (London: Hutchinson, 1972), pp. 17-68;

J. Ann Hone, "William Hone (1780-1842), Publisher and Bookseller: An Approach to Early 19th Century London Radicalism," *Historical Studies* (University of Melbourne), 16 (April 1974): 55-70;

Edgell Rickword, *Radical Squibs & Loyal Ripostes* (Bath: Adams & Dart, 1971);

James Routledge, *Chapters in the History of Popular Progress Chiefly in Relation to The Freedom of the Press and Trial by Jury, 1660-1820, With an Application to Later Years* (London: Macmillan, 1876), pp. 364-492;

John Wardroper, *Kings, Lords and Wicked Libellers: Satire and Protest 1760-1837* (London: John Murray, 1973), pp. 197-200, 202-203, 218-219;

William H. Wickwar, *The Struggle for the Freedom of the Press, 1819-1832* (London: Allen & Unwin, 1928), pp. 58-59, 163-165, 265-267.

**Papers:**

The most important collection, in the British Library, comprises the extensive materials passed down through Hone's family and used by Frederick William Hackwood in his biography. Other notable collections are to be found in the Berg Collection, New York Public Library; Washington State University Library; and the Library of University College London.

# William Howitt

*(18 December 1792 - 3 March 1879)*

and

# Mary Howitt

*(12 March 1799 - 30 January 1888)*

Nicholas R. Jones
*Oberlin College*

SELECTED BOOKS:

**By William and Mary Howitt:**

*The Forest Minstrel and Other Poems* (London: Baldwin, Cradock & Joy, 1823);

*The Desolation of Eyam: The Emigrant, a Tale of the American Woods: and Other Poems* (London: Wightman & Cramp, 1827);

*The Literature and Romance of Northern Europe: Constituting a Complete History of the Literature of Sweden, Denmark, Norway and Iceland*, 2 volumes (London: Colburn, 1852);

*Stories of English and Foreign Life* (London: Henry G. Bohn, 1853);

*Ruined Abbeys and Castles of Great Britain* (London: A. W. Bennett, 1862).

**By William Howitt:**

*A Poet's Thoughts at the Interment of Lord Byron* (London: Printed for Baldwin, Cradock & Joy, 1824);

*The Book of the Seasons; or, The Calendar of Nature*, by William Howitt, with contributions by Mary Howitt (London: Henry Colburn & Richard Bentley, 1828; Philadelphia: Carey & Lea, 1831);

*A Popular History of Priestcraft in All Ages and Nations* (London: E. Wilson, 1833); republished as *History of Priestcraft in All Ages and Nations* (London: E. Wilson / New York: Reprinted for the booksellers, 1833);

*Pantika: or, Traditions of the Most Ancient Times*, 2 volumes (London: Whitaker, 1835);

*The Rural Life of England*, 2 volumes (London: Longman, Orme, Brown, Green & Longmans, 1838);

*Colonization and Christianity: A Popular History of the Treatment of the Natives by the Europeans in All Their Colonies* (London: Longman, Orme, Brown, Green & Longmans, 1838);

*The Boy's Country-book: Being the Real Life of a Country Boy Written by Himself, exhibiting all the Amusements, Pleasures, and Pursuits of Children in the Country* (London: Longman, Orme, Brown, Green & Longmans, 1839; New York: S. Colman, 1840);

*Visits to Remarkable Places; Old Halls, Battlefields and Scenes illustrative of Striking Passages in History and Poetry*, 2 volumes (London: Longman, Brown, Green & Longmans, 1840, 1842; Philadelphia: Carey & Hart, 1841, 1842);

*The Student-Life of Germany* (London: Longman, Orme, Brown, Green & Longmans, 1841; Philadelphia: Carey & Hart, 1842);

*The Rural and Domestic Life of Germany: with Characteristic Sketches of its Cities and Scenery. Collected in a General Tour, and During a Residence in the Country in 1840, 41 and 42* (London: Longman, Brown, Green & Longmans, 1842; Philadelphia: Carey & Hart, 1843);

*German Experiences: Addressed to the English: Both Stayers at Home and Goers Abroad* (London: Longman, Brown, Green & Longmans, 1844);

*The Life and Adventures of Jack of the Mill: commonly called Lord Othmill; A Fireside Story*, 2 volumes (London: Longman, 1844; New York: Harper, 1844);

*The Aristocracy of England: A History for the People*, as John Hampden, Junr. (London: Chapman, 1846);

*Homes and Haunts of the Most Eminent British Poets*, 2 volumes (London: R. Bentley, 1847; New York: Harper, 1847);

*The Hall and the Hamlet, or, Scenes and Characters of Country Life*, 2 volumes (London: H. Colburn, 1848);

*The Year-Book of the Country; or, The Field, the Forest, and the Fireside* (London: H. Colburn, 1850);

*William and Mary Howitt*

*Madam Dorrington of the Dene. The Story of a Life*, 3 volumes (London: H. Colburn, 1851);

*A Boy's Adventures in the Wilds of Australia; or, Herbert's Note-Book* (London: Routledge, 1854; Boston: Ticknor & Fields, 1855);

*Land, labour, and gold: or, Two years in Victoria: with visits to Sydney and Van Dieman's Land*, 2 volumes (London: Longman, Brown, Green & Longmans, 1855; Boston: Ticknor & Fields, 1855);

*Cassell's Illustrated History of England*, volumes 3-8 (London: Cassell, Petter & Galpin, 1856);

*Tallangetta, the Squatter's Home: a Story of Australian Life*, 2 volumes (London: Longman, Brown, Green, Longmans & Roberts, 1857);

*The Man of the People*, 3 volumes (London: Hurst & Blackett, 1860);

*The History of the Supernatural in All Ages and Nations, and in All Churches, Christian and Pagan: Demonstrating a Universal Faith*, 2 volumes (London: Longman, Green, Longman, Roberts & Green, 1863; Philadelphia: Lippincott, 1863);

*The History of Discovery in Australia, Tasmania, and New Zealand, from the Earliest Date to the Present Day*, 2 volumes (London: Longman, Green, Longman, Roberts & Green, 1865);

*Woodburn Grange: a Story of English Country Life*, 3 volumes (London: C. W. Wood, 1867; Philadelphia: T. B. Peterson, 1867);

*The Northern Heights of London; or Historical Associations of Hampstead, Highgate, Muswell Hill, Hornsey, and Islington* (London: Longmans, Green, 1869);

*The Mad War-Planet; and Other Poems* (London: Longmans, Green, Reader & Dyer, 1871).

**By Mary Howitt:**

*The Seven Temptations* (London: R. Bentley, 1834);

*Sketches of Natural History* (London: Darton & Co., 1834; Philadelphia: Conrad & Parsons, 1834);

*Tales in Verse* (London: Wm. Darton & Son, 1836; Boston: Weeks, Jordan, 1839);

*Tales in Prose: for the Young* (London: Wm. Darton & Son, 1836; Boston: Weeks, Jordan, 1839);

*Wood Leighton: or, A Year in the Country*, 3 volumes (London: R. Bentley, 1836; Philadelphia: Carey, Lea & Blanchard, 1837);

*Birds and Flowers, and Other Country Things* (London: Darton & Clark, 1838; Boston: Weeks, Jordan, 1839);

*Hymns and Fireside Verses* (London: Darton & Clark, 1839);

*Hope on, Hope Ever, or, The Boyhood of Felix Law* (London: Thomas Tegg, 1840; Boston: James Munroe, 1840);

*Strive and Thrive: A Tale* (London: Thomas Tegg, 1840; Boston: James Munroe, 1840);

*Sowing and Reaping: or, What Will Come of It?* (London: Thomas Tegg, 1841);

*Which is the Wiser; or, People Abroad. A Tale for Youth* (London: Thomas Tegg, 1842; New York: D. Appleton, 1842);

*Little Coin, Much Care: or, How Poor Men Live. A Tale* (London: Thomas Tegg, 1842; New York: D. Appleton, 1842);

*Work and Wages: or, Life in Service* (London: Thomas Tegg, 1842; New York: D. Appleton / Philadelphia: G. S. Appleton, 1843);

*Love and Money: An Every Day Tale* (London: T. Tegg, 1843; New York: D. Appleton, 1844);

*Alice Franklin: A Tale; Another Part of "Sowing and Reaping"* (London: Thomas Tegg, 1843; New York: D. Appleton / Philadelphia: George S. Appleton, 1843);

*No Sense like Common Sense; or, Some Passages in the Life of Charles Middleton, Esq.*, credited to Mary Howitt but actually written by William Howitt (London: Thomas Tegg, 1843; New York: D. Appleton, 1843);

*My Uncle the Clockmaker; A Tale*, credited to Mary Howitt but actually written by William Howitt (London: Thomas Tegg, 1844; New York: D. Appleton, 1845);

*Fireside Verses* (London: Darton & Clark, 1845);

*My Own Story; or, The Autobiography of a Child* (London: Thomas Tegg, 1845);

*Ballads and Other Poems* (London: Longman, Brown, Green & Longmans, 1847; New York: Wiley & Putnam, 1847);

*The Children's Year* (London: Longman, Brown, Green & Longmans, 1847; Philadelphia: Lea & Blanchard, 1848);

*The Heir of Wast-Wayland: A Tale* (London: Simms & M'Intyre, 1847; New York: D. Appleton, 1851);

*The Childhood of Mary Leeson* (London: Darton, 1848; Boston: Crosby, Nichols, 1854);

*Our Cousins in Ohio* (London: Darton, 1849; New York: Collins, 1849);

*How the Mice Got out of Trouble, and Other Tales. From the "Dial of Love"* (London: Darton, 1850);

*The Picture Book for the Young* (London: Low & Son, 1855; Philadelphia: Lippincott, 1856);

*Mary Howitt's Illustrated Library for the Young*, two series (London: W. Kent, 1856);

*Marien's Pilgrimage: A Fire-Side Story, and Other Poems* (London: Darton, 1859);

*A Popular History of the United States of America, from the Discovery of the American Continent to the Present Time*, 2 volumes (London: Longman, Brown, Green, Longmans & Roberts, 1859; New York: Harper, 1860);

*The Blackbird, the Parrot, the Cat, and Other Stories. A Picture Book for the Young* (London: Dean, 1861);

*Lillieslea; or, Lost and Found: A Story for the Young* (London & New York: G. Routledge & Sons, 1861);

*Little Arthur's Letters to his Sister Mary. A Pleasing Picture Book for Young Folks* (London, 1861);

*A Treasury of New Favorite Tales, for Young People* (London: James Hogg & Sons, 1861);

*The Poet's Children* (London: A. W. Bennett, 1863);

*The Story of Little Cristal* (London: Alfred W. Bennett, 1863);

*The Cost of Caergwyn*, 3 volumes (London: Hurst & Blackett, 1864);

*Stories of Stapleford*, 2 parts (London: A. W. Bennett, 1864);

*Our Four-Footed Friends* (London: S. W. Partridge, 1867);

*John Oriel's Start in Life* (London, 1868);

*Pictures from Nature* (London & New York: George Routledge & Sons, 1869);

*Vignettes of American History* (London: S. W. Partridge, 1869);

*A Pleasant Life* (Edinburgh & London: Gall & Inglis, 1871);

*Birds and their Nests* (London: S. W. Partridge, 1872);

*Natural History Stories for My Juvenile Friends* (London: S. W. Partridge, 1875);

*Tales for All Seasons* (London & Guildford: F. Warne, 1881);

*Tales of English Life, including Middleton and the Middletons* (London: F. Warne, 1881);

*Mary Howitt; an Autobiography*, 2 volumes, edited by Margaret Howitt, with a chapter of autobiography by William Howitt (London: W. Isbister, 1889).

OTHER: *Fisher's Drawing Room Scrap-Book*, edited by Mary Howitt (London: Fisher, Son & Jackson, 1840-1842);

Fredrika Bremer, *The Neighbours: A Story of Every-Day Life*, translated by Mary Howitt (2 volumes, London: Longman, Brown, Green & Longmans, 1842; 1 volume, New York: Harper, 1843);

Bremer, *The Home: or, Family Cares and Family Joys*, translated by Mary Howitt (2 volumes, London: Longman, Brown, Green & Longmans, 1843; 1 volume, New York: Harper, 1843);

Bremer, *The President's Daughters; including Nina*, translated by Mary Howitt (3 volumes, London: Longman, Brown, Green & Longmans, 1843; 1 volume, New York: Harper, 1844);

Adelbert von Chamisso, *The Wonderful History of Peter Schlemihl*, translated by William Howitt (London: Longman, Brown, Green & Longmans, 1843; New York: Burgess & Stringer, 1843);

Anders Fryxell, *The History of Sweden*, 2 volumes, translated by Anne von Schaultz, edited by Mary Howitt (London: R. Bentley, 1844);

Emilie Smith Flygare-Carlen, *The Rose of Tistelon: A Tale of the Swedish Coast*, translated by Mary Howitt, 2 volumes (London: Longman, Brown, Green & Longmans, 1844);

Bremer, *New Sketches of Every-Day Life: A Diary. Together with Strife and Peace*, translated by Mary Howitt (2 volumes, London: Longman, Brown, Green & Longmans, 1844; 1 volume, New York: Harper, 1844);

Bremer, *Domestic Life, or, The H---- Family*, translated by Mary Howitt (London: T. Allman, 1844);

Christoph von Schmid, *The Picture of the Virgin*, translated and adapted by Mary Howitt (London: Wm. S. Orr & Co., 1844);

Wilhelm Hey, *The Child's Picture and Versebook: Commonly Called Otto Speckter's Fable Book*, translated by Mary Howitt (London: Longman, Brown, Green & Longmans, 1844; New York: D. Appleton / Philadelphia: George S. Appleton, 1850);

C. Stoeber, *The Curate's Favourite Pupil*, translated by Mary Howitt (London: Orr, 1844);

Bremer, *Life in Dalecarlia: the Parsonage of Mora*, translated by William Howitt (London: Chapman & Hall, 1845; New York: Harper, 1845);

Hans Christian Andersen, *Only a Fiddler! and O. T.: or, Life in Denmark*, 3 volumes, translated by Mary Howitt (London: R. Bentley, 1845);

Andersen, *The Improvisatore*, translated by Mary Howitt (2 volumes, London: R. Bentley, 1845; 1 volume, New York: Harper, 1845);

Andersen, *Wonderful Stories for Children*, translated by Mary Howitt (London: Chapman & Hall, 1846; New York: Wiley & Putnam, 1846);

Henriette Wach von Paalzow, *The Citizen of Prague*, 3 volumes, translated by Mary Howitt (London: H. Colburn, 1846);

Adalbert Stifter, *Pictures of Life*, translated by Mary Howitt (London: Simms & M'Intyre, 1847);

Alphonse de Lamartine, *Genevieve: a Tale*, translated by Mary Howitt (London: Simms & M'Intyre, 1847);

Andersen, *The True Story of My Life: A Sketch*, translated by Mary Howitt (London: Longman, Brown, Green & Longmans, 1847; Boston: James Munroe, 1847);

Joseph Ennemoser, *The History of Magic*, 2 volumes, translated by William Howitt, with an appendix by Mary Howitt (London: H. G. Bohn, 1847);

*Howitt's Journal of Literature and Popular Progress*, 3 volumes, edited by William and Mary Howitt (London: Willoughby, January 1847 - June 1848);

Bremer, *Brothers and Sisters: A Tale of Domestic Life*, translated by Mary Howitt (London: Henry Colburn, 1848; New York: Harper, 1848);

Sofia Margareta Zelow Knorring, *The Peasant and His Landlord*, translated by Mary Howitt (New York: Harper, 1848);

Bremer, *The Midnight Sun: A Pilgrimage*, translated by Mary Howitt (London: H. Colburn, 1849);

Bremer, *An Easter Offering*, translated by Mary Howitt (London: Henry Colburn, 1850);

*Biographical Sketches of the Queens of Great Britain from the Norman Conquest to the Reign of Victo-*

*Mary Howitt's birthplace (illustration from chapter two of "Some Reminiscences of My Life" by Mary Howitt,* Good Words and Sunday Magazine, *July 1885)*

*ria: or, Royal Book of Beauty*, edited by Mary Howitt (London: Colburn, 1851);

Meir Goldschmidt, *Jacob Bendixen, the Jew*, 3 volumes, adapted by Mary Howitt (London: Colburn, 1852);

Bremer, *The Homes of the New World; Impressions of America*, translated by Mary Howitt (3 volumes, London: A. Hall, Virtue, 1853; 2 volumes, New York: Harper, 1853);

*The Dial of Love: A Christmas Book for the Young*, compiled by Mary Howitt (London: Darton, 1853);

*Pictorial Calendar of the Seasons Exhibiting the Pleasures, Pursuits, and Characteristics of Country Life for Every Month in the Year*, edited by Mary Howitt (London: Henry G. Bohn, 1854);

Elihu Burritt, *Thoughts and Things at Home and Abroad*, includes a memoir by Mary Howitt (Boston: Phillips, Sampson, 1854; London: Cassell, Petter & Gilpin, 1868);

Bremer, *Hertha*, translated by Mary Howitt (London: Arthur Hall, Virtue, 1856; New York: Putnam, 1856);

Bjornstjerne M. Bjornson, *Trust and Trial: A Story from the Danish*, translated by Mary Howitt (London: Hurst & Blackett, 1858);

Bremer, *Father and Daughter*, translated by Mary Howitt (London, 1859);

Bremer, *Two Years in Switzerland and Italy*, 2 volumes, translated by Mary Howitt (London: Hurst & Blackett, 1861);

Bremer, *Travels in the Holy Land*, 2 volumes, translated by Mary Howitt (London: Hurst & Blackett, 1862);

Bremer, *Greece and the Greeks. The Narrative of a Winter Residence and Summer Travel in Greece and Its Islands*, 2 volumes, translated by Mary Howitt (London: Hurst & Blackett, 1863);

Epes Sargent, *Peculiar: A Tale of the Great Transition*, 3 volumes, edited by William Howitt (London: Hurst & Blackett, 1864);

Margaret Howitt, *Twelve Months with Fredrika Bremer in Sweden*, 2 volumes, includes a preface by Mary Howitt (London: Jackson, Walford & Hodder, 1866);

Friedrich Wilhelm Hackländer, *Behind the Counter*, translated by Mary Howitt (Leipzig: Bernhard Tauchnitz / London: Sampson Low / Paris: C. Reinwald, 1867);

Samuel Richardson, *The History of Sir Charles Grandison*, abridged by Mary Howitt (London: G. Routledge, 1873);

*The Religion of Rome*, translated by William Howitt (London: Balliere, Tindall & Cox, 1873).

Mary and William Howitt, now almost wholly forgotten, deserve attention for the volume and range of their work and for the degree to which they mirror the concerns of their age. Part of nineteenth-century literary life throughout Romanticism and Victorianism, this married couple reflected the transition in literary taste during these crucial decades. Provincial in background, they nonetheless reached well beyond the borders of England to the writers of Germany and Scandinavia. William was one of the first English authors to travel in and write about the newly settled lands of Australia and New Zealand. Both Howitts knew well the ever-widening range of religious ideologies, from Quaker to spiritualist to Roman Catholic. Read and admired by old-style Tories, the Howitts nonetheless lived and wrote by a reformist, even Chartist, creed fueled by sensitivity to the abuses of the old systems.

William Howitt was an indefatigable walker around England, both literally and figuratively, recording like William Cobbett in passionate outbursts of prose the complex and changing landscapes about him; William's genius was primarily encyclopedic and assertive. Mary Howitt saw and shaped her work with more focus and with a more muted tone; her poems of natural history for children, her literary ballads, and her wry and unassertive tales have an attractive sensitivity and insight, moralizing without heaviness or monotony.

The Society of Friends was the dominant influence in the early lives of both Mary and William Howitt, fostering their independence, their work for political and social reform, their libertarian activism, their spiritualism, their horror of war. Only in opposition to Quaker codes of silence, however, did the two develop careers as prolific writers of imaginative literature. Fortunately, Mary's loquacious nursemaid told her tales of sprites and elves, and both Mary and William attended schools which, though run in the Friends manner, did not successfully suppress their voracious reading habits.

William, the elder by six years, grew up in the area of Nottingham. The son of Phebe Tatum Howitt and Thomas Howitt, a mine superintendent, he spent much of his childhood roaming the countryside he was later to celebrate in his most remembered book, *The Rural Life of England* (1838). As a youth, he was apprenticed to a cabinetmaker in Mansfield. His favorite memory of this period was a day in 1810 when he went to nearby Newstead Abbey to work on the house of his poetic hero, George Gordon, Lord Byron, who, unfortunately, was absent. On finishing his indentures William gave up cabinetwork and began to learn pharmacy on his own; though for his whole life he thought of himself as a writer, his occupation until 1836 was as an apothecary.

The daughter of Samuel and Ann Wood Botham, Mary Botham grew up in Uttoxeter, Staffordshire, where her father was active first in the iron industry and later in land surveying. She and her sister Anna (with whom she was to conduct a voluminous correspondence most of her life) attended elementary schools at home and away and shared a growing passion for reading poetry, especially ballads and Byron. She and William married on 16 April 1821. After living briefly in Hanley, where William bought a chemist's shop and ran it for seven months, they went to live temporarily with his parents. Then in summer 1822 they set up home and shop in the growing city of Nottingham, where they were to stay for fourteen years while their family grew and their literary careers began.

Mary was pregnant for nearly all of the first eighteen years of her marriage. She bore seven children (of whom only four outlived childhood, and only two outlived their mother) and lost several others by miscarriage. Even with intense dedication to family, the Howitts participated actively in the rich, though provincial, cultural life of Nottingham, increasingly contributed to national literary and reform activities, and went on frequent walking expeditions through England and Scotland.

Their first publication was a small volume of Romantic—primarily Wordsworthian—verse,

*Illustration from chapter three of "Some Reminiscences of My Life" by Mary Howitt* (Good Words and Sunday Magazine, *August 1885)*

*The Forest Minstrel* (1823), which was noticed well in the reviews but not at the booksellers. They began to contribute poems to the popular gift-book annuals and had soon collected enough for a second joint volume of verse, *The Desolation of Eyam* (1827). One poem of William's included in this second volume had already appeared separately—an outpouring of emotion at Byron's funeral (1824), which William attended. Most of the poems in *The Desolation of Eyam* are typical of the sort published in the annuals, nostalgic lyrics on aspects of natural history. The volume was well reviewed and sold well enough to go into a second edition.

The Howitts' real success in this vein came with *The Book of the Seasons* (1828), a kind of combination of John Clare and a farmers' almanac. It is a calendar of the months with articles on each season, mixing information and essays on natural history (on topics such as migration of birds) with Mary's nature poems, and other literary pieces. This easygoing and thoroughly rural compilation, evoking a green England fast disappearing as the Midlands became industrialized, caught the reviewers' and the public's approving eye: Carl Woodring reports seventeen or more large editions of the work. Christopher North (John Wilson), the eccentric *Blackwood's* reviewer, reflected warmly on the Howitts' achievement; their goal, as he saw it, had been to lay before the reader each month "all the objects and appearances which the month would present, in the garden, in the field, and the waters; yet confining itself solely to those objects." His shepherd comments, "And nae insignificant aim either, sir. Hae they hit it?" To which North securely replies, "They have" (April 1831). *The Book of the Seasons* made its publisher a good deal of money, but the Howitts gained little because they had sold the copyright to their publisher. William, feeling angry for decades after, made copyright abuse a recurring issue in his writing.

The book's popularity, like that of later books by the Howitts, seems linked to shifting taste, as the intensity of early and high Romanticism gave way to the lusher tones of Victorianism. As in the annuals, nostalgia and sentiment had become all-important. The Howitts were an active part of an ever-expanding literary network of writers in a similar vein; their friends were part of the circle of Felicia Hemans, at the height of her popularity—the young editor of annuals Alaric Watts (whose son was later to marry the Howitts' daughter Anna), the musician and Germanist Henry Chorley, poets Letitia Elizabeth Landon (L.E.L.), S. C. Hall, and Allan Cunningham. In 1831, unannounced, a greater poet made their acquaintance: William Wordsworth, traveling with his family, knocked on the Howitts' door in Nottingham to ask for help in nursing his wife, stricken with a sudden attack of lumbago. The families got along well, and much later William Howitt was to write an account of his call at Rydal Mount in August 1836, when on a rainy afternoon the two Williams joined forces in an argument with a proslavery general from the American South.

In contrast to the pastoral and often precious qualities of the "annuals" group, the Howitts, with their Quaker conscience, were attentive to issues of poverty and injustice as well as to birds and flowers. Nottingham was becoming a factory town with obvious problems of unemployment and labor abuse, and in 1831 the city was the scene of disastrous rioting, including the burning of Nottingham Castle (those scenes were later to be part of one of Mary's best fictions, *Little Coin, Much Care* [1842]). William, in response to the workers' needs, began a lifelong career of outspoken political agitation; the anti-Reform coalition of peers and bishops in the House of Lords, assembled to combat the Reform Bill of 1832, incensed William to a fierce disestablishmentarian rhetoric. Readers in the national market were presumably surprised and shocked at the contrast between the bucolic *Book of the Seasons* and his next publication, the indignant *Popular History of Priestcraft* (1833). This volume traces idolatry from its phallic and orgiastic roots through its pagan, Jewish, Catholic, and finally Anglican manifestations. In tones reminiscent of Milton's St. Peter (in "Lycidas"), Howitt decries a clergy "Lukewarm in their duties; and proudly cold in their intercourse with the poor of their flocks," and a church stubborn in "Adhering to its most absurd, and most impolitic institutions, rites, and dogmas." Howitt boldly took the fight for disestablishment to an interview with the surprised prime minister, Charles, Earl Grey, who declined to advocate the idea.

In 1834 Mary published volumes on her own for the first time, two books of verse. *The Seven Temptations* is a series of seven dramatic poems set in exotic locations such as the "north woods." In each of the poems a Satanic figure, Achzib, in various guises tempts the protagonists to sin. The attempt to delineate Byronic emotions and situations is inappropriate to Mary's basically English imagination and experience; the formality of the seven-part scheme, based loosely on Joanna Baillie's *Plays on the Passions* (1798-1812), further constricts the poems, which gained mixed reviews.

Far more successful and significant was her *Sketches of Natural History* (1834). These brief lyrics, written in a vein that Mary was to continue with *Tales in Verse* (1836) and *Birds and Flowers, and Other Country Things* (1838), were originally written for her own children; they transcend didactic juvenile poetry by displaying wit, whimsy, multiplicity, and depth. "The Stormy Petrel," surely a poem to be seen as a conscious contribution to the tradition of Romantic bird poems, uses the bird to convey mysterious knowledge normally inaccessible to humans, knowledge of storms, of wrecks at sea, and of the presence of God. With its combination of a sense of underlying violence in the world with a faith in God's control, the poem does far more than "moralize" the natural image. "The Fossil Elephant," though pre-Darwinian, brings to the reader the sense of vast time and (as yet unnamed) cataclysm that will characterize nature in Alfred Tennyson and Thomas Hardy: "And the Dragons lie in the mountain-rock, / As if for eternity!" "The Sea-gull" is an especially energetic poem, representing in the verse the raucous qualities of the wild, free, and ravenous bird. Howitt's verse, invested with urgency and excitement, takes traditionally didactic subjects—the monkey, the eagle, the nettle—and develops both their particularity and their symbolic resonances.

Her best-known poem in the juvenile vein is "The Spider and the Fly," which though saddled with a disappointingly moralistic ending, wittily and vivaciously tells a fable of heartless entrapment and ineffective resistance:

> "I'm sure you must be weary, dear, with soaring up so high;
> Will you rest upon my little bed?" said the Spider to the Fly.
> "There are pretty curtains drawn around; the sheets are fine and thin,
> And if you like to rest awhile, I'll snugly tuck you in!"
> "Oh, no, no," said the little Fly, "for I've often heard it said,
> They never, never wake again, who sleep upon your bed!"

In the 1840s, Mary's works in verse included ballads, culminating in her *Ballads and Other Poems* (1847). Drawing on Samuel Taylor Coleridge's "Rime of the Ancient Mariner," Mary's "Old Man's Story," a story of the curse on a sea captain who has thrown a rich passenger overboard, was particularly well received. "American," a story narrated by a Quaker woman, takes a tough stance within the sentimental pioneer genre, steadily resisting the popular stereotypes of the Native American, both the bloodthirsty and the noble savage.

In the mid 1830s, both Howitts began to expect their writing to bring in income, especially after William left his chemist's shop in 1836, and they moved to Esher, in Surrey, to be nearer the London bases of the publishing industry. In 1836 Mary proudly reported the £150 she made from *Wood Leighton*, a three-volume novel based on scenes of life in Uttoxeter, where she had grown up. By 1839 Mary had signed on with Cheapside publisher Thomas Tegg for a series of thirteen short prose tales on domestic virtue. These, published over the next five years, were known as "Tales for the people and their children." One, *Love and Money* (1843), bears the subtitle "*An Every Day Tale*," an indication of the antiromance intentions of these narratives. They are unpretentious, straightforward, didactic narratives about the interaction of morality and economics. Employment, savings, trade, and expenditure are key themes, intermixed with the proper handling of courtship, parenthood, friendship, and other domestic themes. In nearly all cases the incidents are—perhaps deliberately—characterized by steadiness rather than excitement. Didactic structures leavened by wry observation dominate the tales, as in the double plot of *Love and Money*, where two inherently strong women, each involved in a different crisis, befriend one another in order to compensate for one another's deficiencies. The steady values preached by Mary's tales are well illustrated by the elder of these characters, Ellen Morland, who saves her improvident husband from financial and personal bankruptcy by mastering the careful, patient operation of the perfume distillery he has bought and is totally unsuited to run. As she tells her younger friend, Mary Wheeler—who must learn to survive being jilted by an impetuous and undependable man—the key is in quiet efficiency:

> "Such, dearest Mary," said Mrs. Morland, "has been my life; there is no romance in it; but please God only that I rightly make use of the lessons it has given me. I shall not be altogether useless in my sphere, be it large or be it small."

As admirers of Byron, the Howitts could not totally leave out Romanticism, however, and the tales are shaped with romance underpinnings—dangerous fevers, life-threatening betrayals, fiercely abusive guardians. Their position as transition pieces between Romantic and Victorian is evident in the dual focus of the last scene of *Love and Money*, where Mary Wheeler, having survived being jilted, finds security at the home of her eccentric and benevolent uncle, who was also her first music teacher. There she accepts the proposal of her new lover, a prosperous and morally upright doctor who attended her through the fever (and refused to charge a fee for it). After dinner Mary begins to play the piano for her fiancé but, being understandably nervous, bungles the Mozart. Her uncle facilitates her removal to her properly domestic place on the sofa, while he supplies the entertainment, the Romantic Sturm und Drang of his favorite composer—Beethoven:

> My uncle grew almost angry, and seating himself at the piano, played magnificently. Our little parlour reverberated the almost deafening sounds, for my uncle was doing his grandest; my aunt was enchanted with his performance, and we two [Mary and her fiancé] sat side by side on the little sofa, his arm round my waist, and my head resting upon his bosom.

Along with Mary's poems for children and a few of the ballads, the tales Thomas Tegg published for Mary are among her most interesting work, and deserve more attention than they have received. She should be remembered not only as the poet of juvenile natural history but also as a fic-

*William Howitt*

tion writer of unusual sympathy with the systems of early-Victorian economics and family.

Perhaps William's most successful and interesting work also dates from the late 1830s. *The Rural Life of England* (1838), describing country life among rich and poor, became a favorite with readers longing to preserve "Old England"; appealing to conservative nostalgia, the book therefore oddly allied itself with that Tory squirearchy who would have hardly wanted to be bedfellows with the radical Howitt. The conservative appeal is real: Howitt mourns the passing of an older, greener age. But there is a more radical side, characteristic of Howitt's observant and sympathetic eye for poverty and injustice. As he recounts what he and Mary saw on their many long-distance rambles, the Dickensian specters of industrial ugliness intrude. For Howitt ugliness is not merely scenic, it implies the "grinding and oppression of the poor" and the reforms that ought to ameliorate it.

Oppression and reform were the themes of a scathing work published in the same year as *The Rural Life of England*, but in an entirely different vein. *Colonization and Christianity* (1838) is a fiercely ironic critique of Christian justifications for the European spread of empire. The radical who had five years earlier attacked the established Anglican church by associating it with paganism now even more directly accuses the entire Christian religion of sordid and bloodthirsty hypocrisy:

> We have long laid to our souls the flattering unction that we are a civilized and a Christian people. We talk of all other nations in all other quarters of the world, as savages, barbarians, un-

> civilized.... We shudder at the war-cries of naked Indians, and the ghastly feasts of Cannibals; and bless our souls that we are redeemed from all these things, and made models of beneficence, and lights of God in the earth! ... how is it that these tribes know *us*? ... They know us chiefly by our crimes and our cruelty. It is we who are, and must appear to them the savages.

The fury of William's Quaker pacifism emerged again in his last publication. Late in life, in his long poem *The Mad War-Planet* (1871), he surveyed the modern war machine of the war of 1871 and again condemned the hypocrisy and mass destructiveness of humankind.

William's appetite for walking, observing, and reporting facts of topography and description characterizes the bulk of his extensive prose productions after *The Rural Life of England*. These include the popular and autobiographical *Boy's Country-book* (1839); *Visits to Remarkable Places; Old Halls, Battlefields and Scenes illustrative of Striking Passages in History and Poetry* (1840, 1842), a two-volume sequel to *Rural Life*; the very successful *Homes and Haunts of the Most Eminent British Poets* (1847), with its particular success in anecdotes based on Howitt's genial snooping around the homes of his literary heroes; a volume jointly written with Mary, *Ruined Abbeys and Castles of Great Britain* (1862); and the much later *Northern Heights of London* (1869), an attempt to chronicle the historical and literary geography of Hampstead and Highgate, fast disappearing under the onslaught of suburban London. His busy pen produced volume after volume; on some days, he claimed, he wrote as many as sixteen hours. When Mary and William took their family to Germany in 1840-1843, William produced three descriptive volumes on German life. When in 1852 the indefatigable (and almost sixty-year-old) William went to Australia in search of gold and adventure, the inevitable result was a series of books about the colonies, culminating in the two-volume *History of Discovery in Australia, Tasmania, and New Zealand* (1865).

Mary's work, after the tales for Tegg, continued with a steady output of juvenile fiction and poetry, as well as an occasional work of adult fiction, such as the three-volume novel of Welsh life, *The Cost of Caergwyn* (1864). Her most significant literary contribution in later years, however, was her substantial work in translation: she translated several works from German, including the poems of Adalbert Stifter (1847), and (with William) a lengthy history of magic by Joseph Ennemoser (1847). During the Howitts' German years, Mary was learning Swedish in order to translate the stories of Fredrika Bremer, a writer of sketches and fiction of village life. Mary was to become a good friend of Bremer, working in close collaboration to translate her books without delay for eager English and American audiences. The appearance of unauthorized and competitive translations unfortunately diminished Mary's financial rewards from her extensive work on Bremer—fourteen books in all, plus one translated by William. From 1845 to 1847 Mary translated four works by Hans Christian Andersen and was the first to make his stories accessible in English. Again, circumstances—including Andersen's unpleasant personality—prevented Mary from becoming sole translator and caused her to miss out on the forthcoming vogue for Andersen's stories.

Moving gradually closer to London during their married lives, the Howitts increasingly shed provincial and Quaker manners and society. They were gregarious people, and they befriended many artists and writers whose lifestyles and literary concerns were far from those of the Society of Friends: Alfred Tennyson, Elizabeth Barrett Browning, Coventry Patmore, Charles Dickens, Dinah Craik, Holman Hunt, Dante Gabriel Rossetti. William claimed to have encouraged Elizabeth Gaskell to become a writer, and consequently felt paternalistic pride for *Mary Barton* (1848), her first novel.

Mary and William were continually contributing to the burgeoning London periodical market, including Dickens's *Household Words*. Their most active periodical involvement occurred in the late 1840s, when William joined the staff of, and then invested in, the *People's Journal*, which soon folded, causing the Howitts a substantial financial loss. After this failure they founded and edited *Howitt's Journal of Literature and Popular Progress* (January 1847 - June 1848). The journal was dedicated to the amelioration of the life of the working classes, with a loosely Chartist agenda and an intense interest in cooperative principles. Articles on issues of politics and welfare alternated with cultural material: the journal gave positive reviews to humanitarian writers such as George Sand, the early Anthony Trollope, and Currer Bell (Charlotte Brontë). *Howitt's Journal* collapsed after a year and a half, in part because of the intensity of the Howitts' public quarrel with John Saunders, the proprietor of the *People's Journal*, in part because of the press of new periodicals in mid-century London.

In the 1850s and 1860s, Mary and William were involved in political reform issues—in particular, abolition and woman's rights. They were active in hosting American reformers such as Lucretia Mott and Harriet Beecher Stowe. Gradually, however, as they grew older, spiritualism—including experiments with mesmerism and mediums—took precedence over their social concerns. As always, William wrote about his interests, producing *The History of the Supernatural . . . Demonstrating a Universal Faith* (1863); interest in the spiritual led him in 1870 to recognize Walt Whitman as a "great and original poet" whose work was "alive with that fresh, new, piquant, magical life that no mere poet of the world . . . has" (review of *Leaves of Grass, Spiritual Magazine*, January 1870).

In that same year the Howitts left England for good, to divide their time between Rome and the Tyrol. William died in Rome in 1879 and was buried in the Protestant cemetery, where Keats—whose poetry he loved—also lay. Mary, accompanied by her daughter Margaret, lived on in Europe for almost another decade. The one-time Quaker became a Roman Catholic in 1883, and received an audience with Pope Leo XIII just weeks before her death in Rome in 1888. She was buried beside her husband. Her last literary project was an unfinished autobiography, later edited and published by her daughter. Since then, except for a pair of biographical works by Amice Lee and Carl Ray Woodring in the 1950s, the Howitts—such prolific publishers throughout their long lifetimes—have been practically neglected in literary studies.

**Bibliographies:**

Carl R. Woodring, "William and Mary Howitt and Their Circles," Ph.D. dissertation, Harvard University, 1949;

Woodring, "William and Mary Howitt: Bibliographical Notes," *Harvard Library Bulletin*, 5 (Spring 1951): 251-255.

**Biographies:**

James Britten, *Mary Howitt* (London: Catholic Truth Society, 1890);

Carl Ray Woodring, *Victorian Samplers: William and Mary Howitt* (Lawrence: University of Kansas Press, 1952);

Amice Lee, *Laurels and Rosemary: The Life of William and Mary Howitt* (London, New York & Toronto: Oxford University Press, 1955).

**References:**

James A. Butler, "Wordsworth's funeral: a contemporary report," *English Language Notes*, 13 (September 1975): 127-129;

H. B. de Groot, "R. H. Horne, Mary Howitt, and a Mid-Victorian Version of 'The Ecchoing Green,' " *Blake Studies*, 4 (Fall 1971): 81-88;

R. H. Horne, "William and Mary Howitt," in *A New Spirit of the Age*, 2 volumes, edited by Horne (London: Smith, Elder, 1844), I: 177-198;

Konrad F. Kienesberger, "Mary Howitt und ihre Stifter-Übersetzungen: Zur Rezeption des Dichters in victorianischen England," *Adalbert Stifter Institut des Landes Oberösterreich: Vierteljahrsschrift*, 25 (1976): 13-55;

Kent Ljungquist, "Howitt's 'Byronian Ramblers' and the Picturesque Setting of 'The Fall of the House of Usher,' " *ESQ: A Journal of the American Renaissance*, 33, no. 4 (1987): 224-236;

Mary Howitt Walker, *Come wind, come weather: a biography of Alfred Howitt* (Carlton, Victoria: Melbourne University Press, 1971);

Anna Mary Howitt Watts, *The Pioneers of the Spiritual Reformation* (London: Psychological Press Association, 1883);

C. R. Woodring, "Charles Reade's debt to William Howitt," *Nineteenth-Century Fiction*, 5 (June 1950): 39-46.

**Papers:**

The Howitt papers are scattered among private collections and public libraries including those of the University of Nottingham, Harvard University, Dove Cottage, the Mitchell Library (Sydney), the National Library of Scotland, the Nottingham Public Libraries, the John Rylands Library, and the Library of the Society of Friends (London). In her biography Amice Lee (Mary Howitt's grandniece) has drawn on the family collection of Mary Howitt's letters to her sister Anna Harrison.

# Leigh Hunt

*(19 October 1784 - 28 August 1859)*

David R. Cheney
*University of Toledo*

See also the Hunt entry in *DLB 96: British Romantic Poets, 1789-1832: Second Series.*

BOOKS: *Juvenilia* (London: Printed by J. Whiting, 1801; Philadelphia: Printed & published by H. Maxwell, 1804);

*Critical Essays on the Performers of the London Theatres* (London: Printed by & for John Hunt, 1807);

*An Attempt to Shew the Folly and Danger of Methodism* (London: Printed for & sold by John Hunt, 1809);

*The Prince of Wales V. the Examiner: a Full Report of the Trial of John and Leigh Hunt* (London: Printed by & for John Hunt, 1812);

*The Feast of the Poets, With Notes, and Other Pieces in Verse* (London: Printed for James Cawthorn, 1814; New York: Printed & published by Van Winkle & Wiley, 1814; enlarged edition, London: Gale & Fenner, 1815);

*The Descent of Liberty, a Mask* (London: Printed for Gale, Curtis & Fenner, 1815; Philadelphia: Printed for Harrison Hall, 1816);

*The Story of Rimini* (London: Printed by T. Davison for J. Murray; W. Blackwood, Edinburgh; and Cummings, Dublin, 1816; Boston: Published by Wells & Lilly and M. Carey, Philadelphia, 1816);

*Foliage, or Poems Original and Translated* (London: Printed for C. & J. Ollier, 1818; Philadelphia: Published by Littell & Henry and Edward Earle, printed by W. Brown, 1818);

*Hero and Leander, and Bacchus and Ariadne* (London: Printed for C. & J. Ollier, 1819);

*The Poetical Works of Leigh Hunt,* 3 volumes (London: C. & J. Ollier, 1819);

*The Months, Descriptive of the Successive Beauties of the Year* (London: C. & J. Ollier, 1821);

*Ultra-Crepidarius: a Satire on William Gifford* (London: Printed for John Hunt, 1823);

*Lord Byron and Some of His Contemporaries* (London: H. Colburn, 1828; Philadelphia: Carey, Lea & Carey, 1828);

*Christianism: or Belief and Unbelief Reconciled* (London: Bradbury, 1832); revised and enlarged as *The Religion of the Heart: a Manual of Faith and Duty* (London: John Chapman, 1853; New York: Printed by J. J. Reed, 1857);

*The Poetical Works of Leigh Hunt* (London: Edward Moxon, 1832);

*Sir Ralph Esher: or Adventures of a Gentleman of the Court of Charles II,* 3 volumes (London: Henry Colburn & Richard Bentley, 1830-1832 [i.e., 1832]);

*The Indicator and the Companion: A Miscellany for the Fields and for the Fireside,* 2 volumes (London: Published for Henry Colburn by R. Bentley, 1834); republished as *The Indicator: A Miscellany for the Fields and for the Fireside,* 1 volume (New York: Wiley & Putnam, 1845);

*Captain Sword and Captain Pen: A Poem, With some Remarks on War and Military Statesmen* (London: Charles Knight, 1835);

*A Legend of Florence, A Play in Five Acts* (London: Edward Moxon, 1840);

*The Seer: or, Common-places Refreshed,* 2 parts (London: E. Moxon, 1840; Boston: Roberts Brothers, 1864);

*Essays by Leigh Hunt: The Indicator, The Seer* (London: E. Moxon, 1841);

*The Palfrey: A Love Story of Old Times* (London: How & Parsons, 1842);

*The Poetical Works of Leigh Hunt* (London: Edward Moxon, 1844);

*Rimini and Other Poems* (Boston: William D. Ticknor, 1844);

*Stories from the Italian Poets: with Lives of the Writers,* 2 volumes (London: Chapman & Hall, 1845; New York: Wiley & Putnam, 1846);

*Men, Women, and Books: a Selection of Sketches, Essays and Critical Memoirs,* 2 volumes (London: Smith, Elder, 1847; New York: Harper, 1847);

*A Jar of Honey from Mount Hybla* (London: Smith, Elder, 1848);

*Leigh Hunt (portrait by Benjamin Robert Haydon; National Portrait Gallery, London)*

*The Town: Its Memorable Characters and Events: St. Paul's to St. James's,* 2 volumes (London: Smith, Elder, 1848);

*The Autobiography of Leigh Hunt, With Reminiscences of Friends and Contemporaries* (3 volumes, London: Smith, Elder, 1850; 2 volumes, New York: Harper, 1850; revised edition, 1 volume, London: Smith, Elder, 1860);

*Table-Talk* (London: Smith, Elder, 1851; New York: Appleton, 1879);

*The Works of Leigh Hunt,* 4 volumes (Philadelphia: Willis P. Hazard, 1854);

*Stories in Verse; Now First Collected* (London & New York: Routledge, 1855);

*The Old Court Suburb: or, Memorials of Kensington, Regal, Critical, and Anecdotical,* 2 volumes (London: Hurst & Blackett, 1855; enlarged, 1855);

*The Poetical Works of Leigh Hunt. Now First Entirely Collected, Revised by Himself,* edited by S. Adams Lee (Boston: Ticknor & Fields, 1857);

*The Poetical Works of Leigh Hunt, Now Finally Collected, Revised by Himself,* edited by Thornton Hunt (London & New York: Routledge, Warne & Routledge, 1860);

*A Saunter Through the West End* (London: Hurst & Blackett, 1861);

*A Day By the Fire; and Other Papers Hitherto Uncollected,* edited by Joseph Edward Babson (London: Sampson Low, Son & Marston, 1870; Boston: Roberts Brothers, 1870);

*The Wishing-Cap Papers,* edited by Babson (Boston: Lee & Shepard, 1873; London: Sampson Low, Marston, Low & Searle, 1874);

*Tales by Leigh Hunt, Now First Collected,* edited by William Knight (London: W. Paterson, 1891);

*Hunt at seventeen (engraving after a miniature by R. Bowyer)*

*Musical Evenings, or Selections, Vocal and Instrumental,* edited by David R. Cheney (Columbia: University of Missouri Press, 1964);

*Hunt on Eight Sonnets of Dante,* edited by Rhodes Dunlap (Iowa City: University of Iowa School of Journalism, 1965).

**Editions:** *The Works of Leigh Hunt,* 7 volumes (London: Smith, Elder, 1870-1872);

*Leigh Hunt as Poet and Essayist,* edited by Charles Kent (London & New York: Warne, 1889);

*The Poetical Works of Leigh Hunt,* edited by H. S. Milford (London & New York: Oxford University Press, 1923).

PLAY PRODUCTIONS: *A Legend of Florence,* London, Theatre Royal, Covent Garden, 7 February 1840;

*Lovers' Amazements,* London, Lyceum Theatre, 20 January 1858.

OTHER: *Classic Tales, Serious and Lively on the Merits and Reputations of the Authors,* 5 volumes, includes critical essays by Hunt on five of the authors (London: J. Hunt & C. Reynell, 1807);

William Hazlitt, *The Round Table: a Collection of Essays on Literature, Men, and Manners,* 2 volumes, includes twelve essays by Hunt (Edinburgh: Printed for Archibald Constable and Longman, Hurst, Rees, Orme & Brown, London, 1817);

*Amyntas, a Tale of the Woods: from the Italian of Torquato Tasso,* translated, with notes, by Hunt (London: T. & J. Allman, 1820);

*Bacchus in Tuscany, a Dithyramic Poem from the Italian of Francesco Redi,* translated by Hunt (London: Printed for John & H. L. Hunt, 1825);

*The Masque of Anarchy, a Poem by Percy Bysshe Shelley, Now First Published with a Preface by Leigh*

*Hunt* (London: Edward Moxon, 1832);

*The Dramatic Works of Wycherley, Congreve, Vanbrugh, and Farquhar,* includes biographical and critical notices by Hunt (London: Edward Moxon, 1840);

*The Dramatic Works of Richard Brinsley Sheridan,* edited, with a biographical and critical sketch, by Hunt (London: Edward Moxon, 1840);

*One Hundred Romances of Real Life,* edited and annotated by Hunt (London: L. Whittaker, 1843);

*Imagination and Fancy: or, Selections from the English Poets with an Essay in Answer to the Question What is Poetry?,* edited, with commentary and an introductory essay, by Hunt (London: Smith, Elder, 1844; New York: Wiley & Putnam, 1845);

*Wit and Humour, Selected from the English Poets with an Illustrative Essay,* edited, with introductory essay, by Hunt (London: Smith, Elder, 1846; New York: Wiley & Putnam, 1847);

*A Book for a Corner, or Selections in Prose and Verse from Authors the Best Suited to That Mode of Enjoyment,* edited, with an introduction and comments, by Hunt (2 volumes, London: Chapman & Hall, 1849; 1 volume, New York: G. P. Putnam, 1852);

*Readings for Railways: or, Anecdotes and Other Short Stories, Reflections, Maxims, Characteristics, Passages of Wit, Humour and Poetry, etc.,* selected by Hunt (London: C. Gilpin, 1849);

*Beaumont and Fletcher, or The Finest Scenes, Lyrics, and Other Beauties of Those Two Poets,* includes preface by Hunt (London: Henry G. Bohn, 1855);

*The Book of the Sonnet,* 2 volumes, edited by Hunt and S. Adams Lee, with an essay on the sonnet by Hunt (Boston: Roberts Brothers, 1867; London: S. Low, Son & Marston, 1867).

SELECTED PERIODICAL PUBLICATIONS—UNCOLLECTED: "Memoir of James Henry Leigh Hunt written by himself," *Monthly Mirror,* 7 (April 1810): 243-248;

"The Works of Henry Howard, Earl of Surrey, and of Sir Thomas Wyatt the Elder," edited by George Frederick Nott, *Edinburgh Review,* 27 (December 1816): 390-422;

"The Family Journal," *New Monthly Magazine and Literary Journal,* 13 (January 1825): 17-28; (February 1825): 166-176; (March 1825): 276-282; (April 1825): 353-369, 419-423; (May 1825): 457-466; (June 1825): 548-555; 14 (July 1825): 41-45; (September 1825): 199-206; (October 1825): 323-332; (November 1825): 429-431; (December 1825): 514-518;

"The Wishing Cap," *Tait's Edinburgh Magazine,* 2 (January 1833): 435-442; (March 1833): 689-693; 3 (April 1833): 141-148; (June 1833): 275-280; (July 1833): 417-421; (September 1833): 695-701;

"Lady Mary Wortley Montagu, Letters and Works, edited by Lord Wharncliffe," *London and Westminster Review,* 37 (April 1837): 130-164;

"Memoirs of the Colman Family, by R. B. Peake," *Edinburgh Review,* 73 (July 1841): 389-424;

"The Life, Journal and Correspondence of Samuel Pepys, Esq. by the Rev. John Smith," *Edinburgh Review,* 74 (October 1841): 105-125;

"Madame Sevigne and her Contemporaries," *Edinburgh Review,* 76 (October 1842): 203-236;

"George Selwyn and his Contemporaries, by John H. Jesse," *Edinburgh Review,* 80 (July 1844): 1-42.

Leigh Hunt was known primarily in his own time as a poet, but today he is recognized more for his contributions in prose. He wrote critical articles on plays, operas, and literature; reviews of books; newspaper editorials; essays; a novel; and an autobiography. In the early nineteenth century only William Hazlitt surpassed Hunt as a critic, but no one has surpassed him in the discovery of new literary talent. Here he was all but infallible in the early recognition of great English writers from John Keats and Percy Bysshe Shelley to Robert Browning and Alfred, Lord Tennyson. As editor of the weekly *Examiner* from 1808 until 1821, Hunt exerted considerable influence on journalism, particularly with his liberal political editorials. But Hunt's greatest contribution to prose was to the personal essay. Of his contemporaries, probably only Charles Lamb wrote better essays, and Hunt's influence on the development of the form has been greater than that of any other writer. Particularly notable is the ease and clarity with which he imbued it. Hunt himself was a man of natural gaity and a lively conversationalist. He was courageous, sensitive, hardworking, and a man of exemplary private deportment.

*Marianne Hunt (drawing by an unknown artist; University of Iowa Libraries, Iowa City)*

Hunt's father and mother, Isaac and Mary Shewell Hunt, were Americans, and his six older brothers and sisters were born in America. The family was Tory, however, and, at the beginning of the Revolutionary War, Hunt's father was forced to steal away to England on one of his father-in-law's merchant ships to escape being tarred and feathered by patriots. A few months later he was joined by his wife and children, and their first child to be born in England was James Henry Leigh Hunt.

Hunt was fortunate in his schooling. His father, a popular Anglican preacher, was financially unable to send him to public school but somehow managed to get him admitted to Christ's Hospital school, where from 1791 to 1798 he got a solid education in the classics, read widely, and was trained to write carefully. His first book, published in 1801 when he was seventeen, was *Juvenilia,* a volume of poems written during his school years. After leaving school, he was apprenticed to his barrister brother Stephen for a while as a legal clerk. Then, in 1805, he became drama reviewer on his brother John's weekly *News.* Some of his reviews, which were quite popular and won him a reputation for being perceptive and impartial at a time when impartiality was rare, were collected in *Critical Essays on the Performers of the London Theatres* (1807).

In 1808 Hunt became editor of the *Examiner,* begun by his brother John in that year. As editor until 1821, Hunt developed a wide reputation for his political articles and critical essays. Particularly notable are those later collected with William Hazlitt's in *The Round Table* (1817).

On 3 July 1809, after several years of courtship, Hunt married Marianne Kent, daughter of a court milliner. Marianne was ill with tuberculosis and rheumatism through much of her life and was apparently an alcoholic in her later years. In spite of these problems and a basic incompatibility, Hunt remained loyal to her until her death in 1857.

Intending the other day to go by the two-o'clock stage to a village near the metropolis, & arriving a few minutes too late, ~~which forced me to wait for the three~~ I found myself in the tiresome situation of being obliged to wait for the three. The day was very wet: I had no book with me: and was forced either to sit in a smoking-room, or to stand gaping about me in the door-way of a tap. ~~Mo~~ Some of our readers are doubtless acquainted with this posture of things, & know how greedily a man looks round for a little entertainment. I would have bolted for a bookseller's or a picture-shop, but there was no such thing near, and the rain came down in torrents. The hackney-coaches (all hired) went by, glistening with the drenching rain; the gutters tumbled with it; the umbrellas as they rapidly passed the door, roared with it.

What was to be done?

I went back into the smoking-room, a place of rickety old tables, hard bitter-bottomed chairs, and sanded floor. Not a picture was ~~there~~ on the wall; not even a portrait of a hunter, or Cribb, or the Duke of Wellington. But there was an atmosphere in it, able to make the ~~ten~~ next visitors smoky. ~~I came out &~~

I came out again, & ventured to ask for a book. Not ~~even~~ a book was to be had. "What have you no book at all?" Not even a Whole Duty of Man, or an Army List, or the Report of the Publicans' Committee?" No. "There were books," the landlady said; "but she believed, for her part, a lodger had pawned them, Bible & all." – Oh for an Army List, thought I, or a Navy, ~~&~~ or a Court-Calendar! A Racing Calendar would be too good

*Page from a manuscript for an essay written circa 1824 (MS H94i, University of Iowa Libraries, Iowa City)*

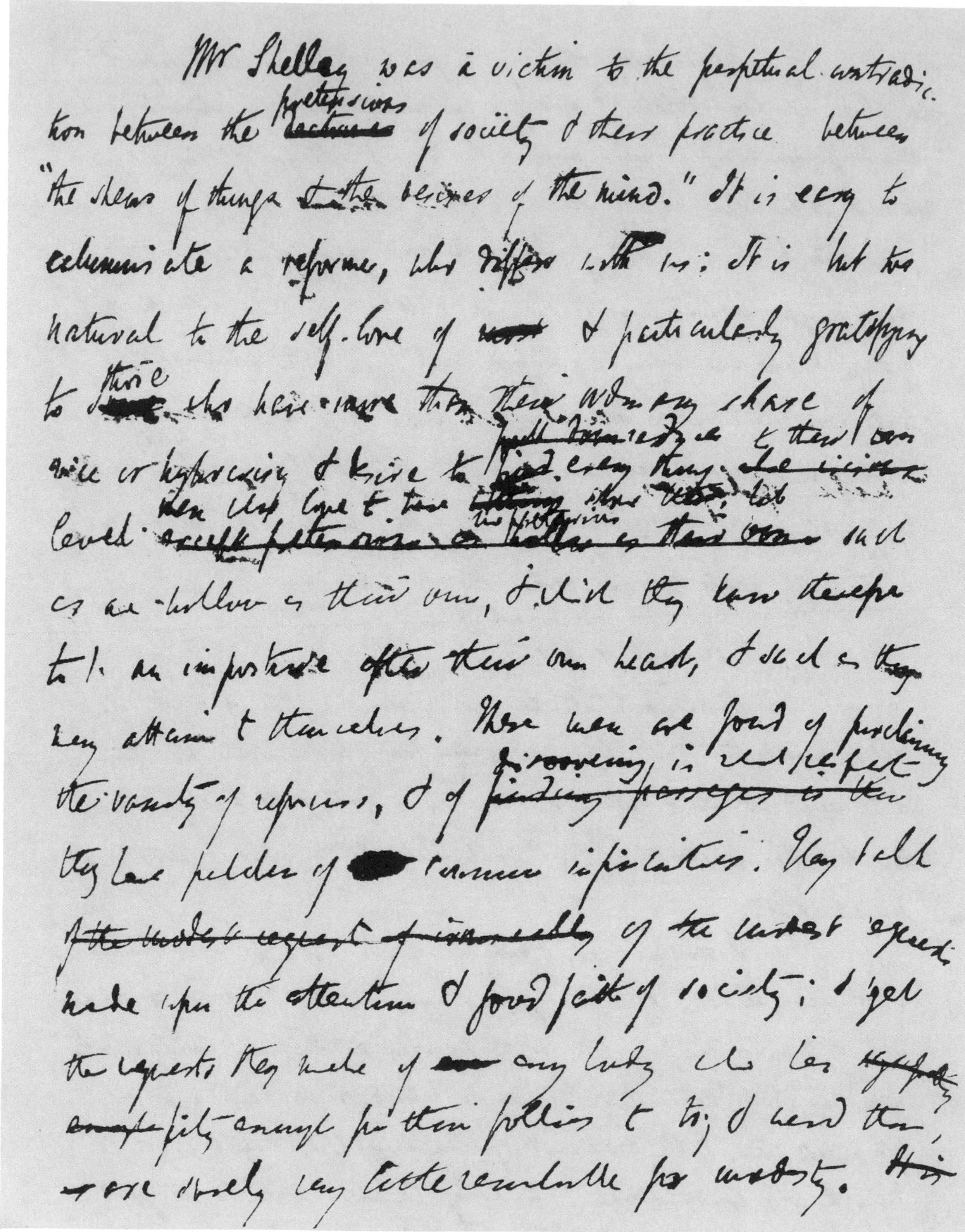
Mr Shelley was a victim to the perpetual contradiction between the pretensions of society & their practice between "the shews of things & the desires of the mind." It is easy to calumniate a reformer, who differs with us: it is but too natural to the self-love of & particularly gratifying to those who have ... any share of wit or hypocrisy & have to ... every thing ... level ... such as are hollow as their own, & which they know therefore to be an importance ... their own heads, & such as they may attain to themselves. These men are fond of proclaiming the vanity of reformers, & of discovering in what respect they have followers of ... common inferiorities. They talk of the ... expedients made upon the attention & good faith of society; & yet the requests they make of any body who has ... pity enough for their follies to try, & need them, have surely very little resemblance for modesty.

*Draft paragraph for the chapter on Shelley, mounted in a copy of* Lord Byron and Some of His Contemporaries *(828 .B996Bhu 1828 v. 1 copy 1, University of Iowa Libraries, Iowa City)*

Hunt's earliest familiar essays appeared in the *Reflector,* a magazine he edited during 1811 and 1812 primarily as a political magazine. In 1812 Hunt was convicted of slandering the Prince Regent as a fat "Adonis" of fifty in the 22 March 1812 issue of the *Examiner* and was sent to jail for two years (3 February 1813 - 2 February 1815). Surprisingly he was allowed to continue to edit the *Examiner* while he was in prison. Also he was able to have his family live with him, to paint the ceiling of his room with a blue sky and clouds and the walls with a rose trellis, and to bring in a pianoforte. Among those who visited him were Charles Lamb, Hazlitt, Thomas Moore, and George Gordon, Lord Byron, whom he met for the first time while in prison.

After Hunt's release from jail came the most exciting and productive years of his life. During this period he published his three best-known poems, most of which he had written in prison, "The Feast of the Poets" (1814), *The Descent of Liberty* (1815), and *The Story of Rimini* (1816). In 1815 Hunt met John Keats and renewed his acquaintance with Percy Bysshe Shelley, whom he had met briefly in 1811. He had close relationships with both during the next few years, until Shelley left for Italy for financial and health reasons in 1818 and Keats left for Rome because of his health in 1820.

Hunt published essays in the *Literary Pocket-Book,* which he edited from 1818 to 1822, and he reached his peak as a personal essayist while editing the *Indicator* during the years 1819 to 1821. Lamb thought so highly of the essays that he hailed the *Indicator* with a sonnet, and Hunt commented that his friends thought his *Indicator* essays were the best writing he had ever done. These essays are typical of the personal essays Hunt wrote over a period of about fifty years. They are always pleasant and frequently delightful; their topics are wide-ranging: activities from dancing to pig driving, real and imaginary people, everyday life, and places from Pisa to St. Paul's. But mostly he wrote about nature—hot days, cold days, rainy days, May days—and literature. His best essays combine close social observation with self-revelation. His persona tends to be less than courageous and not at all ambitious, but he is always friendly and optimistic and encourages the reader to experience life with him. In some of his essays Hunt introduces passages from his favorite authors, as in "Mists and Fogs" (31 November 1819) and "Spring Daisies" (19 April 1820). Sometimes he inserts a masterly short tale. In essays such as "On the Household Gods of the Ancients" (10 November 1819) he draws on antiquities. Hunt is often witty, as in "Far Countries" (8 December 1819), where he comments on the limited imagination of the French by saying, "the greatest height they go is in a balloon." One of his finest essays, "Coaches and Their Horses," extends over two issues of the *Indicator* (23 and 30 August 1820). As in his other treatments of such topics, he analyzes the various types of coaches and their attendant horses and then discusses the process of entering, riding in, and dismounting from a coach.

Shelley kept pressing Hunt to join him in Italy, but Hunt did not decide to go until September 1821. He finally arrived in Italy on 1 July 1822, and on 8 July, just a week later, Shelley was drowned in a sudden squall while returning home to Lerici in his sailboat after welcoming Hunt to Italy. Shelley had intended to support the Hunts until the magazine he, Hunt, and Byron planned was flourishing, but his death left Hunt stranded and at the mercy of Byron, who did not really care for Hunt and loathed his wife and children.

Hunt did what he could to establish the magazine they named the *Liberal.* With the help of Byron and some pieces Shelley had already written, the journal was begun. In the four published issues (1822-1823), Hunt wrote, besides a few poems, several essays including four "Letters from Abroad," describing with copious detail places he had seen and experiences he had had in Italy. Unfortunately for Hunt, though the magazine promised well and had a very satisfying sale of four thousand copies for the first number, Byron became interested in the Greek struggle for independence and left Italy in 1823. Without him the *Liberal* collapsed, but Hunt was forced to remain in Italy for two more years for want of enough money to return to England. Finally in 1825 publisher Henry Colburn advanced him the necessary money on a book to be written about Byron.

After his arrival in London on 14 October 1825, Hunt continued writing essays for the *New Monthly Magazine* through 1827 while he completed *Lord Byron and Some of His Contemporaries,* which came out in 1828. The book, which later became the basis for Hunt's *Autobiography* (1850), caused a storm of protest. After dying in 1824 in the cause of Greek freedom, Byron was a national celebrity, and the public resented what it perceived to be a scathing attack. Hunt did write

*Hunt in 1837 (unfinished portrait by Samuel Lawrence; from Luther A. Brewer,* My Leigh Hunt Library, *1932)*

some harsh things, but he was disgusted by the completely uncritical adulation of someone whom he knew intimately to be no saint. Also, Colburn may have convinced him that a more sensational book would sell better. Moreover, there were those who did not doubt the truth of the presentation but considered it in poor taste for Hunt to say, among other things, that Byron was "ill-tempered," "ill-educated," and "ungenerous" after he had generously taken Hunt in when Hunt was desperate.

The 1830s were probably the time of Hunt's lowest reputation and his greatest financial difficulty. He became a hack writer just to keep alive and wrote numerous essays for various magazines. He also started journal after journal, but none of them was successful. In 1828, for example, he started a new magazine, the *Companion,* which lasted less than seven months. He started another magazine, the *Chat of the Week,* in 1830, but in less than three months he changed its name to the *Tatler.* The *Tatler* lasted only from 4 September 1830 to 31 March 1832. Hunt demonstrated his endurance and fertile invention by writing almost every word of its daily four folio pages of essays and criticism during its nineteen-month existence under his editorship. He introduced perhaps his best magazine during the years 1834-1835; yet *Leigh Hunt's London Journal* lasted less than two years because it was apparently too refined for ordinary tastes. Hunt also edited the *Monthly Repository* during eleven months of 1837 and 1838. The magazine was given to him in the hope that he could prevent it from failing, but he was unable to rescue it even with contributions from such writers as Thomas Carlyle, Robert Browning, and Walter Savage Landor.

In 1832 Hunt published his only novel, *Sir*

Chapter the First

Lauder. Dr Franklin.

The author's birth & family. The Indians attempt to carry off one of his brothers. American Revolution. Perilous situation of his father. He flies to England. Noble conduct of his mother, who follows him. Anecdote of Sheridan's father. A West-Indian out of his sphere. Kinsmen and early acquaintances. A lively old lady of the last century. Wilkes & the author's father. Infant church-militant

An author has so many good reasons now-a-days for writing his life, provided a bookseller offers them, that I am luckily relieved from the necessity of making the usual apologetical exordium; the reader of which never believes it, and the writer not often.

The lives of men of letters are said to be less interesting than those of other men, because they are passed in the closet. This is a common-place, that may fairly be laid on the shelf with other common-places upon writing; such as, that authors are always poor; that they cannot write well when they are in trouble &c. An author sees as many adventures as most people, professed adventurers excepted. He does not live more in his closet, than many stirring men do in theirs; & if he did, & his authorship is at all worth listening to, he can raise more interest out of the little he has to tell, by reason of the very sensibility that has made him an author. Besides, there is hardly a human being in existence, whose life would not be worth hearing, if he would tell it as plainly & truly. I claim an interest for my own, much more on this account than on any other. For as an author, I know how many surpass me; but as a man, I have partaken pretty deeply of the pains & the pleasures, the strength & the weaknesses of my nature, & I will yield to nobody in the sincerity with which I speak of them. To tell every thing, a man in the present state of society has no right; but

*Page from a draft for* The Autobiography of Leigh Hunt *(Ms H94au2, University of Iowa Libraries, Iowa City)*

*Ralph Esher,* a historical novel set in the time of Charles II. While receiving mixed reviews, it went through three editions in four years. In a further desperate attempt to relieve his poverty, Hunt hit on the scheme of collecting in book form essays published previously in periodicals. Thus in 1834 he published *The Indicator and the Companion,* a selection of his essays from his two periodicals of those names. The result was sufficiently satisfactory that the gambit was repeated several more times. In 1840 Hunt published *The Seer,* a collection of his essays published previously in various of his periodicals, principally *Leigh Hunt's London Journal.* It was followed in 1841 by *Essays by Leigh Hunt: The Indicator, The Seer,* a selection from that journal and volume. In 1847 appeared *Men, Women, and Books,* with essays by Hunt from magazines such as the *Edinburgh Review, Westminster Review,* and *New Monthly Magazine.* This collection was followed by two more in the next year: *A Jar of Honey from Mount Hybla,* with essays from *Ainsworth's Magazine,* and *The Town: Its Memorable Characters and Events,* with essays from *Leigh Hunt's London Journal. The Old Court Suburb,* published in 1855, includes essays concerning Kensington taken in part from *Household Words* (August 1853 - February 1854).

Hunt's fortunes seemed to be changing when, in February 1840, his first play, *A Legend of Florence,* was produced to considerable acclaim. Queen Victoria attended twice and later requested a command performance at Windsor Castle. Unfortunately, the leading lady, Ellen Tree, had to withdraw from the production because of previous commitments, so the play, which promised a long run, ran only a few days. It was not until 1844 that Hunt's deepest poverty ended; on the death of Shelley's father Hunt was awarded £120 annually. In 1822 Shelley had promised Hunt a legacy of £2,000, but family financial reverses had decreased the amount. In 1847 Hunt's basic needs were finally satisfied with a Civil List Pension of £200 annually for his services to literature. He still was not well off, but he was finally in little danger of debtor's prison.

Hunt's *Imagination and Fancy* (1844), an anthology of works by English poets, contains, besides Hunt's critical comments on the poets, a critical essay expressing Hunt's philosophy of poetry. "What is Poetry" is probably Hunt's best work of theoretical criticism.

Perhaps Hunt's most significant prose was his *Autobiography,* published in 1850 with a revised edition appearing in 1860. Some critics have called it the best autobiography of the century. The early parts are based largely on his *Lord Byron and Some of His Contemporaries,* but the ascerbity of the earlier volume is gone. The most interesting part concerns his association with the young Romantic poets Keats and Shelley. There is little about Hunt's later life, but the volume is filled with portraits of ordinary as well as famous people such as Byron, Charles Lamb, Thomas Carlyle, Samuel Taylor Coleridge, and Wordsworth. The work is graceful and interesting, and Hunt comes through as cheerful, impulsive, and good-natured.

By the last decade of his life Hunt's reputation had changed from reforming editor of the *Examiner* to gentle essayist, poet, and critic. One last journal, called *Leigh Hunt's Journal,* was published in 1850, but it lasted fewer than four months. The young publisher had unrealistic ideas about financing a publication and ceased publication when he did not start making money immediately.

In 1852 Hunt was devastated by the death of his youngest son, Vincent, after a long illness with tuberculosis. As a kind of consolation, Hunt revised *Christianism* (1832) and published it in 1853 as *The Religion of the Heart,* a distillation of his liberal religious philosophy. While still in mourning, Hunt was hurt further by his friend Charles Dickens, who satirized him as Skimpole in *Bleak House* (1853). Hunt, however, accepted Dickens's explanation that the satire was unintentional, and the affair ended amicably.

Hunt's American reputation hit its apex during the 1850s with the publication in America of *The Works of Leigh Hunt* (1854), followed by a second edition in 1856 and *The Poetical Works of Leigh Hunt* in 1857. Essays in Dickens's *Household Words* and the *National Magazine* in 1857, *Fraser's Magazine* in 1858, and the *Spectator* in 1859 concluded Hunt's career as a prose writer. Hunt died on 28 August 1859 in Putney, where he had gone on 9 August for his health.

Hunt's essays continue to be an influence on magazine journalists. Though they may be uneven and lack depth and though they may not have Lamb's humor and pathos, many are delightful and still may be enjoyed. It is unfortunate for Hunt that the essay is held in such low regard today. If this form were more highly valued, Hunt too would be more highly valued.

**Letters:**

*The Correspondence of Leigh Hunt,* 2 volumes, edited by Thornton Hunt (London: Smith, Elder, 1862);

*My Leigh Hunt Library: The Holograph Letters,* edited by Luther A. Brewer (Iowa City: University of Iowa Press, 1938);

Charles Richard Sanders, "The Correspondence and Friendship of Thomas Carlyle and Leigh Hunt," *Bulletin of the John Rylands Library,* 45 (March 1963): 439-485; 46 (September 1963): 179-216;

David R. Cheney, *The Correspondence of Leigh Hunt and Charles Ollier in the Winter of 1853-54* (London: Keats-Shelley Memorial Association, 1976).

**Bibliographies:**

Alexander Ireland, *List of the Writings of William Hazlitt and Leigh Hunt* (London: John Russell Smith, 1868);

Alexander Mitchell, "A Bibliography of the Writings of Hunt," *Bookman's Journal,* 15 (1927): 3-19;

Luther A. Brewer, *My Leigh Hunt Library* (Cedar Rapids, Iowa: Privately printed by the Torch Press, 1932);

Louis Landré, *Leigh Hunt (1784-1859): Contribution à l'histoire du romantisme anglais,* 2 volumes (Paris: Société d'Edition "Les Belles Lettres," 1936), II: 483-595;

David Bonnell Green and Edwin Graves Wilson, *Keats, Shelley, Byron, Hunt, and Their Circles: A Bibliography* (Lincoln: University of Nebraska Press, 1964);

Carolyn Washburn Houtchens and Lawrence Huston Houtchens, *The English Romantic Poets and Essayists: A Review of Research and Criticism,* revised edition (New York: Published for the Modern Language Association of America by New York University Press, 1966), pp. 255-288;

O. M. Brack and D. H. Stefanson, *A Catalogue of the Leigh Hunt Manuscripts in the University of Iowa Libraries* (Iowa City: Friends of the University of Iowa Libraries, 1973);

Robert A. Hartley, ed., *Keats, Shelley, Byron, Hunt, and Their Circles. A Bibliography: July 1, 1962-December 31, 1974* (Lincoln: University of Nebraska Press, 1978);

Timothy J. Lulofs and Hans Ostrom, *Leigh Hunt: a Reference Guide* (Boston: G. K. Hall, 1985);

John L. Waltman and Gerald G. McDaniel, *Leigh Hunt: a Comprehensive Bibliography* (New York & London: Garland, 1985).

**Biographies:**

Charles and Mary Cowden Clarke, *Recollections of Writers* (London: Sampson, Low, Marston, Searle & Rivington, 1878), pp. 190-272;

Cosmo Monkhouse, *Life of Leigh Hunt* (London: Walter Scott, 1893);

Edmund Blunden, *Leigh Hunt: a Biography* (London: Cobden-Sanderson, 1930);

Louis Landré, *Leigh Hunt (1784-1859): Contribution à l'histoire du romantisme anglais,* volume 1 (Paris: Société d'Edition "Les Belles Lettres," 1936);

Molly Tatchell, *Leigh Hunt and His Family in Hammersmith* (London: Hammersmith Local History Group, 1969);

Richard Russell, *Leigh Hunt and Some of His Contemporaries* (London: C. J. Creed, 1984);

Ann Blainey, *Immortal Boy: a Portrait of Leigh Hunt* (London & Sydney: Croom Helm, 1985).

**References:**

H. Allingham and D. Radford, eds., *William Allingham: A Diary* (London: Macmillan, 1907);

William Baker, "Leigh Hunt, George Henry Lewes and Henry Hallam's *Introduction to the Literature of Europe,*" *Studies in Bibliography,* 32 (1979): 252-273;

Ernest Bernbaum, *Guide Through the Romantic Movement,* revised and enlarged edition (New York: Ronald Press, 1949);

Edmund Blunden, *Leigh Hunt's "Examiner" Examined* (London: Cobden-Sanderson, 1928);

Kenneth Neill Cameron, "Leigh Hunt (19 October 1784-28 August 1859)," in *Romantic Rebels: Essays on Shelley and His Circle,* edited by Cameron (Cambridge, Mass.: Harvard University Press, 1973), pp. 146-160;

David R. Cheney, "Leigh Hunt Sued for Debt by a Friend," *Books at Iowa,* 27 (November 1977): 30-56;

Paul M. Clogan, "Chaucer and Leigh Hunt," *Medievalia et Humanistica,* new series 9 (1979): 163-174;

Donald H. Ericksen, "Harold Skimpole: Dickens and the Early 'Art for Art's Sake' Movement," *Journal of English and Germanic Philology,* 72 (January 1973): 48-59;

Theodore Fenner, "Ballet in Early Nineteenth

*Hunt circa 1850 (engraving by J. C. Armytage, after a portrait by W. F. Williams)*

Century London as Seen by Leigh Hunt and Henry Robertson," *Dance Chronicle,* 1 (1977): 75-95;

Fenner, *Leigh Hunt and Opera Criticism: The "Examiner" Years (1808-1821)* (Lawrence: University Press of Kansas, 1972);

Walt Fisher, "Leigh Hunt as Friend and Critic of Keats: 1816-1859," *Lock Haven Review,* no. 5 (1963): 27-42;

Stephen F. Fogle, "Leigh Hunt and the End of Romantic Criticism," in *Some British Romantics: A Collection of Essays,* edited by James V. Logan, John E. Jordan, and Northrop Frye (Columbus: Ohio State University Press, 1966), pp. 119-139;

William Hazlitt, *The Spirit of the Age* (London: Henry Colburn, 1825);

R. H. Horne, *A New Spirit of the Age* (London: Smith, Elder, 1844);

[Thornton L. Hunt], "A Man of Letters of the Last Generation," *Cornhill Magazine,* 1 (January 1860): 85-95;

Ian Jack, *English Literature 1815-1832* (Oxford: Oxford University Press, 1963);

Reginald Brimley Johnson, *Leigh Hunt* (London: Swan Sonnenschein, 1896);

Johnson, ed., *Shelley-Leigh Hunt: How Friendship Made History: and Extended the Bounds of Human Freedom and Thought* (London: Ingpen & Grant, 1928);

Kenneth E. Kendall, *Leigh Hunt's "Reflector"* (The Hague: Mouton, 1971);

Louis Landré, *Leigh Hunt (1784-1859): Contribution à l'histoire du romantisme anglais,* 2 volumes (Paris: Société d'Edition "Les Belles-Lettres," 1936);

Marie Hamilton Law, *The English Familiar Essay in the Early Nineteenth Century: The Elements, Old and New, Which Went into Its Making as Exemplified in the Writings of Hunt, Hazlitt, and Lamb* (Philadelphia: University of Pennsylvania Press, 1934);

William Maginn, "Leigh Hunt," in *The Maclise Portrait Gallery of "Illustrious Literary Characters," With Memoirs,* edited by William Bates (Lon-

don: Chatto & Windus, 1883), pp. 242-256;
William Marshall, *Byron, Shelley, Hunt, and "The Liberal"* (Philadelphia: University of Pennsylvania Press, 1960);
Barnette Miller, *Leigh Hunt's Relations with Byron, Shelley, and Keats* (New York: Columbia University Press, 1910);
Bryan Waller Proctor, *An Autobiographical Fragment and Biographical Notes* (Boston: Roberts Brothers, 1877);
H. E. Rollins, *The Keats Circle: Letters and Papers and More Letters and Poems of the Keats Circle,* 2 volumes (Cambridge, Mass.: Harvard University Press, 1948);
David H. Stam, "Leigh Hunt and *The True Sun:* A List of Reviews, August 1833 to February 1834," *Bulletin of the New York Public Library,* 77 (Summer 1974): 436-453;
George Dumas Stout, "Leigh Hunt's Money Troubles: Some New Light," *Washington University Studies,* 12 (April 1925): 221-232;
James R. Thompson, *Leigh Hunt* (Boston: Twayne, 1977);
Clarence Dewitt Thorpe, "An Essay in Evaluation: Leigh Hunt As Man of Letters," in *Leigh Hunt's Literary Criticism,* edited by Lawrence Huston Houtchens and Carolyn Washburn Houtchens (New York: Columbia University Press, 1956), pp. 3-73;
Jack Welch, "The Leigh Hunt-William Moxon Dispute of 1836," *West Virginia University Philological Papers,* 18 (September 1971): 30-41;
Stanley Wells, "Shakespeare in Leigh Hunt's Theatre Criticism," *Essays and Studies,* 33 (1980): 119-138;
Carl R. Woodring, "Leigh Hunt as Political Essayist," in *Leigh Hunt's Political and Occasional Essays,* edited by Lawrence Huston Houtchens and Carolyn Washburn Houtchens (New York: Columbia University Press, 1962), pp. 3-71.

**Papers:**

Hunt materials are scattered around the world. The largest collection of correspondence and manuscripts is in the Luther A. Brewer Collection, University of Iowa Libraries. Among other important collections are those at the British Library, the University of Leeds Library, the Carl H. Pforzheimer Library, the Berg Collection of the New York Public Library, the Houghton Library at Harvard University, and the Henry E. Huntington Library and Art Gallery.

# John Keats

*(31 October 1795 - 23 February 1821)*

James Kissane
*Grinnell College*

See also the Keats entry in *DLB 96: English Romantic Poets, 1789-1832*.

BOOKS: *Poems* (London: Printed for C. & J. Ollier, 1817);

*Endymion: A Poetic Romance* (London: Printed for Taylor & Hessey, 1818);

*Lamia, Isabella, The Eve of St. Agnes, and Other Poems* (London: Printed for Taylor & Hessey, 1820).

**Collections:** *The Poetical Works of Coleridge, Shelley, and Keats* (Paris: A. & W. Galignani, 1829; Philadelphia: Stereotyped by J. Howe, 1831);

*Life, Letters, and Literary Remains of John Keats*, edited by Richard Monckton Milnes, Lord Houghton (London: Moxon, 1848; Philadelphia: Putnam, 1848);

*The Poetical Works and Other Writings of John Keats*, 4 volumes, edited by Harry Buxton Forman (London: Reeves & Turner, 1883);

*The Poems of John Keats*, edited by Miriam Allott (Harlow, U.K.: Longman, 1970; New York: Norton, 1970);

*The Poems of John Keats*, edited by Jack Stillinger (Cambridge, Mass.: Belknap Press of Harvard University Press, 1978).

It is of course as a poet of major stature that John Keats belongs among the literary figures of English Romanticism; but his importance as a prose writer is hardly less evident. That is so almost entirely on the strength of his remarkable letters, some 240 of which have been preserved either in the author's hand or as transcriptions from originals no longer extant. Keats penned his letters hastily; they represent in most cases his spontaneous and passing thoughts on life, poetry, and his personal affairs and affections expressed to close friends, fellow artists of his acquaintance, members of his family, and the young woman with whom he was in love near the end of his short and ill-starred life. None of these letters was written with any eye to that eventual fame Keats so ardently wished for his poems; yet to many readers they constitute an indispensable human accompaniment to and commentary upon the poetry itself. One of his biographers, Robert Gittings, asserts that through his letters Keats became a great writer of prose even before he had achieved true greatness as a poet; yet it was many years after Keats's death before any of these letters was published and longer still before their extraordinary value, to an understanding of both Keats's art and his rich and appealing personality, was adequately appreciated. Certainly it is because of his letters that we have a more exact and vivid view of John Keats than of any other Romantic poet (even George Gordon, Lord Byron). Indeed, there must be few historical figures of any sort who have left so complete and so revealing a glimpse into their genius and so compelling a record of their personalities and the texture of their daily lives as Keats has bequeathed us through his letters. Moving and engrossing in their own right, they are the unintended but essential complement to Keats's poetry.

John Keats was born in London on 31 October 1795, the eldest of five children (one of whom died in infancy) born to Thomas and Frances Jennings Keats. When Keats was eight his father, a stable keeper, died after a fall from his horse; when the future poet was fourteen, his mother, after an evidently unsuccessful remarriage, died of tuberculosis. Both John and George (1797-1841) and later their younger brother Tom (1799-1818) had been sent to John Clarke's school at Enfield, where Keats benefited from the guidance, encouragement, and friendship of his teacher, Charles Cowden Clarke, son of the headmaster and a person of strong literary interests and radical political sympathies. When Keats left the Clarkes' school in the summer of 1811 to enter an apprenticeship with an Edmonton surgeon and apothecary named Thomas Hammond, he had already formed a keen taste for poetry, classical mythology, and

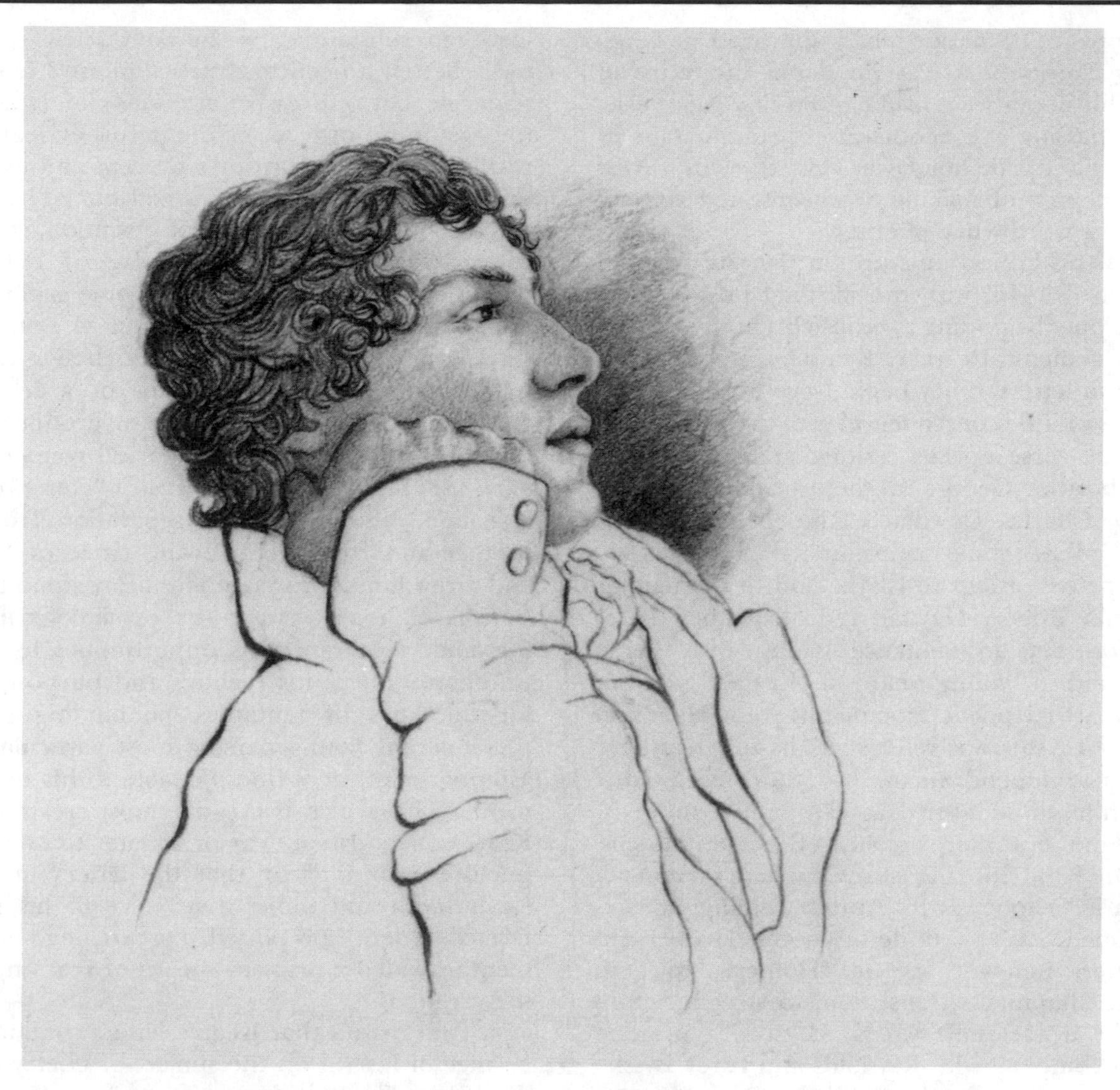

*John Keats, summer 1819 (drawing by Charles Brown; National Portrait Gallery, London)*

tales of history and romance. Existing evidence, however, suggests that John Keats was an outgoing, high-spirited, and even somewhat pugnacious schoolboy rather than a dreamy or moody one. Those who recorded their impressions of Keats during this period and throughout his life were more struck by his stalwart bearing than his small stature. (Full grown he stood less than one inch over five feet tall.) However it was made, the vocational decision resulting in Keats's medical apprenticeship and his subsequent training at Guy's Hospital in south London (which began in October of 1815) was certainly no unreasonable plan, both from the standpoint of Keats's social and economic circumstances and in terms of his own nature. The details of Keats's inheritance, left in trust to him at the death of his maternal grandmother, Alice Jennings, in 1814, are somewhat murky; but it seems clear that in light of Keats's financial expectations, not a life of leisure but certainly a comfortably established profession was an entirely practical objective for him. Moreover, his studies at Guy's and his work as a "dresser" in the hospital wards reflected Keats's aptitude and purposefulness, even as the lure of poetry and the society of literary people increasingly attracted him. On 25 July 1816 Keats passed the licensing examination at Apothecaries' Hall, making him eligible (when he reached the legal age of twenty-one at the end of October) to practice as an apothecary-surgeon. However, for a couple of years he had been writing poems. During his year at Guy's Hospital a friendship with another aspiring poet, George Felton Mathew, encouraged and intensified this growing interest; and in May of 1816 Keats's first published poem, the sonnet "O Solitude," had appeared in Leigh Hunt's *Examiner*. It was no doubt indicative of where his hopes were leading him that Keats celebrated passing the apothecaries' examination by going on a seaside holiday at Margate with the explicit purpose of making a concentrated attempt at writing worthwhile poetry.

At this critical juncture, in the late summer and fall of 1816, with the startling possibility of being a poet beginning to eclipse his newly won access to a medical career, Keats began to record his life in letters. They begin (save for a few earlier ones of little consequence) with two rather self-conscious verse epistles written at Margate, one to his brother George in August and one to his mentor Charles Cowden Clarke in September. Then follow some conventional and slightly stilted prose jottings to Clarke and to the painter Benjamin Robert Haydon (20 November 1816) whose recent acquaintance (along with Leigh Hunt and a young man of Keats's age but greater actual poetic attainment, John Hamilton Reynolds) Keats was relishing. These letters have little to commend them, but they mark what Keats himself identified as "an Era in my existence," the "era" more notably reflected in the sonnet "On First Looking into Chapman's Homer," written in October 1816. At this seemingly propitious time Keats's poetic destiny seemed to be rushing upon him—or, as did Homer's epics in George Chapman's translation, to stretch before him like a vast new world. Hunt was praising him, in company with Reynolds and Percy Bysshe Shelley, in a critical essay on "Young Poets" (*Examiner*, 1 December 1816) and sending his Chapman sonnet to William Wordsworth for a confirming judgment. Haydon was including Keats's intent profile in one of his massive canvases, *Christ's Entry into Jerusalem* (1820), and capturing those same features in a life mask. That winter there were sonnet-writing contests with Hunt, whose *Examiner* printed more of Keats's poems, dinners with Shelley and Reynolds, and, later on, an inspiring visit with Haydon to those relics of masterful Greek sculpture known as the Elgin Marbles. The culmination of these initiatory adventures was the appearance of Keats's *Poems* on 3 March 1817, a slender collection of thirty-one poems published by Charles and James Ollier and dedicated to Leigh Hunt.

Gratifying to a twenty-one-year-old as was this rapid introduction to a world of the arts and of literary achievement, Keats's accomplishments as a poet by the spring of 1817 were more promising than substantial, as he well knew. Instinctively he felt a need to distance himself from the flattering but oppressive attentions of Hunt and to enact in his own terms the heroic endeavors to which the painter Haydon's precept and example somewhat grandiloquently urged him. The result was a poetic project, a "trial of invention," that occupied Keats from the late spring of 1817 into the following year (counting the time spent in revising and copying), took him out of London to the Isle of Wight, back to Margate, then to Canterbury, on to the college rooms of a friend at Oxford (Benjamin Bailey), and produced the four-thousand-line erotic/allegorical romance *Endymion* (1818). This "test" of Keats's "Powers of Imagination" also entailed a separation from his brother and from his growing circle of friends and threw him more than heretofore upon the resources of letter writing—its psychological comfort and reassurance, its opportunities for fruitful expression of his feelings and purposes, and for the kind of tentative, nonbinding self-exploration any young person, most particularly an aspiring artist, may find valuable to his development. "That which is creative must create itself," Keats would write a year or so later to one of his publishers. It is clear that the letters in which Keats more and more gave voice to his many-faceted, ardent, and poised yet searching temperament provided a primary means of realizing such self-creation.

One reason that Keats's letters contain such a range of insight on the subject of poetry is that they were directed at people to whom Keats had different things to say. Naturally, during his protracted struggles with *Endymion*, that poem was never far from his mind; but in discussing it and related matters Keats had in his various correspondents a variety of perspectives and experience to which he could appeal, and he made the most of that fact. That variety included his brothers' familial pride and affectionate loyalty, the practical understanding of more-established artists such as Hunt and Haydon, the respect of the articulate and congenial Reynolds and his playful sisters, the intellectual bent of the morally serious and philosophic Benjamin Bailey, and the admiring receptivity of Keats's young sister, Fanny. As the year 1817 drew to a close and the draft of *Endymion* neared completion, Keats's reflections on the poetic character and the nature of creativity achieve moments of striking penetration and felicity. In a notable letter to Bailey of 22 November, Keats turns his thoughts to "Genius and the

*Silhouettes of Georgiana and George Keats, circa 1830 (from Robert Gittings,* John Keats, *1968)*

*Tom Keats (sketch by Joseph Severn; Keats-Shelley Memorial House, Rome) and Fanny Keats in her forties (Keats House, Hampstead)*

*Life mask of Keats made by Benjamin Robert Haydon on 14 December 1816 (from the cast at Keats House, Hampstead; photograph copyright Christopher Oxford)*

Heart" and declares his faith in "the authenticity of the Imagination." In words that look ahead to the concluding utterance in the "Ode on a Grecian Urn" (written in May 1819) Keats asserts that "What the imagination seizes as Beauty must be truth—whether it existed before or not." He goes on to compare the imagination to Adam's dream of Eve, which in John Milton's *Paradise Lost* (1667) prefigured the reality of the living woman. These essentially aesthetic reflections lead Keats into a more religious realm of speculation, to a sketchy but provocative "conviction that Imagination and its empyreal reflection is the same as human Life and its spiritual repetition." "We shall enjoy ourselves here after by what we call happiness on Earth repeated in a finer tone." It is in the context of this "favorite speculation" that Keats's accompanying exclamation "O for a Life of Sensations rather than of Thoughts" should be understood, not as the expression of a mindless hedonism which some Victorian readers of this letter took it to be. Indeed, there is in this same letter a passage of moving, almost stoic, detachment and characteristic selflessness. "I scarcely remember counting upon any Happiness," Keats reveals to Bailey. "I look not for it in the present hour—nothing startles me beyond the Moment. The setting sun will always set me to rights—or if a Sparrow come before my Window I take part in its existence and pick about the Gravel." He has sounded in this one letter themes that inform some of his finest poetry: the validating power of imaginatively intense perception; the capacity of a truly creative nature to participate sympathetically or empathically in existences beyond the borders of the ordinary self.

On 21 December Keats wrote from Hampstead (north of London, where he had made his home with George and Tom) to his brothers, who were visiting in Devonshire. He mentions having seen a painting by Benjamin West and finding it lacking in the quality William Hazlitt, whom Keats was then reading, would call "gusto" (a term Keats himself later borrowed). "It is a wonderful picture . . . ; But there is nothing to be intense upon; no woman one feels mad to kiss. . . . the excellence of every Art is its intensity, capable of making all disagreeables evaporate, from their being in close relationship with Beauty & Truth." Keats appears to have found such a quality in the acting of Edmund Kean, whose performances he was reviewing for the *Champion*, and his reflections on this distinctive trait of quickening and encompassing nonassertiveness led him then to coin a term that is one of his most distinctive contributions to aesthetic discourse: *negative capability*. It is a concept Keats identifies as that "quality" belonging to "a Man of Achievement especially in Literature & which Shakespeare possessed so enormously." This *negative capability* is present, Keats explains, "when man is capable of being in uncertainties, Mysteries, doubts, without any irritable reaching after fact & reason." Perhaps Keats himself provided the best gloss on this term when he wrote, in a marginal jotting on a passage in *Paradise Lost*, of "the intense pleasure of not knowing[,] a sense of independence, of power, from the fancy's creating a world of its own by the sense of probabilities."

Keats spent the winter and spring (1818) following the completion of *Endymion* in preparing it for the press, attending the theater, resuming a social life that included evenings in the company of Wordsworth and Charles Lamb as well as with his more intimate circle of friends, writing to his brothers in Devonshire, hearing Hazlitt lecture on the English poets, deepening his love of Shakespeare, and pondering his next major attempt in poetry. In early March, in order that George could return to London, Keats joined his ailing brother Tom in Teignmouth, Devonshire. Before he returned to Hampstead in early May, *Endymion* had been published, and Keats had finished *Isabella* (1820), his poem based on a tale from Giovanni Boccaccio's *Decameron* (1353).

The most considerable of Keats's few efforts in prose other than letters belong to this period and should be briefly mentioned. (Students of Keats should also know of his notes and marginalia on Shakespeare, on Milton's *Paradise Lost*, and on Robert Burton's *Anatomy of Melancholy*, 1621.) As a stand-in for his friend Reynolds, who was the regular dramatic critic for the *Champion*, Keats wrote three reviews in December of 1817. One of these dealt with Edmund Kean as a Shakespearean actor (21 December) and gave Keats an opportunity to air his admiration for Kean's work in a manner that consciously and effectively captures much of Hazlitt's flair as a critic. The other two (4 January 1818) are understandably less congenial reactions to an undistinguished melodrama called "Retribution" and to a typical Christmas pantomime. The two prefaces Keats wrote to *Endymion* are a fascinating instance of contrasting attitudes toward both the poet's own work and its prospective public. In neither preface does Keats make high claims for *Endymion*, but in the original he effects a kind of curt but stilted offhandedness, a stance of almost haughty contempt that awkwardly masks his anxiousness and vulnerability: "I have written to please myself and in hopes to please others, and for love of fame; if I neither please myself, nor others nor get fame, of what consequence is Phraseology?" Reynolds and his publishers persuaded Keats this would not do, and his second effort, even shorter, strikes an equable note of candid self-assessment free of both prickliness and false modesty. "There is not a fiercer hell than the failure in a great object," Keats wrote, anticipating how he would later insist that even his unkindest critics were hardly as severe with his poem's genuine faults as he was himself. There is a characteristic mixture of wistfulness and magnanimity in this preface, with its perceptive remarks contrasting the healthy imagination of both a boy and a mature man with the "mawkishness" of the "soul in ferment" that endures the "space of life between."

Keats would think yet more deeply on the stages that make up mortal existence, in the individual but also in the collective sense. In a long letter to Reynolds of 3 May 1818 he sought to "put down a simile of human life as far as I now perceive it." As he developed his simile of a "Mansion of Many Apartments," with the "thoughtless Chamber" of infancy opening on to a "Chamber of Maiden-Thought," thence into those dark passages of tragic life he felt himself beginning to ex-

*Some of Keats's friends: (top) Charles Cowden Clarke (portrait by an unknown artist; National Portrait Gallery, London), Charles Brown in 1828 (bust by Andrew Wilson; Keats House, Hampstead); and (bottom) Charles and Maria Dilke (portraits by unknown artists; from Robert Gittings,* John Keats, *1968)*

plore, Keats recognized the resemblance of his conception to that in Wordsworth's great poem "Tintern Abbey," with its sense of "the burden of the Mystery." Keats had been developing for Reynolds some of his notions about Wordsworth's genius in contrast to Milton's, and despite his reservations about Wordsworth—crucially articulated in a letter to Reynolds three months earlier (3 February), in which he contrasts Wordsworth's modern egotism with Shakespeare's unobtrusiveness—Keats concluded that Wordsworth, though surely no more gifted than Milton, thought more deeply into the human heart. For all his attraction to the older poets and his considerable antipathy to a modern world shorn of heroism and romance, Keats attributed Wordsworth's superiority to "the general and gregarious advance of intellect"—the historical process by which older forms of understanding give way to newer, more enlightened ones.

Such ideas found their way into Keats's next major poetic undertaking, *Hyperion*, his imitation of and challenge to Miltonic epic. The second preface to *Endymion* looks ahead to another reworking of "the beautiful mythology of Greece." It was partly with a view to collecting scenic impressions of suitable grandeur for this new poem that Keats decided to accompany his friend Charles Armitage Brown on a walking tour of the Lake District and Scotland during the summer of 1818. The trip was also a poetic pilgrimage to the haunts of Wordsworth and of Robert Burns, and it gave Keats a chance to see his brother George and his bride, Georgiana Wylie, off on their voyage from Liverpool to America, where George hoped to improve his fortunes. Keats's letters during the nearly two months of this northern journey form a travelogue, punctuated with the poems he attempted under the inspiration of literary landmarks and Highland scenery, out of whimsy, or in spite of fatigue. Keats's hopes for this trip were not perfectly realized. The weather was bad, and he returned early with a sore throat; the poetry he wrote was far from his best, and the travel was more physically exhausting than spiritually stimulating. The most striking touches in the resulting letters are not especially picturesque. He describes for his brother Tom the revolting yet fascinating grossness of a hideous Irish crone, whom he calls "the Duchess of Dunghill." "What a thing would be a history of her life and sensations," he suddenly reflects (9 July). His meditations on Robert Burns are not entirely the conventionally sentimental ones: "he talked with Bitches—he drank with Blackguards, he was miserable" (to Reynolds, 13 July).

Returning home to Hampstead in mid August, Keats encountered two troubling and spirit-testing matters: his brother Tom's tubercular condition had become much worse, and the critical reviews of *Endymion* Keats soon saw were headed by the savage and personally demeaning attacks in *Blackwood's* (August) and the *Quarterly Review* (April). Yet the surprising truth is that Keats then entered upon a year of astonishing productivity, perhaps the most concentrated period of supreme creativity any English poet has known. His letters, especially one to his friend and neighbor Charles Dilke (20, 21 September 1818), show Keats facing courageously the burden and anguish of nursing Tom in his illness, feeling "the hateful siege of contraries" between his duty to his brother and the demands of his new poem. *Hyperion* was a "feverous relief " from Tom's "voice and feebleness." "His identity presses upon me so all day that . . . I am obliged to write, and plunge into abstract images to ease myself of his countenance. . . . if I think of fame of poetry it seems a crime to me, and yet I must do so or suffer." As for the devastating reviews of *Endymion*, Keats's friends rallied in defense and support; and it is in reassuring them of his own staunchness that Keats's letters exhibit his character in its finest light, especially—and paradoxically—in his assertion to Richard Woodhouse on 27 October that a poet of his sort is *without* "character." "As to the poetical Character itself . . . it is not itself—it has no self. . . . A Poet is the most unpoetical thing in existence; because he has no Identity."

Tom Keats died on 1 December 1818, and *Hyperion* remained unfinished. Keats's sorrow and bereavement were intensified by his separation from George and his wife, Georgiana, for whom John Keats had an affectionate kindred feeling. However, from the fall of 1818 until George's brief return home more than a year later (followed almost immediately by the collapse of Keats's health that reduced and redirected his letter writing) Keats produced a wonderful series of long journal-like letters for his brother and sister-in-law in Kentucky. These contain an invaluable record of the poet's life and the contours of his thought during the most fruitful phase of his career. Another kind of compensation for Tom's loss entered Keats's life at about this time. During the previous summer his friend Brown had rented his half of a double house that he shared with Charles and Maria Dilke to the

*Fanny Brawne, 1833 (Collection of Robert Goodsell)*

Brawnes, a widow and her children who had continued to visit the Dilkes after Brown returned home. After Tom's death, Keats went to live with Brown in this house in Wentworth Place, Hampstead. He became acquainted with the Brawnes and attached to the eighteen-year-old daughter, Fanny. About Christmas time of 1818, almost in spite of himself, he fell helplessly in love with her.

We have no epistolary record of the first stages of this love affair. It is unfortunate that none of Fanny Brawne's letters to Keats survive; his first extant letter to Fanny was written from the Isle of Wight on 1 July 1819. Through the earlier part of that year, perhaps in reaction to Tom's death, much of Keats's correspondence was directed to his sister and to George and Georgiana. Indeed, the massive journal-letter Keats wrote to his brother and sister-in-law, extending from 14 February to 3 May 1919, memorably records Keats's life and thought—and much of his poetic output—during that interval. It begins with reference to the just-completed "Eve of St. Agnes" and transcribes near its end the "Ode to Psyche," the first-written of the five great odes that belong to May of 1819. We learn much else from this journal-letter besides what poems Keats was writing: his partiality to claret, his black eye from playing cricket, his yielding to varieties of indolence, his anger at learning of a cruel joke played on poor Tom, a chance conversation with Samuel Taylor Coleridge. Its high point may well be the extended reflections in which he opposed a "superstitious" conception that life is a vale of tears with "a grander system of salvation than the [Christian] religion—or rather it is a system of spirit-creation." Keats elected to "Call the world if you Please 'The vale of Soul-making.' " He was grappling in his way to make constructive sense out of tragic experience, to affirm "how necessary a World of Pains and troubles is to school an Intelligence and make it a soul." The passage may be seen as a substantial enriching of Keats's notion of "the camelion Poet," an *identity-less* creative capability, in the direction of a more positive spiritual self-realization as the possible response to life's intractable circumstances. As such, it moved Keats closer to that conception of the excruciating but humane self-creation of the poet he engrafted upon *Hyperion* when he returned to his epic later that year and rewrote it as the Dantean dream-vision we know as *The Fall of Hyperion*.

Keats continued to mine a rich poetic vein through the summer and into the fall of 1819, as *Lamia*, the superb ode "To Autumn," and his work on the *Hyperion* material attest. But he seemed in the main increasingly dissatisfied with what he had accomplished. Hoping to produce a lucrative stage success, he facilely scribbled away at an unlikely collaboration with Brown, the verse play *Otho the Great*; and he wrote to various friends of turning to some more hopeful occupation than poetry. These appear to be the signs that Keats was reassessing his prospects and could not see how he was ever to live with Fanny Brawne or without her.

It is not surprising that his letters to Fanny have affected readers in strongly different ways; they reveal the many and even contradictory sides of Keats's complex nature and the conflict he felt between a lover's yearning to possess and be possessed and the artist's fierce need to be free and unattached. It should also be remembered that this relationship must have become different after Keats had vomited the blood he recognized to be his "death warrant" from what it was in 1819, when his life still held a poet's ambitions and a lover's usual hopes. In any case, his suspicious accusations of Fanny's fickleness when he was well, and his self-centered envy of her freedom while he was sick and housebound, can both diminish for some readers the high drama and pathos of these letters. Matthew Arnold wrote in 1880 that they "ought never to have been published," and other Victorian guardians of a sentimental and idealized image of Keats felt the love letters lacked a proper reticence, dignity, and good breeding. But it is surely hard to deny that posterity's portrait of Keats would remain seriously incomplete and, after all, less humanly appealing without the letters to Fanny Brawne. They give us (despite the truth of the saying that the words "I love you" are *always* in quotation marks) the authentic flavor of Keats's desperate ardor: "I have two luxuries to brood over in my walks, your Loveliness and the hour of my death. . . . I will imagine you Venus to night and pray, pray, pray to your star like a Hethen" (25 July 1819). There are also candor, realism, and consideration: "really what can I do? Knowing well that my life must be passed in fatigue and trouble, I have been endeavouring to wean myself from you: for myself alone what can be much of a misery?" (13 September 1819). "Perhaps on your account I have imagined my illness more serious than it is: how horrid was the chance of slipping into the ground instead of into your arms—the difference is amazing Love" (March[?] 1820). Best of all, perhaps, Keats could write to "My dearest Girl," even in the face of his ruined health, with a kind of humorous and self-deprecating jauntiness: "I fear I am too prudent for a dying kind of Lover. Yet there is a great difference between going off in warm blood like Romeo, and making one's exit like a frog in a frost" (March [?] 1820).

The year of what Keats called his "posthumous existence," 1820, began with George's visit to England in an attempt to bolster his financial resources. There was a round of parties with members of his and John's circle of friends, but on 3 February, only days after George said good-bye, Keats suffered a hemorrhage that signaled an advanced stage of tuberculosis. His life as a poet was effectively ended, though the volume *Lamia, Isabella, The Eve of St. Agnes, and Other Poems*, containing the bulk of Keats's claim to immortality, was published that July. There are letters recording this final year, including especially the notes Keats wrote to Fanny Brawne (who since May 1819 had been living with her family in the Dilkes' half of the house) while he was confined to Brown's side, struggling with his illness. But equally poignant in some respects are the letters Keats did *not* write. Bailey had already dropped out of Keats's life, and there is only a single letter to Reynolds (28 February); sadder still is the fact that the correspondence with George and Georgiana apparently stopped entirely. Part of the explanation is surely that long letters were physically too taxing, and nearer the end Keats

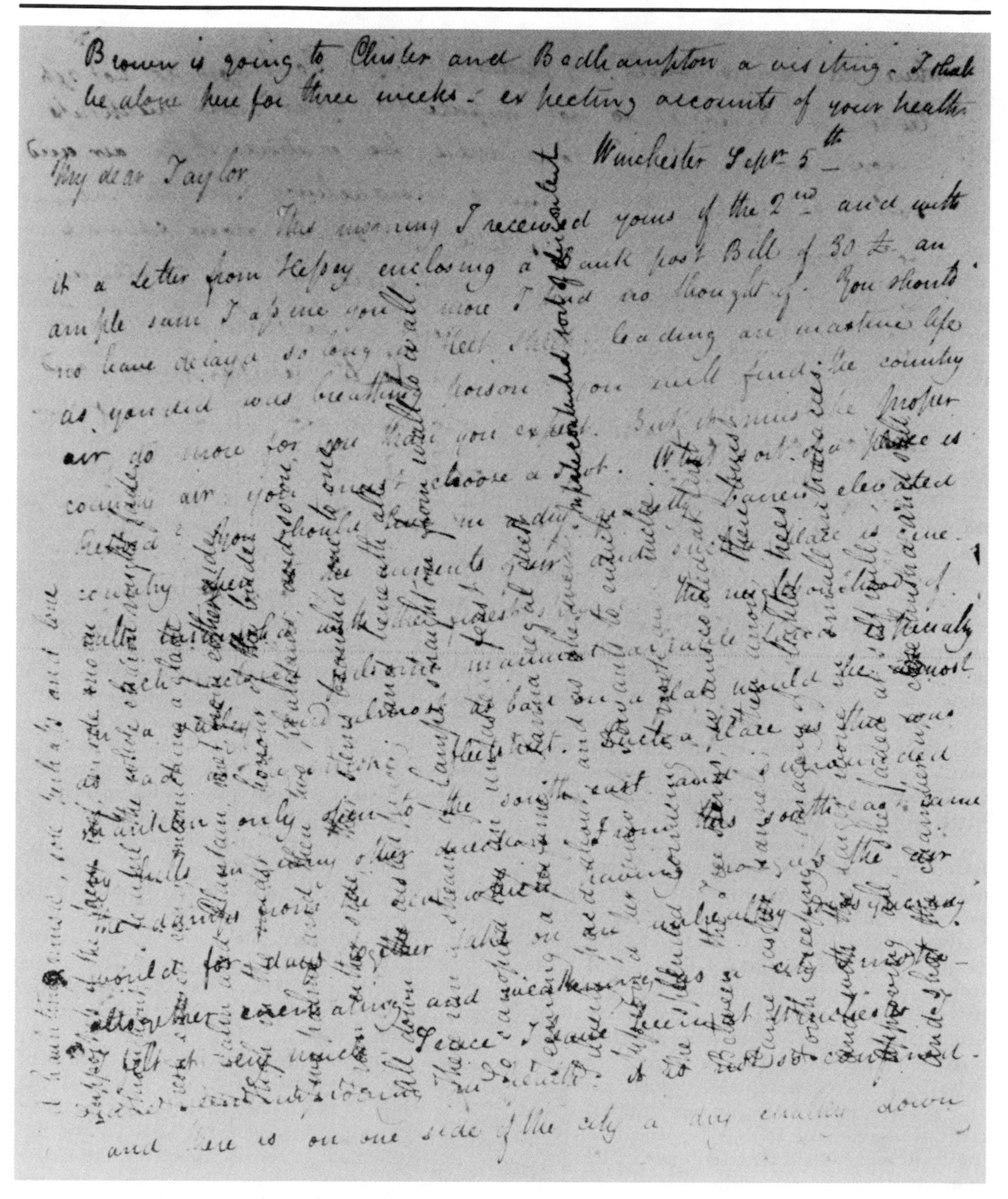

Brown is going to Chister and Bedhampton a visiting. I shall be alone here for three weeks – expecting accounts of your health.

Winchester Sept^r 5th

My dear Taylor

This morning I received yours of the 2nd and with it a Letter from Hessey enclosing a Bank post Bill of 30 £ an ample sum I assure you more I had no thought of. You should not have delayed so long in Fleet St. leading an inactive life as you did was breathing poison: you will find the country air do more for you than you expect. But it must be proper country air. you must choose a spot. What sort of a place is Retford?

*Page from Keats's 5 September 1819 letter to John Taylor, in which Keats wrote lines from a draft for* Lamia *across the text of the letter (Harvard Keats Collection). He omitted these lines from the final draft.*

was emotionally unable to write to those who meant most to him. Before his September departure for Italy, in a desperate venture to recover his health in a milder climate, Keats wrote to his sister that further news of him would come from "a friend." That was Fanny Brawne, to whom also Keats could no longer bear to write directly. (His one letter to her mother, 24[?] October 1820, contains the painful postscript, "Good bye Fanny! god bless you.") Before he left England, Keats did write one of his best-known letters, the one to Shelley on 16 August thanking his fellow poet for the offer of hospitality in Italy and including the bold advice that Shelley "might curb your magnanimity and be more of an artist, and 'load every rift' of your subject with ore."

Shortly before he died in Rome on 23 February 1821, attended by the painter Joseph Severn, who had shared the ordeal of a difficult voyage and his friend's distressing last days, Keats judged himself as "one whose name was writ in water." His poetry was known to few and by many of those lightly regarded; it was, of course, unsuspected that the story of his career and an unforgettable image of his character had been preserved in his letters. How the letters were brought before the public and the part they played in the evolution of Keats's critical reputation during the century after his death is itself an engrossing subject. In more recent times the preponderant estimate has been that Keats's letters constitute a literary treasure hardly less valuable than the poems themselves. T. S. Eliot's reference to the "brilliance and profundity" to be found in the letters and W. H. Auden's characterization of them as Shakespearean in their vigor represent this drastic reversal from the way they were generally dismissed or disparaged by Keats's more immediate successors (not least those who admired his poetry). In fact, some critics, such as F. R. Leavis, have felt it necessary to remind students of Keats that it is, after all, the poems which continue to count most.

Keats's letters are an invaluable supplement to his poems because the letter writer gives us rare access to the absorbing mind, the many-sided character, and the courageous spirit of a major poet. They are an intense and extended meditation on the art of poetry. In them also we make the acquaintance of an individual it is a pleasure to know. Keats's deep seriousness about the aims and nature of poetry is never in doubt; but for him it is a natural, if exalted, human activity, too real and important to be treated with pompous solemnity. What he says on the subject comes in his letters almost modestly and by the way, as if it is by no means offered as the whole truth. Even as he reverences poetry, Keats is usually aiming essentially to demystify it. Perhaps that is because Keats wrote about poetry to particular people, most of whom he knew well and liked and trusted.

His finest letters are those most marked by what one finds to some degree in any good letter: a sense of being written for an actual reader. This is not a matter of trimming or tempering but of writing in a way that acknowledges another "presence." Knowing his readers, Keats in his letters was able to speak himself; they contain so much that is memorable—and from the full extent of Keats's character and experience. They show us his playfulness as he and Maria Dilke from next door engage in a mock duel with celery stalks (to George and Georgiana Keats, 4 January 1819); they also depict the real heroism of Keats, mortally sick, facing his desperate voyage to Italy "with the sensation of marching up against a Batterry" (to John Taylor, 13 August 1820). Most characteristically they reveal what Keats called a "feeling for light and shade"—his keen and simultaneous sensitivity to exquisite joy and excruciating sorrow.


**Letters:**

*The Letters of John Keats*, 2 volumes, edited by Hyder Edward Rollins (Cambridge, Mass.: Harvard University Press, 1958);

*Letters of John Keats: A New Selection*, edited by Robert Gittings (London, Oxford & New York: Oxford University Press, 1970).

**Bibliographies:**

J. R. MacGillivray, *Keats: A Bibliography and Reference Guide* (Toronto: University of Toronto Press, 1949);

David Erdman, *The Romantic Movement: A Selective and Critical Bibliography*, 10 volumes to date (New York: Garland, 1980- );

Jack Stillinger, "Keats," in *The English Romantic Poets: A Review of Research and Criticism*, edited by Frank Jordan, fourth edition (New York: MLA, 1985).

**Biographies:**

Richard Monckton Milnes, Lord Houghton, Biography of Keats, in *Life, Letters, and Literary Remains of John Keats*, edited by Milnes (Lon-

*Keats on his deathbed (drawing by Joseph Severn, Keats-Shelley Memorial House, Rome)*

don: Moxon, 1848; Philadelphia: Putnam, 1848);

Sidney Colvin, *John Keats: His Life and Poetry* (London: Macmillan / New York: Scribners, 1917);

Amy Lowell, *John Keats* (New York & Boston: Houghton Mifflin, 1925);

Aileen Ward, *John Keats: The Making of a Poet* (New York: Viking, 1963; revised edition, New York: Farrar, Straus & Giroux, 1986);

Walter Jackson Bate, *John Keats* (Cambridge, Mass.: Harvard University Press, 1963; revised edition, New York: Oxford University Press, 1966; revised again, Cambridge, Mass.: Harvard University Press, 1979; London: Chatto & Windus, 1979);

Hyder Edward Rollins, ed., *The Keats Circle: Letters and Papers and More Letters and Papers of the Keats Circle*, revised edition, 2 volumes (Cambridge, Mass.: Harvard University Press, 1965);

Robert Gittings, *John Keats* (Boston: Little, Brown, 1968).

**References:**

Douglas Bush, *John Keats: His Life and Writings* (New York: Macmillan, 1966);

Morris Dickstein, *Keats and His Poetry: A Study in Development* (Chicago: University of Chicago Press, 1971);

T. S. Eliot, "Shelley and Keats," in his *The Use of Poetry and the Use of Criticism* (Cambridge, Mass.: Harvard University Press, 1933), pp. 78-94;

Walter Evert, *Aesthetic and Myth in the Poetry of Keats* (Princeton, N.J.: Princeton University Press, 1965);

Marjorie Levinson, *Keats's Life of Allegory* (Oxford: Blackwell, 1988);

G. M. Matthews, ed., *Keats: The Critical Heritage* (New York: Barnes & Noble, 1971);

Christopher Ricks, *Keats and Embarrassment* (Oxford: Clarendon Press, 1974);

Robert M. Ryan, *Keats: The Religious Sense* (Princeton, N.J.: Princeton University Press, 1976);

Ronald A. Sharp, *Keats, Skepticism, and the Religion of Beauty* (Athens: University of Georgia Press, 1979);

Stuart Sperry, *Keats the Poet* (Princeton: Princeton University Press, 1973);

Jack Stillinger, "The Manuscripts of Keats's Letters: An Update," *Keats-Shelley Journal*, 36 (1987): 16-19;

Clarence De Witt Thorpe, *The Mind of John Keats* (New York: Oxford University Press, 1926);

Lionel Trilling, "The Poet as Hero: Keats in His Letters," in his *The Opposing Self* (New York: Viking, 1955), pp. 3-49;

Earl Wasserman, *The Finer Tone* (Baltimore: Johns Hopkins University Press, 1953);

Susan J. Wolfson, "Keats the Letter-Writer: Epistolary Poetics," *Romanticism Past and Present*, 6, no. 2 (1982): 43-61.

**Papers:**

The largest collection of Keats letters, manuscripts, and other papers is in the Houghton Library at Harvard University. Other collections of such material will be found at the British Library; Keats House, Hampstead; Keats-Shelley Memorial House, Rome; and the Pierpont Morgan Library in New York.

# John Gibson Lockhart

*(14 July 1794 - 25 November 1854)*

Richard D. McGhee
*Arkansas State University*

BOOKS: *Peter's Letters to his Kinsfolk,* as Peter Morris (3 volumes, Edinburgh: Printed for William Blackwood, 1819; 1 volume, New York: Printed by C. S. Van Winkle for A. T. Goodrich, Kirk & Mercein, C. Wiley, W. B. Gilley, and James Olmstead, 1820);

*Valerius. A Roman Story* (3 volumes, Edinburgh, W. Blackwood, 1821; 2 volumes, Boston: Wells & Lilly, 1821; revised edition, Edinburgh & London: W. Blackwood & Sons, 1842);

*Letter to the Right Hon. Lord Byron. By John Bull,* sometimes attributed to Lockhart (London: Printed by & for William Wright, 1821);

*Some Passages in the Life of Mr. Adam Blair* (Edinburgh: A. Blackwood / London: T. Cadell, 1822; Boston: Wells & Lilly, 1822);

*Reginald Dalton* (3 volumes, Edinburgh: W. Blackwood / London: T. Cadell, 1823; 2 volumes, New York: E. Duyckinck, 1823);

*The History of Matthew Wald* (Edinburgh: W. Blackwood / London: T. Cadell, 1824; New York: E. Duyckinck, Collins & Hannay, 1824);

*Life of Robert Burns* (Edinburgh: Constable, 1828; New York: W. Stodart, 1831);

*The History of Napoleon Buonaparte,* 2 volumes (London: John Murray 1829; New York: J. & J. Harper, 1830);

*The History of the late War; Including Sketches of Bonaparte, Nelson, and Wellington For Children* (London, 1832);

*Memoirs of the Life of Sir Walter Scott, Bart.*, 7 volumes (Edinburgh: R. Cadell, 1837-1838); abridged as *Narrative of the Life of Sir Walter Scott, Bart.,* 2 volumes (Edinburgh: R. Cadell, 1848);

*The Ballantyne-Humbug Handled* (Edinburgh: R. Cadell, 1839);

*Theodore Hook, A Sketch* (London, 1852).

**Editions:** *Lockhart's Literary Criticism,* edited by M. Clive Hildyard (Oxford: Blackwell, 1931);

*John Bull's Letter to Lord Byron,* edited by Alan Lang Strout (Norman: University of Oklahoma Press, 1947).

OTHER: *The History of the Ingenious Gentleman, Don Quixote of La Mancha; translated from the Spanish by Motteux. A new edition with copious notes; and an essay on the Life and Writings of Cervantes, by J. G. Lockhart,* 5 volumes (Edinburgh: A. Constable / London: Hurst, Robinson, 1822);

*Ancient Spanish Ballads: Historical and Romantic,* translated by Lockhart (Edinburgh: W. Blackwood / London: T. Cadell, 1823; revised edition, London: John Murray, 1841; New York: Wiley & Putnam, 1842);

*Janus, or the Edinburgh Literary Almanack,* includes contributions by Lockhart (Edinburgh: Oliver & Boyd, 1826);

*The Poetical Works of Sir Walter Scott, Bart.*, 12 volumes, edited by Lockhart (Edinburgh: Robert Cadell, 1833-1834);

*The Complete Works of Lord Byron,* includes notes by Lockhart (Paris: A. & W. Galignani, 1835);

John Wilson, *The Noctes Ambrosianæ of Blackwood,* 4 volumes, includes contributions by Lockhart (Philadelphia: Carey & Hart, 1843).

Held responsible by some for the early death of John Keats and by others for the duel in which *London Magazine* editor John Scott was killed, John Gibson Lockhart was so effective a satirist, his scorn so painful, that early in his career he was known as the "Scorpion" to readers of *Blackwood's Magazine.* He had difficulty outgrowing this reputation, and perhaps he never was free from the taint. Indeed, he added to his stained reputation with the scandalous stories of an adulterous minister and a bloody madman. As the son-in-law of the famous novelist Sir Walter Scott, Lockhart had to find new literary fields for himself. He earned credit for his work as a scholar of Spanish literature and for his sustained good work as editor of the *Quarterly Review* from 1825 to 1853. Finally he achieved positive success as the biographer of Robert Burns in 1828 and Sir Walter Scott in 1837-1838.

*John Gibson Lockhart (portrait by Sir Francis Grant; Scottish National Portrait Gallery)*

The eldest son of Reverend John Lockhart and his second wife, Elizabeth Gibson Lockhart, John Gibson Lockhart was born in Lanarkshire, Scotland, on 14 July 1794. The next year his father, a Presbyterian minister, moved to Glasgow, where Lockhart attended Glasgow High School from 1800 to late 1805, when he entered the University of Glasgow. He won prizes for his work in Greek, Latin, and logic. One of his prizes, called the "Latin Blackstone," brought him a scholarship, a Snell Exhibition to attend Balliol College, Oxford, which he entered in 1808. At Balliol he studied Italian, Spanish, and Portuguese. He took his degree with first-class honors at age nineteen, in 1813. He returned to Glasgow, writing frequently to his Oxford friend Jonathan H. Christie to describe his life of reading and contemplating a career. He began a novel in 1814, calling it "The Romance of the Thistle," but he may have destroyed his manuscript before going to Edinburgh in November 1815, where he studied to become an advocate, an attorney of Scottish law. He was called to the bar in late 1816.

He met John Wilson in Edinburgh and began a career of literary journalism. He contracted with William Blackwood, a bookseller, to translate August Wilhelm von Schlegel's *Lectures on the History of Literature* after a trip to Germany in summer 1817, when he met Johann Wolfgang von Goethe at Weimar. Earlier that year Lockhart had published an essay on Greek tragedy in *Blackwood's Magazine* (April 1817), which

*Self-portrait by Lockhart, October 1816 (from Andrew Lang,* The Life and Letters of John Gibson Lockhart, *1897)*

he signed Z, a pseudonym he and others used for several articles published in that journal. Then in October he had a hand in the writing of "Translation from an Ancient Chaldee Manuscript," a playful satirical piece in *Blackwood's,* causing scandal but bringing success for the magazine. With Wilson and James Hogg, Lockhart had set out to satirize the bookseller Archibald Constable, but they managed to offend nearly everyone in Edinburgh as they parodied the Bible and poked fun at many, including Walter Scott. Because of this piece Lockhart acquired the name of the "Scorpion."

In May 1818 Lockhart met Scott, who was amused by Lockhart's satire but concerned that it would get Lockhart into trouble. Lockhart shared with Scott, however, a common ground for attacking the *Edinburgh Review,* whose liberal and Whig views invited sharp correction by conservatives and Tories. Writing under such pseudonyms as Baron von Lauerwinkel and William Wastle, Lockhart cut away at the *Edinburgh* for its supposedly unchristian principles, through a vigorous assault on the conduct of Reverend Professor Playfair, a contributor to the *Edinburgh,* in the September 1818 issue of *Blackwood's.* Lockhart's other notorious essays in *Blackwood's* began with "The Cockney School of Poetry" (October 1817), to continue through some seven more (and written by several hands), until August 1825. These include the infamous attack on Keats in the fourth article (August 1818), written probably (though not certainly) by Lockhart.

*Lockhart's sketch of himself (center) riding with a man believed to be Sir Walter Scott (left; Collection of Mrs. Maxwell Scott of Abbotsford)*

Lockhart's first significant literary project, whose title he borrowed from Scott, was *Peter's Letters to his Kinsfolk,* published in 1819. It is a series of sketches by one Peter Morris, M.D., written during his supposed visit to Edinburgh and Glasgow while on vacation from his home in Wales. Peter examines the characters of many representative Scots; his favorite is Francis Jeffrey, editor of the *Edinburgh Review*: "Of all the celebrated characters of this place, I rather understand that Jeffrey is the one whom travellers are commonly most in a hurry to see—not surely, that the world, in general, has any such deep and abiding feeling of admiration for him." Although Jeffrey is kindly, Peter cannot restrain his contempt for this man, whose "business [is] to bamboozle." He finds Jeffrey at a celebration dinner for the memory of Robert Burns, whom Jeffrey had savagely attacked. Peter reports that some "regard Mr. Jeffrey as having been the enemy of his country, and as meriting, in all succeeding generations, the displeasure of high-minded and generous Englishmen." Peter contrasts the unattractive though courteous Jeffrey with the attractive Walter Scott, whose "works are altogether the most remarkable phenomenon in this age of wonders." Most interesting is Peter Morris's description of his meeting with John Gibson Lockhart himself! He concludes that Lockhart "may soon find that there are much better things in literature than satire."

One of the satisfied readers of *Peter's Letters to his Kinsfolk* was Walter Scott's daughter Sophia, who married Lockhart on 29 April 1820 at Abbotsford. By the time their first child, John Hugh, was born on 14 February 1821, Scott's old worries about Lockhart's reputation were renewed by Christie's duel with John Scott. The duel, which ended in John Scott's death, followed by the flight and eventual acquittal of Christie, arose from John Scott's attack on Lockhart as the "secret" editor of *Blackwood's* (*London Magazine*, January 1820).

Yet Lockhart was indeed turning from sarcasm to do "better things" in his writing. He wrote *Valerius. A Roman Story* (1821). In this novel

Valerius, son of a Roman patrician and a British lady, writes in old age of his visit to Rome in the time of Trajan. There to claim an inheritance, Valerius had rescued the Christian Athanasia and become a Christian himself, before marrying Athanasia and escaping with her back to Britain. While Sir Walter Scott told Lockhart he was delighted with the "reality" of the Romans in the novel, most of the reading public was less impressed, and the novel did not have much success. Criticism in the *Edinburgh Review* (October 1824) was not overly harsh in describing it as a secondary Scottish novel. Nevertheless, Lockhart was proceeding with his next novel, *Adam Blair,* which he would finish after publishing a new edition of *Don Quixote,* to which he added a "Life of Cervantes" and explanatory notes, in 1822. Again, Lockhart's published work was not very successful, but he persisted, bringing forward *Adam Blair,* for which Blackwood paid him five hundred pounds, later that year.

Set in the 1750s, *Adam Blair* describes how Blair, a Presbyterian minister and widower, follows once-divorced Charlotte Campbell to the Highlands, where he consummates his sexual passion for her. Filled with guilt and remorse, he rages and loses consciousness; when he wakes, he discovers Charlotte has died. Adam resigns his ministry and disappears into the countryside for ten years. His congregation petitions him to return, which he does, remaining until his death and frequently using his own life as a moral example in his sermons. *Adam Blair* caused a stir with its mixture of religion with sex, and it did well enough for Blackwell to offer Lockhart a substantial one thousand pounds for a new novel, *Reginald Dalton: A Story of University Life* (1823), which had considerable staying power the rest of the century. Fantasizing over inheriting the Dalton estate, Grypherwast-Hall, Reginald becomes a companion of Frederick Chisney, with whom he goes to Oxford. Reginald, who has fallen in love with mysterious Ellen Hesketh, discovers Frederick trying to assault her, and the two men fight a duel. Reginald is kicked out of Oxford, and Frederick tries to subvert Reginald's happiness by marrying the supposed heiress of the Dalton estate. It is discovered that the estate really belongs to Reginald's father, who marries Reginald to Ellen in Grypherwast-Hall.

Though *Reginald Dalton* had some success with readers, the work which established Lockhart's favorable reputation was his *Ancient Spanish Ballads: Historical and Romantic* (1823), published, unlike all of his other works, under his name. In his introduction Lockhart, who translated and edited the ballads, says the old Spanish ballads disprove the prevailing impression that Spain has always been intolerant: "We have been accustomed to consider the modern Spaniards as the most bigoted, and enslaved, and ignorant of Europeans; but we must not forget, that the Spaniards of three centuries back were, in all respects, a very different set of beings. . . . But the strongest and best proof of the comparative liberality of the old Spaniards is, as I have already said, to be found in their Ballads."

His translations of the Spanish ballads showed Lockhart's talent for poetry, and he contributed a body of verse, mainly satiric, to *Blackwood's.* He also had some skill as a sketch artist, putting together a small collection of drawings to entertain his family. In 1824 he published his fourth and last novel, *The History of Matthew Wald,* for which Blackwood paid him only four hundred pounds, despite the relative success of *Reginald Dalton.* One reason Lockhart may have written no more novels after *Matthew Wald* is that Sir Walter thought the book was disagreeable, though powerful. Certainly the novel was a miserable failure with the public. In this Gothic romance of blood and madness, Matthew Wald's father has mysteriously left his property to his niece Katharine rather than to Matthew, who has fallen in love with his cousin. Away at school, Matthew has learned that Katharine married snobbish George Lascelyne. Matthew marries, passes medical exams, and thrives in his country practice. Then he goes to London as an M.P., taking his pregnant wife with him. Discovering Matthew with Katharine one night, his wife bears a stillborn child and then dies herself. Later, Matthew brutally murders Lascelyne and shows the bloody sword to Katharine, who then dies. Matthew goes mad and spends time in a dungeon, where he hallucinates about his dead wife and child.

Despite his lack of success as a novelist, Lockhart suddenly had the great opportunity which would define the remaining work of his life. Publisher John Murray offered him the editorship of the *Quarterly Review* and some additional salary to contribute to Murray's new (though short-lived) venture in newspaper journalism, the *Representative.* On 20 October 1825, Lockhart signed contracts to accept these appointments. This work took him to London, where he established his home for the remainder of his life. At first, old enemies resisted Lockhart's edi-

*John Gibson Lockhart, 1830 (portrait by H. W. Pickersgill, R.A.; John Murray Collection)*

torship but he surprised all when he performed his duties with little of his youthful sarcasm. Lockhart contributed two articles to the first number of the *Quarterly Review* published under his editorship (March 1826), a review of the *Memoirs of Sheridan* and an analysis of the conditions of slavery in the West Indies. Lockhart would continue to contribute to the *Quarterly* as he continued to be its editor until 1853. His articles range from essays on the art of fiction to the condition of the Church in India, from the methodology of natural science to biographies of prominent people in all walks of life.

His most enduring literary interest was in biography. In 1828 he published the *Life of Robert Burns* for the Constable's Miscellany series. Drawing upon Burns's letters and journals as well as notes by the poet's brother Gilbert, Lockhart efficiently narrates the life of the poet as a genius of his art. Nevertheless, certain features of Burns's life could not be ignored, though they were sensitive subjects, including Jean Armour's premarital pregnancies and the difficulties of Burns's courtship before their official marriage. Lockhart presents the matter as resolved in the end by Burns's "tenderness and manliness." Another delicate topic was the persistent belief that Burns was dissipated by chronic alcoholism. Lockhart argues vigorously against this belief, as he does in favor of Burns's patriotism. Lockhart felt he must clear Burns's name to examine his achievement as a poet clearly. Though Lockhart deplores Burns's poverty in his last years, the biographer nevertheless praises his countrymen for

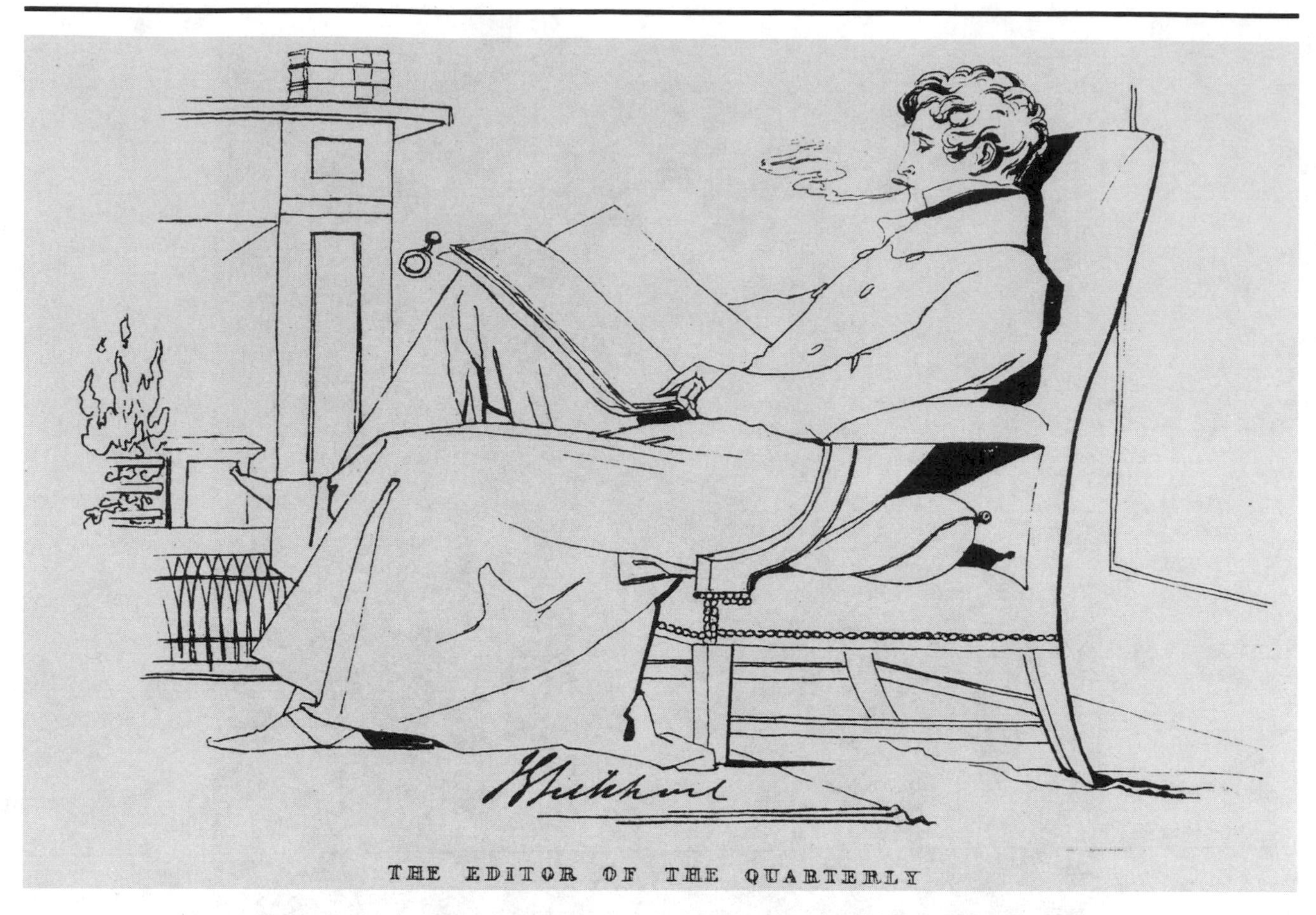


*Portrait by Daniel Maclise in the* Fraser's Magazine *"Gallery of Illustrious Literary Characters" (1830-1838)*

having recognized greatness in Burns before his death. In addition, Lockhart asserts, "On one point there can be no controversy; the poetry of Burns has had most powerful influence in reviving and strengthening the national feelings of his countrymen."

The biography of Burns was well received (despite Thomas Carlyle's strong criticism in the *Edinburgh Review* [1828]), and Lockhart had good reason to be pleased with its success. At the same time he had to contend with the bad news that his first son was losing his battle with disease in the summer of 1828. At the end of 1831 John Hugh (whom the family called Littlejohn) died, and, not long after, in September 1832, so did Sir Walter Scott. Lockhart immediately began the mammoth task of preparing all Scott's works for a new edition. This work created the context within which Lockhart initiated his greatest literary project, the *Memoirs of the Life of Sir Walter Scott, Bart.*, first published in seven volumes in 1837-1838.

Uniquely qualified, as a writer and as the son-in-law of his great subject, Lockhart had to overcome several serious problems to produce his masterpiece. He had first to gather an enormous amount of material and arrange it in unified form, keeping his subject in focus. While he had to resist temptations to exaggerate the virtues of Scott's personal life as explanations for his public success, at the same time Lockhart had to resist temptations to satisfy curiosity about weaknesses in Scott's character that might cut the legend down to the size of the merely human. Lockhart saw his challenge as one of balance, and he realized that his close personal knowledge might become a liability. He solved his problems by letting Scott speak for himself as often as possible, quoting at length from Scott's voluminous letters, from others' letters to Scott, and, most important, from Scott's *Journal.* There are lively interruptions of objectivity when Lockhart narrates events to which he was a witness or even an active participant, such as his first visit to Abbotsford and his journey with Scott to Ireland in the summer of 1825.

For those years before Lockhart met Scott in 1818, the biographer depended upon Scott's brief "Autobiography," which he used to open the book. Lockhart provides several early chapters as "illustrations" of the "Autobiography." Scott's most important characteristic, which emerged from his early life, was his pride in his ability to conduct a life of "business" while practicing his art of poetry and fiction. Scott thought "that to spend some fair portion of every day in any matter of fact occupation, is good for the higher faculties themselves in the upshot. In a word, from beginning to end, he piqued himself on being *a man of business;* and did—with one sad and memorable exception—whatever the ordinary course of things threw in his way, in exactly the business-like fashion which might have been expected from the son of a thoroughbred old Clerk to the Signet, who had never deserted his father's profession."

Lockhart identified what would prove to be the most difficult of issues for him. The "one sad and memorable exception" to Scott's successful application of his "business" tenet was the dreadful bankruptcy of his finances in 1826. Like almost everyone else, Lockhart had had no idea his father-in-law was so deeply involved in the financial dealings of publisher Archibald Constable and printers James and John Ballantyne. The *Memoirs,* then, reads at times as a detective's attempt to find out the "mystery" of Scott's financial failure. He returns to the nagging question again in the conclusion, where he speculates that Scott sought to conceal the "machinery" of his means to realize a grand ambition, to create the romanticism of his novels in his life at Abbotsford. Out of pride, then, Scott concealed his money deals, and that led, consequently, to a tragic fall, as the hero was victimized by the Ballantynes in a "fatal connexion with merchandise."

Lockhart then surveys his subject as a tragic figure, whose stature was achieved by great merit but whose fall into financial ruin was brought about because of a tiny flaw in his character, which allowed other, lesser men to bring him down with them. The assignment of blame on the Ballantynes would cause Lockhart to spend considerable effort defending his book over the next years, but there is little doubt the *Memoirs* constituted the great achievement of Lockhart's career. He would go on to write nothing else of importance, though he continued to serve ably as the editor of the *Quarterly Review* nearly to the end of his life. His last years were melancholy, for his wife died in May 1837, and his son Walter Scott Lockhart (born 16 April 1826) was a chronic concern, beginning with his failure to enter Oxford in 1844, continuing with his restless wandering after he inherited Abbotsford in 1847, and ending only with his death at Versailles in 1853. At that time, Lockhart's son-in-law, J. R. Hope, took the name Hope-Scott, his wife, Charlotte (born 1 January 1828), being the last lineal descendant of Sir Walter Scott. On 25 November 1854, Lockhart died while visiting his daughter at Abbotsford. He was buried in Dryburgh Abbey, near Sir Walter Scott.

John Gibson Lockhart worked long and hard to escape his reputation as the "Scorpion." His labors as editor of the *Quarterly Review* for more than a quarter of a century should have released him from that burden of notoriety. His scholarship in Spanish literature should have purged some of the taint on his honor. His solid and sensitive biography of Robert Burns, whose own reputation Lockhart helped to rescue from suspicion, may have taken him toward redemption. But something of the old Scorpion returned when he attacked the Ballantynes for the fall of Sir Walter Scott, and so finally Lockhart had to accept his fate as one whose sharp tongue could not be blunted. Other scholars and editors have come and gone since his death; others have written better biographies of both Burns and Walter Scott. Lockhart remains what he was in the beginning, the "Scorpion" whose sting could not discriminate John Keats from all the other "Cockney" poets of the age.

**Bibliography:**

M. Clive Hildyard, "Bibliography of Lockhart's Critical Writings," in *Lockhart's Literary Criticism,* edited by Hildyard (Oxford: Blackwell, 1931), pp. 153-164.

**Biography:**

Andrew Lang, *The Life and Letters of John Gibson Lockhart,* 2 volumes (London: Nimmo / New York: Scribners, 1897).

**References:**

M. F. Brightfield, "Lockhart's Quarterly Contributors," *PMLA,* 59 ( June 1944): 491-512;

James C. Corson, "Lockhart the Scorpion: An Unpublished Manuscript," *Studies in Scottish Literature,* 1 ( January 1964): 197-201;

F. Ewen, "John Gibson Lockhart, Propagandist of German Literature," *Modern Language Notes,* 49 (April 1934): 260-265;

Francis R. Hart, *Lockhart as Romantic Biographer* (Edinburgh: Edinburgh University Press, 1971);

M. A. Hassan, "Lockhart's 'Life' of Defoe," *Notes and Queries*, new series 20 (August 1973): 294-296;

M. C. Hildyard, "J. G. Lockhart," *Cornhill Magazine,* 72 (1932);

Ian Jack, "Two Biographers: Lockhart and Boswell," in *Johnson, Boswell and Their Circle: Essays presented to Lawrence Fitzroy Powell in Honour of His Eighty-Fourth Birthday* (Oxford: Clarendon Press, 1965), pp. 268-285;

Joseph Kestner, "Defamiliarization in the Romantic Regional Novel: Maria Edgeworth, Walter Scott, John Gibson Lockhart, Susan Ferrier, and John Galt," *Wordsworth Circle,* 10 (Autumn 1979): 326-330;

Kestner, "Lockhart's *Peter's Letters to His Kinsfolk* and the Epistolary Genre," *Wordsworth Circle,* 11 (Autumn 1980): 228-232;

Marion Lockhead, *Lockhart* (London: Murray, 1954);

Gilbert Macbeth, *John Gibson Lockhart: A Critical Study* (Urbana: University of Illinois, 1935);

Peter F. Morgan, "Lockhart's Literary Personality," *Scottish Literary Journal,* 2 ( July 1975): 27-35;

Thomas C. Richardson, "Character and Craft in Lockhart's *Adam Blair,*" in *Nineteenth-Century Scottish Fiction: Critical Essays,* edited by Ian Campbell (Totowa, N.J.: Barnes & Noble, 1979), pp. 51-67;

Patrick Story, "A Neglected Cockney School Parody of Hazlitt and Hunt," *Keats-Shelley Journal,* 29 (1980): 191-202;

Virginia Woolf, "Lockhart's Criticism," in her *The Moment and Other Essays* (London: Hogarth Press, 1947).

# William Maginn

*(10 July 1794 - 21 August 1842)*

John H. Rogers
*Vincennes University*

SELECTED BOOKS: *Whitehall: or, The Days of George IV* (London: W. Marsh, 1827);
*Magazine Miscellanies* (London, 1841);
*John Manesty, The Liverpool Merchant*, 2 volumes, completed by Charles Ollier (London: J. Mortimer, 1844);
*Maxims of Sir Morgan O'Doherty, Bart.* (Edinburgh & London: William Blackwood, 1849);
*Shakespeare Papers: Pictures Grave and Gay* (London: Richard Bentley, 1859; enlarged, 1860);
*A Gallery of Illustrious Literary Characters (1830-1838) drawn by the late Daniel Maclise, R.A., and accompanied by notices chiefly by the late William Maginn*, edited by William Bates (London: Chatto & Windus, 1873).
**Collections:** *Miscellaneous Writings of the late Dr. Maginn*, 5 volumes, edited by Shelton Mackenzie (New York: Redfield, 1855-1857);
*Miscellanies: Prose and Verse*, 2 volumes, edited by R. W. Montagu (London: Sampson, Low, Marston, Searle & Rivington, 1855);
*Ten Tales By Dr. William Maginn* (London: Eric Partridge, 1933).

OTHER: John Wilson, *The Noctes Ambrosianæ of "Blackwood,"* 4 volumes, includes contributions by Maginn (Philadelphia: Carey & Hart, 1843);
*Homeric Ballads*, translated by Maginn (London: J. W. Parker, 1850).

It is the unhappy fate of some once-well-known writers to be completely forgotten; it is the perhaps unhappier fate of others to achieve a certain dubious immortality not through their own work but as "characters" in the anecdotes, memoirs, and fiction of their contemporaries. Such is the case of William Maginn, who is now known, if at all, as what Michael Sadleir termed a "pungent marginal note in the lives of other men" or as the purported original of Capt. Charley Shandon in William Makepeace Thackeray's *Pendennis* (1848-1850). Yet in his own time Maginn was among the most feared, respected, and influential journalists in England.

William Maginn was born on 10 July 1794 at Marlboro's Fort, Cork, Ireland, to Anne Eccles Maginn, descendant of an old Scottish family, and John Maginn, who ran a private school on Marlboro Street, where, he said, he tried to teach boys to think rather than become students who "crawled like a snail over the facts." Maginn began his education at his father's school, where he soon proved himself a prodigy. He was fluent in Latin, Greek, and Hebrew by the time he entered Trinity College, Dublin, in 1806. He received his A.B. in 1811 and became a teacher in his father's school; he became head of the school after his father's death in 1813 and continued to run it successfully for the next ten years. Maginn, who was always known as "the Doctor" to his journalistic colleagues, received his LL.D. from Dublin University in 1819, the youngest person ever to receive this degree. Like his two younger brothers, Maginn was trained for the Church; he soon realized that he did not have the vocation and apparently hoped for an academic career, but during his years as schoolmaster he also began sending anonymous contributions to various periodicals, thus beginning the journalistic career in which he would continue for the rest of his life.

Maginn's first contributions, under the pseudonym of R. T. Scott, were sent in early 1819 to William Jerdan, an editor of abundant mediocrity whose *Literary Gazette* was nonetheless among the first of the influential literary weeklies. More important, later that year Maginn also contributed, under the name P. P. Crossman, to *Blackwood's Magazine*. William Blackwood, who at this time relied almost totally on John Gibson Lockhart and John Wilson for his copy, gladly accepted a "few short things" from Maginn, who soon became a mainstay of the magazine. His early articles for *Blackwood's* are characteristic in both their uneven quality and in their result. The contributions in-

cluded a brilliant translation of "Chevy Chase" into doggerel Latin verse and a vicious attack on the philosopher and mathematician John Leslie for "sarcasms on the language of the Bible," which resulted in the first of several libel suits. Maginn's contributions to the magazine soon became so important that, according to Margaret Oliphant, at one time he produced half the articles and nearly half the verse for some issues. Maginn's most notable contribution to *Blackwood's*, however, was the suggestion for the *Noctes Ambrosianæ*, or "Nights at Ambrose's Tavern," a series of imaginary conversations among a group of friends—largely based on such real people as Lockhart, Christopher North (Wilson), the "Ettrick Shepherd" (James Hogg), and Sir Morgan O'Doherty (Maginn)—who discuss a wide range of topical issues while also presenting a romantic view of Scotland. Most of the later notes of this extremely popular series were written by Wilson, but Maginn wrote the first, which appeared in March 1822, and under his favorite pseudonym of Sir Morgan O'Doherty, Adjutant, he contributed several of the earlier and more spirited dialogues. Some were indeed so spirited that Blackwood explained to Wilson that he had written to Maginn, explaining, "it really will not do to run a-muck in this kind of way."

Maginn for some time continued to send his contributions from Cork, but in 1823 he decided to leave Ireland and his school to become a full-time journalist. Theodore Hook, whom Maginn may have assisted on his newspaper *John Bull*, at this time planned a second weekly paper, which he wanted Maginn to edit. John Wilson Croker, thinking Maginn would be a useful political writer, apparently used this venture to entice him to England. On 31 January 1824 Maginn married Ellen Cullen, daughter of an Irish clergyman, and in February of that year they settled in London, where Maginn became—and for the next decade remained—one of the leading figures in British journalism.

Upon Maginn's arrival in London, Croker introduced him to John Murray, who was so impressed that he gave him George Gordon, Lord Byron's papers and asked him to write the poet's life. Maginn, who disliked and often parodied Byron's poetry, was impressed by his memoirs and letters, the only Byron writings, he found, that "give me, in the least degree, the notion of a fine creature enjoying the full and unrestrained swing of his faculties." Maginn told his friend E. V. Kenealy that Byron's personal writings revealed his false character, and that he would use these writings to present "a picture of the man, unvizored and unrobed, in his true and natural colors." One feels that Byron, to say nothing of most modern biographers, would have heartily approved this approach, but Murray did not. Dissuaded by Byron's friends, he burned the poet's memoirs and entrusted the biography to Thomas Moore, who produced the safe, emasculated work that remained the standard life of Byron until well into the next century.

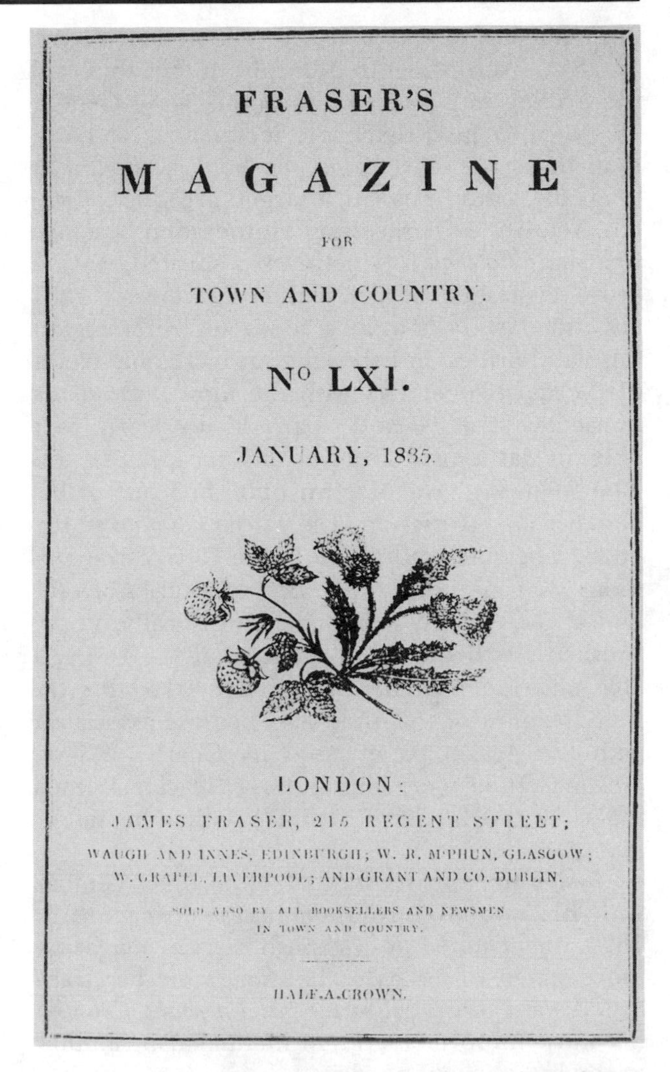
FRASER'S

MAGAZINE

FOR

TOWN AND COUNTRY.

No LXI.

JANUARY, 1835.

LONDON:

JAMES FRASER, 215 REGENT STREET;

WAUGH AND INNES, EDINBURGH; W. R. M'PHUN, GLASGOW;
W. GRAPEL, LIVERPOOL; AND GRANT AND CO. DUBLIN.

SOLD ALSO BY ALL BOOKSELLERS AND NEWSMEN
IN TOWN AND COUNTRY.

HALF-A-CROWN.

*Cover for an issue of the magazine Maginn and Hugh Fraser founded in 1830, after approaching their publisher because they liked his name*

The biographical episode having proved abortive, Murray sent Maginn to Paris as correspondent for the *Representative*, a daily Tory newspaper Murray had started. It was a choice assignment, but the irresponsibility and dissipation that led to the nickname "Maginn and Water" (and were ultimately to destroy Maginn) were already much in evidence. Just before he left, Lockhart wrote Wilson in December 1825 that "Maginn is off for Paris, where I hope he will behave himself. He has an opportunity of retrieving much if he will use it." The hope was forlorn, the opportunity lost. During his short time in Paris Maginn did begin a serious novel, which he did not complete and is now lost, but for the most part, reported Samuel Smiles, he "proved better at borrowing money than writing articles" and fell ever deeper into drunkenness. Murray brought Maginn back to London to edit the "lighter side" of the paper, at a salary of seven hundred pounds. Maginn wrote humorous pieces but also sharper, more offensive articles, including, according to S. C. Hall, an account of a fancy dress ball at the Opera House, written "as if it had taken place among the thieves and demireps of Whitechapel."

Such humorous but imprudent articles probably hastened the end of the *Representative* in July 1826, but this period was one of Maginn's most productive and successful as a writer. On his return from Paris he became assistant to Stanley Lees Gifford, editor of the *Standard*, at a salary of four hundred pounds a year. In 1827 he published, anonymously and perhaps in collaboration with Lockhart, *Whitehall: or, The Days of George IV*, his longest satirical work. This parody of currently popular historical romances, specifically Horace Smith's *Brambletye House* (1826), purports to be a historical novel written in the year

2227 but in fact concerns the people and events of 1827. According to Kenealy, it includes "all the leading characters of the time, from George IV down to Jack Ketch the hangman." At more than three hundred pages the book is much too long, and many of its satiric targets are long forgotten. Yet, while the incessant vituperation becomes wearing, *Whitehall* is nonetheless a spirited, extravagant grotesque of the eighteenth-century variety, filled with pompous footnotes referring to false authorities and showing an incredible blend of the most sober fact with the most outrageous nonsense (one is not surprised to learn that Maginn was a great admirer of Laurence Sterne). The following year Maginn published one of his better short stories in *The Literary Souvenir* for 1828. The stark moral tale "The City of the Demons" was intended as the first of a series of rabbinical tales which were, characteristically, never finished. With the usual mixture of the respectable and the reprehensible that marked his career, Maginn at this time also became associated with the *Age*, a paper used by Charles Malloy Westmacott, its scurrilous editor, to blackmail leading citizens who were afraid of what he might print.

Maginn apparently had some disagreement with Blackwood and left *Blackwood's Magazine* in 1829, determined to establish a new magazine more suited to his style. The magazine he established was *Fraser's Magazine For Town and Country*, his most important and influential contribution to the literature of his day.

The origin of *Fraser's* was characteristic both of Maginn and of the less-than-formal style of the magazine during its formative years. Maginn and Hugh Fraser, a wealthy young man with literary aspirations, completed enough material for the first number and began looking for a publisher. As they walked down Regent Street, Maginn stopped before James Fraser's bookshop and declared, "Fraser! here is a namesake of yours—let us try him." James Fraser agreed to publish the new magazine, but had no interest in the editorial side (the magazine was named for Hugh Fraser, not the publisher), thus giving Maginn a free hand to create the kind of magazine he wished. Although the magazine itself later declared that Maginn was never officially its editor—probably because he did not read proof—the early issues of *Fraser's*, beginning with the first in February 1830, were almost entirely manifestations of his style and spirit. *Fraser's* was a family magazine, so it included reviews, fiction, light verse, and articles to appeal to every family member, but it was its emphasis on politics and literature that made *Fraser's* the most brilliant periodical of the 1830s, one that, according to Michael Sadleir, "roused more excited enthusiasms; contained more brilliant, but irresponsible and often caddish writing, [and] provoked more angry retaliation" than any other nineteenth-century magazine.

The mixture of brilliance and irresponsibility that was so striking a feature of the early *Fraser's* and its founder was evident from the first, in Maginn's ploy to attract attention and readership for his new venture. Remembering the success of the infamous "Chaldee Manuscript" by Lockhart and Wilson in launching *Blackwood's* in 1817, he began writing a series of articles on the "Election of Editor," announcing that the magazine would poll the country to discover "the very first genius of the age" to edit *Fraser's*. Maginn then wrote candidacy speeches for such London celebrities as Arthur Wellesley, Duke of Wellington; Sir Robert Peel; Samuel Taylor Coleridge (described as the "first genius of the age" but whose speech is interrupted by heckling from William Cobbett); Wilson; William Hazlitt ("the king of cockaigne"); and Blackwood. At the conclusion of these speeches, which are brilliant parodies of the writers' ideas, styles, and opinions, the search ends when the fictional Oliver Yorke is elected with shouts of "Noll Yorke and *Regina* forever! Noll Yorke and the Queen of Magazines!"

The queen of magazines soon attracted a remarkable staff of writers, including Lockhart, John Galt, Croker, Robert Southey, James Hogg, Barry Cornwall (Brian Waller Procter), and Coleridge, who contributed rarely but whose thought exerted a profound influence on the staff. The two best-known Fraserians were Thomas Carlyle, who had an intense aversion to the forced bohemianism of the staff and thought the magazine itself a "chaotic, fermenting dung-hill heap of compost" but who also found its pages open to so strange and novel a work as his *Sartor Resartus* (published in *Fraser's* during 1833 and 1834); and Thackeray, an acknowledged disciple of Maginn in his early career whose later writing bears more traces of *Fraser's* and its editor than he cared to acknowledge in his later, more fastidious days. Despite the brilliance of its staff, however, for its first six years the heart and soul of *Fraser's* was William Maginn, who laid about him, with great gusto, at most of the fashionable ideas, politicians, and writers of the time.

While it was not an acknowledged political organ, there was no doubt where the loyalties of *Fraser's* lay. The magazine's writers, regardless of their subject, continually inserted attacks on Whigs, laissez-faire principles, and political economy in what amounted to a continuous Tory polemic. Maginn was a fierce and dedicated Tory, but his Toryism had a strongly humanitarian cast. He had spent much time in the London and Paris slums talking with workers and criminals, and his conversations had convinced him that "the source of crime, the fountainhead of pauperism and its consequences—is POVERTY!" Maginn had developed great sympathy for the oppressed, and felt that the political economists indulged Malthusian theories at the expense of humanity. He continually attacked their idea that all poorhouses, charity hospitals, alms, and other aid to the poor be abolished, writing that "The feelings of these political economists toward the people, are just the same as those entertained three thousand years ago by Pharaoh toward the children of Israel. . . . And there are those among ourselves, who, if they dare, would gladly employ the same means with those adopted by Pharaoh." Maginn's outcries against political corruption were not only heartfelt but also influential. When some of his political articles attacking Whigs and economic radicals and advocating the restructuring of the Tory party were reprinted as pamphlets, they sold, according to *Fraser's*, in the tens of thousands, and may have helped prepare the proper political climate for Disraeli.

The literary onslaughts of *Fraser's* were as lively as, and more entertaining than, its political diatribes. Its attacks centered on the fashionable historical novelists of the time, epitomized by Edward Bulwer-Lytton, whose status as a novelist and as editor of the staunchly Whig *New Monthly* made him a prime satiric target. Beginning with a caustic but reasonably accurate attack on "Fashionable Novels," Maginn and the Fraserians launched the longest, most sustained assault in the history of literary journalism. Maginn himself relented slightly after Bulwer resigned from the *New Monthly* in 1833, but Thackeray, under the name of Michael Angelo Titmarsh, resumed the attack on "Bulwig" which ended only with the first "Novels By Eminent Hands" in *Punch* in 1847. This "baiting of Bulwer," with Bulwer's reference to the Fraserians as the "great unwashed" and their characterization of him as "a silver fork polisher" and leader of "the footman school of novelists," is certainly less than elevated literary criticism, and one may sympathize with poor Bulwer's later complaint, reported in his grandson's biography, that Maginn and Thackeray attacked him "not in any form that can fairly be called criticism, but with a kind of ribald impertinence offered, so far as I can remember, to no other writer of my time." Still, for a modern reader the strictures against Bulwer's novels seem no more than just—if sharply exaggerated—criticism, and much of the "ribald impertinence" is, despite its undeniable crudeness and vulgarity, wonderfully funny.

In addition to his continual, joyfully vicious assaults on Bulwer, "Pimpled Hazlitt," and other writers, Maginn also throughout his career provided literary criticism in the form of such parodies and burlesques as "Don Juan Unread"; "Moore-ish Melodies," in which such a sentimental poem as Thomas Moore's "The Last Rose of Summer" becomes "The Last Glass of Claret" and "The Last Lamp in the Alley"; and Maginn's most sustained parody, the transformation of John Wilson's then-popular poem "Unimore" into "Barney Moore, A Vision of Covent Garden and St. Giles." His most important literary contribution to *Fraser's* was the "Gallery of Illustrious Literary Characters" (1830-1838). This series of eighty-one representations of well-known writers and politicians of the day, which consists of slightly mocking but accurate drawings by Daniel Maclise, with brief and informative—though also sharply satiric, sometimes too "knowing," and entirely too personal—paragraph biographies by Maginn, soon became the most popular feature of *Fraser's*.

These years with *Fraser's* were the climax of Maginn's career, a time when his reputation was at its peak and his output was prodigious. In addition to his "Gallery" biographies and a minimum of four to five articles for each issue of the magazine, in 1834 *Blackwood's* published his two best short stories. "The Story Without a Tail" is a plotless narrative in which a group of Irishmen, after a long night of serious drinking, tries, with no success whatever, to remember Humpy Harlowe's "tale of wondrous length" but can recall only the opening words "Humphries Told Me." The second is Maginn's comic masterpiece, "Bob Burke's Duel With Ensign Brady of the 48th," the story of Bob's money-inspired devotion to Dosy Macnamara and his reluctant duel with his equally reluctant romantic rival Ensign Brady. These first-person monologues, written in a racy Irish vernacular and filled with Hibernian hyperbole, make

*Maginn and Hugh Fraser with contributors to their magazine (drawing by Daniel Maclise)*

one regret that his personal excesses and the demands of journalism prevented Maginn from writing more in this form.

From his arrival in London Maginn had been a success, but in 1836 a series of public and private disasters began a steady personal and professional decline. As early as 1834 Maginn's irresponsibility had led to his dismissal from the *Standard*, his main source of income; he had been forced to escape his creditors by hiding in a garret in Wych Street and was later placed in a sponging house. Lockhart and other friends sent Maginn to Belgium until they could raise one thousand pounds to pay his debts. In August 1836 Maginn reviewed, anonymously, for *Fraser's* the Honorable Grantley Berkeley's novel *Berkeley Castle*. He rightly declared that "In everything the novel is stupid, ignorant, vulgar and contemptible," but also in the review he attacked Berkeley personally and made several snide references to some of his less than illustrious ancestors. The enraged Berkeley and his brother Craven responded by attacking James Fraser with a loaded riding crop, a nearly lethal attack from which the publisher never fully recovered. After the assault Maginn immediately acknowledged the review and challenged Berkeley to a duel. The men exchanged three rounds of shots without effect, thus ending the last documented literary duel in England.

After the Berkeley affair Maginn left the staff of *Fraser's*, and by 1837 drink, dissipation, and insolvency became paramount in his life. He remained, however, the leading journalist in England, evidenced by his being asked in 1837 to write the prologue to *Bentley's Miscellany*, to which he also contributed essays on Shakespeare. These, with his "Consideration of Farmer's *Essay on the Learning of Shakespeare*" (*Fraser's*, September, October, and December 1839), are the best examples of Maginn's more serious work. His Shakespeare criticisms offer several sound insights, particularly regarding the characters of Falstaff, Jacques, and Bottom, but even here Maginn was too much the journalist to develop his ideas fully. As Augustus Ralli remarks, his "inspiration is momentary, but the moment is a precious one." In 1838 Maginn also began to publish in *Fraser's* his "Homeric Ballads." These poems, which were extremely popular and went through several editions, are well evaluated in Matthew Arnold's *On Translating Homer* (1861), where he judged that the ballads are "vigorous and genuine poems in their own way," but that as translations they are "not at all Homeric, they have not the least in the world the manner of Homer."

Then, in 1838, came the death of Letitia Elizabeth Landon. L.E.L., the most popular female poet in England and the most important early reviewer for the *Literary Gazette*, had formed a lasting attachment with Maginn on their meeting in 1821. Despite unsupported allegations by Maginn's enemies, their deep friendship seems to have been precisely that, but it led to gossip and personal problems for both. When Ellen Maginn found some letters by Landon and her husband, she took them in a jealous rage to John Forster, Landon's fiancé, who then broke off the engagement. Ellen Maginn's jealous act apparently estranged Maginn, who spent most of the next two years away from home. When Landon, who had married George Maclean and moved to West Africa, died under mysterious circumstances from an overdose of prussic acid, Maginn was insensible for days afterward, and shortly before his own death he thought he saw Letitia sitting reproachfully at his bedside.

Landon's departure and death hastened Maginn's now precipitate decline, and his last few years offer a sad spectacle of debt, drink, and depression. In 1839, again to escape his creditors, he moved to Liverpool to edit the *Lancaster Herald*. He stayed in the city only long enough to gather material for—rather surprisingly in light of his earlier savage criticisms of the form—an historical novel set in Liverpool in the eighteenth century. *John Manesty, The Liverpool Merchant*, left unfinished at Maginn's death, was completed by Charles Ollier and published, with illustrations by George Cruikshank, in 1844. Maginn continued to write for the *Age*, the *Argus*, and even a radical paper, the *True Sun*, and published two works which further damaged his already tattered reputation.

"The Tobias Correspondence," which Maginn later jokingly termed "the whole art and mystery of editing a newspaper," is a clever demonstration of how a clever journalist can manipulate facts, arguments, and statistics to support either side of a topic. First published in the July and August 1840 issues of *Blackwood's*, "The Tobias Correspondence" is in fact a trenchant satire on the lies and venality of the contemporary newspaper world, but it has too often been taken as a serious statement of Maginn's own methods. Such an interpretation enhanced Maginn's undeserved reputation as an unprincipled journalist and gives point to Miriam Thrall's pungent remark that "The danger of being a satirist has long been recognized, and it is well known that Daniel Defoe was not the only innocent man pilloried for supposing the reading public to be intelligent."

In 1841 Maginn had published *Magazine Miscellanies*, a cheap, shoddy collection of his work which embarrassed his friends and remained unbought and unread. The collection, meant to salvage his fortunes, instead destroyed them. The publisher sued to recover his losses, and at the beginning of 1842 Maginn was arrested for debt and placed in Fleet prison. Lockhart and other friends, fearful for his health, pleaded for his release on the grounds of illness. The release was granted in the spring of 1842. After leaving prison Maginn, his wife, and their three children moved just outside London to the village of Walton-on-Thames, where he died on 21 August 1842 at the age of forty-eight. When he died *Punch*, to which he was one of the first contributors, used its now-famous black border for the first time, and *Fraser's* published a sympathetic and complimentary eulogy to its founder, but Maginn left his family in such financial straits that the *Fraser's* staff blended the usual encomiums with a delicate request for funds for his family. Maginn was buried in Walton-on-Thames in a grave that remained unmarked until a Celtic cross was placed on it in 1926.

Maginn's literary reputation remains buried and unmarked. The complete neglect into which his work has fallen is not altogether just, but for this neglect Maginn himself, whose talent for journalism was equaled by his talent for self-destruction, is largely to blame. His contributions were diverse and in their time significant. In addition to his work on Shakespeare and Homer, Maginn was among the first to write genuine Irish songs as opposed to the sentimentalities he had attacked in his essay "On Irish Songs"; he was an early critic of Irish literature and an early compiler, with Crofton Croker, of Irish folklore; and his character Sir Morgan O'Doherty is the prototype of William Hamilton Maxwell and Charles James Lever's later drunken, joking military heroes. Maginn was an adept writer of, appropriately, such drinking songs as "The Pewter Quart" and "A Twist-imony in Favour of Gin Twist," while "The Story Without a Tail" and "Bob Burke's Duel With Ensign Brady" show him to be a master of a certain kind of short story. His work with *Blackwood's* and especially with *Fraser's* places him among the founders of magazine jour-

*Portrait by Daniel Maclise in the* Fraser's Magazine *"Gallery of Illustrious Literary Characters" (1830-1838)*

nalism. But Maginn's was an ephemeral brilliance, thoughtlessly expended on topics of little interest in a style too hasty and careless. Maginn, who often called himself "a mere scrap writer" and had an "almost irresistible impulse" to throw his magazine and newspaper writing into the fire, was sufficiently aware of his personal and professional faults that he would probably have agreed with the *Fraser's* obituary that he "resembled Swift not merely in his wit, but in the utter carelessness with which he regarded the fate of the productions of his genius. If they served the purpose of the moment, whether it were to make a minister tremble or a lady smile, 'the Doctor' never troubled himself further about his thunder or his jest." Maginn gave no thought to posterity, and posterity has so fully repaid the compliment that, despite the value of some aspects of his work, he is likely to be remembered not as a scholar, a writer, or a journalist, but as the subject of Lockhart's ruefully affectionate epitaph:

Here, early to bed, lies kind William Maginn,
Who, with genius, wit, learning, life's trophies to win,
Had neither great lord nor rich cit of his kin,
Nor discretion to set himself up as to tin;
So his portion soon spent, like the poor heir of Lynn,
He turned author while yet was no beard on his chin;
And whoever was out, or whoever was in,
For the Tories his fine Irish brains he would spin,
Who received prose and rhyme with a promising grin,
"Go ahead, you queer fish, and more power to your fin,"
But to save from starvation stirred never a pin.
Light for long was his heart, though his breeches were thin,
Else his acting for certain was equal to Quin;
But at last he was beat and sought help from the bin,
(All the same to the Doctor, from claret to gin),
Which led swiftly to gaol with consumption therein.

It was much when the bones rattled loose in his skin,
He got leave to die here out of Babylon's din.
Barring drink and the girls, I ne'er heard of a sin—
Many worse, better few, than bright, broken Maginn!

**Biographies:**

E. V. Kenealy and D. M. Moir, "William Maginn, LL.D," *Dublin University Magazine*, 23 (1844);

Shelton Mackenzie, "Memoir," in *Miscellaneous Writings of the Late Dr. Maginn*, 5 volumes, edited by Mackenzie (New York: Redfield, 1855-1857);

R. W. Montagu, "Memoir," in *Miscellanies: Prose and Verse by William Maginn*, 2 volumes, edited by Montagu (London: Sampson, Low, Marston, Searle & Rivington, 1885), I: viii-xix.

**References:**

Matthew Arnold, *On Translating Homer* (London: Longman, Green, Longman & Roberts, 1861);

Grantley Berkeley, *My Life and Recollections*, 4 volumes (London: Hurst & Blackett, 1865-1866);

Malcolm Elwin, *Victorian Wallflowers* (London: Cape, 1934);

R. P. Gillies, *Memoirs of a Literary Veteran*, 3 volumes (London: Bentley, 1851);

John Gross, *The Rise and Fall of the Man of Letters* (New York: Macmillan, 1969);

S. C. Hall, *A Book of Memories of Great Men and Women, From Personal Acquaintance* (London: Virtue, 1871);

Hall, *Retrospect of a Long Life, From 1815 to 1883* (London: Bentley, 1883);

William Jerdan, *The Autobiography of William Jerdan, With His Literary, Political and Social Reminiscences and Correspondence During the Last Fifty Years*, 4 volumes (London: A. Hall, Virtue, 1852-1853);

E. V. Kenealy, *Brallaghan: or, The Deipnosophists* (London: E. Churton, 1845);

"The Late William Maginn, LL.D.," *Fraser's*, 26 (September 1842);

John Gibson Lockhart, "The Doctor," *Fraser's*, 2 (January 1831): 716;

Michael Monahan, "Doctor Maginn," in his *Nova Hibernia: Irish Poets and Dramatists of Yesterday and Today* (New York: Kennerley, 1914), pp. 203-235;

D. J. O'Donoghue, "Irish Wit and Humour," in *Irish Literature*, 10 volumes, edited by Justin Mccarthy and others (Philadelphia: J. D. Morris, 1904);

O'Donoghue, *The Poets of Ireland*, 3 parts (London: Printed for the author, 1892-1893; Dublin: Hodges, Figgis, 1912);

Margaret Oliphant, *Annals of a Publishing House: William Blackwood and His Sons, Their Magazine, and Friends*, 3 volumes (Edinburgh: William Blackwood, 1897-1898);

Augustus Ralli, *A History of Shakespearian Criticism*, 2 volumes (London: Oxford University Press, 1932), pp. 193-197;

Michael Sadleir, *Bulwer: A Panorama, 1803-1806* (Boston: Little, Brown, 1931);

Sadleir, *XIX Century Fiction: A Bibliographical Record Based on His Own Collection*, 2 volumes (London: Constable, 1951);

Sadleir, *Things Past* (London: Constable, 1944);

George Saintsbury, *A History of Nineteenth Century Literature (1780-1895)* (New York & London: Macmillan, 1896);

Saintsbury, "Three Humourists: Hook, Barham, Maginn," in his *Essays in English Literature, 1780-1860*, second series (New York: Scribners, 1895), pp. 270-302;

Samuel Smiles, *A Publisher and His Friends: Memoirs and Correspondence of the Late John Murray, With an Account of the Origin and Progress of the House*, 2 volumes (London: John Murray, 1891);

Logan Pearsall Smith, *Reperusals and Re-Collections* (London: Constable, 1936);

M. H. Speilman, *The History of Punch* (London: Cassell, 1895);

K. D. Thomson, "Dr. Maginn," in her *Recollections of Literary Characters and Celebrated Places*, 2 volumes (London: Bentley, 1854), I: 1-12;

Miriam M. H. Thrall, *Rebellious Fraser's: Noll Yorke's Magazine in the Days of Maginn, Thackeray, and Carlyle* (New York: Columbia University Press, 1934);

"Tragedy of A Writer: William Maginn, 1793-1842," *Times Literary Supplement*, 22 August 1942, p. 418;

R. M. Wardle, "Outwitting Hazlitt," *Modern Language Notes*, 57 (1942): 459-462.

# Mary Russell Mitford

*(16 December 1787 - 9 January 1855)*

Nicholas R. Jones
*Oberlin College*

BOOKS: *Poems* (London: Printed by A. J. Valpy & sold by Longman, Hurst, Rees & Orme, 1810; enlarged edition, London: Printed by A. J. Valpy & sold by F. C. & J. Rivington, 1811);

*Christina, The Maid of the South Seas; A Poem* (London: Printed by A. J. Valpy for F. C. & J. Rivington, 1811);

*Watlington Hill; A Poem* (London: Printed by A. J. Valpy, 1812);

*Narrative Poems on the Female Character in the Various Relations of Human Life*, volume 1 [no more published] (London, 1813; New York: Eastburn, Kirk, 1813);

*Julian, A Tragedy in Five Acts* (London: G. & W. B. Whittaker, 1823; New York: W. B. Gilley, 1823);

*Our Village: Sketches of Rural Character and Scenery*, volume 1 (London: G. & W. B. Whittaker, 1824); volumes 2 and 3 (London: G. B. Whittaker, 1826, 1828); volumes 1-3 (New York: E. Bliss, 1828); volumes 4 and 5 (London: Whittaker, Treacher, 1830, 1832); volume 4 (New York: E. Bliss, 1830);

*Foscari: A Tragedy* (London: Printed for G. B. Whittaker, 1826);

*Dramatic Scenes, Sonnets, and Other Poems* (London: G. B. Whittaker, 1827);

*Rienzi: A Tragedy, in Five Acts* (London: J. Cumberland, 1828; Baltimore: Printed & published by J. Robinson, 1829; Boston: Press of the Boston Daily Advertiser, 1829; New York: Elton & Perkins, 1829);

*Charles the First, An Historical Tragedy, in Five Acts* (London: J. Duncombe, 1834);

*Sadak and Kalasrade; or, The Waters of Oblivion. A Romantic Opera in Two Acts* (London: Fairbrother, 1835);

*Belford Regis; or, Sketches of a Country Town* (3 volumes, London: R. Bentley, 1835; 1 volume, Philadelphia: Carey, Lea & Blanchard, 1835);

*Country Stories* (London: Saunders & Otley, 1837; Philadelphia: Carey, Lea & Blanchard, 1838);

*The Works of Mary Russell Mitford: Prose and Verse* (Philadelphia: Crissy, 1841);

*Inez de Castro: A Tragedy in Five Acts* (London: John Dicks, 1841);

*Recollections of a Literary Life; or, Books, Places, and People* (London: R. Bentley, 1852; New York: Harper, 1852);

*Atherton, and Other Tales* (3 volumes, London: Hurst & Blackett, 1854; 1 volume, Boston: Ticknor & Fields, 1854);

*The Dramatic Works of Mary Russell Mitford*, 2 volumes (London: Hurst & Blackett, 1854).

PLAY PRODUCTIONS: *Julian*, London, Theatre Royal, Covent Garden, 15 March 1823;

*Foscari*, London, Theatre Royal, Covent Garden, 4 November 1826;

*Rienzi*, London, Theatre Royal, Drury Lane, 9 October 1828;

*Charles the First*, London, Royal Victoria Theatre, 2 July 1834;

*Sadak and Kalasrade*, with music by Charles Parker, London, English Opera House, 20 April 1835;

*Inez de Castro*, London, Royal City of London Theatre, 12 April 1841.

OTHER: *Stories of American Life; by American Writers*, 3 volumes, edited by Mitford (London: H. Colburn & R. Bentley, 1830);

*American Stories for Little Boys and Girls, Intended for Children under Ten Years of Age*, 3 volumes, edited by Mitford (London: Whittaker, Treacher, 1831); republished as *Stories, for Little Boys and Girls: Intended for Children under Ten Years of Age. Selected from American Writers*, first series, 3 volumes (London: Printed for Whittaker, 1835) and *Tales for Young People. Above Ten Years of Age. Selected from American Writers*, second series, 2 volumes (London: Whittaker, 1835);

*Lights and Shadows of American Life*, 3 volumes, edited by Mitford (London: H. Colburn & R. Bentley, 1832);

*Mary Russell Mitford (engraving after a portrait by Benjamin Robert Haydon)*

*Finden's Tableaux. A Series of Picturesque Scenes of National Character, Beauty, and Costume. From Paintings, by Various Artists, after Sketches by W. Perring*, edited by Mitford (London: C. Tilt, 1838);

*Finden's Tableaux of the Affections; A Series of Picturesque Illustrations of the Womanly Virtues. From Paintings by W. Perring*, edited by Mitford (London: C. Tilt, 1839).

Famous in her day for what she herself considered one of her lesser accomplishments, Mary Russell Mitford deserves attention as one of the first women successfully to enter the expanding nineteenth-century marketplace of prose and as the virtual founder of the local-color movement of regional fiction. Her finest work, *Our Village* (1824-1832), five volumes of sketches of English country life, became a local and international success and generated large numbers of imitations and descendants through the century, both in England and America.

Like many other writers of the later Romantic period, Mitford's literary life spanned many genres; she only reluctantly engaged in the prose work that alone brought her financial success. Mitford began her publishing career with an extensive production of poetry between 1810 and 1813; at the time, she was living in an elegant house outside of Reading, with her father and mother, in relative middle-class comfort. But the family had not always been—nor was it to remain—well off. In 1785 her mother, Mary Russell, a distant relative of the dukes of Bedford, had inherited a substantial estate; the thirty-six-year-old heiress almost immediately married George Mitford, a surgeon ten years younger, already addicted to high spending and gambling. They settled in the market town of Alresford, in Hampshire, in a gentility apparently little disturbed by Dr. Mitford's slight practice of medicine. Mary, their only surviving child, was born two years after the marriage, and grew up precocious, reading and reciting poetry from the age of three, the companion of her father on many excursions in the countryside. Her father's extravagance quickly consumed his wife's property and, in the mid 1790s, led him away from rural Alresford to the more sophisticated seaside resort of Lyme Regis. Setting up in grand style, he tried for about a year to recoup his fortunes at gambling. When the attempt failed, the family fled to uncomfortable lodgings (and possibly debtors' prison) in London, where Dr. Mitford tried to piece together a living with odds and ends of a practice.

On Mary's tenth birthday, she playfully selected a lottery ticket for her father; the twenty-thousand-pound prize enabled the family to resettle, this time in the prosperous town of Reading. Mitford was sent for four years to the fashionable Abbey School in London—whose alumnae included L.E.L. (Letitia Elizabeth Landon, the poet) and the future Caroline Lamb. Here Mitford excelled in languages (including Latin) and literary studies, but she was summoned home in 1802 to grace the parlor at her father's newest folly, a grand mansion on parklike grounds just outside Reading. Here, with occasional trips to London and Northumberland, Mitford lived for the next two decades. Always an avid reader, she kept an extensive correspondence on literary and local topics, and before long she began to compose poetry with an eye to publication. As the family money inevitably disappeared and life grew shabbier, Mitford tried to earn an income with her poems. *Poems* (1810), the first production, was a small volume of miscellaneous poems about nature and flowers, combined with poems of praise for her father's Whig friends. Encouraged by Sir William Elford, an elderly man of letters with whom she carried on a lengthy correspondence, Mitford took on a full-length narrative poem about the newly revealed fate of the Bounty mutineers on Pitcairn Island. Both Elford and, through him, Samuel Taylor Coleridge took an active role in seeing this poem, *Christina, The Maid of the South Seas*, into print in 1811; it met with considerable success in Britain and the United States. As the family furniture and eventually the house itself were put up for sale, Mitford began to voice her hope that her publications might bring in substantial revenues. In 1812 she published a poem of country life, *Watlington Hill*, concentrating on descriptions of country-house scenery and hunting. A year later, inspired by the poems of Sir Walter Scott and Robert Southey, she wrote and published *Narrative Poems on the Female Character in the Various Relations of Human Life*, comprising two ambitious poems—"The Rival Sisters" and "Blanche of Castille," capitalizing on the current English interest in Spain. Although this volume appeared to promise a sequel, it apparently never saw light.

*Miniature of Mitford at age four (from Constance Hill,* Mary Russell Mitford and Her Surroundings, *1920)*

By 1820 Dr. Mitford's lottery winnings had been spent, and the family was forced to sell their mansion. They moved to a cottage outside Reading, on the turnpike road at Three Mile Cross, the village Mitford was to make famous as "our village." Though life in the tiny cottage could not have been easy, with a demanding and still-extravagant father, Mitford kept up a significant literary activity, not only engaging in an extensive and witty correspondence, but also actively pursuing income in two new fields, drama and prose. As she later wrote, the alternative would have been to leave her family and become a schoolteacher or governess.

For a prolific and imaginative author in need of funds, the stage held great attraction. Mitford had made an abortive try at stage writing in 1813, but only after the move to Three

Mile Cross did she turn to it in earnest, with the diary prayer, "God grant I may make some money of it" (20 December 1820). Her first manuscript, "Fiesco," was rejected after some interest by the actor-manager William Macready. With the advice of a younger author and critic, Thomas Talfourd—friend of William Wordsworth, Charles Lamb, Coleridge, and William Hazlitt, and intimate of the London theaters—Mitford persisted, and by 1825 she had written four tragedies, all on historical themes in the heroic Romantic mode: *Foscari* (1826), *Julian* (1823), *Charles the First* (1834), and *Rienzi* (1828). Only one of these saw timely production, however, the rest being delayed by theatrical infighting and—in the case of *Charles the First*—a licensing ban. The eight-day run of *Julian* in March 1823 brought Mitford a welcome two hundred pounds, but also a fierce critical attack. Mitford seems to have agreed with Macready that the review was sexist, and at once she proclaimed her intention to continue to write on themes of grand historical tragedy. *Foscari*, delayed at first by the coincidence of George Gordon, Lord Byron's simultaneous presentation of a tragedy on the same subject, was further delayed by quarrels with the actor Charles Kemble, who eventually played the lead in a run of fifteen nights in November and December 1826.

Mitford's most substantial theatrical success was *Rienzi*, which she finished by early 1825. A nasty series of private and public squabbles delayed its production; at last the play was produced in October 1828 at Drury Lane theater, with an unknown young actress, Louisa Anne Phillips, as the heroine. *Rienzi* ran to considerable critical praise, was often republished, and eventually became a popular vehicle for the American actress Charlotte Cushman; Edward Bulwer-Lytton referred to it with warm praise in the preface to his novel on the same subject (*Rienzi*, 1835). But even with this success, which kept the Mitford household from dissolution, dramatic work cost Mitford, as she wrote in a 4 December 1825 letter to Talfourd, "perpetual anxiety & constant disappointment." Even so, she kept writing for the stage: three more plays (*Inez de Castro* [1841] and two that remained unperformed—*Gaston de Blondeville* and *Otto of Wittlesbach*, both first published in *Dramatic Works* [1854]). She also wrote a libretto for an opera (*Sadak and Kalasrade*, 1835). The music for the opera was written by a young Reading amateur, Charles Parker, and achieved something less than success.

The period of Mitford's struggles to make a living through the theater was also the period of her most productive work in prose. She briefly considered writing novels, but gave up, imagining them compared to the prose of Jane Austen: "I know how utterly contemptible they will be," she wrote to Talfourd on 29 July 1825. In 1821, on Talfourd's advice (and conscious of Washington Irving's success in *Geoffrey Crayon's Sketch Book*, 1819, 1820), she began to turn her considerable skill as a letter writer—her letters are witty, observant, epigrammatic, engaging—to production of prose pieces for the magazines. Four early sketches were published by Thomas Campbell in the *New Monthly Magazine* in 1821, but Campbell subsequently rejected Mitford and Talfourd's proposal for a series of sketches on village life. The first pieces of *Our Village* were therefore published in 1823 in an obscure journal, the *Lady's Magazine*, where their popularity significantly enlarged the magazine's subscriptions. When the editor absconded owing Mitford some forty pounds, she began to think of publishing the prose pieces herself, to recoup her loss. By mid 1824 the first volume of *Our Village*, containing twenty-four sketches, was published, and it sold well from the first. By September 1824 the publisher asked her for a second series, which was in print by 1826; there were eventually to be five volumes published at two-year intervals until 1832.

In *Noctes Ambrosianæ*, Christopher North's "Shepherd" characterized the remarkable combination of wit and tenderness found throughout *Our Village*: "She has an ee like a hawk's, that misses naething, however far aff—and yet like a dove's, that sees only what is nearest and dearest, and round about the hame-circle o' its central nest" (*Blackwood's Magazine*, March 1829). Indeed, this observer of village life—as indistinguishable from the real Mitford as Childe Harold from Byron—is vital, social, chatty, acute, caring. Her personal life—a father to care for, a cottage and its garden to tend, her former home in all its grandeur not far off—is present but not consuming, for it is the lives of others that fill these sketches: blacksmith, cobbler, cricketers, farmers, maids, tradesmen, odd-jobbers. Like the journals of Dorothy Wordsworth, Mitford's sketches are filled with the stories of those she encounters on walks, social calls, and errands; unlike the journals, of course, these stories are developed over time, anecdotes that become narrations, fleshed out with beginnings, middles, and endings. Harriet Martineau, in her memoir of Mitford, as-

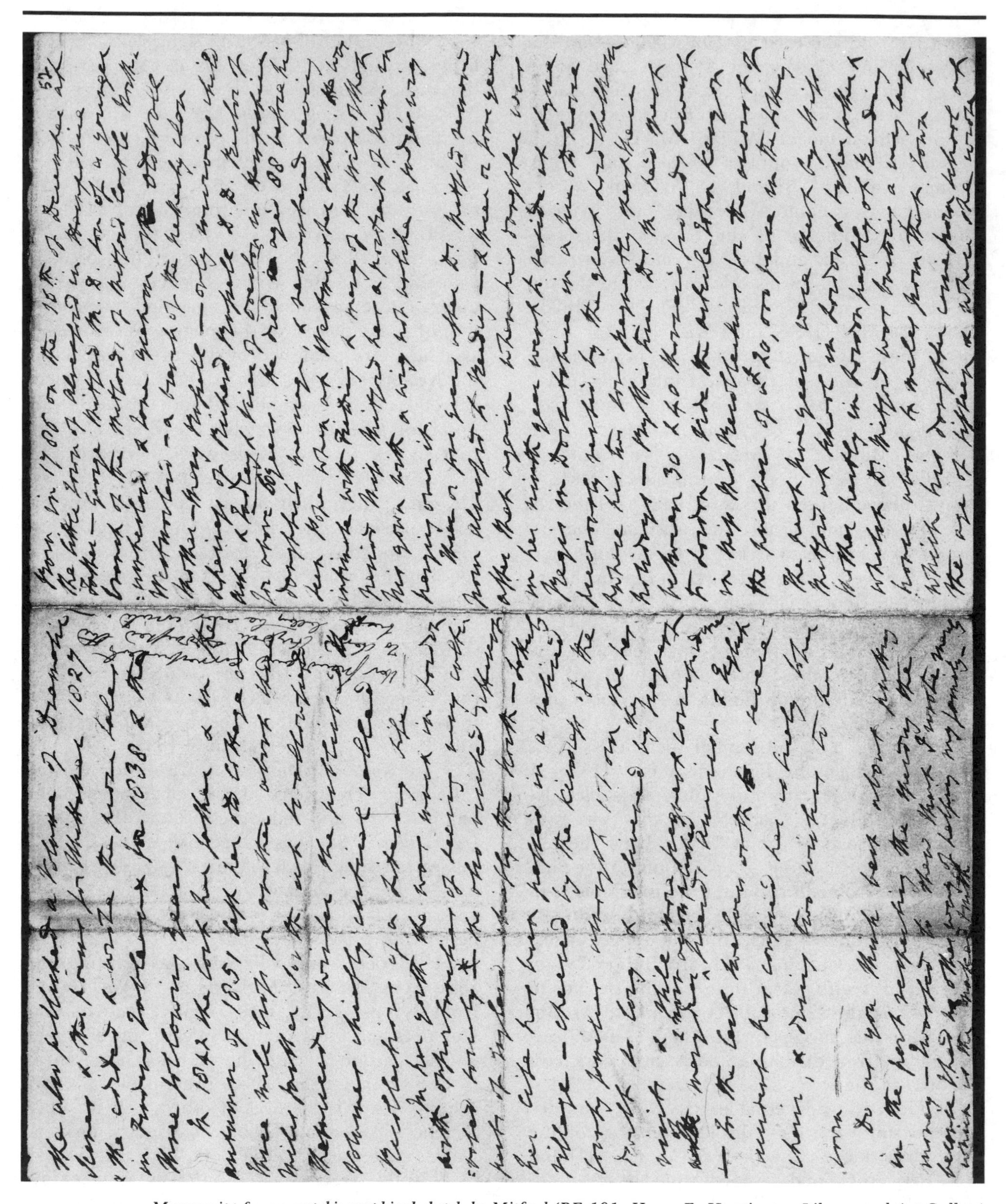

*Manuscript for an autobiographical sketch by Mitford (BE 101; Henry E. Huntington Library and Art Gallery)*

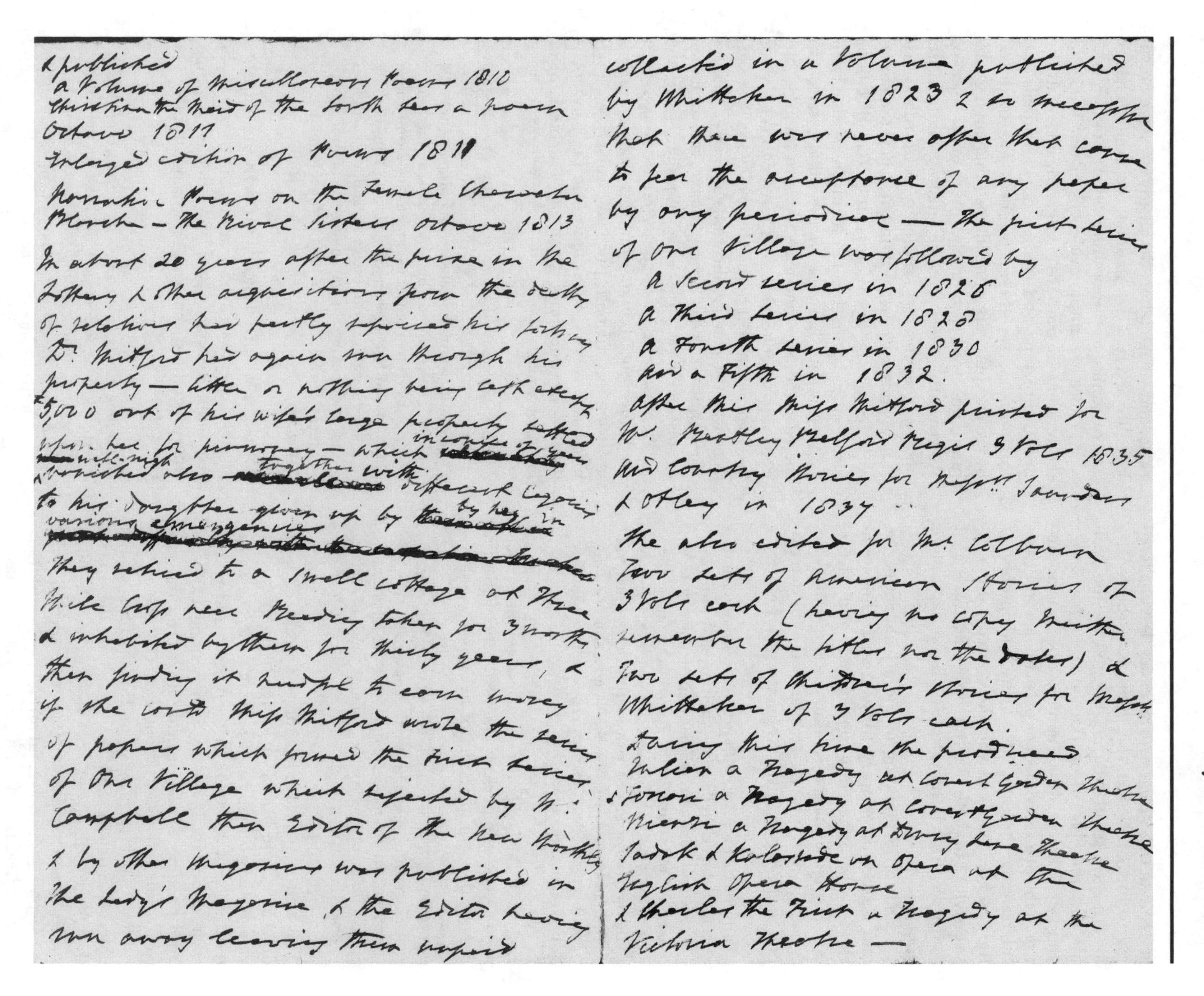

& published
a Volume of Miscellaneous Poems 1810
Christina the Maid of the South Seas a poem
Octavo 1811
Enlarged edition of Poems 1811
Narrative Poems on the Female Character
Blanch — The Rival Sisters Octavo 1813
In about 20 years after the prize in the
Lottery & other acquisitions from the death
of relations had partly repaired his fortune
Dr. Mitford had again run through his
property — little or nothing being left except
5,000 out of his wife's large property settled
upon her for pin money — which in course of years
was well-nigh vanished also together with different legacies
to his daughter given up by her in
various emergencies
They retired to a small cottage at Three
Mile Cross near Reading taken for 3 months
& inhabited by them for thirty years, &
then finding it needful to earn money
of the world Miss Mitford wrote the series
of papers which formed the first series
of Our Village which rejected by Mr.
Campbell then Editor of the New Monthly
& by other Magazines was published in
the Lady's Magazine & the Editor having
run away leaving them unpaid

collected in a Volume published
by Whittaker in 1823 & so successful
that there was never after that cause
to fear the acceptance of any paper
by any periodical — The first series
of Our Village was followed by
A Second series in 1826
A Third series in 1828
A Fourth series in 1830
and a Fifth in 1832.
After this Miss Mitford printed for
Mr. Bentley Belford Regis 3 Vols 1835
and Country Stories for Messrs Saunders
& Otley in 1837
She also edited for Mr. Colburn
Two sets of American Stories of
3 Vols each (having no copy neither
remember the titles nor the dates) &
Two sets of Children's Stories for Messrs
Whittaker of 3 Vols each.
During this time she produced
Julian a Tragedy at Covent Garden Theatre
Foscari a Tragedy at Covent Garden Theatre
Rienzi a Tragedy at Drury Lane Theatre
Sadak & Kalasrade an Opera at the
English Opera House
& Charles the First a Tragedy at the
Victoria Theatre —

serted that *Our Village* uses an easier, less challenging form than fiction, that there is in the form a lowering of standards, necessitated by the real-life demands placed on the writer by her father and her finances. But this view does not do justice to the precise control of point of view, the careful framing through the activity and interest of the observer-persona, and the craftedly unobtrusive style. Elizabeth Barrett Browning's praise of Mitford's "Dutch minuteness" is perhaps more apt.

Mitford's updating of the urbane wit of the mid eighteenth century forms a surprising vehicle for the inherently sentimental and picturesque subject matter—country scenery and life. A cottage in the forest receives a skillful description in the mode of the Romantic picturesque:

> a picture of a place, with its French windows and verandahs, its trellis and porch covered with clematis and jesamine, its baby-house conservatory and its miniature lawn. It was situated in the midst of woody, winding lanes, lost, as it were, in the labyrinths of our rich and intricate country, with an open grove of noble beeches on one side of it, and a clear stream, crossed by a winding bridge, on the other.

But after this obviously warm observation of a pretty scene, the persona pointedly and wittily undercuts the sentimentality of her description:

> It seemed a spot made expressly for brides and bridegrooms, doomed, by the inexorable laws of fashion, to four weeks of connubial felicity, to get creditably weary of solitude and of each other.

This acute narrator takes subjects of apparent ordinariness (the life of an insignificant crossroads village, the courtships of servant girls, the short-term lease of a cottage in the woods) and reveals their importance, not by commenting explicitly but by telling the stories that lie behind the subjects. The important themes of *Our Village* are found, not surprisingly, in the interests of the observer-narrator and developed in the stories she tells: the dignity of working-class life; the difficulties of courtship and marriage choices for servant women; the powerful influence of marital status on individuals of both genders and all classes; the importance of age—childhood, adolescence, young adulthood, old age—in the moral and economic choices of everyday life; the difficult interaction between established gentry, urban nouveau riche, and village labor; the steady pressure on village life exerted by national economic change and proximity to the swelling city of London.

There are ample evidences in *Our Village* of the tensions of post-1815 England, above all the pressure of time and change on individuals and communities; yet these evidences are mediated by the exceptionally calm, almost unchanging narrator, one who, not unlike the poetic voice of Wordsworth, feels change deeply and insists upon a compensatory continuity. Mitford's sketch "Lucy" ends with such a moment: Lucy, the narrator's servant, a lively, gossiping and flirtatious girl, is jilted by her beau, a handsome tailor from London whose business in the village fails. On the rebound, she marries a pleasant enough, but pedantic, schoolteacher and moves to the city of S--- [old Sarum?]. There "Mitford" visits her, saddened at the change she finds in Lucy: "She, a schoolmistress, a keeper of silence, a maintainer of discipline, a scolder, a punisher! Ah! she would rather be scolded herself; it would be a far lighter punishment." But this change, though involving loss for both Lucy and herself, is recognized as necessary, for it has made Lucy independent of servitude and given her the pleasure of her own house:

> What a pleasure it is to see Lucy presiding in that parlor, in all the glory of her honest affection and warm hospitality, making tea for the three guests whom she loves best in the world, vaunting with courteous pride her home-made bread and her fresh butter, yet thinking nothing good enough for the occasion; smiling and glowing, and looking the very image of beautiful happiness. Such a moment almost consoles us for losing her.

After tea, Mitford walks us through the old ruins in which the town of S--- and Lucy's new home are built, evoking again the themes of time, change, and loss, but this time romantically. The essay ends:

> Nothing can be finer than the mixture of those varied greens, so crisp and life-like, with the crumbling grey stone; nothing more perfectly in harmony with the solemn beauty of the place, than the deep cooings of the wood-pigeons, who abound in the walls. I know no pleasure so intense, so soothing, so apt to bring sweet tears into the eyes, or to awaken thoughts that "lie too deep for tears," as a walk around the old city on a fine summer evening. A ride to S--- was always

*Mitford's cottage at Three Mile Cross, circa 1836 (lithograph by E. Havell)*

delightful to me, even before it became the residence of Lucy; it is now my prime festival.

The quote from *Lyrical Ballads*, followed by the echo of the Immortality Ode in the final word of the essay ("festival"), implies that these sketches are structured on an aesthetic more demanding than may be apparent from their "charming" appearance.

Mitford's work in the prose sketch continued after the five volumes of *Our Village*, with *Belford Regis; or, Sketches of a Country Town* (1835) and *Country Stories* (1837). Neither is as inventive or as aptly composed as *Our Village*, though both met with decent commercial and critical success and helped to keep the wolf from the cottage door. The project of *Belford Regis*—the description of life in nearby Reading—is interesting as a precursor of later nineteenth-century market-town fictions, but the sketches, while in places witty and observant like those of *Our Village*, seem less convincing as a whole, missing the truth of their overall subject, a rapidly growing trading town not far from London. Mitford was hampered by the frenetic and demanding conditions of life at the cottage, with an ever more demanding father. Her mother died in January 1830, but Dr. Mitford lived on in the care of his daughter until 1842. She may also have been restricted by nostalgia, writing with, as she says, "the peculiar tastes and old-fashioned predilections" of one who remembers the Reading of forty years earlier.

Other literary enterprises of her later years include the editing of several volumes of stories about life in the United States. Mitford's strong interest in American literature led also to correspondence and visits with American men and women of letters, many of whose careers were advanced by Mitford's essays and anthologies; these American connections included James Greenleaf Whittier, Oliver Wendell Holmes, Henry Wadsworth Longfellow, Daniel Webster, Catharine Maria Sedgwick, and Nathaniel Hawthorne, whose work Mitford actively promoted and whose visit she was disappointed to miss. Increasingly connected and recognized in the literary world, Mitford became a close and confidential friend of Elizabeth Barrett (though not of her husband, Robert Browning), and their extensive correspondence, which began in 1836, is well known. Edmund Gosse claimed that Mitford was responsible for the first publication, in 1847, of Barrett's *Sonnets to the Portuguese* (1850), but John Carter and Graham Pollard's bibliographic investigations have revealed this "publication" to be a forgery by T. J. Wise. A less disputed connection with

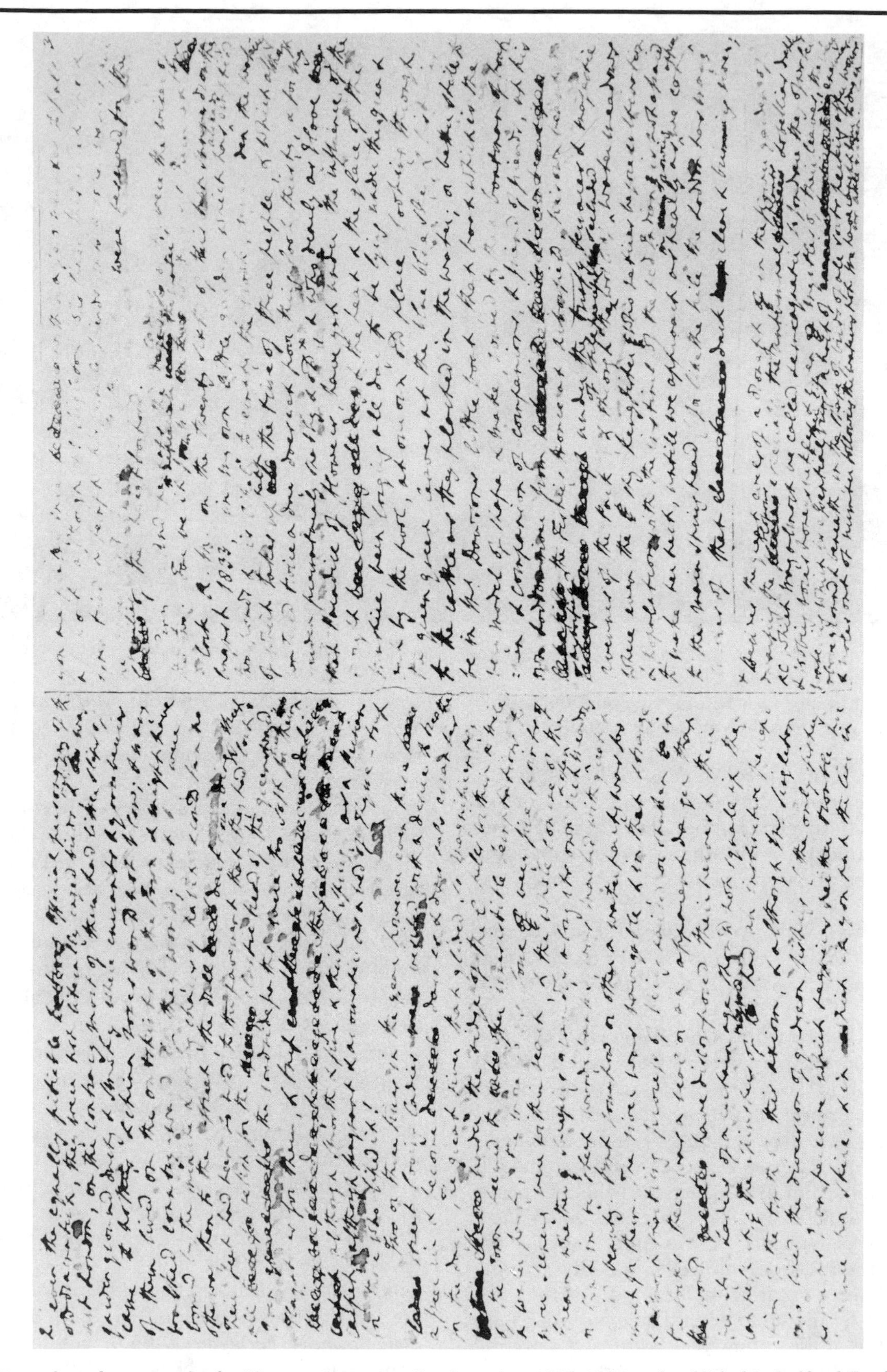

*Pages from the manuscript for "Country Excursions," written circa 1833-1834 and published in* Belford Regis *(MA 2346, Pierpont Morgan Library)*

Barrett is that the famous lapdog Flush began domestic literary life at Three Mile Cross and went to Wimpole Street as a gift from Mitford.

In 1837 Mitford was asked to edit *Finden's Tableaux,* a series of elegant "coffee-table" anthologies of poems, sketches, and engravings, drawing on her widening circle of literary friends for material. In the same year Mitford was given a state pension, and in 1842 a private subscription was raised to help her pay the debts left after her father's death; the last decade of her life was relatively free of financial worries. Her beloved cottage, however, had so deteriorated that by 1851 she had to abandon it for another in Swallowfield, about three miles further from Reading. Invalided by an accident in her pony chaise, she continued an active correspondence with many friends until her death in January 1855. Her final literary projects include the publication in 1852 of *Recollections of a Literary Life,* a volume of personal and anecdotal essays about her reading and her acquaintances with literary figures, both English and American, and in 1854 of her longest prose narrative, *Atherton,* comprising the first of three volumes, of which the other two were fugitive stories. *Atherton,* on which she had worked sporadically and reluctantly for years, finds its strength in the descriptive vein of the village sketches rather than in mastery of plot, incident, or character development.

Remembered largely in terms such as "charming" and "pleasant," Mitford's prose sketches are probably best seen not merely in such nostalgic perspectives, but also as precursors of the fictions of community that were to find their English masters in such writers as Charles Dickens and Elizabeth Gaskell, and a strong American life in the local-color writings of Harriet Beecher Stowe and Sarah Orne Jewett.

**Letters:**

*The Life of Mary Russell Mitford Related in a Selection from Her Letters to Her Friends,* 2 volumes, edited by A. G. L'Estrange (London: Bentley, 1870; revised, 1870; New York: Harper, 1870);

*Memoirs and Letters of Charles Boner . . . with Letters of Mary Russell Mitford to Him during Ten Years,* 2 volumes, edited by R. M. Kettle (London: Bentley, 1871);

*Letters of Mary Russell Mitford, Second Series,* 2 volumes, edited by Henry Chorley (London: Bentley, 1872);

*The Friendships of Mary Russell Mitford as Recorded in Letters from her Literary Correspondents,* edited by L'Estrange (2 volumes, London: Hurst & Blackett, 1882; 1 volume, New York: Harper, 1882);

*Mary Russell Mitford: Correspondence with Charles Boner & John Ruskin,* edited by Elizabeth Lee (London: Unwin, 1914; Chicago: Rand, McNally, 1915);

*The Letters of Mary Russell Mitford,* edited by R. Brimley Johnson (London: John Lane, 1925; New York: MacVeagh, 1925).

**Bibliography:**

R. J. Hart, "Mary Russell Mitford, 16 December 1787 - 9 January 1855: A Bibliography," Thesis, American Library Association, 1981.

**Biographies:**

M. O. Oliphant, "Mary Russel [*sic*] Mitford," *Blackwood's Magazine,* 75 (June 1854): 658-670;

Harriet Martineau, Sketch of Mitford, in her *Biographical Sketches* (London: Macmillan, 1869);

Oliphant, "Miss Austen and Miss Mitford," *Blackwood's Magazine,* 107 (March 1870): 290-313;

William Maginn, Sketch of Mitford, in *A Gallery of Illustrious Literary Characters, Drawn by the late Daniel Maclise, R.A., and accompanied by notices chiefly by the late William Maginn,* edited by William Bates (London: Chatto & Windus, 1873);

W. J. Roberts, *Mary Russell Mitford: The Tragedy of a Blue Stocking* (London: A. Melrose, 1913);

Constance Hill, *Mary Russell Mitford and Her Surroundings* (London & New York: John Lane, 1920);

Marjorie Astin, *Mary Russell Mitford: Her Circle and Her Books* (London: Noel Douglas, 1930);

Vera Watson, *Mary Russell Mitford* (London: Evans Bros., 1949);

Caroline Mary Duncan-Jones, *Miss Mitford and Mr. Harness; Records of a Friendship* (London: S.P.C.K., 1955).

**References:**

James Agate, "Mary Russell Mitford," in *English Wits,* edited by Leonard Russell (London: Hutchinson, 1941), pp. 329-349;

Lucien A. Agosta, " 'The Inconvenience of Celebrity': An Unpublished Letter from Elizabeth Barrett Browning to Mary Russell Mitford,"

*Browning Society Notes*, 8, no. 1 (1978): 11-13;

W. L. Bond, "Incomparable Old Maid: Letters of Mary Russell Mitford," *English*, 2, no. 11 (1938): 304-309;

John Carter and Graham Pollard, *An Enquiry into the Nature of Certain XIX Century Pamphlets* (London: Constable, 1934; New York: Scribners, 1934);

W. A. Coles, "Magazine and Other Contributions by Mary Russell Mitford and T. N. Talfourd," *Studies in Bibliography: Papers of the Bibliographical Society of the University of Virginia* (Charlottesville: Bibliographical Society of the University of Virginia, 1959), pp. 218-226;

Coles, "Mary Russell Mitford: the Inauguration of a Literary Career," *Bulletin of the John Rylands Library*, 40 (September 1957): 33-46;

Helen Gray Cone and Jeannette L. Gilder, eds., *Pen-Portraits of Literary Women, by Themselves and Others* (New York: Cassell, 1887);

Thomas Crofton Croker, *My Village, versus "Our Village"* (London: H. Fisher, R. Fisher & P. Jackson, 1833);

M. H. Dodds, "Mary Russell Mitford and Jane Austen," *Notes and Queries* (29 April 1950): 189;

James Thomas Fields, *Yesterdays with Authors* (Boston & New York: Houghton, Mifflin, 1900);

Edmund Gosse, *Books on the Table* (New York: Scribners, 1921);

Pamela Horn, "Alresford and Mary Russell Mitford," *Hatcher Review*, 22 (Autumn 1986): 86-94;

Shelagh Hunter, "George Sand and Mary Russell Mitford: Politics and Poetry," in her *Victorian Idyllic Fiction: Pastoral Strategies* (London: Macmillan, 1984), pp. 59-76;

John L. Idol, Jr., "Mary Russell Mitford: Champion of American Literature," in *Studies in the American Renaissance*, edited by Joel Myerson (Charlottesville: University Press of Virginia, 1983), pp. 313-334;

R. B. Johnson, *The Women Novelists* (London: Collins, 1919);

Stanley Jones, "B. R. Haydon on Some Contemporaries: A New Letter," *Review of English Studies*, 26 (May 1975): 183-189;

M. Kent, "Mary Mitford's Letters," *Cornhill Magazine*, 159 (June 1936);

Charles E. Lauterbach, "Let the printer do it," *Notes and Queries*, new series 10 (January 1963): 17-18;

Jenny Lewis, "Mary Russell Mitford Letters," *British Museum Quarterly*, 29 (Winter 1965): 6-10;

Anne Manning, "M. R. Mitford," *Macmillan's Magazine*, 21 (February 1870): 346-354;

Betty Miller, ed., *Elizabeth Barrett to Miss Mitford; The Unpublished Letters of Elizabeth Barrett Browning to Mary Russell Mitford* (London: J. Murray, 1954);

"Miss Mitford's Recollections," *Blackwood's Magazine*, 71 (March 1852): 259-272;

J. C. Owen, "Utopia in Little: Mary Russell Mitford and *Our Village*," *Studies in Short Fiction*, 5 (Spring 1968): 245-256;

James Payn, *Some Literary Recollections* (New York: Harper, 1884);

"R. H. Horne on Miss Mitford after Forty Years," *Notes and Queries*, 190 (9 March 1946): 101;

Meredith B. Raymond, "A Report on the Published and Unpublished Letters of Elizabeth Barrett Browning to Mary Russell Mitford," *British Institute Studies*, 1 (1973): 37-62;

Raymond and Mary Rose Sullivan, eds., *The Letters of Elizabeth Barrett Browning to Mary Russell Mitford, 1836-1854*, 3 volumes (Waco, Tex.: Armstrong Browning Library of Baylor University / New York: Browning Institute / Winfield, Kans.: Wedgestone Press / Wellesley, Mass.: Wellesley College, 1983);

Michael Sadleir, *XIX Century Fiction: A Bibliographical Record, Based on His Own Collection*, 2 volumes (London: Constable / Berkeley: University of California Press, 1951);

Virginia Woolf, *The Common Reader* (New York: Harcourt, Brace, 1925).

**Papers:**

There are letters in the Becks County Library, Reading; the John Rylands Library; the Harvard University Library; the Bodleian Library; and the Huntington Library. The British Library has Mitford's diary for 1819-1823.

# Mary Wollstonecraft Shelley

*(30 August 1797 - 1 February 1851)*

John R. Holmes
*Franciscan University of Steubenville*

BOOKS: *Mounseer Nongtongpaw; or, the Discoveries of John Bull in a Trip to Paris* (London: Proprietors of the Juvenile Library, 1808);

*History of a Six Weeks' Tour through a part of France, Switzerland, Germany, and Holland, with Letters Descriptive of a Sail Round the Lake of Geneva, and of the Glaciers of Chamouni*, by Mary Shelley, with contributions by Percy Bysshe Shelley (London: Published by T. Hookham, jun., and C. & J. Ollier, 1817);

*Frankenstein; or, The Modern Prometheus* (3 volumes, London: Lackington, Hughes, Harding, Mavor & Jones, 1818; revised edition, 1 volume, London: Henry Colburn & Richard Bentley, 1831; 2 volumes, Philadelphia: Carey, Lea & Blanchard, 1833);

*Valperga: or, the Life and Adventures of Castruccio, Prince of Lucca, by the Author of 'Frankenstein,'* 3 volumes (London: G. & W. B. Whittaker, 1823);

*The Last Man, by the Author of 'Frankenstein'* (3 volumes, London: Henry Colburn, 1826; 2 volumes, Philadelphia: Carey, Lea & Blanchard, 1833);

*The Fortunes of Perkin Warbeck, by the Author of 'Frankenstein'* (3 volumes, London: Henry Colburn & Richard Bentley, 1830; 2 volumes, Philadelphia: Carey, Lea & Blanchard, 1834);

*Lodore, by the Author of 'Frankenstein'* (3 volumes, London: Richard Bentley, 1835; 1 volume, New York: Wallis & Newell, 1835);

*Lives of the Most Eminent Literary and Scientific Men of Italy, Spain, and Portugal*, volumes 86-88 of *The Cabinet of Biography*, Lardner's Cabinet Cyclopedia, conducted by Reverend Dionysius Lardner (London: Printed for Longman, Orme, Brown, Green & Longman and John Taylor, 1835-1837); republished in part as *Lives of the Most Eminent Literary and Scientific Men of Italy*, 2 volumes (Philadelphia: Lea & Blanchard, 1841);

*Falkner: A Novel by the Author of 'Frankenstein,' 'The Last Man,' etc.* (3 volumes, London: Saunders & Otley, 1837; 1 volume, New York: Harper & Brothers, 1837);

*Miniature of Mary Shelley, painted after her death by Reginald Easton, who based this portrait on a sketch made by Edward Ellerker Williams in 1821 or 1822, Mary Shelley's death mask, and the advice of her son and daughter-in-law (Bodleian Library, Oxford)*

*Lives of the Most Eminent Literary and Scientific Men of France*, volumes 102 and 103 of *The Cabinet of Biography* (London: Printed for Longman, Orme, Brown, Green & Longman, 1838, 1839); republished in part as *Lives of the Most Eminent French Writers*, 2 volumes (Philadelphia: Lea & Blanchard, 1840);

*Rambles in Germany and Italy, in 1840, 1842, and 1843, by Mrs. Shelley*, 2 volumes (London: Edward Moxon, 1844);
*Proserpine & Midas: Two Unpublished Mythological Dramas by Mary Shelley*, edited by A. Koszul (London: Humphrey Milford, 1922);
*Mathilda*, edited by Elizabeth Nitchie (Chapel Hill: University of North Carolina Press, 1959);
*Mary Shelley: Collected Tales and Stories, with Original Engravings*, edited by Charles E. Robinson (Baltimore & London: Johns Hopkins University Press, 1976);
*The Journals of Mary Shelley*, 2 volumes, edited by Paula R. Feldman and Diana Scott-Kilvert (Oxford: Clarendon Press, 1987).

OTHER: *Posthumous Poems of Percy Bysshe Shelley*, edited by Mary Shelley (London: Printed for John & Henry L. Hunt, 1824);
*The Poetical Works of Percy Bysshe Shelley*, 4 volumes, edited by Mary Shelley (London: Edward Moxon, 1839);
*Essays, Letters from Abroad, Translations and Fragments, By Percy Bysshe Shelley*, 2 volumes, edited by Mary Shelley (London: Edward Moxon, 1840).

The most eloquent summary of Mary Wollstonecraft Shelley's position in English letters is still Leigh Hunt's much-quoted couplet from "The Blue-Stocking Revels": "And Shelley, four-fam'd,—for her parents, her lord, / And the poor lone impossible monster abhorr'd." Though recent studies have shown some appreciation of Mary Shelley by her own lights, the four "fames" Hunt mentioned have tended to outshine them. When not known as the wife of the poet Percy Bysshe Shelley, she is recognized as the daughter of the celebrated radical writer Mary Wollstonecraft and the equally well-known novelist and political philosopher William Godwin. Even the sole recognition won by her own efforts, the "monster abhorr'd" of her great novel *Frankenstein* (1818), is tainted by popular associations with stage and cinema versions of the monster which have little to do with her "Modern Prometheus." Yet this "four-famed" woman was also a skilled editor and critic, an influential travel writer, a literary historian, a devoted mother, and a dabbler in verse as well as in the new genre of the short story.

There is some warrant for seeing Mary Shelley as a reflection of her parents, for both mother and father were extraordinary. Her mother, Mary Wollstonecraft, published the classic manifesto of sexual equality, *A Vindication of the Rights of Woman* (1792). Her father, William Godwin, established his preeminence in radical British political thought with his *Enquiry Concerning Political Justice* (1793) and won a permanent place in literary history with his novel *Caleb Williams* (1794), often considered the first English detective novel. The toast of radical social circles, the two were bound to meet. When they did, in the summer of 1796, an immediate mutual attraction began, and they were married on 29 March 1797. On 30 August of that year Mary Wollstonecraft Godwin was born. Complications from her birth resulted in her mother's death 10 September.

In 1801, when little Mary was four, Godwin remarried. The only memories of her stepmother that Mary recorded are bad ones. Godwin's second wife, Mary Jane Clairmont, brought her own children, Charles and Jane, into the family, and young Mary felt displaced. A son, William, born in 1803, furthered the girl's sense of alienation, and she felt driven to compete, not only with the other children but also with the second Mrs. Godwin, for her father's affection.

Godwin's second wife was not of Mary Wollstonecraft's intellectual stature. Still, entering a literary household, she developed a literary pursuit of her own. In 1805 she persuaded Godwin to found a publishing house in her name, M. J. Godwin, to publish children's books under the imprint of the Juvenile Library. In 1808, at the age of eleven, Mary Wollstonecraft Godwin published a booklet in the series, a rhymed children's tale called *Mounseer Nongtongpaw; or, the Discoveries of John Bull in a Trip to Paris*.

Threatened by her stepdaughter's attention to Godwin, especially when adolescence transformed the child into a beautiful image of the first wife, Mary Jane Godwin sent the teenaged Mary to Scotland on 7 June 1812, ostensibly for the girl's health. In addition to further isolating her from the father she loved, the two years in Scotland nurtured Mary's literary imagination, as she records in her 1831 preface to the single-volume, Standard Novels edition of *Frankenstein*:

> They were my eyry of freedom, and the pleasant region where unheeded I could commune with the creatures of my fancy. I wrote then—but in a most common-place style. It was beneath the trees belonging to our house, or on the bleak sides of the woodless mountains near, that my true compositions, the airy flights of my imagination, were born and fostered.

In this period, during a brief visit home on 11 November 1812, Mary first met Percy Bysshe Shelley, who was in the company of his first wife, Harriet Westbrook.

By March of 1814, however, when Mary returned to England to stay, Shelley's marriage was troubled, and Mary had become a lovely young woman, almost seventeen. On 5 May Shelley saw her for the first time in two years; a swift summer courtship led to elopement on 28 July (though without a divorce Shelley was not free to marry), a quick tour of the Continent, and the raw material for Mary Shelley's first adult publication, *History of a Six Weeks' Tour* (1817).

From the start, Percy Shelley encouraged Mary to write. When they eloped, they carried with them a box of her early writings, which were lost in Paris during the trip. Mary responded to the loss by beginning immediately a novel called "Hate," and, when back in England, she started an historical novel, "The Life of Louvet." Neither novel was ever finished, as pregnancy and illness stole her energy. On 22 February 1815 her first daughter was born prematurely, and died 6 March.

In August the Shelleys moved to Bishopsgate, where, on 24 January 1816, Mary gave birth to a son, named William after Grandfather Godwin. On 3 May the Shelleys, including the boy William, and Mary's stepsister, Jane Clairmont (who had come to be known as Claire) left for Geneva to meet George Gordon, Lord Byron. There, with the promise of a lengthier stay on the Continent, and in the company of the most celebrated literary figure in Europe, Mary began to write her masterpiece, *Frankenstein*.

The story of the composition of *Frankenstein* is often told, though it is hardly ever told the same way twice. Though critics have called some of its details into question, the best account of the novel's genesis is Mary's own, in her preface to the 1831 edition. Sometime in mid June, the literary discussion of the Shelley-Byron party turned toward German ghost stories. Byron suggested each member of the group (Shelley, Byron, Claire Clairmont, Mary, and Dr. John William Polidori) write a ghost story in the same vein. In the next few weeks Mary produced a short story which, when expanded, became *Frankenstein*.

The Geneva idyll ended 29 August 1816, when the Shelleys returned to England. Then came a series of shocks: Mary's half sister, Fanny Imlay (daughter of Mary Wollstonecraft and Gilbert Imlay), committed suicide on 9 October; a month later Shelley's wife, Harriet, drowned herself. Harriet's death left Shelley free to marry; on 20 December he and Mary were wed at St. Mildred's Church on Bread Street, London.

*Mary Shelley circa 1814 (sketch by an unknown artist; St. Pancras Public Libraries)*

By May of 1817 Mary had finished writing *Frankenstein*. Knowing that the public had a romantic interest in their elopement and that it would take some time to see her novel through the press, Mary prepared an account of her romantic summer of 1814, padded with Shelley's *Mont Blanc*, written at that time, and a few of the poet's letters. *History of a Six Weeks' Tour* appeared in November of 1817, almost two months after the birth of Clara Everina Shelley on 2 September.

Though the year 1818 opened with the publication of *Frankenstein* on New Year's Day, and the Shelleys began a much longer stay on the Continent, this period saw another series of emotional shocks to Mary Shelley: in September her daughter, barely a year old, died in Venice, and the following June her son died in Rome. By the end of the summer she was able to return to writing, producing the novella *Mathilda.* The birth of her fourth and last child, Percy Florence Shelley, in November made it difficult for her to see to its publication; it did not appear in print until 1959. Moreover, she had all but abandoned her shorter work in order to begin historical research for a much longer novel, *Valperga* (1823).

In the spring of 1820, Mary Shelley also made an attempt at writing drama, producing two short blank-verse adaptations from Ovid, *Proserpine* and *Midas.* The first appeared in an annual during her lifetime; the second was not published until 1922. Both blank-verse dramas include brief lyrical pieces by Percy Shelley.

In 1821 the Shelleys settled in Pisa, and by the end of the year Byron had joined them. Once again, as in Geneva five years earlier, the Shelleys enjoyed stimulating literary fellowship. But again Mary's joy was cut short. On 16 June 1822 she suffered a miscarriage, and on 8 July Percy Shelley drowned while sailing in the Gulf of Spezia.

Grief so debilitated her, as her letters and journals attest, that the first year after her husband's death should have been Mary Shelley's least productive period, but her novel *Valperga* had been completed for more than a year and was ready for press, and bereavement drove her to express her grief in verse, a medium she normally avoided. "I can never write verses," she wrote to Maria Gisborne on 11 June 1835, "except under the influence of a strong sentiment & seldom even then." Furthermore, the need to support her surviving child and limits on her support from her father-in-law, Sir Timothy Shelley, made writing a practical need rather than a personal indulgence.

Thus, in February of 1823, *Valperga* appeared in three volumes, and the first of Mary's periodical essays—a review of the Florentine Chronicles of Giovanni Villani—appeared in Byron and Leigh Hunt's magazine *The Liberal.* Knowing of the strong marketability of her late husband's works, she immediately returned to England and began editing his remaining manuscripts. Sir Timothy, however, cut off that avenue of income: his angry reaction to the appearance of *Posthumous Poems* in 1824 forced Mary to agree not to publish any more of her late husband's writings in Sir Timothy's lifetime. Sir Timothy had also threatened to withdraw all support for his grandchild, Percy Florence Shelley, unless Mary surrendered the boy to his care, but when Mary categorically refused Sir Timothy relented, sending an allowance of £100 per year beginning in 1823, increased to 200 the following year, 250 in 1827, 300 in 1829, and 400 in 1841.

Thrown back on her own literary resources, Mary began writing *The Last Man,* published in February of 1826. The public was anxious for works from her pen; the immense popularity of *Frankenstein* had been increased even more by several stage productions: Richard Brinsley Peake's *Presumption; or the Fate of Frankenstein,* which Shelley herself saw, was one of six different versions in 1823 alone. As she wrote to Leigh Hunt on 9 September, after seeing the drama: "lo and behold! I found myself famous." The title pages of all of her later novels carry the phrase "by the author of 'Frankenstein.' "

In September of 1826 Charles Bysshe Shelley, son of the poet by his first wife and heir to Sir Timothy Shelley's title, died. Thus Mary's son, Percy, the only surviving male named Shelley, became heir to the baronetcy just before his seventh birthday.

Once again Mary Shelley had the financial means to travel to the Continent: she visited Paris in April of 1828, meeting General Lafayette and the rising young novelist Prosper Merimée. The meeting with Merimée, though brief, must have been stimulating: their literary conversation continued in letters after Mary's return to England. The trip was not all pleasant, however: contracting smallpox, she returned to England six weeks after she left.

Though faithful to the letter of her agreement with Sir Timothy not to publish any of her husband's works, Mary Shelley did continue to assist in the editorial work of others. Most of the latter half of 1829 was devoted to helping Cyrus Redding with the Paris edition of Shelley's collected poems, as well as completing the writing and research for *Perkin Warbeck,* which appeared in May of 1830. That March she had the peculiar experience of reviewing her father's novel *Cloudesley* in *Blackwood's Edinburgh Magazine.* As one might expect, the review was overwhelmingly favorable, describing Godwin's work in superlatives and explicating his theory of the novel. In November of 1831 *Frankenstein* appeared in a best-selling single-volume edition, for which Mary Shelley wrote a new preface. She also published her drama *Proserpine* in a Christmas annual, *The Winter's Wreath* for 1832.

Percy Florence Shelley, almost thirteen, began public school at Harrow in September of

1832. His mother's letters reveal a touch of wistfulness at letting him go, but the separation did create more writing time for her. Sometime in 1834 the Reverend Dionysius Lardner commissioned Mary Shelley to write biographical sketches for his popular *Cabinet Cyclopedia*. Doubtless, he had read her essays on Italian literature in the *Westminster Review*, and requested similar work for his series. The connection with Lardner proved fruitful for Mary: after the appearance of the first volume of *Lives of the Most Eminent Literary and Scientific Men of Italy, Spain, and Portugal* in February of 1835, another in October, and the third two years later, Mary went on to produce a similar work covering French authors, appearing in two volumes in 1838 and 1839. This period also saw the publication of Mary Shelley's last novel, *Falkner*, and Percy Florence Shelley's matriculation to Cambridge, both in 1837.

As Mary concluded the *Cyclopedia* series, Sir Timothy Shelley rescinded his prohibition against publishing his son's works. Although 1839 began a period of declining health for Mary Shelley, she began a complete edition of her late husband's poems in four volumes, the last of which appeared in May. In November she produced a single-volume edition of the same work, and her edition of Percy B. Shelley's *Essays, Letters from Abroad, Translations and Fragments* was reviewed in December.

Recovering somewhat from her illness, and in hopes of gaining even more strength from a milder climate, Mary Shelley began a tour of the Continent with her son and his college friends; a second trip with the same company lasted more than a year, June 1842 to August 1843. Keeping a journal and copies of all her letters from both journeys, she turned them to profit as a travel book, much as she had with her elopement tour some thirty years earlier. *Rambles in Germany and Italy*, published in two volumes in July of 1844, was to be her last book.

Mary Shelley's primary concern of her widowed life—the care of her son—was relieved at this time, but other worries soon followed. On 24 April 1844 Sir Timothy Shelley died, leaving his estate and title to Percy Florence Shelley; but in the following year two blackmail schemes against her came close to crushing her spirit. Near the end of her Continental excursion in 1843, Mary Shelley had befriended in Paris a down-and-out Italian political exile named Ferdinando Gatteschi. It was for him that she wrote her *Rambles*, and she sent him the proceeds, as well as a continual flow of caring, supportive letters. The language of these heartfelt letters, however, was so sentimental that Gatteschi, realizing that the tone could be misconstrued as seductive, demanded further payment from Mary Shelley to keep them from the press. She was saved by another acquaintance from her travels, who had the Parisian police seize all Gatteschi's papers and retrieved the letters. Another attempt at blackmail by a literary forger known as George Byron, who claimed to be the poet's son, was also thwarted.

The last six years of Mary Shelley's life were spent in relative peace and retirement. She lived to see her son married on 22 June 1848, now secure as Sir Percy Shelley. On 1 February 1851 Mary Shelley died in London at the age of fifty-three.

Though *Frankenstein* assures Mary Shelley a permanent place in literary history and though some of her other novels are praised by critics, her nonfiction prose, particularly in the forms of biography and travel essay, ranks with some of the best writing in those genres. Indeed, when *Rambles* and her *Cyclopedia* biographies are considered next to her fiction of the period after 1830, it must be admitted that the nonfiction is superior writing. Mary Shelley herself thought so: near the end of her literary career, she told her husband's publisher, Edward Moxon, "I should prefer quieter work . . . such as my lives for the Cyclopedia . . . which I think I do *much* better than romancing . . . " (20 September 1843).

Mary Shelley's first adult work, *History of a Six Weeks' Tour* (1817), introduced her into the peculiar genre of travel writing almost by accident. Though Mary Shelley knew that much of the interest in the work would be based on hopes of catching glimpses of her husband's life, the book's main strength is the vivid description that had become a hallmark of Romanticism. Moreover, the description is of that essentially Romantic type which describes the observer as much as the scene, and senses a supernatural presence in nature. In her preface she tells the reader:

> Those whose youth has been past as theirs (with what success it imports not) in pursuing, like the swallow, the inconstant summer of delight and beauty which invests this visible world, will perhaps find some entertainment in following the author, with her husband and friend, on foot, through part of France and Switzerland, and in sailing with her down the castled Rhine, through scenes beautiful in themselves, but which, since

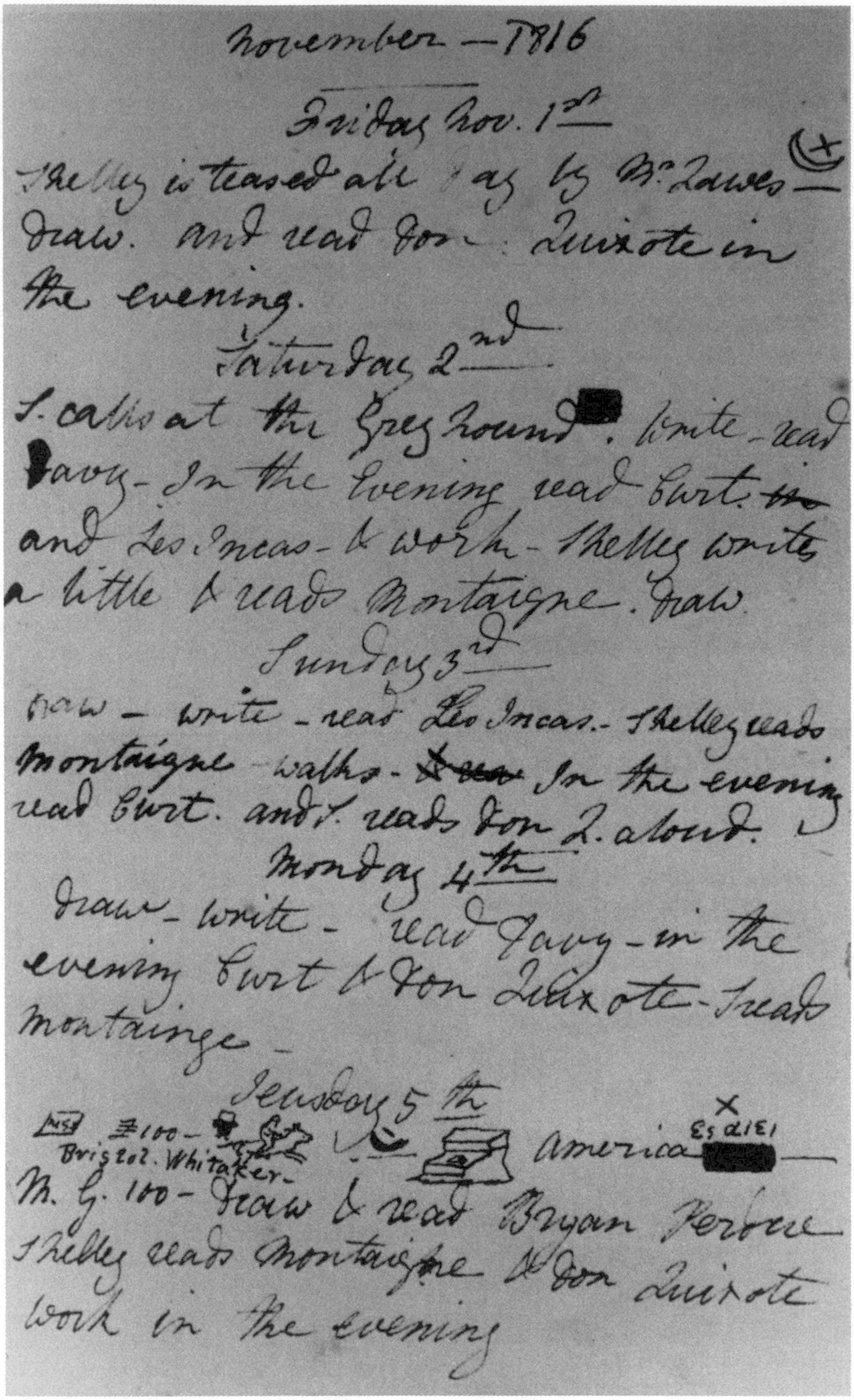

November — 1816

Friday Nov. 1st

Shelley is teased all day by Mr Lawes — Draw. and read Don Quixote in the evening.

Saturday 2nd

S. calls at the Greyhound. Write — read Davy — In the evening read Curt. and Les Incas — & work — Shelley writes a little & reads Montaigne. Draw.

Sunday 3rd

Draw — write — read Les Incas. — Shelley reads Montaigne — walks — In the evening read Curt. and S. reads Don Q. aloud.

Monday 4th

Draw — write — read Davy — in the evening Curt & Don Quixote — S reads Montainge —

Tuesday 5th

MSS £100 — Bristol. Whitaker — america —

M. G. 100 — Draw & read Bryan Perdue Shelley reads Montaigne & Don Quixote Work in the evening

*Page from the journal Mary Shelley kept from 21 July 1816 to 7 June 1819 (Bodleian MSS Abinger Dep. d.311, Bodleian Library, Oxford). She used the crescent moon symbol in her journals to indicate trouble. When the first entry on this page was written, Percy Bysshe Shelley was in the technical custody (under legal supervision) of the Honorable Edward Law for failure to pay a debt.*

> she visited them, a great poet has clothed with the freshness of a diviner nature.

That "great poet," of course, is her husband, and the reference is to his blank-verse masterpiece *Mont Blanc*, which was first published in this book. In her preface she is acknowledging that travel writing is not poetry, but that it is more than just clinical and objective description: it is an attempt to bring the reader imaginatively into scenes described. Mary Shelley's English audience, starved for real experience of the Continent (Napoleon's wars made travel there dangerous until the peace of 1814), was eager for new accounts of travel there.

Mary Shelley's literary career began and ended with travel books. Of all of her writings, her last, *Rambles in Germany and Italy* (1844), suffers most from the constraint of writing for money. Pushed into writing by a need for money for Gatteschi, Mary Shelley's heart was not always in what she wrote. Nevertheless, there are passages in which her heart was too much with her: again and again a scene would remind her of how she first saw it with her husband. Yet she does not allow the reminiscence to obscure the description for the reader. This work too has affinities to descriptive-meditative verse. It maintains the sense of a supernatural presence behind nature:

> It has seemed to me—and on such an evening, I have felt it,—that this world, endowed as it is outwardly with endless shapes and influences of beauty and enjoyment, is peopled also in its spiritual life by myriads of loving spirits; from whom, unawares, we catch impressions, which mould our thoughts to good, and thus they guide beneficially the course of events, and minister to the destiny of man. Whether the beloved dead make a portion of this holy company, I dare not guess; but that such exists, I feel.

There is also a political element to the book, consisting mostly of laments over the increasing oppression of Italy under Austria, but this part owes most to Gatteschi, and is not Mary Shelley's best writing.

When she breaks away from Italian politics and writes of Italian literature, Mary Shelley is at her best, and some sections dealing with Italian culture are as good as her periodical essays on Italy or her *Cyclopedia* entries on Italian writers. Letter XVI, in the second volume of *Rambles in Germany and Italy*, is a complete history of Italian literature: she is particularly eloquent in her discussion of the Italian Romantics, using military language to describe the struggle between classic and romantic.

> It began in 1818, when Berchet, a poet of merit, descended suddenly into the arena, throwing, by way of challenge, a translation of the Leonora of Burgher, accompanied by an essay, discarding the old models and planting a new banner....

There is a fair portion of art criticism in the book as well, but it is not as good as her literary history.

Mary Shelley's periodical essays of the 1820s establish her as a leading ambassador of Italian culture in England. Her very first published essay was a review of the Italian historian Giovanni Villani's *Chroniche Fiorentine*. Her focus is telling: after a vigorous defense of modern writers (as opposed to classical; that is, since Dante), she praises Villani for his illumination of the places and people mentioned in Dante's *Divine Comedy*. She presents Villani as the very type of narrator she has been in her travel writing,

> the writer who makes the persons of Dante's Spirits familiar to us; who guides us through the unfinished streets and growing edifices of Firenze la bella, and who in short transports us back to the superstitions, party spirit, companionship, and wars of the thirteenth and fourteenth centuries.

Mary Shelley's poetics in the opening paragraphs are squarely Romantic: citing Madame Germaine de Staël's distinction of classic and romantic without commenting on its validity, she laments the folly of systematizing genius.

More than any other topic, Mary Shelley's articles through the 1820s dealt with presenting Italy and its culture to English readers. "Recollections of Italy" in the *London Magazine* for January 1824 combined her Italophilia with travel writing. Her "Defense of Velluti" in the *Examiner* for 11 June 1826 was signed "Anglo-Italicus," another indication of the extent to which Italy became a part of her literary identity.

A review article in the October 1826 *Westminster Review* examining three English travel books about Italy shows how well Mary Shelley understood the genre, and the confidence with which she judged the expertise of other "authorities" on Italy. A similar essay in the same magazine three years later (July 1829) reviewed two books for English travelers in Italy. What is striking about these essays, as criticism, is one judgment which is out of line with those of her day and ours. It is the identification of a genre she terms "Anglo-Italian literature," inaugurated, she says in the first article, by Byron's "Beppo" and represented by the five books she reviews in both essays. The fact that Mary Shelley discerned a "school" of English expatriate authors writing in and about Italy suggests one reason for her preoccupation with Italy in her nonfiction: she saw Anglo-Italian literature as a category as distinct as biography or travel writing. These two essays, "The English in Italy" and "Modern Italy," form an important link between her travel writing and her writings about Italy, having elements of both.

Mary Shelley's book reviews of non-Italian topics are not nearly as engaging, but they are of some biographical interest when the reader speculates how peculiarly fitting each is to her personality, and how each in some way illuminates her other work. Her essay "On Ghosts" (*London Magazine*, March 1824) strikes those who know Mary Shelley only through *Frankenstein* as very much a part of her Gothic sensibility, and captures the mood that must have presided over that ghost-story session with Byron at Lake Geneva in 1816. Yet its tone is analytical, and it presents the Gothic as a yearning for a lost innocence of superstition. She suggests a central tenet of Romanticism and Gothicism: the Enlightenment did not totally exorcise the supernatural from human consciousness, and that is a good thing. "But do none of us believe in ghosts?" she continually asks.

Each of the remaining essays bears some connection with an aspect of Mary Shelley's life. Her review of two works by Merimée in the October 1929 *Westminster Review* recalls her visit to the young poet the previous year. Her review, in the same issue, of *The Loves of the Poets*, by Anna Brownell Jameson, is poignant with the unstated realization that she too would be the subject of just such literary biography: the definition of love she cites is from her husband's essay "On Love." The definition of a poet is her own, and is worthy of being placed beside those of the other Romantics, especially as hers is not well known:

> What is a poet? Is he not that which wakens melody in the silent chords of the human heart? A light which arrays in splendor things and thoughts which else were dim in the shadow of their own significance. His soul is like one of the pools in the Ilex woods of the Maremma, it reflects the surrounding universe, but it beautifies, groups, and mellows their tints, making a little world within itself, the copy of the outer one; but more entire, more faultless. But above all, a poet's soul is Love; the desire of sympathy is the breath that inspires his lay, while he lavishes on the sentiment and its object, his whole treasure-house of resplendent imagery, burning emotion, and ardent enthusiasm. He is the mirror of nature, reflecting her back ten thousand times more lovely; what then must not his power be, when he adds beauty to the most perfect thing in nature—even Love.

Mary Shelley's review of Thomas Moore's *Life and Death of Lord Edward Fitzgerald* (1831) in the January 1832 *Westminster Review* is interesting as a gauge of her demands on biography, the genre which would absorb most of her literary energies for the next decade. Her review of her father's novel *Cloudesley* in *Blackwood's Edinburgh Magazine* for May 1830 holds a twofold interest: as her only public critical comment on a work of fiction not her own and as a sign of her affection for her father, a glimpse at the critical biography that she planned but never finished (though portions of it appear in Kegan Paul's biography of Godwin).

The review also illuminates Mary Shelley's own thoughts on novel writing. It begins with a summary of the theory of the novel presented in Godwin's preface to *Cloudesley*, supported by lengthy quotations. Shelley then contrasts Godwin's theory with Edward Bulwer-Lytton's, as expressed in his preface to *Pelham* (1828). The comparison serves to assert Godwin's supremacy in the art of the novel. "Mr. Bulwer," Shelley states, "gives us . . . himself, his experience, his opinions, his emotions. The high-wrought and noble tone of his mind spreads a sacred and even mysterious grandeur over his pages."

On the other hand Godwin, his daughter tells us, brings himself into his novels only by entering into his characters:

> By dint of the mastery of thought, he transfuses himself into the very souls of his personages; he dives into their secret hearts, and lays bare, even to their anatomy, their workings; not a pulsation escapes him,—while yet all is blended into one whole, which forms the pervading impulse of the individual he brings before us.

*Cloudesley* is then presented as "a fresh example of what we have been saying."

*Mary Shelley, 1840 (portrait by Richard Rothwell; National Portrait Gallery, London)*

Shelley's contrast of the two styles reveals some of her own view of the novelist's craft. Her image of Bulwer-Lytton's is very like the Victorian age caricature of Romanticism: overrich, grandiose, overstuffed with the author's ego. Her concept of her father's practice represents what the Romantics themselves thought they were doing: balancing reason and emotion, subject and object, classical form and "Gothic" ornament. "The mere copying from our own hearts," she concludes, "will no more form a first-rate work of art, than will the most exquisite representation of mountains, water, wood, and glorious clouds, form a good painting, if none of the rules of grouping and colouring are followed."

Mary Shelley's biographical sketches in Lardner's *Cabinet Cyclopedia* may be, as she thought they were, her very best writing; ironically, they are the least read. There is little to lament in this irony: the type of work these sketches form may be best termed "serviceable." They are lively and readable, but they are intended to be reference works. Mary Shelley's studies of the great men of Italy, Spain, Portugal, and France display a Romantic tendency to explore the inner workings of the subject's mind, insofar as they can be discerned. This imaginative quality in her biographies makes them more compelling than others before her time; yet there is no lack of hard fact or logical analysis in these accounts.

The last genre attempted by Mary Shelley is in many ways a continuation of her work in biography and literary history, for her notes and prefaces to Shelley's poems are mostly biographical rather than critical. There is varying critical opinion today concerning how careful Mary Shelley was as an editor, but most of the cavils—silent emendation, or even suppression of some material—are the result of demanding twentieth-century editorial values of a nineteenth-century editor. Her last paragraph in the preface to *Posthumous Poems* may be a key to the lack of any evaluative tone in her notes:

> I do not know whether the critics will reprehend the insertion of some of the most imperfect among them; but I frankly own that I have been more actuated by the fear lest any monument of his genius should escape me than the wish of presenting nothing but what was complete to the fastidious reader.

Since the Oxford and other standard editions of Percy Shelley's works have incorporated all "Mrs. Shelley's" notes and prefaces, it may be that, after *Frankenstein*, the most-read works from her pen are her editorial works, which provide the most thorough and reliable biographical background to Shelley's poems of any single source.

Mary Shelley's letters and journals must be evaluated by different criteria, as they were not written for publication. This is not a universal rule: many of her literary contemporaries wrote each slightest note with an eye toward the public, and it was not unusual to prepare one's own letters and journals for publication. To some extent, Mary Shelley did this with her travel journals and related letters. But with those excepted, most of her letters and journals are personal, showing the verbal shorthand one uses with close friends.

The journals are not typical of Shelley's prose style: they are more memoranda than diaries; telegraphic and abbreviated for the most part. Two exceptions are notable: travel entries, especially her descriptions of Geneva in 1816; and the melancholy entries following the three-month gap in her journal after Percy Shelley's death in 1822. Here she confides to herself the minutest feelings that had been previously found only in letters, and rarely there. Perhaps it was her husband's death that unleashed this eloquent self-communion, since her ideas and feelings before had always been tested against his. She says in the first entry (2 October) after the poet's death on 8 July:

> For eight years I communicated, with unlimited freedom, with one whose genius, far transcending mine, awakened and guided my thoughts. I conversed with him; rectified my errors of judgment; obtained new lights from him; and my mind was satisfied. Now I am alone—oh, how alone! The stars may behold my tears, and the winds drink my sighs; but my thoughts are a sealed treasure, which I can confide to none. But can I express all I feel? Can I give words to thoughts and feelings that, as a tempest, hurry me along? Is this the sand that the ever-flowing sea of thought would impress indelibly? Alas! I am alone.

Yet it is out of this solitude that Mary Shelley forged some of her greatest writing.

The extent to which Mary Shelley's mind was connected with her husband's before his death can also be seen in their letters. Many of her letters in the eight years of her marriage were postscripts to her husband's. Virtually every variety of style may be read in her letters. There is a breathless, precipitous jumble of emotions and half-uttered sentiments in her billets-doux to Shelley, such as this letter of 25 October 1814, when he was running to escape imprisonment for debt:

> For what a minute did I see you yesterday—is this the way my beloved that we are to live till the sixth in the morning I look for you and when I awake I turn to look on you—dearest Shelley you are solitary and uncomfortable why cannot I be with you to cheer you and to press you to my heart oh my love you have no friends why then should you be torn from the only one who has affection for you . . . ?

In contrast is the florid "Continental" ornament of her formal epistles to French and Italian correspondents, such as this 11 November 1830 letter to Lafayette:

> Pardon a woman, my dear and most respected General, for intruding these observations. I was the wife of a man who—held dear the opinions you espouse, to which you were the martyr and are the ornament; and to sympathize with successes which would have been the matter of such delight to him, appears to me a sacred duty—and while I deeply feel my incapacity to understand or treat such high subjects, I rejoice that the Cause to which Shelley's life was devoted, is crowned with triumph.

Yet another style is the respectful, almost deferential balance of dignity and humility in her formal letters to those she thought to be above her station, either in society or in letters. Consider this 25 May 1829 request to Sir Walter Scott for help on her research for *Perkin Warbeck*:

*Sir Percy Florence Shelley and Jane, Lady Shelley (Alexander Hay Collection, Mitchell Library, State Library of New South Wales, Sydney)*

> I hope you will forgive my troubling you—it is almost impertinent to say how foolish it appears to me that I should intrude on your ground, or to compliment one all the world so highly appretiates—but as every traveller when they visit the Alps, endeavours however imperfectly, to express their admiration in the Inn's Album, so it is impossible to address the Author of Waverly [*sic*] without thanking him for the delight and instruction derived from the inexhaustible source of his genius. . . .

Mary Shelley's business correspondence is pointed, succinct, and direct, as we see in this 6 August 1835 query to Charles Ollier about royalties:

> What of Lodore—Do you remember that when 700 are sold I am to have £50—? Will 700 never be sold—I am very unlucky; praised & noticed as it has been. You promised me to look after my interests in this particular and I trust you, because I think you will feel more sympathy with a *poor Author* than a *rich Publisher*.

Virtually all of the Shelley circle were Mary Shelley's correspondents (Lord Byron, Maria Gisborne, Claire Clairmont, Edward John Trelawny), as well as other important Romantic writers (Leigh Hunt, Thomas Love Peacock, Henry Crabb Robinson), editors, and publishers (Thomas Campbell, Edward Moxon, John Murray, Charles Ollier). Mary Shelley's letters are of interest not only as sources for biography, but also as further indications of her literary skill. For whichever of her "four fames" draws us to her—her mother, her father, her husband, or her monster—everything from Mary Shelley's pen claims for her prodigious territory in English Romantic prose.

**Letters:**

*The Letters of Mary Wollstonecraft Shelley*, 3 volumes, edited by Betty T. Bennett (Baltimore: Johns Hopkins University Press, 1980, 1983, 1988).

**Bibliographies:**

W. H. Lyles, *Mary Shelley: An Annotated Bibliography* (New York: Garland, 1975);

Clement Dunbar, *A Bibliography of Shelley Studies, 1823-1950* (New York: Garland, 1976).

**Biographies:**

Elizabeth Nitchie, *Mary Shelley* (New Brunswick: Rutgers University Press, 1953);

Sandra Gilbert and Susan Gubar, *The Madwoman in the Attic* (New Haven: Yale University Press, 1979);

Anne K. Mellor, *Mary Shelley: Her Life, her Fiction, her Monsters* (New York: Methuen, 1988);

Emily W. Sunstein, *Mary Shelley: Romance and Reality* (Boston, Toronto & London: Little, Brown, 1989).

**References:**

Christopher Small, *Ariel Like a Harpy: Shelley, Mary and Frankenstein* (London: Gollancz, 1972);

Muriel Spark, *Mary Shelley* (New York: Dutton, 1987);

William Veeder, *Mary Shelley & Frankenstein: The Fate of Androgyny* (Chicago: University of Chicago Press, 1986);

William A. Walling, *Mary Shelley* (New York: Twayne, 1972).

**Papers:**

Mary Shelley's journals, workbooks, unpublished papers, and much of her correspondence is in the Abinger Collection, on deposit at the Bodleian Library, Oxford. Other significant collections of letters are in the Carl H. Pforzheimer Library, New York Public Library; the Huntington Library; and the British Library.

# Percy Bysshe Shelley

*(4 August 1792 - 8 July 1822)*

John R. Greenfield
*McKendree College*

See also the Shelley entry in *DLB 96: British Romantic Poets, 1789-1832: Second Series.*

BOOKS: *Zastrozzi, A Romance* (London: Printed for G. Wilkie & J. Robinson, 1810);

*Original Poetry; by Victor and Cazire,* by Percy Bysshe Shelley and Elizabeth Shelley (Worthing: Printed by C. & W. Phillips and sold by J. J. Stockdale, London, 1810);

*Posthumous Fragments of Margaret Nicholson; Being poems found amongst the papers of that noted female who attempted the life of the King in 1786. Edited by John Fitzvictor,* by Shelley and Thomas Jefferson Hogg (Oxford: Printed & sold by J. Munday, 1810);

*St. Irvyne; or, The Rosicrucian. A Romance,* as a Gentleman of the University of Oxford (London: Printed for J. J. Stockdale, 1811);

*The Necessity of Atheism* (Worthing: Printed by C. & W. Phillips, 1811);

*An Address, to the Irish People* (Dublin, 1812);

*Proposals for An Association of those Philanthropists, Who Convinced of the Inadequacy of the Moral and Political State of Ireland to Produce Benefits which Are Nevertheless Attainable Are Willing to Unite to Accomplish Its Regeneration* (Dublin: Printed by I. Eton, 1812);

*A Letter to Lord Ellenborough, Occasioned by the Sentence which He Passed on Mr. D. I. Eaton, As Publisher of the Third Part of Paine's Age of Reason* (Barnstaple: Printed by Syle, 1812);

*Declaration of Rights* [broadside] (Dublin, 1812);

*Queen Mab; a Philosophical Poem: with Notes* (London: Printed by P. B. Shelley, 1813; New York: Printed by W. Baldwin, 1821);

*A Refutation of Deism: in a Dialogue* (London: Printed by Schulze & Dean, 1814);

*Alastor; or, The Spirit of Solitude: and Other Poems* (London: Printed for Baldwin, Cradock & Joy and Carpenter & Son, by S. Hamilton, 1816);

*A Proposal for Putting Reform to the Vote Throughout the Kingdom,* as The Hermit of Marlow (London: Printed for C. & J. Ollier, 1817);

*Laon and Cythna; or, The Revolution of the Golden City: A Vision of the Nineteenth Century* (London: Printed for Sherwood, Neely & Jones and C. & J. Ollier, by B. M'Millan, 1818 [i.e., 1817]); revised as *The Revolt of Islam; A Poem, in Twelve Cantos* (London: Printed for C. & J. Ollier by B. M'Millan, 1817);

*Rosalind and Helen, A Modern Eclogue; with Other Poems* (London: Printed for C. & J. Ollier, 1819);

*The Cenci. A Tragedy, in Five Acts* (Leghorn, Italy: Printed for C. & J. Ollier, London, 1819);

*Prometheus Unbound. A Lyrical Drama in Four Acts, With Other Poems* (London: C. & J. Ollier, 1820);

*Oedipus Tyrannus; or, Swellfoot the Tyrant. A Tragedy. In Two Acts. Translated From the Original Doric* (London: Published for the author by J. Johnston, 1820);

*Epipsychidion. Verses Addressed to the Noble and Unfortunate Lady Emilia V____ Now imprisoned in the Convent of ____* (London: C. & J. Ollier, 1821);

*Adonais: An Elegy on the Death of John Keats, Author of Endymion, Hyperion etc.* (Pisa: With the types of Didot, 1821; Cambridge: Printed by W. Metcalfe & sold by Gee & Bridges, 1829);

*Hellas: A Lyrical Drama* (London: C. & J. Ollier, 1822);

*Posthumous Poems of Percy Bysshe Shelley,* edited by Mary Wollstonecraft Shelley (London: Printed for John & Henry L. Hunt, 1824);

*The Masque of Anarchy. A Poem,* edited by Leigh Hunt (London: Edward Moxon, 1832);

*Essays, Letters from Abroad, Translations and Fragments,* 2 volumes, edited by Mary Shelley (London: Edward Moxon, 1840);

*The Wandering Jew. A Poem,* edited by Bertram Dobell (London: Shelley Society, 1887);

*Note books of Percy Bysshe Shelley, From the Originals in the Library of W.K. Bixby,* 3 volumes, edited by H. Buxton Forman (St. Louis: Privately printed, 1911);

*Percy Bysshe Shelley in 1819 (portrait by Æmelia Curran, completed in 1822 or 1823; National Portrait Gallery, London)*

*A Philosophical View of Reform*, edited by T. W. Rolleston (London: Oxford University Press, 1920);

*The Esdaile Notebook. A volume of early poems*, edited by Kenneth Neale Cameron from the manuscript in the Carl H. Pforzheimer Library (New York: Knopf, 1964);

*The Esdaile Poems*, edited from the manuscripts by Neville Rogers (Oxford: Clarendon Press, 1966);

*The Manuscripts of the Younger Romantics. Shelley*, 3 volumes: *The Esdaile Notebook, The Masque of Anarchy, Hellas: A Lyrical Drama*, edited by Donald H. Reiman (New York & London: Garland, 1985).

**Editions:** *The Poetical Works of Percy Bysshe Shelley*, edited by Mary Shelley (4 volumes, London: Edward Moxon, 1839; 1 volume, Philadelphia: Porter & Coates, 1839);

*The Poetical Works of Percy Bysshe Shelley: Including Various Additional Pieces From MS. and Other Sources*, 2 volumes, edited by William Michael Rossetti (London: E. Moxon, 1870; New York: T. Crowell, 1878);

*The Complete Poetical Works of Shelley*, edited by Thomas Hutchinson (Oxford: Clarendon Press, 1904); revised by G. M. Matthews (London: Oxford University Press, 1969);

*The Complete Works of Percy Bysshe Shelley*, The Julian Edition, 10 volumes, edited by Roger Ingpen and Walter Edwin Peck (London: Ernest Benn, 1926-1930);

"Shelley's Translations from Plato: A Critical Edition," in James Notopoulous, *The Platonism of Shelley: A Study of Platonism and the Poetic Mind* (Durham, N.C.: Duke University Press, 1949);

*Shelley's Prose; or The Trumpet of a Prophecy*, edited by David L. Clark (Albuquerque: University of New Mexico Press, 1954; corrected 1966);

*Shelley as a child (artist unknown; Pierpont Morgan Library)*

*Posthumous Poems of Shelley: Mary Shelley's Fair Copy Book, Bodleian Ms. Shelley Adds. d.9 Collated with the Holographs and the Printed Texts*, edited by Irving Massey (Montreal: McGill-Queen's University Press, 1969);

*Shelley's Poetry and Prose*, edited by Donald Reiman and Sharon Powers (New York: Norton, 1977).

OTHER: *Essay on Christianity*, in *Shelley Memorials*, edited by Jane, Lady Shelley (London: Smith, Elder, 1859).

While Percy Bysshe Shelley's reputation rests primarily on his considerable accomplishments as one of the great English Romantic poets, he left a substantial body of prose writings, among them one of the great documents on the Romantic endeavor, *A Defence of Poetry*. Shelley's prose writings, which span his whole productive career, cover a wide range of topics: philosophical questions raised from Plato's time to his own, religion and belief, politics and society, and the value and uses of literature. In addition to his prose essays Shelley also wrote suggestive prefaces to many of his longer poems and a smattering of reviews, as well as engaging in correspondence with several of his contemporaries, including George Gordon, Lord Byron; John Keats; Leigh Hunt; William Godwin; and Thomas Love Peacock. Shelley's essays, prefaces, and letters, aside from their intrinsic interest, have the added benefit of allowing the reader to see Shelley's mind at work and of providing glosses for many of his more difficult poems.

Born on 4 August 1792 to Sir Timothy and Elizabeth Shelley, Percy Bysshe Shelley (the "Bysshe" from his grandfather, a peer of the realm) was the elder son among one brother, John, and four sisters, Elizabeth, Mary, Margaret, and Hellen. Young Percy faced the pleasant prospect not only of inheriting his grandfather's considerable estate one day but also of sitting in the House of Lords. Percy's active imagination was fueled by his early reading of many Gothic romances and was manifested by the ghost stories with which he thrilled his enrapt sisters. His formal schooling began with his attendance at Syon House Academy (1802-1804), where his lifelong interest in science began with the lively lectures of Adam Walker. Sir Timothy prepared his son for his eventual responsibilities by putting him on the aristocratic educational track of a notable public school, Eton, and then Oxford.

It is not surprising that Shelley became an accomplished prose writer, for his thinking was shaped by his voracious reading of many of the great thinkers in prose as well as in poetry. Shelley's reading extended far beyond the prescribed curriculums at both Eton College, which he attended from 1804 to 1810, and Oxford University, where he attended University College for less than a year in 1810 and 1811. From his teens onward Shelley was reading Plato, the Greek tragedians and historians, Francis Bacon, John Locke, Sir William Drummond, David Hume, the philosophes, Jean-Jacques Rousseau, Mary Wollstonecraft, William Godwin, and many other writers.

While at Oxford, Shelley continued his literary pursuits by writing Gothic novels and romantic and political poetry. However, it was his writing of a philosophical essay at this time that was to prove fateful in changing the course of his life. *The Necessity of Atheism* (1811), Shelley's first published essay, composed at Oxford in consultation with his fellow student and close friend Thomas Jefferson Hogg, had a profound effect on the rest of his life. Employing premises derived from skeptical philosophy, Shelley argues what is essentially an agnostic position: that existing evidence cannot support belief in a deity. Shelley's and Hogg's ill-advised decision to distribute copies of the pamphlet to several dons and bishops at Oxford led to their expulsion. Sir Timothy Shelley had the influence to get his son reinstated if he would only recant the pamphlet, but as a matter of principle Shelley would not give in and so became estranged from his family at the cost of his financial well-being, at least until he came of age.

After his elopement in August 1811 with the sixteen-year-old Harriet Westbrook, whom he married on the twenty-eighth or twenty-ninth, Shelley met Robert Southey, whom he came to dislike for his patronizing attitude and his political apostasy. Shelley's exposure in his youth to the Foxite Whigs, the more radical wing of the opposition party, along with his reading of writers such as Godwin and Thomas Paine—and his own rebellious personality—led him to adopt radical political stances. One of the first causes he took up was the Irish movement, including Catholic emancipation, in *An Address, to the Irish People* (1812). Fired with the enthusiasm of becoming a practical reformer, Shelley, Harriet, and her sister, Eliza, traveled to Dublin in February of 1812. He distributed about fifteen hundred copies of the pamphlet and delivered a version of it on 28 February at an Irish nationalist rally. Mindful of Godwin's admonitions against advocating or inciting violence, Shelley stressed the concept of universal brotherhood and the importance of nonviolent methods of achieving much-needed reforms. Indicative of the way Shelley's mind worked, the pamphlet moves from the specific grievances of the Irish to a call for the liberation and happiness of all mankind: "I write now not only with a view for Catholic Emancipation but for universal emancipation." The reform of individual minds and "intellectual resistance" to tyranny will gradually but eventually result in a "millenium of virtue."

While in Dublin, Shelley also wrote and published another "Irish" pamphlet, *Proposals for An Association of those Philanthropists, Who Convinced of the Inadequacy of the Moral and Political State of Ireland to Produce Benefits which Are Nevertheless Attainable Are Willing to Unite to Accomplish Its Regeneration* (1812), and a polemical broadside, the *Declaration of Rights* (1812). The *Proposals* reiterates many of the same arguments of *An Address, to the Irish People*, but this second pamphlet is directed toward intellectuals and urges them to use their powers of persuasion and their altruistic feelings of social love to create an international community of brotherhood. He urges them to seize the occasion of the Irish crisis not to foment violent revolution but to "excite the benevolent passions, that generalize and expand private into public feelings, and make the hearts of individuals vibrate not merely for themselves, their families, and their friends, but for posterity, *for a people*, till their country becomes the world and their family the sensitive creation." Before he left Dublin

*Silhouette of Thomas Jefferson Hogg as an Oxford undergraduate (Collection of Reverend Dr. W. S. Scott)*

later in 1812 to set up a household in Wales, Shelley distilled the arguments of Paine's *Rights of Man* (1791-1792), Rousseau's *Social Contract* (1762), and other similar documents treating the relationship between government and the people, as well as of his two "Irish" pamphlets, into his *Declaration of Rights*. The political broadside calls for a society based upon the principles of universal liberty, equality, and brotherhood, held together by a belief in reason and a reliance upon truth. Shelley was administered a strong lesson in the state's power to resist these universal rights when his servant Daniel Hill (or Healey) was arrested in Wales for distributing copies of the broadside.

This incident, along with his outrage over the arrest of Daniel Isaac Eaton for publishing part three of Paine's *The Age of Reason*, spurred Shelley to write another pamphlet, *A Letter to Lord Ellenborough* (1812), an eloquent argument in defense of freedom of speech and press. After a brief discussion of justice and law, Shelley begins the letter by asking Edward Law, first Baron Ellenborough, the lord chief justice and attorney general, on what grounds he presumes to judge and punish Eaton. He accuses Ellenborough of punishing Eaton simply over religious differences, the former's Christianity versus the latter's Deism. Reiterating the argument of *The Necessity of Atheism*, Shelley avers that to force someone to believe in something unprovable is an unreasonable position. Shelley concludes the letter with a prediction that the various religious beliefs and preferences that separate humanity will soon be overcome in the spirit of "charity and brotherly love."

During his Wales period, Shelley began an intense correspondence with Elizabeth Hitchener, a fellow freethinker who conducted a school at Hurstpierpoint. During this correspondence, Shelley and Hitchener, who was ten years

# DECLARATION OF RIGHTS.

GOVERNMENT has no rights; it is a delegation from several individuals for the purpose of securing their own. It is therefore just, only so far as it exists by their consent, useful only so far as it operates to their well-being.

2

IF these individuals think that the form of government which they, or their forefathers constituted is ill adapted to produce their happiness, they have a right to change it.

3

Government is devised for the security of rights. The rights of man are liberty, and an equal participation of the commonage of nature.

4

As the benefit of the governed, is, or ought to be the origin of government, no men can have any authority that does not expressly emanate from their will.

5

Though all governments are not so bad as that of Turkey, yet none are so good as they might be; the majority of every country have a right to perfect their government, the minority should not disturb them, they ought to secede, and form their own system in their own way.

6

All have a right to an equal share in the benefits, and burdens of Government. Any disabilities for opinion, imply by their existence, barefaced tyranny on the side of government, ignorant slavishness on the side of the governed.

7

The rights of man in the present state of society, are only to be secured by some degree of coercion to be exercised on their violator. The sufferer has a right that the degree of coercion employed be as slight as possible.

8

It may be considered as a plain proof of the hollowness of any proposition, if power be used to enforce instead of reason to persuade its admission. Government is never supported by fraud until it cannot be supported by reason.

9

No man has a right to disturb the public peace, by personally resisting the execution of a law however bad. He ought to acquiesce, using at the same time the utmost powers of his reason, to promote its repeal.

10

A man must have a right to act in a certain manner before it can be his duty. He may, before he ought.

11

A man has a right to think as his reason directs, it is a duty he owes to himself to think with freedom, that he may act from conviction.

12

A man has a right to unrestricted liberty of discussion, falsehood is a scorpion that will sting itself to death.

13

A man has not only a right to express his thoughts, but it is his duty to do so.

14

No law has a right to discourage the practice of truth. A man ought to speak the truth on every occasion, a duty can never be criminal, what is not criminal cannot be injurious.

15

Law cannot make what is in its nature virtuous or innocent, to be criminal, any more than it can make what is criminal to be innocent. Government cannot make a law, it can only pronounce that which was law before its organization, viz. the moral result of the imperishable relations of things.

16

The present generation cannot bind their posterity. The few cannot promise for the many.

17

No man has a right to do an evil thing that good may come.

18

Expediency is inadmissible in morals. Politics are only sound when conducted on principles of morality. They are in fact the morals of nations.

19

Man has no right to kill his brother, it is no excuse that he does so in uniform. He only adds the infamy of servitude to the crime of murder.

20

Man, whatever be his country, has the same rights in one place as another, the rights of universal citizenship.

21

The government of a country ought to be perfectly indifferent to every opinion. Religious differences, the bloodiest and most rancorous of all, spring from partiality.

22

A delegation of individuals for the purpose of securing their rights, can have no undelegated power of restraining the expression of their opinion.

23

Belief is involuntary; nothing involuntary is meritorious or reprehensible. A man ought not to be considered worse or better for his belief.

24

A Christian, a Deist, a Turk, and a Jew, have equal rights: they are men and brethren.

25

If a person's religious ideas correspond not with your own, love him nevertheless. How different would yours have been, had the chance of birth placed you in Tartary or India.

26

Those who believe that Heaven is, what earth has been, a monopoly in the hands of a favored few, would do well to reconsider their opinion: if they find that it came from their priest or their grandmother, they could not do better than reject it.

27

No man has a right to be respected for any other possessions, but those of virtue and talents. Titles are tinsel, power a corruptor, glory a bubble, and excessive wealth, a libel on its possessor.

28

No man has a right to monopolize more than he can enjoy; what the rich give to the poor, whilst millions are starving, is not a perfect favour, but an imperfect right.

29

Every man has a right to a certain degree of leisure and liberty, because it is his duty to attain a certain degree of knowledge. He may before he ought.

30

Sobriety of body and mind is necessary to those who would be free, because, without sobriety a high sense of philanthropy cannot actuate the heart, nor cool and determined courage, execute its dictates.

31

The only use of government is to repress the vices of man. If man were to day sinless, to-morrow he would have a right to demand that government and all its evils should cease.

Man! thou whose rights are here declared, be no longer forgetful of the loftiness of thy destination. Think of thy rights; of those possessions which will give thee virtue and wisdom, by which thou mayest arrive at happiness and freedom. They are declared to thee by one who knows thy dignity, for every hour does his heart swell with honorable pride in the contemplation of what thou mayest attain, by one who is not forgetful of thy degeneracy, for every moment brings home to him the bitter conviction of what thou art.

*Awake!—arise!—or be for ever fallen.*

*The 1812 broadside in which Shelley outlined his philosophy of government* his senior, developed the idea of soul mates, which became an important concept in Shelley's philosophy of love. However, as Shelley discovered more than once, reality had a difficult time living up to the ideal, for shortly after Hitchener came to live with the Shelley household in 1812, Shelley became disillusioned with her, and she and Shelley parted ways amid local gossip about an immoral household. Shelley had also begun a correspondence with his political father, William Godwin, who had faded into such obscurity that Shelley had originally assumed that he was dead. Godwin's view of political action had become tempered with age, and he tried to moderate Shelley's youthful enthusiasm for radical action. Shelley was ultimately disillusioned with Godwin because he did not appear to practice what he preached—particularly in his advocacy of free love except when it applied to his own daughter, Mary—and because Godwin would finally become a nagging financial burden to Shelley for the rest of his life.

During his Wales-London period of 1812-1813, Shelley's major poetic project was the political epic *Queen Mab* (1813). In addition to several short explanatory notes and quotations, Shelley appended to this long poem six lengthy notes, really essays, on political, philosophical, religious, social, and moral issues that were uppermost in his mind at this time: "A Vindication of Natural Diet," an essay advocating vegetarianism; "There is No God," an essay reiterating the skeptical arguments of *The Necessity of Atheism*; "I Will Beget a Son," a redaction of the *Letter to Lord Ellenborough* in its discussion of the injustice of forcing belief in an unprovable system of belief; "Necessity! Thou Mother of the World!," an essay on the power of Necessity, or cause and effect, in governing belief and action; "And Statesmen Boast of Wealth," a short essay on the labor theory of value closely following ideas in Adam Smith's *The Wealth of Nations* (1776) and Godwin's *Political Justice* (1793); "Even Love Is Sold," an attack on the injustice of laws governing marriage—which should be a matter of personal decision based on mutual feelings of love, not an institution enforced by laws—and divorce. Though only a few copies of *Queen Mab* were distributed at the time it was privately printed for Shelley by his friend Thomas Hookham in 1813, pirated editions of the poem began appearing in 1821, and it became a radical bible to many Chartists during the 1830s and 1840s.

From the time *Queen Mab* was printed (May or June 1813) to 1815, Shelley was largely preoccupied with personal affairs and had little time to devote to literary projects. As a frequent visitor to the Godwin household, Shelley met and fell in love with Mary Godwin. As the daughter of William Godwin and Mary Wollstonecraft (who died soon after giving birth to Mary in 1797), she embodied to Shelley the offspring of two great intellects. The two engaged in passionate discussions by the grave of Mary's mother, and before long Mary replaced Harriet as the object of Shelley's highest love. Following the principles of free love that he had read in Godwin's writings, Shelley eloped with Mary to the Continent, accompanied by her half sister, Jane (Claire) Clairmont. The result was Harriet's estrangement and eventual suicide, Godwin's hostility until Mary and Percy were married in December 1816, and greater financial difficulties until Shelley's grandfather Bysshe died in 1815.

During this period of personal upheaval Shelley's only publication was *A Refutation of Deism: in a Dialogue* (1814). Reiterating many of his antidoctrinal arguments from his earlier critiques upon the problem of religious belief, Shelley also attacks Deism, the last bastion for intellectuals who wanted to retain some vestige of belief in a deity. Shelley employs two disputants, Eusebes, the supposed spokesperson for Christianity, and Theosophus, the defender of Deism, to debate the grounds of their beliefs and to find the weak points in the grounds of the other's belief. By the end of the debate both positions have been destroyed, leaving only deep skepticism or atheism as viable, rational positions. Shelley came increasingly to believe that before a new era of freedom and equality could take hold, the old superstructure of rigid thought and moribund institutions would have to be swept away.

Shelley's career as a great Romantic poet may be said to begin in earnest with the writing and publishing of the volume of poetry titled *Alastor; or, The Spirit of Solitude: and Other Poems* (1816). It is also with *Alastor* that Shelley begins a practice of writing prose prefaces for his longer and more difficult poems, perhaps because he felt that he had often been misunderstood. As good prefaces should, Shelley's prefaces do not explain the poem's meaning but provide suggestive ideas for thinking about various themes in the poem. During 1816 also, Shelley, Mary, and Claire made their second trip to the Continent, this time to commune with Byron in the sublime scenery around Lake Leman (now Lake Geneva) and in the Alps. The two poets were stimulated by one another's presence, as well as by the magnificence of the natural environment and the associations it had with Rousseau, especially his *Julie; ou la Nouvelle Héloïse* (1761). Out of this adventure Byron produced Canto III of *Childe Harold's Pilgrimage*; Shelley produced the great philosophical poem *Mont Blanc*; and Mary produced what is possibly the most-popular and best-known work of the age, *Frankenstein* (published in 1818). Shelley wrote the preface for *Frankenstein*, which Mary was motivated to write as a result of a ghost-story contest proposed by Byron.

After the Shelleys (married on 30 December 1816) settled in Marlow in March of 1817, Shelley's attentions again turned to politics. The liberal to radical politics espoused by Shelley's circle of friends—which at this time included Godwin, Thomas Love Peacock, Leigh Hunt, Horace Smith, and John Keats—along with the wave of political reaction that followed the defeat of Napoleon in 1815 led Shelley to address the current crisis in two pamphlets and an epic-length political poem: *A Proposal for Putting Reform to the Vote Throughout the Kingdom, An Address to the People on the Death of the Princess Charlotte*, and *The Revolt of Islam; A Poem, in Twelve Cantos*.

Knowing that his own name had already become a synonym for radical politics and atheism and that signing the pamphlets would ensure their condemnation, Shelley signed both pamphlets "The Hermit of Marlow." The main argument of *A Proposal for Putting Reform to the Vote* is that increased suffrage, along with annual parliaments, would make the government more representative of the people without yet going the full way to the eventual but inevitable goal of universal suffrage. As mild as Shelley's proposals are, the necessary first step toward needed reforms was postponed until the passage of the 1832 Reform Bill. In *An Address to the People on the Death of the Princess Charlotte* (no copies of the first edition are extant), Shelley reveals himself to be a master of rhetorical strategy in prose. Shelley takes an occasion for public mourning, the untimely death of Princess Charlotte, and turns it into an occasion for political awareness. Using Paine's famous line from *The Rights of Man*—"We pity the plumage but forget the dying bird"—Shelley explains that while even the liberals have been mourning the death of the princess, they have ignored the injustice perpetrated in the executions of three laborers—Isaac Ludlam, Jeremiah Brandreth, and William Turner—who in turn become symbols of the plight of the poor and unrepresented masses. In his peroration, Shelley reveals that the true mourning should be for the death of Liberty itself and concludes with a prophecy of Liberty's resurrection as queen.

Three essays of uncertain date (unpublished during Shelley's lifetime) are important to an understanding of the development of Shelley's thought: the *Essay on Christianity*, the "Essay on Love," and the "Essay on Life." In the *Essay on Christianity*, probably written in 1817 or earlier, Shelley distinguishes between the oppressive institutions of Christianity and the figure of Jesus Christ, whom Shelley greatly admires as a poet and self-sacrificing reformer. Shelley compares Christ to Rousseau and finds in the teachings of both the social love that could be the fabric of a harmonious society. The fragmentary "Essay on Love," which Donald H. Reiman believes was written in the summer of 1818, builds upon the ideas on love first developed in Shelley's correspondence with Elizabeth Hitchener during 1811-1812. This essay may provide a gloss for some of Shelley's difficult poetry on the theme of love, such as *Epipsychidion* (1821). Beginning with the concept of love as sympathy, Shelley adds that real love brings forth our ideal selves (the "soul within our soul") and helps us realize our highest potential. In "Essay on Life," Shelley synthesizes apparently opposing systems of thought, such as idealism and skepticism, and emphasizes that there is no real distinction between objects and ideas or between individual minds and the one mind. Shelley left several other essays or fragments of essays, some serious, some playful, and others speculative, on various topics, including marriage, the ancient Greeks, a future state, morals, and religion.

In March of 1818 the Shelleys and their children William and Clara, together with Claire and Allegra (her child by Byron), set out for Italy. Shelley would never see England again. Through reading the liberal Hunt brothers' *Examiner* and through his correspondence, he maintained a lively interest in the English political scene, such as the Manchester or "Peterloo" Massacre of 1819, which provides the topic for Shelley's radical political poem *The Masque of Anarchy* (not published until 1832), as well as an intense enthusiasm for favorable political movements such as Spanish revolution and the Greek war for independence. His interest in these events—as well as his long-range hope for the improvement of hu-

*Pages from the notebook in which Shelley drafted* A Philosophical View of Reform *(from Ruth S. Granniss,* A Descriptive Catalogue of the First Editions in Book Form of the Writings of Percy Bysshe Shelley, Based on a Memorial Exhibition Held at the Grolier Club from April 20 to May 20, 1922, *1923)*

manity, the establishment of a just society, the transcendence of poets and poetry, and the triumph of love over the destructive feelings—is reflected in many of the great poems he wrote during the time he lived in Italy, from 1818 until his death in July 1822, including *The Cenci* (1819), *The Masque of Anarchy*, *Prometheus Unbound* (1820), *Hellas* (1822), and *The Triumph of Life*. Though Shelley felt isolated in Italy, which he described as the "paradise of exiles," the Shelleys' "Pisan circle," in addition to good friends (John and Maria Gisborne, Edward and Jane Williams, and others), included Byron and Edward John Trelawny and would have included Keats, whose untimely death in 1821 provided the subject for Shelley's great elegy *Adonais* (1821), and Hunt, who arrived in Italy a few days before Shelley died.

Neither of the two longest and most important essays Shelley wrote during his residence in

Italy was published during his lifetime: *A Philosophical View of Reform* (written in 1819-1820) and *A Defence of Poetry* (written in 1821). In *A Philosophical View of Reform,* Shelley returns to the political theme of the need for an expansion of suffrage that he had addressed at various other points in his career. But this essay goes beyond the earlier ones in its broad historical scope and in the way Shelley synthesizes various strains of his philosophical, cultural, and political thinking. Shelley's emphasis on gradual reform, rather than revolution, is evident in his appeal to increase suffrage without demanding universal suffrage until such time as more individual reform has occurred. After criticizing the corrupting influences of the class system, religious bigotry and intolerance, the system of paper money, the tyranny of unrepresentative government, the "aristocracy of attorneys" and others who prey upon the common people and diminish the cultural quality of life, Shelley concludes by calling for various "poets, philosophers, and artists" sympathetic to the cause of reform, such as Godwin, William Hazlitt, Jeremy Bentham, and Hunt, to write petitions urging the cause of reform.

In 1821 Shelley was stirred to write *A Defence of Poetry* as a response to his friend Peacock's lighthearted assessment of the decline of poetry in "Four Ages of Poetry," which appeared in the only issue of *Ollier's Literary Miscellany* (June 1820). Shelley's efforts to get *A Defence of Poetry* published quickly so that it would appear as a refutation came to no avail because of the failure of Ollier's magazine and because of Shelley's own untimely death. *A Defence of Poetry* was not published until 1840, when Mary Shelley included it in *Essays, Letters from Abroad, Translations and Fragments.* Shelley's brilliant synthesis of the various strains of his thought in arguing the moral and social utility of poetry, as well as in expanding on definitions of the poet and poetry and in commenting on how poetry gets written, extends far beyond a refutation of Peacock's semiserious essay and makes *A Defence of Poetry* one of the seminal prose documents of English Romanticism, along with William Wordsworth's preface to the 1800 edition of *Lyrical Ballads* and Samuel Taylor Coleridge's *Biographia Literaria* (1817).

Shelley counters Peacock's argument that poetry has lost its utility because it has been superseded by economics and social sciences with the idea that poetry—with its capacity to shape feelings, beliefs, and therefore ultimately actions—does have moral and social utility. Shelley begins the essay by distinguishing between reason and imagination, not to diminish the importance of reason but to show the importance of and the need for imagination. Poetry, then, is defined broadly as "the expression of the Imagination," and is evident in the order and rhythm possessed by, as well as the delight given by, all the creative arts. Synthesizing both the imaginative or visionary powers of the poet with the social or political utility of poetry, Shelley argues that the poet "comprises and unites both these characters" of legislators and prophets. The poet's visionary powers enable him or her to apprehend, however briefly, a transcendent and permanent realm of order and beauty. This transcendence and permanence endow poetry with a higher moral truth than reason or science can apprehend. By relating the influence poetry exerts to his theory of morals, and specifically to his theory of love, Shelley explains how poetry is able to effect social benefits. "[Poetry] awakens and enlarges the mind itself by rendering it the receptacle of a thousand unapprehended combinations of thought." The expanded consciousness allows us to transcend our petty and selfish concerns and to feel sympathy with others:

> The great secret of morals is Love; or a going out of our own nature, and an identification of ourselves with the beautiful which exists in thought, action, or person, not our own. A man, to be greatly good, must imagine intensely and comprehensively; he must put himself in the place of another and of many others.

Shelley's distinction between material progress and moral progress not only refutes Peacock's argument concerning the relative uselessness of poetry but sets the grounds of the general debate between the value of culture and inner progress versus material progress that would become important to the great Victorian prose writers such as Thomas Carlyle, John Ruskin, and Matthew Arnold: "We want the creative faculty to imagine that which we know; we want the generous impulse to act that which we imagine; we want the poetry of life; our calculations have outrun our conception.... The cultivation of those sciences which have enlarged the limits of the empire of man over the external world has for want of the poetical faculty proportionally circumscribed those of the internal world; and man, having enslaved the elements, remains himself a slave." According to Shelley, the greatest poetry, even against the conscious wishes of the individual

*Pages from a 29 November 1821 letter to John Keats's friend Joseph Severn, in which Shelley enclosed a copy of* Adonais *and commented that since he and Keats shared one "accidental" quality—a lack of public recognition—this elegy on Keats was unlikely to "excite any attention" (MA 790; Pierpont Morgan Library)*

poet, transforms the world into something better. Poetry does not function didactically but works upon the consciousness unawares. Shelley concludes *A Defence of Poetry* with a high social claim: "Poets are the unacknowledged legislators of the world." This statement, while consistent with his argument of how poetry effects moral and social improvement, also conveys a sense of Shelley's frustration with his own failure to be acknowledged by the reading public at large.

In one of the ironies that seem to permeate Shelley's life, his powers as a poet seemed to be reaching a higher plateau, in his writing of the visionary poem *The Triumph of Life*, at the time of his death. This fragmentary poem ends with "Then what is Life?," the last line of poetry Shelley is known to have written before his legendary death by drowning at the age of twenty-nine. The circumstances of Shelley's death and cremation have helped to contribute to the legend of Shelley as an otherworldly or almost supernatural being. The Shelleys and their intimate friends Edward and Jane Williams had rented Casa Magni on the Bay of San Terenzo, near Lerici, in May 1822. Here Shelley and Edward Williams could spend the summer sailing their new boat, the *Don Juan*, in the Gulf of Spezia. In early July 1822 they sailed to Leghorn to meet Leigh Hunt, who, accompanied by his family, had come to Italy to begin a new journal, the *Liberal*, with Byron and Shelley. After getting the Hunts settled, Shelley and Williams set sail on the return trip to Lerici on 8 July, but a sudden squall enveloped and overcame the *Don Juan*, and the two bodies were washed ashore ten days later. In accordance with Italian quarantine laws of the time, Shelley's and William's bodies were cremated. Byron, Hunt, and Trelawny attended their friend's cremation, and Trelawny contributed to the legend of Shelley's otherworldliness when he plucked Shelley's heart—said to be too pure to burn—from the fire. He later arranged for Shelley's ashes to be buried near Keats's grave in the Protestant Cemetery in Rome. Trelawny and Hunt each provided an epitaph for Shelley's gravestone: the former, three lines from *The Tempest*: "Nothing of him that doth fade / But doth suffer a sea-change / Into something rich and strange"; the latter, the Latin inscription: "Cor Cordium."

*A Philosophical View of Reform* and *A Defence of Poetry*, along with the prefaces to several of his last great poems, such as *Prometheus Unbound*, *The Cenci*, and *Adonais*, represent Shelley's highest achievements in prose. His claim to greatness as a prose writer rests in his ability to synthesize various, even apparently opposing, strains of his reading and thinking, such as skepticism and idealism, into something new that is wholly his own. Shelley's prose writings, because they reveal the philosophical, social, and even the poetical development of his thought, can be studied independently, but they are more productively read in conjunction with his poetry. Despite vicissitudes in his reputation during the nineteenth century and the early part of the twentieth century, Shelley's hope that he would become one of the immortals has been realized. Unappreciated by all but a few friends and enlightened individuals in his own day, he has been vindicated according to his criteria in *A Defence of Poetry*: "The jury which sits in judgment upon a poet, belonging as he does to all time, must be composed of his peers; it must be empanelled by time from the selectest of the wise of many generations."

**Letters:**

*Select Letters of Percy Bysshe Shelley*, edited by Richard Garnett (London: Kegan Paul, Trench, 1882);

*Letters From Percy Bysshe Shelley to Elizabeth Hitchener*, 2 volumes, edited by T. J. Wise and Harry Buxton Forman (London: Privately printed, 1890);

*Letters from Percy Bysshe Shelley to William Godwin*, 2 volumes, edited by Wise and Forman (London: Privately printed, 1891);

*The Shelley Correspondence in the Bodleian Library: Letters of Percy Bysshe Shelley and others, mainly published from the collection presented to the library by Lady Shelley in 1892*, edited by H. R. Hill (Oxford: Printed for the Bodleian Library by John Johnson, 1926);

*Shelley and His Circle, 1773-1822*, The Carl H. Pforzheimer Library, 8 volumes, volumes 1-4, edited by Kenneth Neill Cameron; volumes 5-8, edited by Donald H. Reiman (Cambridge, Mass.: Harvard University Press, 1961-1986);

*The Letters of Percy Bysshe Shelley*, 2 volumes, edited by Frederick L. Jones (Oxford: Oxford University Press, 1964).

**Bibliographies:**

David Bonnell Green and Edwin Graves Wilson, eds., *Keats, Shelley, Byron, Hunt, and Their*

*Mary Shelley's 1829 sketch of her husband (Harry Ransom Humanities Research Center, University of Texas at Austin)*

*Circles. A Bibliography: July 1, 1950 - June 30, 1962* (Lincoln: University of Nebraska Press, 1964);

A. C. Elkins and L. J. Forstner, *The Romantic Movement Bibliography 1936-1970*, 7 volumes (Ann Arbor, Mich.: Pierian Press, 1973);

Clement Dunbar, *A Bibliography of Shelley Studies: 1823-1950* (New York & London: Garland, 1976);

Robert A. Hartley, ed., *Keats, Shelley, Byron, Hunt and Their Circles. A Bibliography: July 1, 1962 - December 31, 1974* (Lincoln: University of Nebraska Press, 1978);

David Erdman, *The Romantic Movement: A Selective and Critical Bibliography*, 10 volumes to date (New York: Garland, 1980- );

Stuart Curran, "Percy Bysshe Shelley," in *The English Romantic Poets*, edited by Frank Jordan, fourth edition (New York: MLA, 1985);

Karsten Klejs Engelberg, *The Making of the Shelley Myth: An Annotated Bibliography of Criticism of Percy Bysshe Shelley 1822-1860* (London: Mansell / Westport, Conn.: Meckler, 1988).

**Biographies:**

Leigh Hunt, *Lord Byron and Some of His Contemporaries; with Recollections of the Author's Life, and of His Visits to Italy* (London: Colburn, 1828);

Thomas Medwin, *The Shelley Papers; Memoir of Percy Bysshe Shelley* (London: Whittaker Treacher & Co., 1833); revised and enlarged as

*The Life of Percy Bysshe Shelley*, 2 volumes (London: Thomas Cautley Newby, 1847);

Thomas Jefferson Hogg, *The Life of Percy Bysshe Shelley*, 2 volumes (London: Edward Moxon, 1858);

Edward John Trelawny, *Recollections of the Last Days of Shelley and Byron* (London: Edward Moxon, 1858);

Thomas Love Peacock, "Memoirs of Percy Bysshe Shelley," *Fraser's Magazine*, 57 (June 1858): 643-659; part 2, *Fraser's Magazine*, 61 (January 1860): 92-109; "Percy Bysshe Shelley, A Supplementary Notice," *Fraser's Magazine*, 65 (March 1862): 343-346; republished in *Peacock's Memoirs of Shelley with Shelley's Letters to Peacock*, edited by H. F. B. Brett-Smith (London: Henry Frowde, 1909);

William Michael Rossetti, *Memoir of Shelley* (London: Moxon, 1870);

George Barnett Smith, *Shelley: A Critical Biography* (Edinburgh: David Douglas, 1877);

John Addington Symonds, *Shelley* (London: Macmillan, 1878);

John Cordy Jeaffreson, *The Real Shelley. New Views of the Poet's Life*, 2 volumes (London: Hurst & Blackett, 1885);

Edward Dowden, *The Life of Percy Bysshe Shelley*, 2 volumes (London: Kegan Paul, Trench, Trübner, 1886);

A. Clutton-Brock, *Shelley: The Man and the Poet* (London: Methuen, 1910);

Francis Gribble, *The Romantic Life of Shelley and the Sequel* (London: Eveleigh Nash, 1911);

Walter E. Peck, *Shelley: His Life and Work*, 2 volumes (Boston & New York: Houghton Mifflin, 1927);

Newman Ivey White, *Shelley*, 2 volumes (New York: Knopf, 1940);

Edmund Blunden, *Shelley: A Life Story* (New York: Viking, 1947);

C. L. Cline, *Byron, Shelley, and Their Pisan Circle* (Cambridge, Mass.: Harvard University Press, 1952);

Jean Overton Fuller, *Shelley: A Biography* (London: Cape, 1968);

Richard Holmes, *Shelley: The Pursuit* (London: Weidenfeld & Nicolson, 1974).

**References:**

Lloyd Abbey, *Destroyer and Preserver: Shelley's Poetic Skepticism* (Lincoln: University of Nebraska Press, 1979);

James O. Allsup, *The Magic Circle: A Study of Shelley's Concept of Love* (Port Washington, New York & London: Kennikat Press, 1976);

Matthew Arnold, "Shelley," *The Nineteenth Century*, 23 (January 1888): 23-29;

Edward Aveling and Eleanor Marx Aveling, *Shelley's Socialism. Two Lectures* (London: Privately printed, 1888);

Carlos Baker, *Shelley's Major Poetry: The Fabric of a Vision* (Princeton: Princeton University Press, 1948);

James E. Barcus, *Shelley: The Critical Heritage* (London & Boston: Routledge & Kegan Paul, 1975);

Stephen Behrendt, *Shelley and His Audiences* (Lincoln: University of Nebraska Press, 1989);

Kim Blank, *Wordsworth's Influence on Shelley: A Study of Poetic Authority* (New York: St. Martin's Press, 1988);

Blank, ed., *The New Shelley: Later Twentieth-Century Views* (New York: St. Martin's Press, 1991);

Harold Bloom, *Shelley's Mythmaking* (New Haven: Yale University Press, 1959);

Bloom, ed., *Percy Bysshe Shelley* (New York: Chelsea House, 1985);

Stopford Augustus Brook, *The Inaugural Address to the Shelley Society* (London: Privately printed, 1886);

Nathaniel Brown, *Sexuality and Feminism in Shelley* (Cambridge, Mass.: Harvard University Press, 1979);

Robert Browning, Introduction to *Letters of Percy Bysshe Shelley* (London: Edward Moxon, 1852);

Peter H. Butter, *Shelley's Idols of the Cave* (Edinburgh: Edinburgh University Press, 1954);

Kenneth N. Cameron, *Shelley: The Golden Years* (Cambridge, Mass.: Harvard University Press, 1974);

Cameron, *The Young Shelley: Genesis of a Radical* (New York: Macmillan, 1950);

Judith Cherniak, *The Lyrics of Shelley* (Cleveland: Press of Case Western Reserve University, 1972);

Timothy Clark, *Embodying Revolution: The Figure of the Poet in Shelley* (Oxford: Clarendon Press, 1989);

Richard Cronin, *Shelley's Poetic Thoughts* (New York: St. Martin's Press, 1981);

Nora Crook and Derek Gruton, *Shelley's Venomed Melody* (Cambridge: Cambridge University Press, 1986);

Stuart Curran, *Shelley's Annus Mirabilis: The Maturing of an Epic Vision* (San Marino, Cal.: Huntington Library, 1975);

Curran, *Shelley's Cenci: Scorpions Ringed with Fire* (Princeton: Princeton University Press, 1970);

P. M. S. Dawson, *The Unacknowledged Legislator: Shelley and Politics* (Oxford: Clarendon Press, 1980);

Roland A. Duerksen, *Shelley's Poetry of Involvement* (New York: St. Martin's Press, 1988);

Edward Duffy, *Rousseau in England: The Context for Shelley's Critique of the Enlightenment* (Berkeley: University of California Press, 1979);

Kelvin Everest, ed., *Shelley Revalued: Essays from the Gregynog Conference* (Leicester: Leicester University Press, 1983);

Nancy Fogarty, *Shelley in the Twentieth Century: A Study of the Development of Shelley Criticism in England and America 1916-1971* (Salzburg, Austria: Institut für Englische Sprache und Literatur, 1976);

Paul Foot, *Red Shelley* (London: Sidgwick & Jackson, 1980);

Christine Gallant, *Shelley's Ambivalence* (New York: St. Martin's Press, 1989);

Carl Grabo, *The Magic Plant: The Growth of Shelley's Thought* (Chapel Hill: University of North Carolina Press, 1936);

John P. Guinn, *Shelley's Political Thought* (The Hague: Mouton, 1969);

Jean Hall, *The Transforming Image: A Study of Shelley's Major Poetry* (Urbana: University of Illinois Press, 1980);

Terence Allan Hoagwood, *Skepticism and Ideology: Shelley's Political Prose and Its Philosophical Context from Bacon to Marx* (Iowa City: University of Iowa Press, 1988);

Jerrold E. Hogle, *Shelley's Process: Radical Transference and the Development of His Major Works* (New York: Oxford University Press, 1988);

A. M. D. Hughes, *The Nascent Mind of Shelley* (Oxford: Clarendon Press, 1947);

Carol Jacobs, *Uncontainable Romanticism: Shelley, Bronte, Kleist* (Baltimore: Johns Hopkins University Press, 1989);

William Keach, *Shelley's Style* (New York & London: Methuen, 1984);

Benjamin P. Kurtz, *The Pursuit of Death: A Study of Shelley's Poetry* (New York: Oxford University Press, 1933);

Angela Leighton, *Shelley and the Sublime: An Interpretation of the Major Poems* (Cambridge: Cambridge University Press, 1984);

Gerald M. McNiece, *Shelley and the Revolutionary Idea* (Cambridge, Mass.: Harvard University Press, 1969);

John Stuart Mill, "The Two Kinds of Poetry," *Monthly Repository and Review of Theology and General Literature*, n.s. 7 (October 1833): 714-724;

John V. Murphy, *The Dark Angel: Gothic Elements in Shelley's Works* (Lewisburg, Pa.: Bucknell University Press, 1975);

Sylva Norman, *Flight of the Skylark: The Development of Shelley's Reputation* (Norman: University of Oklahoma Press, 1954);

James A. Notopoulos, *The Platonism of Shelley: A Study of Platonism and the Poetic Mind* (Durham, N.C.: Duke University Press, 1949);

Michael O'Neill, *The Human Mind's Imaginings: Conflict and Achievement in Shelley's Poetry* (Oxford: Clarendon Press, 1989);

O'Neill, *Percy Bysshe Shelley: A Literary Life* (New York: St. Martin's Press, 1990);

Julie Power, *Shelley in America in the Nineteenth Century: His Relation to American Critical Thought and His Influence* (Lincoln: University of Nebraska Press, 1940);

C. E. Pulos, *The Deep Truth: A Study of Shelley's Scepticism* (Lincoln: University of Nebraska Press, 1954);

Donald H. Reiman, *Percy Bysshe Shelley* (New York: Twayne, 1969);

Reiman, ed., *Shelley, Keats, and London Radical Writers*, 2 volumes, part C of *The Romantics Reviewed: Contemporary Reviews of British Romantic Writers* (New York & London: Garland, 1972);

Seymour Reiter, *A Study of Shelley's Poetry* (Albuquerque: University of New Mexico Press, 1967);

George Ridenour, ed., *Shelley: A Collection of Critical Essays* (Englewood Cliffs, N.J.: Prentice-Hall, 1965);

James Rieger, *The Mutiny Within: The Heresies of Percy Bysshe Shelley* (New York: Braziller, 1967);

Charles E. Robinson, *Shelley and Byron: The Snake and Eagle Wreathed in Fight* (Baltimore: Johns Hopkins University Press, 1976);

Ivan Roe, *Shelley: The Last Phase* (London: Hutchinson, 1953);

H. S. Salt, *A Shelley Primer*, Shelley Society Publications, fourth series, no. 4 (London: Reeves & Turner, 1887);

Earl J. Schulze, *Shelley's Theory of Poetry: A Reappraisal* (The Hague: Mouton, 1966);

Michael Henry Scrivener, *The Philosophical Anarchism and Utopian Thought of Percy Bysshe Shelley* (Princeton: Princeton University Press, 1982);

Melvin T. Solve, *Shelley: His Theory of Poetry* (Chicago: University of Chicago Press, 1927);

Stuart Sperry, *Shelley's Major Verse: The Narrative and Dramatic Poetry* (Cambridge, Mass.: Harvard University Press, 1988);

Floyd Stovall, *Desire and Restraint in Shelley* (Durham, N.C.: Duke University Press, 1931);

Ronald Tetreault, *Shelley and Literary Form* (Toronto: University of Toronto Press, 1987);

Earl R. Wasserman, *Shelley: A Critical Reading* (Baltimore & London: Johns Hopkins University Press, 1971);

Bennett Weaver, *Toward the Understanding of Shelley* (Ann Arbor: University of Michigan Press, 1932);

Timothy Webb, *Shelley: A Voice Not Understood* (Manchester, U.K.: Manchester University Press, 1977);

Webb, *The Violet in the Crucible: Shelley and Translation* (Oxford: Clarendon Press, 1976);

Andrew J. Welburn, *Power and Self-Consciousness in the Poetry of Shelley* (New York: St. Martin's Press, 1986);

Newman I. White, *The Unextinguished Hearth: Shelley and His Contemporary Critics* (Durham, N.C.: Duke University Press, 1938);

Milton Wilson, *Shelley's Later Poetry: A Study in His Prophetic Imagination* (New York: Columbia University Press, 1959);

R. B. Woodings, ed., *Shelley Modern Judgements* (London: Macmillan, 1968);

Ross Woodman, *The Apocalyptic Vision in the Poetry of Shelley* (Toronto: University of Toronto Press, 1964);

John W. Wright, *Shelley's Myth of Metaphor* (Athens: University of Georgia Press, 1970).

**Papers:**

The three great repositories for manuscripts and letters by Shelley and his circle are the Bodleian Library, Oxford: Lord Abinger's collection (on deposit at the Bodleian); and the Carl H. Pforzheimer collection, now in the New York Public Library. In addition, there are notebooks and manuscripts in the Huntington Library, the British Library, the Pierpont Morgan Library, Harvard University, the Library of Congress, the University of Texas, Texas Christian University, and the Keats-Shelley Memorial House in Rome.

# Edward John Trelawny

*(13 November 1792 - 13 August 1881)*

Paula R. Feldman
*University of South Carolina*

BOOKS: *Adventures of a Younger Son* (3 volumes, London: Henry Colburn & Richard Bentley, 1831; 2 volumes, New York: J. & J. Harper, 1832);

*Recollections of the Last Days of Shelley and Byron* (London: Edward Moxon, 1858; Boston: Ticknor & Fields, 1858); revised and enlarged as *Records of Shelley, Byron and the Author* (London: Pickering, 1878; New York: Scribners, 1887).

Despite little formal education, Edward John Trelawny was a riveting storyteller with a prodigious imagination who managed to insinuate himself into the lives of some of the most important literary figures of nineteenth-century Britain. He was the intimate friend, confidant, and correspondent of Lord Byron, Percy Bysshe Shelley, Mary Wollstonecraft Shelley, Claire Clairmont (the subject of Henry James's short story "The Aspern Papers," 1888), William Michael Rossetti, Prince Aléxandros Mavrokordátos (hero of the Greek war of independence), and Fanny Kemble (British Shakespearean actress and author), among others.

It was his good fortune to live long enough to regale the Victorians with firsthand accounts of long-dead Romantic writers. Robert Browning marveled, "Ah did you once see Shelley plain / And did he stop and speak to you." In later life Trelawny became known as "the friend of Byron and Shelley," though, in truth, he had known Shelley for only six months when the poet drowned at sea, and his association with Byron was only of eighteen months' duration. Some even said he had been a friend of Keats though, in fact, he had never met Keats. But it was Trelawny who cremated Shelley's body on the beach at Viareggio in August of 1822 (an act immortalized in the 1869 painting by Louis-Edouard Fournier and Jean-Léon Gérôme) and Trelawny who snatched the poet's heart from the flames of the funeral pyre.

Not a great deal is known about Trelawny's childhood. He was born on 13 November 1792 probably in Cornwall to Charles and Maria Hawkins Trelawny, a lieutenant colonel and an heiress living in straitened circumstances. In 1798 his father came into an inheritance, changed his name to Brereton, and moved the family to London. All six children disliked and feared their father, who was subject to rages. Trelawny would later describe him as "tyrannical," "stern and unforgiving," and "selfish." From age eight to ten Trelawny attended a boarding school run by Rev. Samuel Seyer but was expelled after attacking the headmaster's assistant and deliberately setting fire to the building. Branded as rebellious and ungovernable, he was made to join the Royal Navy at age twelve. During his seven-year naval career, he cruised the Indian Ocean and saw Bombay, Madras, and Java. Wounded in the invasion of Mauritius and subsequently contracting cholera, he returned to England where his family nursed him back to health. But, when he was nineteen, his naval career was at an end.

The next year he married Caroline Addison and settled with her in London, where their first child was born in 1814. After giving birth to a second child, Caroline ran off with a Captain Coleman in December 1816. Trelawny obtained a divorce in 1819. With an annual allowance of three hundred pounds, he left for Paris that autumn and was in Switzerland by the next summer.

His flair for the dramatic evinced itself in many ways. He had read Byron's *Corsair* (1814) and was so taken with the work and its hero that he determined to get to know its author personally. Byron, whom he met in January 1822, and his circle in Italy were enthralled by Trelawny's stories of his early life as a privateer, stories that were almost total fabrications. In an unfinished tragedy about Trelawny, Shelley remarks, "Some said he was a man of blood and peril, / And steeped in bitter infamy to the lips." Walter Savage Landor and Byron also found him interest-

*Edward John Trelawny in Italy, 1822-1823 (portrait by W. E. West; private collection; from William St. Clair,* Trelawny: The Incurable Romancer, *1977). This depiction of Trelawny as a Byronic hero helped to establish his Romantic image among his contemporaries.*

ing enough to make him the subject of literary works. On 21 July 1823 Trelawny accompanied Byron to fight in the Greek war of independence.

Trelawny's exploits in Greece earned him a certain celebrity. After a brief trip back to England in 1828, during which he proposed to the widowed Mary Shelley and was politely refused, he settled in Florence. At first he lived with Keats's friend Charles Armitage Brown in a house once belonging to Petrarch, not too far from Joseph Severn and Landor. Later he took a villa overlooking the city. There Trelawny resolved to write a book about his life, to include not only his early life but also a memoir of Shelley and Byron. When Mary Shelley, fearing she would jeopardize her income from Shelley's disapproving father, refused to supply the necessary documents and anecdotes, Trelawny decided to end his narrative before he met Shelley.

Charles Armitage Brown took the rough draft of the book Trelawny had titled "A Man's Life" and helped him get it in shape for a publisher. According to William St. Clair, Trelawny's best and most recent biographer,

> Trelawny began his book with (reasonably) factual events of his childhood and naval experiences and ended with (reasonably) factual events about his return to England, but for the interven-

> ing period he composed a romantic fantasy with imaginary characters and events which projected his own masthead dreams of the young corsair at the side of the legendary Surcouf. It is a good story, wild, violent, and prejudiced, representing in style and arrangement as well as in plot the character which the author had so successfully assumed.

Mary Shelley agreed to locate a publisher and to take care of the details of seeing it through the press. She supplied missing epigraphs for many of the chapters and successfully urged Trelawny to tone down and, in a few instances, delete the most offensive passages. Henry Colburn paid three hundred pounds and, over Trelawny's objections, changed the title to *Adventures of a Younger Son* (1831). Declaring the book "an honest confession of my life," Trelawny insisted on anonymity even with the publisher for fear, he said, of family reprisal. But early reviewers blew his thin cover, with Colburn soon following their lead, printing Trelawny's name in advertisements.

Nineteenth-century readers believed in the historical truth of this "autobiography," and credulous critics applauded it, despite its violence and the shocking nature of some of its incidents. Walter Savage Landor compared it to the *Iliad*. William Michael Rossetti called it "wonderfully vivid, full of the passion of maritime enterprise and saturated with the fierce, semi-barbaric chivalry of its author's character. Some of its passages of description and of narrative are not to be surpassed, and have seldom been rivalled. . . ." Post-Freudian critics, however, armed with documentary evidence, have seen it in a far different light. For example, Thomas Philbreck, in *Nineteenth Century Fiction* (1975), calls the book "one of the most impressive nineteenth century examples of the pornography of violence because it is so obsessively imagined." St. Clair calls attention to the pattern of mythological and psychological themes such as the protagonist's

> urge towards sexual conquest, self-assertion against established authority, terror of unknown monsters. The world is a rich and fruitful garden where every desire can be fulfilled and every appetite sated. . . . [for] a man with sufficient ruthlessness. The *Adventures* is a celebration of rape and plunder. Anything which stands in the way of self-gratification can be violently smashed aside, and human beings are treated no differently from the exotic beasts and monsters which guard the jungle orchard. In the *Adventures* women do not give birth, they whelp and litter. . . .

For nineteenth-century readers, however, the *Adventures* reinforced the erroneous view that Trelawny was the original of the Byronic hero, the real-life Lara, the authentic Corsair. Trelawny would exploit this false impression for the rest of his long life.

After a brief stay in England to enjoy his newfound literary fame, Trelawny set sail in 1833 for America, where civil war seemed imminent. Though disappointed in his hopes of seeing battle, he did meet James Fenimore Cooper, romance Fanny Kemble, and, the evidence suggests, try to establish a community of freed slaves in Virginia.

Back in England by 1835, after the apparent failure of his utopian dreams, Trelawny, the notorious womanizer who had fathered several children, both legitimate and illegitimate, married Augusta Goring and settled down to a life of domesticity at Usk. This marriage lasted nearly two decades before being shattered when Trelawny brought home a mistress.

In 1856 Lady Shelley, wife of the Shelleys' only surviving son, decided that the time had come for an authorized biography. She invited to her home (which doubled as a shrine to the poet) several prospective biographers who had known Shelley, including Thomas Love Peacock, Thomas Jefferson Hogg, and Trelawny. Though her husband, Percy Florence, traveled to Usk to talk with Trelawny about the project, in the end Trelawny refused to participate. Even so, though he had been in literary retirement for nearly a quarter century, he began to think of writing his own, unauthorized book. He had made some notes and gathered materials in 1829, when he had approached Mary Shelley unsuccessfully. Now he wrote asking for reminiscences and anecdotes to Daniel Roberts, the retired naval officer who had been part of the Shelley circle in Italy, and to Claire Clairmont, mother of Byron's child Allegra and stepsister to Mary Shelley, who had accompanied the Shelleys on their elopement in 1814 and remained a part of their household on and off for some years after.

Lady Shelley commissioned Thomas Jefferson Hogg to write the biography. He had been the poet's schoolmate and close friend and, after Shelley's death, had established a household with Jane Williams, widow of Edward Williams and the object of Shelley's last romantic passion.

The Cremation of Shelley's Body *(1869), by Louis-Edouard Fournier and Jean-Léon Gérôme (Walker Art Gallery, National Museums and Galleries on Merseyside). In this romanticized portrait Byron, Leigh Hunt, and Trelawny stand beside the funeral pyre while Mary Shelley (who did not attend her husband's cremation) kneels behind them.*

When the first two volumes came out, however, portraying Shelley as the comic companion of Hogg's school days rather than the angelic and ethereal poet Lady Shelley pictured, she was outraged. Amid threats of lawsuits, a third volume was suppressed and a fourth never completed.

Lady Shelley now turned to the eminent scholar Richard Garnett to produce a more acceptable book, published in 1859 under her name as *Shelley Memorials*. Peacock, too, was persuaded to set down his memories (1858-1862), and another biography, by Charles Middleton, came out in 1858. However, most observers agreed with William Michael Rossetti that Trelawny's *Recollections of the Last Days of Shelley and Byron* (1858) "is certainly the best account of Shelley as a mature man which any contemporary has handed down to us. The style of writing, too, is in essential respects excellent."

Trelawny brings his subjects vividly, convincingly to life, mythologizing as he goes, recasting conversations with Shelley and Byron through the dual lenses of memory and imagination, augmented by the anecdotal and the apocryphal. This narrative picks up where the *Adventures* had left off. In the summer of 1820 Trelawny and his friend Roberts are in Switzerland, where Trelawny meets Edward Williams and Thomas Medwin, who has just received a copy of *The Cenci* (1819) from its author, Medwin's cousin. The three friends decide to meet the following spring in Italy for a holiday with Shelley. The momentous meeting with Shelley takes place on 14 January 1822, and another with Byron follows the next day. The book recounts the adventures of Shelley, Byron, and their circle at Pisa, the events surrounding the death at sea of Williams and Shelley, the cremation at Viareggio, the trip to Greece with Byron, their exploits in the war, Byron's death, and more of Trelawny's Greek exploits up through 1825.

The *Recollections* not only made Trelawny once more the center of literary attention, but established him as *the* authority on Shelley. The competition for the title was gradually dying off, leaving Trelawny as the last remnant of a bygone era. The temper of the times had changed, though, since Trelawny's first experience with literary celebrity. In the *Adventures*, he had claimed to have been a pirate, a thief, even a murderer and a traitor, but no one had been much bothered by these "confessions." Now, however, the public was scandalized by a much milder "revelation," one whose truth is as suspect as much else in the book. According to Trelawny, three days after Byron's death at Missolonghi, Byron's valet Fletcher ushered Trelawny into the room where the poet lay. Alone with the corpse, he lifted the shroud to discover which of Byron's feet was deformed. The Victorian public was revolted by what they considered a gross gesture of disrespect toward the dead.

But they came increasingly to hear Trelawny, the old raconteur, in his eighties now, tell stories about Byron and Shelley, stories that grew increasingly elaborate and dramatic as the years drew on. In 1878, at the urging of William Michael Rossetti, Trelawny published *Records of Shelley, Byron and the Author*, a reworking of the *Recollections*. Not only does "the author" command a notably larger and more central role in the narrative this time, but stories are added and revised. Since publishing the earlier work, he had learned that Byron had laughed at him behind his back. Now he could even the score. Byron becomes proud, vain, cheap, jealous, a poor swimmer, an even poorer boxer—in short, much Shelley's inferior. And Trelawny had a score to settle with Mary Shelley too. It was one thing to have denied him access to the documents he asked to see in 1829 and quite another for her to have turned around and offered these same documents to Thomas Moore for his biography of Byron. Later the two quarreled when Trelawny accused her of failing to help the Radical cause and of conforming to the conventional values Shelley hated. Even though Mary assured him that Shelley himself approved the changes, Trelawny still could not forgive Mary for having omitted some of the notes to *Queen Mab* and the dedication to Shelley's first wife, Harriet, in the edition of Shelley's poems Mary painstakingly edited and published in 1839. Perhaps, as the years passed, her rejection of his marriage proposal rankled as well. At any rate, in the *Records*, his portrayal of Mary Shelley is not only unkind but vengefully untruthful. She becomes a slave to conformity, a shrew, a conventional churchgoer, betrayer of her dead husband's values, undeserving of him and unequal to him in nearly every way. Because of Trelawny's presumed authority, this cruel caricature was destined to stick and would seriously damage Mary Shelley's reputation for the next hundred years.

But Trelawny's reputation continued to prosper. Rossetti described him as "Tameless in youth . . . [and] untamed in age. Of iron firmness, at once vehement and stoical, outspoken and often overbearing, despising the conventions and the creeds of society. . . ." In his "Lines on the Death of Edward John Trelawny," A. C. Swinburne calls him the:

> Last high star of the years whose thunder
> Still men's listening remembrance hears,
> Last light left of our fathers' years.

By virtue of longevity, Trelawny's distorted and self-serving vision was to triumph. He would have the last word of any of his generation and the privilege of remaking Romantic literary history with his "eye-witness" accounts. True to form, when he died at age eighty-eight, at his request his remains were transported from England to the Protestant Cemetery in Rome. There, nearly sixty years after their brief friendship, he was buried next to Shelley, whose words he had earnestly chosen for his tombstone, intending no irony:

> These are two friends whose lives were undivided.
> So let their memory be now they have glided
> Under the grave: let not their bones be parted
> For their two hearts in life were single-hearted.

**Letters:**

*Letters of Edward John Trelawny*, edited by H. Buxton Forman (London & New York: Henry Frowde, Oxford University Press, 1910);

*The Collected Letters of Edward John Trelawny*, edited by Paula R. Feldman (Kent, Ohio: Kent State University Press, forthcoming 1992).

**Biographies:**

Lady Anne Hill, *Trelawny's Strange Relations* (Stanford, Dingley, U.K.: Mill House Press, 1956);

William St. Clair, *Trelawny: The Incurable Romancer* (London: John Murray, 1977).

**References:**

Margaret Armstrong, *Trelawny: A Man's Life* (New York: Macmillan, 1941);

Richard Edgcumbe, "Talks with Trelawny," *Temple Bar*, 89 (May 1890): 29-42;

Paula R. Feldman, "Letters Unravel the Mystery of Trelawny's American Years," *Manuscripts*, 32 (Summer 1980): 168-185;

R. Glynn Grylls, *Trelawny* (London: Constable, 1950);

Lady Anne Hill, "Trelawny's Family Background and Naval Career," *Keats-Shelley Journal*, 5 (1956): 11-32;

Frederick L. Jones, "Trelawny and the Sinking of Shelley's Boat," *Keats-Shelley Memorial Bulletin*, 16 (1965): 42-44;

Samuel J. Looker, *The Worthing Cavalcade, Shelley, Trelawny and Henley: A Study of Three Titans* (Worthing, Sussex: Aldridge, 1950);

Leslie A. Marchand, "Trelawny on the Death of Shelley," *Keats-Shelley Memorial Bulletin*, 4 (1952): 9-34;

H. J. Massingham, *The Friend of Shelley: A Memoir of Edward John Trelawny* (London: Cobden-Sanderson, 1930);

Joaquin Miller, *Trelawny with Shelley and Byron* (Pompton Lakes, N.J.: Biblio Co., 1922);

William Michael Rossetti, "Talks with Trelawny," *Athenæum*, no. 2855 (15 July 1882): 78-79; no. 2857 (29 July 1882): 144-145; no. 2858 (5 August 1882): 176-177.

**Papers:**

Trelawny materials are scattered around the world, chiefly in England, the United States, Italy, and Greece. The manuscripts for *Adventures of a Younger Son* and *Records of Shelley, Byron and the Author* are in the Houghton Library, Harvard University. Major collections of letters and other related documents are in the British Library; the Bodleian Library, Oxford; the Keats-Shelley Memorial Library, Rome; the Carl H. Pforzheimer Collection at the New York Public Library; Archives of the London Greek Committee, National Library, Athens; collection of Mr. John Murray, London; collection of Lord Abinger, on deposit at the Bodleian Library, Oxford.

# John Wilson (Christopher North)

*(18 May 1785 - 3 April 1854)*

Thomas L. Blanton
*Central Washington University*

BOOKS: *Lines Sacred to the Memory of the Reverend James Grahame* (Glasgow: Printed for John Smith & Son, Glasgow; A. Constable & Co., Manners & Miller, W. Blackwood, and J. Ballantyne & Co., Edinburgh; Hurst, Rees, Orme & Brown, London, 1811);

*The Isle of Palms and Other Poems* (Edinburgh: Printed by James Ballantyne for Longman, Hurst, Rees, Orme & Brown, London; John Ballantyne & Co., Edinburgh; and John Smith & Son, Glasgow, 1812; New York: James Eastburn, 1812);

*The Magic Mirror* (Edinburgh: Printed by James Ballantyne & Co., 1812);

*The City of the Plague and Other Poems* (Edinburgh: Printed by George Ramsay & Co. for Archibald Constable & Co.; John Smith and Son, Glasgow; Longman, Hurst, Rees, Orme & Brown, London, 1816);

*Lights and Shadows of Scottish Life* (Edinburgh: William Blackwood and T. Cadell, London, 1822; Boston: C. Ewer, 1822);

*The Trials of Margaret Lyndsay* (Edinburgh: William Blackwood and T. Cadell, London, 1823; Boston: Wells & Lilly, 1823; New York: E. Bliss & E. White, 1823);

*The Foresters* (Edinburgh: William Blackwood and T. Cadell, London, 1825; New York: Wilder & Campbell, 1825; Philadelphia: J. Gregg, T. Desilver, 1825);

*Poems by John Wilson, in Two Volumes* (Edinburgh: William Blackwood and T. Cadell, London, 1825);

*Janus; or, The Edinburgh Literary Almanack*, by Wilson and John Gibson Lockhart (Edinburgh: Oliver & Boyd, 1826);

*Some Illustrations of Mr. M'Culloch's Principles of Political Economy. By Mordecai Mullion, Private Secretary to Christopher North* (Edinburgh: William Blackwood and T. Cadell, London, 1826);

*The Poetical Works of Milman, Bowles, and Wilson, and Barry Cornwall* (Paris: Published by A. & W. Galignani, 1829);

*The Recreations of Christopher North* (3 volumes, Edinburgh & London: William Blackwood, 1842; 1 volume, Philadelphia: Carey & Hart, 1845);

*The Noctes Ambrosianæ of "Blackwood,"* 4 volumes (Philadelphia: Carey & Hart, 1843); republished as *Noctes Ambrosianæ* (Edinburgh & London: William Blackwood, 1855-1856);

*The Works of Professor Wilson of the University of Edinburgh. Edited by his son-in-law Professor Ferrier*, 12 volumes (Edinburgh & London: William Blackwood & Sons, 1855-1858).

**Edition:** *Noctes Ambrosianæ*, 5 volumes, edited, with memoirs and notes, by R. Shelton Mackenzie (New York: Redfield, 1854).

John Wilson was born on 18 May 1785 in Paisley, near Glasgow, to John Wilson, a wealthy gauze manufacturer, and Margaret Sym Wilson, a woman known for her elegance and extraordinary beauty. Wilson, the first son, had three elder sisters and seven younger brothers and sisters, among whom James, the youngest, became a noted naturalist and ornithologist. After two years of primary education in Paisley, John was sent for more rigorous schooling at the manse in the nearby parish of Mearnes, a rural setting of extraordinary beauty. It is likely that Wilson's lifelong love of nature had its beginnings at Mearnes, where he remained until 1796, when he was called home on the death of his father. Shortly after, he entered Glasgow University, as was common at the time, to continue his secondary-school education.

At Glasgow he resided with George Jardine, professor of logic and rhetoric, who found Wilson a bright boy with both athletic ability and intellectual potential. In addition to classical studies and athletics, Wilson found time for reading po-

*John Wilson, 1832 (portrait by R. Scott Lauder; Scottish National Portrait Gallery)*

etry and writing verse with remarkable facility. With fellow pupil Thomas Campbell, he attempted to write an epic poem of twenty-four books, the "Tarquiniad," on an episode in Roman history. The project failed after Wilson had dashed off a thousand or more lines to Campbell's none, the effort ending in laughter as Campbell read aloud in a tone of mock seriousness the fledgling poet's heroic verses. The incident is important for what it suggests of Wilson's characteristic fluency as a writer and his tendency to collaboration. Further evidence of the latter is revealed in Wilson's 24 May 1802 letter to William Wordsworth, written on behalf of himself and a group of young poetry enthusiasts. The third edition of *Lyrical Ballads* had been published in that year to little acclaim, but to Wilson and his college friends it signaled Wordsworth's emergence as a great, new talent. Dorothy Wordsworth recorded in her journal the receipt of the letter and how she and her brother drafted a detailed reply (5-7 June 1802). Wilson's letter is noteworthy both for its self-confidence and for its pointed criticism of Wordsworth's poetry. The seventeen-year-old praised Wordsworth for the depth of feeling in the poems, but he also took him to task for selecting subjects, such as the "idiot boy," which are not pleasing and thereby, Wilson argued, inappropriate for poetry. Wilson's enthusiasm for Wordsworth was echoed by a fellow student, Alexander Blair, Wilson's lifelong friend, who would be ever ready to provide him with the critical prose or the structure of thought to convey Wilson's enthusiasm for whatever he undertook as a writer or critic.

In 1803 the eighteen-year-old Wilson completed his studies at Glasgow, and with his inheritance of fifty thousand pounds he went down to

Oxford a very wealthy young man. He entered Magdalen College as a gentleman-commoner, a category reserved for moneyed students, who formed the social and economic elite of the university. Wilson was not the typical playboy that gentlemen-commoners tended to be. He was serious enough about his studies to win in 1806 the first Newdigate Prize for a verse essay, "A Recommendation of the Study of the Remains of Ancient Grecian and Roman Architecture, Sculpture and Painting." His examination for the B.A. in 1807 was judged just short of the miraculous by his Oxford examiners, who responded with rare "public approbation and thanks"—a reaction which helped to make credible Wilson's later reputation as a scholar.

At Oxford, as at Glasgow, Wilson was perhaps best known for his athletic prowess, especially his spectacular feats of leaping—in meadows and over canals—and other gymnastic achievements. Known also for his capacity for drink, as well as for his careless dress and appearance, Wilson was a familiar campus figure at Oxford, with a reputation as an eccentric given to long solitary walks during vacations and periods of boredom. Unlike that other nature lover and would-be poet, Wordsworth, who had found the Cambridge of a decade earlier an uncongenial place, Wilson seems to have thrived in the Oxford of his day. He left Oxford in 1807 (he was awarded the M.A. in 1810) with the Lake Country his destination.

Drawn, no doubt, to the region by its natural beauty, Wilson was also attracted by the presence of Wordsworth. The Wordsworths were living in Dove Cottage when Wilson arrived, and they soon moved to Allan Bank. Through Wordsworth, Wilson met Thomas De Quincey, Robert Southey, Samuel Taylor Coleridge, and Charles Lloyd—all of whom lived nearby. Wilson's property on Lake Windermere, Elleray, with its small cottage, had been purchased with a portion of his inheritance while he was still a student at Oxford. When he became a full-time resident at the lake, he adopted a life-style that included outdoor sport and recreation, enjoyment of nature for its own sake, and literary enthusiasm—especially for the new poetry he associated with Wordsworth. He fished, chased bulls, took long walks in the mountains, wore sporting jackets and dressed with a Byronic flair, wrote poetry, and within a year spent a good deal of time with Wordsworth, who read his poems to the young admirer. Wilson was a patron of wrestling and cock fighting, and he assembled a fleet of seven or more boats for sailing on the lake. He became a "squire" of rural sports and pastimes, a landowner who worked hard to improve his property, and a bon vivant whose name was known to everyone in the polite society of the district. He abandoned a romantic scheme for travel on the Continent in 1810 when it became clear that Englishmen on a walking tour might be seen as spies by the agents of Napoleon. The aborted plan, however, suggests Wilson's restlessness in a life Dorothy Wordsworth described as one "idly spent in the pursuit of idle enjoyments." At the same time Wilson wrote in a letter to a friend that "I do not, I hope, want either ballast or cargo or sail, but I do want an anchor most confoundedly, and, without it, shall keep beating about the great sea of life to very little purpose."

More purpose was soon evident following his meeting Jane Penny of nearby Ambleside. The daughter of a Liverpool merchant who, with his family, had come to the district the same year Wilson moved to Elleray, Jane was, according to De Quincey, the "leading belle of the Lake Country." After a brief engagement, John Wilson and Jane Penny were married in May 1811. Contrary to one of the most persistent, sentimental myths about Wilson, the young couple did not go on a honeymoon walking tour of the remote Highlands. The couple went directly to settle at Elleray.

About the time of his marriage, Wilson was completing a collection of poems—some of them dating from the beginning of his years at Elleray—which would become *The Isle of Palms and Other Poems*. Some of the earliest poems were sonnets written in the descriptive-meditative manner of William Lisle Bowles, whose slim volume of sonnets (1789) had inspired young Coleridge to write in a similar vein. While *The Isle of Palms* was in press Wilson wrote an elegy on James Grahame, which appeared in 1811. This poem caught the attention of Sir Walter Scott, who wrote to Joanna Baillie that the author was "a young man of very considerable poetical powers . . . an eccentric genius, and . . . an excellent, warm-hearted, enthusiastic young man: something too much, perhaps, of the latter quality, places him among the list of originals."

*The Isle of Palms and Other Poems* appeared in February 1812 to less than resounding acclaim. Nevertheless, Francis Jeffrey's review in the next issue of the *Edinburgh Review* did not reflect that formidable critic's general contempt for the poets

*Wilson circa 1805 (portrait by Sir Henry Raeburn; Scottish National Portrait Gallery)*

of the Lake School, with whom Wilson obviously wished to identify. The title poem, which Scott had described to Baillie as "something in the style of Southey," disappointed readers because it did not appear to be the product of the man they knew. Wilson was a social animal and a large man, lively, physical, witty, boisterous, an immensely energetic being. There was no wit nor humor nor laughter in his long narrative title poem. In it, as Elsie Swann writes, "immaculate beings of unearthly refinement move delicately amid exotic scenes of tropical luxuriance and splendour, attended by none of the discomforts of so equitorial a climate, but blissful on the isle of Palms as the first young lovers in pre-Satanic Eden." After miraculously surviving a shipwreck, two marooned lovers live for several years in a state of nature on the beautiful island. They are eventually rescued by an English man-of-war and restored to home and family. Henry Crabb Robinson described the poem in 1814 as having "a plentiful lack of thought, with great delicacy, and even elegance of taste, but with no riches or strength of imagination. I could never get on with it though the poetry is pretty."

In spite of the tepid reception of *Isle of Palms* Wilson was not deterred from publishing *The Magic Mirror* (1812), a poem that had appeared two years earlier in the *Edinburgh Annual Register*, and dedicating it to Sir Walter Scott. But study for the Scottish bar delayed any further attempts at publication. In his quest for admission to the bar, Wilson followed a practice which he would rely on later as critic and professor, of soliciting ideas, even whole essays, from his friends and acquaintances. As always, Wilson depended on Alexander Blair for such support. A letter to Thomas De Quincey (17 December 1813), in which Wilson asks for "a few hints" to help him prepare for a debate at the Speculative Society, reveals his method of operation: "The whole principal of such a Debating Society as this is very absurd, but as my friends and acquaintances will be present on this occasion, and as a little quackery is useful in this world, I would prefer making a good speech to a bad one, and really without your assistance and advice I fear that this will not be in my power. On the same night I must also read an essay on some political or philosophical subject. I find that I have not time, inclination, nor ability to write one. If therefore you have any essay by you that you think would surprise a Scottish intellect, or if you could direct me to one not likely to be known here, I can inform you of the effect your reasoning produces in the Metropolis of Scotland. . . ." At least with his friends, Wilson showed a disarming candor.

In 1814 Wilson met James Hogg, the Ettrick Shepherd, in Edinburgh, and the two exchanged visits at Elleray and Altrive Lake Farm, Hogg's rural home. They got along well from the first, their friendship forming the basis for the literary collaboration that was soon to begin and that would continue to Hogg's death. In 1815 Wilson suffered the loss of most of his fortune as the result of the dishonesty of an uncle who managed his estate. Consequently, the Wilsons left Elleray—while still retaining the property—for a new home in Edinburgh.

About this time Thomas Carlyle, then a student at the University of Edinburgh, had his first glimpse of John Wilson. Carlyle's description conveys the impact Wilson had on those he met: "A very tall, strong-built and impetuous-looking young man, age perhaps about twenty-eight, with a profusion of blond hair, with large flashing countenance of the statuesque sort, flashing pair of blue eyes, which were fixed as if on something far off, was impetuously striding along, regarding nobody to right or left, but gently yet rapidly clearing the press, and with large strides stepping along, as if too late for some appointment far ahead. His clothing was rough (I think some loose, whitish jacket of kersey-stuff), hat of broadish brim, on the big massive head, flanked with such overplus of strong, unclipt flaxen hair, seemed to have known many showers in its time; but what struck one most was the glance of those big blue eyes, stern yet loving, pointing so authentically to something far away—a human character of fine and noble elements, thought I, but not at one with itself; an exuberant enough, leafy and tropical kind of tree rather exhaling itself in balmy odours than producing fruit."

In 1815 Edinburgh was in the process of transforming itself into the "Modern Athens" it claimed to be. It was also about to become the center for a new literary journalism, among whose practitioners John Wilson, as Christopher North, would become a leading figure. To become a full-fledged member of the social aristocracy a man had to be a member of the bar, so Wilson qualified in 1815 along with John Gibson Lockhart, who, like Wilson, did not enter practice. In July of the same year, Wilson and his wife set out on a walking tour of the Highlands, covering 350 miles between 5 July and 25 August and thereby proving to the more sedate members of Edinburgh society how eccentric the charismatic Wilson and his wife could be. Wilson had more than tales of his Highland ramble in mind when he returned to the city—namely a new volume of poetry. After a series of maneuvers to find a new publisher, Wilson brought out *The City of the Plague and Other Poems* in 1816. This time the reviews were favorable, including a positive notice by Francis Jeffrey in the influential *Edinburgh Review* (June 1816).

In fact, *The City of the Plague* is an uninspired poem of interminable length set in the London of 1665. Although Wilson published individual poems in later years, he ended his attempt at a career as a poet with this volume. Other, more congenial occupations were at hand for Wilson, and by mid summer 1817, after some reviewing for *Edinburgh Monthly Magazine*, he was asked by Jeffrey to write for the *Edinburgh Review*. Wilson wrote only one piece for the *Edinburgh*, a review of George Gordon, Lord Byron's *Childe Harold, Canto IV* (June 1818), once again with a major assist from his obliging friend Blair. (If, over the years, Blair's letters to Wilson had gone into print instead of providing his friend with unacknowledged matter for his reviews, essays, and lectures, Blair might have become a well-known reviewer and essayist.) As it happened, Wilson was now on course, for 1817 saw the beginning of *Blackwood's Magazine* with which Wilson was associated for the rest of his life.

An ambitious bookseller, publisher, and would-be rival of Archibald Constable (the publisher of Scott's novels and founder in 1802 of the Whiggish *Edinburgh Review*), William Blackwood inaugurated the Tory *Edinburgh Monthly Magazine* in April 1817. Like the *Edinburgh Review*, the *Monthly* would be a journal of opinion about literature and politics and would be determinedly au courant. The new magazine had a rocky beginning with Blackwood almost immediately falling out with the two editors, Thomas

*Portrait by Daniel Maclise in the* Fraser's Magazine *"Gallery of Illustrious Literary Characters" (1830-1838). Wilson was never officially the editor of* Blackwood's.

Pringle and James Cleghorn—their partnership ending with the sixth number. John Wilson contributed to these issues, most notably a two-part review of Thomas Moore's *Lalla Rookh* (August 1817), an article that impressed Francis Jeffrey sufficiently to ask Wilson to write for him. After Blackwood's break with Pringle and Cleghorn, Wilson encouraged Blackwood to continue with a reorganized and renamed publication, *Blackwood's Edinburgh Magazine*—especially since the publisher could depend on Wilson, as well as his friends Lockhart and Hogg, to contribute the kind of lively, partisan material which would be sufficient to challenge the *Edinburgh Review*.

The first issue of *Blackwood's* (October 1817, the retitled, seventh number of the magazine) created a sensation in Edinburgh and beyond. Three of its articles were clearly meant to establish the publication as a wickedly satirical journal whose contributors would go to any verbal length to lampoon their victims. Personal ridicule and ad hominem criticism were common enough in the literary and political journalism of the day, but the *Blackwood's* staff appeared determined to set a new high—or low—in this kind of verbal abuse. Coleridge was attacked in a review of his *Biographia Literaria*; Leigh Hunt was maligned in another article; and the issue concluded with the *Chaldee Ms.* Although it cannot be determined with certainty who was responsible for any given article—the evidence clearly points to collaboration in these and the other sensational pieces in the early years of *Blackwood's*—Wilson and Lockhart, with ample assist from Hogg, seem to have been largely responsible for them.

The attack on Coleridge seems particularly strange because Wilson had agreed not long before to write a favorable review of Coleridge for the *Edinburgh Review.* Whether it reflected the need to be consistently mean at the time or whether it was the result of collaboration by a group intoxicated with the power of language to debunk and deflate, Coleridge did not continue to be an object of ridicule in subsequent issues. Leigh Hunt did, however, and the attack on him by "Z"—usually identified as Lockhart—was the first of seven notorious assaults on Hunt and the "Cockney School of Poetry." The article was ostensibly a review of Hunt's poem *The Story of Rimini* (1816), but it was nothing but a slanderous attack on the man whose poetry "is that of a man who has kept company with kept-mistresses. He talks indelicately like a tea-sipping milliner girl." In subsequent assaults on the "Cockney School," William Hazlitt is described as "pimpled Hazlitt," and Keats is advised that "it is a better and a wiser thing to be a starved apothecary than a starved poet, so back to the shop, Mr John, back to 'plasters, pills and ointment boxes, etc.' But for heaven's sake, young Sangrado, be a little more sparing of extenuatives and soporifics in your practice than you have been in your poetry." The attack broadened to include, among others, Benjamin Robert Haydon, who was tagged the "Cockney Raphael." Lockhart gets the credit for these articles, but they should be thought of as the product of a shared outlook as well as sessions where wine punch flowed and raucous laughter punctuated the reading and revising of scurrilous prose.

William Maginn joined Wilson and Lockhart two years after the first issue of *Blackwood's,* bringing his delight for parody, ridicule, and personal abuse to the joint effort. In December 1821, for example, a review of Percy Bysshe Shelley's *Adonais* includes a parody with the title "Elegy on My Tom Cat," probably by Maginn, and the observation that this work shared Shelley's "odiferous, colorific, and daisy-enamoured style." Such verbal extravagance calls into question the taste, if not the character of all who shared in the joke. The snobbery and intellectual arrogance behind Lockhart's (or Z's) attacks must also be judged the shared responsibility of the entire group, including Wilson. In the first "Cockney School" article, Lockhart wrote, "All the great poets of our country have been men of some rank in society, and there is no vulgarity in any of their writings, but Mr Hunt cannot utter a dedication, or even a note, without betraying the shibboleth of low birth and low habits. He is the ideal of a Cockney poet." In these words—and those by Wilson and the others—is embodied the elitism of the Tory intellectual who believes he has all the right credentials to enable him to stand above and censure any lesser beings who dare to aspire to achievement.

The pièce de résistance of the first issue of *Blackwood's* was the *Chaldee Ms.*, a parody of biblical apocalyptic literature and an allegory of the contemporary literary scene in Edinburgh as viewed by the Blackwood establishment. The idea for the piece may have been Hogg's, but the text was largely by Wilson and Lockhart. The early history of *Blackwood's* is depicted, including beasts representing the original editors, who defected to the enemy camp. Blackwood is introduced, standing at the door of his shop: "And I looked, and beheld a man clothed in plain apparel . . . and I saw his name, and the number of his name; and his name was as it had been the colour of ebony. . . ." Two more beasts, representing Wilson and Lockhart, are called to service by a "veiled editor," and thus, allegorically, they rescue the enterprise. Wilson is represented as a "beautiful leopard, from the valley of the palm trees, whose going forth was comely as the greyhound, and his eyes like the lightning of fiery flame." Lockhart is "the scorpion, which delighteth to sting the faces of men, that he might sting sorely the countenance of the man who is crafty [Constable], and of the two beasts [Pringle and Cleghorn]." Hogg is the "great wild boar from the forests of Lebanon . . . whetting his dreadful tusks for the battle." Numerous other well-known persons are represented in the vision. As in most topical satires, the names and issues are of little meaning to most people who now attempt to read the work, but when the *Chaldee Ms.* was published, Edinburgh was, according to an observer, "in an uproar." Libel actions were immediately brought and many local notables, even those not attacked, were not amused. Sir Walter Scott influenced Blackwood to suppress the *Chaldee Ms.*, and it was omitted from the second printing of the issue. In addition, the publisher was so chastened by the uproar that he had the text of the "Cockney School" article revised to make it less libelous. Nevertheless, a spectacular beginning had been achieved for the new magazine, and copies of the original printing of the October 1817 issue—with marginal notes to identify the characters in the allegory—were in great demand. The

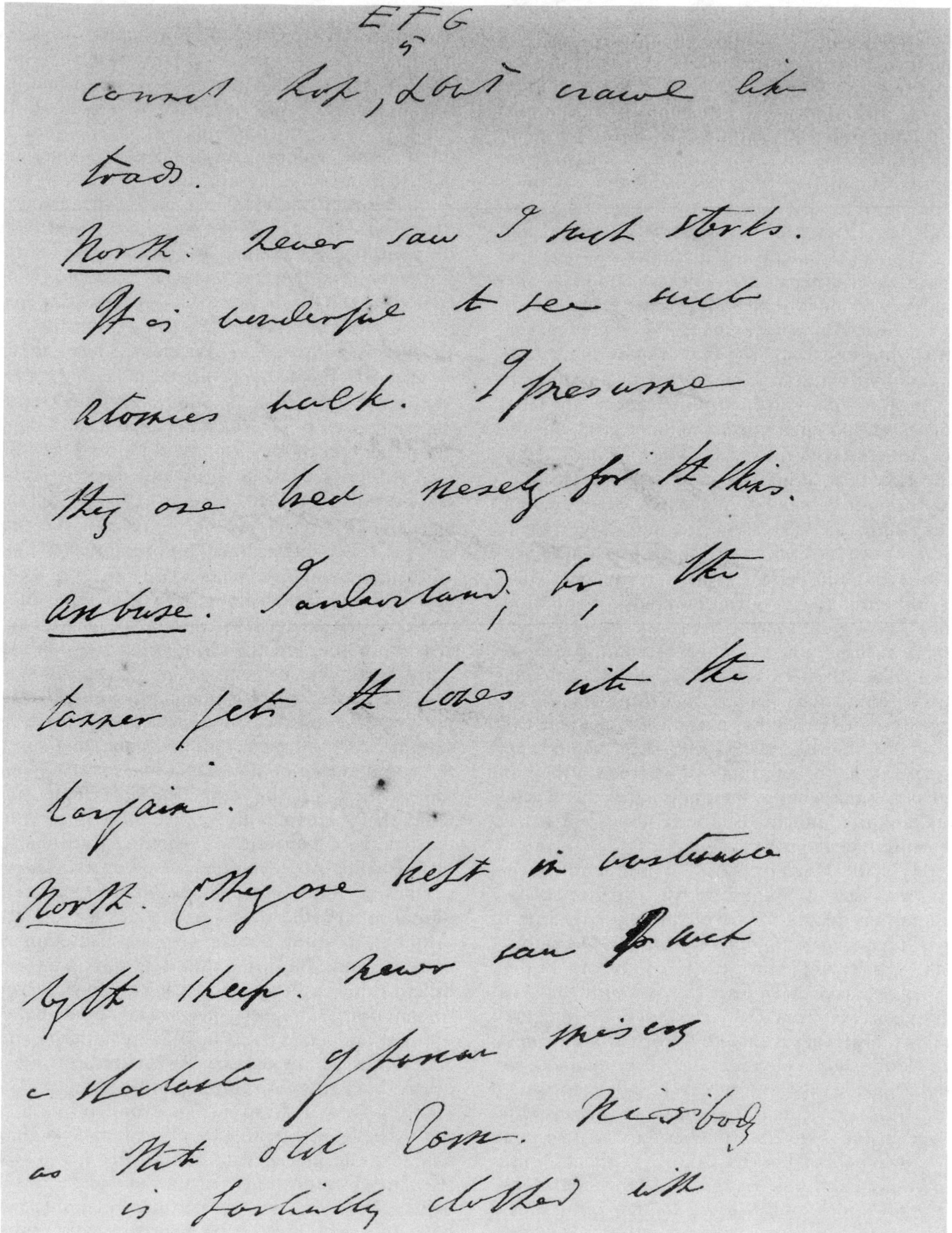

*Page from Wilson's manuscript for the February 1832 installment of* Noctes Ambrosianæ *(from R. Shelton Mackenzie, ed.,* Noctes Ambrosianæ*, volume two, 1854)*

first victims of the Leopard, the Scorpion, and the Wild Boar all survived the assault, but a member of the opposition, John Scott, the editor of the *London Magazine*, was fatally wounded some months later in a duel with a representative of Lockhart, thus ending a continuing conflict that had begun with the Cockney School articles. Others were less fatally injured in the early years of *Blackwood's*, including hapless victims such as Dr. James Scott, a dentist who was portrayed as the Odontist, a local poet responsible for verses actually written by Lockhart and others, or a Professor Playfair, a clergyman and holder of the chair of natural philosophy at the University of Edinburgh who was accused of apostasy in an article on the irreligiousness of the *Edinburgh Review* (*Blackwood's*, September 1818). One finds in the harmless foolery of transforming an unlettered dentist into a poet and in the mean-spirited, partisan, and baseless attack on the professor, both the "laughing and the lashing" characteristic of the early *Blackwood's* style of Lockhart and Wilson.

It is not surprising that the two were attacked in kind in an anonymous pamphlet, *Hypocrisy Unveiled and Calumny Detected, in a Review of "Blackwood's Magazine"* (1818). The Leopard and the Scorpion sent challenges to their assailant, thereby dropping their anonymity. Jeffrey notified Wilson that he was no longer interested in his writing for the *Edinburgh Review*. Some years later Wilson tried to play down the personal abuse of the early issues of *Maga*, as *Blackwood's* was called, by claiming that the writing was not only harmless but had the effect of raising the general level of criticism. But Lockhart's reflections, twenty years later, in a 11 July 1838 letter to Benjamin Robert Haydon, are probably closer to the truth: "I was a raw boy, who had never had the least connection with politics or controversies of any kind, when, arriving in Edinburgh in October 1817, I found my friend John Wilson (ten years my senior) busied in helping Blackwood out of a scrape he had got into with some editors of his Magazine, and on Wilson's asking me to try my hand at some squibberies in his aid, I sat down to do so with as little malice as if the assigned subject had been the Court of Pekin. But the row in Edinburgh, . . . was really so extravagant that when I think of it now, the whole story seems wildly incredible." He went on to reflect that because Wilson was considered an eccentric, he had been "allowed to get off comparatively scot-free, while I, by far the youngest and least experienced of the set, and who alone had no personal grudges against any of Blackwood's victims, remained under such an accumulation of wrath and contumely, as would have crushed me utterly, unless for the buoyancy of extreme youth"—and perhaps the callous indifference of a young Tory snob who equated intelligence and a quick wit with moral superiority. The Blackwoodians were right in declaring that their methods were no different from those of their Whig opponents at the *Edinburgh Review* and those of periodical writers generally. There was nothing gloomy about these Tory satirists. For a brief while self-confident youth, intellectual snobbery, like-mindedness, abundant wit, and the "chemistry" of collaboration brought success and notoriety to all concerned at *Blackwood's*. Such collaborations rarely last for long, and Wilson and his friends soon turned to other occupations.

Apart from establishing *Blackwood's* as a no-holds-barred publication, the *Chaldee Ms.* also was responsible for the continuing guessing game about editorial authority at the publication. The "veiled editor" of the *Chaldee Ms.* was variously identified, with John Wilson the prime candidate. Wilson's association with the magazine was substantial, and while he was never the editor—William Blackwood exercised that authority—he was a mainstay, eventually writing the copy for entire numbers. But the work which is his chief claim to our attention today did not begin until 1822. That year saw the beginning of a series of dialogues published as *Noctes Ambrosianæ* (Ambrosial Nights). Eventually, as the series developed, Wilson adopted as his own the pseudonym Christopher North, which originally had been the common property of the anonymous collaborators at *Blackwood's*.

Whoever originated the idea—Wilson, Lockhart, Maginn, or another—the *Noctes Ambrosianæ* series of seventy-one dialogues, running from 1822 until 1835, did more than all of the sensationalism of the first years to secure fame and future for *Blackwood's*. Its beginning may be found in "Christopher in the Tent," a narrative with dialogue which filled the entire August 1819 issue of the magazine. The account purported to describe a hunting and fishing excursion of the "eight principal supporters of *Blackwood's Magazine*" on the property of the earl of Fife "at the head of the Dee." The group pitched a tent which served as their gathering place for conversation, food, and drink. Scattered throughout the narrative are conversations on topics familiar to readers of earlier issues of the magazine—including a good deal of literary shoptalk and exchanges about current books and their authors—along with poems and songs. All was done in a light and easy manner without the savagery or libel of the "Cockney School" articles.

Ambrose's inn is the setting for the celebrated dialogues, which took for their subjects anything of interest to the company assembled, but principally the people and events of the literary and political beaux mondes. As Elsie Swann writes, "The continuity attained by the evenings at Ambrose's, where the merry circle was supposed to assemble, made the *Noctes Ambrosianæ* an admirable medium for characterisation and 'criticism of life,' as well as a most popular series of periodical literary sketches. This contemporary commentary of the *Noctes Ambrosianæ* had for its chief interlocutors Christopher North, Timothy Tickler, and the Ettrick Shepherd. . . . It was the light and rapid survey in racy dialogue of public events, books and people, by an easy tribunal that delighted most in the ludicrous side of life. The writers of the magazine here appeared in their different individualities, a gay and reckless band, always ready for light-hearted personal sallies and attacks, with instant retaliation and wild horse-play."

The first of the *Noctes* appeared in March 1822, opening with a rapid-fire conversation between Christopher North, identified as editor, and Ensign Morgan Odoherty, lately arrived from London (or, as the editor opines, from the Fleet, a debtors' prison). Lockhart is thought to be the principal author of this initial dialogue, and its lampooning references to Leigh Hunt and the "Cockneys" support the contention, but William Maginn was very likely a party to the effort. It is gossipy and filled with conversational quips (Horace Walpole is "a most malicious, prying, lying old fox;" the first two volumes in a life of William Pitt, by Sir George Pretyman Tomline, Bishop of Winchester, "are not quite *the potato*"). References abound to writers, journals and magazines, and the book trade. The works of *Blackwood's* insiders are puffed. Most of the names and events require explanatory notes today, but in places the text is as accessible today as it was in 1822—especially where the author (Lockhart, very likely) delivers himself of critical opinions. Byron receives a good deal of space and praise, often at the expense of other writers: "Editor. Byron is a prince; but these dabbling dogglerers destroy every dish they dip in. . . . Imagine Shelley, with his spavin, and Hunt with his stringhalt, going in the same harness with such a caperer as Byron, three-a-breast! He'll knock the wind out of them both the first canter." Or this remark, attributed to Coleridge, that "an essay, in a periodical publication [is] merely 'a say' for the time—an ingenious string of sentences, driving apparently, with great vehemence, towards some object, but never meant to lead to anything, or to arrive at any conclusion (for in what conclusion are the public interested but the abuse of individuals)."

By March 1825, Wilson's participation in *Noctes* had reached a point where not only had the series become largely his but also the character of Christopher North. From the nineteenth number of *Blackwood's* in 1825 to its final appearance in 1835, the *Noctes* dialogues were mainly Wilson's creations, with his chief accomplishment the character of the Ettrick Shepherd, the fictional double of James Hogg. The Shepherd speaks frequently in authentic Scots dialect, the creation of which must be seen as one of Wilson's achievements as a writer. Like "Christopher in the Tent," the *Noctes* abound in topical references and are characterized by sudden shifts of topic or outlook. The March 1825 *Noctes*—usually thought to be the first in the series written by Wilson—may be considered illustrative.

The dialogue features North, the Ettrick Shepherd, and, sleeping most of the time, Timothy Tickler. The setting is Ambrose's; the time the wee hours of the morning. The conversation progresses from sleep and dreaming, poetical and otherwise (with the Shepherd punctuating his talk with measures of Glenlivet from a jug), to what purports to be a poem by the Shepherd ("Hymn to the Devil"), to such contemporaries as Barry Cornwall (Bryan Waller Procter) and on to the Reverend C. Colton, Jack Thurtell, Thomas Grattan and other forgotten Whigs of the day. Talk of Dr. Samuel Hibbert's treatise on apparitions precedes Tickler's musing in his sleep on an actress, Miss Laeticia Foote—with comments by North and the Shepherd. The conversation takes a literary turn when North asks the Shepherd for a pamphlet he wishes to use in lighting a cigar—a pamphlet by the Reverend William Lisle Bowles from the interminable battle of the pamphlets about the poetry of Alexander Pope, with Bowles on the negative side and Thomas Campbell, Lord Byron, and others on the affirmative. The Shepherd (perhaps speaking for Wilson) says of Bowles's poetry, "Lisle Bolls is a poet o' real genius. I never could thole [endure] a sonnet till I read his." In the course of the subsequent conversation, Bowles is chided for his obstinacy, while Pope is praised for his character and awarded the prize in the controversy over his genius and character. From Pope the conversation turns to Wordsworth with North exclaiming, 'Look at the nerveless laxity of his *Excursion!*—what interminable prosing!—the language is out of condition:—fat and fozy, thick-winded, purfled and plethoric. Can he be compared with Pope?—Fie on't! no, no, no!—Pugh, pugh!" In turn, Southey, Coleridge, and Moore are similarly dismissed as "all deficient in sense, muscle, sinew, thews, ribs, spine." The Lake Poets as a group are condemned for "this senseless clamour against the genius of Pope," but in the end Bowles and the others are toasted by North: "Here's their healths in a bumper. (*Bibunt Omnes*)." Political talk is followed by reflections by the Shepherd on poultry, and with two of his songs the dialogue draws to a close.

One curious feature of this dialogue is the ridicule of Wordsworth, who had been the object of the youthful Wilson's adulation and with whom Wilson continued to associate on periodic visits to the Lake Country. The September 1825 *Noctes* included jabs at Wordsworth shortly after Wilson had been his guest at Rydal Mount. Owing to the outraged response of another man who was lampooned in the same issue and was threatening legal action, Wilson was in danger of being unmasked as the author of the commentary on Wordsworth. A letter of his to Blackwood confirms his responsibility and reveals his fear of exposure—as well as his agitated, confused state of mind. Even Lockhart was hard pressed to explain his friend's action and, in an apparent attempt to protect Wilson, wrote an article for the next issue explaining the attacks as "Midsummer Madness." The episode points to an enigmatic dimension of Wilson's character which has never been accounted for or explained away.

In April 1820 the holder of the chair of moral philosophy at the University of Edinburgh died, and immediately there were ready aspirants to the professorship—including John Wilson. One might rightly wonder what Wilson's credentials were for such a post and indeed some—including James Mill—questioned his qualifications. But his Tory affiliation and the presence of a Tory majority on the Edinburgh Town Council (the governing body of the university) were enough, eventually, to secure the position for him. His cause was aided by a thick bundle of testimonials written by former teachers and tutors at Glasgow and Oxford, the strong support of Sir Walter Scott, and even an equivocal letter of support from Wordsworth. Scott realized that Wilson had no achievements to argue for his election, but he wrote to Lockhart on 30 March 1820 that if Wilson were to turn from his career as the chief writer at *Blackwood's*, he might find his appointment to a university chair "a pledge for binding down his acute and powerful mind to more regular labour than circumstances have hitherto required of him. . . . and give him the consistence and steadiness which are all he wants to make him the first man of the age." After his election in July, however, Wilson was even more involved with *Blackwood's*, especially when he took over responsibility for *Noctes Ambrosianæ*, and would remain involved for the rest of his life. The story of Wilson's professorship, which came clearly to light only in 1934, with the publication by Elsie Swann of Wilson's correspondence with Alexander Blair, is the account of Wilson's acquiring yet another pseudonym and persona—The Professor. Indeed, the letters largely refute Wilson's nineteenth-century reputation as a man of great intellect and nullify most of what had been written about his academic career and serious writing. Once elected to the professorship, the unqualified Wilson had suddenly to think of whole courses of lectures that were his responsibility. In a 29 July 1820 letter to Scott, he boldly proclaimed his intention of composing "thirty or forty lectures." He then asks Scott, "Have you anything to recommend during a leisure hour regarding books? Or would you write me a letter or two on a plan of lectures?" But it was to Blair that Wilson once again turned to bail him out in a time of distress, Wilson's July 1820 letter to Blair essentially tells the story of Wilson's professorship, his scholarship, and his subsequent efforts as a writer on serious topics: "One thing is certain, that if I can get through the *first course of Lectures* with reputation, my future life may glide on usefully and respectably. . . . Three months only have to elapse till I begin to lecture, and at this moment I have not a single lecture—nor yet anything like a plan of Lectures in my head. Now, Blair, you know me, and I venture to ask you, by every thought that may endear us to each other, in a future world, *to come down to Scotland and stay with me for those three months!* . . . You know *that I by myself* am unable to proceed, and that disgrace must ensue, indeed utter and fatal failure. . . . I know that *together we can do this thing*. . . . Trust-

*Wilson circa 1844 (calotype by D. O. Hill)*

ing that you who have before this saved my soul, will now come down to save it once more, and to bless my family with unspeakable blessings—I am, my dearest friend, yours with all love and affection, . . ."

To Wilson's credit, he was—thanks to Blair—able to get his lectures together, and he delivered them well. What he lacked in intellectual power or scholarly aptitude he more than made up for as an orator. As the years went on, Blair continued to supply Wilson with material for lectures which were impressive in the delivery but, as one former student observed, less impressive on second thought. Wilson's letters to Blair, often written in an imploring and desperate tone, called for specific and detailed written responses to particular questions and problems Wilson could not hope to confront on his own. It may be unfair to dwell on Wilson's acting the role of professor, since what he accomplished at the lectern was what other, perhaps equally inept or incompetent, academics could not do—namely do a convincing job of acting out the part. Christopher North as Professor was popular with the students who packed the halls to hear him. He was an impressively eccentric figure—tall and shaggy, with ruddy good looks, flashing eyes, and unkempt in a Byronic sort of way. He became one of Edinburgh's best-known "characters." Carlyle, not generally sympathetic to Wilson, wrote of The Professor more than a decade after Wilson's death: "Thrice or so I have strayed in, as an accidental auditor, and heard him lecture. . . . He stood erect like a tower; cloudy energy, determination, and even sincerity (or the visible wish to be sincere) looking out from every feature of him; giving you, among his chaos of papers there, assurance of a man. One of the times, and one only, he had got some rather strictly scientific or metaphysical point to handle, or to tide over in some plausible way. His internal embarrassment and yet determined outer onrush in this troublesome matter, I still remember well; and how with wild strokes he plunged about, like a whale among tubs, hither, thither, churning the ocean into foam, for a length of time, and at last in some good way got floated over into more genial waters. All the other times I found him dealing with human life in the concrete; and this in a style, and with a stormful opulence of faculty, great and peculiar. Glowing pictures dashed off in rapid powerful strokes, often of a fine poetic and emphatic quality, this, I could see, was his favourite mode of illustrating and teaching."

Thomas De Quincey, writing in 1850 of Wilson's lectures, defended their lack of originality as contributions to philosophy by claiming, "it would be no just blame, but the highest praise, to Professor Wilson, if his lectures really *did* wear the character imputed to him—of being rich and eloquent abstracts, rather than scholastic exercitations in untried paths." Ironically, Wilson had asked De Quincey in a June 1829 letter to write of his lectures as "thoroughly logical and argumentative" rather than as the "glowing pictures" Carlyle found them to be. "Yet," Elsie Swann concludes, "if Moral Philosophy be considered not as an exact science, but as an art, and more particularly an art that is best presented as an individual expression of the highest and completest approximation to the ideal of the art of living—an art that is poetic and needs to possess a subjective personal character, with the real value of philosophy not in the pretended reasoning, but in the exposition in one form or other of a certain view of life—then Wilson, in spite of his limitations of knowledge, his lack of complete philosophical system, his lack of detachment, was genuinely of value as a Professor of Moral Philosophy."

Wilson's works of fiction and poetry of the 1820s and later are of little note and have not been long remembered. He published three volumes of fiction, each of which is of interest today only to the historian of sentimental literature. The first of these, *Lights and Shadows of Scottish Life* (1822), includes stories originally published in *Blackwood's* under the pseudonyms Alfred Austin and Eremus. Homely tales of Scottish rural life, these stories may have been intended as prose equivalents to the poems on humble lives in *Lyrical Ballads*. Short on plot but long on pathos, the twenty-four stories in this collection became a popular success, with the volume going through several editions in Wilson's lifetime. When the work was republished in 1834, more than four thousand copies were sold in a month—what one might expect of a London best-seller. *The Trials of Margaret Lyndsay, An Orphan* (1823) is a sentimental tale of the suffering and eventual triumph of the humble Margaret. Wordsworth was not amused by Wilson's "borrowing" in this instance, writing to Henry Crabb Robinson, "Have you ever peeped into his Trials of Margaret Lyndsay? You will see there to what extent he had played the plagiarist with the very tale of Margaret in The Excursion which he abuses; and you will also, with a glance, learn what passes with him for poetical Christianity. More mawkish stuff I never encountered." Yet he might have, had he read *The Foresters* (1825), another tale of "familiar life." Finally a collected edition of Wilson's poems appeared in 1825. In these poems are to be found echoes of Bowles, Coleridge, Wordsworth, and Southey, to name the most obvious sources for Wilson's muse.

Wilson's most productive period as a writer for *Blackwood's* was the decade from 1825 to 1835, when he produced more than half of the seventy-one dialogues in the *Noctes Ambrosianæ* series. In 1833-1834 he wrote fifty-four articles for *Maga*. James Hogg's death in 1835, however, seems to have brought the end of the *Noctes* dialogues, and the death of William Blackwood in 1834 and Wilson's wife in 1837 each, in its own way, curtailed Wilson's career as a periodical writer. The original circle of collaborators had already been broken when Lockhart left *Blackwood's* in 1825 to assume the editorship of the *Quarterly Review*. Declining health—including a disabling paralysis of his right hand in 1840—became an increasingly serious problem for Wilson. He continued to be in demand as a public speaker, and contemporary accounts of events such as the Burns Festival of 1844 are reminders of just how well known and popular he was in his day as The Professor and Spellbinding Orator.

Later in life, he returned to earlier triumphs and produced for *Blackwood's* in May 1849 *Christopher under Canvas*, "a sort of *Noctes*," he said, which continued under the series title *Dies Boreales* (Northern Days) since the dialogues were conducted in the daylight and in the outdoors rather than at Ambrose's. In writing the ten *Dies Boreales* papers Wilson, as always, depended on Alexander Blair for much of the con-

1

Notes on Living Writers.

Robert Chambers.

Few of the popular writers of the present day have been more successful in every point of view than the gentleman whose name stands at the head of this paper. That success, however, though mainly the result of the intrinsic merit of his varied contributions to our popular literature was quite as much the reward of a prompt use of remarkably favorable and inviting opportunities.

Prior to the birth of that very popular, ably written, and carefully conducted miscellany with wh. Mr Chambers's name is associated with that of his brother as editor, he had acquired no mean reputation in a branch of literature requiring more severe labour and attainments, namely, biography, history, & archaeology. The work wh. brought his name early and prominently before the public, & besides introducing him to the society of men of established reputation, gained him the valuable friendship of Sir Walter Scott, was his "Traditions of

*Pages from the manuscript for Wilson's 1852 biographical essay on Edinburgh publisher Robert Chambers, founder of* Chambers's Edinburgh Journal *(1832-1938) and well known to his contemporaries as the author of* Traditions of Edinburgh *(1825),* A Biographical Dictionary of Eminent Scotsmen *(1832-1835), and* Vestiges of the Natural History of Creation *(1844; HM 156; Henry E. Huntington Library and Art Gallery)*

2/ Edinburgh"—a work written in a very pleasing style, and treating a subject of more than ordinary interest and attraction for a people so noted for their nationality as the Scotch; but beyond this it possessed little merit, and involved no great acquirements or any remarkable antiquarian research.

This work at once enabled him to surmount the difficulties with wh all men of original humble position are doomed for a longer or shorter period to struggle. Through the interest of Sir Walter Scott he ~~was recommended~~ obtained the editorship of the Edinburgh Advertiser, wh however he relinquished after a very brief period. He subsequently failed to obtain the editorship of the "Edinburgh Courant," in competition with Mr Buchanan, a gentleman of varied and extensive acquirements, though hardly known beyond the bounds of the Scottish metropolis and its literary coteries.

The Traditions were succeeded by the "Lives of Illustrious Scotsmen", a work of higher aim and pretension, and equally successful. But with this production his contributions to the catalogue of distinct works ceased.

tent, for reflections on *Paradise Lost* and other literary and philosophical topics.

In 1851, after ill health forced Wilson to retire from his university post, he was awarded a pension of three hundred pounds a year. On 1 April 1854 he suffered a stroke and died two days later. In his *Fraser's* "Portrait Gallery" series (1830-1838), Maginn had asked, "What can be said of Professor Wilson worthy of his various merits?" His answer covers Wilson's achievements as poet, "moral professor," orator, and novelist—but ends with the man himself: "a sixteen stoner . . . , an out and outer, a true, upright, knocking-down, poetical, prosaic, moral, professorial, hard-drinking, fierce-eating, good-looking, honourable, straightforward Tory. . . . A Gipsy, a magazine, a wit, a six-foot club man, an unflinching ultra in the worst of times! In what is he not great?"

**Biographies:**

R. Shelton Mackenzie, "Life of Professor Wilson," in *Noctes Ambrosianæ*, 5 volumes (New York: Redfield, 1854), II: iii-xxxvi;

Elsie Swann, *Christopher North ( John Wilson)* (Edinburgh: Oliver & Boyd, 1934).

**References:**

David Daiches, "Christopher North," in his *Literary Essays* (Edinburgh: Oliver & Boyd, 1956 corrected, 1966);

Thomas De Quincey, "Literary and Lake Reminiscences," in volume 2 of *The Collected Writings of Thomas De Quincey*, edited by David Masson (Edinburgh: Adam & Charles Black, 1889), pp. 113-454;

De Quincey, "Professor Wilson: Sketch in 1829; Sketch in 1850," in volume 5 of *The Collected Writings of Thomas De Quincey*, edited by Masson (Edinburgh: Adam & Charles Black, 1890), pp. 259-302;

Malcolm Elwin, "Christopher North," in his *Victorian Wallflowers: A Panoramic Survey of the Popular Literary Periodicals* (London: Cape, 1934), pp. 25-84;

Ian Jack, *English Literature, 1815-1832* (Oxford: Oxford University Press, 1963);

William Maginn, "John Wilson," in *A Gallery of Illustrious Literary Characters*, edited by William Bates (London: Chatto & Windus, 1873);

Margaret Oliphant, *Annals of a Publishing House: William Blackwood and His Sons, Their Magazine and Friends*, 3 volumes (Edinburgh & London: William Blackwood & Sons, 1897);

D. J. Pohn, "The Life, Work and Literary Career of John Wilson (Christopher North)," Ph.D. dissertation, University of Dundee, 1976;

Alan Lang Strout, "Hunt, Hazlitt, and *Maga*," *English Literary History*, 4 (March 1937): 151-159;

Strout, "John Wilson, 'Champion' of Wordsworth," *Modern Philology*, 31 (May 1934): 383-394;

William S. Ward, "Wordsworth, the 'Lake' Poets, and Their Contemporary Magazine Critics, 1798-1820," *Studies in Philology*, 42 ( January 1945): 87-113.

# Appendix

# Literary Reviewing

# La Belle Assemblée

*(February 1806 - June 1837)*

Becky W. Lewis

*La Belle Assemblée or Bell's Court and Fashionable Magazine* was published by John Bell, whom Stanley Morison has called "the most resourceful and inventive bookseller of his generation." In his *Autobiography* (1850) Leigh Hunt said that Bell "instinctively felt the importance to appeal to the intellect or to the appetite for gossip and scandal, news and notions, curious facts and extravagant fancies." *La Belle Assemblée*, which Alison Adburgham calls a "landmark in the history of magazine publishing," was one of Bell's most successful projects. When G. and W. B. Whittaker took over the magazine in 1821, they made few changes.

The title page for *La Belle Assemblée* states that it is "Addressed Particularly to The Ladies." His goal, Bell said, was to lay "the foundation of a Work, which, in the comprehensiveness of its instruction, the variety of its amusements, and the elegance of its embellishment, has had no parallel in the history of periodical publications" (February 1806). Adburgham has described *La Belle Assemblée* as a fashion magazine, and Donald H. Reiman has said that it is "without intellectual pretensions." Yet the magazine follows the tradition of women's magazines begun in the eighteenth century, promoting the intellectual equality of women by providing general education material. The magazine also reflects the Romantic belief in the power of the mind to improve the human condition.

Robert D. Mayo notes that *La Belle Assemblée*

> avoided the numerous puerilities of the *[Lady's Monthly] Museum*, adopting a more dashing approach to high life and pretending to a larger sphere of interest. It was allegedly addressed to older women who sought a more intimate acquaintance with London society, with new fashions, travel, polite literature, the theater, and chitchat of the bon ton.

*La Belle Assemblée* was also a new, more professional type of women's magazine. Priced at three shillings, each issue comprised sixty-four pages and a table of contents, as well as two separate supplements for each volume. The first supplement was a "Monthly Compendium of Literary, Fashionable, and Domestic Advertisement . . . addressed to the Elegant, Polite, and Economical" (March 1806). The reader was expected to save each monthly part of this supplement and bind them together after the concluding issue in each semiannual volume. The other supplement was literary, including the "Critical Review of the Most Distinguished Works of Literature" for the year, as well as extracts from recently published works and literary classics, called "Beauties of the British Poets." James Thomson's *The Seasons* (1726-1730), John Milton's *Paradise Lost* (1667), and Edward Young's *Night Thoughts* (1742-1745), for example, are printed in their entirety in these literary supplements.

The periodical clearly seeks to provide an intellectual as well as a fashionable window to the world. It has an instructional tone, open and for the most part politically nonpartisan. Its contents, which display a remarkable eclecticism and variety, are relevant to both sexes. The magazine typically opens with a section called "Biographical Sketches of Distinguished and Illustrious Characters," which includes a full-page engraving of an "illustrious character" and a short biography. Actresses, such as Mrs. Garrick (a distant relative of David Garrick) and Nell Gwyn, are popular subjects as are aristocrats, especially members of the royal family. The section also features writers such as Hannah More, Mary Russell Mitford, Jane Porter, and George Gordon, Lord Byron—even Washington Irving.

In the first issue, Bell encouraged reader contributions:

> We flatter ourselves that we have introduced a material improvement, so far as method, arrangement, and elegance of display, which may be considered as enticements to writers in periodical publications. Communications, and correspondence, therefore, are ardently invited.

*John Bell, founder and publisher of* La Belle Assemblée *(lithograph by G. Arnold)*

Reader contributions—including novels, short stories, nonfiction prose, lessons, and letters—were published in a section called "Original Communications," often in serial form. The periodical's interest in female education is apparent in a March 1806 letter from a male reader. Considering the "present mode of female education," he supports the idea of male-female equality: "As beings endowed with reason, and consequently capable of the highest degree of intellectual improvement, the female sex is in no respect inferior to our own." He goes on to cite the error of female education:

> more attention [is] paid to the graces, accomplishments, and decorations of the person and the fashion of the times, than to the virtues of the heart, the correctness of judgment, or the energies of the mind.

He ends his letter by reminding the reader that the female is responsible for the education and guardianship of the young.

In the custom of the period contributions are signed with initials or pen names such as Stella, Belinda, and M. N. O. One frequent contributor is E. R. (possibly Emma Roberts), whose "Novels and Romances With a Cursory Review of the Literary Ladies of Great-Britain" (November 1806) begins as an early defense of novel reading: "In the present state of society, it appears that women should read Novels, notwithstanding what has been said by professed moralists on that subject." She discusses Ann Radcliffe, Fanny Burney, Elizabeth Inchbald, Mary Robinson, Joanna Baillie, and Hannah More. Holding Ann Yearsley up as the greatest literary lady of the past, she observes that the greatest contemporary woman author is Anna Laetitia Barbauld. She ends with a discussion of Mary Wollstonecraft's *Vindication of the Rights of Woman* (1792), exclaiming, "What energetic and original, what clear and never exaggerated ideas she has thrown upon the dignity and the destination of women!"

*La Belle Assemblée* promoted the fine arts, publishing series on the history of music and lives of composers, and original musical scores appear in many issues. The supplement to volume three (December 1807) includes commentary and engravings of seven cartoons by Raphael on exhibition in the Royal Palace of Hampton Court.

The "Monthly Miscellany," a regular section, tells what is going on in London, French, and American theaters and includes reviews of important musical performances, art exhibitions in London, and book reviews. Mary Shelley's *Frankenstein* (1818) was well received in the March 1818 issue, in a review that also includes a plot summary and extensive quotations from the novel. The reviewer calls it "very *bold* fiction" and recommends it as "a work which, from its originality, excellence of language, and peculiar interest is likely to be very popular. . . ." The reviewer also reassures readers that, while the novel is dedicated to William Godwin, this former radical, "however he once embraced novel systems, is, we are credibly informed, happily converted to what he once styled *ancient prejudices*." In the supplement for 1819 *La Belle Assemblée* reviewed John William Polidori's *Vampyre* (1819), written as part of the same ghost-story-writing contest that produced *Frankenstein*.

Poetry appears in every issue, and "poetical correspondents" are reminded that only poetry "of a very high quality indeed, can obtain admission into this work" (September 1806). Often there are several pages of "Original and Select Poetry" or "Fugitive Poetry" from readers. In the March 1818 issue, Thomas Love Peacock's *Rhododaphne* (1818) is reviewed as an "elegant and well written poem." A summary and extracts from the poem are also included. William Wordsworth's *Excursion* (1814) and *White Doe of Rylstone* (1815) are favorably reviewed, with extensive extracts, in May and July 1815, respectively. Both Byron and Sir Walter Scott were popular poets with *La Belle Assemblée*. A January 1810 review of Sir Walter Scott's *Lady of the Lake* (1810) perceptively observes:

> The characteristic feature of Walter Scott is, that he possesses a great susceptibility of mind, the images of nature present themselves strongly and clearly to his imagination, he sees distinctly, he conceives with the spirit and vigour of a Poet, and he knows how to select. His fault is a namby pamby kind of versification, sometimes extended through a whole Canto, the inanity of which is concealed from himself, and from superficial readers, by an antiquated jargon, a nomenclature of words, which being out of date, and some of which, perhaps, never in use, give a meaning of images which, dominated by their usual name, would be trite and familiar.

The names of the departments in *La Belle Assemblée* often changed, but the magazine retained much the same format and content during its thirty-year run. In June 1832 *La Belle Assemblée* became the *Court Magazine and Belle Assemblée* and, for the first time, listed the name of its editor, "the Honorable Mrs. Norton" (Caroline Norton). In 1837 the periodical became the *Court Magazine and Monthly Critic*.

Literature was always given a high priority in *La Belle Assemblée*, but, as Reiman observes, the book reviews "tend to be long on excerpts and plot summaries, short on literary theorizing and practical criticism." When the Whittaker family became publishers of the magazine in 1821, literary criticism was given slightly more emphasis. For example, in 1822 and 1823, a regular series on poetry, "Strictures on the Poets of the Present Day," included separate articles on Scott (September 1822), Wordsworth (November 1822), Leigh Hunt (January 1823), Samuel Taylor Coleridge (February 1823), Robert Southey (June 1823), John Clare (September 1823), and others. In 1824 the periodical featured a regular series on "Shakespeare's Females."

*La Belle Assemblée* was a popular women's magazine with a large circulation, which included readers as far away as Russia, the West Indies, Quebec, Halifax, and New York. While it may have appealed to an elite group of fashionable women, it had more intellectual and literary content than any fashion magazine in the later nineteenth or twentieth centuries.

**References:**

Alison Adburgham, *Silver Fork Society: Fashionable Life and Literature from 1814 to 1840* (London: Constable, 1983);

Adburgham, *Women In Print, Writing Women and Women's Magazines From the Restoration to the Accession of Victoria* (London: George Allen & Unwin, 1972);

Robert D. Mayo, *The English Novel in the Magazines, 1740-1815* (London: Oxford University Press, 1962);
Stanley Morison, *John Bell, 1745-1831* (Cambridge: Cambridge University Press, 1930);
Donald H. Reiman, ed., *The Romantics Reviewed; Contemporary Reviews of British Romantic Writers*, 9 volumes (New York & London: Garland, 1972);
Alvin Sullivan, ed., *British Literary Magazines: The Romantic Age, 1789-1836* (Westport, Conn.: Greenwood Press, 1983);
Cynthia White, *Women's Magazines 1693-1968* (London: Joseph, 1970).

# Blackwood's Edinburgh Magazine

*(October 1817 - December 1980)*

Richard D. McGhee
*Arkansas State University*

William Blackwood began publishing the *Edinburgh Monthly Magazine* in April 1817 as the Edinburgh Tory answer to Archibald Constable's increasingly influential Whig periodical, the *Edinburgh Review*, but the editors, James Pringle and Thomas Cleghorn, proved unable to capture sufficient attention for the magazine. After the September 1817 issue, Blackwood put himself in charge and changed the name. *Blackwood's Edinburgh Magazine* began appearing in October and continued publication under this name through December 1980. William Blackwood continued as editor and publisher until 1834, when Alexander Blackwood assumed the editorship, which he retained until 1845.

Typically, *Blackwood's* offered a variety of prose and some poetry in each issue, along with regular sections of information such as "Literary and Scientific Intelligence," a "Monthly Register" of "Foreign Intelligence," "Meteorological Reports," and "Births, Marriages, and Deaths." Each issue contains a wide variety of essays, such as "Observations on Coleridge's Biographia Literaria," "Meteorological Phenomena observed in Argyllshire," "Alarming Increase of Depravity among Animals," and "Verses written at Killarney" in the October 1817 issue. In the March 1822 issue the reader would find "The Widow's Tale, and other poems," "A Key to the Mythology of the Ancients," and the first number of *Noctes Ambrosianæ*. Or, in the May 1824 issue one could read "Sketches of the Five American Presidents," a review of "Works on Ireland," and "On the Metaphysics of Music."

Because Blackwood wanted his publication to offer a different menu of reading—as well as presenting a Tory political viewpoint—he sought fiction, poetry, humorous essays, and other informal and personal prose. Thus, he enlarged the scope of the periodical beyond that of the *Edinburgh Review*, which was dominated by the review-essay. Among the most successful of *Blackwood's* authors were Edward Bulwer-Lytton, George Eliot, Anthony Trollope, and Joseph Conrad; during the Romantic period there were Thomas De Quincey and John Galt.

Controversial and popular *Blackwood's* writers John Gibson Lockhart, John Wilson, and James Hogg used satire to criticize many of their contemporaries in Edinburgh society through invention of a supposedly newfound "Translation from an Ancient Chaldee Manuscript," which they published in the October 1817 issue of *Blackwood's*. Using biblical language and described as a translation of a manuscript found in a Parisian library, it presents a narrator "in the midst of a great city," where he beholds "a man clothed in plain apparel" and "two beasts [who] came from the lands of the borders of the South." One of the beasts was "like a lamb, and the other like a bear; and they had wings on their heads." The "man" is Blackwood, the two "beasts" are Pringle

*William Blackwood, founder and publisher of* Blackwood's Edinburgh Magazine *(etching by F. Huth, after a miniature)*

and Cleghorn. The two "beasts" offered to "put words into the Book," and "the man hearkened unto their voice, and he took the Book and gave them a piece of money." The "beasts," however, "put no words in the Book; and the man was astonished and waxed wroth." Thus was Blackwood disappointed with the work of Pringle and Cleghorn. The publisher Constable is described as "the Crafty," a man who "had a notable horn in his forehead with which he ruled nations." Walter Scott is presented as the "Magician" to whom "the Crafty" applied for a remedy to combat the "Book" of Blackwood. Scott's humorous reaction to this caricature was an exception to the general rule of angry responses from most who saw themselves in the satire of the Chaldee. This piece caused legal trouble for Blackwood, but it also brought his new magazine great popularity, and it reached multitudes of readers in a short time. The "Ancient Chaldee Manuscript" included introductions of its own authors: Wilson as "the beautiful leopard from the valley of the palmtrees," Lockhart as "the scorpion, which delighteth to sting the faces of men," and Hogg as "the great wild boar from the forest of Lebanon."

At the same time as the "Chaldee Manuscript," Lockhart began his infamous series of essays "On the Cockney School of Poetry," under the signature "Z," which continued until 1825. In his first essay on the "Cockney School" (October 1817) Lockhart attacked Leigh Hunt's *Story of Rimini* (1816) as an exercise in "exquisitely bad taste" by a man "of little education." Furthermore, Hunt disqualified himself as a poet because he lacked "religious feeling" and "patriotic feeling," showing no reverence "for God or Man." While there is much of the ad hominem in Lockhart's attack, there is more expression of disgust for aesthetic incompetence. This is the basis for all of Lockhart's essays in this series, even when he focuses on the "immorality" of the poems, as in the second essay (November 1817), where he contrasts George Gordon, Lord Byron's handling of the incest theme in his *Parasina* (1816) with Hunt's in *The Story of Rimini*; the poet who "prostitutes his talents" (as did Hunt and his protégés, including John Keats) is to be condemned.

That Lockhart should have attacked the poetry of Keats in the fourth "Cockney School of Poetry" essay (August 1818) is not surprising, since Keats followed Hunt in practicing an art of "vulgarity," according to Lockhart's aesthetic principles. Again, Lockhart said in this consideration of Keats's *Poems* (1817) and *Endymion* (1818), here was a poet of some talent, but one who was misguided by his mentor (Hunt) and models. For Lockhart, Keats lacked judgment and decorum, which perhaps he did at the time. The style and tone of Lockhart's essay are so biting and sarcastic that his main points are likely to be lost upon the modern reader, who is accustomed to thinking that Keats is a consummate poet. In his close analysis of Keats's diction, Lockhart scores some critical hits, particularly against the "Cockney rhymes" of *Endymion*. In the sixth essay (October 1819) Lockhart pretends that Leigh Hunt is dead and treats his *Foliage* (1818) as a "posthumous publication" in the care of "the author's executors," including John Keats, who is once again condemned for his adulation of Hunt. For the May 1819 issue Lockhart wrote a "Letter From Z to Leigh Hunt, King of the Cockneys," in which he accused Hunt of being an aesthetic coward—one who attacks his critics rather than defending his art.

Lockhart championed the poetry of both Byron and Percy Bysshe Shelley, although he deplored the association of both with the Cockneys. For most of the reviewers in *Blackwood's* Byron was a great poet of strong passions and mysterious powers. Lockhart took some interesting critical approaches to Byron's art, particularly when that art came under widespread attack after Byron's divorce and during publication of the cantos of *Don Juan* (1819-1824). Lockhart recognized the brilliance of the poem, but it was an assault on the social and moral values which Lockhart always used to measure the aesthetic worth of poetry. In August 1821 he may have had a hand in the attack on Cantos III-V (1821), as he may also have helped to write the sharp review of Cantos VI-VIII (1823) in July 1823. Nevertheless, in September 1823 Lockhart wrote of Cantos IX-XI (1823) that, whatever else one might say of Byron's poetry, these cantos included, one could never call them "dull."

Attitudes toward Byron and Shelley are interesting touchstones for examining the character of *Blackwood's*. Each reviewer found much to praise and admire in Byron's poetry, until his divorce and the beginning of his publication of *Don Juan*. Then the magazine (especially its publisher) accused Byron of betraying his talent; there was division among the reviewers, however. Lockhart, for example, tried to separate himself from the magazine's condemnation of the reprobate Byron. To appreciate the complicated character of *Blackwood's*, one must take into account its critical attitude toward Shelley, whose aristocratic background and elitist taste were (like Byron's) congenial to the magazine's principles, but whose radical politics and demanding, individual poetic style often challenged conservative *Blackwood's* reviewers to reconsider their aesthetic principles.

In his January 1819 review of Shelley's *Revolt of Islam* (1818) Lockhart recognized evidence of "a powerful and vigorous intellect," despite Shelley's "Cockney" principles of social and political egalitarianism. Lockhart is impressed with Shelley's style of intensity, but he is puzzled by the obscurity of the poem. Clearly what attracted his notice is Shelley's ability to use language for achieving concentrated emotional responses: Shelley displays "a mind intensely poetical" through "an exuberance of poetic language." Underlying Lockhart's analysis is his basic respect for Shelley as "a scholar, a gentleman, and a poet."

Although Shelley's theme of incestuous love disturbed Lockhart, it was not as egregious a fault as it was in Hunt's *Story of Rimini*. In his June 1819 review of Shelley's *Rosalind and Helen* the limit of Lockhart's tolerance for Shelley's moral "waywardness" was nearly reached, so that Lockhart was forced to observe, "there is no great moral flow in his poetry." Nevertheless (and this is the strength of Lockhart's critical attitude), he praises the "mastery" of the "softer strings of pathos and tenderness" in Shelley's "little eclogue." Shelley's technique is compared, for high praise, with the techniques of Byron and Scott. Later, in his November 1819 review of *Alastor* (1816), Lockhart defended Shelley against the attacks he suffered from reviewers in other magazines, such as the *Quarterly Review*.

In September 1820 Lockhart admired Shelley's audacity in challenging Aeschylus. The peculiar feature of this review of Shelley's *Prometheus Unbound* (1820) was Lockhart's diversion to defend his criticism of Keats, whose death he deplored but whose poetry he continued to believe had been corrupted by the influence of Leigh Hunt. When Shelley's *Adonais* (1821) was to be reviewed, Lockhart deferred to George Croly, whose biting criticism in the December 1821 issue was far different from the attitude toward Shelley that readers were used to finding in *Blackwood's*. Lockhart's next opportunity to examine Shelley came in February 1822, when he joined with Charles Ollier to review Shelley's *Epipsychidion* (1821). Ostensibly writing a "Letter from London" to "C. North" (John Wilson) in Edinburgh, Ollier offers a "report" on current tastes in London, including the interest excited by *Epipsychidion,* a poem of "threefold curiosity": "impenetrable mysticism," "delicious beauty," and advocacy of incest. Lockhart's footnote says he is at the end of his tether with Shelley, who insists on wasting his great talent on such an immoral theme. Even Byron, Lockhart notes, has begun to show evidence of corruption by his association with the Cockney gang.

*Blackwood's* was therefore a major force in the critical reception of the "new" authors who would be called "Romantic," including William Wordsworth and Samuel Taylor Coleridge, William Godwin, Keats and Shelley, as well as Byron, William Hazlitt, and Scott. In addition, the magazine (often referred to as *Maga*) helped create interest in German literature of the Romantic era. Again Lockhart was the major author for these essays, although others, including Thomas De Quincey, contributed at times. *Blackwood's* also contributed to public awareness of a distinctively American literature, publishing several essays by John Neal, a young American author who succeeded in getting his pieces printed in several British journals.

In his *Blackwood's* series, Neal pretended to be an Englishman who observed with a critical eye what was happening in American letters. He wrote five essays titled "American Writers" for *Blackwood's* (September 1824 - February 1825) and a sixth titled "Late American Books" (September 1825). In these essays Neal arranged commentaries on American writers in alphabetical order, "so that those who happen to know the name of any American author, may be able to tell, at a glance, what he has written." In the first essay Neal asserts that the popularity of certain authors is no reliable sign of good writing in their works; he appeals to a "law of nature, which governs alike through all creation. . . . That which is a given time in coming to maturity, shall abide a like time without beginning to decay." Most popular American writers sound too much like Englishmen, states Neal; only two or three authors are distinctively American: James Kirke Paulding, James Neal, and Charles Brockden Brown.

Among the most popular works appearing in the magazine were the imaginary conversations of the *Noctes Ambrosianæ* (March 1822 - February 1835). These essays were initially the work of several hands, but gradually they became the responsibility of John Wilson, a major author for *Blackwood's* during the Romantic era. He showed his versatility, his ability to extend his range of taste, in his reviews of Wordsworth's writings. Wilson wrote disparagingly of Wordsworth in his June 1817 review (in the *Edinburgh Monthly Magazine*) of Wordsworth's *Letter to a Friend of Robert Burns* (1816), but in July 1818 Wilson praised Wordsworth's *White Doe of Rylstone* (1815) and called Wordsworth one of "the three great master-spirits of our day, in the poetical world" (Scott and Byron being the other two). He accused Coleridge of obscurity and egotism, however, for publishing the *Biographia Literaria* (1817). In a carefully reasoned and learned review (October 1817) Wilson made a point often repeated since: "in a literary point of view, the work is most execrable. He rambles from one subject to another in the most wayward and capricious manner." Wilson contrasts Coleridge's egotism (a trait of the "original members of the Lake School") with the "dignified" modesty of Scott, Thomas Campbell, and Thomas Moore.

Wilson also wrote some of the attacks on the "Cockney School of Poetry." In the August 1825 issue he declares that Leigh Hunt is incurable, despite the best efforts of *Blackwood's* to "purge," "bleed," "blister," and "bandage" him.

Like Lockhart, Wilson admired the writing of Lord Byron. In June 1817 Byron's *Manfred* (1817) was the occasion for Wilson to praise the poet for his ability to look deeply "into the soul of man."

Wilson also wrote light, humorous review-essays, as in June 1826, when he used the occasion of examining Mrs. Margaret Dod's *The Cook and Housewives Manual* to discourse on the art of "carving," good Scotch dishes (including haggis), and social manners at dinner parties. In the next number (July 1826) Wilson took on the role of tour guide, throwing out "Hints for the Holidays," especially focused on the Lake District. Wilson often praised the pleasures derived from nature, as in February 1826, when he wrote a gracefully informal essay on "Birds." While there is little that is distinctive about this piece—it classifies favorite "birds of Scotland," from the blackbird to the "Grey Lintie," that is, the linnet—it displays Wilson's typically self-referential manner: the introduction announces, "We are never the same Magazine for two months together."

After Lockhart left Edinburgh in late 1825 to assume editorship of the *Quarterly Review* in London, Blackwood directed his magazine in new, less satirical and less critical, directions. It began its Victorian existence as a quieter, still conservative, and increasingly less strident voice for literary and social Britain. There were still pieces by Walter Scott (such as his scholarly account of Lord Pitsligo in May 1829), and there were still satirical pieces by William Maginn, although his writing sounded tame by comparison with the early essays of Lockhart and Wilson. For example, the August 1826 issue included Maginn's satirical essay "First Love," in which he recalls how his discovery of the combined effects of tobacco and rum came on the occasion of his first falling in love while at Trinity College, Dublin; he has never recovered the joy of that experience, either in the smoking and drinking or in the romantic love—he concludes, "I was born to be unhappy."

Beginning in 1831, Archibald Alison was an increasingly frequent contributor to *Blackwood's*. Marked by the "high seriousness" which would distinguish much Victorian writing, his essays are weighted with erudition, written in a complicated style to express complex thought. In March 1832 he wrote of François-Auguste-René de Chateaubriand as "the most eloquent writer of the present age," and he introduced his subject with a diatribe against literary journals!

> It is one of the worst effects of the vehemence of faction, which has recently agitated the nation, that it tends to withdraw the attention altogether from works of permanent literary merit, and by presenting nothing to the mind but a constant succession of party discussions, both to disqualify it for enjoying the sober pleasure of rational information, and render the great works which are calculated to delight and improve the species known only to a limited class of readers.

Alison uses his position as author of journal articles to discourage readers from relying too much on such pieces for substantial literature. Journalism, he says, undermines conservative principles and encourages "the lurid flame of democratic flattery." To Alison praising a French author proves his own objectivity because it is the French who have done the most to threaten conservative standards. To illustrate his point, Alison gives, in his August 1838 review of the first part of Thomas Arnold's *History of Rome* (1832-1842), the example of Rome, "which underwent exactly the same changes, and suffered the consequences of the same convulsions" as contemporary Britain. Democratic energy requires aristocratic control, Alison asserted, as anyone who observes events in America could easily recognize. In his January 1836 review of the first part of Alexis de Tocqueville's *Democracy in America* (1835, 1840) he expressed admiration for the "ambition" of American democracy but cautioned against its damaging effects on British stability. Through voices such as Alison's in *Blackwood's*, Romantic energy was giving way to Victorian restraints.

One Romantic writer whose Tory principles brought him to the service of *Blackwood's* was Thomas De Quincey. His series of essays on "The Caesars" (October and November 1832; January 1833; and June, July, and August 1834) clearly complements Alison's essays, although De Quincey strikes a distinctive tone and theme in his attention to the ironies of great power: "There was no escape open, says Gibbon, from Caesar: true; but neither was there any escape for Caesar." The power of passion to drive men and nations into terror and madness was a constant attraction to De Quincey. For *Blackwood's* in 1831 he had written a series of papers on "Dr. Parr and His Contemporaries" (January, February, May, and June), analyzing the career of Dr. Samuel Parr, who in 1812 had acquired fame as "the mere football of passion." De Quincey said Parr was "brilliant" as a scholar, "but he consumed his power in gladiatorial displays." Many conservative writers would use this example, in *Blackwood's* and elsewhere, to warn Victorians against the evils of a rising democratic tide that had its origins in the Romantic energies of an earlier generation (whence De Quincey himself derived). The most interesting of De Quincey's writings for *Blackwood's* may be in his tales and romances, such as "The Avenger" (August 1838). Like most of his writing, this tale mixes fascination and fear of the powers unleashed by (especially erotic) passion. It is a version of Romantic entertainment that would dominate much Victorian literature, both popular and elitist, for a long time afterward.

An example of the mildly humorous writing which began to appear in *Blackwood's* during the onset of the Victorian era is the essay which immediately followed Maginn's in August 1826: "The Man With the Nose," by Robert Macnish (who signed himself as "A Modern Pythagorean"), an insipid dream sequence of social tension created by a mysterious stranger whose nose seems to grow longer as he smokes. The hallucinogenic effects of tobacco are put to literary uses in this vapid and pointless anecdote, perhaps an imitation of writings on opium which had been popular during the Romantic era. The somewhat humorous treatment of human character through concentration on a part of human anatomy was undertaken again in "A Dialogue between the Marquis of Angelsea, and the Ghost of His Leg," by Samuel O'Sullivan (signed "Glanlville Redivivus") in November 1831. It is tiresomely tendentious in its use of a humorous notion for a long diatribe against the Reform Bill then under debate in Parliament.

The author who made the social and political debates of the late Romantic and early Victorian periods into serious art for *Blackwood's* was John Galt, who wrote both fictional and nonfictional prose for the magazine. His social and political prejudices were often quite clear, as in his October 1825 essay calling for an "Oriental College in England" to propagate English and Protestant values to counter the successful efforts of the Roman church in the Orient. Sometimes signing himself "Bandana," he would discuss more immediate issues, such as political representation or emigration ( January and April 1824). Galt's best writing, however, is his fictional prose, where he created vivid characters who spoke a vigorous Scots-English dialect. In "Our Borough" (October 1832) his narrator, called Robin Gables, describes how the Whigs gave Radicals "head-rope enough to work meikle mischief," and Robin's wife expostulates with him, " 'Nane of your fleechings, Robin; ye're just fou', and tavert, and that's what has put it into your head to gar ayou think ye can blaw wind in my lug." Galt employed a style of speaking made popular by Walter Scott, using it to paint portraits of grotesque people (anticipating Charles Dickens) and for narratives of contemporary social relevance to Victorian audiences (in a manner more profoundly pursued by George Eliot). Thus did *Blackwood's* continue to provide its readers with variety, prose, and poetry for pleasure and profit, in styles adjusted to changing tastes, but always in conformity with high standards of conservative aesthetics, cautious social principles, and concerned Tory politics.

**References:**

Margaret Oliphant, *Annals of a Publishing House: William Blackwood and His Sons: Their Magazine and Friends*, 3 volumes, volume 3 completed by Mrs. Gerald Porter (Edinburgh & London: William Blackwood & Sons, 1897, 1898);

Donald H. Reiman, ed., *The Romantics Reviewed: Contemporary Reviews of British Romantic Writers*, 9 volumes (New York & London: Garland, 1972);

A. L. Strout, *A Bibliography of Articles in "Blackwood's Magazine." Volumes I Through XVIII. 1817-1825, Library Bulletin*, no. 5 (Lubbock: Texas Technological College, 1959);

Roger P. Wallins, "Blackwood's Edinburgh Magazine," in *British Literary Magazines. The Romantic Age, 1789-1836*, edited by Alan Sullivan (Westport, Conn.: Greenwood Press, 1983), pp. 45-53.

# The British Critic

*(May 1793 - October 1843)*

James C. McKusick
*University of Maryland, Baltimore County*

The *British Critic* was founded in 1793 by a small group of Anglican clergy. Distressed by the radical tone of many recent publications, these clergymen first met together in late 1791 at the Suffolk County vicarage of William Jones of Nayland, a provincial curate who shared their respect for traditional values and their contempt for the egalitarian principles of the French Revolution. Designating themselves a "Society for the Reformation of Principles," this group published a bold proclamation on 1 January 1792 defending their conservative ideology and calling for the publication of a new review. Their *Proposal for the Reformation of Principles* set forth the rationale for this new review: it was intended to remedy "the corruption, which prevails among scholars, and persons of the higher orders of life, from evil *principles*, and what may be called *a monopoly of the press*." The editorship of the *British Critic* was undertaken by two Anglican clergymen, Robert Nares (1753-1829) and William Beloe (1756-1817), who served as coeditors from 1793 through 1813. Nares was the author of two antireforming pamphlets and various philological works, including a comprehensive glossary of Elizabethan literature. He advanced moderate and ecumenical views in his controversial writings, and a similar tone was often apparent in reviews of theological works that appeared in the *British Critic* during his editorship. Beloe was a talented classical scholar with a more strictly orthodox mentality. In his autobiography, *The Sexagenarian* (1817), Beloe stated that the *British Critic* enjoyed the support of Charles Moore, Archbishop of Canterbury, and Beilby Porteus, Bishop of London. The *British Critic* was published by the house of Rivington, which for almost a century had sold mostly books on the Church of England.

*Robert Nares, who edited the* British Critic *with William Beloe from the founding of the magazine through 1813 (engraving by S. Freeman, after a painting by J. Hoppner)*

The Tory government of William Pitt provided covert financial assistance to the editors of this new periodical; Nares received fifty pounds from the secret-service funds in March 1792 and another fifty pounds the following year. Meanwhile the main competitor of the *British Critic* was subjected to legal harassment by the attorney general, who threatened to prosecute the *Monthly Review* in January 1793 for its allegedly treasonous review of Nares's *Principles of Government Deduced from Reason* (1792). The reviewer of this pamphlet had criticized Nares's unconditional support for the monarchy, asserting instead that a nation may "dismiss or controul its king, whenever it thinks fit" (October 1792). Although the threat of prosecution was not carried out, it clearly served its purpose of intimidating the *Monthly Review* and thereby stifling its competitive response to the *British Critic*, which first appeared in May

1793. This new review was an immediate success among the more conservative sectors of the British reading public; its subscribers included prominent members of the aristocracy, gentry, and clergy, along with wealthy professionals and merchants; it was also received by many circulating libraries, which presumably extended its influence among middle-class readers. By 1797 the *British Critic* had achieved a circulation of approximately thirty-five hundred copies, making it one of the most widely read reviews of the period; only the *Monthly Review* surpassed this figure with an estimated circulation of five thousand. The extensive circulation of the *British Critic* was probably achieved at the expense of the *Monthly Review*; in 1795 William Jones reported that the *British Critic* was having "the good effect of lessening the sale of the *Monthly Review* to the value of 1000 copies a month, which is a circumstance worth all the trouble I took in giving birth to the undertaking."

While making inroads upon the readership of the rival reviews, the *British Critic* also attracted some of their most talented contributors. Several of these anonymous contributors have been identified by Derek Roper in his meticulous study *Reviewing Before the Edinburgh, 1788-1802* (1978). According to Roper, the Swiss geologist Jean André Deluc and the Orientalist Joseph White, both of whom had previously written articles for the *Monthly Review*, now began to contribute to the *British Critic*. The antiquarian and political pamphleteer John Whitaker, formerly a paid contributor to the *English Review*, agreed to write for the *British Critic* "gratuitously, and merely to support it as an orthodox and constitutional journal of literature." Samuel Partridge, a prominent cleric, also declined payment for his articles. Reviewers for the *British Critic* included some of the leading intellectual figures of the late eighteenth century, such as Thomas Percy, compiler of the *Reliques of Ancient English Poetry* (1765); Samuel Parr, a renowned classical scholar; John Brand, a political economist; John Hellins, a mathematician and astronomer; Richard Polwhele, a prolific poet, critic, and local historian; and William Vincent, a classical linguist and ancient geographer. Other likely contributors were Thomas Maurice, a pioneering Sanskrit scholar, and Thomas Rennell, a respected theologian. All of these contributors (with the exception of Deluc) were ordained clergy of the Church of England, and their shared intellectual outlook is apparent in the high moral tone of the *British Critic*. Throughout its publication history, this review gave great prominence to religious topics; works of "Divinity" were always listed first in its biannual survey of important publications. Novels, by contrast, were considered intellectually frivolous and received critical approval only if they were deemed "favourable to the interests of morality" (preface to volume four of the *British Critic*, July-December 1794). Under the editorship of Nares and Beloe, the *British Critic* displayed an exemplary moderation and tolerance in its reviewing of theological works; for example, it welcomed books by John Knox (in September 1796) and William Wilberforce (in September 1797) that expressed "sound and genuine Christianity" despite occasional deviations from strict Anglican orthodoxy. Under subsequent editors, however, the *British Critic* became more narrowly sectarian; by 1833 it had become virtually an organ of the Oxford Movement under the editorship of John Henry Newman and others.

In its general organization and layout, the *British Critic* closely resembled the *Monthly Review*; it attempted an encyclopedic breadth of coverage that would enable its readers to judge the intellectual and literary merits of all current publications. However, the *British Critic* was unique among contemporary monthly reviews in having an explicit political agenda: it openly and consistently advocated a conservative ideology summed up in the slogan, "Church and Constitution" (preface to volume sixteen of the *British Critic*, July-December 1800). This staunch Tory outlook was especially apparent in its reviews of works on politics and religion, but it also extended to the reviewing of poetry and novels, which were closely examined for their political opinions, whether expressed or implied. Such intense political scrutiny was not uncommon among the other four monthly reviews of the time (the *Monthly*, the *English*, the *Analytical*, and the *Critical*); but by 1793 all four of these journals had taken on a reformist or Dissenting outlook, and their political views, though not distinctly avowed as a matter of editorial policy, were widely believed to determine the tone of their articles. The *British Critic* was created in order to resist what its founders regarded as the dissemination of subversive principles by the existing reviews and to uphold traditional values at a time of severe national crisis. The historical circumstances of its founding are vividly described in the preface to the July-

December 1800 volume, probably written by Nares and Beloe:

> We have seen a century close, the last years of which have been such as hardly any century has produced. At a time of gloom and apprehension, when Faction and Impiety had grown insolent and menacing, and those principles which our Church and Constitution support, however numerous their private friends, had scarcely any public advocates;—among those who revised new publications, not even one;—at that moment of real, not of feigned alarm, when they who avowed themselves loyal were tauntingly accused of forming lists of condemnation for themselves; at that period, though little inclined to assume a public situation, we strongly felt, that duty bid us quit our private walk, to do our utmost for the general cause.

The conservative outlook of the *British Critic* stemmed from the anxiety and turmoil of the years immediately following the French Revolution, when foreign invasion and domestic subversion were regarded as serious threats to the established order.

The *British Critic* nevertheless aspired to be more than just a conduit for official propaganda. Like the *Monthly Review*, the *British Critic* professed to be consistent and impartial in its coverage of books from all points of the political spectrum. It attempted to engage seriously with viewpoints radically opposed to its own, and it tried to maintain at least the appearance of critical neutrality and gentlemanly decorum. But how could the *British Critic*'s claim of impartiality be reconciled with its overt political stance? The preface to the first volume (May-August 1793) attempts, not altogether successfully, to answer this question:

> With respect to the nature of our design, we know but of one objection, even of apparent weight, that has been urged against it: which is, that we began by professing partiality. That this was an improper construction of the words of our Prospectus has been, we trust, sufficiently evinced by the actual execution of our work, so far as it has yet proceeded; in which it may be seen, that writers of all classes and descriptions obtain a fair consideration; and that censure, if it has appeared necessary, has been given sometimes with reluctance, and generally with a degree of delicacy in the manner, which might palliate, in some degree, the harshness of the matter.

These claims are to some extent justified by the critical practice of the *British Critic*. Certainly it did review "writers of all classes and descriptions," although with varying degrees of fairness; and certainly it did maintain a certain degree of restraint even in its harshest criticism, generally avoiding crude personal attacks of the sort launched by its political ally, the *Antijacobin Review*.

The *British Critic*'s rules of literary decorum are further specified in a January 1800 review of a vitriolic pamphlet by Jacob Bryant:

> The just limits of controversy are as clearly defined by the courtesy of letters, as legitimate war is distinguished from piracy by the law of nations. Wit, humour, sarcasm, and irony, are within the bounds prescribed; gross language, invective, and calumny, are as much forbidden, as poisoned weapons are in war.

The *British Critic* was always careful to avoid these "poisoned weapons," but such critical restraint did not, in practice, guarantee fairness in reviewing. It was often blind to the merits of works published by its political adversaries, especially such radicals as Thomas Paine, William Godwin, and Mary Wollstonecraft. Nor were books of poetry exempt from unfair treatment; the *British Critic* denounced John Keats's *Endymion* (1818) largely on the ground of his affiliation with the radical Leigh Hunt, and for several years it carried on an implacable feud with George Gordon, Lord Byron, condemning virtually all of his works for their insidious moral and political tendencies.

However, the judgment of the *British Critic* was not automatically determined by an author's political views; in some cases the journal was surprisingly sympathetic to works by authors known to be hostile to its own conservative outlook. Perhaps the most striking instance of such critical indulgence may be found in its review of *Lyrical Ballads* (1798), published anonymously but known to be partly the work of Samuel Taylor Coleridge. Although the *British Critic* had harshly condemned Coleridge's political pamphlets in 1796, it responded quite sympathetically to *Lyrical Ballads*, praising his linguistic virtuosity and making constructive suggestions for revision. Even in the case of Byron, the condemnation of the *British Critic* was not simply a knee-jerk reaction; each new work was thoroughly appraised, and two of Byron's later narrative poems, *Beppo* (1818) and *The Island* (1823), received critical approval. In the case of Keats, the *British Critic* published an apology for its unfair treatment of *Endymion* and reviewed his last volume, *Lamia, Isabella, The Eve of St. Agnes, and Other Poems* (1820), more sympathetically. On the whole, the *British Critic* usually managed to provide its readers with an open-minded response to works of poetry and fiction, even if certain parts of those works offended against the prevailing political orthodoxy. Indeed, some of the most interesting reviews to appear in this journal are those in which the political views of the reviewer are manifestly in conflict with his sense of a work's literary merit. This latent tension between political and literary values, which recurs in various forms throughout the history of the *British Critic*, provides an opportunity for modern readers to observe the genesis and development of a Romantic conception of poetry within a wider social context.

The conservative political outlook of the *British Critic* is characteristically revealed in its review of William Godwin's *Enquiry concerning Political Justice* (1793), a utopian treatise that exerted a profound influence on the English Romantic poets, especially Coleridge and Percy Bysshe Shelley. While the *Monthly*, *Analytical*, and *Critical* reviews gave this work various degrees of qualified approval, the *British Critic* greeted it with unmitigated scorn and ridicule, taking it as the point of departure for a lively and entertaining essay on the follies of "this enlightened age." The reviewer laments the tendency of radical thinkers to reject the accumulated wisdom of previous generations, evidently believing "that a casual thought upon an abstruse subject decides it better than a profound enquiry; and that wisdom and knowledge come to *enlightened ages*, like Sir Andrew Aguecheek's reading and writing, *by nature*." The reviewer acknowledges Godwin's exceptional philosophical talent, but regrets that it is woefully misdirected:

> we would not be so dishonest as to say, or imply, that the author is deficient in natural powers. . . . A weak man cannot produce a long work of connected subtilty and argument. It is the property of a very different state of mind to take for granted one or two extravagant absurdities, and then to reason justly and correctly from them, as though they were truths.

The main tactic of this review is to state Godwin's premises reductively in order to reveal their alleged implausibility:

> The principles then, taken for granted as axioms, on which the whole is founded, are these; 1. The omnipotence of truth;—2. The *perfectibility* (as it is expressed) of man; probably by means of this omnipotent truth;—3. That man is a mere machine;—and, 4. That his actions, as well as every thing that happens in this universe, are the result of *absolute necessity*.

Each of these premises is criticized in turn, with particular scorn heaped upon the atheistic implications of the "omnipotence of truth," a doctrine that arrogantly rejects the traditional religious conception of God, yet covertly attributes quasi-divine power to an abstract notion of "truth":

> Why then is this abstract matter erected into a divinity? Gentle reader, you shall know. It is because Mr. G. has discarded all other divinity from his system, and nothing can be carried on, by any system-maker, without the intervention of some omnipotence.

Tracing Godwin's philosophical premises back to their historical origin in the ideology of the French Revolution, the *British Critic* argues that Godwin has only succeeded in exposing the absurdity of this foreign intellectual tradition:

> The true light, therefore, in which we ought to regard this book is, as a complete refutation of Helvetius, Rousseau, the author of Systeme de la Nature, and some English writers of equal extravagance, by a fair *reductio ad absurdum*; by showing demonstratively, to what nonsense and extravagance their doctrines, when pursued, must lead.

Although it is obviously unsympathetic to Godwin's democratic idealism, this review is nonetheless remarkably successful in revealing the main structure of his argument and his place in the history of radical thought. Appearing in the first volume of the *British Critic* (July 1793), this review serves as a critical manifesto; it is precisely the kind of essay, broad in scope and forceful in argument, that attracted readers away from the more insipid reviews of its competitors. In its derisive tone and its indiscriminate attack on a variety of targets, it also foreshadows the aggressive tactics of the *Edinburgh Review*.

The *British Critic* responded with similar hostility to Godwin's novel *Caleb Williams* (1794), dismissing it in the July 1794 issue with a curt paragraph that condemned its moral and political philosophy but nevertheless admitted that Godwin was an author of "considerable talents."

Stung by this review and a subsequent anonymous letter to the *British Critic* (April 1795) that attacked his handling of legal matters in *Caleb Williams,* Godwin replied in a letter published in the July 1795 issue that defended his novel as essentially utopian, rather than strictly realistic. He stated that his intention was not to attack "the laws of my country," but more generally "to expose the evils which arise out of the present system of civilized society." This letter was followed by an anonymous rejoinder in the February 1796 issue that cast further aspersions on Godwin's legal knowledge and political principles. Although the *British Critic* certainly gained the upper hand in this debate, it is remarkable that the editors even condescended to print Godwin's letter, since it was virtually unprecedented for any review to allow authors to reply to unfavorable criticism. The entire episode suggests that the *British Critic* was seeking to engage in political dialogue, rather than simply impose official dogma upon its readers. Once again the openness of the journal to dissenting viewpoints speaks well for the tolerant attitude of its editors.

The *British Critic* responded with initial hostility to the early prose works of Coleridge, who in 1795 had delivered a series of lectures in Bristol attacking the established Church and advocating democratic principles. Two of these lectures were published in 1796 as pamphlets, *The Plot Discovered* and *Conciones ad Populum, or Addresses to the People*. The *British Critic* responded to the first of these pamphlets with predictable antagonism in a review of May 1796:

> We abhor, not only as critics, but as men of morals, the custom which has late prevailed among certain individuals, of taking a detached sentence from a speech or publication, and commenting upon it, without any consideration of the context. Mr. Coleridge, whom we have commended as a poet, has done this with respect to an expression of the Bishop of Rochester, which, when explained, was found not only to be harmless, but truly constitutional. The violence of this pamphlet supersedes all criticism; it breathes all the petulance and irritability of youth, assertion without proof, and the absurdest deductions from the most false and unreasonable premises.

Its June 1796 review of *Conciones ad Populum* was also antagonistic, seeking to discredit Coleridge's democratic convictions with heavy sarcasm:

> These addresses are by the same author, whose address to the people on a supposed plot, we noticed last month. They contain similar sentiments and are expressed with similar consistency and similar elegance. His tender and compassionate anxiety for the welfare of mankind, he dwells upon through many pages, and with that spirit of patriotism, which has frequently actuated the writers of his party, attempts to ascribe the murders of Robespierre, and all the horrors acted in France, to the obstinate hostility of this country. When shall we cease to see this nonsense repeated, which the best informed even of our French enemies have again and again contradicted?

These two reviews show the *British Critic* at its most inflexible and dogmatic.

The *British Critic* responded with surprising indulgence to Coleridge's early volumes of poetry, reviewing them favorably despite his known political sentiments. In the May 1796 issue appeared a generally positive review of Coleridge's *Poems on various Subjects* (1796):

> This collection is marked by tenderness of sentiment, and elegance of expression, neither sufficiently chastened by experience of mankind, or habitude of writing. . . . Mr. C. does not, in this volume, betray much of his politics, except in his violent rant to Lord Stanhope.

The terms "tenderness" and "elegance" are evidently used without sarcasm here, although this reviewer clearly disapproves of Coleridge's political values. A similar incongruous mixture of literary praise and political condemnation appears in the June 1799 review of Coleridge's next volume of poetry, *Fears in Solitude* (1798):

> We by no means deny this writer the praise of sensibility and poetic taste, and, on this account, we the more seriously lament his absurd and preposterous prejudices against his country, and give a decided preference to the last of these compositions [that is, "Frost at Midnight"], as having no tincture of party.

The reviewer goes on to specify his grievances against the poem "Fears in Solitude": it denounces the British government as "tyrannous" and describes the English people as "a selfish, lewd, effeminated race" that is "passionate for war." The *British Critic* replies: "Now all this we deny, and consider it as the hasty emotion of a young man, who writes without experience of facts." But despite his doubts of Coleridge's patriotism, this reviewer has some kind words for his poetic talent: "The Poem called Frost at Midnight, not being defaced by any of these absurdities, is entitled to much praise. A few affectations of phraseology, are atoned for by much expressive tenderness."

This indulgent attitude toward Coleridge's poetry, regardless of his obnoxious political opinions, is even more apparent in the review of *Lyrical Ballads* (1798) that appeared in the October 1799 issue of the *British Critic*. This was the earliest and most sympathetic review of *Lyrical Ballads* to appear in any of the monthly journals. Although the volume was published anonymously, the reviewer surmised that it was by Coleridge. The review is almost entirely favorable, giving a lucid account of the theoretical foundation of the poems and providing constructive criticism of particular passages. No reference is made to political considerations until the final sentence of the review, which states that the volume is free of "any offensive mixture of hostility to present institutions, except in one or two instances, which are so unobtrusive as hardly to deserve notice." It is difficult for a modern reader to determine whether the *British Critic* regarded the *Lyrical Ballads* as genuinely inoffensive, or whether it was willing to overlook the implicit political agenda of the book because of its unusual literary merit. In any case, the review begins by lavishing praise upon the attempted reform of poetic diction:

> The attempt made in this little volume is one that meets our cordial approbation; and it is an attempt by no means unsuccessful. The endeavour of the author is to recall our poetry, from the fantastical excess of refinement, to simplicity and nature. The account of this design, and its probable effects upon modern readers, is so very sensibly given in the Introduction, that we shall insert the passage at large.

At this point the reviewer quotes several paragraphs of the introductory "Advertisement," including the statement that "the following Poems are to be considered as experiments. They were written chiefly with a view to ascertain how far the language of conversation in the middle and lower classes of society is adapted to the purposes of poetic pleasure." The reviewer clearly approves of this experiment:

> In the collection of poems subjoined to this introduction, we do not often find expressions that we esteem too familiar, or deficient in dignity; on the contrary, we think that in general the author has succeeded in attaining that judicious degree of simplicity, which accommodates itself with ease even with the sublime. It is not by pomp of words, but by energy of thought, that sublimity is most successfully achieved; and we infinitely prefer the simplicity, even of the most unadorned tale in this volume, to all the meretricious frippery of the *Darwinian* taste.

In preferring the simplicity of the *Lyrical Ballads* to the "meretricious frippery" of Erasmus Darwin, the *British Critic* unequivocally endorses the emerging Romantic standard of taste. Its reactionary political opinions clearly did not blind it to the revolutionary literary implications of the *Lyrical Ballads*. Throughout the Romantic period, the *British Critic* was consistently the strongest advocate for the poetry of Wordsworth and Coleridge, frequently defending their work against persistent attacks by the *Edinburgh Review* and other journals.

The *British Critic*'s lavish praise for *Lyrical Ballads* is combined with constructive criticism of particular poems. Its remarks on "The Rime of the Ancyent Marinere" are especially cogent:

> The Poem of "the Ancyent Marinere," with which the collection opens, has many excellencies, and many faults; the beginning and the end are striking and well-conducted; but the intermediate part is too long, and has, in some places, a kind of confusion of images, which loses all effect, from not being quite intelligible. The author, who is confidently said to be Mr. Coleridge, is not correctly versed in the old language, which he undertakes to employ. "Noises of a *swound*," p. 9, and "broad as a *weft*," p. 11, are both nonsensical; but the ancient style is so well imitated, while the antiquated words are so very few, that the latter might be entirely removed without any detriment to effect of the Poem. The opening of the Poem is admirably calculated to arrest the reader's attention, by the well-imagined idea of the Wedding Guest, who is held to hear the tale, in spite of his efforts to escape. The beginning of the second canto, or fit, has much merit, if we except the very unwarrantable comparison of the Sun to that which no man can conceive:—"like God's own head," a simile which makes a reader shudder; not with poetic feeling, but with religious disapprobation.

Coleridge's revisions to this poem for the 1800 edition of *Lyrical Ballads* were made partly in response to these suggestions. He removed most of the antique idioms, including the words *swound* and *weft* (although these two words are perfectly valid English vocabulary), evidently agreeing that they impeded the reader's comprehension of the poem without adding anything to its authenticity. He also deleted several stanzas, streamlining the narrative and helping to preclude the alleged "confusion of images." However, he did not alter the phrase, "like God's own head," perhaps judging that the doctrinal squeamishness of the *British Critic* was not shared by many of his readers and that this expression was entirely appropriate to the literal-minded Mariner. Aside from his retention of this phrase, Coleridge's revisions incorporated all of the suggestions made by the *British Critic*. Since these revisions are now generally regarded as improvements, it would appear that the *British Critic* deserves some credit for its role in shaping one of the finest and most familiar Romantic poems.

The *British Critic* reviewed the second edition of *Lyrical Ballads* (1800) in February 1801. This is one of the few literary reviews in the *British Critic* whose authorship can be definitely attributed; it was written by John Stoddart, a London lawyer and journalist who was a friend of Wordsworth and Coleridge and had recently visited them in the Lake District. Stoddart was not a regular reviewer, but, probably at Wordsworth's suggestion, he wrote a review of the new edition and offered it to the *British Critic*, which promptly accepted it for publication. This review begins by acknowledging Wordsworth's share in the composition of *Lyrical Ballads* and praising his stylistic development:

> His style is now wholly changed [since the publication of *Descriptive Sketches* and *An Evening Walk*], and he has adopted a purity of expression, which, to the fastidious ear, may sometimes sound poor and low, but which is infinitely more correspondent with true feeling than what, by the courtesy of the day, is usually called poetical language. . . . The author has thought for himself; he has deeply studied human nature, in the book of human action; and he has adopted his language from the same sources as his feelings.

Stoddart then comments perceptively on Wordsworth's famous preface:

> This Preface, though written in some parts with a degree of metaphysical obscurity, conveys much penetrating and judicious observation. . . . He declares himself the Poet chiefly of low and rustic life . . . and he pourtrays it, not under its disgusting forms, but in situations affording, as he thinks, the best soil for the essential passions of the heart, incorporated with a durable state of manners, and with the beautiful and permanent forms of nature.

Quoting extensively from the preface, Stoddart summarizes the main tenets of Wordsworth's poetic theory, with particular attention to his conception of rustic language as "a more permanent, and a far more philosophical, language, than that which is frequently substituted for it by poets." Stoddart praises several of the poems first published in this edition, including "Michael" and "The Brothers," and he quotes in full "Strange fits of passion I have known" and "She dwelt among th'untrodden ways." In his final appraisal, Stoddart admits "that sometimes [Wordsworth] goes so far in his pursuit of simplicity, as to become flat or weak; but, in general, he sets an example which the full-dressed poet of affectation might wish, but wish in vain, to follow." By publishing this review, the *British Critic* deepened its commitment to the new Romantic aesthetic represented by *Lyrical Ballads*, while it completely disregarded any political implications that were not in harmony with its own views.

The *British Critic* continued to grant wholehearted critical approval to Wordsworth for the rest of his career, standing firm against the attacks of the *Edinburgh Review* and a host of other detractors. Wordsworth's resolute conversion to a conservative political and religious outlook was undoubtedly instrumental in sustaining the support of the *British Critic*, but its editors also found his newfangled theory of poetic diction congenial to their own sense of literary value. The *British Critic*'s most notable account of his later work occurs in a May 1815 review of *The Excursion* (1814), written partly in response to Francis Jeffrey's famous attack in the *Edinburgh Review* (November 1814). This lengthy review, extending over some nineteen pages, defends Wordsworth's political and religious views, laying particular stress on his orthodoxy; it criticizes some "occasional lapses into childish and trivial allusion," but it concludes with warm praise for his poetic ability and his sublime representation of the natural world:

> Who can estimate the advantage which would result to mankind, if all men endowed with Mr. Wordsworth's talents would devote them to the expression, by their life and writings, of sentiments pure and ennobling like these? Is it indeed for purposes of vanity or applause, or to be the plaything of an idle hour, that Poetry was sent into

> the world? that a few are gifted above their fellows with eyes that can see deep into their own minds, and wide around them on the operations of Nature and Providence: with a tongue that can wield all the powers of language for gracefulness or terror: with the port and march almost of superior beings, bowing all hearts to receive their words as it were an oracle?

The same anonymous critic contributed a twenty-page review of *Peter Bell* (1819) to the June 1819 issue of the *British Critic*; once again he defends Wordsworth against his detractors, commending his poetry in the highest possible terms:

> We think there is no one of the present day, and none but the few giants of the preceding ages, who have excelled him in some of his productions; in these and parts of others he has displayed a splendour and purity of diction, a force, and skilful harmony of measure, with a depth, a truth, a tenderness, and a solemn sublimity of sentiment, which in their union remind us forcibly of the happiest, and most golden moments of the immortal Petrarch.

There follows a detailed exegesis of Wordsworth's poetic theory, stressing its moral and religious aspects, but also defending the presentation of everyday occurrences in ordinary language:

> We see no cause for departing from the account which we have before given of the principles, on which Mr. Wordsworth's poetical system is built; they seem to us to be two in number, with an important corollary deducible from them; we perfectly agree in the truth and importance of the two first, and we are precluded from denying the abstract truth, though we doubt of the practical expediency of the last. The principles are, first, that "whatsoever material or temporary exists before our senses, is capable of being associated in our minds with something spiritual and eternal;" and, secondly, that it is the business of the poet to see all things with a view to this capability of association, and to familiarize the process to his own, and to his reader's mind; the corollary is, that if all things are equally capable of the process, and in the availing itself of that capability, the true and essential excellence of poetry consists, then the commonest external thing, the most every day occurrence of life, or the meanest appearance of nature is equally capable of being made the ground-work or subject of poetry with the noblest and the most uncommon.

Although this sanctimonious view of Wordsworth's poetry may seem reductive to modern readers, we should nevertheless recognize that the *British Critic* was making a bold and principled stand on behalf of a poet who was often reviled in the popular press. While the *British Critic* may have undervalued some of Wordsworth's playful vernacular experiments, it still managed to keep his literary reputation alive during some of its darkest hours.

The *British Critic* also did what it could to enhance Coleridge's reputation, publishing a generally favorable review of his *Sibylline Leaves* (1817) and *Biographia Literaria* (1817) in its November 1817 issue. This twenty-two-page review perceptively analyzes Coleridge's prose style, noting his reliance on such seventeenth-century writers as Jeremy Taylor and Richard Hooker. While the reviewer deplores Coleridge's penchant for metaphysical obscurity, he finds that Coleridge's observations on other topics are "often just and striking, and invariably display a tone of mind that is both scholarlike and amiable." The reviewer particularly admires the second volume of the *Biographia Literaria*, which includes

> one of the fairest and most able reviews of the peculiarities of Mr. Wordsworth's poetry, that we have met with. Mr. Coleridge's observations upon the diction of Mr. Wordsworth, contain many just and striking thoughts; and the analytical criticisms which occur in various parts of the discussion, upon one or two of the poems contained in the "Lyrical Ballads," impressed us with a very favourable opinion of his good taste and discrimination.

This review marks the inception of a view of the *Biographia Literaria* that prevailed well into the twentieth century and is still held by some scholars: that its philosophical speculations are worthless, but its practical criticism is of great value.

The *British Critic* devotes great attention to an aspect of the *Biographia Literaria* not often discussed by modern critics, namely its recurrent obsession with periodical reviewers. Taking as his point of departure the spiteful reviews of the Lake School by Francis Jeffrey, Coleridge denounces the practice of anonymous reviewing and suggests that it is the province of intellectual eunuchs. The *British Critic* responds to these charges at some length, and its response is of particular interest since it leads to a frank discussion of the practice of reviewing and a defense of partisan advocacy. The *British Critic* agrees that the

*Edinburgh Review* has transgressed standards of critical decorum in its relentless vilification of Wordsworth, Coleridge, and Robert Southey; but it seeks to exonerate critical partisanship in principle, since only through the clash of contrary opinions can truth emerge:

> If one party condemn in excess, another will generally be found to praise in an equal excess; and after the first fermentation of contending opinions has a little subsided, the real truth gradually separates itself from the errors, with which it had been mixed, and becomes perhaps better and more certainly distinguishable, than by almost any process, to which it could have been subjected. As in our courts of justice, one advocate is paid, to say all that can be said in favour of one side of the question; another, to urge in like manner all that can be said against it, the decision meanwhile resting with the jury: so it is with the jury: so it is with us critics; one review is set up by men strongly biassed in favour of one system of principles; another starts in opposition to it by men as warmly favourable to the opposite; both of them, indeed, affect to speak with the authority, that belongs to the judicial office; but they are listened to as judges, only by those of their own party; the public knows well, that they are mere advocates, hired by their prejudices to plead the cause of a particular sect; and by listening to both sides, is much more likely to be put in possession of all the arguments in favour of each, than if it implicitly trusted to the impartiality, with which any single review could state them.

This candid admission of critical bias, and the corresponding doubt thrown upon any claim of critical impartiality, seems a more honest appraisal of the adversarial role of contemporary reviews, and especially of the avowedly partisan *British Critic*, than any of its previous statements of editorial policy.

If the critical bias of the *British Critic* was beneficial in enabling it to stand firm in its generous appraisal of Wordsworth and Coleridge, such bias had the more insidious effect of blinding this review to the emerging talents of the second generation of Romantic poets. Its reviews of Byron and Shelley are laced with such venom, and display such a fundamental lack of critical understanding, that they hardly merit detailed analysis. A few examples, however, may serve to illustrate the prevailing tone of these reviews. In a sarcastic account of Shelley's *Alastor* (1816), published in the May 1816 issue, the *British Critic* praises him for reaching a sublime level of nonsense:

> If this gentleman is not blessed with the inspiration, he may at least console himself with the madness of a poetic mind. In the course of our critical labours, we have been often condemned to pore over much profound and prosing stupidity; we are therefore not a little delighted with the nonsense which mounts, which rises, which spurns the earth, and all its dull realities. . . . We cannot do sufficient justice to the creative fancy of our poet. A man's hair singing dirges, and a boat pausing and shuddering, are among the least of his inventions; nature for him reverses all her laws, the streams ascend. The power of the syphon we all know, but it is for the genius of Mr. Shelley to make the streams run up hill. But we entreat the pardon of our readers for dwelling so long upon this *ne plus ultra* of poetical sublimity.

This curt dismissal of *Alastor* is the only significant review of Shelley's poetry to appear in the *British Critic*; his later works were passed over in silence, doubtless reflecting the journal's severe disapproval of his radical politics and scandalous life-style. Many years later, in an October 1834 review of Coleridge's *Poetical Works* (1834), the *British Critic* contrasted the "profound and meditative" Christian beliefs of Coleridge with the militant atheism of Shelley, lamenting that the younger poet was so bereft of moral and religious values:

> This poem ["Religious Musings"] suggests an instructive comparison between Mr. Coleridge and Mr. Shelley. They both professed to breathe intensely what they each called a love of universal nature. But the former traced the true source of this feeling to a knowledge of the God of Revelation, of "God in Christ." The Atonement was to his mind an irrefragable proof of the infinite love of God. It taught him that the evils and woes in the universe would, though this economy, be no impeachment of the Divine Wisdom. But here Mr. Shelley failed: if he deified any abstract notion at all; if he attributed to it any intelligence, it was that of simple nature, beneath whose sway sorrows and anguish were permitted without any future remedial provision. And surely such a view as this is wholly incompatible with unalloyed complacency in the universe.

For the *British Critic*, Coleridge served as a touchstone of poetic excellence, despite what it regarded as the "injuriously latitudinarian" tendencies of his religious doctrines. Shelley, on the other hand, exemplified all that was wrong with the younger generation of poets; and the evident "complacency" of the *British Critic* induced it to pass over his poetry in silence, confident that his literary reputation would eventually decline into oblivion.

This tactic of silent rejection could not possibly have worked against Lord Byron; it was impossible to ignore the most prominent poet of the age, although his reputation for loose living and his liberal Whig politics were hardly likely to appeal to the *British Critic*. The journal granted generally favorable reviews to some of Byron's early works, particularly the first two cantos of *Childe Harold* (1812); but it soon turned against him, and by 1816 its reviews of his works had become exercises in savage abuse and invective. The *British Critic* was outraged by the first two cantos of *Don Juan* (1819), denouncing their "degrading debauchery" and "gross impiety" in a review of August 1819. It concludes:

> Upon the indecency, and the blasphemy which this volume contains, a very few words will suffice. The adventures which it recounts are of such a nature, and described in such language, as to forbid its entrance within the doors of any modest woman, or decent man. Nor is it a history only, but a manual of profligacy. Its tendency is not only to excite the passions, but to point out the readiest means and method of their indulgence.

This was the most unremittingly negative review of *Don Juan* to appear in any of the monthly reviews, and it was followed in September 1821 by an even more fiercely abusive review of Cantos 3-5 of that poem:

> It is the eft, and toad, and lizard, . . . the slimy, and creeping, and venomous tribes, which shrink from observation, and bring forth in covert. The Poem before us is one of these hole and corner deposits; not only begotten but spawned in filth and darkness. Every accoucheur of literature has refused his obstetric aid to the obscure and ditch-delivered foundling; and even its father, though he unblushingly has stamped upon it an image of himself which cannot be mistaken, forbears to give it the full title of avowed legitimacy.

The *British Critic* refers here to the anonymous publication of *Don Juan*, suggesting that the poem, and its author, are of such a vile nature that no decent person would dare to approach them. Such mean-spirited vilification of Byron's lighthearted satirical poem bespeaks a massive failure of critical judgment on the part of the *British Critic*.

The case of Keats, however, is more interesting. In its June 1818 review of *Endymion* (1818), the *British Critic* denounced the poem in typically sarcastic fashion, mocking its overwrought diction and its adolescent eroticism, both allegedly imitated from the poetry of Leigh Hunt:

> Mr. Keats is not contented with a half initiation into the school he has chosen. And he can strike from unmeaning absurdity into the gross slang of voluptuousness with as much skill as the worthy prototype whom he has selected. We will assure him, however, that not all the flimsy veil of words in which he would involve immoral images, can atone for their impurity; and we would not disgust our readers by retailing to them the artifices of vicious refinement, by which, under the semblance of "slippery blisses, twinkling eyes, soft completion of faces, and smooth excess of hands," he would palm upon the unsuspicious and the innocent imaginations better adapted to the stews.

Presuming that since Keats imitated Hunt's style, he must also share his "jacobinical" politics, the reviewer condemned the poem largely on the ground of its supposed radical tendencies. But the *British Critic* reversed its judgment in a September 1820 review of Keats's next volume, *Lamia, Isabella, The Eve of St. Agnes, and Other Poems* (1820), giving it a more balanced appraisal and even making the rare gesture of apologizing for its previous review. Its awkward explanation allows a revealing glimpse into the politics of reviewing:

> If there be one person in the present day, for whom we feel an especial contempt, it is Mr. Examiner Hunt; and we confess that it is not easy for us to bring our minds to entertain respect for any one whose taste, whether in morals, in poetry, or politics, is so exceedingly corrupt as that person's must be supposed to be, who is willing to take such a man for his model. It was for this reason that Mr. Keats fell under our lash, so severely, upon the occasion of his poem of Endymion. Upon recurring to the poem, we are not unwilling to admit, that it possesses more merit, than upon a first perusal of it we were able to perceive, or rather than we were in a frame of mind to appreciate. We can hardly doubt as to that poem having been corrected by our modern Malvolio [that is, Hunt], and projected by his advice and under his superintendence;—so full was it, of all the peculiari-

> ties of that ingenious gentleman's ideas. The effect of this upon Mr. Keats's poetry, was like an infusion of ipecacuanha powder in a dish of marmalade.

The rest of the review, despite its stern criticism of Keats's "innovations of language," is quite receptive to the merits of his style, and especially commends his chaste Miltonic manner in "Hyperion." Although this review is hardly a model of objective criticism, it does indicate that the *British Critic* was capable of admitting error and responding sympathetically to a poet of genuine talent, regardless of his political views.

The *British Critic* enjoyed wide circulation and influence during the Romantic period, especially in the decade before the founding of the *Edinburgh Review* in 1802. The *Edinburgh* incorporated some of the most successful features of the *British Critic*: its overt partisanship (though from an opposing point of view), its lively attacks on supposed adversaries, and its extension of the scope of review essays to include more general reflections on topics suggested by the book in hand. As the *Edinburgh Review* developed these features far beyond anything attempted by its predecessors, the *British Critic* found its influence waning, and it retreated into a more narrowly partisan and sectarian viewpoint than it had held during the heyday of its popular appeal. This narrowing of perspective was no doubt related to the departure of its two original editors, Nares and Beloe, in 1813; their more tolerant attitudes were evidently incompatible with the revised political agenda of the journal. A new tone of dogmatic severity became apparent, especially in its hostile rejection of Shelley and its extended feud with Byron. Even such narrow-mindedness, however, can reveal a great deal about the contemporary reception of the works under discussion.

Throughout the Romantic period, the composition of poetry was an activity fraught with political significance. Yet the precise political tendency of any particular poem is difficult for modern readers to reconstruct, often being a matter more of allusion and innuendo than of manifest ideological content. The *British Critic* provides fascinating insights into the politics of reviewing during the Romantic period, and its reviews may help modern readers to situate particular poems in their social context and to analyze their reception by contemporary audiences. Affirming its political bias as a matter of editorial policy, the *British Critic* often condemned works for reasons that had little to do with their literary merit; but it also displayed surprising receptiveness to works by authors whose political beliefs were opposed to its own. Its warm response to *Lyrical Ballads* is perhaps the most significant example of such critical indulgence; and its reversal of judgment on Keats suggests that it could sometimes approve innovation, even by "jacobinical" poets, during its later, less tolerant phase. After the departure of Nares and Beloe, the *British Critic* continued to be one of the most eloquent defenders of the new Romantic aesthetic, especially in its detailed and sympathetic reviews of Wordsworth's *Excursion* and Coleridge's *Biographia Literaria*. The *British Critic* remains of interest to modern readers, not for its dubious attempts at critical impartiality, but because of the latent tension between its conservative political stance and its commitment to the most progressive forms of literature.

**References:**

Donald H. Reiman, ed., *The Romantics Reviewed: Contemporary Reviews of British Romantic Writers*, 9 volumes (New York & London: Garland, 1972);

Derek Roper, *Reviewing Before the Edinburgh, 1788-1802* (London: Methuen, 1978);

Alvin Sullivan, ed., *British Literary Magazines*, 4 volumes (Westport, Conn.: Greenwood Press, 1983-1986).

# The British Review and London Critical Journal

*(March 1811 - November 1825)*

Thomas L. Blanton
*Central Washington University*

Of the sixty-three British periodical reviews John O. Hayden lists for the period 1802-1824, the *Edinburgh Review* set the standard for subsequent rivals or challengers such as the *Quarterly Review* and *Blackwood's Edinburgh Magazine*. Beginning with the *Edinburgh* in 1802, book reviews were no longer notices to benefit booksellers or summaries of books for prospective readers. Instead, the review (today's equivalent would be the essay-review) afforded the reviewer an opportunity to address both books and subjects occasioned by them. As different as the *Edinburgh*, the *Quarterly*, and *Blackwood's* were in politics, in style, and in the writers they favored and those they ridiculed and damned, they were remarkably similar in origin—all revealing the importance reviewing had assumed in the Romantic period. They came into being as the creations of enterprising publishers and booksellers, writers with literary ambitions, and a growing number of well-educated men who found reviewing—either as occupation or avocation—a satisfying means for venting their literary and political opinions. The collective influence of these reviews must be kept in mind if the history of a lesser quarterly such as the *British Review* is to be properly understood.

Details about the origin of the *British Review and London Critical Journal* are scant, but it appears to have been founded as a new voice to challenge the authority of the *Edinburgh Review* and the *Quarterly*. In spite of the affiliation of its founders with the evangelical wing of the Church of England, it was meant to be a general literary review as free from church influence as from the influence of government and party. Thus it would differ from the *Christian Observer* and the *Eclectic Review*, monthlies with a markedly religious emphasis. While the *British Review* may have lived up to its promise to be free from government and party influence, it was no more successful than the *Edinburgh Review* and the *Quarterly* in avoiding a reputation for editorial bias. Just as the *Edinburgh Review* came to be seen as Whig in outlook and the *Quarterly* as Tory, the *British Review* within five years of its inception was judged by the *Augustan Review* to be written "by evangelical lawyers."

Two of these lawyers, John Weyland and William Roberts, seem to have been present at the creation of the *British Review*. Weyland is usually identified as principal founder and was, for a brief time, the first editor. Of Roberts, John O. Hayden writes, "The *British* probably more than any other journal of the period was the work of one man—William Roberts, the editor. According to his son, Roberts wrote most of the leading articles and often four or five reviews in a number (i.e., almost half ), not to mention extensive revision of articles contributed by others. In 1823, when he was no longer editor, Roberts told a correspondent that the spirit of the *British* was 'peculiarly my own', as it must have been." The first number of the *British Review and London Critical Journal* appeared in March 1811—two years after the first issue of the *Quarterly* and not quite ten years after the *Edinburgh* made its appearance. In the range of books reviewed, the subjects covered in articles, and the length of the reviews, it clearly invited comparison with these established leaders. Furthermore, it did so in its first article, "Advice to a Young Reviewer," a piece as much about the excesses of contemporary reviewing as it was a declaration of intent for the new review.

William Roberts (1767-1849) was educated at Eton and Corpus Christi College, Oxford, where he received his B.A. in 1787 and M.A. in 1791. At Oxford he gained some experience as a writer for the elder John Murray's *English Review*, and from March to December 1792 Roberts was responsible for a biweekly periodical, the *Looker-On*, writing under the pseudonym of Reverend Simeon Olive Branch. Later he studied law, becoming a barrister in 1806. For the balance of his life he published treatises on legal subjects, held government posts until a change in government led to his dismissal, became the friend of important evangelicals, and edited the *British Review* for most of its existence. He was a biographer of Hannah More (1745-1833), a playwright and prominent religious writer. In a preface to the second edition of *Memoirs of the Life and Correspondence of Mrs. Hannah More* (1834) he answered complaints that he had revealed unsaintly aspects of his subject's life by declaring it had been "his duty" to disclose "the stages of the Christian's advancement under divine teaching, from small beginnings, and through various trials, to victory and security." Furthermore, in a statement which suggests his sense of duty as editor of the *British Review*, he concludes, "If laws are becoming weak, and opinion strong—if power is gradually passing from the few to the many, leaving its ancient settlements to go with the throng in the great levelling march of its numerical and aggregate force, whatever has a tendency to rectify the common judgment, to lead the people to clearer perceptions of what belongs to their peace, and to counteract the effects of wicked counsel, deserves to be candidly, if not favourably received by the parent, the patriot, and the philanthropist."

Roberts assumed the editorship of the *British Review* shortly after the first issue (March 1811) and remained in control until the fortieth number was printed in 1822. Publication of the review was erratic between December 1812 and 1814 when it stopped altogether, resuming in August 1815. Following Roberts's departure as editor in 1822 (he continued to be a contributor) there was another gap in publication. A forty-first number appeared in August 1823 with the announcement that "The readers of the British Review will perceive that it has passed into the hands of new conductors. Further, it is intended, that, as the Public have long considered the British Review to be a Literary work, of a character decidedly Religious, it shall now take the full advantage of this understanding, by rendering to the cause of Religion, all the service of which it can be made capable. And this, without at all abandoning its station in the general field of Literature, or suffering one publication of general utility or interest to pass unnoticed." In two years (November 1825) the *British Review* abruptly ceased publication, having become almost exclusively devoted to religious publications and subjects, thereby abandoning its founders' claim for it as a comprehensive review.

Volume one, number 1, of the *British Review* includes twelve articles totaling 135 octavo pages. Following the lead article, "Advice to a Young Reviewer, with a Specimen of the Art," are review articles on economics, politics, travel, mathematics, 16 pages treating "Florin grass," and "The Pleader's Guide, a didactic Poem in two Parts, containing Mr. Sur-rebutter's Poetical Lectures on the Conduct of a Suit at Law; including the Arguments of Counsellor Bother'um and Counsellor Bore'um, in an Action for Assault and Battery between John A-Gull and John A-Gudgeon. By J. Anstey, Esq." The final two articles, requiring 30 pages, treat religious issues: "Grounds of Union between the Churches of England and Rome" and "Hints on Toleration: in five Essays." Although the issue begins with a discussion of reviewing, there are no literary reviews. The second number (June 1811) is nearly as innocuous in content, beginning with a life of Thomas Paine, more on the "Bullion Question" which occupies several pages in the first number, a review of Hannah More's *Practical Piety* (1811), and accounts of experiments on the ascent, descent, and motion of sap in trees. The only literary review treats *Cottage Dialogues Among the Irish Peasantry* (1811), by Mary Leadbeater. A 20-page "Charge delivered to the Clergy of the Diocese of London" by the bishop was "Published at the Request of the Clergy."

By June 1812 Roberts was reviewing major literary works, particularly the first of a long series of reviews of works by George Gordon, Lord Byron, which would give the *British Review* its place in the history of reviewing and criticism in the period. The August 1815 issue, the first after a break in publication, includes reviews of William Wordsworth's *Excursion* (1814), *The Lord of the Isles* (1815) by Sir Walter Scott, and Byron's *Hebrew Melodies* (1815) along with review articles on a variety of subjects, including "Negotiations on the Slave Trade" and "A brief Account of the Jesuits." The next issue (number 12) includes reviews of Robert Southey's *Roderick, the Last of the Goths* (1814) and Wordsworth's *The White Doe of Rylstone* (1815). Canto IV of Byron's *Childe Harold's Pilgrimage* is the subject of the lead review in the August 1818 issue (number 23). The next two issues contain no literary reviews although they treat the usual variety of books and subjects. Number 26 (May 1819) devotes nearly 40 pages to "The Late Antinomian Secession," along with 36 pages to a comprehensive review of four major works by William Hazlitt. In addition, briefer note is given to *Human Life: a Poem* (1819), by Samuel Rogers, and *Florence Macarthy* (1818), by Sydney, Lady Morgan. The lead review in the May 1819 issue of 265 pages treats the letters of Horace Walpole with other review articles devoted to "Savings Banks and Friendly Societies," "Contagion, of Plague, and Policy of the Quarantine Laws," and "Actual Condition of the United States." The last two issues edited by Roberts (numbers 39 and 40) in 1822 review two dramatic poems, *The Martyr of Antioch* (1822) and *Belshazzar* (1822), by the Reverend H. H. Milman, professor of poetry at Oxford University; Southey's *Remains of Henry Kirke White* (1807); poems by the Quaker poet Bernard Barton; Wordsworth's *Memorials of a Tour on the Continent, 1820* (1822); and, as the final review article in number 40, Thomas De Quincey's *Confessions of an English Opium Eater* (1822). By this time Roberts had suffered the frustration and humiliation of an exchange in print with Byron, which appears to have led him to withdraw as editor. He did not lose his sense of duty, however, for his final efforts as editor preserved the curious blend of books and subjects, religious and secular, which sustained the claim of the *British Review* to be a general review.

*Advice to a Young Reviewer* by Edward Copleston, Bishop of Llandaff (Wales), a seventeen-page pamphlet published in Oxford in 1807, provided the text for the self-promotion of the *British Review* as it entered into the competitive arena of early-nineteenth-century reviewing. The founders of the new review, having promoted "ourselves by our own authority to the office of Reviewers," announced that "the great object we proposed to ourselves was no less than to fill up a chasm in this department of literature, by endeavoring to lay before the public such observations upon books, *and upon the subjects* of which they treat, as our means of information, and judgment *unbiassed by party views, or private objects of ambition*, might suggest." Since readers would find this a familiar disclaimer, the writer adds, "We could not but observe, that every one of our contemporaries had set out with the professing, and of course with *intending* the same objects; yet had, almost without exception, entirely deviated from it." To avoid a similar fate, "It became . . . a matter of utmost concern to us, to discover by what fatality this deviation had been so occasioned, in hopes that we might ourselves avoid so common, yet apparently so disgraceful a failure." Discovery of the pamphlet under review "at once afforded a solution of our difficulties, and a vindication of our contemporaries." As a "tolerably complete specimen of that style in composition which the French call 'persiflage;' a style of which we confess ourselves, in general, not to be great admirers," *Advice to a Young Reviewer* offers a tongue-in-cheek account of contemporary reviewing and reviewers, an account the writer of the review begs to challenge while at the same time offering views of his own, especially in the latter portion of the review which purports to update the pamphlet. Beyond its pious claims for the high calling of reviewing and its obvious commentary on partisanship, the article advertises the moral purpose and high seriousness of the founders of the *British Review*.

*Advice to a Young Reviewer* proposes that he should write what will sell for "popularity cannot be attained without humouring the taste and inclinations of men." Further, he should not see himself as a magistrate but rather as a "cross-examining pleader" who may, as the reviewer observes, "put an end to all compunctious visitings of conscience," thereby becoming "exonerated from all *moral duties*, which we foolishly conceived to be attached to our office." In updating the pamphlet, the reviewer advises, "do not suppose that you are bound by any ties of justice or morality to undeceive *the public*. Your utility depends upon your influence: and your influence would be destroyed by so grievous a sin against your first principles, and so impolitic a sacrifice at the shrine of justice." Finally, the reviewer turns to religion and the claim on the public's attention of a literary review such as the *British*. "I cannot permit you to depart without a word or two of advice upon the subject of Religion. True it is, that nothing would contribute more to public utility than a Review, in which great talents were joined to liberal and honest views of improving the religious opinions and moral conduct of our countrymen." Of course, he continues in the ironic mode of *Advice to a Young Reviewer*, the way of the reviewing world offers little hope for anyone who would as a reviewer set out to support the cause of religion or to do good in the world. Dropping the ironic mask and his version of "persiflage," the reviewer concludes, "We are convinced that this whole system of modern reviewing, as explained in the preceding pages, is a gross libel upon the sound understandings and good dispositions of the well educated part of the people of England. We think that we perceive a confirmation of this opinion in the regret that we continually hear expressed, at the lamentable influence which the 'advice' above detailed has had upon this department of literature. And we should not prognosticate unfavourably of the public reception which would be given to a Review, conducted upon directly opposite principles; to one that is really honest and impartial in its intentions, and free from all selfish views and wilful perversions of truth. . . ." That the *British Review* survived for as long as it did was very likely owing to Roberts's belief that he and his quarterly had lived up to these guiding principles.

How effective the *British Review* had become by 1819 in "improving the religious opinions and moral conduct of our countrymen" cannot be measured, but the review of four major prose volumes by William Hazlitt in May of that year suggests how seriously the review went about its professed aim of undeceiving the public. The reviewer—almost surely William Roberts—considers Hazlitt as critic, lecturer, and moral essayist, but his subject throughout is Hazlitt the man, who, as writer, expresses ideas that are blasphemous, profane, and immoral and who, as thinker and stylist, is vulgar, inconsistent, and unintelligible. Yet it was not Hazlitt's apparent "notoriety, if not popularity, as a writer" that prompted an inquiry "into the validity of his pretentions. A stronger reason . . . has induced us to bestow some attention upon an author, whom as such we cannot but consider as below serious refutation. He is looked upon, if we are not mistaken, as one of the most promising representatives of a class of writers, whose aim appears to be to destroy the very foundations of morality and decorum, by a series of periodical attacks on all received opinions, and by the systematic ridicule of everything that is serious or respectable. Such at least is the obvious tendency of his loose manner of treating subjects which all good men think of with awe, and discuss with reverence; of the exaggerated importance which he attaches to things of, at most, but secondary consequence; and of the high colouring with which he represents ideas affecting the senses only, and in no way connected with the nobler purposes of man's existence." Hazlitt's claim for the stage as a primary source for refined manners and moral awareness leads the reviewer to chastise him for his taste in drama and for daring to claim "so foul a libel" as to suggest that Shakespeare "was 'the least moral of all writers.' " Hazlitt's taste in poetry he dismisses as merely conventional, and the passages he cites are to be "found in the common-place book of every intelligent school-boy." But if Hazlitt's favorite poets are everyone's, his attempts to write about poetry defy comprehension. To illustrate his contention, the reviewer offers—not altogether unjustly—a medley of quotations showing Hazlitt's excesses of language and concludes sarcastically, "all this may be very good, but we confess it is above the level of our tastes, capacities and feelings." Continuing the attack, he mocks Hazlitt's claim that he spent two years reading Jean-Jacques Rousseau's *Confessions* (1781-1788): "If some enemy to Mr. Hazlitt had told this to the world, he would have been accused of illiberality and misrepresentation; but the fact stands on his own authority, an earnest of his diligence, and a token of the liberal cultivation of his mind, though, for his own sake, we would hope that the recording angel, to borrow the image of Sterne, 'will drop a tear upon the page in which it is registered, to blot it from the history of his life for ever.' " Such moments of successful ridicule yield to lengthy and heavier-handed assaults on Hazlitt as an imposter posing as a connoisseur of painting and as an unpatriotic Jacobin.

But Hazlitt is chiefly offensive "in his character as a moral essayist" for "of all infidels, a scoffing infidel is, in our opinion, the most insufferable." He who "will not stop to be serious on the subject of religion, but jests and laughs at every thing that is sacred . . . has more to answer for than the argumentative unbeliever, or the reasoning holder of atheistical principles." Hazlitt's "worn out tirades against priests and priestcraft are light in the balance when compared with [his] profane flippancy, in daring to write that 'the first Methodist on record was David.' He chooses to represent him as being the first 'who made a regular compromise between religion and morality, between faith and good works. After any trifling peccadillo in point of conduct, as a murder, adultery, perjury, or the like, he ascended with his harp into some high tower of his palace, and having chaunted, in a solemn tone of poetical inspiration, the praises of piety and virtue, made his peace with heaven and his own conscience.' We will not pollute our pages with what follows and still less do we think it necessary to vindicate 'the man after God's own heart' from these random blasphemies"—yet that is precisely what the humorless evangelical reviewer, as defender of the innocent reader, does for nearly a page. After rescuing David from Methodism the reviewer asks in a final, patronizing appeal, "Will Mr. Hazlitt permit us in conclusion to say one word to him personally . . . ? There must have been a time when he was emulous of better things than would appear to be the case at present, . . . before his taste and feeling were perverted. We would intreat him, therefore, to consider for a moment whether he may not one day be called upon to answer for the impressions made by him on the minds of his readers, by presenting objects to their imaginations through delusive media, and in painted disguises.... Should Mr. Hazlitt live to be old, let him think on the decline of life he is preparing for himself, when his Mahometan paradise will be fast fading from before his eyes.... Lastly, let him take in good part our observations on the tendency of his writings, in the assurance that not one word of what we have felt it our duty to offer has been set down in malice, but has been written more in sorrow than in anger."

If the reviewer of Hazlitt wished to repeat John Gibson Lockhart's (1794-1854) first assault in *Blackwood's Edinburgh Magazine* (October 1817) against Leigh Hunt and the "Cockney School of Poetry" he fell short of his goal. Throughout Lockhart took aim at the literary pretensions of Hunt, but in several passages he outdid the *British Review* in defending values sacred to it in language as memorable as that of the *British Review* is forgettable. Setting aside questions about Lockhart's sincerity, his prose does more damage to his victim in a few witty thrusts than Roberts is able to achieve in pages of pious denunciation. The *British Review* had, from the beginning, rejected "persiflage" as its style in favor of a serious, more lofty tone, but given the twin aims of advancing a "true cause" and discrediting one's opponents, the witty maliciousness of a Lockhart is surely more effective—and surely more honest in its refusal to appear to be fair—than the manner of an editor and reviewer Donald H. Reiman has characterized as "a self-satisfied, humorless pedant," whose typical review Douglas K. Morris has summed up as having "top-heavy introductions only obliquely related to the book under consideration, ... moralistic digressions, ... animadversions on non-British cultures, and ... [a] lordly tone." While Roberts and the *British Review* deserve to be so described, it should also be noted that in his unfavorable reviews Roberts labors to suggest a balanced estimate of the work under consideration—a tactic Byron identified as that of a "Wolf in sheep's cloathing"—and solemnly prays that the offending writer will mend his ways and achieve the renown his genius seems to promise. This final characteristic, perhaps more than any other single feature of style, gives the *British Review* its distinctive voice.

Lockhart's second "Cockney School" article in *Blackwood's* (November 1817) focused on Leigh Hunt's *Story of Rimini* (1816). The treatment of that work in the *British Review*—when it is compared to reviews of the poem in *Blackwood's*, the *Quarterly*, and the *Edinburgh*—further suggests the distinctive style and bias of the *British*. The review by John Wilson Croker and William Gifford in the January 1816 number of the *Quarterly Review* antedates by more than two years Croker's famous April 1818 critique of Keats's *Endymion* (1818) in the same publication. Croker and Gifford's review of *The Story of Rimini* is remarkably similar in content, although considerably more effective in execution, to the May 1816 review of Hunt's book in the *British Review*. While each review praises portions of the poem (in this Roberts is seemingly more generous than Croker), they both attack Hunt personally, and he is taken to task for his deficiencies as poet and theorist about poetry. Croker censures Hunt for advancing a new principle of versification that he finds nothing more than an attempt to justify "an inaccurate, negligent, and harsh style of versification...." He turns next to Hunt's claim that "the proper language of poetry is in fact nothing different from that of real life" and finds "this passage, compared with the verses to which it preludes, affords a more extraordinary instance of self-delusion than even Mr. Hunt's notion of the merit of his versification; for if there be one fault more eminently conspicuous and ridiculous in Mr. Hunt's work than another, it is,—that it is full of *mere vulgarisms* and *fugitive phrases*, and that in every page the language is—not only not *the actual, existing language*, but an ungrammatical, unauthorised, chaotic jargon, such as we believe was never before spoken, much less written."

Roberts, in his wordy, circumvolutory way, makes a similar point: "As Mr. Hunt, we believe, is no great admirer of dignities and distinctions in political life, so neither will he allow any artificial difference between the language of poetry and of ordinary life. According to his theory we have all been poets without knowing it, and our common table-talk, if sufficiently animated, has in it all the elements of poetical composition." He further observes that "Mr. Hunt is, however, in happy contradiction to himself, in many passages of his little poem, which display a richness of expression, a vivacity in the colour of his words, and a chaste use of appropriate ornament, which show him to feel that poetry is an art, notwithstanding his industrious affection to hide it." Just as Roberts has discovered that Hunt is a poet in spite of himself, he also hopes "that one day or another we shall see Mr. Hunt emancipated from these very silly prejudices, and acknowledging in every language a diction of common use, and a diction of poetry;—a truth which every school-boy with good natural taste is sensible of almost as soon, and almost as distinctly, as he knows the difference between plain and plum pudding." Unfortunately, Roberts cannot stop after making his point in this homely way. Dropping his avuncular tone, he instructs Hunt about "vain affections" as "the great error of modern poetry" and further, "we warn him, too, against giving to gross nature the attractions of poetry, and conjure him not to add in future to the practice of borrowing from the passions assistance to poetry, instead of using poetry to elevate and purify the passions." He allows that Hunt has told the story of Paolo and Francesca "with great address," and even though it "has not a very delicate foundation, . . . it must be admitted, to his honour, that the superstructure which he has raised upon it is not a temple to licentious love, and that he has touched with as much decency, as the conduct of the story would admit, the crime of which he has pointed the consequences in the language of virtue." As psychologist and storyteller, Hunt deserves praise: "The slow underworking, the imperceptible progress of criminal passion, and the flattering security of conscious virtue, are represented with great truth and knowledge of nature, and convince us that Mr. Hunt might become a poet, if he would be content with being what he is, and divest himself of his retrograde ambition." Hunt is, however, guilty of numerous poetical sins: "He has also a very insipid affectation of trifling minuteness in collateral and mere circumstantial description, a certain garrulous prolixity of narration, which, in the favourite familiar idiom of this writer, degenerates almost into gossip." Roberts offers readers "a few out of a multitude of specimens of this familiar style" and then, in a typical volte-face, quotes a descriptive passage which illustrates that "Mr. Hunt can do better things." For a valedictory, Roberts again wishes "the author a safe deliverance from that silly scheme of poetical reform of which he vainly aspires to be the founder."

Roberts's review of Hunt's poem follows in the same article a review of Byron's *Parisina* (1816), a gloomy tale of incest that Byron expects readers of "delicacy or fastidiousness" to find "unfit for the purposes of poetry." Roberts, including himself in this group, drops any pretense of judicial reviewing and pronounces ex cathedra that "Lord Byron need not be told that his Poem of 'Parisina' is read in domestic circles, where parent and child, and brother and sister, are assembled to hear a tale of unnatural prostitution. We solemnly proscribe this poem from the English fire-side, and summon all that religion, morality, and policy enjoin, to give authority to the interdict." Relieved of the responsibility to acknowledge poetic merit the reviewer is "happy to be able to say in this instance, that the subject is not more objectionable than the poetry is contemptible."

In the *Quarterly* review of *The Story of Rimini* Croker, unlike Roberts in the *British*, remains focused, for the most part, on Hunt's poetry, noting when appropriate Hunt's ignorance of literature and his arrogance in presuming to address the subject of poetry. When he turns to Hunt's story he does not mention incest and adultery. Rather, he shows how lamely Hunt has versified passages in prose that he "found in the Specimens of Early English Romances." For Croker, the original prose "has far more of poetry, of sentiment and of nature" than what he describes as Hunt's "metrical adjustments" of it. He concludes his review with a backhanded compliment that does not appear to contradict his otherwise negative treatment of the poem: "We have but one word more to say of Mr. Hunt's poetry; which is, that amidst all his vanity, vulgarity, ignorance, and coarseness, there are here and there some well executed descriptions, and occasionally a line of which the sense and the expression are good. . . ."

Roberts and Croker very likely agreed about Hunt, both as a man and as a poet, because they shared conservative, eighteenth-century critical opinions about such matters as poetic diction, as well as Tory assumptions about church and nation. Yet as reviewers they differ not only in style but also in the concern they show for violations of what seem to them to be the canons of good art. As magistrate in the ecclesiastical court of public morality, Roberts always has his judicial robe at hand. Croker, as guardian of the membership lists of an exclusive club of literati, is ever vigilant against the incursions of imposters and upstarts who would dare to enter without a proper invitation. As evidence of this, in an epilogue to his review he notes that "Mr. Hunt prefixes to his work a dedication to Lord Byron, in which he assumes a high tone, and talks big of his '*fellow-*

*dignity*' and independence: what fellow dignity may mean, we know not . . . but this we will say, that Mr. Hunt is not more unlucky in his pompous pretension to versification and good language, than he is in that which he makes, in this dedication, to *proper spirit*, as he calls it, and *fellow-dignity*; for we never, in so few lines, saw so many clear marks of the vulgar impatience of a low man, conscious and ashamed of his wretched vanity, and laboring, with coarse flippancy, to scramble over the bounds of birth and education, and fidget himself into the *stout-heartedness* of being familiar with a LORD."

A similar hauteur and snobbery pervades Lockhart's "Cockney School" pieces, of which the first two deal with Hunt and *The Story of Rimini*. These review articles from the early numbers of *Blackwood's* are masterpieces of character assassination and make Roberts's ad hominem efforts fade by comparison. *Blackwood's* achieved instant fame and notoriety by being outrageous. In its early years—when John Wilson, John Gibson Lockhart, James Hogg, and William Maginn were contributors—it put style before principle and raised—or lowered—reviewing to a new level of personalism. In this league Roberts was no competitor not only for his style, which tended to heavy-handedness, but also because he took seriously his duty as spokesman for good manners, morality, and true religion. One wonders how the *British Review* might have fared had it been willing or able to employ a Lockhart who would write in defense of the principles of English Evangelicalism. In his October 1817 "Cockney School" article in *Blackwood's* Lockhart wrote, "Mr. Hunt is not disqualified by his ignorance and vulgarity alone, for being the founder of a respectable sect in poetry. He labours under the burden of a sin more deadly than either of these. The two great elements of all dignified poetry, religious feeling, and patriotic feeling, have no place in his writings. His religion is a poor tame dilution of the blasphemies of the *Encyclopaedie*—his patriotism a crude, vague, ineffectual, and sour Jacobinism. His works exhibit no reverence either for God or man; neither altar nor throne have any dignity in his eyes." At this point, Lockhart's flight of wit and ridicule carried him beyond religion and politics, ending eventually with a comparison of Hunt and Shakespeare's Bottom. It was meant to be fun, malicious fun perhaps, and not a straight-faced indictment of a man devoid of proper Tory religious or political feelings. Lockhart never lets his reader believe him to be capable of Roberts's high censoriousness. Yet, in his treatment of Hunt's *Story of Rimini* in the second "Cockney School" article, Lockhart subjects Hunt's poem to detailed criticism, including a comparison of it to other works of literature, including Byron's *Parisina*, which have incest as a theme. Unlike Roberts, who "solemnly proscribes" Byron's poem, Lockhart offers both an analysis which places Hunt's poem in historical and critical perspective and a detailed commentary on the poem itself. As Reiman notes, "Lockhart's substantive critical points on *The Story of Rimini* were so well taken that Hunt in his later revisions of the poem . . . corrected it to meet these objections." There is no evidence to suggest that Roberts had a comparable influence on any writer whose work he found objectionable.

The attacks on Leigh Hunt and other "Cockneys" in the *Quarterly Review*, *Blackwood's*, and in lesser reviews such as the *British Review* document the emphasis, in the period, on partisan, "slashing" criticism. Reviewing periodicals of the period were known for the writers they condemned, ridiculed, and maligned as well as those they praised and promoted. Francis Jeffrey and the *Edinburgh*, for example, consistently gave unfavorable reviews to the "Lake School." William Roberts, in the *British Review*, consistently praised congenial writers such as Joanna Baillie and Hannah More as well as a host of the long forgotten. Of the Romantic writers considered to be major figures today, William Wordsworth received favorable treatment by the *British Review*. For example, *The Excursion* (1814)—which Jeffrey greeted with his famous remark, "This will never do"—was praised in an April 1815 review in the *British Review*. The reviewer ("surely not William Roberts," according to Reiman) observes that the poem is a "sealed volume" for readers (presumably those like Jeffrey) who are unable to bring to its reading "a portion of the same meditative disposition, innocent tastes, calm affections, reverential feelings, philosophic habits, which characterize the poet himself; for readers of another kind we greatly fear, (and we deeply sympathize in the author's shame and mortification) that this poem 'will never do.' " In its length, its extensive quotations, and its systematic attention to the text, *The Excursion* review in the *British* resembles more clearly the example of Jeffrey than it does the typical Roberts review. Lacking Roberts's sanctimoniousness or patronizing tone, it offers readers a view of a poem which it praises throughout as poetry rather than a piece of morally correct literature. The review concludes by recapitulating its opening theme: "We end with the opinions with which we set out: this poem 'will never do' for persons without poetical enthusiasm, nor for persons without devotional warmth. 'The great, vulgar, and the small,' will not understand it; and by consequences it will not please them." The religious and political bias of this observation differs not a whit from the "position" of Evangelical Tories such as Roberts, but it is expressed simply and directly and in the context of a literary analysis. As such, it comes closer than Roberts typically does to the aim of the quarterly as expressed in the "Advice to a Young Reviewer" article of the first number. The reviewer's final observation on Wordsworth is based on a concept of critical relativism quite alien to Roberts's outlook: "But the writer [Wordsworth] may watch with calmness and confidence the fluctuations of taste; and despise, without any emotion of anger, the sarcasms of petulant conceit, sitting in judgment on superior intellect. If the present age be not fitted to receive his poem with reverence and gratitude, that age assuredly will come."

A similarly well-considered treatment of Wordsworth's *River Duddon* volume (1820) appeared in the September 1820 number of the *British Review* (very likely written, according to Reiman, by the "unidentified reviewer" who wrote on *The Excursion*). Wordsworth is praised for his poetical powers but taken to task for excess in his emphasis on simplicity. "We always leave Mr. Wordsworth with regret, but on no occasion have we left him with so much regret as on the present. He has touched in these poems some of the finest springs of natural pathos; and we do really think that there is enough in the collection before us to fix the wreath upon his brows too firmly to be torn off by his own hands in any of his fits of prosaic depression or temporary rage for simplicity"—a critical view which has surely stood the test of time better than the partisan judgments of the *Edinburgh Review*.

The *British Review* devoted more than two hundred pages to reviews of works by Byron during Roberts's tenure as editor. All of these reviews have been attributed to Roberts, and they reveal—perhaps more than any other of his writings—his sense of the critic as defender of good taste, morality, and decency. A June 1812 review of *Childe Harold's Pilgrimage*, Cantos I and II (1812), opens with an interminable preamble, the point of which is obscure but seems to be a resolve on the part of the reviewers of the *British Review* strictly to adhere "to the motto of their publication," *Fiat Justicia* (let there be justice), and to perform "their duty like gentlemen." After two pages devoted to the meaning of the words *childe* and *romance* the reviewer asserts, "the Childe Harold is no child of chivalry. Neither virtue nor enterprise is his. He has scarcely the qualifications of a paynim knight. He is in truth a mere son of sensuality, who has finished a long career of gross and selfish enjoyment by the notable discovery that nothing is good enough for him; and so resolves to travel for the sake of some refreshment to his jaded appetites, and to see if there be anything new under the sun. . . . But it is really too much to be told by this sort of man, with the authority of a preacher, that all is vanity, because, forsooth, he has chosen to abuse the capacities of his nature, and to despise the dictates of reason and religion. . . . But nothing is more sickening and insufferable than the whining morality of those, who, because they have placed their whole dependance upon enjoyments below the dignity and destination of man, and have had experimental proof of their inanity, affect the tone of philosophers, and talk with fastidious refinement of all sublunary pleasures." In spite of his disgust with the poem's hero, Roberts offers in the next eighteen pages numerous passages "to justify our general admiration of the genius displayed" in a poem containing language that, "though in general pure and grammatical, is disfigured by some negligencies, and some vulgarities." The review ends with a "sincere declaration of our respect for [Lord Byron's] genius and his talents" and with a Tory hope that young nobles entering public life will maintain the "dignity of the peerage by nobility of conduct; and to preserve it in its true elevation, the age of chivalry must partially return; without its ceremonies and its superstitions, indeed, but with that pure honour, that religious sentiment, and those high thoughts, which render an aristocracy the living rampart of the state, the throne, and the church."

In his February 1817 review of *Childe Harold's Pilgrimage. Canto the Third* (1816), Roberts censures Byron for the sameness of the Byronic Hero, the poem's unintelligibility, and its "nauseating topics." In his treatment of Waterloo in the poem, "Lord Byron seems to think that we have gained nothing by the victory of Waterloo except that military renown which it suits either his poetical or philosophical spleen magnanimously to despise." In spite of the poem's "vigorous and beautiful imagery," it is "wretchedly poor and vulgar in point of reasoning and reflection." Notwithstanding its unfavorable beginning, Roberts's review fluctuates between praise for passages of poetic merit and expressions of contempt for the poem's false and subversive ideas as well as the cynicism of "this authoritative castigator . . . that there may be some sincerity amongst us, though he has found it not,—that there may be two, or at least one, who 'are almost what they seem.'" The devout Tory solemnly goes on to "wish that Lord Byron, instead of reprobating us in terms so severe, would try to make us better. He has a powerful engine of moral persuasion in his hands, and might do much at this moment in diffusing among us the virtues of which we stand most particularly in need—loyalty, patriotism, charity, and content." Concluding, he gives Byron his due as a poet second only to Edmund Spenser for "variety of expression, boldness of imagery, and a certain opulence of expression derived from native resources," yet in a characteristic turn confesses "that there is in this poem neither the elevation of thought nor strength of delineation which are found in the Castle of Indolence, nor that picturesque display of character, and delicacy of touch in moral point, by which the Minstrel is distinguished, wherein is described the early call of the poet of nature to the fulfilment of his destiny, with the vigour and vivacity of conscious genius, and with the intelligence of an initiated votary, to whom the mysteries of poetic inspiration were known by experience."

In review after review, Roberts continued to single out lines and stanzas for praise while continuing to condemn Byron's ideas, his hero, and his failure to reform himself as a poet. In an August 1815 review of Byron's *Hebrew Melodies* (1815), a collection of lyric poems he found "obscure in expression," Roberts observed that "Lord Byron is not very likely to accept advice from the British Review. . . . But if he *would* take our advice, he would tell his minstrels to hang their 'harps upon the trees,' and would refuse to write any more Hebrew melodies." With uncharacteristic humor he wrote in an August 1817 review of *Manfred* (1817) that "as we have long considered Lord Byron as our patient, every resource of our medical skill has been tried from a soothing syrup, to a blistering plaster; but since this poem of 'Manfred' has appeared, we doubt whether any thing less potent than hellebore will prove efficacious." The *Manfred* review concludes, "We trust we have done justice to this little poem, which, as a drama, or as a whole we cannot praise; as a repetition of the old story of one of Lord Byron's pleasant fellows, full of crime, and yet full of conscious superiority, we cannot but condemn; but which, for its particular passages of poetical excellence, we consider as worthy of the fame of the author."

Roberts had not been so generous in his review of *The Siege of Corinth* (1816)—included in the same May 1816 review with Byron's *Parisina* and Hunt's *Story of Rimini*. Weary of the Byronic Hero and an unrepentant Byron as a negative influence on "Britannia's sons and daughters," the *British Review* wished "ardently . . . that we could prevail upon the noble poet whose work we are now considering to put in execution the promised retirement of his muse" or alternatively "if Lord Byron could be persuaded to expand his capabilities, and raise his poetical thoughts to their proper standard, he might soon perhaps be able to afford to abandon to their due condemnation all those miserable compositions which have flowed from his pen since the appearance of the Childe Harold and give us a hero instead of a malefactor." Byron, however, would neither retire as poet nor reform, thereby ensuring that Roberts would be forced to continue to do his duty and review each new work in turn. *Beppo* (1818), he asserted in a May 1818 review, is "an apparent parody on Lord Byron's poetry," a "bantering poem" in its treatment of adultery and the "product of a mind careless, cold and callous"—another threat to the moral well-being of Britannia's sons and daughters. Roberts concluded his discussion of *Beppo* with a promise to review the forthcoming canto of *Childe Harold*—an advertisement meant, perhaps, to attract prospective readers who might look forward to another installment in his continuing series on Byron, the misguided genius. He wrote, "We shall be happy to find in it [*Childe Harold*] some reparation for the injury done to the cause of virtue and religion by those [earlier cantos] which have appeared; and dread for [Byron's] sake, the accumulation of that fearful accountability which accompanies the gift of such great talents as unquestionably belong to him. We shall not fail to bestow on it that honest criticism which the important productions of genius have, we are sure, always experienced from us, whose pens are obedient to no motives or influences but the love of our dear country, its mind, and its character."

When the promised review of *Childe Harold's Pilgrimage. Canto the Fourth* (1818) appeared (August 1818), readers might well have agreed with Roberts when he wrote, "Those who have perused our former examination of Lord Byron's several poems, . . . will wonder what we have yet to say on this exhausted subject." What Roberts has to "say" on Byron's poem and on John Cam Hobhouse's *Dissertation on the Ruins of Rome; and an Essay on Italian Literature* (1818) required thirty-four pages to complete before ending on almost an elegiac note: "Our duty has been a painful one" for "nothing in either of the works we have been reviewing afford us a hope of our ever being made better or wiser by the intellectual exertions of either of these friends." Roberts views Byron "with less despair" than he does Hobhouse. The former is "many cubits higher in the stature of his capacity." In a final flourish of Roberts's pen, Byron the poet becomes Byron the Philistine hero who is opposed by God's champion, the true believer as David: "The staff of his spear is like a weaver's beam, and one bearing a shield goes before him. Against this giant and his armour-bearer, however, we have a humble assurance in our minds that God will still appropriate the victory to those who rely on his protection, believe in his word, and contend with his weapons."

Within a year Cantos I and II of Byron's *Don Juan* had appeared, and Roberts discovered what it was like to be one of the "giant's" victims. Stanzas 209 and 210 of Canto I include these lines:

> For fear some prudish readers should grow skittish,
> I've bribed my grandmother's review—the British.
>
> I sent it in a letter to the editor,
> Who thank'd me duly by return of post—
> I'm for a handsome article his creditor;
> Yet if my gentle Muse he please to roast,
> And break a promise after having made it her,
> Denying the receipt of what it cost,
> And smear his page with gall instead of honey,
> All I can say is—that he had the money.

Roberts replied in a three-page review (August 1819), in which no passage from the poem could be printed "without insult to the ear of decency, and vexation to the heart that feels for domestic or national happiness." Byron, he proclaims in a clumsy mixture of irony and self-justification, could not have been the author of the anonymous poem, for "it can hardly be possible for an English nobleman, even in his mirth, to send forth to the public the direct and palpable falsehood contained in the 209th and 210th stanzas of the first canto of this work. . . . No peer of the British realm can surely be capable of so calumnious a falsehood, refuted, we trust, by the very character and spirit of the journal so defamed. . . . Lord Byron could not have been the author of this assertion concerning us . . . not only because he is a British peer, but because he has too much discernment not to see how little like the truth such a statement must appear concerning a Review which has so long maintained, in the cause of public and private virtue, its consistency and purity, independently of all party and of all power. He knows in what a spirit of frankness and right feeling we have criticised his works, how ready we have been to do justice to their great poetical merit. . . ." Poor Roberts. Like William Lisle Bowles, another self-righteous apologist who was currently engaged with Byron and others in a pamphlet war over the issue of Alexander Pope's character and achievement as a poet, Roberts failed to see that Byron could not be answered without his victim appearing even more ridiculous.

On reading Roberts's review, Byron wrote to John Cam Hobhouse on 23 August 1819: "Had you any conception of a man's tumbling into such a trap as Roberts has done? Why it is precisely what he was wished to do." In a letter to John Murray of the same date Byron included a mock-serious letter ostensibly from an admirer and supporter of Roberts: "Letter to the Editor of 'My Grandmother's Review' " by Wortley Clutterbuck, posted from "Little Pidlington." To Murray he wrote, "I have had many proofs of man's absurdity but he [Roberts] beats all, in folly. —Why, the Wolf in sheep's cloathing has tumbled into the very trap.—We'll strip him." In another letter to Murray written the next day he added, "I wrote to you by last post—enclosing a buffooning letter for publication addressed to the buffoon Roberts—who has thought proper to tie a cannister to his own tail." More than a year later (8 October 1820) Byron wrote to Murray, "To be sure I took in the British Roberts finely—he fell precisely into the glaring trap laid for him—it was inconceivable how he could be so absurd as [to] think us serious with him." In the Clutterbuck letter Byron had great fun "explaining" the ambiguity in the reference to "my Grandmother's Review": "Some thought the allusion was to the *British Critic*; others, that by the expression, 'my Grandmother's Review,' it was intimated that 'my grandmother' was not the reader of the review, but actually the writer; thereby insinuating, my dear Roberts, that you were an old woman." On the question of the bribe he wrote: "I don't mean to insinuate, God forbid! but if, by any accident, there should have been such a correspondence between you and the unknown author, whoever he may be, send him back his money: I dare say he will be very glad to have it again: it can't be much, considering the value of the article and the circulation of the journal; and you are too modest to rate your praise beyond its real worth." Byron succinctly described the effect of his exchange with Roberts by concluding, "I cannot believe in the first instance, that you would receive a bribe to praise any person whatever; and still less can I believe that your praise could ever produce such an offer. You are a good creature, my dear Roberts, and a clever fellow; else I could almost suspect that you had fallen into the very trap set for you in verse by this anonymous Wag, who will certainly be but too happy to see you saving him the trouble of making you ridiculous." Byron's Clutterbuck letter was not immediately published. According to Thomas Moore, the letter was printed for Murray in a pamphlet of twenty-three pages, but not published until it appeared in the first issue of Leigh Hunt's *Liberal* (October 1822).

Roberts seems not to have recovered from the encounter although he continued to review or refer to Byron and his works in the *British Review*: twice in 1821 (June and December); twice in 1822 (March and December), the second in the final number he brought out as editor; in November 1824; and finally in May 1825, six months before the *British Review* ceased publication. To the last Roberts continued to damn Byron and to lament sanctimoniously the failure of the poet to achieve the greatness his genius portended. In his November 1824 review following Byron's death, he both praises that genius and warns, as self-professed "watchman for the moral weal of the community," of the tragedy in store for followers of Lord Byron. Earlier, in his review of *Don Juan, Cantos III, IV, and V* (December 1821), Roberts, after making his case against the poem, proposes to "add only two or three words principally respecting ourselves. Let us not be suspected of any feelings of hostility towards this anonymous author; nor even that we have treated his production with severity as a practical confutation of the lines in the former part of this work which charged us with having received a present from the author as a bribe to commend his performances. Such a nonsensically wicked assertion we felt it almost beneath us to contradict. The earth could not contain a man so stupid or so malignant as to give it credence. It carried in itself its own contradiction: no man offers a bribe, and then tells of it. To the stanza alluded to, therefore, our only answer shall be, that all who know us, or know how the British Review has at various times treated the poems of one who writes exactly in the style of this anonymous writer, must, we flatter ourselves, be satisfied that we can neither be bribed nor despised by the author of Don Juan."

Roberts was right. Byron neither bribed nor, it would appear, despised the *British Review*, but because Roberts could not take a joke—or leave it alone—he ensured that his cherished *British Review* would be known henceforth as "my grandmother's review—the British."

**References:**

John O. Hayden, *The Romantic Reviewers, 1802-1824* (Chicago: University of Chicago Press, 1969);

William H. Marshall, *Byron, Shelley, Hunt, and* The Liberal (Philadelphia: University of Pennsylvania Press, 1960);

Douglas K. Morris, Entry on the *British Review*, in *British Literary Magazines*, 4 volumes, edited by Alvin Sullivan (Westport, Conn.: Greenwood Press, 1983-1986), II: 68-76;

Donald H. Reiman, ed., *The Romantics Reviewed: Contemporary Reviews of British Romantic Writers*, 9 volumes (New York & London: Garland, 1972);

Arthur Roberts, *The Life, Letters, and Opinions of William Roberts* (London: Seeleys, 1850);

W. S. Ward, "The 'Lake' Poets and Their Contemporary Magazine Critics, 1798-1820," *Studies in Philology*, 42 (January 1945): 87-113;

Ward, "Lord Byron and 'My Grandmother's Review,' " *Modern Language Notes*, 64 (January 1949): 25-29;

Ward, "Some Aspects of the Conservative Attitude Toward Poetry in English Criticism," *PMLA*, 60 (June 1945): 386-398.

# The Eclectic Review

*(January 1805 - December 1868)*

Dana S. Litherland

In the early nineteenth century, periodical publications became a major form of religious expression for Evangelicals in England. The *Eclectic Review* originated in 1805 as an Evangelical counterpart to the *Edinburgh* and *Quarterly* reviews. Remembered today mainly by theological historians, the Evangelicals who conducted the publication were fundamental in establishing the moral tone of the magazine, which provided a forum for their sermons and essays dealing with various aspects of Nonconformity. From its inception the magazine foreshadowed the repressive moral climate of the Victorian era, and it flourished well into that period. Evangelical moral principles determined what type of literature was reviewed and how it was received. Yet, aside from the moral slant of its reviews of Romantic poets and prose writers, the magazine demonstrated a more comprehensive coverage of literature than many other religious periodicals, and it also covered a variety of intellectual topics, which encouraged a broad secular circulation.

Few of the Evangelicals associated with the *Eclectic Review* were particularly well known outside religious circles. The *Eclectic* was edited in 1805 by a Dissenting preacher named Samuel Greatheed. Though he conducted the *Eclectic* for only one year, his influence endured. It was Greatheed who determined that the magazine would "pursue a different track from that in which Reviews have hitherto been conducted." In the prospectus to the inaugural issue (January 1805) he explained that the main objective of the *Eclectic* was "to blend with impartial criticism an invariable regard to moral and religious principle." What he meant by "impartial" is uncertain, since most reviews in the magazine were heavily disposed to moralizing. Greatheed went on to comment on the reviewing of some contemporary periodicals: "If warped by *interested motives*, or *contaminated* with *important errors*, works of periodical criticism become *baneful* instead of *beneficial*, in proportion to the talents of their conductors; and to the extent of their circulation."

The magazine was, however, able to exist "free of the influence of party-spirit." Editorials fostered religious unity, and the editors were determined to avoid confrontations between various religious sects. As Greatheed eloquently summarized the political policy of the magazine in January 1805, "Neither excluding nor admitting indiscriminately the sentiments of any party, religious or political . . . (we) select from all whatever appears . . . to be sanctioned by reason, experience, and revelation. Things in which we differ from each other, we agree to leave undecided."

In 1806 Greatheed was succeeded by fellow Dissenter Daniel Parken, who edited the *Eclectic* until his death in 1812. He was responsible for attracting reviewers John Foster and James Montgomery to the magazine. Theophilus Williams, a Dissenter who later conformed and took orders, edited the *Eclectic* from 1812 to 1814, a period in which the faltering *Eclectic* was nearly condemned to extinction. The next editor was Josiah Conder, a writer and bookseller, who became highly regarded in Evangelical circles as the *Eclectic* matured under his management, which continued through the end of 1836.

The *Eclectic Review* was piloted by Conder and Foster throughout most of the Romantic era. Both proprietor and editor of the magazine, Conder was a Nonconformist whose dedication to the cause of religious freedom was reflected in his book *On Protestant Nonconformity* (1818) and in the *Patriot*, a weekly Evangelical newspaper which he began editing in 1832. He was respected in contemporary literary circles as well as among Evangelicals, corresponding frequently with Robert Southey and James Montgomery. John Foster, a Baptist minister, compiled some of his 184 articles in *Contributions, Biographical, Literary, and Philosophical, to the Eclectic Review* (1844). Deeply concerned about the intellectual alienation of Evangelicals in society, Foster also wrote an essay titled

"On Some of the Causes by Which Evangelical Religion has been Rendered Less Acceptable to Persons of Cultivated Taste" (1826). While the articles in many Evangelical periodicals were almost exclusively theological, Conder and Foster aimed to unite religion and learning in their magazine, which, because of its intellectual seriousness, ranked as one of the most cultured Evangelical publications. Both Conder and Foster wrote literary reviews for the magazine.

Beginning in 1806, James Montgomery, whose poetry was especially admired by Evangelicals, was a principle literary reviewer for the *Eclectic*. Later in his life he remarked that he had reviewed "every contemporary of note except Byron" in its pages. Montgomery was not a particularly insightful critic, and though he has been praised for impartiality, he tended to judge literary works in terms of his own moral and religious beliefs, as did Conder.

In general reviewers for the *Eclectic* agreed with the philosophy of the *Christian Observer*, which concluded that "a poem must, after all be criticised as a work of taste; and there is one rule for the appreciation of moral and another for that of literary excellence." The criticism found in the *Eclectic* combined Evangelical morality and comprehensive analysis in a manner which was unparalleled in most contemporary Evangelical reviews. Like secular periodicals such as the *Edinburgh* and *Quarterly* reviews, the *Eclectic Review* adhered to eighteenth-century Neoclassical criteria in its literary criticism. The *Eclectic*, however, put a stronger emphasis upon morality than these magazines. The reviewers for the *Eclectic* lamented that few modern writers showed any real awareness of eternity. John Foster once commented that most polite literature was hostile to Christianity. In addition, one reviewer for the magazine commented that "there is a great deal of modern poetry, that is ill-adapted to make its readers either the wiser, the better, or the happier" (February 1821). Yet the magazine's attitude toward contemporary literature was best summarized by a reviewer in June 1826:

> We deeply lament the grossness which so far deteriorates their high qualities, as to exclude a large portion of our wealthiest literature from the staple of safe and commendable reading. Still they must, to a certain extent, be studied by all, who are anxious to ascertain the finest characteristics of English style, or the complete range of English genius.

While many Evangelical magazines refused to review secular literature or offered only condemnations, the *Eclectic* differentiated between the inherent literary value and moral values.

This policy toward secular literature was not always consistently applied, however. In January 1805 the *Eclectic* echoed a common belief among Evangelicals, that "the habit of perusing novels . . . tends to dissipate, and commonly mislead the mind." This distrust of the novel may be traced to the eighteenth-century belief that novel reading created false expectations in young girls, aroused their passions, and encouraged loose living in general. Also denouncing "the refuse of the circulating-library and of the theatre," the *Eclectic* (in January 1805) preferred to focus on "vehicles of useful information and rational entertainment," expressing the attitude that eventually led to censorship of popular fiction, or "Grundyism," in the Victorian period.

By the third decade of the nineteenth century, novels were becoming legitimized, with secular magazines such as the *Quarterly Review* commenting in 1821, "The times seem to be past when an apology was requisite for condescending to notice a novel." While many Evangelical magazines continued to maintain moral prejudices against novels, the *Eclectic* was gradually influenced by contemporary attitudes toward fiction. Magazines such as the *Christian Observer* blamed Sir Walter Scott for the increasing number of Evangelical novel readers, and the *Eclectic* continued to maintain that the genre was "a class of works which has but doubtful claim on our notice" (June 1820). Yet, unlike the *Christian Observer*, they spoke highly of Scott and quoted at length from his works. In a November 1819 critique of Scott's *Tales of my Landlord*, the reviewer conceded, "We will not dispute that a service is rendered to the lovers of light reading, by writers of superior talent . . . who furnish the public with amusements more deserving of the name intellectual, than the generality of novels." The *Eclectic* commended Scott's endeavors: "Tales of this Author will at any rate have one good effect, that of inducing a taste for intellectual excitement of a higher order, which shall render the trash of circulating libraries, the inane productions of the needy panders to sentimentalism, no longer palatable." By the Victorian era, as Evangelicals became novel readers, circulating libraries had changed to accommodate the Evangelicals' taste for moral fiction.

The *Eclectic Review* reflected the Evangelicals' classical tastes for poetry that was designed "to please, to gratify the imagination, and to touch the softer feelings." They read descriptive poetry because it was unlikely to instill immoral ideas or to inflame the passions. Sir Walter Scott and Robert Southey were the contemporary poets most admired by Evangelicals, and the *Eclectic* praised them. Josiah Conder favored Scott's poetry over that of the metaphysical poets because in Scott "there is, perhaps, scarcely a sentiment expressed, or a feeling described, which the humblest intellect would find it difficult to understand" (January 1816). By contrast, he asserted the metaphysicals tended to alienate readers with their abstractions. The *Eclectic* accused Southey of using myth and allegory too often while lacking feeling on religious subjects. Yet they found much to praise in his works. Conder's July 1816 review of Southey's *Poet's Pilgrimage to Waterloo* declared that "whatever he writes is at least interesting . . . it bears the stamp of character,—of the man and of the poet." Evangelicals often had difficulty distinguishing between art and life, tending to believe that a poet always spoke in his own voice rather than adopting a persona. They often compared poetry with sermons, and thus expected poets to be preachers of moral wisdom. Judging by the reviews in the *Eclectic*, the poetry of Scott and Southey came closest to meeting these demands.

William Wordsworth was highly esteemed by the *Eclectic* reviewers, although they strongly encouraged him to replace metaphysical objects with moral ones in his poetry. In the eyes of Evangelicals, Wordsworth's talents qualified him as a spokesperson for their moral ideology. James Montgomery spoke with conviction in January 1815, when he declared that "no one living is more eminently gifted . . . than Mr. Wordsworth." However, Montgomery's religious biases were evident throughout this review of *The Excursion* (1814). He encourages the poet to "sing of Christ's Kingdom," and he criticizes Wordsworth for concealing his Christian faith. Montgomery also feels that Wordsworth's reverence for nature is extreme, "difficult to distinguish from . . . the homage due to the Supreme alone." He maintains that "a Philosophical Poem, containing views of *Man*, *Nature*, and *Society*, would be miserably imperfect if it involved no contemplations on the eternal destiny of man." Notwithstanding his dislike of what he considered Wordsworth's impious subjects, Montgomery's review of *The Excursion* is more positive than criticism offered by Sir Francis Jeffrey in the *Edinburgh Review* (November 1814). In general, the *Eclectic* accorded more praise to Wordsworth than most contemporary reviews. Referring to the *Lyrical Ballads* in a January 1808 review of Wordsworth's *Poems* (1807), Montgomery praised him as "one of the boldest and most fortunate adventurers in this age of poetical experiment." Moreover, Josiah Conder demonstrated an open-minded attitude toward Wordsworth's innovative genius in his January 1816 review of *The White Doe of Rylstone* (1815). He remarked that the poet's "bold and determined nonconformity to the creeds and rules of established usages, marks him out as a poetical schismatic." In a portion of his lengthy commentary: Conder was critical of the contemporary reaction to Wordsworth:

> Strictly speaking, it will generally, perhaps always, be found, that a writer's peculiarities are his faults: in their excellencies, men resemble each other. . . . From a character with which ordinary persons cannot sympathize, of the inner springs of which they can know little—and such a character, judging from his productions, we must conceive Mr. Wordsworth's to be—we may naturally expect a degree of singularity in its productions, which ill deserves to be submitted to the flippancy of opinion, but which must, nevertheless, interfere with the impression that their excellencies are adapted to produce.

Conder was less appreciative of Samuel Taylor Coleridge's talents. Like most of his contemporaries, Conder, reviewing *Christabel. Kubla Khan, A Vision: The Pains of Sleep* (1816) for the June 1816 issue, found *Kubla Khan* incomprehensible. The opium vision prompted Conder to urge Coleridge to "break off his desultory and luxurious habits and to brace his mind to intellectual exertion." Not all of the magazine's reviews of Coleridge were totally impercipient, however. In his *Coleridge: The Critical Heritage* (1970), J. R. de J. Jackson recognizes the insight of the review of *The Friend* (1809-1810) that appeared in the October 1811 issue:

> During these early years appreciative comments were rare. One of the few was a long, detailed, and enthusiastic review of *The Friend*, which appeared in the *Eclectic Review*. The review deserves a careful reading as the first description of Coleridge's thought and prose style, and for its anticipation of later apologists. . . . More than

> ten years were to pass before Coleridge was to be served as well by a reviewer.

The reviewer has since been identified as John Foster, who—of all the members of the *Eclectic* staff—was best suited to evaluate "the distinguishing properties of *The Friend's* intellectual and literary character." He distinguishes Coleridge from his contemporary poets: "He always carries on his investigation at a depth, and sometimes a profound depth, below the uppermost and most accessible stratum; and is philosophically mining among its most recondite principles of the subject, while ordinary intellectual and literary workmen . . . are pleasing themselves and those they draw around them, with forming to pretty shapes or commodious uses, the materials of the surface." Foster's review is one of the finest examples of the comprehensive literary analyses that appeared in the *Eclectic Review*.

Reviews of the Lake poets contrasted sharply with reviews of George Gordon, Lord Byron in the *Eclectic*. Yet despite "the prominence which is given to voluptuous themes and visions, and the licentious manner in which they are frequently celebrated" in Byron's poetry, the *Eclectic* reviewed his works more than those of any other major Romantic writer. In the November 1807 critique quoted above of *Hours of Idleness* (1807) an unidentified reviewer served Byron "with a few admonitions which he is not very likely to hear from any other quarter." Two pages of the three-page review are devoted to reforming the "Noble Lord," as the reviewer encourages the poet to be "upright, moral, humane, and religious." In a 20 January 1808 letter to R. C. Dallas, Byron responded to the criticism by calling the review "a furious Philippic, not against the book but the author." The *Eclectic* refused to review *Don Juan*, Cantos I and II (1819), commenting in its August 1819 review of Byron's *Mazeppa*:

> Poetry which it is impossible not to read without admiration, yet, which it is equally impossible to admire without losing some degree of self-respect; such as no brother could read aloud to his sister, no husband to his wife;—poetry in which the deliberate purpose of the Author is to corrupt by inflaming the mind, to seduce to the love of evil which he has himself chosen as his good; can be safely dealt with in one way, by passing it over in silence.

The *Eclectic* reviewers actually held a "very high opinion of the genius" of the poet whom they found morally offensive. The early cantos of *Childe Harold's Pilgrimage* (1812), *The Gaiour* (1813), and *The Corsair* (1814) were praised highly by the magazine in June 1812, November 1813, and April 1814, respectively. Moreover, in his review of *The Corsair* Conder disagreed with contemporaries who believed that his poems led to the corruption of readers' morals:

> If in any degree they may lessen our abhorrence of vice, by making our sympathy predominate over the principle, rather than by counteracting its influence, they at the same time, deepen our conviction of the miseries inseparably connected with a departure from virtue. . . .
>
> . . . It is but justice to say, that there is nothing, so far as we recollect, in his poems, which displays any design, or which is in itself calculated to corrupt the virtuous mind, to raise a guilty glow of pleasure, or to delude the imagination into a love of splendid crime. There is, at least, a highly moral lesson to be deduced, *if the readers please*, from his poetry.

While the *Eclectic* offered fewer condemnations of Byron's poetry than most Evangelical periodicals, it shared the Evangelical belief that writers such as Byron, who perpetuated an anti-Christian view of life, must be motivated by the desire for fame. The magazine predicted that the popularity of his works would continue precisely because they satisfied society's immoral curiosities.

The *Eclectic* criticized John Keats severely. In a September 1817 review Conder conceded to "an immature promise of possible excellence" evident in Keats's *Poems* (1817), but, Conder adds, "Unless Mr. Keats has designedly kept back the best of his mind, we must take the narrow range of ideas and feelings in these Poems, as an indication of his not yet having entered in earnest on the business of intellectual acquirement, or attained the full development of his moral faculties." Conder, himself an aspiring poet, regrets that he has "the power, to dash to the ground, by his pen, the innocent hopes of a youth struggling for honourable distinction." He adds, however, that when a young man has been "flattered into the resolution to publish verses, of which a few years hence he shall be glad to escape remembrance. The lash of a critic is the thing least to be dreaded, as the penalty of premature publication." Bitter attacks on *Endymion* (1818) which appeared in the *Quarterly Review* (April 1818) and *Blackwood's* (August 1818) influenced Conder's second and final review of Keats, in September 1820. He was unable to divorce the image of Keats as the "unfortunate 'Author of Endymion' " from his criticism. Of the now-celebrated lines from *Ode on a Grecian Urn*—" 'Beauty is truth, truth beauty,'—that is all / Ye know on earth, and all ye need to know"—Conder comments, "That is all that Mr. Keats knows or cares to know.—But till he knows more than this, he will never write verses fit to live." Throughout Keats's mythological work *Lamia* ("decidedly the best" of the longer poems), Conder finds a "school boy taste" for classics: "Had he passed through the higher forms of liberal education, . . . he would have known that the last use which a full-grown scholar thinks of making of his classical acquirements, is to make a parade of them either in prose or verse." For Evangelicals, a knowledge of the classics was essential for reading scriptures. Some asserted that classical training was conducive to morality. Conder's reproval of the poet's use of his classical education derived from these views. Conder also severely denounced Keats and his works on moral grounds, describing the poet as being "in a diseased state of feeling, arising from the want of . . . the regulating principle of religion." Similarly, his productions had an apparent "sickliness" about them, "which shews that there is mischief at the core." From a modern vantage point, Conder was obviously mistaken when he declared that Keats's immortal verses "will not live very long." He failed to judge Keats independently from the blemished reputation he obtained by the association of his name with Leigh Hunt's. For this reason, the *Eclectic* ranks among the contemporary publications whose bitter attacks were blamed for Keats's early demise.

Probably because his attitude toward religion so opposed the Evangelical views of the magazine, Percy Bysshe Shelley was reviewed only once in the *Eclectic*, in October 1816, when Conder chose to review *Alastor* (1816). He acknowledged the poet's "very considerable talent for descriptive poetry," but faulted the morality of the poem: "It exhibits utter uselessness of imagination, when wholely undisciplined, and selfishly employed for the mere purposes of luxury, without reference to those moral ends which it was designed to be subservient." Conder believed that Shelley, whose antireligious sentiments were widely known, had "a genius which might be turned to much better account." That is, he wished Shelley's poetry could be morally useful. What Shelley offered instead, "such heartless fictions as *Alastor*, fail in accomplishing the *legitimate purposes* of *poetry*." Shelley's works did not qualify as examples of the morally didactic poetry that the *Eclectic* wished to recommend for its readers.

Similarly, the *Eclectic* could not recommend Thomas De Quincey's controversial autobiography, *Confessions of an English Opium Eater* (1822). The work includes "so much that is objectionable and positively disgusting," that the *Eclectic* almost passed it over. Yet the reviewer (April 1823) set aside moral prejudices and approached the work in the context of a medical documentary on opium addiction. De Quincey, the "patient," is compared to other addicts, and expert testimony on opium addiction is provided from the London College of Physicians. Compared to the doses taken by "Mustapha the Smyrna Opium Eater," who reportedly consumed three drams a day, De Quincey's daily opium consumption, recorded in the autobiography, was minimal. The reviewer felt that a more accurate title for the work would have been "*Confessions of an English Laudanum Drinker*," given the fact that De Quincey "never ate a grain of opium in his life." Had he not painted such a "seductive picture" of his habit, De Quincey might have been given "credit for intending by this volume to make some atonement for the misspent and irrevocable past." The reviewer determined, however, that the work might encourage readers to pursue the habit and therefore denounced it as "quite worthless." Instead of focusing on the literary merit of the work, the *Eclectic* chose to expose "factual" contents.

The conductors of the *Eclectic* communicated a wide variety of information to educate its readership. In addition to literature, the *Eclectic* reviewed books in history, philosophy, science, mathematics, astronomy, natural history, anatomy, medicine, and other fields. The diversity of the magazine was enhanced by contributors such as Olinthus Gilbert Gregory, a prominent mathematician, scientist, and theologian, and Isaac Taylor, an artist, author, and inventor. Utilitarian philosopher James Mill frequently contributed articles and reviews. Another contributor was artist-antiquary James Douglas, who traveled around the world, discovering valuable relics from ancient Celtic, British, Roman, and Danish ceremonies in Great Britain. Numerous contributions from experts on world affairs and travel enabled the *Eclectic* to maintain an international scope. American literature, Latin poetry, Chinese language and culture, and histories of Europe, the Middle East, and Africa are only a sample of the international subjects in the publication. More general information was offered by the *Eclectic* than any other Evangelical periodical in the nineteenth century. The *Eclectic Review* lived up to its title.

Because of its wide-ranging articles, the *Eclectic Review* was one of the few Evangelical magazines which appealed to secular tastes. Its popularity in the secular world undoubtedly enhanced the magazine's longevity. Yet his biographer quotes Conder as lamenting the lack of support the magazine received from Evangelicals: "It is thrown away upon the Dissenters. They prefer the *Evangelical Magazine* and the *Congregational*. . . . I am continually receiving testimonies from those who are *without*."

The magazine appealed to a highly literate audience, and the social restrictions on education for Dissenters may explain why many of them read other religious periodicals and ignored the cultured *Eclectic*. Excluded, because of their religious beliefs, from taking degrees at Oxford or Cambridge until 1854, many Evangelicals managed to reach the middle class through manufacturing and business endeavors. Aimed at this social group, not the aristocracy, the *Eclectic* promoted respectability and cultivated literary tastes. In January 1805 its founder sought "numerous and respectable classes of society . . . possessed of general intelligence, and laudably desirous of practical information." Efforts were continually made to keep the price within the budgets of the middle and lower-middle classes. The low price facilitated circulation, helping the *Eclectic Review* "to unite the advancement of literature with the welfare of mankind."

The *Eclectic Review* thrived well into the Victorian era, surviving many contemporary secular and religious periodicals. When he resigned from his editorship in December 1836, Conder marveled at the demise of several established periodicals, including *Blackwood's*, the *Quarterly Review*, and the *Christian Review*, all of which were outlived by the *Eclectic*. His observation inspired the question, "where is the literary world into which we entered?" Since the *Eclectic* was founded in 1805, the literary world had changed dramatically. Yet the stability of the *Eclectic* was enhanced rather than hindered by the Victorian age. In fact, its popularity with secular readers, which predated the Victorian era, contributed to the shift in moral climate during the Victorian period, and its Evangelical morality ensured its continued appeal in Victorian society. The *Eclectic Review* never wavered from its design to "employ the influence of literature in promoting the prevalence of true religion and morality."

**References:**

Eustace R. Conder, *Josiah Conder: A Memoir* (London: J. Snow, 1857);

Gary Kelly, *English Fiction of the Romantic Period* (London: Longman Group, 1989);

Donald H. Reiman, ed., *The Romantics Reviewed*, 9 volumes (New York & London: Garland, 1972);

Doreen M. Rosman, *Evangelicals and Culture* (London: Croom & Helm, 1984), pp. 166-222;

Jonathan Edwards Ryland, *The Life and Correspondence of John Foster* (London: Jackson & Walford, 1846);

Joan Shattock and Michael Wolff, eds., *The Victorian Periodical Press: Samplings and Surroundings* (Leicester: Leicester University Press, 1982);

Alvin Sullivan, ed., *British Literary Magazines: The Romantic Age, 1789-1836* (Westport, Conn.: Greenwood Press, 1983);

David M. Thompson, *Nonconformity in the Nineteenth Century* (London: Routledge & Kegan Paul, 1972).

# The Edinburgh Review

*(October 1802 - October 1929)*

Thomas L. Cooksey
*Armstrong State College*

"I think the commencement of. the Edinburgh Review an important epoch in periodical criticism," declared Samuel Taylor Coleridge in the *Biographia Literaria* (1817), reflecting on the early reception of William Wordsworth and himself. He suggested that the *Edinburgh Review* had initiated the scheme of reviewing only those books which merited critical commentary, ignoring the rest, and replacing them with "original essays on the most interesting subjects of the time, religious, or political; in which the titles of the books or pamphlets prefixed furnished only the name and occasion of the disquisition." Coleridge went on to complain that the *Review* was often guilty of ad hominem attacks on him and others, and that they had failed to appreciate the true significance of Wordsworth. In his notebooks, he also confided his distrust of the authority of the "High & Mighty Edinburghers" as the "Guardians & Overseers of Taste & Poetry," comparing them to the tone-deaf Saint Cecilia. Whatever his doubts about merits of the "Edinburghers," Coleridge's estimate of their place in literary history was both perceptive and accurate. The publication of the first issue of the *Edinburgh Review* in October 1802 initiated a new kind of literary journalism. It established itself and its editor in the role of cultural arbiter, a role held by it and similar journals for the rest of the century. When James Hogg called editor Francis Jeffrey "an intellectual Buonaparte," he commented both on his intellectual merits and on his power and influence in the realm of letters. By the middle of the nineteenth century it had become such an important cultural institution in its own right that Walter Bagehot could quip in the *National Review* (October 1855) that the younger generation "has always regarded the appearance of that periodical as a grave constitutional event (and been told that its composition is intrusted to Privy Councillors only)." Given such a venerable and dignified reputation, it was surprising, Bagehot noted, to realize that the *Review* was once looked upon as an "incendiary publication."

The *Edinburgh Review* was founded in 1802 by four young men. The Reverend Sidney Smith (1771-1845) was the oldest at thirty-one; Francis Jeffrey (1773-1850) was twenty-nine; Francis Horner (1778-1817) and Henry Brougham (1778-1868) were both twenty-four. Born in Scotland, and educated at the University of Edinburgh, Jeffrey, Horner, and Brougham were lawyers with a taste for philosophical speculation, literature, and political economy. Smith, by contrast, was English, educated at Winchester and New College, Oxford, and had come to Edinburgh as the tutor of Michael Hicks-Beach, who was then studying at the university. Smith enjoyed the city, finding that it combined the amenities of invigorating climate, good libraries, learned men, and "large healthy virgins." It was among the literary circles and debating societies such as the Speculative Society and the Academy of Physics that Smith made the acquaintance of Jeffrey and the others, eventually proposing to them the idea of establishing a periodical. In 1802 Scottish political life was under the control of Henry Dundas, Viscount Melville, who had been home secretary, secretary of war, and a lord of the Admiralty in the administration of William Pitt. In his capacity as home secretary, Dundas ruled Scotland, and the Tories dominated the Edinburgh bar, with the result that Whigs or Whig sympathizers had little opportunity for preferment or political office. Deeply imbued with the principles and spirit of the Scottish Enlightenment—and its sympathy both to the French Enlightenment and much of the French Revolution—that they had received under their professor Dugald Stewart, Jeffrey, Horner, and Brougham styled themselves as "philosophical Whigs." They saw a periodical as a vehicle to advance their political and philosophical ideas as well as their careers. While Jeffrey remained initially skeptical of the prospects for such a project, and Brougham, calculating the political advantages, withdrew from the first issues only to return later, arrangements for publication were made with the Edinburgh publisher Archibald

*The first publisher of the* Edinburgh Review

Constable, who already published the *Farmer's Almanac* and the *Scots Magazine*. (The *Review* was distributed in England by the London publisher Thomas Norton Longman, who took over full publication and distribution in 1827.) Sporting a blue-and-buff cover, the colors of the Foxite Whigs, and carrying the motto "*Judex damnatur cum nocens absolvitur*" ("The judge is condemned when a criminal is set free"), by the Roman writer Publius Syrus, 750 copies of the first number of *Edinburgh Review* appeared on 10 October 1802 at five shillings a copy. (Smith had first proposed *Tenui musam meditamur avena* [We cultivate literature on a little oatmeal] for the motto.) These copies proved so successful that additional editions of the first number were in press by November. In Edinburgh alone, it sold some 2,150 copies. Thereafter, the *Review* appeared in January, April, July, and October until it ceased publication in October 1929, after some 250 issues. By 1813 it boasted about twelve thousand subscribers, reaching a maximum of about thirteen thousand in 1814. (In contrast the London *Times* had only eight thousand subscribers in 1814.) The *Review* inspired several competitors that imitated its format and challenged its politics. These included most notably the *Quarterly Review* to its right, founded in 1809 by Sir Walter Scott, George Ellis, John Murray, and others, and the *Westminster Review* to its left, founded in 1824 by Jeremy Bentham and James Mill. Other imitators included the *Annual Review* (founded 1803), *Eclectic Review* (founded 1805), the *London Review* (founded 1809), and *Blackwood's Edinburgh Magazine* (founded 1817).

The first issue, the product of "all gentlemen, and no pay," was edited by Smith, with contributions from the other founders. When it became clear that the *Review* would be successful, Smith negotiated with Constable to pay the editor and contributors and convinced Jeffrey to take over the role of editor. The editor received the generous pay of fifty pounds an issue (two hundred per volume), while a contributor received ten pounds a sheet (sixteen printed pages). In a 21 January 1831 letter to his brother John, Thomas Carlyle explained his preference for writing for the magazine: "There is no periodical so steady as the *Edinburgh Review*, the salary fair, the vehicle respectable." Jeffrey recollected that while hesitant to take on the responsibilities of sole editorship, "300 pounds a year is a monstrous bribe to a man in my situation." Jeffrey held the editorship from January 1803 to June 1829, when he relinquished it to his son-in-law Macvey Napier (1776-1847) in order to become dean of the Faculty of Advocates. Napier held the position from October 1829 until January 1847.

Several factors contributed to the early success of the *Edinburgh Review*. While it was not the first general periodical, it differed from its chief competitors, the *Monthly Review*, the *Critical Review*, and the *British Critic*, in at least three regards. First, it proposed to alter the basic conception of the literary journal. The traditional reviews aimed at an inclusive digest of information. "They were conceived," says Derek Roper, "as installments of a continuous encyclopedia, recording the advance of knowledge in every field of human enterprise." The ever-increasing flow of information and the crush of new publications undermined this enterprise, making inclusiveness impossible. Instead, the *Edinburgh Review* developed a principle of selectivity, commenting on those books that had already established themselves. As the "Advertisement" in the first issue declared,

> the Conductors of the Edinburgh Review propose to carry this principle of selection a good deal farther; to decline any attempt at exhibiting a complete view of modern literature; and to confine their notice, in great degree, to works that either have attained, or deserve, a certain portion of celebrity.

As a result, the magazine decreased the number of books reviewed, and increased the length of the individual reviews. The issue that appeared in October 1802 had twenty-nine articles. By contrast the *Monthly Review* had forty-four that month; the *Critical* had sixty; and the *British Critic* had seventy-five. As the format of the *Edinburgh Review* became more fixed, the number of articles averaged nine to fifteen per issue. The principle of selection, coupled with the expanded space allotted to each article, shifted the tone and focus of the book reviews, pointing to a second contributing factor for the magazine's success.

The *Review* instituted a lively style of reviewing atypical of the traditional reviews. Aspiring to entertain as well as inform, the early contributors developed the "essay review" and the "review essay," often written with a vigorous, contentious, and acerbic wit that aimed to engage and perhaps enrage the reader. Jeffrey's infamous "This will never do," opening his November 1814 review of Wordsworth's *Excursion* (1814), is exemplary of this style of writing, as is the opening of Smith's review, in the first issue, of Dr. Samuel Parr's published sermon:

> Whoever has had the good fortune to see Dr. Parr's wig, must have observed, that while it trespasses a little on the orthodox magnitude of perukes in the interior parts, it scorns even Episcopal limits behind, and swells out into boundless convexity of frizz, the *mega thauma* of barbers, and the terror of the literary world. After the manner of his wig, the Doctor has constructed his sermon.

Wordsworth, Coleridge, and others condemned what they took to be the "slashing" style of essay or review, dismissing it as a device for selling copies of the *Review*. Explaining the success of the magazine in an 18 November 1808 letter to George Ellis, Sir Walter Scott suggested that "the *Edinburgh* folks squeezed into their sauce plenty of acid, and were popular from novelty as well as from merit." The reviewers on the other hand saw it as a way of holding up to ridicule what they perceived to be folly or dogmatism. Commenting on the "savageness" of many of the essays, Smith told Harriet Martineau, "we *were* savage ... I remember how Brougham and I sat trying one night how we could exasperate our cruelty to the utmost." He explained with glee, "We had got hold of a poor nervous little vegetarian who had put out a poor silly little book; and when we had done our review [April 1803] of it, we sat trying to find one more chink, one more crevice, through which we might drop in one more drop of verjuice, to eat into his bones." In addition to writing entertaining, if savage, essays, the *Review* also proposed to go beyond merely summarizing and judging the merits of the work at hand.

The book review became a vehicle for exploring the philosophical background of the work, or the social and political issues of current interest. In some cases the work in question was only nominally discussed. Sydney Smith once joked "that he never read a book before reviewing it because it prejudiced a man so." Henry Brougham often submitted his contributions with the top left part of the first page blank to be filled in with some appropriate book title. This practice of "essay-reviews" continued with the second generation of reviewers. Thomas Babington Macaulay contributed essentially as an essayist, selecting books that allowed him to write on a subject that interested him. Similarly, Thomas Carlyle's 1831 assignment to review Thomas Hope's *Essay on the Origin and Prospects of Man* (1831) and Friedrich von Schlegel's *Philosophische Vorlesungen* (1830) for the December 1831 issue became his famous essay "Characteristics." Indeed, Carlyle was only able to have a cursory glance at Hope's book in the British Museum, review copies being rarely provided at the time.

A third factor contributing to the success of the *Edinburgh Review* relates to changes in the reading public. In his essay "The Periodical Press" (*Edinburgh Review*, May 1823), William Hazlitt suggested that the new periodical criticism both suited "the spirit of the times," and advanced it. Expanding on this theme in 1855, Walter Bagehot observed that part of the popularity of the reviews was related to the accelerated pace and business of the modern age. "In truth review-writing but exemplifies the casual character of modern literature. Everything about it is temporary and fragmentary." To this he added, "people take their literature in morsels, as they take sandwiches on a journey." Underlying the fragmentation, Bagehot suggested, the reviews functioned to digest, analyze, and synthesize information for a busy reading public that lacked a comprehensive education:

> In this transition from ancient writing to modern, the review-like essay and the essay-like review fill a large space. Their small bulk, their slight pretension to systematic completeness, their avowal, it might be said, of necessary incompleteness, the facility of changing the subject, of selecting points of attack, of exposing only the best corner for defence, are great temptations.

By contrast, James Mill saw in the success of both the *Edinburgh* and *Quarterly* a studied attempt by a class of technocrats, between the landed aristocracy and the masses, to curry favor with both sides through dissembling and equivocation. Examining the *Edinburgh Review* in the April 1824 issue of the radical *Westminster Review*, Mill argued, "a periodical publication is interested in going to the full length of the existing prejudices; but it lies under no inducement to go beyond them." Summarizing, he declared, "it will never do anything to set the reader right—to correct his errors—to overcome his prejudices. When he is right already, it will be right along with him: a poor merit!"

Until as late as July 1912 contributions to the *Edinburgh Review* were published anonymously, though in many cases the identities of specific reviewers were in little doubt. Thomas Moore, taking offence at a negative notice of his poetry in the July 1806 issue, challenged Jeffrey to a duel. Jeffrey accepted, but the late arrival of the seconds, who were followed by the police, turned the affair into a farce, especially when it was learned that the lead shot had accidently fallen out of both men's pistols. Moore and Jeffrey soon became close friends. George Gordon, Lord Byron commemorated the duel in *English Bards, and Scotch Reviewers* (1809):

> But Caledonia's Goddess hovered o'er
> The field, and saved him [Jeffrey] from the wrath of MOORE;
> From either pistol snatched the vengeful lead,
> And strait restored it to her favourite's head.

After reading these lines, Moore challenged Byron to a duel, which had a similar outcome.

At the early stages of the magazine the four founders wrote most of the contributions, especially Jeffrey and Brougham, who each often contributed three or more essays to an issue. Indeed, it was Brougham's willingness and ability to write on almost any topic (sometimes with disastrous results) that at times provided sufficient copy to complete an issue. Other early contributors included Thomas Brown, Thomas Thomson, John Thomson, and John A. Murray, as well as the founders' old mentor, Dugald Stewart. It should also be noted that all of the contributors, including Jeffrey, prepared their reviews in the midst of active professional careers.

Sir Walter Scott was an early supporter of the *Edinburgh Review*, until Jeffrey's unfavorable notice of *Marmion* (1808) in April 1808. Jeffrey complained of the elaborate descriptions, "which render so many notes necessary, and are, after all, but imperfectly understood by those to whom chivalrous antiquity has not hitherto been an object of particular attention." When Jeffrey and Brougham published their review "Don Pedro Cevallos on the French usurpation in Spain" (October 1808), an article that seemed to praise popular revolt against monarchies, Scott broke entirely with the magazine, and helped found the *Quarterly Review* as a political counterweight. The furor over "Don Pedro Cevallos" proved to be the only serious crisis in the early history of the *Edinburgh Review*. Sydney Smith described it in a letter to Lady Holland, "you have no idea of the consternation which Brougham's attack upon the titled orders has produced: the Review not only discontinued by many, but returned to the booksellers from the very first volume: the library shelves fumigated, etc.!—" In *English Bards, and Scotch Reviewers*, Byron quipped,

> Yet mark one caution ere thy next Review
> Spread its light wings of Saffron and of Blue,
> Beware lest blundering BROUGHAM destroy
> the sale,
> Turn Beef to Bannocks, Cauliflowers to Kail.

Early in the second decade William Hazlitt (1778-1830) also became an important contributor, despite his opposition to the work of another contributor, Thomas Robert Malthus (1766-1834). Hazlitt was particularly important in smoothing Jeffrey's reception of Keats, as well as contributing essays on Coleridge and Shelley, among others.

Jeffrey once remarked to Scott that the *Edinburgh* had "two legs to stand on, literature no doubt is one of them, but its Right leg is politics." The founders had early on declared their political sympathies with the Whig cause, terming themselves "philosophical Whigs" and showing the colors of the Foxites. In its later history the *Edinburgh Review* became an important mouthpiece for the Whig party, advocating political reform and serving as an important tool for the passage of the Parliamentary Reform Bill in 1832. In 1802, however, the Whigs were predominantly divided among three factions with little in common aside from their opposition to William Pitt and their support for Catholic Emancipation. These groups included the Grenvillites, the Foxites (who were associated with Henry Vassall Fox, Lord Holland, and Holland House), and a left wing known as "the Mountain." While Francis Horner eventually found his way into Parliament through the good offices of Holland House, Brougham flirted with the Tories before eventually linking himself with "the Mountain." Philosophical Whiggism should not, therefore, be understood as narrow party allegiance. Rather, as Biancamaria Fontana argues, "the *Review* itself ought principally to be regarded not as an instrument for the promotion of a clearly defined, preexisting ideology but rather as the locus within which a new ideology was tentatively given shape." Underlying this ideology was a socioeconomic interpretation of history and a vision of commercial society derived from the writings of David Hume, Adam Smith, and other members of the Scottish Enlightenment and transmitted through the lectures on political economy of Dugald Stewart, which Jeffrey, Horner, and Brougham had attended from 1799 to 1801. It was to prepare an English edition of the works of the French physiocrat and minister of Louis XVI, Anne Robert Turgot (1727-1781), that Jeffrey, Horner, and Brougham had first come together. The name of the *Edinburgh Review* was itself significant, echoing that of a short-lived journal founded by Adam Smith and Allan Ramsay in 1755. Between 1802 and 1850, the *Review* published more than 250 articles on various aspects of political economy, and included contributions on and by Malthus and David Ricardo (1772-1823). In their reviews they advocated an economic rationalization of society, favoring free trade and commercial interests. Thomas Love Peacock satirized the intellectual pretensions of Jeffrey and the *Review* in the character Mr. MacQuedy (Mac Q.E.D.—"son of demonstration"), in his 1831 novel, *Crotchet Castle*. "Morals and metaphysics, politics and political economy, the way to make the most of all the modifications of smoke, steam, gas, and paper currency," MacQuedy declares. "You have all these to learn from us; in short, all the arts and sciences. We are the modern Athenians."

The passion of the founders of the *Review* was with politics and political economy. Their interest and appreciation of the literary movements of the day, and especially Romanticism, was at best limited. While, for instance, they praised Scott, Byron, Samuel Rogers, Thomas Campbell, and Felicia Hemans with reservations, they recognized John Keats and Percy Bysshe Shelley only belatedly, and ignored Jane Austen and Mary Shelley entirely. Most notably, they attacked Wordsworth, Coleridge, and the Lake Poets for some twenty years. "One's chief feeling about the early reviewing of the *Edinburgh* and the *Quarterly*," suggests Derek Roper, "must be regret for opportunities wasted."

While Jeffrey evoked Shakespeare and the Elizabethans as the standards of poetic excellence, his aesthetic and critical principles were derived from David Hume and the Scottish Enlightenment, though perhaps not as explicitly or as dogmatically as were his principles of politics and political economy. In the review of Robert Southey's *Thalaba the Destroyer* (1801), which appeared in the first issue of the *Edinburgh Review*, Jeffrey asserts the existence of fixed poetic standards. In a move typical of his reviews (and condemned by Coleridge), he shifts from work to author, concluding: "All the productions of this author, it appears to us, bear very distinctly the impression of an amiable mind, a cultivated fancy, and a perverted taste." In his October 1807 review of *Poems* (1807) by Wordsworth, Jeffrey asserts, "The end of poetry, we take it, is to please—and the name, we think, is strictly applicable to every metrical composition from which we receive pleasure . . . This pleasure, may, in general, be analyzed into three parts—that which we receive from the excitement of Passion or emotion—that which is derived from the play of Imagination, or the easy exercise of Reason—and that which depends on the character and qualities of the Diction."

Underlying Jeffrey's critical assumptions is a sort of political economy of aesthetics derived from Hume. The beauty or value of an object relates not to some intrinsic quality, but through the effect produced by subjective associations in the mind of the observer. Some associated ideas will arouse a feeling of beauty, while others will not. Reviewing with favor (May 1811) the associationalist aesthetics found in Archibald Alison's *Essays on the Nature and Principles of Taste*, Jeffrey declares that the artist must "employ only such objects as are the *natural* signs, or the inseparable concomitants of emotions, of which the greater part of mankind are susceptible." Going a step further, he adds, "his taste will *then* deserve to be called bad and false, if he obtrude upon the public, as beautiful, objects that are not likely to be associated in common minds with any interesting impressions." If beauty is derived from an association of ideas, it follows that many associations will necessarily be private, the result of personal ("accidental") associations and individual tastes. Nevertheless, some associations will also be shared, rendering them objective by their intersubjectivity. These, Jeffrey suggests, are what artists must try to arouse and what critics must judge in the artist. In effect, aesthetic value is equivalent to an economic exchange value in which the worth of a work of art is backed up by a common currency of associations shared by artists and their audience. Bad art for Jeffrey and the other early reviewers derived either from associations too personal to be meaningful to anyone but the individual, or from associations that were inconsistent, unnatural, or incongruous. These for Jeffrey were the chief faults of Southey, Wordsworth, and the other Lake Poets.

Wordsworth's poetry exemplified for Jeffrey everything that was wrong with modern poetry. In Wordsworth's appeal to simple diction, Jeffrey found a "mannered" affectation. Underlying that was a jarring incongruity between his diction and subject matter. The simple folk he affected to represent spoke and thought in a fashion that was not natural to them. This diction compared sharply with the more natural treatment found in the poetry of Robert Burns, a poet Jeffrey deeply admired. In turn, Jeffrey charged Wordsworth with appealing to exaggerated sentiments out of proportion with nature. The effect was to subvert any true association with the sublime. While recognizing that Wordsworth had talent, and even acknowledging some fine lines and phrases, Jeffrey found his work distorted and ultimately ruined by his theory. In the review of *Poems*, he lamented,

> When we look at these, and many still finer passages, in the writings of this author, it is impossible not to feel a mixture of indignation and compassion, at that strange infatuation which has bound him up from the fair exercise of his talents, and withheld from the public the many excellent productions that would otherwise have taken the place of the trash now before us.

Jeffrey's critical response to Coleridge was little different.

His approach to Coleridge was marked by sarcasm and dismissal. In a September 1816 review of *Christabel: Kubla Khan. A Vision. The Pains of Sleep* (1816), Jeffrey began by surveying what he took to be the extravagance of the Lake Poets. Supposing that the extreme of "untamed effusion" had been reached, he then declared, "forth steps Mr. Coleridge, like a giant refreshed with sleep." In a telling remark, Jeffrey grants some slight merit to the Lake Poets: "The other productions of the Lake School have generally exhibited talents thrown away upon subjects so mean, that no power of genius could ennoble them; or perverted and rendered useless by a false theory of poetical composition." "Christabel," on the hand, he found, "utterly destitute of value." In a November 1822 review of Wordsworth's *Memorials of a Tour on the Continent* (1822) Jeffrey could not resist taking one last swipe at "Christabel," suggesting that it had helped to undermine the Lake School: "Coleridge, who had by far the most original genius among its founders, has long ceased to labour for the fraternity, and gave their reputation a most unkind cut at parting, by publication of his 'Christabell' [*sic*],—which they had all been lauding, while it remained unprinted, as the crowning glory of their sect." Hazlitt, perhaps expressing his disappointment in Coleridge, took up Jeffrey's theme of dismissal in his review of *The Statesman's Manual* (December 1816) and in his review, probably coauthored with Jeffrey, of *Biographia Literaria* (August 1817). In the former, evoking the principle that the privilege "of talking, and even publishing nonsense, is necessary in a free state; but the more sparingly we make use of it, the better," Hazlitt declares, "Mr. Coleridge has here availed himself of this privilege,—but not sparingly."

In his November 1822 review of Wordsworth's *Memorials of a Tour on the Continent*, Jeffrey sounded what he took to be the death knell of the Lake Poets. Summarizing their achievements, he concluded: "The great characteristic of these works is a sort of emphatic inanity—a singular barrenness and feebleness of thought, disguised under a sententious and assuming manner and style beyond example verbose and obscure." Echoing Horace Walpole's famous dismissal of heroic epic as the art of making a dull story long, he suggested that their efforts exemplified "nothing but the very worthless art of saying ordinary things in an unintelligible way."

The relationship between the *Review* and Lord Byron differed sharply from its relationship with Wordsworth and the Lake Poets. Brougham instigated the first attack on Byron when he reviewed Byron's *Hours of Idleness* (1807) in the January 1808 issue. Finding little merit in the work, Brougham dismissed it as the amateurish effusions of a young nobleman which had received notice only by virtue of his titles: "The poesy of this young lord belongs to the class which neither gods nor men are said to permit." With a final note of sarcasm Brougham concluded, "but whatever judgment may be passed on the poems of this noble minor, it seems we must take them as we find them, and be content; for they are the last we shall ever have from him." In retrospect, the note sounded against Brougham. Byron responded to Brougham's attack with his *English Bards, and Scotch Reviewers*, in which he pilloried his critics, especially Jeffrey and the *Edinburgh Review*. The satire hit its target. Jeffrey opened his February 1812 review of *Childe Harold's Pilgrimage*, Cantos I and II (1812), with the conciliatory note that "Lord Byron has improved marvelously since his last appearance at our tribunal," adding that the poem worked despite its lack of the "ordinary ingredients of interest or poetical delight." Between the first note in 1808, and its final notice of Byron in February 1823, the *Edinburgh* published some eleven reviews on Byron's work, more than on any other single author during the Romantic period.

In his December 1816 piece on the third canto of *Childe Harold's Pilgrimage*, Jeffrey offers an insight into what he took to be the merit of Byron, whom he judged to be the great poet of the age.

> If the first poetry be that which leaves the deepest impression on the minds of its readers—and this is not the worst test of its excellence—Lord Byron, we think, must be allowed to take precedence of all his distinguished contemporaries. He has not the variety of Scott—nor the delicacy of Campbell—nor the absolute truth of Crabbe—nor the polished sparkling of Moore; but in force of diction, and inextinguishable energy of sentiment, he clearly surpasses them all.

While Jeffrey was disturbed by the gloomy, misanthropic Byronic persona, Byron nonetheless had the ability to create powerful associations. In this regard, Byron's poetic production was consistent with Jeffrey's associationalist aesthetics.

The treatment of John Keats and Percy Bysshe Shelley appeared late, and then largely through the efforts of Hazlitt. Jeffrey offered a sympathetic and encouraging review of Keats's *Endymion* (1818) in August 1820. While acknowledging the extravagance of this poem, which John Wilson Croker had criticized in his infamous attack in the *Quarterly Review* (April 1818), Jeffrey found a spirit of poetry in *Endymion* that suggested to him a feeling for the "true genius of English poetry." Jeffrey saw in Keats an affinity for his favorite Elizabethans, especially John Fletcher and Ben Jonson, as well as Shakespeare and Milton. Admiring Keats's imagination and diction, Jeffrey concludes with the friendly warning that "he must learn not to misuse or misapply these advantages; and neither to waste the good gifts of nature and study on intractable themes, nor to luxuriate too recklessly on such as are more suitable."

Hazlitt published his review of the *Posthumous Poems* (1824) of Shelley in the July 1824 issue of the *Edinburgh Review*. The importance of this essay is less in the insights it offers than in its setting the tone and tenor for the subsequent reception of Shelley. Anticipating Matthew Arnold's 1888 characterization of Shelley's weak grasp of the actual as "a beautiful and ineffectual angel, beating in the void his luminous wings in vain," Hazlitt declares, "Mr. Shelley's style is to poetry what astrology is to natural science—a passionate dream, a straining after impossibilities, a record of fond conjectures, a confused embodying of vague abstractions." In short, "Mr. Shelley is the maker of his own poetry—out of nothing." Explaining, Hazlitt adds, "his Muse offers her services to clothe shadowy doubts and inscrutable difficulties in a robe of glittering words, and to turn nature into a brilliant paradox." Hazlitt closes his review with a suggestive, if implicit, comparison of Shelley and Christopher Marlowe's Dr. Faustus, with that character's "love of learning, his philosophic dreams and raptures, his religious horrors and melancholy fate, with appropriate gloom or gorgeousness of colouring."

In a 3 January 1825 letter to John Allen, Jeffrey asked, "Can you lay your hands on some clever young men who would write for us. The original supporters of the work are getting old and either too busy or too stupid, and here the young men are mostly Tories." Three new contributors—who were to carry the *Review* into the early Victorian era and to initiate a new epoch in its history—came forward: William Empson, a professor at the India College at Haileybury, who would become the editor of the *Review* on the death of Napier in 1847; Thomas Carlyle, who had published reviews of Burns and various topics on German literature; and Thomas Babington Macaulay, who emerged as the rising star of the *Review* in the 1830s and 1840s, eclipsing Brougham in contributions and influence. Empson, Carlyle, and Macaulay mark the transition in the history of the *Edinburgh Review* from the Romantic era to the Victorian.

Jeffrey, Smith, and Brougham lived well into the reign of Victoria. The periodical they founded took on a life and reputation of its own, becoming—like its founders—a venerable institution, influencing the tone and shape of Victoria's century. Thomas Love Peacock's Mr. Crotchet, standing at the edge of the new era in 1831 and looking at the ferment of the day, sighed:

> The sentimental against the rational, the intuitive against the inductive, the ornamental against the useful, the intense against the tranquil, the romantic against the classical; these are great and interesting controversies, which I should like, before I die, to see satisfactorily settled.

These were among the conflicts that the *Edinburgh Review* and its founders had helped to raise, and, though the ferment had not been settled before they had died, they had helped to generate a new world.

**References:**

Walter Bagehot, "The First Edinburgh Reviewers," in volume 1 of *The Collected Works of Walter Bagehot*, edited by Norman St. John-Stevas (Cambridge, Mass.: Harvard University Press, 1965), pp. 308-341;

Ruth Berman, "Critical Reactions to Fantasy in Four Nineteenth-century Periodicals: *Edinburgh Review, Blackwood's, Fraser's*, and *Cornhill*," *Sphinx: A Magazine of Literature and Society*, 4, no. 1 (1981): 1-37;

David Bromwich, "Romantic Poetry and the *Edinburgh* Ordinances," *Yearbook of English Studies*, 16 (1986): 1-16;

John Clive, "The Edinburgh Review, 150 Years After," *History Today*, 2 (December 1952): 844-850;

Clive, *Macaulay: The Shaping of the Historian* (New York: Random House, 1973);

Clive, *Scotch Reviewers: The Edinburgh Review, 1802-1815* (London: Faber & Faber, 1956);

Stefan Collini, Donald Winch, and John Burrow, *That Noble Science of Politics: A Study in Nineteenth-Century Intellectual History* (Cambridge: Cambridge University Press, 1983);

Philip Flynn, *Francis Jeffrey* (Newark: University of Delaware Press, 1978);

Biancamaria Fontana, *Rethinking the Politics of Commercial Society: The Edinburgh Review 1802-1832* (Cambridge: Cambridge University Press, 1985);

Walter Graham, *English Literary Periodicals* (New York: Nelson, 1930);

James A. Greig, *Francis Jeffrey of the Edinburgh Review* (Edinburgh: Oliver & Boyd, 1948);

John Gross, *The Rise and Fall of the Man of Letters: A Study of the Idiosyncratic and the Humane in Modern Literature* (New York: Collier Books, 1970);

John O. Hayden, *The Romantic Reviewers, 1802-1824* (Chicago: University of Chicago Press, 1969);

Raymond N. MacKenzie, "Romantic Literary History: Francophobia in *The Edinburgh Review* and *The Quarterly Review*," *Victorian Periodicals Review*, 15 (Summer 1982): 42-52;

Muriel J. Mellowin, "Francis Jeffrey, Lord Byron, and *English Bards, and Scotch Reviewers*," *Studies in Scottish Literature*, 16 (1981): 80-90;

Michael Munday, "The Novel and its Critics in the Early Nineteenth Century," *Studies in Philology*, 79 (Spring 1982): 205-226;

Derek Roper, *Reviewing Before the Edinburgh: 1788-1802* (Newark: University of Delaware Press, 1978);

Joanne Shattock, "Politics and Literature: Macaulay, Brougham, and the Edinburgh Review Under Napier," *Yearbook of English Studies*, 16 (1986): 33-50;

Shattock, *Politics and Reviewers: The Edinburgh and the Quarterly in the Early Victorian Age* (London: Leicester University Press, 1989);

René Wellek, *The Romantic Age*, volume 2 of *A History of Modern Criticism, 1750-1950* (Cambridge: Cambridge University Press, 1981), pp. 110-121.

# The Examiner

*(3 January 1808 - 26 February 1881)*

David R. Cheney
*University of Toledo*

The *Examiner*, a weekly newspaper published on Sundays, was founded in 1808 by brothers Leigh and John Hunt. It began primarily as a political journal which covered national and foreign affairs. In his *Autobiography* (1850) Leigh Hunt stated his aims as "reform in Parliament, liberality of opinion in general . . . and an infusion of literary taste into all subjects whatsoever." Though the paper was not associated with any political party, it was early identified with radical politics and was consequently subjected in its first years to several libel suits by the government. Indeed, because of an attack on the Prince Regent on 12 March 1812 the Hunt brothers spent two years in prison, and each paid a five-hundred-pound fine. Interestingly enough, Leigh Hunt was allowed to edit the paper while he was in prison (3 February 1813 - 2 February 1815). Though the circulation dropped, the *Examiner* continued to be an influential journal and remained so during its first fourteen years, while Leigh Hunt was editor and John Hunt was publisher. Its circulation by the end of the first year was twenty-two hundred, and it continued to rise to a high of seven thousand in 1812. Its audience was intelligent, liberal, and literate.

The *Examiner* became also a literary journal, which published original poems, essays, and reviews of books and theatricals. Influential in gaining public acceptance of Romantic literature, it introduced John Keats and Percy Bysshe Shelley to the public by publishing, among other poems, Keats's "To Solitude" (5 May 1816, his first appearance in print) and Shelley's "Hymn to Intellectual Beauty" (19 January 1817), "Ozymandias" (11 January 1818), and "To a Skylark" (1822). Hunt also published some of his own poems and essays, as well as poems by William Wordsworth, including the sonnets "How clear, how keen, how marvellously bright" (28 January 1816) and "While not a leaf seems faded" (11 February 1816), and essays by Charles Lamb and William Hazlitt.

In "The Periodical Press" (*Edinburgh Review* May 1823) Hazlitt wrote:

> The *Examiner* stands next to Cobbett in talent, and is much before him in moderation and

> steadiness of principle. It has also a much greater variety both of tact and subject. Indeed an agreeable rambling scope and freedom of discussion is so much in the author's way, that the reader is at a loss under what department of the paper to look for any particular topic. A literary criticism perhaps insinuates itself under the head of the Political Examiner, and the theatrical critic, or lover of Fine Arts, is stultified by a *tirade* against the Bourbons. If the dishes are there it does not much signify in what order they are placed. With the exception of a little egotism and *twaddle*, and flippancy, and dogmatism about religion or morals, and mawkishness about firesides, and furious Bonapartism, and a vein of sickly sonnet-writing, we suspect the *Examiner* must be allowed (whether we look to the design or execution of the general run of articles in it) to be the ablest and most respectable of the publications that issue from the weekly press.

The *Examiner* did not really become a literary journal until 1814, when Hunt published some of his sonnets on Hampstead and his long review of Maria Edgeworth's 1814 novel, *Patronage* (27 February and 6 March); when Charles Lamb contributed a long article on *Debtor and Creditor*, a play by James Kenney (8 May), and an epigram on actors Charles Kemble and Edmund Kean (6 March); and particularly when Hazlitt reviewed Wordsworth's *Excursion* (1814), the first nontheatrical review by Hazlitt to appear in the *Examiner* (21 and 28 August and 2 October). Hazlitt had already written theatrical reviews for the *Examiner* while Hunt was in prison, including one on a production of *Othello* (24 July and 7 August 1814). In 1813 he had contributed to the "Table Talk" section, intended to be a series of anecdotes but actually a series of brief essays.

Hazlitt begins his long, three-part review of *The Excursion* with an overall assessment:

> In power of intellect, in lofty conception, in the depth of feeling, at once simple and sublime, which pervades every part of it, and which gives to every object an almost preternatural and preterhuman interest, this work has seldom been surpassed. If the subject of the Poem had been equal to the genius of the Poet, if the skill with which he has chosen his materials had accorded with the power exerted over them, if the objects (whether persons or things) which he makes use of as the vehicle of his feelings had been such as immediately and irresistibly to convey them in all their force and depth to others, then the production before us would indeed "have proved a monument," as he himself wishes it, worthy of the author, and of his country.

Hazlitt's main objection to the poem was that, as a philosophical poem, it should have had a philosophical form:

> There is in his general sentiments and reflections on human life a depth, an originality, a truth, a beauty, and grandeur, both of conception and expression, which place him decidedly at the head of the poets of the present day, or rather which place him in a totally distinct class of excellence. But he has chosen to encumber himself with a load of narrative and description, which, instead of assisting, hinders the progress and effect of the general reasoning.

In 1815 Hunt, Hazlitt (who became the drama critic for the *Examiner* in March), and Thomas Barnes (later editor of the *Times*), wrote twenty-eight articles for the series called *The Round Table*, a group of essays supposed to be in the style of Joseph Addison and Richard Steele, which was published as a book in 1817.

During 1815 Hunt met Wordsworth, whom he had hailed in the first edition of his *Feast of the Poets* (1814) as "Prince of Bards." At first they were on generally good terms, but Hunt objected to Wordsworth's politics and thus to the lines in his 1816 sonnets on Waterloo, where he called the French army an "impious crew" and the battle itself "a victory sublime" (18 February). Hunt also thought that George Gordon, Lord Byron's *Monody on the Death of Sheridan* (1816), written for delivery at the Drury Lane theater, was unsuccessful because oratorical poetry did not fit Byron's talents (22 September). More important was Hunt's short article on the "Young Poets" (1 December 1816), which hailed the arrival of John Keats, Percy Bysshe Shelley, and John Hamilton Reynolds as the second wave of Romantic poets. Hunt called Shelley "a very striking and original thinker," while Keats was remarkable for his "truth . . . and ardent grappling with Nature." Reynolds was a young man with talent, but he later turned away from poetry to more lucrative pursuits. Hunt ended the article with the first publication of Keats's sonnet "On First Looking into Chapman's Homer."

The 2 June 1816 issue of the *Examiner* includes Hazlitt's review of Samuel Taylor Coleridge's *Christabel: Kubla Khan, A Vision; The Pains of Sleep* (1816), a volume made up of two unfinished poems and a fragment, which led Hazlitt to write that "the fault of Mr. Coleridge is, that he comes to no conclusion. He is a man of that university of genius, that his mind hangs suspended between poetry and prose, truth and falsehood, and an infinity of other things, and from an excess of capacity, he does little or nothing." Of "Christabel" he says "there is a great deal of beauty, both of thought, imagery, and versification; but the effect of the general story is dim, obscure, and visionary," while "Kubla Khan" "only shews that Mr. Coleridge can write better *nonsense* verses than any man in England."

It was in October 1817 that John Gibson Lockhart of *Blackwood's Edinburgh Magazine*, following the lead of the *Quarterly Review*, began his attacks on Hunt, Keats, Shelley, and Hazlitt, whom Lockhart dubbed "The Cockney School of Poetry." Except for a fruitless demand at the outset, in the 2 November 1817 issue of the *Examiner*, that the anonymous writer of the attacks in *Blackwood's* reveal his identity, Hunt did not answer save in defense of Keats and Shelley. Earlier that year, Hunt had written a three-part review (1 June, 6 and 13 July 1817) of Keats's *Poems* (1817), describing Keats as "a young poet giving himself up to his own impressions, and revelling in real poetry for its' own sake." Although the volume was dedicated to Hunt, he gave as much space to Keats's faults as to his virtues.

> The very faults indeed of Mr. Keats arise from a passion for beauties, and a young impatience to vindicate them; and as we have mentioned these, we shall refer to them at once. They may be comprised in two;—first, a tendency to notice every thing too indiscriminately and without an eye to natural proportion and effect; and second, a sense of the proper variety of versification without a due consideration of its principles.

Hunt insisted, however, that these faults of youth would disappear with time, adding that the poems had many beauties, "and the reader will easily perceive that they not only outnumber the faults a hundred fold, but that they are of a nature decidedly opposed to what is false and inharmonious. Their characteristics indeed, are a fine ear, a fancy and imagination at will, and an intense feeling of external beauty in it's [*sic*] most natural and least expressible simplicity." During 1817 Hunt also reviewed favorably Hazlitt's 1817 book *Characters of Shakespeare's Plays* (26 October, 2 and 23 November).

During that year Hazlitt continued his attacks on Coleridge and Robert Southey. For example, in his 4 May review of the poet laureate's *Letter to William Smith* (1817), Hazlitt wrote devastatingly: "Mr. Southey publicly exposes his mind to be anatomised while he is living. He lays open his character to the scalping knife, guides the philosophic hand in its painful researches, and on the bald crown of our *petit tondu*, in vain concealed under withered bay-leaves and a few contemptible grey hairs, you see the organ of vanity triumphant—sleek, smooth, round, perfect, polished, horned and shining, as it were in a transparency."

On 28 December 1817 the *Examiner* published Shelley's typically poetic and imaginative review letter of William Godwin's *Mandeville* (1817). For example, Shelley describes the meeting of Henrietta and Mandeville: "an occurrence resplendent with the sunrise of life; it recalls to the memory many a vision,—or perhaps but one. —which the delusive exhalations of unbaffled hope has invested with a rose-like lustre as of morning, yet, unlike morning, a light, which, once extinguished, never can return. . . . There is a mist of dazzling loveliness which encircles her, and shuts out from the sight all that is mortal in her transcendant charms. But the veil is gradually withdrawn, and she 'fades into the light of common day.' "

In 1818 Hunt reviewed Shelley's *Revolt of Islam* (1818) in three articles (1 and 22 February and 1 March), defending Shelley's philosophy, poetry, and person. He pointed out at the beginning of his review that "This is an extraordinary production," but, he added,

> The ignorant will not understand it; the idle will not take the pains to get acquainted with it; even the intelligent will be startled at first with it's [*sic*] air of mysticism and wildness; the livelier man of the world will shake his head at it good naturedly; the sulkier one will cry out against it; the bigot will be shocked, terrified, and enraged . . . but we will venture to say, that the intelligent and the good, who are yet healthy-minded, and who have not been so far blinded by fear and self-love as to confound superstition with desert, anger and hatred with firmness, or despondency with knowledge, will find themselves amply repaid by breaking through the outer shell of this production.

Again, as in his review of Keats's *Poems*, after describing *The Revolt of Islam*, discussing its philosophy, comparing Shelley's genius to the "two very opposite ones" of Lucretius and Dante, Hunt mentions the faults of the poem:

> Mr. Shelley's defects as a poet are obscurity, inartificial and yet not natural economy, violation of costume, and too great a sameness and gratuitousness of image and metaphor, and of image and metaphor too drawn from the elements, particularly the sea. The book is full of humanity; and yet it certainly does not go the best way to work of appealing to it, because it does not appeal to it through the medium of it's [*sic*] common knowledges. It is for this reason that we must say something, which we would willingly leave unsaid, both from admiration of Mr. Shelley's genius and love of his benevolence; and this is, that the work cannot possibly become popular. It may set others thinking and writing, and we have no doubt will do so; and those who can understand and relish it, will relish it exceedingly; but the author must forget his metaphysics and sea-sides a little more in his future works, and give full effect to that nice knowledge of men and things which he otherwise really possesses to an extraordinary degree. We have no doubt he is destined to be one of the leading spirits of his age, and indeed has already fallen into his place as such; but however resolute as to his object, he will only be doing it justice to take the most effectual means in his power to forward it.

In 1819 the popularity of *The Examiner* continued as the quality of writing remained high. Hunt and Hazlitt kept writing for it; Lamb contributed frequent sonnets, parodies, theatrical and literary reviews; and Keats made his only prose contribution to the *Examiner*, his brief favorable review of Reynolds's parody of Wordsworth's *Peter Bell*, where Keats contrasts "the sad embroidery of the *Excursion*" with "the coarse samples of Betty Foy and Alice Fell" (25 April).

In 1819 Hunt defended Shelley (26 September; 3 and 10 October) against John Taylor Coleridge's scathing review of Shelley's *Revolt of Islam* in the April issue of the *Quarterly Review*. Hunt noted that "the *Quarterly Review* . . . ought to be ashamed of the one it has written upon Mr. Shelley" and described the review as "heavy, and swelling, and soft with venom, [creeping] through the middle of it [the *Review*] like a skulking toad." In the same year Hunt also reviewed Hazlitt's recently published *Lectures on the English Comic Writers* (18 April and 6 June). In the second of the two articles devoted to the book, Hunt expressed his view of Hazlitt as a writer.

> If Mr. Hazlitt is not the most popular writer of the day, he yields only to some of the great poets and novelists, and he is at the head of a class in which our most ambitious wits are anxious to be enrolled. His knowledge of the drama, the fine arts, works of fancy and fiction, and other departments of polite literature, taken severally, may not equal that of some other persons, but, taken altogether, is certainly unrivalled. His writings are full of spirit and vivacity; he has the ease and gaiety of a man of the world; and there is, at the same time, an intensity in his conceptions which embodies ideas that are so volatile and fugitive as to escape the grasp of a slower but profounder intellect. He professes to throw aside the formality and prudery of authorship, and to give his best thoughts to the world with the freedom and frankness of old Montaigne, without submitting to assume the mask of current opinions or conventional morality. In discussing any subject he disregards logical methods, but pursues the tract that leads him into the most interesting vein of thinking, and concludes when all his best things are said, at whatever stage that may be. He feels sure that every fault will be pardoned but dulness; and providing he can bear the reader along with him, he is not very scrupulous about the means he employs, or the course he steers. His beauties are procurred [*sic*] by a great expenditure of thinking; and some of his single strokes or flashes reveal more to the reader's understanding than whole pages of an ordinary writer. The great fault of his works arises from a surcharge of excellence. He is too uniformly emphatic and dazzling, and fatigues us by placing all objects in the strongest lights, without any space for shade or repose. His love of effect betrays him into paradox and caricature; but his thoughts are crowded together rather than grouped; and though they please individually by their poignancy, it often happens that we lay down the book with a sense of satiety and exhaustion.

Also in 1819 Hunt reviewed Cantos I and II of Byron's *Don Juan* (1819), defending the morality of the poem but objecting to Byron's attacks on conventional sentiment (31 October). He concludes his answer to the charge that *Don Juan* is immoral with "The fact is . . . that many things are made vicious, which are not so by nature; and many things made virtuous, which are only so by calling and agreement: and it is on the horns of this selfcreated dilemma, that society is continually writhing and getting desperate."

By 1819 Hunt's friendly feeling for Wordsworth had evaporated. In his 2 May review of Wordsworth's *Peter Bell* (1819) he called it "another didactic little horror of Mr. Wordsworth's, founded on the bewitching principles of fear, bigotry, and diseased impulse." The next year the 30 July issue of the *Examiner* included Lamb's fine criticism of Keats's *Lamia, Isabella, The Eve of St. Agnes, and Other Poems* (1820), reprinted from the *New Times*. Of *The Eve of St. Agnes*, Lamb says: "such is the description which Mr. Keats has given us, with a delicacy worthy of *Christabel*, of a high-born damsel, in one of the apartments of an old baronial castle, laying herself down devoutly to dream, on the charmed Eve of St. Agnes; and like the radiance, which comes from those old windows upon the limbs and garments of the damsel, is the almost Chaucer-like painting, with which this poet illumines every subject he touches. We have scarcely any thing like it in modern description." As for *Isabella*, Lamb quotes the three stanzas describing Isabella's digging up the body of her love, Lorenzo, and says "there is nothing more awfully simple in diction, more nakedly grand and moving in sentiment in Dante, in Chaucer, or in Spenser." Lamb found *Lamia* even "more exuberantly rich in imagery and painting. . . . It is of as gorgeous stuff as ever romance was composed of."

Hunt notes in his *Autobiography* that in 1820 "receipts of the *Examiner* [were] now declining under the twofold vicissitude of Triumphant ascendency in the Tories, and the desertion of reform by the Whigs." It was Hunt's last full year as editor of the *Examiner*, during which he noted Keats's *Lamia, Isabella, The Eve of St. Agnes, and Other Poems*, which he pronounced "a fine volume of poetry, 'good and true' " (30 July) and Shelley's tragedy *The Cenci* (1819), which he described as "undoubtedly the greatest dramatic production of the day" (19 March).

In autumn 1821 Hunt left for Italy to help Byron and Shelley establish a journal to be called the *Liberal*. His editorship of the *Examiner* passed on to Henry Leigh Hunt, son of his brother John. In 1822 Leigh Hunt submitted a review of Byron's *Cain* (2 June) and of Shelley's *Adonais* (7 July) and *Prometheus Unbound* (16 and 23 June). On 5 January 1823 the *Examiner* published Hunt's humorous "Arrival of Don Juan at Shooter's Hill." Hunt ended his relationship with the *Examiner*, at least while it was still in the hands of the Hunts, with the publication of his series of thirty-two articles called "The Wishing Cap Papers" during 1824-1825. He did have a poem and some essays published in the *Examiner* in the 1830s when it was under the editorship of Albany W. Fonblanque, but his days as editor had ended in a bitter dispute with his brother John who insisted against Hunt's belief that Hunt had forfeited both his part ownership and editorship by being away in Italy so long.

Because of low circulation (it had continued to decline from three thousand in 1821 when Leigh Hunt left the paper), Henry Leigh Hunt, publisher as well as editor of the *Examiner* since 1828, was forced in 1830 to declare bankruptcy. The paper passed into the hands of Albany Fonblanque who had been chief political editor of the paper since 1826. Fonblanque remained editor until 1847. Succeeding editors were: John Forster (1847-1855), Marmion W. Savage (1856-1859), Henry Morley (1859-1867?), and William Minto (1874-1878). Because of declining circulation, a note in the *Examiner* for 26 February 1881 stated that it would be "temporarily discontinued," but it never appeared again.

**References:**

Edmund Blunden, *Leigh Hunt and His Circle* (New York & London: Harper, 1930);

Blunden, *Leigh Hunt's "Examiner" Examined* (New York: Harper, 1928);

Leigh Hunt, *The Autobiography of Leigh Hunt*, 3 volumes (London: Smith, Elder, 1850);

Donald H. Reiman, *The Romantics Reviewed: Contemporary Reviews of British Romantic Writers*, 9 volumes (New York & London: Garland, 1972);

George Dumas Stout, *The Political History of Leigh Hunt's "Examiner"* (St. Louis, Mo.: Washington University Press, 1949);

Alvin Sullivan, *British Literary Magazines*, 4 volumes (Westport, Conn.: Greenwood Press, 1983-1986);

James R. Thompson, *Leigh Hunt* (Boston: Twayne, 1977).

# The Literary Chronicle and Weekly Review

*(22 May 1819 - 26 July 1828)*

Leslie Haynsworth

The *Literary Chronicle and Weekly Review*, published every Saturday between 22 May 1819 and 26 July 1828, announced in its subtitle that it would offer "an Analysis and General Repository of Literature, Philosophy, Science, Arts, History, the Drama, Morals, Manners, and Amusements." Covering such a wide range of subjects was an ambitious undertaking for a sixteen-page weekly review, but with a variety of departments, some of which included all sorts of miscellany, the *Literary Chronicle* did indeed manage to survey the topics it promised to include. The editors of the *Literary Chronicle* saw their journal as departing radically from the reviewing pattern followed by their contemporaries: often long-winded discourses about morals, manners, and politics as they relate to particular authors and their work. Rather than sermonizing about what literature ought to be, they announced in their first annual "Address to the Public" (22 May 1819), the *Literary Chronicle* would strive above all to be "Impartial in its criticisms, diversified in its contents, and regular in its publication." For the most part, the review was successful in meeting these goals throughout its uninterrupted ten-year run. Its contents were certainly diverse, and—if its literary critiques were at times less strictly impartial than promised—they were still generally more objective and more concerned with literary merits, as opposed to morality, than the reviews found in many other leading journals of the time.

The concept of a weekly, rather than monthly, book review was a fairly novel one in 1819, but the editors of the *Literary Chronicle* felt that weekly publication was justified because it afforded an opportunity to provide the public with "an Analytical Review of every new work of value or interest, as soon as published." This goal again differentiated the *Literary Chronicle* from the monthlies of that time, which published much longer reviews and were therefore more selective about which new works would receive their attention. Not only did the editors of the *Literary Chronicle* seek to broaden readers' literary horizons by reviewing more books than their rivals did, they also sought—by charging the moderate fee of sixpence an issue and by adopting an overall tone for their journal which was generally both straightforward and pleasantly anecdotal—to reach a larger audience than that which traditionally subscribed to literary reviews. In an era when the field of journalistic literary criticism was dominated by weighty periodicals such as the *Quarterly Review* and the *Westminster Review*, the chatty and relatively undemanding reviewing style of the *Literary Chronicle* earned it a fairly lowbrow reputation; even its chief weekly rival, the *Literary Gazette*, was more highly regarded.

Yet it is precisely the "lowbrow" nature of the *Literary Chronicle and Weekly Review* which makes the journal worthy of attention today. While it reviewed many of the same books as the prestigious monthlies, the *Literary Chronicle* directed its critiques to a different audience, providing the modern scholar with a more comprehensive picture of mainstream literary tastes in early-nineteenth-century England than the serious, intellectual journals.

The nonliterary departments in the *Literary Chronicle* are also good resources for gauging the tastes and interests of Regency England. Regular columns such as "Literary and Scientific Intelligence" catalogue interesting and curious bits of information about topics ranging from accounts of the latest scientific advancements to advice about how to preserve vegetables. "The Bee" offers a selection of humorous anecdotes akin to those found in *Reader's Digest* today. The editors also published "Original Correspondence," letters which express opinions—often rather unorthodox—on a variety of subjects. The first issue, for example, includes a letter titled "Cockneyism Vindicated," in which the author argues that, far from having corrupted proper English diction as they are generally believed to have done, those who speak the cockney dialect have actually preserved the English language in the closest existing approximation of its original form. Whether

# THE LITERARY CHRONICLE

## And Weekly Review;

*Forming an Analysis and General Repository of Literature, Philosophy, Science, Arts, History, the Drama, Morals, Manners, and Amusements.*

This Paper is published at Six o'Clock every Saturday Morning; and forwarded, Weekly or Monthly, to all Parts of the United Kingdom.

No. 7. LONDON, SATURDAY, JULY 3, 1819. Price 6*d*.

### Review of New Books.

*Mazeppa, a Poem.* By Lord Byron. 8vo. pp. 69. London, 1819.

THE poetry of Lord Byron is too well known, and has been too often criticised, to render many remarks necessary. An intimate acquaintance with the human heart and character; a power of description, at once forcible and eloquent, but too deeply tinged with melancholy; a felicitous manner of depicting the worse passions of human nature, and displaying, in the whole, an inexhaustible store of mental reflection, are the peculiar features of Lord Byron's muse; and, prolific as his pen has been, these are the characteristics of the whole of his poems. The story of Mazeppa is one well suited to the talents of his lordship, and much expectation was raised, when it was known, that it was to form the subject of his long announced poem; nor do we think its readers will be disappointed.

The poem is founded on an incident, in the early life of Mazeppa, which is related by Voltaire, in his History of Charles XII, and by Lesur, in his *Histoire des Kosaques*. Mazeppa was born in the Palatinate of Podolia, and being of a good family, was made page to Jean Casimir, King of Poland, at whose court, he acquired some knowledge of the belles lettres; but, having been discovered in an intrigue with the wife of a Polish nobleman, he was scourged, and then tied on a wild horse, from the Ukraine, which carried him into the desert. Here, perishing with fatigue and hunger, some peasants came to his assistance, and he recovered. He enrolled himself among the Cossacks, soon distinguished himself by his bravery and superior talents, and became Hettman of the Cossacks and Prince of the Ukraine. At the battle of Pultowa, Mazeppa, who had taken part with Charles XII, was present with a troop of Cossacks, and after that fatal defeat, he retired with the king to Bender, where he died, at the age of eighty, but whether he poisoned himself, or died of sorrow, is doubtful. It is during the retreat of the army, and while the Swedish monarch, wounded and fatigued, is reclining at the foot of a tree, that Mazeppa is made to relate the story of his early life. The poem opens finely :—

> 'Twas after dread Pultowa's day,
> When fortune left the royal Swede,
> Around a slaughter'd army lay,
> No more to combat and to bleed.
> The power and glory of the war,
> Faithless as their vain votaries, men,
> Had pass'd to the triumphant Czar,
> And Moscow's walls were safe again,
> Until a day more dark and drear,
> And a more memorable year,
> Should give to slaughter and to shame
> A mightier host and haughtier name;
> A greater wreck, a deeper fall,
> A shock to one—a thunderbolt to all.'

VOL. I.

While the wounded monarch is laid at the foot of a tree, surrounded by a band of chiefs, Mazeppa first attends to his courser, which is described as 'shaggy and swift, and strong of limb,' and then joins the group, offering his whole stock of provisions, from his haversack, to the monarch and his men; Charles partook of it,

> 'And then he said—"Of all our band,
> Though firm of heart and strong of hand,
> In skirmish, march, or forage, none
> Can less have said or more have done
> Than thee, Mazeppa! On the earth
> So fit a pair had never birth,
> Since Alexander's days till now,
> As thy Bucephalus and thou.
> All Scythia's fame to thine should yield
> For pricking on o'er flood and field."
> Mazeppa answer'd—"I'll betide
> The school wherein I learn'd to ride!"
> Quoth Charles—"Old Hettman, wherefore so,
> Since thou hast learn'd the art so well?"'

Mazeppa then begins the story of his life, which, however unfortunate, was the precursor of his great success afterwards. He describes himself as in his twentieth spring, when he became acquainted with the wife of a Polish count, who was rich, and proud of his ancestry :—

> '"His wife was not of his opinion—
> His junior she by thirty years—
> Grew daily tired of his dominion;
> And, after wishes, hopes, and fears,
> To virtue a few farewell tears,
> A restless dream or two, some glances
> At Warsaw's youth, some songs, and dances,
> Awaited but the usual chances,
> Those happy accidents which render
> The coldest dames so very tender,
> To deck her Count with titles given,
> 'Tis said, as passports into heaven;
> But, strange to say, they rarely boast
> Of these who have deserved them most.'

The description of his mistress, and of their first interview, is a luxuriant one, and in the best style of the noble bard :—

> '"But let me on: Theresa's form—
> Methinks it glides before me now,
> Between me and yon chesnut's bough,
> The memory is so quick and warm;
> And yet I find no words to tell
> The shape of her I loved so well:
> She had the Asiatic eye,
> Such as our Turkish neighbourhood
> Hath mingled with our Polish blood,
> Dark as above us is the sky;
> But through it stole a tender light,
> Like the first moonrise at midnight;
> Large, dark, and swimming in the stream,
> Which seem'd to melt to its own beam;
> All love, half languor, and half fire,
> Like saints that at the stake expire,

H

*First page from an early issue of Thomas Byerley's literary review* or not the reader comes away convinced of the merits of cockneyism, he or she has certainly learned a great deal about the etymology of the English language. In this respect all of the seemingly extraneous departments in the *Literary Chronicle* are similar; while sometimes eccentric, each of them is educational and thought provoking.

The bulk of each issue of the *Literary Chronicle* was, however, devoted to reviewing new books. The journal examined a wide range of works—including novels, volumes of poetry, travelogues, memoirs, and biographies—by famous authors and relatively unknown, but promising, writers. The editors also ran a weekly column about interesting recent developments in foreign literature. The reviews in the *Literary Chronicle* are generally not dominated by the reviewer's opinion of a work or its author. The first "Address to the Public" suggests that this departure from the reviewing style of magazines such as the *Edinburgh Review* is hardly accidental. The *Literary Chronicle*, they proclaim,

> will differ widely from such of its contemporaries as merely take the title of a book for a text, and enter into long disquisitions, in which the author and his work are alike forgotten; or, if the former be remembered, it is only to indulge in splenitive invectives against his political opinions or private errors. On the contrary, our great objective will be, to put our readers in possession of such an abstract as will, in some measure, enable them to form their own opinion of the merits of the work under consideration.

With this aim in mind, reviewers discussed the basic story line and main characters of a novel, the style and themes of a book of poetry, and the places visited in a travelogue. Long excerpts from the text under review are frequently included so that the reader may, as the editors promise, form his or her own opinions about whether the book is to his or her particular taste. In a 1 December 1821 review of Shelley's *Adonais* (1821), for example, the critic provides background information to the poem's subject and comments: "Of the beauty of Mr. Shelley's elegy we shall not speak; to every poetic mind, its transcendent merits must be apparent." He then concludes the review by quoting the entire poem. While hardly rigorous commentary, the review does serve its purpose: introducing the reader to the poem and placing it in a meaningful context.

The editors of the *Literary Chronicle* also proclaimed that the journal was not a "bookseller's rag." They wished to make it quite clear from the start that their journal did not exist for the purpose of promoting sale of certain books through favorable reviews. Not all literary reviews of the period were quite so removed from the business side of the book trade. The overall tone of careful impartiality in the *Literary Chronicle* served to reassure readers that their opinions of the books under review were not being manipulated by publishers eager for their money.

At times, however, the reviews in the *Literary Chronicle* were not as strictly objective or as plainly descriptive as the editors claimed. Far from letting the reader make up his or her own mind about the merits of Byron's *Don Juan*, Cantos I and II (1819) for example, the reviewer remarks that "the very subject of this tale is censurable, but particularly so when it is made the vehicle of indecent allusions, double entendres, and a mockery of religion; that there are many beautiful passages in it we admit, but they will but ill compensate for the many objections that may justly be made to it." Such remarks are certainly intended to sway the reader's opinion, and are, moreover, just the sorts of attacks on the moral character of an author and his text from which the *Literary Chronicle* promised to abstain. Nevertheless, this commentary appears in the last paragraph of a fairly extended review (17 and 24 July 1819) in which, for the most part, the reviewer has confined himself to tracing the story line of the poem and quoting representative passages from it, after warning that "the pruning-knife has been applied to it before it was deemed proper to send it forth to the public." The review opens with a brief account of the sensation publication of the poem has caused and goes on to examine the ways in which Byron's text has departed from the traditional Don Juan legend. The reviewer then states that "For the present, we shall abstain from any critical remarks on the poem, and shall merely detach a few passages, written with much spirit and much humor; we may, however, remark, en passant, that this is in many respects a satirical poem. . . ." Thus, until the end of his review, the reviewer, for the most part, leaves his audience to judge Byron's verse for themselves. The review is much more informative than it is critical, and, in this respect, it is a fairly representative sample of the typical *Literary Chronicle* review.

The *Literary Chronicle* was sometimes, however, entirely unobjective in its reviews, as was the case when the subject was William Wordsworth's *Peter Bell* (1819), reviewed in the 29 May 1819 issue. The reviewer's tone is openly scornful from start to finish; he begins by dismissing Wordsworth's poetic philosophy as "frigid and extravagant," and goes on to ridicule both the subject and style of the poem: "All that is called poetic diction, Mr. Wordsworth carefully shuns and despises, convinced that a poet may give all the pleasure he wishes to do without its assistance, and yet he adds that 'from the tendency of metre to divest language in a certain degree of its reality, . . . there is little doubt that more painfully pathetic incidents and situations may be endured in verse, especially in rhymed verse than in prose.' This we suppose is Mr. Wordsworth's defence for writing in rhyme and measure; but although metre may make us endure 'painfully pathetic incidents and situations,' yet we cannot easily tolerate painfully ludicrous ones, and such this poet has contrived to introduce into many of his poems." The review concludes with an eloquent statement of thorough disgust:

> Of all Mr. Wordsworth's poems, this is decidedly the worst; it possesses all the faults of the Lake school without any of its beauties . . . nor will any defence of it which Mr. Wordsworth or his admirers can set up, ever make Peter Bell fill a permanent situation in the literature of the country, as its author has the vanity to anticipate, unless indeed the public taste should become so far perverted, as not to distinguish between the puerilities of some modern poets and the lofty and impassioned diction of those whose works have stood the test of ages, and who will be read with delight when Mr. Wordsworth and the Lake school will be entirely forgotten.

Such a strong negative reaction to a book and its author is quite unusual in the *Literary Chronicle*. More often when a reviewer makes adverse comments about a work, these remarks are counterbalanced by praise of some sort.

The only other literary figure who was subject to such frequent and strong attack in the pages of the *Chronicle* was Sir Walter Scott, who, like Wordsworth, had become a highly regarded author by the time the *Literary Chronicle* was founded. Yet its reviewers often proclaimed that novels such as *Ivanhoe* (1820) were not as good as Scott's earlier fiction. These reviews of Wordsworth and Scott, however, are atypical of the general tone of the *Literary Chronicle*.

The *Literary Chronicle* was founded by Thomas Byerley, who was its editor until his death in 1826. Byerley also edited the *Mirror of Literature, Amusement and Instruction*, and assisted in editing an evening newspaper, the *Star*. He was not closely associated with any of the leading men of letters of the day, and those anonymous reviewers who have been identified are all relatively obscure. In an age when the leading literati frequently reviewed one another in the leading periodicals, the *Literary Chronicle* could boast of no well-known critics of its own. Nevertheless, its reviewers were clearly well-educated men who kept abreast of the latest literary developments.

When Byerley died, the editorship of the *Chronicle* was taken over by John Watson Dalby, who had been a contributor of original verse to the magazine. Dalby did little to change the journal, which he edited through April 1828. He was at this time a young man, and, although he later became an intimate friend of Leigh Hunt, at the time he directed the *Chronicle* he had none of the literary connections which might have served to enhance the journal's reputation.

In May of 1828 the *Chronicle* was purchased by a consortium, one of whom, Frederick Denison Maurice, edited it until July 1828, when it was merged with the *Athenæum*, a journal run by Maurice's friend John Silk Buckingham. Maurice, who was only twenty-three at the time, was already regarded as one of the leading intellectuals of his generation, and he had contributed several times to the *Westminster Review*. During his short proprietorship, Maurice was even more broadly tolerant of different moral and political philosophies than Byerley and Dalby. He assumed the editorship of the newly merged *Athenæum and Literary Chronicle*, a title which lasted through December 1829, at which time Maurice resigned to go to Oxford, where he studied for the priesthood. He eventually became a leading Christian Socialist. The new management of the magazine shortened its name to the *Athenæum*.

**References:**

John O. Hayden, *The Romantic Reviewers, 1802-1824* (Chicago: University of Chicago Press, 1969);

Donald H. Reiman, ed., *The Romantics Reviewed*, 9 volumes (New York & London: Garland, 1972);

Alvin Sullivan, ed., *British Literary Magazines*, 4 volumes (Westport, Conn.: Greenwood Press, 1983-1986).

# The London Magazine

*(January 1820 - June 1829)*

Linda Mills Woolsey
*King College*

The *London Magazine* entered the field of nineteenth-century periodicals with a sense of risk and high adventure, its "Prospectus" declaring, "Opinion now busies itself with more venturous themes than of yore; discussion must start fleeter and subtler game; excitement must be stronger; the stakes of all sorts higher; the game more complicated and hazardous." These were to prove prophetic words for the early years of the *London Magazine*, as its contributors poured out witty, poignant, and frequently experimental prose, and its first editor died seeking to defend his ideals of literary responsibility. Leaving the newspapers to cover "what is merely intelligence," the *London Magazine* addressed itself to "the *spirit* of things generally, and above all, of the present time." For writers and editors in the magazine's early years this meant the cultivation of an urbane and urban perspective, the exploration of subjective responses to a changing era, and the creation of a literary criticism freed from narrow political and commercial constraints.

The pages of the *London Magazine* give twentieth-century readers a lively and compelling picture of early-nineteenth-century London, that " 'mighty heart' whose vast pulsations circulate life, strength and spirits throughout this great Empire." More important, the early years of the *London Magazine* mark a pioneering effort in literary criticism as its reviewers followed John Scott, the magazine's first editor, in creating reviews which focused on the literary work itself, rather than on the author's politics or personal life. While the *London Magazine* adopted the miscellany format of its rival, *Blackwood's*, it deliberately avoided the party politics and sensational criticism that had made *Blackwood's* famous. As Josephine Bauer has suggested, Scott believed that the critic had "a dual responsibility: that to the public and that to the author." For Scott, the critic was not a judge but an interpreter, with a moral responsibility not only to point out weaknesses but to recognize merit.

The advent of the *London Magazine* was announced to the public in *Baldwin's Weekly Journal* in November 1819. Since the *London Magazine* was originally published by the firm of Baldwin, Cradock, and Joy, it was first called Baldwin's *London Magazine* to distinguish it from the *London Magazine and Monthly Critical and Dramatic Review*, which also began publication in January 1820. In John Scott, publishers Baldwin, Cradock, and Joy found a capable and experienced editor to launch the magazine. Scott, a native of Aberdeen, had edited Drakard's *Stamford News* from 1809 to 1813 and his own liberal weekly, the *Champion*, from 1817 to 1819. He was also a writer whose *A Visit to Paris in 1814* (1815) and *Paris Revisited in 1815* (1816) won praise from William Wordsworth and William Thackeray. Despite his initial reluctance to enter again upon what he termed "the anxieties of literary gladiatorship," Scott threw himself into the work of editing the *London Magazine*.

In his brief term as editor, Scott wrote ably on political and literary issues, advocating reforms and practicing the sort of fair-minded criticism he expected from his contributors. Unlike many editors of his day, Scott did not shrink from publishing articles he disagreed with and refrained from retailoring submissions to bring them into line with his own point of view. Instead, he inserted notes stating his editorial position or commenting on the argument at hand, sometimes with a touch of humor. When—for the sake of conserving space or keeping an article in line with the tone or principles of the magazine—he felt changes were necessary, Scott generally consulted with the writer. He encouraged his writers to carry out their own friendly exchanges, so that the early issues of the magazine sometimes have the atmosphere of a convivial dinner party.

While Scott was by no means a radical, or even, for that matter, a political theorist, his belief in British integrity and in the national character enabled him to espouse reforms that would

*John Scott, the first editor of the* London Magazine *(pencil sketch by Seymour Kirkup; Scottish National Portrait Gallery)*

eradicate abuses in the electoral system, promote a free press, improve British commerce and agriculture, and create a more humane penal code. He encouraged his writers to speak to contemporary issues, even in reviews. Scott himself was an able critic, and his series on "Living Authors" demonstrates a balance between openness to Romantic tendencies in contemporary literature and an appreciation of the neoclassical heritage. In the first article in this series (January 1820) Scott discussed "The Author of the Scotch Novels," comparing the anonymous author of the *Waverley* novels to Shakespeare and ending his article with the suggestion that Sir Walter Scott might indeed be the "Great Unknown." John Scott's discussion of the *Waverley* novelist emphasizes the healthy, moral quality of his work as well as his "intense feeling for natural truth."

Scott urged *London Magazine* writers and their readers to reform contemporary literary criticism. In his April 1820 review of John Keats's *Endymion* (1818), Peter George Patmore seconds Scott, declaring that "the periodical criticism of the present day, *as* criticism, enjoys but a slender portion of public respect—except among mere book-buyers and blue-stockings." In place of an "impertinent" and blighting criticism, Scott and his compatriots wrote reasonably and sympathetically, without neglecting to point out weakness where they saw it. In the second article of his "Living Authors" series (March 1820), despite what he considered the democratic excesses in William Wordsworth's choice of language and circumstance, Scott could admire his poetry as "a delightful text-book to nature herself," exhibiting a "perfect harmony in the elements of moral and physical beauty." Patmore, too, could find promise in Keats's *Endymion*—which, though "not *a poem* at all" is "an ecstatic dream of poetry"—suggesting that it "was born while his muse was his mistress, and he her rapturous lover. He will marry her by and by . . . and then he may chance to love her *better* than ever; but he will cease to be *her lover*." In so doing, the critic suggests, Keats will become a mature poet, fulfilling the promise of his early work.

As an editor, Scott followed many of the practices of his leading contemporaries, including anonymous and pseudonymous publication, paying his contributors well, and seeking out and encouraging well-educated and talented writers such as William Hazlitt, Charles Lamb, and Thomas Griffiths Wainewright. Under Scott's direction, the *London Magazine* devoted nearly half its pages to reviews, including notices of new works, discussions of Elizabethan literature, foreign literature, and the modern periodical press.

Treatment of foreign literature was wide-ranging, covering works from Batavia, Denmark, Iceland, the Netherlands, Russia, Serbia, Spain, and the United States, as well as French, German, and Italian literature. Although Scott found much modern French thought and writing problematic, he began a ground-breaking series of discussions of "The Early French Poets" (March 1820) later continued by Henry Francis Cary. This series initiated the practice of including translations of foreign texts in *London Magazine* reviews. From the beginning, *London* contributors were enthusiastic about Italy and its writers. John Scott, Henry Francis Cary, and Ugo Foscolo particularly commended the works of Petrarch and Dante to the magazine's readers. Scott also valued German literature, seeing it as a model of a nation's writers shaking off the influence of the French; he was among the first English reviewers to recognize the power and genius of Johann Wolfgang von Goethe's *Faust* (1808).

Under Scott, the *London Magazine* not only provided its readers with a "Monthly Register" of information about foreign affairs, commerce, agriculture publishing, deaths, births, marriages, and bankruptcies, but also let them into the convivial circle of the magazine with its "Lion's Head" column, in which the editorial staff declare themselves "Valiant as a Lion, and wondrous affable." The "Lion's Head," begun in July 1820, provides a running commentary on the state of the magazine and epigrammatic messages to correspondents and would-be contributors. Under Scott the magazine began publishing tales of romance, high-risk adventure, and mysterious powers, often modeled on folk narratives and containing ballads and other verse.

In its early days the *London Magazine* also established itself in the realm of fine-arts criticism, with regular reviews of plays, concerts, and exhibitions. The dramatic criticism of William Hazlitt, Thomas Noon Talfourd, and John Hamilton Reynolds relies heavily on description. Hazlitt's essays re-create the ambiance of the London theater world, and his successors focused on productions of old plays, preferring works of the "Elizabethan revival" to contemporary dramatists. The articles on music provide a record of middle- and upper-class taste of the period, fretting a little about the neglect of English composers and admiring the work of Wolfgang Amadeus Mozart and Gioacchino Antonio Rossini. The *London Magazine* carried many perceptive reviews of sculpture and painting, often focusing on subjective response more than on technique. The Elgin marbles provided a touchstone for many of the *London Magazine* perspectives on art, for those works, according to one writer, taught viewers that "the great secret is to recur at every step to nature" and reminded them that ideal form "is nothing but a selection of fine nature" (February 1822).

From the magazine's earliest days, its writers were travelers, giving their readers glimpses of places as accessible as Italy and as remote as Persia. Their articles tended to focus on people and customs, but they also described familiar and exotic scenes with careful, evocative detail. Some of them delighted in pointing up the contrast between idealized distant landscapes and firsthand experience. In March 1822, for instance, one traveler in Italy comments: "Who would suppose, that the swimming skiff, which looks so pretty, and so inviting at a distance, with its puffed white sail and painted side, could be such a nest of filth and misery within?"

Perhaps the most striking characteristic of the *London Magazine* group, established and encouraged by Scott, was the writers' exploration of memory, feeling, and identity. Months before the appearance of Thomas De Quincey's *Confessions of an English Opium Eater* in the September and October 1821 issues of the *London*, they were examining their responses to common objects and people, celebrating the mysterious powers of metropolitan London, confessing their weaknesses and eccentricities, and speculating about hypochondriasis and the effects of "Diseased Imagination."

Scott's tenure as editor was brief, but it established a momentum that was to carry the magazine through the crisis of his death. The rivalry with *Blackwood's* that ended in Scott's fatal duel with J. H. Christie began as a friendly competition between the two magazines. After the first issue of the *London Magazine* came out, *Blackwood's* proclaimed it a "promising publication." Scott returned the compliment in the February 1820 issue, thanking "our brethren Editors . . . for a *civil notice* in their last Number" and declaring it "far more agreeable (to both parties, we presume) than a *civil war*." Even in the May 1820 article in which Scott criticized *Blackwood's* and the *Quarterly Review* for their rough handling of the "Cockney School," he ended on a friendly note designed to cast his criticism in the light of gentlemanly exchange.

No one at *Blackwood's* seemed to take offense. Then, in October, the anonymous editors of "Maga" wrote "of Baldwin's new bang-up concern we, at present, civilly ask the Jehu, John Scott, to keep to his own side of the road—not to be so fond of running races—and not to abuse the passengers who prefer going by another conveyance." John Scott responded in November with a strong article on *Blackwood's*, using his pen as an "instrument of justice" against critics whose "poison in jest" threatened to corrupt the manly and honorable principles of British literature and literary criticism. Yet, even as he castigates the "brazen insolence" and "meanest hypocrisy" of the *Blackwood's* crew, Scott recognizes their ability. For him the very genius and education of his rivals make their betrayal more insidious.

The resulting exchange of accusations and justifications, carried out in the pages of the two rival magazines and in correspondence between John Scott and John Gibson Lockhart, came to a head with Scott challenging Lockhart to confess publicly to his role as one of *Blackwood's* "Mohocks" (January 1821). Lockhart failed to do so in the statement he sent Scott, though, in a statement published in *Blackwood's*, Lockhart did acknowledge his authorship of articles for the magazine but denied (correctly) that he was its editor. Although Lockhart's friend and message bearer J. H. Christie attributed the initial omission to an oversight, there was a further exchange of heated letters. In the February issue Scott published a statement of his side of the story, including correspondence. This action angered Christie, who then challenged Scott to a duel. They met at the Chalk Farm on the evening of 16 February to settle the matter. On the first round, Christie fired into the air, but, in the darkness, Scott was evidently not aware of this. Scott's second urged that they fire another round, and Christie's second urged him to take aim at Scott in self-defense. Scott was mortally wounded and died on 27 February 1821.

While the *London Magazine* group mourned the passing of their editor, Robert Baldwin and John Hamilton Reynolds carried on the work of the magazine. By May, Baldwin had decided to sell, and the publishing firm of Taylor and Hessey was interested in buying. The July 1821 issue was the first to bear Taylor and Hessey's imprint. John Taylor had considered asking Henry Francis Cary, a translator of Dante, to edit the magazine, but decided, instead, to do the work himself. Taylor served as editor of the magazine from July 1821 to December 1824, with Thomas Hood assisting him from 1821 to 1823. Taylor made few substantial changes, continuing the format and features that characterized Scott's magazine. In early 1821 the *London* became an illustrated magazine, publishing engravings of art works of contemporary interest.

John Taylor and his partner James Hessey retained many of the original contributors and added other talented writers, instituting regular contributors' dinners at Waterloo House that further encouraged camaraderie and intellectual interchange among the *London Magazine* writers. Under Scott, Charles Lamb's Elia essays and William Hazlitt's *Table-Talk* had come into being; both series continued under Taylor. After Taylor published the first installment of *The Confessions of an English Opium Eater* in the September 1821 issue, Thomas De Quincey became an important contributor. During the first five years of its existence, the *London Magazine* featured the work of poets such as John Clare, Thomas Hood, and John Keats. Allan Cunningham wrote regularly on traditional English literature, and Henry Francis Cary wrote on foreign literature. As Edward Herbert, John Hamilton Reynolds contributed witty and amusing sketches of travels in England and eyewitness accounts of important events.

As Egomet Bonmot, Cornelius Van Vinkbrooms, and Janus Weathercock, Thomas Griffiths Wainewright wrote lighthearted, yet sometimes telling, articles on the arts that, in many ways, embodied the venturesome and convivial spirit of the magazine. Wainewright was one of few in that decade to notice and admire the work of William Blake. Through his three personae, Wainewright could create rivalries and exchanges that echoed the dialogue of the *London* writers while it poked fun at critical and moral pretensions. Hartley Coleridge, George Darley, C. A. Elton, Octavius Gilchrist, B. W. Proctor (as Barry Cornwall), Horace Smith, and Thomas Noon Talfourd were also regular contributors. In 1823 Thomas Carlyle, Julius C. Hare, and Mary Shelley joined the *London* band of writers. Thus, under the direction of Scott, Taylor, and Hood, the *London Magazine* became a veritable "who's who" of the writing world.

Despite its energy and its talent, the *London Magazine* evidently never enjoyed great financial success. In early 1821 the magazine had a circulation of sixteen hundred which increased to seventeen hundred by August of that year. In November 1822 circulation was holding steady, but Hessey was discouraged. The current circulation, he declared, "will not pay expenses" and, "whether we are too good for the Age, or the Age is not good enough for us, I know not, but so it is that we seem rather on the decline than the increase." Nevertheless, the magazine did survive through most of the decade, with the circulation holding steady at sixteen hundred in 1825.

Estimates of Taylor's work as an editor are mixed. While he did manage for a time to keep and even enlarge upon the *London* writers' sense of community, he gradually alienated some of the important early contributors, including William Hazlitt. Although Taylor and Hessey often dealt very generously with writers—putting up with the procrastination of Thomas De Quincey and paying even young unknowns well—Taylor was decided in his political opinions, less venturesome than Scott in addressing current controversies, and less adept at gauging public taste. Taylor was also apt to cut contributors' manuscripts in ways that provoked their ire. By the end of 1821, Hazlitt shifted his *Table-Talk* to the *New Monthly* and the *London* began devoting greater space to sober articles on topics such as "Paper Currency" while the number of literary reviews dwindled.

Taylor's tendency to rely on editorial assistants may also have caused some difficulties among the *London* writers. The "Lion's Head" for December 1822 jokes that the magazine has a dozen editors, divided eleven to one about the authorship of a particular poem, and "Our Eleven, as Mary-le-bone cricketers call themselves, pin their faith upon the passages in italics." By January 1823 Wainewright, as Janus Weathercock, was playfully declaring, "As to the Editor, I am doubtful. He is without form—I can't make up my mind to believe in such a *nominous umbra*." In 1823 Thomas Hood left the magazine, apparently disgruntled with both Taylor and Hessey. Without Hood, Taylor's subeditors were able, but lacked the creativity, energy, and wit that had marked Hood's work. Among Hood's successors between 1823 and 1825 were Charles Wentworth Dilke, Harry Stoe Van Dyk, and Henry Hunt. While the magazine of these years lacks the gusto of its early days, it was still attracting important contributors, among them Thomas Carlyle and Stendhal (Henri Beyle). In 1824 Carlyle was asked to contribute an article on Friedrich Schiller for a series of portraits of great men; as he worked on the article it became a series on the life and work of Schiller. As "Grimm's Grandson," Stendhal wrote a regular series—notable for its disparagement of Victor Hugo—on contemporary France and its literature in 1825 and 1826.

By 1825 Taylor and Hessey were looking for a buyer. At the same time, John Stuart Mill, John Hamilton Reynolds, and Henry Southern were looking for a magazine to embody their political and social ideals. Reynolds pulled out in June of 1825 and in August, the firm of Hunt and Clarke began to publish the *London Magazine*, now owned and edited by Henry Southern. With many of the old *London* contributors (such as Lamb, Hazlitt, De Quincey, and Cunningham) gone, Southern did much of the writing himself, focusing on principles of economy and plans for public projects such as the Thames Quay. Despite his sometimes flippant tone, Southern took a serious view of the magazine's public responsibility, and the contents were often informative and practical but hardly imaginative.

In 1828 Charles Knight bought the *London Magazine* and, assisted by Barry St. Leger, edited it for its last two years. Under Knight's direction, politics and practical concerns were the focal point of the magazine, reflecting Knight's firm utilitarian perspective. Knight used the magazine as a platform to promote his favorite cause—education for the masses. While the *London* still continued to run interesting articles, in its last years it had lost the energy, wit, and broadness of political and aesthetic vision that marked its early days. One telling indication of the shift in the *London Magazine* under Knight is its reversal of opinion about German literature. Scott had praised German literature highly; under Taylor,

De Quincey attacked Goethe but enthusiastically introduced readers to other German writers including Jean-Paul Richter and Immanuel Kant. Under Southern, the magazine continued to summarize and print abstracts from German work, with little critical commentary. During Knight's tenure as editor, the magazine denigrated German literature for its lack of utility and its tendency to obscurity and mysticism.

The magazine that had begun as an adventure had become, finally, cautious, narrow, and pedestrian. The *London Magazine* of 1820-1823 is, in many ways, an embodiment of a politically minded, but not narrowly political, Romanticism—urban, reasonable, and energetic. Its prose is mobile, reflective, and marked by sensibility. Its writers explore the solitary responses of the individual, yet feel themselves a company—not exiles but a band of adventurers. This is the magazine that served as a catalyst for Romantic prose, calling up table talk and confessions, the gentle voice of Elia and the wild dreams of the Opium-Eater.

**References:**

Herschel Baker, *William Hazlitt* (Cambridge, Mass.: Harvard University Press, 1962);

Josephine Bauer, *The London Magazine 1820-1829* (Copenhagen: Rosenkilde & Bagger, 1953);

Edmund Charles Blunden, *Keats's Publisher: A Memoir of John Taylor* (London: Cape, 1936);

Elmer L. Brooks, "Byron and the *London Magazine,*" *Keats-Shelley Journal*, 5 (1956): 49-67;

Jonathan Curling, *Janus Weathercock: The Life of Thomas Griffiths Wainewright, 1794-1847* (New York: Nelson, 1938);

Thomas De Quincey, "Charles Lamb," in volume 5 of *The Collected Writings of Thomas De Quincey*, edited by David Masson (Edinburgh: Adam & Charles Black, 1890);

Helen B. Ellis, Entry on the *London Magazine*, in *British Literary Magazines*, 4 volumes, edited by Alvin Sullivan (Westport, Conn.: Greenwood Press, 1983-1986), II: 288-296;

John O. Hayden, *The Romantic Reviewers, 1802-1824* (Chicago: University of Chicago Press, 1968);

William Hazlitt, "The Periodical Press," in volume 16 of *The Complete Works of William Hazlitt*, edited by P. P. Howe (London & Toronto: Dent, 1933);

Humphry House, *All in Due Time* (London: Hart-Davis, 1955);

Ian Jack, *English Literature 1815-1832*, The Oxford History of English Literature, edited by F. P. Wilson and Bonamy Dobree (London: Clarendon Press, 1963);

Charles Knight, *Passages of a Working Life During Half a Century*, 3 volumes (London: Bradbury & Evans, 1864-1865);

Peter F. Morgan, "Taylor and Hessey: Aspects of Their Conduct of the *London Magazine,*" *Keats-Shelley Journal*, 7 (Winter 1958): 61-68;

Donald H. Reiman, ed., *The Romantics Reviewed*, 9 volumes (New York & London: Garland, 1972);

Alan Lang Strout, "*Blackwood's Magazine*, Lockhart, and John Scott. A Whig Satirical Broadside," *Notes and Queries*, 180 (11 January 1941): 22-24;

Jacob Zeitlin, "The Editor of the *London Magazine,*" *Journal of English and Germanic Philology*, 20, no. 3 (1921): 328-354.

# The Monthly Review

*(May 1749 - December 1844)*

Jennifer Viereck

Prior to the establishment of the *Monthly Review* in May 1749, there were no regular literary magazines in existence in Great Britain. Some earlier periodicals were collections of abstracts, or digests, of scholarly works which the editors considered "learned," but they were not literary journals in the modern sense. They were not read by the general public, and they made no attempt to evaluate books. The *Monthly Review* discussed relative merits of literary works and covered a broader range of books than earlier periodicals. These two factors combined to make the *Monthly* one of the most successful reviews of late-eighteenth- and early-nineteenth-century England, with a run of nearly one hundred years.

The title page for the first issue of the *Monthly Review* proudly boasts that it will give "An Account, with proper Abstracts of, and Extracts from, the New Books, Pamphlets, & c. as they come out," while "Advertisement" in that issue promises a "compendious account of those productions of the press, as they come out that are worth notice." Ralph Griffiths, the original publisher and editor of the *Monthly*, did indeed attempt to evaluate all works which came out within a given month—a tradition which was carried on by his son, George Edward Griffiths, who took over publication on his father's death in 1803. The inclusion of notices for popular literature perhaps accounted for the success of the *Monthly* as much as any change in approach to literary works. The *Monthly* attempted to direct readers toward works of merit, but offered little in the way of critique, until Samuel Badcock, a writer for the magazine, suggested to Ralph Griffiths in 1783 that reviews should be more than mere abstracts. Griffiths evidently agreed, and the periodical began offering more criticism in its reviews.

The list of contributors to the *Monthly Review* is impressive. Oliver Goldsmith contributed more than twenty articles between April 1757 and December 1758. Thomas Denman, who became chief justice in 1832, reviewed many of the works of George Gordon, Lord Byron; Thomas Campbell, George Crabbe, and Charles Lamb. William Gilpin, William Norwich, Charles Burney, and Thomas Holcroft were all regular contributors. Little circulation information is available, but in 1817 the *British Stage* contended that the *Monthly* had a "circulation more extensive than that of all its rivals combined."

The format established by 1790 includes an initial spate of long reviews (ten to fifteen pages), followed by a "Monthly Catalogue" of shorter treatments. Most monthly reviews established in the eighteenth century, including the *Critical Review* (established in 1756) and the *Analytical Review* (established in 1788), adopted this format, as well as the goal of reviewing each new work that was published in a given month. Not until the *Edinburgh Review* was established in 1802 did a periodical attempt more selectivity of subject matter.

The *Monthly Review* was essentially liberal in its outlook, prompting Samuel Johnson to tell James Boswell on 10 April 1776 that its reviewers were "Christians with as little christianity as may be; and are for pulling down all establishments." In a November 1801 letter to Robert Southey, William Taylor stated that "Both the Monthly and the Critical are in the main well conducted, and as low in their politics as the times will yet patronize."

The *Monthly* expressed attitudes considered liberal in the eighteenth and early nineteenth centuries. Its June 1792 review of Mary Wollstonecraft's *Vindication of the Rights of Woman* (1792) is radical for its time. The anonymous reviewer (Dr. William Enfield) claims that "In the class of philosophers, the *'author'* of this treatise—whom we will not offend by styling, authoress—has a right to a distinguished place," but he is careful to acknowledge the validity of her claims throughout. The one exception the reviewer takes to Wollstonecraft's ideology is with its imple-

*William Taylor, a principal reviewer for the* Monthly *during the Romantic period (engraving by J. Thomson)*

mentation: "We do not, however, so zealously adopt Miss W.'s plan for a REVOLUTION in female education and manners, as not to perceive that several of her opinions are fanciful, and some of her projects romantic. We do not see, that the condition or the character of women would be improved, by assuming an active part in civil government. . . . Certain associations, now firmly established, forbid us to think that women are degraded by the trivial attention which the men are inclined to pay them. . . . Notwithstanding all this, however, we entirely agree with the fair writer that both the condition and character of women are capable of great improvement; and that, by means of a more rational plan of female education . . . women might be rendered at once more agreeable, more respectable, and more happy in every station of life."

The views expressed in the *Monthly* were consistent largely because of the editorial policy of the Griffiths, who believed that a review should reflect a corporate opinion, with the publisher accepting sole responsibility for that opinion. For this reason, most of the reviews were anonymous and employed the pronoun *we* when expressing an opinion. At the same time, Griffiths did allow his reviewers a degree of latitude. In his *Spirit of the Age* (1825) William Hazlitt credits William Taylor, a frequent contributor to the *Monthly*, with developing "philosophical criticism."

This type of criticism was also employed by Enfield, who began his September 1794 review of William Godwin's *Caleb Williams* (1794) by saying that, "Between fiction and philosophy there seems to be no natural alliance:—yet philosophers, in order to obtain for their dogmata a more ready reception, have often judged it expedient to introduce them to the world in the captivating dress of fable." He then goes on to critique Godwin's novel, both in terms of its literary merit and its philosophical orientation. He praises Godwin for his creation of character, calling Falkland a "visionary character [who] is drawn with uncommon strength of conception and energy of language." He then suggests that one of Godwin's objectives in writing the novel was "to exhibit an example of the danger of indulging an idle curiousity, merely for its own gratification. . . . The general result is a forcible conviction of the hazard of suffering any foolish desire, or curiousity, (that restless propensity,) to creep into the mind." He also points out, "This narrative seems, moreover, intended to give the author an opportunity of making an indirect attack on what he deems vulgar prejudices, respecting religion, morals, and policy," and he concludes by labeling *Caleb Williams* "a work in which the powers of genius and philosophy are strongly united."

This consideration of the literary merits of a work as an issue apart from its morality gave the *Monthly* an objectivity of tóne unusual for the time. Of M. G. Lewis's *The Monk* (1796), Taylor stated in August 1797 that although the novel in a sense plagiarizes its story line, characters, and setting from other works, it is still praiseworthy. Despite his conclusion that the novel is obscene in parts and therefore "totally unfit for general circulation," he nonetheless defends it on the grounds of its literary merit: "The great art of writing consists in selecting what is most stimulant from the works of our predecessors, and in uniting the gathered beauties in a new whole. . . . All invention is but new combination. To invent well is to combine the impressive."

Similarly, the July 1819 review of Byron's *Don Juan*, Cantos I and II (1819), expresses the hope "that his readers have learnt to admire his genius without being in danger from its influence; and we must not be surprised if a poet *will* not always write to instruct as well as to please us." The *Monthly*, which began to tire of *Don Juan* as subsequent cantos appeared, reviewed Byron's work extensively, finding fault with his solipsistic tendencies, more because of their infringement on his literary genius than for any possible influence on readers' morals. In November 1818 the reviewer of *Childe Harold's Pilgrimage*, Canto IV (1818), asserts: "Lord Byron seems not to be aware that the popularity of his early poems was, in a great degree, owing to the strong contrast which they bore to the mawkish sentimentality and vapid whinings of a different race of verse-writers, with whom the public had been recently nauseated. . . . The author, however, unfortunately imagined that peculiarities, which were tolerated for the excellences that seemed to accompany them, were in themselves the object of admiration." The reviewer also chastises Byron for addressing the ocean "as if it were some untameable and savage monster that played with human power as a bauble: rather than as an element which, from an immensity of years, has been rolling its fathomless billows in obedience to some superior laws. . . ." Inherent in this criticism is a belief in a supreme being who has established a natural order. Yet the reviewer faults Byron for his poetic ineptness in describing the ocean, rather than for not sharing his religious beliefs. This insistence on recognizing the literary merit of a work despite any of its perceived moral failings was one of the trademarks of the *Monthly Review*.

Griffiths was also known for his strict reviewing ethics. Reviewers could not review their own works or those of their friends. This policy helped to make the review popular. Yet, in the end, the uniformity of opinion and the wide range of works reviewed—which had made the periodical so successful—were instrumental in its downfall. In 1821 its readership began to fall off, and in 1825 George Edward Griffiths sold the magazine. Periodicals such as the *Edinburgh Review* focused selectively on subjects of current interest, and presented a variety of opinions. Also, the *Monthly* addressed the university-educated gentry while the *Edinburgh Review* and periodicals styled after it were written for the rising tradesman and the newly educated working class as well. The *Monthly Review* printed its last issue in December 1844. The rise and fall of the *Monthly Review* epitomize the changing tastes and ideals of the English reading public.

**References:**

Richmond P. Bond, *Studies in the Early English Periodical* (Chapel Hill: University of North Carolina Press, 1957);

Walter Graham, *English Literary Periodicals* (New York: Nelson, 1930);

John O. Hayden, *The Romantic Reviewers, 1802-1824* (Chicago: University of Chicago Press, 1968);

Jon P. Klancher, *The Making of the English Reading Audiences: 1790-1832* (Madison: University of Wisconson Press, 1987);

Donald H. Reiman, ed., *The Romantics Reviewed: Contemporary Reviews of British Romantic Writers*, 9 volumes (New York & London: Garland, 1972);

Derek Roper, *Reviewing before the* Edinburgh, *1788-1802* (London: Methuen, 1978);
Alvin Sullivan, ed., *British Literary Magazines*, 4 volumes (Westport, Conn.: Greenwood Press, 1983-1986).

# The New Monthly Magazine

*(February 1814 - January 1884)*

Martin A. Cavanaugh
*Washington University*

Henry Colburn founded the *New Monthly Magazine and Universal Register*, with Frederic Shoberl as editor, to offer a "Tory, anti-Jacobin, anti-Napoleonic" rebuttal to Richard Phillips's *Monthly Magazine*. The political conservatism of Colburn's magazine colored many of its literary reviews during the early years. The major poets of the period were often looked upon with disfavor because of their liberal political or social views. George Gordon, Lord Byron; Percy Bysshe Shelley; and William Wordsworth all received negative reviews in the pages of the *New Monthly*.

The work of Byron received more extensive attention from the *New Monthly* than that of any other Romantic poet. Thirteen reviews of his works appeared between 1814 and 1823. The first of these was a notice of *The Corsair, a Tale* (1814) in March 1814, which made little critical comment. Six months later the *New Monthly* reviewed the sequel, *Lara, a Tale* (1814), and the reviewer bemoaned the lack of moral direction shown in the work, "still mystery and murder, without cause or consequence, obscure and deform this sequel of the story, which, like the former part, possesses many beauties, unhappily allied to extravagance and immorality." This focus on Byron's immorality became a recurring theme in the *New Monthly* reviews of his work.

In a much more critical tone the *New Monthly* reviewed Byron's *The Siege of Corinth, a Poem; Parasina, a Poem* (1816) in March 1816. The reviewer again criticized the lack of morality in the work: "But though we are ready to admit the poetic claims of Lord Byron to the fullest extent, justice compels us to call in question the moral tendency of them. None of the pieces that we have read can be said to elevate the mental dignity of man, by exhibiting the inward beauty of virtue, and the real deformity of vice. He delights in subjects that are revolting to humanity, and in drawing characters that ought, if possible, to be burned in darkness."

The May 1816 review of *Poems on his own Domestic Circumstances* (1816) continued the assault on Byron's lack of morals and began, "We have repeatedly been compelled, by the indignant feelings of loyalty and virtue, to enter our strong protest against the pernicious tendency of Lord Byron's productions." The reviewer went on to criticize Byron's hypocritical attitude toward those who are born lower than he. This negative view of Byron's work persisted in a February 1817 review of *The Prisoner of Chillon, and other Poems* (1816): "There breathes in this slight performance, as in all the productions of the noble author, a wild and gloomy tincture of misanthropy, which gives, indeed, uncommon force to the representations, but raises in the mind of the reader no sublime emotions." According to the reviewer, Byron missed a golden opportunity to exhibit the "finest sentiments of morality and patriotism.... Lord Byron is successful in describing scenes of suffering agony; but he fails in delineating and expressing the virtues by which the immortal mind is enabled to triumph over misery."

A rare complimentary review of Byron's *Childe Harold's Pilgrimage, Canto the Fourth* (1818) appeared in September 1818, breaking the string of disapproving reviews that the *New Monthly* had published during the previous four years. The reviewer concurs with Byron's own opinion that it is "the most thoughtful and comprehensive of all his compositions." He is much more sympathetic to Byron's emotive language than previous review-

*Portrait by Daniel Maclise in the* Fraser's Magazine *"Gallery of Illustrious Literary Characters" (1830-1838)*

ers and, in fact, focuses on the language as a strength in the poet's work: "No poet was ever gifted with so powerful a talisman for discerning the intenser passions of the heart, as Lord Byron. He reveals to us thoughts and sensations, of which we scarcely believed ourselves capable, and teaches us that we are indeed, 'fearfully and wonderfully made.' "

A balanced appraisal of Byron's *Mazeppa, a Poem* (1819) appeared in August 1819. The reviewer praised Byron's ability to involve the reader in the poetry: "Lord Byron possesses, in a superior degree, the power of exciting the attention, of touching the sympathies, and rousing the passions. He, as it were, burns in our blood, and moulds our spirit to his own likeness and purpose." However, the reviewer lamented the lack of moral sensibility in Byron, whose hero is a criminal, worthy of punishment, not sympathy. Distinct from the previous *New Monthly* reviews is this reviewer's technical analysis of the poetry, criticizing forced rhymes and obsolete vocabulary.

The disapproval of the unvirtuous elements in Byron's poetry reappeared in the August 1819 review of *Don Juan*, Cantos I and II (1819). The reviewer lamented "to behold so much fervid genius, elegant literature, and knowledge of the world, united with a spirit of libertinism and infidelity, and employed to corrupt senses." After quoting a passage concerning Donna Julia's efforts to suppress her passion, the reviewer bemoaned, "We cannot read these passages without being touched by their exquisite beauty, and wishing that a poet so full of the true inspiration had devoted his powers to the cause of virtue." This reviewer presented a treatise on the dissolute character of Byron's poetry and concluded, "A certain degree of fleeting reputation may be acquired by ministering to the fashionable follies and corruptions of the age; but no British poet can obtain a universal and permanent fame, excepting by the devotion of his muse to the interests of truth and justice, and the delineation of examples conducive to social happiness and virtue."

In 1821 Colburn changed his publication from a political organ to a more mainstream literary journal and renamed it *The New Monthly Magazine and Literary Journal.* To promote the new literary emphasis, he hired poet Thomas Campbell as editor. Campbell was in reality a figurehead editor, whose name on the masthead was credited with doubling the circulation of the magazine. After the first issue, Cyrus Redding carried on the day-to-day editorial responsibilities until his resignation in September 1830.

As the *New Monthly* moved away from politically reactionary diatribe to literary commentary, its reviewers moderated their appraisal of Byron. The first review of a Byronic work to appear in the *New Monthly* after its reorganization was a neutral review of *The Prophecy of Dante* (1821) in the June 1821 issue. The reviewer found one major fault: Byron's forced imitation of Dante's versification, which was unsuitable for the English language.

A generally favorable review of Byron's *Heaven and Earth; A Mystery* (1823) appeared in April 1823. The reviewer, perhaps recalling earlier negative responses to the poet's works, made a lengthy argument for accepting a poet's stylistic uniqueness, rather than evaluating each poet according to some presumedly fixed laws of poetry. In this vein the reviewer maintained a sympathetic ear for Byron's work and concluded, "That it has faults must be obvious to every reader: prosaic passages, and too much tedious soliloquizing. But there is the vigour and force of Byron to fling into the scale against these. There is much of the sublime in description, and the beautiful in poetry. Prejudice or ignorance, or both, may condemn this poem. But while true poetical feeling exists amongst us, it will be pronounced not unworthy of its distinguished author."

*The Island; or, Christian and His Comrades* (1823) was the last of Byron's works reviewed in the *New Monthly*. Appearing in August 1823, the review proclaimed, "Whereas, of all the numerous fragments which this extraordinary writer has put forth, if there is one which indicates the true nature of the poetical structure he is capable of raising, and (we are determined to hope and expect) he some day or other *will* raise, to the glory of his art and the immortal honour of his name—it is this."

The first of Wordsworth's works reviewed by the *New Monthly Magazine* was *The Excursion* (1814). In the September 1814 issue, the reviewer announced, "Mercy upon the reader, and still more upon the reviewer! for it seems this ponderous volume is only the prelude to two others of an equal size, and similar materials." The reviewer's major criticism focused on the metaphysical nature of the content and the "hobbling kind of measure."

An insignificant notice of *The White Doe of Rylstone* (1815) appeared in July 1815 with little commentary. A short notice of *The Waggoner* (1819) in August 1819 lamented, "As we would much rather be pleased than displeased, it is with concern that truth compels us to express the disappointment which we have felt on laying down the present poem of four cantos, containing the simple history of a good-natured waggoner, who loses his place on account of his incorrigible propensity to nut-brown ale."

Leigh Hunt, radical editor of the *Examiner*, was the object of some of the *New Monthly* reviewers' most caustic remarks. A short notice of *The Feast of the Poets* (1814) in the August 1814 issue proclaimed, "the writer who can commit to paper such jargon as this ought to receive the horsewhip." A review of *The Story of Rimini* (1816) in March 1816 complained, "Of the book itself we shall only say, that the subject is taken from an episode in Dante; but most miserably expanded in the present version." The most biting comments appeared in a September 1818 review of *Foliage, or Poems Original and Translated* (1818), which alluded to Hunt's libel of the prince regent: "How can so contemptible a being as the editor of the Examiner newspaper, presume to talk of his poetical capabilities, when the germ of all true poetry is *religion* and *patriotism?*—How can the man who has dared to pronounce the glorious creed of Christianity '*unattractive,*' and who drivels away what little talents he possesses in the composition of obscene verses, and libels on public characters, pretend to have an eye to the glories of the creation. . . ."

Only one review of a work by Shelley appeared in the *New Monthly*, and that during the journal's early, conservative phase. *The Cenci* (1819) was reviewed in the May 1820 issue and found to be much too vulgar for British literary taste. The reviewer mourned Shelley's misuse of his genius, "The lamentable solution is, that Mr. Shelley, with noble feelings, with far-reaching hopes, and with a high and emphatic imagination, has no power of religious truth fitly to balance and rightly to direct his energies. . . . Thus will he continue to vibrate until he shall learn that there are sanctities in his nature as well as rights, and that these venerable relations which he despises, instead of contracting the soul, nurture its most extended charities, and cherish its purest aspirations for universal good. Then will he feel that his imaginations, beautiful as ever in shape, are not cold, but breathing with genial life, and that the most ravishing prospects of human improvement, can only be contemplated steadily from those immortal pillars which Heaven has provided for Faith to lean on."

In September 1820 the *New Monthly* reviewed John Keats's *Lamia, Isabella, The Eve of St. Agnes, and Other Poems* (1820). This review, contrary to many of the reviews of Byron, Wordsworth, Hunt, and Shelley, was supportive of the poet's work. The reviewer began, "These poems are very far superior to any which their author has previously committed to the press. They have nothing showy, or extravagant, or eccentric about them; but are pieces of calm beauty, or of lone and self-supported grandeur. We have perused them with the heartiest pleasure . . . and we rejoice to find these his latest works as free from all offensive peculiarities—as pure, as genuine, and as lofty, as the severest critic could desire." The reviewer concluded, "We may now take leave of Mr. Keats with wonder at the gigantic stride which he has taken, and with the good hope that, if he proceeds in the high and pure style which he has now chosen, he will attain an exalted and a lasting station among English poets."

Most of the reviews of the major Romantic poets appearing in the pages of the *New Monthly Magazine* came during the early, politically conservative period. This conservatism apparently colored the reviewers' judgments, and many times they attacked the poets' personal lives. When the magazine was reorganized and focused on the literary merits of the poetry it reviewed, the criticism became more moderate, without political acrimony.

In July 1829 the *London Magazine*, which Charles Knight had purchased in April 1828, merged with the *New Monthly*. With Redding's resignation, Colburn hoped Campbell would take over full control of the editorial job, but he proved unable. Colburn replaced Campbell with Samuel Carter Hall in December 1830. Hall, however, was not well known, and Colburn desired a literary name to attract readers. In October 1831 Colburn announced that Edward Bulwer (later Bulwer-Lytton) would be the new editor, with Hall as his subeditor.

Colburn got more than he bargained for in Bulwer, who quickly began transforming the *New Monthly* into a radical-reform periodical. Colburn tolerated Bulwer's political agitation, but in August 1833 Bulwer resigned, to Colburn's relief. Colburn reappointed Hall to the chief editorial position, and he returned the journal to its politically neutral stance.

In January 1837 Colburn, in reaction to Richard Bentley's magazine *Bentley's Miscellany*, again changed the title of his publication, to *The New Monthly Magazine and the Humorist*, added a humor section, and named Theodore Hook editor. Hook served as editor until his death in August 1841. In September 1841 Thomas Hood replaced Hook, but he resigned in August 1843, in part because he could not tolerate Colburn's meddling. Colburn sold the publication to William Harrison Ainsworth in June 1845. According to W. Paul Elledge, "The best days of the magazine were over. Although it was published until 1884, the *New Monthly* never enjoyed the stature or success it had known under Campbell and Bulwer."

**References:**

W. Paul Elledge, Entry on the *New Monthly Magazine*, in *British Literary Magazines*, 4 volumes, edited by Alvin Sullivan (Westport, Conn.: Greenwood Press, 1983-1986), II: 331-339;

Donald H. Reiman, ed., *The Romantics Reviewed: Contemporary Reviews of British Romantic Writers*, 9 volumes (New York & London: Garland, 1972).

# The Quarterly Review

*(February 1809 - October 1967)*

Thomas L. Cooksey
*Armstrong State College*

"The *Quarterly Review* arose out of the *Edinburgh*, not as a corollary, but in contradiction to it," declared William Hazlitt in his essay on Francis Jeffrey in *The Spirit of the Age* (1825). He added cynically, "It was not to be endured that the truth should *out* in this manner, even occasionally and half in jest." Writing in 1818, Thomas Love Peacock saw the two reviews as the "organs and oracles of the two great political factions," suggesting that their success was more attributable to the curiosity of the public to divine the current views of the Whigs and Tories than any inherent literary merit. James Mill shared this view in his April 1824 analysis of the *Edinburgh* and *Quarterly* reviews in the newly founded *Westminster Review*, arguing that they represented the competing interests between two factions of the landed aristocracy. Indeed, from its inception, the *Quarterly* envisioned imitating the format and style of the *Edinburgh* while challenging its politics and providing a sympathetic organ for Tory policies. Locked in a competition that lasted the entire nineteenth century, both magazines transformed the role of general reviews as a cultural force and deeply influenced the development and reception of British Romanticism.

While not the first journal to challenge the *Edinburgh*, the *Quarterly* proved the most successful. Richard Cumberland, with the help of Hewson Clarke and Henry Crabb Robinson, had founded the short-lived *London Review* in 1809, explicitly challenging the *Edinburgh* and its policy of anonymous reviews, and evoking the "genuine spirit of criticism." Begun in the same year, the *Quarterly* lasted until 1967, outliving the *Edinburgh* by some thirty-eight years. While much of its early writing was characterized by its seriousness—even heaviness when compared with the wit and playfulness of the *Edinburgh*—its influence and reputation eclipsed that of the *Edinburgh* midway through the nineteenth century. The motivations that underlay the foundation of the *Quarterly* were complex, mixing politics and business, personal animus and moral principles. The key to its origins, however, involves the convergence of three men: the Tory politician and prime minister in 1823, George Canning (1770-1827); the London publisher John Murray II (1778-1843); and the Scottish novelist Sir Walter Scott (1771-1832).

*William Gifford, the first editor of the* Quarterly Review *(engraving by S. Freeman, after a painting by J. Hoppner)*

Toward the end of the 1790s, Canning and other Tory ministers in the government of Sir William Pitt felt the need for some means of supporting Tory interests against what they took to be Jacobin sympathies in the British press. Aside from the use of licensing, stamp taxes, and libel suits, the king's ministers had few weapons against the press. Support among provincial papers was unreliable, and Pitt's ministry had few friends among the major London papers. Faced with hostile voices in James Harmer's *Weekly Dispatch*, William Cobbett's *Weekly Register*, the Benthamite *Atlas*, and John and Leigh Hunt's *Examiner*, Canning judged that the most effective weapon for the Tories was to sponsor a sympathetic journal of their own. With this in mind, he helped to found the *Anti-Jacobin; or, Weekly Examiner* in November 1797, appointing the scholar and satirist William Gifford as its editor. While the *Anti-Jacobin* terminated the following year, when Canning became Pitt's undersecretary of state for foreign affairs, the experience confirmed for him the advantages of a friendly journal with inside links to the government. This became doubly the case with the foundation and immediate success of the Whig-affiliated *Edinburgh Review* in 1802.

When the *Edinburgh Review* first appeared, Archibald Constable, its Scottish publisher, arranged for its London distribution by the publisher Thomas Norton Longman. In 1806 Constable gave part of the London distribution to John Murray, his friend and occasional business partner. Longman objected. There followed an injunction and a bitter dispute that left Longman the sole London agent and eventually the chief publisher of the *Edinburgh*. While Murray received little compensation for his efforts, he had become aware of the lucrative potential of a successful periodical. Perhaps still smarting from his dealings with Constable, Murray was also distressed by the political leanings of the *Edinburgh*. In a 25 September 1807 letter to Canning, he complained, "the principles of this work [the *Edinburgh*] are, however, so Radically bad that I have been led to consider the effect that such sentiments, so generally diffused, are likely to produce." Developing this theme, he suggested that "some means equally popular ought to be adopted to counteract their dangerous tendency." He went on to state his willingness to promote such a venture, if Canning thought it worthy. Concerned for discretion and secrecy, Canning responded to Murray through his cousin, Stratford Canning (1786-1880). The younger Canning introduced Murray to William Gifford in January 1808, and helped to coordinate plans for a new journal, enlisting a circle of prominent Tories, including Robert Southey and George Ellis (1753-1815).

Sir Walter Scott had been an early backer of the *Edinburgh Review*, contributing several essays. His enthusiasm for the project cooled in April 1808, however, when Jeffrey wrote an unfavorable review of Scott's poem *Marmion* (1808). While Scott took Jeffrey's criticism gracefully, he discontinued his contributions. The crisis broke later that year, when Jeffrey and Henry Brougham published their review "Don Pedro Cevallos on the French Usurpation in Spain" in the October issue. The article seemed to favor popular revolt against monarchies and to anticipate such a revolt against the British crown. Writing to Constable soon after the issue appeared, Scott complained, "The *Edinburgh Review had* become such as to render it impossible for me to become a contributor to it; *now* it is such as I can no longer continue to receive or read it." When Murray and Robert Southey approached Scott about a journal to counterpoint the *Edinburgh*, he joined at once, becoming an active participant.

While Murray hoped that Scott might become the editor of the *Quarterly*, Scott declined. The position was then offered to Gifford, who accepted at once. Scott played an important role, however, in shaping the format and guiding principles for the new journal. Recognizing that much of the success of the *Edinburgh* rested on its free style of writing and independence from the booksellers, he recommended the same for the *Quarterly*. Writing to George Ellis on 2 November 1808, Scott said,

> Now, I think there is balm in Gilead for all this, and that cure lies in instituting such a Review in London as should be conducted totally independent of bookselling influence, on a plan as liberal as that of the *Edinburgh*, its literature as well supported, and its principles English and constitutional.

In a letter to Gifford, written on 25 October 1808, Scott recommended the importance of "impartial disquisition," adding, "From the little observation I have made I think they [the Whigs] suffer peculiarly under cool, sarcastic ridicule. . . ." In matters of literary criticism, Scott recommended liberality: "The common Reviews, before the appearance of the *Edinburgh*, had become extremely mawkish," he wrote to Ellis in November. "The *Edinburgh* folks squeezed into their sauce plenty of acid, and were popular from novelty as well as from merit." That being the case, he nevertheless suggested that the *Quarterly* should rest upon principles "indulgent and conciliatory as far as possible upon mere party questions, but stern in detecting and exploring all attempts to sap our constitutional fabric . . . and not forgetting the Gentleman in the Critic."

The first issue of the *Quarterly Review* appeared in February 1809, with Murray the London publisher and James Ballantyne the Edinburgh agent. It contained eighteen articles, including a piece by Scott on Robert Burns and one by Southey on the Baptist Missionary Society. While the founders had high expectations, the initial response was not overwhelming. Ellis judged the first issue with reservation: "Upon the whole, I am at least *tolerably satisfied.*" Despite a slow start, interest in the *Quarterly* began to increase. By March the initial printing of four thousand issues was sold, and a new edition was printed.

Publication of the early issues was hampered by a combination of delays and complaints about the editor and the books reviewed. The second issue (May 1809), for instance, included a review of a treatise on "the Greek Article," leading to complaints of dullness. Murray thought the third issue (August 1809) was bad; Ellis was blunter, calling it, "most notoriously and unequivocally dull." Defending himself, Gifford complained to Murray, "the delay and confusion which have arisen must be attributed to a want of confidential communication. In a word, you have too many advisers, and I too many masters." Robert Grant's review of *The Character of the Late Charles James Fox* in the fourth issue (November 1809) and Southey's article on Admiral, Lord Nelson, the seed to his later *Life of Nelson* (1813), in the fifth issue (February 1810) caught the attention of the reading public and increased the general interest in the *Quarterly*. While it never sold in the numbers that the early *Edinburgh* did, it achieved a healthy and profitable circulation of about seven thousand in 1813, eventually reaching a maximum of about thirteen thousand.

Murray took an active role in soliciting contributors. Following Scott's advice, they were paid. The original rate was £10 to £25 a sheet, though Southey later regularly received £100 a year. Gifford initially received £200 plus an additional £160 for expenses and contributors. By the end of his tenure, he received £900 a year. With the exception of Scott, Southey, Gifford, and a few others, most of the contributors were professional men, especially lawyers. (Later in the century, Elizabeth Rigby, subsequently Lady Eastlake [1809-1893], became an important and influential contributor.) John Barrow and John Wilson Croker, first secretary of the admiralty for more than twenty years, became part of a stable of regular contributors, often providing three articles an issue, and even assuming editorial duties when Gifford's precarious health prevented him from working. Isaac D'Israeli (1766-1848), the father of the novelist and politician Benjamin Disraeli and a friend and confidant of Murray, was also a regular contributor. In 1818 Thomas Love Peacock dismissed the circle of contributors as "all more or less hired slaves of the Government, and for the most part gentlemen pensioners clustering round a common centre in the tangible shape of their paymaster Mr. Gifford." In *The Spirit of the Age*, Hazlitt offered up a satirical group portrait of the inner circle:

> The poetical department is almost a sinecure, consisting of mere summary decisions and a list of quotations. Mr. Croker is understood to contribute the St. Helena articles and the liberality, Mr. Canning the practical good sense, Mr. D'Israeli the good-nature, Mr. Jacob the modesty, Mr. Southey the consistency, and the Editor himself [Gifford] the chivalrous spirit and the attacks on Lady Morgan.

While the *Quarterly* followed Scott's advice about format and independence, occasionally even damning books that Murray published, it took its tone from Gifford. Sensitive of his humble origins and having built his reputation as the author of the *Maeviad* (1795); the *Baviad* (1791), a biting satire directed against the Della Cruscans; and a translation of Juvenal's satires (1802), Gifford favored a style of criticism marked by abusive, often savage invective, turning frequently into furious ad hominem attacks. "He was," says his biographer R. B. Clark, "utterly unable to take any view except that of the strict Tory and churchman. He was, moreover, swayed by an uncontrollable tendency to lash himself into a fury over what he considered injustices." The result was a criticism markedly different from the "gentleman in the critic" that Scott had envisioned. In his February 1809 review of *Woman: or Ida of Athens* (1809), by Sydney Owenson (later Lady Morgan), he wrote,

> This young lady, as we conclude from her Introduction, is the *enfant gaté* of a particular circle, who see, in her constitutional sprightliness, marks of genius, and encourage her dangerous propensity to publication. She has evidently written more than she has read, and read more than she has thought. But this is beginning at the wrong end.

In his review of her *France* (1817) in the seventeenth issue (April 1817), he blasted her as an "audacious worm," and in his review of her *Italy* (1821) in the twenty-fifth issue (October 1821), he declared that she was "utterly incorrigible," adding that "though every page teems with errors of all kinds, from the most disgusting down to the most ludicrous, they are smothered in such Boethian dulness, that they can do no harm." Lady Morgan, attributing the anonymous reviews to John Wilson Croker rather than Gifford, took her revenge by caricaturing Croker as Conway Crawley in her novel *Florence Macarthy* (1818).

Gifford's "pungent wit and attic salt" flavored many of the *Quarterly's* reviews, earning it a reputation for viciousness. As Thomas Love Peacock quipped in his 1818 "Essay on Fashionable Literature," "This publication contains more talent and less principle than it would be easy to believe coexistent." Sydney Smith (a founder of the *Edinburgh*), by contrast, shrugged off the attack on his *Sermons* in the May 1809 issue, inferring from such an attack that he had hit his mark: "As for the Quarterly Review, I have not read it, nor shall I, nor ought I—where abuse is intended not for my correction but my pain." He added with a sly wink, "I am however very fair game. If the oxen catch a butcher, they have a right to toss and gore him." Others were less sanguine. In his *Letter to William Gifford, Esq.* (1819), Hazlitt seethed, "the dingy cover that wraps the pages of the Quarterly Review does not contain a concentrated essence of taste and knowledge, but is a receptacle for the scum and sediment of all the prejudice, bigotry, ill-will, ignorance, and rancor, afloat in the kingdom."

Because the *Quarterly*, like the *Edinburgh*, chose to publish its reviews anonymously, Gifford, like Jeffrey, was often the target of ridicule and frequently involved in literary feuds. Thus, John Wilson Croker's attack on Leigh Hunt's *Story of Rimini* (1816), reviewed in January 1816, began a feud with Hunt and the *Examiner*, which culminated in Hunt's 1823 poem *Ultra-Crepidarius* (Beyond the Shoe), a satiric portrait of Gifford (a "vile Soul of a Shoe"—a punning allusion to his early apprenticeship as a cobbler) and the circle around the *Quarterly*:

> Adorn thou his [Murray's] door, like the sign of the Shoe,
> For court-understrappers to congregate to;
> For Southey to come, in his dearth of invention,
> And eat his own words for mock-praise and a pension;
> For Croker to lurk with his spider-like limb in,
> And stock his lean bag with way-laying the women;
> . . . . . . . . . . . . . . . . . . . . . . . . . . . . . . . . . . . . . . .
> Be these the Court-critics, and vamp a Review;
> And by a poor figure, and therefore a true,
> For it suits with thy nature, both shoe-like and slaughterly,
> Be its hue leathern, and title the *Quarterly*.

Ironically, Murray once invited Hunt to contribute articles on poetry or literature, an offer Hunt declined through his brother.

James Russell's assault on Hazlitt's *The Round Table* in the August 1817 issue, *The Characters of Shakespeare's Plays* in the June 1818 issue, and *Lectures on the English Poets* in the January 1819 issue also brought responses in the *Examiner*. These were recast and published as a pamphlet by Hazlitt in *A Letter to William Gifford, Esq.*, his longest single work, and a potent counterattack intensified by the second-person point of view:

> You are a little person, but a considerable cat's-paw; and so far worthy of notice. Your clandestine connexion with persons high in office constantly influences your opinions, and alone gives importance to them. You are the *Government Critic*.

This role Hazlitt found to be little better than a government spy. Continuing his theme, Hazlitt added,

> The distinction between truth and falsehood you make no account of: you mind only the distinction between Whig and Tory. Accustomed to the indulgence of your mercenary virulence and party-spite, you have lost all relish as well as capacity for the unperverted exercise of the understanding, and make up for the obvious want of ability by a bare-faced want of principle.

Hazlitt renewed the attack on Gifford in his essay on the editor in *The Spirit of the Age* (1825). Noting that Gifford had long edited the *Quarterly*, he went on to say, "he is admirably qualified for his situation, which he has held for some years, by a happy combination of defects, natural and acquired; and in the event of his death, it will be difficult to provide him a suitable successor." Hazlitt's remarks proved to be ironic. Gifford retired the same year because of poor health. He was succeeded briefly by John Taylor Coleridge, a nephew of the poet, but then by John Gibson Lockhart (1794-1854), whose nickname was "The Scorpion" and who had built a reputation for himself at *Blackwood's*, ridiculing Hazlitt, Hunt, and John Keats as the "Cockney School" of poetry.

Lockhart, the son-in-law of Sir Walter Scott, edited the *Quarterly* from March 1826 until bad health forced his retirement in 1853. Ironically, Lockhart styled himself a "moderate Tory," and had often opposed the judgments of the *Quarterly* when he was a principle contributor with *Blackwood's*. In "Remarks on the Periodical Criticism of England" (*Blackwood's Edinburgh*, March 1818) he compared Jeffrey and Gifford to the Roman emperors Nero and Tiberius: "The former resembles the gay despot of Rome, the latter the bloody and cruel one of Capreæ. Both are men of great talent, and both, I think, are very bad reviewers." He also disliked the ultra-Toryism of Southey and Croker. Croker, who adopted the term *conservative* to characterize his brand of Toryism, had originally opposed the appointment of Lockhart to the editorship and did not contribute again until 1831, when he spearheaded the attack on the Parliamentary Reform Bill that passed the next year. Despite his moderate views, Lockhart did little during his tenure to change the political direction of the *Quarterly*, though he helped to lighten its tone and to expand its literary horizons, instilling his own interest in German literature. Not insignificantly, he also brought more punctuality and regularity to the publication of the *Quarterly*, overcoming problems that had plagued it throughout Gifford's tenure.

The literary relations of the *Quarterly* were originally envisioned as a counterpoint to those of the *Edinburgh*. Thus, while Jeffrey and the *Edinburgh* ridiculed William Wordsworth and the "Lake Poets" for more than twenty years, the *Quarterly*, under the influence of Southey, championed them. On occasion this proved to be difficult. Jeffrey damned Wordsworth's *White Doe of Rylstone* (1815) in an October 1815 review as "the very worst poem we ever saw imprinted in a quarto volume." Reviewing the poem in the October 1815 issue of the *Quarterly*, William Rowe Lyall struggled heroically to praise it:

> It is not, indeed, free from the singularities which arise from the particular point of view in which Mr. Wordsworth likes to look at things; but in the present instance, they fall not unhappily with the whimsical nature of the subject, and give a tone of colouring to the poem, which, however peculiar, is far from being unpleasing.

Despairing, Lyall concluded, "all we can say is, that if he [Wordsworth] is not now or should not be hereafter, a favourite with the public, he can have nobody to blame but himself." The *Quarterly* eventually abandoned the policy of reacting to the *Edinburgh* and followed its own course, often praising or censuring according to political or religious bias. In its early years it supported the Lake Poets, Sir Walter Scott, Lord Byron, Washington Irving, and Jane Austen. Gifford even encouraged Murray to publish Austen's *Emma*, suggesting that he himself would see it through the press. At the same time the *Quarterly* attacked Leigh Hunt, William Hazlitt, John Keats, Charles Lamb, Percy Bysshe Shelley, the novels of William Godwin, and Mary Shelley's *Frankenstein* (1818). Later under Lockhart, it would attack Alfred Tennyson, Thomas Babington Macaulay, Thomas Carlyle, Charles Dickens, and Charlotte Brontë.

The critical principles that informed the reviewing of the *Quarterly* under Gifford and Lockhart are more diffuse then those of the *Edinburgh*. Jeffrey and the early contributors to the *Edinburgh* were deeply imbued with the principles of the Scottish Enlightenment and the aesthetics of David Hume. The reviewers for the *Quarterly* tended to look back to the criticism of Samuel Johnson and the poetry of Alexander Pope for their standards. Croker, for instance, was to prepare an edition (1831) of James Boswell's *Life of Johnson*, and was working on an edition of Pope when he died. Later, the *Quarterly* joined the fray against William Lisle Bowles during the "Pope Controversy." D'Israeli attacked Bowles in his July 1820 review of Spence's *Anecdotes Observations, and Characters of Books and Men* (1820), and Gifford edited Byron's letters on Bowles, published in 1821.

In broad terms, the critical principles of the *Quarterly* combined an appeal to aesthetic formalism and moral character. Richard Whately's January 1821 review of Jane Austen's *Northanger Abbey* and *Persuasion* is indicative of this approach. Comparing Austen's novels to Flemish painting, an image he cribbed from Scott's review of *Emma* in October 1815, he praised her skill in being a moral writer without being didactic. Contrasting her with Maria Edgeworth, Whately wrote, "If instruction do not join as a volunteer, she will do no good service." Turning to Austen, he observes, "the moral lessons also of this lady's novels, though clearly and impressively conveyed, are not offensively put forward, but spring incidentally from the circumstances of the story." In a telling note he adds, "we know not whether Miss Austin [*sic*] ever had access to the precepts of Aristotle; but there are few, if any writers of fiction who have illustrated them more successfully."

John Wilson Croker drew on similar principles to condemn Hunt's *Story of Rimini* (1816) and later Keats's *Endymion* (1818). Croker denied any political bias, though he could not resist noting that Hunt had written most of his poem in Newgate Prison while serving a sentence for libel against the king. He quickly added the disclaimer that "we are as little prejudiced as possible on this subject," adding, "we are to judge him solely from the work now before us." He condemned Hunt, and later Keats and Tennyson, whom he astutely recognized as belonging to Hunt's "school," on the grounds that they were guilty of bad taste, blindly following a theory at the expense of sense. Good art, for Croker and many of the other reviewers for the *Quarterly*, appealed to nature, or at least a certain eighteenth-century conception of nature, while bad art was contrary to nature. Underlying this definition was an equation of the moral with the natural, the immoral with the unnatural or extravagant. Thus linking the moral with the aesthetic, Croker saw in the extravagant or irresponsible artist someone who betrayed his or her trust to shape popular moral character, someone who seemed to challenge the constitutional fabric of society, and therefore someone who was open to moral and critical censure.

The relations of the *Quarterly* with Romanticism are well illustrated in an exchange between Byron and Gifford. In a letter to Murray (15 September 1817), Byron wrote:

> With regard to poetry in general I am convinced the more I think of it—that he and *all* of us —Scott—Southey—Wordsworth—Moore—Campbell—I—are all in the wrong—one as much as another—that we are upon a wrong revolutionary poetical system—or systems—not worth a damn in itself—& from which none but Rogers and Crabbe are free.

Only Pope, Byron concluded, represented a true model and classic. Murray showed the letter to Gifford, who noted approvingly, "there is more good sense, and feeling and judgment in this passage, than in any other I ever read, or Lord Byron wrote."

While the *Quarterly* championed the cause of Wordsworth, Coleridge, and the Lake Poets, it often did so tepidly. Wordsworth complained that *both* Jeffrey and Gifford had ruined any chance for profits to be made from his poetry. Ironically, while the *Quarterly* tended to be indulgent with Coleridge and Wordsworth, it did not hesitate to level criticism against them that was not unlike that of Jeffrey and the *Edinburgh* in substance, if not tone. Specifically, both magazines found the Lake Poets guilty of indulging in such a personal examination of private feelings that they distorted them, and thereby created a poetic language that was too private to be meaningful to a general audience. Looking at the second edition (1814) of his uncle's play *Remorse* in an April 1814 review, John Taylor Coleridge suggested ironically that the Lake Poets' intense examination of nature in fact distorted their perception of nature. Further, he complained that Coleridge and Wordsworth seemed to confuse metaphor with metaphysics, that what was good poetry was not necessarily good philosophy:

> All the features and appearances of nature in their poetical creed possess a sentient and intellectual being, and exert an influence for good upon the hearts of her worshippers. Nothing can be more poetical than this feeling, but it is the misfortune of this school that their very excellences are carried to an excess. Hence they constantly attribute not merely physical, but more animation to nature.

It is not clear whether Coleridge knew the identity of his critic. It was largely to address these concerns, however, to explain and justify his system, that he turned to the composition of the *Biographia Literaria* (1817).

Charles Lamb echoed John Taylor Coleridge's criticisms, though with a more sympathetic tone, in his October 1814 review of Wordsworth's *Excursion* (1814). "He [Wordsworth] walks through every forest, as through some Dodona; and every bird that flits among the leaves, like that miraculous one in Tasso, . . . In his poetry nothing in Nature is dead. Motion is synonymous with life." Lamb saw in Wordsworth's love of nature a surrogate religion:

> In him, *faith*, in friendly alliance and conjunction with the religion of his country, appears to have grown up, fostered by meditation and lonely communions with Nature—an internal principle of lofty consciousness, which stamps upon his opin-

> ions and sentiments (we were almost going to say) the character of an expanded and generous Quakerism.

While Lamb tried to justify the incongruities, distortions, and private associations in Wordsworth's system, the result was to draw attention to them. "The causes which have prevented the poetry of Mr. Wordsworth from attaining its full share of popularity are to be found in the boldness and originality of his genius," he declared. Continuing, Lamb explained, "a writer, who would be popular, must timidly coast the shore of prescribed sentiment and sympathy." William Rowe Lyall drew a similar conclusion in his treatment of *The White Doe of Rylstone*.

The periodical's relationship with Byron was complex. Murray was Byron's publisher, and Byron deeply respected Gifford, looking on him as his mentor. In turn he endeared himself to Gifford when he evoked Gifford's name in *English Bards, and Scotch Reviewers* (1809) as "satire's bard," calling on him to "Make bad men better, or at least ashamed." But while Byron revered the editor of the *Quarterly*, he had little respect for the journal itself. Nevertheless, the *Quarterly* looked on Byron as its protégé, though it tended to hold back its notice until a work had proven itself before the public. George Ellis wrote most of the early reviews of Byron. His approach to works such as *Childe Harold's Pilgrimage*, Cantos I and II (1812) in March 1812, *Giaour* (1813) and the *Bride of Abydoes* (1813) in January 1814, and *The Corsair* (1814) and *Lara* (1814) in July 1814 was reminiscent of an earlier generation, combining urbane paraphrases with occasional quibbles on matters of diction and prosody. *Childe Harold's Pilgrimage* seemed to Ellis to be essentially a poetic travel narrative, while the other works were "tragical love-tales." He saw the public's enthusiasm for Byron as indicative of Byron's talents and by implication a confirmation of the quality of his own judgment.

Ellis was, however, perplexed by the Byronic persona. Looking at the "hero" of *The Corsair*, he expressed the objection "that Conrad is a personage so eccentric, so oddly compounded of discordant qualities, and so remote from common nature, that it is difficult to sympathize in his feelings." He went on to observe that "the affinity of his character to those of the Giaour and Childe Harold, is so marked, as to do away the merit, whatever it may be, of singularity, and to give him the appearance of a mere copy from a capricious original." Ellis tried to account for the Byronic hero by appealing to models derived from Homer's Achilles and the knightly heroes of romance. Coming closer, but finally resisting a connection between Byron and the Byronic hero, Ellis rejected the view of Byron put forward by Jeffrey. Quoting directly from Jeffrey's review of *The Corsair* and *Lara* in the *Edinburgh Review* (April 1814), Ellis noted, "It is contended, on one hand, that for the poetical taste of the present times, 'the minds of the great agents must be unmasked for us—and all the anatomy of their throbbing bosoms laid open to our gaze.' " Dismissing this position, Ellis sniffed, "We think, on the contrary, that this anatomical operation is essentially unpoetical; and that therefore Lord Byron, who is emphatically styled the 'searcher of dark bosoms,' is least attractive, and least popular, when he attempts to execute this special office."

Sir Walter Scott, a better judge both of human character in general and Lord Byron in particular than Ellis, did not hesitate to link poet and persona: "The works before us contain so many direct allusions to the author's personal feelings and private history," he said of *Childe Harold's Pilgrimage. Canto the Third* (1816) in the October 1816 issue, "that it becomes impossible for us to divide Lord Byron from his poetry." He continued this theme in the April 1818 review of the fourth canto (1818). Practicing the sort of tolerant and humane criticism that he had originally envisioned for the *Quarterly*, Scott chided Byron for his skepticism, his praise of Napoleon Bonaparte, and his association with radicals such as John Cam Hobhouse. Offering the friendly admonition that the world is full of trials and disappointments, Scott suggested,

> It is not the temper and talents of the poet, but the use to which he puts them, on which his happiness or misery is grounded. A powerful and unbridled imagination is, we have already said, the author and architect of its own disappointments. Its fascinations, its exaggerated pictures of good and evil, and the mental distress to which they give rise, are the natural and necessary evils attending on that quick susceptibility of feeling and fancy incident to the poetical temperament.

Byron's Childe Harold, like Bunyan's Pilgrim, must exercise patience and preserve his faith even in an imperfect world. "Lord Byron may not have loved the world," Scott concluded, "but the world has loved him, not perhaps with a wide or discriminating affection, but as well as it is capable of loving any one."

While the *Quarterly* felt it could be generous to Byron, its response to Keats, Shelley, and others affiliated with the radical "school" of Leigh Hunt, fell beyond the pale of sympathy. Croker led the assault in his infamous April 1818 review of Keats's *Endymion* (1818). Confessing that he was unable to persevere through the entire work, Croker noted that Keats was a disciple of Hunt:

> It is not that Mr. Keats, (if that be his real name, for we almost doubt that any man in his senses would put his name to such a rhapsody,) it is not, we say, that the author has not powers of language, rays of fancy, and gleams of genius—he has all these; but he is unhappily a disciple of the new school of what has been somewhere called Cockney poetry; which may be defined to consist of the most incongruous ideas in the most uncouth language.

Keats, Croker complained, followed his poetic theory blindly without a grounding in either taste or common sense. The results, he suggested, were incongruous if not incomprehensible. "There is hardly a complete couplet inclosing a complete idea in the whole book. He wanders from one subject to another, from the association, not of ideas but of sounds."

John Taylor Coleridge carried the attack to Shelley the following year, reviewing *Laon and Cythna* (1818), *Revolt of Islam* (1818), and *Rosalind and Helen* (1819) in April 1819. Coleridge focused on Shelley's doctrine and character, dismissing *Laon and Cythna* as "insupportably dull, and laboriously obscure." He attributed Shelley's doctrine to a combination of naïveté and vanity, derived from his inexperience and limited education. He expressed his resentment and indignation at Shelley's presumption: "He has indeed, to the best of his ability, wounded us in the tenderest part." Explaining, Coleridge wrote, "—as far as in him lay, he has loosened the hold of our protecting laws, and sapped the principles of our venerable polity; he has invaded the purity and chilled the unsuspecting ardour of our fireside intimacies; he has slandered, ridiculed and blasphemed our holy religion. . . ." Expressing his pity for Shelley, Coleridge assigned blame to the influence of Leigh Hunt:

> But of Mr. Shelley much may be said with truth, which we not long since said of his friend and leader Mr. Hunt: he has not, indeed, all that is odious and contemptible in the character of that person; so far as we have seen he has never exhibited the bustling vulgarity, the ludicrous affectation, the factious flippancy, or the selfish heartlessness, which it is hard for our feelings to treat with the mere contempt they merit.

Turning specifically to Shelley's character, however, Coleridge added,

> Like him, however, Mr. Shelley is a very vain man; and like most very vain men, he is but half instructed in knowledge, and less than half-disciplined in his reasoning powers; his vanity, wanting the control of the faith which he derides, has been his ruin; it has made him too impatient of applause and distinction to earn them in the fair course of labour; like a speculator in trade, he would be rich without capital and without delay, and, as might have been anticipated, his speculations have ended only in disappointments.

In these criticisms of Shelley's character, Coleridge came close to the Tory complaint against political and economic reform in general.

A final shot at Hunt and his associates was fired by Gifford himself in a short, July 1819 review of Hazlitt's *Political Essays* (1819). Responding to the *Letter to William Gifford*, Gifford began by expressing his "unqualified detestation," of Hazlitt, comparing him to a death's-head hawkmoth: "Its favorite object is, always, the plunder of a hive, and its sole safeguards in accomplishing its purpose are its startling appearance and disagreeable noise." Gifford's approach to Hazlitt amounted to enumerating the names of those eminent Englishmen he had slandered. This was juxtaposed with the dubious list of those Hazlitt claimed to admire. "It will not take up much room," Gifford scoffed, "and comprises, we believe, only Buonaparte, 'the very god,' Mr. Hazlitt says, 'of his idolatry,' Murat, Mr. Cobbett, Mr. John Hunt, Mr. Leigh Hunt, and," alluding to Byron, "one other whom we should wish to see in more respectable company."

With the fall of the Tory government in 1830, the *Quarterly* lost its inside connection with the ministry. In turn, the passage of the Reform Bill of 1832 brought the constitutional revolution that the founders of the *Quarterly* had feared and fought against. Out of the reorientation and revolution emerged a new generation of Tory politicians such as Benjamin Disraeli and "Young England," shifting the ideological base of the party. With this, there were corresponding shifts in the

*Quarterly*, as well, as it moved into the age of Victoria. While Croker, for instance, would continue to publish reviews until 1854, taking on at various times Tennyson, Dickens, and Macaulay, and Elizabeth Rigby would continue this tradition, as in her December 1848 review of Charlotte Brontë's *Jane Eyre* (1847), the tone of most contributions became less strident, and the *Quarterly* became more a cultural commentator than a party instrument. Like the "co-ordinate tribunal" that it had been founded to counterpoint, the *Quarterly Review* helped to transform the face of British culture and tradition, becoming itself a venerable tradition.

**References:**

Ruth Berman, "Critical Reactions to Fantasy in Four Nineteenth-century Periodicals: *Edinburgh Review, Blackwood's, Fraser's,* and *Cornhill*," *Sphinx: A Magazine of Literature and Society*, 4, no. 1 (1981): 1-37;

Myron F. Brightfield, *John Wilson Croker* (Berkeley: University of California Press, 1940);

"The Centenary of 'The Quarterly Review,'" *Quarterly Review*, 210 (April 1909): 731-784; 211 (July 1909): 279-324;

Roy Benjamin Clark, *William Gifford: Tory Satirist, Critic, and Editor* (New York: Columbia University Press, 1930);

E. S. De Beer, "Macaulay and Croker: The Review of Croker's Boswell," *Review of English Studies*, 10, no. 40 (1959): 388-397;

Walter Graham, *English Literary Periodicals* (New York: Nelson, 1930);

John Gross, *The Rise and Fall of the Man of Letters: A Study of the Idiosyncratic and the Humane in Modern Literature* (New York: Collier, 1970);

Francis R. Hart, *Lockhart as Romantic Biographer* (Edinburgh: Edinburgh University Press, 1971);

John O. Hayden, *The Romantic Reviewers, 1802-1824* (Chicago: University of Chicago Press, 1969);

Andrew Lang, *The Life and Letters of John Gibson Lockhart*, 2 volumes (London: Nimmo / New York: Scribners, 1897);

J. G. Lockhart, *Memoirs of the Life of Sir Walter Scott, Bart.* (7 volumes, Edinburgh: Cadell, 1837-1838; revised, 10 volumes, 1839);

Raymond N. MacKenzie, "Romantic Literary History: Francophobia in *The Edinburgh Review* and *The Quarterly Review*," *Victorian Periodicals Review*, 15 (Summer 1982): 42-52;

Peter F. Morgan, "Croker as Literary Critic in the *Quarterly Review*," *Wordsworth Circle*, 8 (Winter 1977): 62-68;

Michael Munday, "The Novel and its Critics in the Early Nineteenth Century," *Studies in Philology*, 79 (Spring 1982): 205-226;

Charles C. Nickerson, "Disraeli, Lockhart, and Murray: an Episode in the History of the 'Quarterly Review,'" *Victorian Studies*, 15 (March 1972): 279-306;

Paul Riley, "John Wilson Croker and Keats' Endymion," *Studies in the Humanities*, 5, no. 2 (1976): 32-37;

Derek Roper, *Reviewing Before the Edinburgh: 1788-1802* (Newark: University of Delaware Press, 1978);

Joanne Shattock, *Politics and Reviewers: The Edinburgh and the Quarterly in the Early Victorian Age* (London: Leicester University Press, 1989);

Shattock, "Showman, Lion-Hunter, or Hack: The Quarterly Editor at Mid-Century," *Victorian Periodicals Review*, 16 (Fall-Winter 1983): 89-103;

Samuel Smiles, *A Publisher and His Friends: Memoir and Correspondence of the Late John Murray*, 2 volumes (London: John Murray, 1891);

René Wellek, *The Romantic Age*, volume 2 of *A History of Modern Criticism, 1750-1950* (Cambridge: Cambridge University Press, 1981): 110-121.

# The Spectator

*(5 July 1828 - )*

Richard D. Fulton
*Clark College*

Throughout most of the nineteenth century, the *Spectator* was viewed by its contemporaries as one of the most influential newspapers in Britain. It earned that reputation through the ability, integrity, and independence of its various editors, including Robert Rintoul (1828-1858), Richard Holt Hutton (1861-1886), and Meredith Townsend (1861-1897). Remarkably, for an era in which the life of tens of thousands of periodicals could be measured in weeks or months no matter how famous the editor or contributors, the *Spectator* was founded by an obscure band of fugitive journalists from the *Atlas* (Rintoul, Douglas Kinnaird, and Joseph Hume), and, according to pioneer press historian James Grant, it was successful from the start: "So early as the first year of its publication, [it] acquired a high reputation, both for the independent course it pursued on political and indeed on all other questions, and the intellectual character of its articles." Its independence in politics set it apart from the other influential periodicals of the day, which were invariably party oriented: *Blackwood's* with the Tories, the *Edinburgh* with the Whigs, *John Bull* with the nationalist ultraconservatives. The readership of the *Spectator* was "chiefly . . . among the men of culture who like to listen to all sides of controversies, provided the argument is conducted with fairness and moderation" (*Spectator*, 1 May 1858). They were liberal in politics, MPs, peers, professional people, and businessmen, in both England and the colonies. They were, in other words, the decision makers and opinion makers of the realm.

Although the *Spectator* was not a literary paper—it called itself "A Weekly Journal of News, Politics, Literature, and Science"—its independence and the quality of the writing in the paper gave it significant influence in literature and the arts as well as in politics. Rintoul's interests generally lay with the significant political issues of the day, but he insisted on applying the same standards to literary reviewing as he did to political critiquing. As a result, the paper's nineteenth-century contemporaries recognized it as a voice to be respected in literary criticism. As the 1857 edition of *The Newspaper Press Directory* noted: "the impartiality that gives so much originality to its political views, imparts immense value to its literary criticism, which never descends into mere eulogy on the one hand, nor abuse on the other: discerning, industrious, painstaking, it elicits every excellence, and exhibits every characteristic feature, of such a work."

In some respects, the *Spectator* might be compared with a contemporary newsmagazine such as *Time* or *Newsweek*. Each issue began with a table of contents, followed by several pages summarizing the important news of the week. Next came summaries of news items from foreign countries (separate listings for Ireland and the various colonies), the metropolis, and the provinces; law reports; church and university news; military news; shipping and business news, including markets; births, marriages, deaths; a postscript which included late-breaking notices; editorials (titled "Topics of the Day"); reviews of art, literature, and music; a gazette; current prices; and several pages of advertising. Some departments were altered or dropped temporarily or permanently, but the paper's basic makeup remained the same. The price was originally ninepence for sixteen pages. On 22 May 1830 the price increased to a shilling and the length to twenty-four pages, and remained thus for the rest of the century.

The literary-review column began as "The Literary Spectator"; in the very first issue (5 July 1828) thirteen novels, seven histories, four travel books, and five biographies received comments of various lengths. Later issues were not quite as ambitious as this first one, but it was a rare issue that carried fewer than four or five substantial essays over two or three pages. In addition to the reviews, in the early issues of the *Spectator* books and periodicals might be noticed either under the "Spectabilia" column (interesting extracts from several books) or in one of the lists of books either about to be published or just out.

*The first editor of the* Spectator *(woodcut by H. Brooke)*

"The Literary Spectator" later became, variously, "New Books," "Reviews of New Books," "Recent Literature," and other variants (one week it was "Books and Booklings"), and gradually the lists of books disappeared. Cogent, incisive essays on current works remained a staple, however, as did quick, paragraph-length notices of what the reviewer considered the important works released during the week.

In reading the early *Spectator* literary pages, one is struck by the numbers of books regularly published in the 1820s and 1830s in Britain: poems and verse; children's tales; travel and geography; memoirs, biography, autobiography; science, medicine, and technology; schoolbooks; indexes and references; periodicals; and of course, novels. After the richness of the first issue, numbers 2-14 seem rather sparse, containing a total of twenty-nine notices of books and periodicals. Number 15, however, began the tradition of long reviews, short notices, and lists that mark both the publishing industry's torrential output and the role of the *Spectator* in recognizing it. The issue includes a four-page review of a novel, John Banim's *The Anglo-Irish of the Nineteenth Century* (1828), and notices of eighteen books on the "eve" of publication plus another thirteen books "subscribed" by the trade, including the fourth volume of William Godwin's *History of the Commonwealth of England*; John Malcolm's *Scenes of War and Other Poems*; *Zillah. A Tale of Jerusalem*, by the author of *Brambletye House* (Horace Smith); and Charles Cowden Clarke's *Readings in Natural Philosophy*—as well as *Life in India, or the English in Calcutta*; *Life of Nollekens the Sculptor*; and *My Grandfather's Farm; or, Pictures of Rural Life*.

The reviewer did his best to keep up with the books pouring in on him. He complained occasionally, and admitted that many worthy books would never see the light of a decent review, but he managed reviews of some 172 books in 1829, 340 in 1830, 270 in 1831, and 234 in 1832; he also listed hundreds of other works without reviewing them. His lists early on were ways of giving books notices without having to write a review—a sort of "Births, Deaths, and Marriages" of the literary world. For scholars searching for publishing histories of obscure works, these lists are rich lodes of information, and far more accurate than the advertisements that were carried in most periodicals associated with the arts.

The literary outlook of the first reviewer set the tone for the first decade. It is important to know that, despite the oft-repeated observation that the *Spectator* under Rintoul was so successful because the entire paper reflected his style and thought, the reviews often showed political and social attitudes diametrically opposed to Rintoul's. For example, Rintoul was a philosophic radical, and from the first the *Spectator* was a reform journal. The paper often attacked the Tories for being too conservative, the Whigs for being out-of-date, and the utilitarians for being out-of-step. Yet the reviewer often directly repeated gospel from these objects of Rintoul's criticism. In the first issue he said, "Since the direct influence of literature upon the well-being of society has been discovered, the practical utility of books is the standard by which they are tried" ("The Works of the Learned for 1827-8").

Where Rintoul was quite liberal in his politics and his social outlook, his reviewer's liberality extended only to the middle and upper classes of England. A key sociopolitical question in the late 1820s concerned the continuation of legalized slavery in the colonies, especially in the sugar islands of the West Indies. The reviewer's position on slavery was carefully outlined in a review of *Sketches and Recollections of the West Indies*, in which he managed a shot at the Irish as well: "When a comfortable Negro operative is told that he is to be emancipated, he straightaway dreams of idleness; an Irish peasant similarly tickles his imagination with low rents and cheap whiskey." With no sense of irony, he described the advantages that slaves had over English laborers: "carelessness of the future, surety of never coming to want, the regular hours, and the advantage of a doctor and an hospital in every case of illness." The life of the West Indian slave was the life of a "merry black, dancing, laughing, pattering, and drumming" (15 November 1828). In a later essay he claimed that "the life of a West Indian slave is a happy one . . . he is subject to few privations . . . his labour is moderate . . . his state of mind is contented, and his body subject to few diseases, and those, when they occur, [are] carefully attended by skillful persons." In fact, he said, the problem was not with the condition of the slaves, but with certain reformers who knew nothing about the true condition of West Indian slaves. It also lay with the word *slave*, which had certain negative connotations. Alexander Barclay, a Jamaican planter and author of *A Practical View of the Present State of Slavery in the West Indies*, supposedly convinced the reviewer (who seemed pretty convinced a month earlier in the review of *Sketches*) that while slavery may be an abstract evil, as it was practiced it was good for everyone, even the slaves. And besides, he added, over a period of time the blacks would become civilized enough to be emancipated (20 December 1828).

A year later, the reviewer continued his cause with an essay under the misleading title "The Death Warrant of Negro Slavery" (7 November 1829). In it he repeated his earlier statement that "no testimony worthy of credit has ever been adduced to show that the condition of the slaves is an unhappy one. On the contrary, those best informed on the subject concurred in describing them as a contented, cheerful race." He continued his arguments that emancipation violated planters' property rights (in the slaves), and a slave rebellion would show once and for all that slaves have no respect for property, and thus could not be trusted to govern themselves. The only answer the reviewer could see as legitimate was a long weaning away from the use of slaves, thanks to the abolition of the slave trade.

Clearly, the issue was too important to be discussed on the literary pages alone; on 21 August 1830, an editorial entitled "Advice to Mr. Brougham" took up the issue and noted, "it is acknowledged on all hands, that Slavery is a great evil, and that it ought to be abated." To argue a proof of that statement would insult the readers. Yet the problems revolved around the compensation of the owners, and the timing of emancipation (that is, women and children first? everyone at once? gradually over several years?) If Henry Peter Brougham could work out answers to those problems, he would be successful in his struggle for emancipation. If not, he had no hope.

By 7 April 1832, the question was no longer "whether West Indian Slavery is worse than African freedom, or whether the owners abuse their property." It was whether or not emancipation would be gradual or sudden, and the editorialist supported only a "sudden redemption of slavery," because "bit-by-bit emancipation will only make things worse" as slaves became free ("Difficulties of the West Indies Question"). The reviewer was not finished fighting his rearguard action, however; in the issue for 2 June 1832, he reviewed two pamphlets on "The West Indian Question." Both were written by Jamaicans, both were "warmly partisan," and both contained truths not being expressed by the abolitionists ("Literary Postscript"). On both 14 July and 1 September 1832 the critic reviewed books dealing with slavery, and in both instances he preached slow movement toward enfranchisement ("Murray on Colonial Slavery," 14 July 1832; "The System," 1 September 1832). The last word was spoken on the editorial page, however; on 8 September, in "Sugar and Slavery," the writer, perhaps Rintoul himself, said, "slavery is an unmanly and a detestable vice of society—let it be extinguished."

While the book reviewer had announced a utilitarian stance in the very first issue, later in the same essay he qualified that position somewhat, stating that in his review of the publications of 1828, he would "estimate them according to the knowledge they have contributed, the pleasure they produce in the perusal, or the ability they display." Thus, he had three critical standards, and not merely the one drawn from the utilitarians.

He told his readers that he would regularly notice novels, because novels were legitimate works of literature: "If we were to exclude novels from the works of the learned, we should be led by an ignorant and vulgar prejudice. In a novel descriptive of national manners, the author must have been a keen observer, and have 'learned' numberless facts—and moreover, have reasoned upon them." He goes on to give as an example of a successful novelist Henry Fielding, whose *Jonathan Wild* (1743) and *Amelia* (1752) both showed learning in the depiction of character. In general, novels which showed "scenes and characters which please the reader, and show intelligence, and sometimes humour in the writer" and novels which were "a close transcript of life in the nineteenth century" would be praised, if not judged worthy of long-term fame. Sadly, his critical criteria did not hold up well when tested: his choice for the classic novel of 1828 was David M. Moir's *Life of Mansie Wauch, Tailor in Dalkeith, Written by Himself*, "the only work of genius . . . this year—excepting, always, any that Sir Walter may have favored the world with" (5 July 1828).

Histories, the reviewer said, must meet the standards of profundity, originality, judgment, and industry. The very best writers on history were those who built on original observation, not the works of others. Any historian whose writing appeared to come easily would be heavily criticized, he said (5 July 1828). He recommended Lord John Russell's *Memoirs of the Affairs of Europe to the Peace of Utrecht* (volume one, 1824) as an example of successful history: "He registers all the principal facts; connects them well together; draws a character with more truth than ambition; and when he does mix up with his narrative a reflection—which is not very often—it is, we may say, always sensible, if not pointed . . . he never fails to introduce the great *mots* of the time—the piquant little anecdotes which illustrate persons and events, or the remarkable sayings which in the mouths of great men sometimes supply a key by which to interpret the meaning of historical transactions." When good sense was characteristic of a historian, his writings "may be recognized by their straightforwardness and simplicity; by the absence of tropes; by the aptness and suitableness, and we may add, the rarity of his remarks; and further, if he should give into the great foible of historians, character-drawing, he will do it plainly and shrewdly" (1 February 1829).

The ever-popular travel books should be full of information, with "wise and liberal suggestions," and "scenes conceived with a poet's fire." Biography should be first of all written on people with good characters—with well-managed historical details, and "novelty." Poetry and criticism had both fallen so far since the death of George Gordon, Lord Byron, that "we have no poetry; and in criticism, much so-called, but nothing that deserves the title. . . . Crudities, miscalled criticism, appear in every shape, from the paragraph puff to the solemn *Quarterly*; but where are the principles applied? on what philosophy are the random remarks founded? and in reference to what end, or by what test, are the productions of literature estimated by our most celebrated critics? Poetry is as rife as criticism, and equally worthless." All works must be pleasing, well-written, and have a "high moral tone." Neither the so-called Cockney school nor affectedness in any way may taint a work; of Edward Bulwer-Lytton's *Pelham* (1828) he said, "there is a coxcombery and an impudence, and oftentimes a silliness, which tasks our patience almost beyond that of any other writer of fiction." All writers must show "the ability to conceive character, to represent scenes dramatically, to reason respecting the motives and actions of human beings, [and] to write . . . sensibly on the affairs of society." In addition, "a knowledge of locale" was indispensable for a travel writer.

The reviewer's job was to advise the reader and, incidentally, to make some formal judgments on particular works. Like all reviewers, this one occasionally failed. However, he had a strong admiration for both Sir Walter Scott and Byron (and Russell's histories), perhaps overstated Mrs. Felicia Hemans's and Robert Southey's talents somewhat, and correctly noted that Alfred Tennyson's 1832 *Poems* showed a falling off in workmanship from his earlier volumes. Some of his judgments exhibited particularly fine marksmanship: of *Zillah* he said, "Of all the awkward botchings up at the end of a tale, from Mrs. Radcliffe to Sir Walter Scott, this of *Zillah* is the most lamentable we have ever seen; and we are only not angry at the clumsiness of the author because he had utterly failed in creating any concern in the fate of his imaginary personages" (22 November 1828). Of *The Protestant*, a historical novel by Mrs. (Anna Eliza) Bray, he said, "her figures do not start from the canvass; we are not much interested in her tale; and we are not aware that she exposes any of the secret springs of history" (20 December 1828). He said of Henry Neele, the author of *Romance of History*: "His industrious habits ruined him: had he been as idle as the generality of poets, he never would have aggravated his mental malady. . . . But he unfortunately took to severe study, and puzzled his brain with a kind of bastard history-writing, for which he was totally unfit. There is little merit in the *Romance of History*—that is to say, little of the merit of talent" (20 December 1828). One entire review, titled "The Worst Novel of the Season," brushed off *Florence, or the Aspirant*, by Mrs. Robertson, thus: "We will not pretend to have read the whole of *Florence, or the Aspirant*: we found it a task beyond our limited powers. This being the case, we ought, perhaps, to say nothing about it; we confess, however, that we felt called upon strongly to advise the author to change his or her occupation, and the publishers to repress as far as they can the propagation of trash" (13 June 1829).

Yet he was not unalloyedly cruel, even toward deserving objects of derision. He concluded his review of *Zillah* with a recommendation that "all persons of leisure" could enjoy the book because it was moral and contained interesting information. And of Neele, author of *Romance of History*, he said, "as a minor poet, Neele must be placed on a level with some very old and respectable authorities; he left several little pieces of great and happy completeness. His name will outlast several existing brilliant reputations." He even let poor Mrs. Bray off the hook in his conclusion, noting that "whoever reads this book attentively through, will not fail to derive matter for reflection, and perhaps a supply of information." And he admitted that "Mrs. Bray is industrious and faithful."

The *Spectator* maintained its political and literary influence throughout the nineteenth century, and enjoys considerable respect to this day. Its approving reviews of Charles Lyell's *Principles of Geology* (7 August 1830, 7 January 1832) helped in the de-religionizing of science. Its admiring acceptance of American literature and American figures such as Thomas Jefferson certainly helped the British to understand and appreciate the United States as a developing independent entity, and as not some kind of scruffy, second-rate England. The *Spectator* was not alone in its positions, of course, but its extraordinary influence gave its positions more impact than those of a lesser journal. Certainly, it is a useful archive of nineteenth-century thought.

**References:**

Ephraim Douglass Adams, *Great Britain and the American Civil War*, 2 volumes (London & New York: Longmans, Green, 1925);

Richard D. Altick, *The English Common Reader: A Social History of the Mass Reading Public 1800-1900* (Chicago: University of Chicago Press, 1957);

Altick, "Nineteenth Century English Periodicals," *Newberry Library Bulletin*, second series 9 (May 1952): 255-264;

W. H. G. Armytage, "The Editor Reflects: Newly Discovered Letters of R. H. Hutton, Editor of the *Spectator* 1861-1897," *Journal of English and Germanic Philology*, 49 (1950): 566-569;

A. Aspinall, "The Circulation of Newspapers in the Early Nineteenth Century," *Review of English Studies*, 22 (January 1946): 29-43;

Aspinall, "Statistical Accounts of the London Newspapers 1800-1836," *English Historical Review*, 65 (July 1950): 372-383;

J. B. Atkins, "Reminiscences of the *Spectator* Office," *Spectator*, 141 (3 November 1928): Centennial Supplement, 17-20;

Paul Bloomfield, "R. S. Rintoul, 1787-1858," *Spectator*, 200 (18 April 1958): 481;

George Boyce and others, *Newspaper History, from the Seventeenth Century to the Present Day* (Beverly Hills, Cal.: Sage, 1978);

J. Buchan, "*Spectator* Memories," *Spectator*, 141 (3 November 1928): Centennial Supplement, 20-21;

Carl L. Cannon, *Journalism: A Bibliography* (New York: New York Public Library, 1924);

Raymond Chapman, *The Victorian Debate: English Literature and Society 1832-1901* (New York: Basic Books, 1968);

Samuel C. Chew, "Swinburne's Contributions to the *Spectator* in 1862," *Modern Language Notes*, 35 (January 1920): 118-119;

Robert A. Colby, " 'How It Strikes a Contemporary': The 'Spectator' as Critic," *Nineteenth Century Fiction*, 11 (June 1956): 182-206;

R. G. Cox, "The Reviews and Magazines," in *From Dickens to Hardy*, edited by Boris Ford, volume 6 of *The Pelican Guide to English Literature* (Harmondsworth, U.K.: Penguin, 1958), pp. 188-204;

David de Laura, ed., *Victorian Prose; a Guide to Research* (New York: Modern Language Association, 1973);

Louis Dudek, *Literature and the Press* (Toronto: Ryerson Press, 1960);

Alvar Ellegård, *The Readership of the Periodical Press in Mid-Victorian Britain* (Göteborg: Göteborgs Universitäts, 1957);

T. H. S. Escott, *Masters of English Journalism* (London: Unwin, 1911);

Roger Fulford, "Through Eight Reigns: 1853," *Spectator*, 190 (15 May 1953): 125th Anniversary Issue, vi;

Richard Fulton, Entry on the *Spectator*, in *British Literary Magazines*, 4 volumes, edited by Alvin Sullivan (Westport, Conn.: Greenwood, 1982-1986), II: 391-398;

Clarence L. F. Gohdes, *American Literature in Nineteenth Century England* (New York: Columbia University Press, 1944);

Walter James Graham, *English Literary Periodicals* (New York: Nelson, 1930);

James Grant, *The Metropolitan Weekly and Provincial Press*, volume 3 of *The Newspaper Press* (London & New York: Routledge, 1872);

C. L. Graves, "The *Spectator* in the Eighties and Nineties," *Spectator*, 141 (3 November 1928): Centennial Supplement, 16-17;

John J. Gross, *The Rise and Fall of the Man of Letters* (London: Weidenfeld & Nicolson, 1969);

A. J. Harrop, "New Zealand and 'The Spectator,' " *Spectator*, 164 (2 February 1940): 146;

Harrop, "Rintoul and Wakefield," *Spectator*, 141 (3 November 1928): Centennial Supplement, 10-11;

Harold Herd, *The March of Journalism: The Story of the British Press from 1662 to the Present Day* (London: Allen & Unwin, 1952);

John Hogben, *Richard Holt Hutton of 'The Spectator'* (Edinburgh: Oliver & Boyd, 1899);

W. E. Houghton, "British Periodicals of the Victorian Age: Bibliographies and Indexes," *Library Trends*, 7 (1959): 554-565;

H. D. Jordan, "The Daily and Weekly Press of England in 1861," *South Atlantic Quarterly*, 28 (1929): 302-317;

John D. Jump, "Matthew Arnold and the *Spectator*," *Review of English Studies*, 25 (1949): 61-64;

Jump, "Weekly Reviewing in the Eighteen-Fifties," *Review of English Studies*, 24 (1948): 42-57;

Jump, "Weekly Reviewing in the Eighteen-Sixties," *Review of English Studies*, new series 3 (1952): 244-262;

Alan J. Lee, *The Origins of the Popular Press in England, 1855-1914* (Totowa, N.J.: Rowman & Littlefield, 1976);

Gaylord C. Leroy, "Richard Holt Hutton," *PMLA*, 56 (1941): 809-840;

"Literary Pages of the *Spectator*," *Spectator*, 141 (3 November 1928): Centennial Supplement, 46-48, 645-646, 690-691;

E. V. Lucas, "Sir Walter Scott and the *Spectator*," *Spectator*, 141 (3 November 1928): Centennial Supplement, 40-41;

Oscar Maurer, "My Squeamish Public: Some Problems of Victorian Magazine Publishers and Editors," *Studies in Bibliography*, 12 (1959): 21-40;

Juliet McMaster, "The Meaning of Words and the Nature of Things: Trollope's *Can You Forgive Her?*," *Studies in English Literature*, 14 (Autumn 1974): 603-618;

"One Hundred Years of the *Spectator*," *Living Age*, 335 (January 1929): 369;

Harold Orel and George Worth, *Six Studies in Nineteenth-Century Literature and Thought*, University of Kansas Humanities Studies, no. 35 (Lawrence: University of Kansas, 1962);

Morton D. Paley, "The Critical Reception of *A Critical Essay*," *Blake Newsletter*, no. 29-30 (Summer-Fall 1974): 33-37;

Patrick Parrinder, *Authors and Authority: A Study of English Literary Criticism and its Relation to*

*Culture, 1750-1950* (London: Routledge & Kegan Paul, 1977);

Alan Porter, "Dickens and the 'Spectator,'" *Spectator*, 141 (15 September 1928): 320;

Peter Quennell, "Through Eight Reigns: 1828," *Spectator*, 190 (15 May 1953): 125th Anniversary Issue, iv;

F. D. Roberts, "Early Victorian Newspaper Editors," *Victorian Periodicals Newsletter*, no. 14 (January 1972): 1-12;

A. L. Rowse, "Through Eight Reigns: 1878," *Spectator*, 190 (15 May 1953): 125th Anniversary Issue, viii;

Charles R. Sanders, *The Strachey Family 1888-1932* (Durham, N.C.: Duke University Press, 1953);

"The 6,000th *Spectator*," *Spectator*, 170 (25 June 1943): 586-587;

David Skilton, *Anthony Trollope and His Contemporaries: A Study in the Theory and Conventions of Mid-Victorian Fiction* (New York: St. Martin's Press, 1972; London: Longman, 1972);

Skilton, "The *Spectator*'s Attack on Trollope's *Prime Minister*: A Mistaken Attribution," *Notes and Queries*, 213 (November 1968): 420-421;

Felix Spa, *The Periodical Press of London, 1800-1830* (Boston: Faxon, 1937);

"The *Spectator*," *Nation and Athenæum*, 44 (November 1928): 168-169;

Amy Strachey, *St. Loe Strachey: His Life and His Paper* (London: Gollancz, 1930);

John Strachey, "J. St. Loe Strachey," *Spectator*, 141 (3 November 1928): Centennial Supplement, 14-16;

John St. Loe Strachey, *The Adventure of Living: A Subjective Autobiography* (London: Hodder & Stoughton, 1922);

Robert H. Tener, "An Arnold Quotation as a Clue to R. H. Hutton's *Spectator* Articles," *Notes and Queries*, 216 (March 1971): 100-101;

Tener, "A Clue for Some R. H. Hutton Attributions," *Notes and Queries*, 207 (October 1967): 382-383;

Tener, "More Articles by R. H. Hutton," *Bulletin of the New York Public Library*, 66 (January 1962): 58-62;

Tener, "R. H. Hutton and 'Agnostic,'" *Notes and Queries*, 209 (November 1964): 429-431;

Tener, "R. H. Hutton: Some Attributions," *Victorian Periodicals Newsletter*, no. 20 (June 1973): 14-31;

Tener, "R. H. Hutton's Editorial Career. III. The 'Economist' and the 'Spectator,'" *Victorian Periodicals Newsletter*, no. 8 (April 1970): 6-17;

Tener, "R. H. Hutton's Essays Theological and Literary: A Bibliographical Note," *Notes and Queries*, 205 (May 1960): 185-187;

Tener, "Richard Holt Hutton," *Times Literary Supplement*, 24 April 1959, p. 241;

Tener, "The *Spectator* Records 1874-1897," *Victorian Newsletter*, no. 17 (1960): 33-36;

Tener, "Spectatorial Strachey," *Times Literary Supplement*, 31 December 1964, p. 1181;

Tener, "Swinburne as Reviewer," *Times Literary Supplement*, 25 December 1959, p. 755;

Tener, "The Writings of Richard Holt Hutton: A Checklist of Identifications," *Victorian Periodicals Newsletter*, no. 17 (September 1972);

*Tercentenary Handlist of English and Welsh Newspapers, Magazines and Reviews* (London: Times Publishing, 1920);

Sir William Beach Thomas, *The Story of the Spectator* (London: Methuen, 1928);

Denys Thompson, "A Hundred Years of the Higher Journalism," *Scrutiny*, 4 (June 1935): 25-34;

C. Townsend, "Meredith Townsend," "R. H. Hutton," and "The Story of the *Spectator*," *Spectator*, 141 (3 November 1928): Centennial Supplement, 1-8, 11-12, 13-14;

Frank Miller Turner, "*Rainfall, Plagues, and the Prince of Wales*: a Chapter in the History of Science," *Journal of British Studies*, 13 (May 1974): 46-65;

A. P. Wadsworth, "Newspaper Circulations 1800-1954," *Transactions of the Manchester Statistical Society* (1955): 1-40;

J. O. Waller, "Edward Dicey and the American Negro in 1862: An English Working Journalist's View," *Bulletin of the New York Public Library*, 66 (January 1962): 31-45;

Wilfrid Philip Ward, *Ten Personal Studies* (London & New York: Longmans, Green, 1908);

William Smith Ward, *Index and Finding List of Serials Published in the British Isles, 1789-1832* (Lexington: University of Kentucky, 1954).

# Tait's Edinburgh Magazine

*(April 1832 - July 1861)*

Linda Mills Woolsey
*King College*

"The times are political, and so, of course, are we." With this notice "To Correspondents," *Tait's Edinburgh Magazine* introduced its first issue to the public in April 1832. From the beginning, William Tait designed his periodical miscellany to emulate the liberal politics of London's *Westminster Review* right under the noses of the well-established Tory wags and pundits of *Blackwood's*. The times were ripe for such a magazine, which first appeared when the Reform Bill hung in the balance, violence threatened in Ireland and the West Indies, and cholera shadowed the cities of Britain. For much of its career *Tait's Edinburgh Magazine* spoke for the politics of reform to a receptive audience in both Scotland and England. Yet, while its primary emphasis was on liberal, even radical politics, *Tait's* did not neglect the world of letters. From its earliest numbers well into the 1840s, *Tait's* featured essays and reviews that often unite a utilitarian demand for instruction with the heritage of a Romantic faith in sympathy, in nature, and in imagination.

Although the opening notice seemed to slight the world of literature with its assertion that "the public at large . . . is too much engrossed with the business of real life to find leisure for imaginative indulgence," even in the heat of the reform crisis, *Tait's* was devoted to freedom in the world of letters. The first issue was dedicated to Leigh Hunt, whose *Examiner* was hailed as a model for holding its course "with courage, perseverance, and single-minded consistency." From the first, the role of *Tait's* in letters, as in politics, was to oppose the "organized system of persecution and calumny" represented by the *Edinburgh Review*, the *Quarterly Review*, and *Blackwood's*. Thus, while the reviewers for *Tait's* often revealed liberal and utilitarian biases, the magazine allowed for a freedom of expression in criticism that embodied its approval of "honest or independent opinion."

William Tait shaped the magazine as an organ of progressive thought for much of its history, serving as publisher from 1832 to 1846 and editing the magazine from its founding until May 1834. *Tait's* magazine was intended for a middle- and working-class audience, which included women subscribers. Under Tait's editorship, the magazine's political fervor permeated its articles, fiction, and poetry, but the earnest and sometimes intense tone of the serious essays was balanced by frequent humorous and satirical pieces—parodies, slapstick narratives, and doggerel verse.

While the prospectus for the magazine had spelled out its political and ideological allegiance, an article on "A Tete a Tete with Mr. Tait" in the first issue refines that position and suggests some of the concerns shaping the particular marriage of Romantic and Utilitarian ideals in the magazine. The article takes the form of a dialogue between a Mr. Smith and Mr. Tait, sparked by the question of whether there is room for another periodical in the crowded field of contemporary publishing. Mr. Tait, of course, asserts that there is not only room, but actually a demand "for a magazine of liberal principles, of independent spirit, bearing upon the times, bringing out the sympathies of mankind" in ways that are reform-minded but not narrow. Such a magazine would recognize change as a positive force, and would "talk of that which living people talk and think about."

While granting that this goal is laudable, Mr. Smith is still a little uneasy, for the prospectus has given him visions of "spinning jennies and steam engines." Mr. Tait's espousal of "utility" seems to promise a dull magazine, devoted only to "that which has a direct and positive tendency to fill the belly or cover the back." Mr. Tait, however, declares that he means the magazine to embody a broader spirit of utility, since "everything that contributes to the enjoyment of our being and the perfection of our nature, is useful."

While "A Tete a Tete with Mr. Tait" is informed at every turn by the language of supply and demand and the economics of usefulness, both are redefined in ways that serve the world

TAIT'S

EDINBURGH MAGAZINE.

No. I.——APRIL, 1832.

CONTENTS.



WILLIAM TAIT, EDINBURGH;

SIMPKIN & MARSHALL, LONDON; AND JOHN CUMMING, DUBLIN.

APRIL, 1832.

*Cover for the first issue of the liberal magazine William Tait founded to challenge the Tory politics of* Blackwood's Edinburgh Magazine *during the final months of debate over the Reform Bill of 1832* of imagination as well as that of commerce. This new definition is particularly evident in the discussion of poetry, which Mr. Tait punctuates by grumbling that there is "no demand for poetry" and that "the world has outgrown poetry." For Mr. Tait, the age of prose has arrived. But the counterarguments of Mr. Smith suggest the ways *Tait's* essayists and reviewers were to qualify the world of supply and demand by their appreciation of poetry and their acknowledgment—and sometimes practice of—a poetry in prose. Smith argues first that "it is the supply that creates the demand." While *Tait's* did not succeed in gracing its pages with the "really sublime and original" poetry Smith envisions, it did publish verse, and for much of its career it demonstrated an appreciation for the Romantic heritage of William Wordsworth, John Keats, and Percy Bysshe Shelley. Smith also defines poetry as "that mental electricity, whereby the heart holds living converse with the soul of nature, and the living invisible spirit of the material and visible world," asserting that this "mental electricity" occurs in the best prose. To this point, Mr. Tait assents. Under William Tait's direction, the magazine encouraged this poetry of prose, valuing not only brevity and substance, but liveliness, imagination, and independence of mind as well.

"A Tete a Tete with Mr. Tait" also suggests the dedication of *Tait's* to fair play. Mr. Tait banks the success of his magazine not only on "the talent of [his] contributors" but also on the "good spirit" of its contents. He lets Smith denigrate the magazines that descend to notices of personal appearance and details of domestic life. Smith says that the writers and reviewers of *Tait's* will be "gentlemen," and he suggests the faith of *Tait's* in the British people and in the reading public: "Depend upon it, Mr. Tait, the public is not an ass, it knows good from bad; some few readers, who cannot think, will read for reading's sake; but they who can think will prefer their own wordless thoughts to others' thoughtless words."

The first year's issues of the magazine demonstrate these principles. Their pages are permeated by the political fervor of the times. Even articles on such topics as the "State of Magic in Egypt—By an Eyewitness" and "A Lawyer's Dream" (both in the April issue) are clearly political, as is much of the poetry. The lead articles for 1832 are by and large political: "The Ministry" (April); "The Second Reading [of the Reform Bill]" (May); "Our Three Days" (June); "The Tories, the Whigs, and the Court" (July); "Parliamentary Candidates" (August and September); "The Ministry and the People" (October). By November, however, with the Reform Bill safely in place and a succession of minor crises in its application passed, *Tait's* could offer lead articles bearing more on general principles than on practical politics, publishing "The Radical Poets" in November and "The Church of England and the Dissenters" in December. Throughout the first year, the political writers of *Tait's* emphasize the importance of education and political understanding and are careful to distinguish, as does the writer of "The Revolution" (April), between revolution as salutary and inevitable change and revolution as violence.

Even in that first heady year of political tensions and opportunities, William Tait seems to have tried to follow the advice Leigh Hunt offered him in a letter written on 9 April 1832: "Politics are undoubtedly the great thing just now, and long may they continue to be so; for when truly great, they include thousands of other fine things; but a magazine, I am sure, is the better for having a good deal of its ground broken up into smaller and more flowery beds." Even the first number, heavily political, includes poetry and amusing character sketches, as well as a twenty-page narrative, "The Ventilators: A Tale of the Last Session," whose mixture of romance and politics, social satire and earnestness is in some ways typical of *Tait's*.

"The Ventilators" also marks *Tait's* as being, from the beginning, aware of women's interest in—and capacity for—political involvement. Margaret Clifford, the heroine of this tale, dodges the wiles of her worldly friend Georgiana (Lady Robert Anson) and her Tory cronies and listens enthralled to the eloquence of that liberal M.P., Mr. Talbot. Miss Clifford also saves the day for reform, breaking her feminine silence to warn some straggling gentlemen that if they wish to vote they must hurry into the House of Commons before the doors are locked. While the ladies of the story watch Parliament as they would a tournament, the tale acknowledges their real, although indirect, influence on political action. At the climax of the narrative, Mrs. Talbot advises her future daughter-in-law of the importance of a woman's learning about politics in order to "discriminate right from wrong" and to separate "her highest public duty" from "her own worldly interest." The heroine faints, of course, after her heroic action, and later admits to having loved Talbot before she heard him speak in Parliament; yet, despite the sentimental conventions of the narrative, the piece gives striking evidence of the early commitment of *Tait's* to practical roles for women in the changing world of the nineteenth century.

The literary articles and reviews of 1832 demonstrate that the role of *Tait's* in literary criticism, though modest, contributed to the survival of a fair-minded criticism, aware of its political ideals but not imprisoned by them. Reviews and literary articles in *Tait's* take several forms made popular by periodicals of the 1820s. These include the balanced overview of a writer's career ("Miss Edgeworth" in June) and the overview as a defense against detractors ("Gothe" [*sic*] in June). Sometimes, as in "The Cultivation of Fancy" (June), the book in hand is merely the excuse for an excursus on a topic suggested by the book. Often, the review attempts to give the reader a concise view of the strengths and weaknesses of a new work, with the author's general assertions illustrated by sizable excerpts from the text (see, for example, the reviews of Fanny Kemble's *Francis I* [1832] and of Harriet Martineau's current volumes of *Illustrations of Political Economy* [1832-1834] in the May "Monthly Register"). While the forms and political outlooks vary, the reviewers are consistently reasonable, making a point of separating the writer's life or politics from his or her writing.

Although the magazine has often been described as liberal, radical, and utilitarian in ways that emphasize its practicality and rationality, the reviewers, on the whole, are clearly influenced by a Romantic heritage. One of the most striking features of these early reviews is the insistence on the importance of imagination and passion, as well as on morality and information. In the "Monthly Register" for May 1832, distinguishing his balanced view from the puffery of public acclaim, the reviewer of Kemble's *Francis I* notes not only its "elaborately polished" language and its author's "natural cleverness and tact," but suggests that the author might have learned from Samuel Taylor Coleridge ways to make "powerful tragic use" out of "the conflict of passions." In the same issue a reviewer, writing about George Cornewall Lewis's *Remarks on the Use and Abuse of Some Political Terms* (1832), presents a view of imagination that was to appear in various guises through many of the issues for 1832: "Men who, for want of cultivation, have the intellects of dwarfs, are of course the slaves of their imagination, if they have any, as they are the slaves of their sensations, if they have not; and it is partly, perhaps, because the systematic culture of the thinking faculty is in little repute, that imagination also is in such bad odour; there being no solidity and vigour of intellect to resist it where it tends to mislead." Here, an informed and guided imagination is seen as central to a world of progress and justice.

In the same issue, an article on "Female Letter Writers" not only seconds "The Ventilators" in celebrating "the passive courage of woman in her hour of fiery trial," but affirms the power of some women's letters as a sort of "natural" literature, defined in what we have come to regard as "Romantic" terms: "In letter-writing, as in everything else, commend us, however, to *words* which are *things*; to the exuberance which throws up from the deep mines of native feeling the rough diamond, together with the embedding soil, and leave conceit leisurely to polish its pebbles."

In June 1832 articles on "Miss Edgeworth's Works," "The Cultivation of Fancy," "Gothe [*sic*]," and "Jean Jacques Rousseau" provide variations on the themes of imagination and feeling. While Maria Edgeworth's fiction is "most useful and practical," the reviewer is critical of her "pattern children" and "docile young women," and the "tinge of pedantry" that mars her work. The reviewer laments her "rigid proscription of all vehement passion and overwhelming feeling," and declares that she ought to make her "pattern ladies" either "a little more feminine—weak we shall not call it" or "pardon her readers for lavishing their affections on her more captivating and piquante naughty ones." In the same issue, a review of James Hogg's *Queer Book* (1832) titled "Cultivation of the Fancy" laments a dearth of appreciation for the fantastic and imaginative, which affects even the young men of the House of Commons. There, the reviewer suggests, "You will find good abilities, solid acquirements; but lumps of lead, in all that pertains to the imagination, and incapable of those flights which, though they seem but the flutterings of sportiveness, often raise the mind to new views, and strike on rich quarries which otherwise would have escaped observation." Thus, he concludes, "it is not enough that the mind is stored with knowledge, but the fancy must be exercised. Error has its fancy, its skill in escaping under false appearances; and the soldiers of truth should be able to combat and defeat it in all its Protean shifts. But nothing is thought of now but solidity. A man's head must be as grave and substantial as a cannon-ball; good for a straight flight at its mark and no more. This is villainous."

The articles on Johann Wolfgang von Goethe and Jean-Jacques Rousseau also seek to strike a balance between excesses of imagination and of utilitarian pragmatism. Against Goethe's detractors, the reviewer defines the German writer's greatness in terms of "the union of an active and almost prodigal imagination, with an intellect, clear, subtle, and commanding." Unlike some earlier critics, this reviewer values not *The Sorrows of Young Werther* (1774), but *Faust* (1808, 1832). The article on Rousseau in the June and October issues attempts to reevaluate a man whose character and work may seem to some readers "an obsolete topic." But, the reviewer argues, "the temper of the present times, the questions that are now being agitated by large classes of the community, are bringing into existence modes of thinking remarkably analogous to those so eloquently propounded by Rousseau." Both this writer and Harriet Martineau in her assessment of Sir Walter Scott in the December issue attempt to understand the genius and the ideas of the writer in terms of the formation of his character and the times in which he wrote, tracing the growth of the writer's mind in ways that reflect Romantic attention to the child as father to the man united with a utilitarian urge to demystify and clarify intellectual greatness.

Harriet Martineau is a visible presence in the first year of *Tait's*, represented by reviews of her work in May and July, in her tale "The English in China" in September, and in her article on Scott in December. In July the reviewer suggests that she is an example of woman's capability—not only in her domestic role, but as a teacher. For this reviewer, political economy is particularly suited to female minds, in part because "the economy of empires is only the economy of families and neighborhoods on a larger scale." Thus, though women lack strength for active governance, "The sentiments and opinions contained in her books shew how lovely a thing the mind of woman may become, when allowed fairly to develope [*sic*] itself. With all man's power of endurance, it has a gentleness and delicacy he never can acquire."

The relatively broad scope of *Tait's* reviewers and their subjects is well illustrated by the October issue, which includes discussions of the work of Jeremy Bentham, Shelley, and Rousseau. Bentham's genius for synthesis makes him the "herald of a new era," whose mind, "attracting to itself, as the magnet does iron filings, all those novelties, remains inaccessible to the worn-out dry husks of old opinion, and compresses by its innate power the hitherto *disjecta membra* into a luminous and convincing system." Here, the language of attraction, organic organization, and radiance—terms that often figure in texts labeled Romantic—is joined to the celebration of eminently practical genius. The article on Shelley acknowledges his wayward life, but celebrates the "maiden purity in his soul," advocating the criticism of a poem as an object: "A poem, to be rightly estimated, must be judged without reference to its author as much as a painting or a statue." Continuing his assessment of Shelley in the November issue, the reviewer praises the dramatic power of *The Cenci* (1819) and the "mine of the richest beauty of poetry" in *Prometheus Unbound* (1819). In the same issue, an article on the Radical poets begins with a recognition of the poetry of prose practiced by Francis Bacon and William Hazlitt, defining poetry (as Ebenezer Elliott might) as "impassioned truth."

Under William Tait's editorship in the 1830s, the magazine attracted some able writers in the service of "impassioned truth," including John Bright, Richard Cobden, Thomas De Quincey, Leigh Hunt, Harriet Martineau, and John Stuart Mill. Ebenezer Elliott, radical author of *Corn Law Rhymes* (1830), was also a frequent contributor. A magazine in which his sympathy for the working class stood shoulder to shoulder with the perspective of a self-proclaimed Tory gentleman such as De Quincey suggests a catholicity of taste in both editors and readers. Despite its relatively high price, the magazine was popular, especially in coffeehouses and workingmen's reading rooms. By the mid 1830s it claimed a circulation of twenty-five hundred. After Tait lowered the price of the magazine in 1834, it rapidly led magazine sales in Scotland and was popular even in England.

In June 1834 *Johnstone's Edinburgh Magazine* merged with *Tait's*, bringing Christian Isobel Johnstone to the editorial staff. While Tait continued to serve as publisher and handled much of the correspondence with contributors, Johnstone took over most of the actual editing. She was an able writer, contributing criticism and fiction, and writing all of the "Literary Register" while she served as editor through December 1846. Under her guidance, literature became more central to *Tait's* and the magazine attracted new contributors. While *Tait's* already reflected the changing times in the space it devoted to reviews of works by women, women played an even more important role as writers during Johnstone's editorship. Harriet Martineau continued to contribute, as well as Marguerite, Countess Blessington; Catherine G. F. Gore and Mary Russell Mitford. While Michael W. Hyde depicts Johnstone as a moderate feminist, Mary Wilson Carpenter argues that Johnstone took a strong position, evidenced in her appeals to the arguments of writers such as Catherine Macaulay and Mary Wollstonecraft. In her July 1844 review of Mrs. Hugo Reid's *Plea for Women* (1844), Johnstone advocated not only woman's rights, but women's need for economic independence. Johnstone's work and writing bear witness to her strength of mind and editorial skills, as well as to her awareness of the concerns of many nineteenth-century women.

Under Johnstone's editorship John Galt and George Gilfillan became regular writers, and De Quincey continued to be a prolific, if irregular contributor. In 1834 De Quincey began a series of "Sketches of Life and Manners; from the Autobiography of an English Opium Eater" that was to run off and on for seven years, including scenes from his life and reading as well as reminiscences of Wordsworth and Coleridge. From 1833 through 1841 and again between 1845 and 1848, De Quincey contributed numerous articles on various subjects, topical and literary. As late as 1851, De Quincey was still a sporadic contributor.

Johnstone continued Tait's emphasis on broad and satiric humor, most notably with William Edmoundstone Aytoun and Theodore Martin's 1841-1844 series of satiric reviews of contemporary annuals and ephemeral publications. With great gusto these satirists wrote parodic prose and poetry mocking the bad taste of the day, which they later collected and published as *The Book of Ballads* (1845).

In 1847 Alexander Alison, an ironmaster, bought the magazine and moved it to Glasgow. During 1847 and 1848 Alison worked with George Troup to continue *Tait's*, shifting its emphasis more firmly toward instruction and information. Troup, an experienced journalist, edited the magazine from 1847 to mid 1861. Despite his skills and the magazine's long-standing reputation, *Tait's* declined during these years. Under Troup, the magazine lacked the variety and energy of its earlier days, perhaps because Troup himself was busy as a lecturer, newspaperman, and political writer in addition to his duties at *Tait's*. But the declining circulation of *Tait's*, like its initial success, was also a sign of the times. The 1830s, with their sense of national crisis and vast possibility, were ripe for a magazine dedicated to reform and to the world of enlightened imagination. The very excitement of the period echoes through the early numbers, as contributors vilify the oligarchy, celebrate reform, and remember the humanizing heritage of Romantic sympathy. By the late 1850s, the heyday of Victorian faith in progress had passed, and the radical ideas of the 1830s had become commonplaces of an entrenched, but not always prosperous, middle class. *Tait's* had, with the reformers, grown a little stodgy, a little dull, and the reading public gradually fell away. Yet *Tait's* had left its mark on British politics and British prose with its championship of liberty, not only for the people, but for the press as well.

**References:**

James Bertram, *Some Memories of Books, Authors, and Events* (London: Constable, 1893);

Odile Boucher, "Le discours sur le roman dans *Tait's Edinburgh Magazine, 1832-1850*," Ph.D. dissertation, University of Nancy, 1980;

Mary Wilson Carpenter, "The Hair of the Medusa: Leigh Hunt, *Tait's Edinburgh Magazine*, and the Criticism of Female Beauty," in *The Life and Times of Leigh Hunt*, edited by Robert A. McCann (Iowa City: Friends of the University of Iowa Libraries, 1985), pp. 17-40;

Michael W. Hyde, "The Role of 'Our Scottish Readers' in the History of *Tait's Edinburgh Magazine*," *Victorian Periodicals Review*, 14 (Winter 1981): 135-140;

James W. Scott, "*Tait's Edinburgh Magazine*," *Scottish Notes and Queries*, 6 (February 1893): 129-132; (March 1893): 150;

George Elmslie Troup, *Life of George Troup, Journalist* (Edinburgh: Macniven & Wallace, 1881);

Mark A. Weinstein, Entry on *Tait's Edinburgh Magazine*, in *British Literary Magazines*, 4 volumes, edited by Alvin Sullivan (Westport, Conn.: Greenwood Press, 1983-1986), II: 401-405.

# The Westminster Review

*(January 1824 - January 1914)*

Michael Laine
*Victoria College, University of Toronto*

The first number of the *Westminster Review,* inaugurated under the influence of Jeremy Bentham and James Mill to represent liberal, indeed radical, political opinion, appeared in January 1824 under the joint editorship of Henry Southern and John Bowring. In May 1823 Southern wrote to William Whewell, "The politics of the Review (party politics being however as much as possible avoided) are to be what are called *liberal*—that is to say, every question will be discussed with a view to the interests of and happiness of mankind at large." Both Bentham and James Mill had contemplated the establishment of such a review for many years, but by the time Bentham, then aged seventy-five, put up the money, Mill felt unable to accept the editorship, feeling that it would conflict with his position in the India Office. He was, however, to edit for it a series of articles analyzing other journals. His own disparaging assessment of the *Edinburgh Review* appeared in the first number and was concluded in the second by his son, John Stuart Mill. This two-part article was in some measure responsible for the success of the first issues. The firm of Longman, Hurst, Rees, Orme, Brown, and Green—which had a half-interest in the *Edinburgh Review*—had nevertheless agreed with Southern to publish the new journal. They had laid out a considerable sum in advertisements and had printed 150,000 copies of the prospectus, but Thomas Longman III recognized, when late in 1823 he saw Mill's article, the extent which the new review would conflict with his interest in the *Edinburgh* and withdrew his support. James Mill then applied for relief to his own publishers, Baldwin, Cradock, and Joy, who agreed to maintain the enterprise.

During the review's early history, contributors were, for the most part, associated with Southern's literary journal, the *Retrospective Review,* but those affiliated with the two Mills remain the best known today. In James Mill's orbit were Charles and John Austin, George and Harriet Grote, the journalist Albany Fonblanque, and from India House, Thomas Love Peacock and his friend Thomas Jefferson Hogg. Prominent among John Stuart Mill's associates were William Ellis, John Arthur Roebuck, and Eyton Tooke. Bentham, up to his death in 1832, contributed only five articles or parts of articles, the last, "Mr. Brougham and Local Judicatories," in October 1830, for which he says that "he sent in the meat for this meal but does not know who did the dressing." James Mill, himself suspicious of Bowring's editorial competence, contributed only nine, ceasing with his article on the ballot in the July 1830 issue. This, the best known of his contributions to the *Westminster,* was published as a pamphlet in that same year and has been frequently republished since. Francis Place, the radical tailor who refused to allow Bowring, the political editor, to tamper with his prose, contributed only two articles, one on Egypt in July 1826 and the other on the history of Parliament in October 1827. John Cam Hobhouse contributed only one. Moreover, there was a certain reluctance on the part of prominent liberals of other than a Benthamite cast of mind to participate. Notable by their absence were Joseph Hume, Robert Owen, John Sterling, and William Cobbett.

Even though Southern acted as literary editor, in its early years the review was never really hospitable to literature. In October of 1824 John Stuart Mill, commenting on David Hume as a historian, offered that Hume's only interest in truth was to demonstrate that it was unattainable. Mill went on to say, "His mind, too, was completely enslaved by a taste for literature; to those kinds of literature which teach mankind to know the causes of their happiness and misery, that they may seek the one and avoid the other; but that literature which without regard for truth or utility, seeks only to excite emotion." In April of the same year, continuing his father's analysis of the *Edinburgh Review,* he suggested that Sir Walter Scott wrote with no moral purpose and that his work shows "no decided leaning between virtue and vice." Mill went on to complain that the

*John Bowring, who edited the* Westminster Review *with Henry Southern during the early years of its existence*

*Edinburgh* has never lamented that Scott's productions "were not useful, as well as agreeable."

Despite its initial success, in good part due to the excitement over the agitation in 1831 for the Reform Bill, the *Westminster* in its early years never really paid its own way and was kept alive by the devotion of its patrons. Estimates of Bentham's support vary between four thousand pounds and ten thousand pounds; Bowring agreed to serve for no pay, and the Mills, who hoped to wrest control from Bowring, offered to edit and write without remuneration stipulating that Bowring resign as editor. Fortunately for Bowring, Thomas Perronet Thompson, a previous associate of his, fell into an inheritance and, abandoning his military career, agreed to rescue the journal. At the close of 1828, Thompson paid the outstanding debts of the *Westminster Review* and became, with Bentham, coproprietor. Bowring remained as a paid editor. Thompson established himself as coeditor and emerged as a principal contributor during the next seven years. The Mills were not happy with this arrangement and withdrew their support and participation. During these years the *Westminster*, as William Thomas says, in "seeking to do good mainly by a gloomy insistence on the prevalence of evil, squandered its popularity." Moreover, the reputation of the review was damaged by the involvement of Bowring, along with Edward and Joseph Hume, in a financial scandal connected with Greek bonds.

In 1835 the Mills, having lost their platform, established the *London Review* with William Molesworth as proprietor. It was designed to promote the views of the Philosophic Radicals under the editorial hand of John Stuart Mill, who was the real editor, although the titular editor was William Falconer. Mill wrote that "The spirit of the new review will be democratic, but with none of the exclusiveness and narrowness of the *Westminster Review*. . . ." Only two issues of the *London Re-*

*view* appeared before it was amalgamated with the *Westminster*. The first issue appeared in April 1836 as the *London and Westminster Review* (a title it kept until June 1840 when it once again became the *Westminster Review*). The first two volumes of the *London and Westminster Review* include six articles by James Mill as well as seven articles and a review by John Stuart Mill, whose contributions include "Tennyson's Poems" (July 1835) and his first essay on Alexis de Tocqueville (October 1835).

James Mill's death in 1836 allowed John Stuart Mill to assume full control over the direction of the journal. He opened its pages to a broader spectrum of liberal opinion. Mill, having come through his "mental crisis" and having discovered through it the value of poetry, published an increasing proportion of articles on science and literature. In addition to reviews and criticism of his own, he included his articles on Bentham (August 1838) and Samuel Taylor Coleridge (March 1840), literary articles and reviews by Edward Bulwer-Lytton and Leigh Hunt, William Makepeace Thackeray's "Parisian Caricatures" (April 1840), and four important articles by Thomas Carlyle. Of Carlyle's article on Mirabeau (January 1837), Mill wrote that it "has been the most popular we ever had in the review."

Molesworth, along with many of Mill's former associates, disagreed with his approach, and Mill assumed the proprietorship in 1838. The times were not right for a radical review, and Mill, discouraged, sold the review in March 1840 to William Cole and Edward Hickson. The first number under their direction appeared in June of that year. Sales had become slow, and Cole soon tired of the enterprise, withdrawing in July and leaving Hickson as editor and sole proprietor. Hickson was a very personal editor providing a good deal of sharp editorial opinion. He continued, through 1851, the reformist agenda of the *Review*: "The cause of the people . . . is still that of *Westminster Review*."

Although Mill's editorial direction ceased, one should remember that the impetus for the foundation of the *London Review* was the desire to provide a periodical which, through the abandonment of anonymous journalism, was to allow the free play of opinion and was "to drop altogether every kind of lying; the lie of pretending that all articles are *reviews* when more than half of them are not; and the lie of pretending that all articles proceed from a *corps*, who jointly entertain all the opinions expressed. There is to be no *we*; but each writer is to have a signature, which he may avow or not as he pleases, but which is, (unless there be special reasons to constitute an exception) to be the *same* for *all* his articles."

For the first six years of Hickson's editorship, the somewhat heavy political and social emphasis of the review was leavened by the contributions of George Henry Lewes, who wrote regular short notices and sixteen full articles ranging widely over literature and history, including two on Shelley, an article on Shakespeare and his editors, one titled "Errors and Abuses of English Criticism," as well as those on French and German literature and philosophy. George Eliot's first contribution, a review of Robert William Mackay's *Progress of the Intellect*, appeared in January 1851. By this time Hickson was negotiating with John Chapman, the publisher, for the sale of the review, which passed into Chapman's hands in October. Chapman, assisted by George Eliot (Mary Ann Evans) until 1854, became editor as well as proprietor. Eliot collaborated with Chapman on the prospectus for the review, and the literary section was conducted under her influence and that of Lewes for the next five years. Under their direction and that of Chapman the *Westminster* retained a distinguished list of reviewers, among them Thomas Henry Huxley on science, Mark Pattison and Havelock Ellis on theology and philosophy, James Anthony Froude on history, and George Eliot and George Meredith on literature.

Chapman sold the review to the newly formed Westminster Review Company in 1887, whereupon the *Westminster* became a monthly rather than the quarterly it had been. Chapman remained as editor to be succeeded, after his death in 1894, by his second wife, Hannah. She retained management control and the editor's chair, later to be assisted by her niece, Nellie Chapman, until the *Westminster* ceased publication in 1914. Although its financial condition had never been really stable, the review maintained its powerful reputation almost to the end. In 1883 George Bernard Shaw wrote that it was first among those "journals which make it a rule not to touch a subject without leaving a mark on it."

**References:**

Joseph Hamburger, *Intellectuals in Politics: John Stuart Mill and the Philosophic Radicals* (New Haven & London: Yale University Press, 1965);

John Stuart Mill, *Additional Letters*, edited by Marion Filipiuk, Michael Laine, and John M.

Robson, volume 32 of *Collected Works of John Stuart Mill* (Toronto: University of Toronto Press, 1991);

Mill, *Autobiography*, edited by Robson and Jack Stillinger, volume 1 of *Collected Works of John Stuart Mill* (Toronto: University of Toronto Press, 1981);

Mill, *Earlier Letters*, edited by Francis E. Mineka, volume 12 of *Collected Works of John Stuart Mill* (Toronto: University of Toronto Press, 1963);

Mill, *Essays on England, Ireland and the Empire*, edited by Robson, with an introduction by Hamburger, volume 6 of *Collected Works of John Stuart Mill* (Toronto: University of Toronto Press, 1982);

James Mulvihill, "The Poetics of Utility: Benthamite Literary Reviewing, 1824-1836," *English Studies in Canada*, 15 (June 1989): 149-161;

George Lyman Nesbitt, *Benthamite Reviewing: The First Twelve Years of "The Westminster Review," 1824-1836* (New York: Columbia University Press, 1934);

William Thomas, "John Stuart Mill and the Crisis of Benthamism," in his *The Philosophic Radicals* (Oxford: Clarendon Press, 1979), pp. 147-205;

Rosemary T. VanArsdel, "Notes on *Westminster Review* Research," *Victorian Periodicals Newsletter*, 1 (January 1968): 21-23;

VanArsdel, "*The Westminster Review*, 1824-57: with special emphasis on Literary Attitudes," Ph.D. dissertation, Columbia University, 1961;

Roger P. Wallins, "The Westminster Review," in *British Literary Magazines*, 4 volumes, edited by Alvin Sullivan (Westport, Conn.: Greenwood Press, 1983-1986), II: 424-433.

**Note:**

Sets of the *Westminster Review* are available in England and in North America in volumes and in microform. John Stuart Mill's marked set ending in 1840 was given as a gift to the Fox family of Falmouth in 1840 and is now at Somerville College, Oxford. Francis Place's annotated set is held in the Thomas Fisher Rare Book Library of the University of Toronto. Another marked set, running from April 1835 to May 1843, is at the Fisher Library, University of Sydney, Australia.

# Books for Further Reading


Abrams, M. H. *The Mirror and the Lamp; Romantic Theory and the Critical Tradition.* New York: Oxford University Press, 1953.

Abrams. *Natural Supernaturalism: Tradition and Revolution in Romantic Literature.* New York: Norton, 1971.

Abrams, ed. *English Romantic Poets: Modern Essays in Criticism.* New York: Oxford University Press, 1960; revised, 1975.

Aers, David, Jonathan Cook, and David Punter. *Romanticism and Ideology: Studies in English Writing 1765-1830.* London & Boston: Routledge & Kegan Paul, 1981.

Ball, Patricia M. *The Central Self: A Study in Romantic and Victorian Imagination.* London: Athlone Press, 1968.

Beaty, Frederick L. *Light from Heaven: Love in British Romantic Literature.* De Kalb: Northern Illinois University Press, 1971.

Bloom, Harold. *The Visionary Company: A Reading of English Romantic Poetry,* revised and enlarged edition. Ithaca, N.Y.: Cornell University Press, 1971.

Bloom, ed. *Romanticism and Consciousness: Essays in Criticism.* New York: Norton, 1970.

Bostetter, Edward E. *The Romantic Ventriloquists: Wordsworth, Coleridge, Keats, Shelley, Byron,* revised edition. Seattle: University of Washington Press, 1963.

Bowra, C. M. *The Romantic Imagination.* Cambridge, Mass.: Harvard University Press, 1950.

Brisman, Leslie. *Romantic Origins.* Ithaca, N.Y.: Cornell University Press, 1978.

Butler, Marilyn. *Romantics, Rebels, and Reactionaries: English Literature and its Background 1760-1830.* Oxford & New York: Oxford University Press, 1981.

Clubbe, John, and Ernest J. Lovell, Jr. *English Romanticism: The Grounds of Belief.* De Kalb: Northern Illinois University Press, 1983.

Cooper, Andrew M. *Doubt and Identity in Romantic Poetry.* New Haven: Yale University Press, 1988.

Curran, Stuart. *Poetic Form and British Romanticism.* New York & Oxford: Oxford University Press, 1986.

Eaves, Morris, and Michael Fischer, eds. *Romanticism and Contemporary Criticism.* Ithaca, N.Y.: Cornell University Press, 1986.

Ellison, Julie K. *Delicate Subjects: Romanticism, Gender, and the Ethics of Understanding.* Ithaca, N.Y.: Cornell University Press, 1990.

Enscoe, Gerald E. *Eros and the Romantics: Sexual Love as a Theme in Coleridge, Shelley and Keats.* The Hague: Mouton, 1967.

Ford, Boris, ed. *From Blake to Byron, New Pelican Guide to English Literature*, volume 5. Harmondsworth, U.K.: Penguin, 1962.

Frye, Northrop. *A Study of English Romanticism*. New York: Random House, 1968.

Frye, ed. *Romanticism Reconsidered*. New York: Columbia University Press, 1963.

Gaull, Marilyn. *English Romanticism*. New York: Norton, 1988.

Gleckner, Robert F., and Gerald E. Enscoe. *Romanticism: Points of View*, second edition. Englewood Cliffs, N.J.: Prentice-Hall, 1970.

Harris, R. W. *Romanticism and the Social Order 1780-1830*. London: Blandford, 1969.

Hoeveler, Diane Long. *Romantic Androgyny: The Women Within*. University Park: Pennsylvania State University Press, 1990.

Jack, Ian. *English Literature 1815-1832*. Oxford: Clarendon Press, 1963.

Jackson, J. R. de J. *Poetry of the Romantic Period*. London & Boston: Routledge & Kegan Paul, 1980.

Jordon, Frank, ed. *The English Romantic Poets: A Review of Research and Criticism*, fourth edition. New York: Modern Language Association, 1985.

Kermode, Frank. *Romantic Image*. London: Routledge & Kegan Paul, 1957.

Klancher, Jon P. *The Making of English Reading Audiences, 1790-1832*. Madison: University of Wisconsin Press, 1987.

Knight, G. Wilson. *The Starlit Dome: Studies in the Poetry of Vision*. London & New York: Oxford University Press, 1941.

Kroeber, Karl. *Romantic Narrative Art*. Madison: University of Wisconsin Press, 1960.

Levinson, Marjorie. *The Romantic Fragment Poem: A Critique of a Form*. Chapel Hill: University of North Carolina Press, 1986.

Levinson and others. *Rethinking Historicism: Critical Readings in Romantic History*. Oxford & New York: Blackwell, 1989.

McFarland, Thomas. *Romantic Cruxes: The English Essayists and the Spirit of the Age*. Oxford & New York: Oxford University Press, 1987.

McFarland. *Romanticism and the Forms of Ruin: Wordsworth, Coleridge, and Modalities of Fragmentation*. Princeton: Princeton University Press, 1981.

McGann, Jerome J. *The Romantic Ideology: A Critical Investigation*. Chicago & London: University of Chicago Press, 1983.

Mellor, Anne K. *English Romantic Irony*. Cambridge, Mass.: Harvard University Press, 1980.

Mellor. *Romanticism and Feminism*. Bloomington: Indiana University Press, 1988.

Metzger, Lore. *One Foot in Eden: Modes of Pastoral in Romantic Poetry*. Chapel Hill: University of North Carolina Press, 1986.

Morse, David. *Romanticism: A Structural Analysis*. Totowa, N.J.: Barnes & Noble, 1982.

Porter, Roy, and Mikulas Teich, eds. *Romanticism in National Context*. Cambridge & New York: Cambridge University Press, 1988.

Prickett, Stephen, ed. *The Romantics*. New York: Holmes & Meier, 1981.

Redpath, Theodore. *The Young Romantics and Critical Opinion, 1807-1824: Poetry of Byron, Shelley, and Keats as Seen by Their Contemporary Critics*. London: Harrap, 1973.

Reed, Arden, ed. *Romanticism and Language*. Ithaca, N.Y.: Cornell University Press, 1984.

Reiman, Donald H. *English Romantic Poetry, 1800-1835: A Guide to Information Sources*. Detroit: Gale Research, 1979.

Reiman. *Intervals of Inspiration: The Skeptical Tradition and the Psychology of Romanticism*. Greenwood, Fla.: Penkevill, 1988.

Reiman. *Romantic Texts and Contexts*. Columbia: University of Missouri Press, 1987.

Reiman, ed. *The Romantics Reviewed: Contemporary Reviews of British Romantic Writers*, 9 volumes. New York & London: Garland, 1972.

Renwick, W. L. *English Literature 1789-1815*. Oxford: Clarendon Press, 1963.

Richardson, Alan. *A Mental Theater: Poetic Drama and Consciousness in the Romantic Age*. University Park: Pennsylvania State University Press, 1987.

Rodway, Allen. *The Romantic Conflict*. London: Chatto & Windus, 1963.

Simpson, David. *Irony and Authority in Romantic Poetry*. London: Macmillan, 1979.

Siskin, Clifford. *The Historicity of Romantic Discourse*. New York: Oxford University Press, 1988.

Sullivan, Alvin, ed. *British Literary Magazines*, 4 volumes. Westport, Conn.: Greenwood Press, 1983-1986.

Swingle, L. J. *The Obstinate Questionings of English Romanticism*. Baton Rouge: Louisiana State University Press, 1987.

Thorburn, David, and Geoffrey Hartman, eds. *Romanticism: Vistas, Instances, Continuities*. Ithaca, N.Y., & London: Cornell University Press, 1973.

Thorlby, Anthony, ed. *The Romantic Movement*. London: Longmans, 1966.

Watson, J. R. *English Poetry of the Romantic Period 1789-1830*. London & New York: Longmans, 1985.

Wilkie, Brian. *Romantic Poets and Epic Tradition*. Madison: University of Wisconsin Press, 1965.

Williams, Raymond. *Culture and Society, 1780-1950*. New York: Columbia University Press, 1958.

Woodring, Carl. *Politics in English Romantic Poetry*. Cambridge, Mass.: Harvard University Press, 1970.

Wordsworth, Jonathan, Michael C. Jaye, and Robert Woof, with the assistance of Peter Funnell. *William Wordsworth and the Age of English Romanticism*. New Brunswick, N.J. & London: Rutgers University Press / Wordsworth Trust, 1987.

# Contributors


Thomas L. Blanton....................*Central Washington University*
Martin A. Cavanaugh....................*Washington University*
David R. Cheney....................*University of Toledo*
Thomas L. Cooksey....................*Armstrong State College*
Paula R. Feldman....................*University of South Carolina*
Richard D. Fulton....................*Clark College*
John Spalding Gatton....................*Bellarmine College*
John R. Greenfield....................*McKendree College*
Leslie Haynsworth....................*Charlottesville, Virginia*
Jonathan E. Hill....................*St. Olaf College*
John R. Holmes....................*Franciscan University of Steubenville*
Nicholas R. Jones....................*Oberlin College*
James Kissane....................*Grinnell College*
Michael Laine....................*Victoria College, University of Toronto*
Becky W. Lewis....................*Columbia, South Carolina*
Dana S. Litherland....................*Clarkston, Michigan*
Richard D. McGhee....................*Arkansas State University*
James C. McKusick....................*University of Maryland, Baltimore County*
John H. Rogers....................*Vincennes University*
Patricia L. Skarda....................*Smith College*
Robert Stewart....................*London, England*
Jennifer Viereck....................*Columbia, South Carolina*
Howard M. Wach....................*Clarkson University*
Linda Mills Woolsey....................*King College*

# Cumulative Index

*Dictionary of Literary Biography,* Volumes 1-110
*Dictionary of Literary Biography Yearbook,* 1980-1990
*Dictionary of Literary Biography Documentary Series,* Volumes 1-8

# Cumulative Index

**DLB** before number: *Dictionary of Literary Biography,* Volumes 1-110
**Y** before number: *Dictionary of Literary Biography Yearbook,* 1980-1990
**DS** before number: *Dictionary of Literary Biography Documentary Series,* Volumes 1-8

## A

## B

## C

## D

## E

## F

## G

## H

## I



## J

## K

## L

## M

## N

## O

## P

## Q



## R

## S

## T

## U

## V



## W

## Y

## Z

**(Continued from front endsheets)**

**80:** *Restoration and Eighteenth-Century Dramatists,* First Series, edited by Paula R. Backscheider (1989)

**81:** *Austrian Fiction Writers, 1875-1913,* edited by James Hardin and Donald G. Daviau (1989)

**82:** *Chicano Writers,* First Series, edited by Francisco A. Lomelí and Carl R. Shirley (1989)

**83:** *French Novelists Since 1960,* edited by Catharine Savage Brosman (1989)

**84:** *Restoration and Eighteenth-Century Dramatists,* Second Series, edited by Paula R. Backscheider (1989)

**85:** *Austrian Fiction Writers After 1914,* edited by James Hardin and Donald G. Daviau (1989)

**86:** *American Short-Story Writers, 1910-1945,* First Series, edited by Bobby Ellen Kimbel (1989)

**87:** *British Mystery and Thriller Writers Since 1940,* First Series, edited by Bernard Benstock and Thomas F. Staley (1989)

**88:** *Canadian Writers, 1920-1959,* Second Series, edited by W. H. New (1989)

**89:** *Restoration and Eighteenth-Century Dramatists,* Third Series, edited by Paula R. Backscheider (1989)

**90:** *German Writers in the Age of Goethe, 1789-1832,* edited by James Hardin and Christoph E. Schweitzer (1989)

**91:** *American Magazine Journalists, 1900-1960,* First Series, edited by Sam G. Riley (1990)

**92:** *Canadian Writers, 1890-1920,* edited by W. H. New (1990)

**93:** *British Romantic Poets, 1789-1832,* First Series, edited by John R. Greenfield (1990)

**94:** *German Writers in the Age of Goethe: Sturm und Drang to Classicism,* edited by James Hardin and Christoph E. Schweitzer (1990)

**95:** *Eighteenth-Century British Poets,* First Series, edited by John Sitter (1990)

**96:** *British Romantic Poets, 1789-1832,* Second Series, edited by John R. Greenfield (1990)

**97:** *German Writers from the Enlightenment to Sturm und Drang, 1720-1764,* edited by James Hardin and Christoph E. Schweitzer (1990)

**98:** *Modern British Essayists,* First Series, edited by Robert Beum (1990)

**99:** *Canadian Writers Before 1890,* edited by W. H. New (1990)

**100:** *Modern British Essayists,* Second Series, edited by Robert Beum (1990)

**101:** *British Prose Writers, 1660-1800,* First Series, edited by Donald T. Siebert (1991)

**102:** *American Short-Story Writers, 1910-1945,* Second Series, edited by Bobby Ellen Kimbel (1991)

**103:** *American Literary Biographers,* First Series, edited by Steven Serafin (1991)

**104:** *British Prose Writers, 1660-1800,* Second Series, edited by Donald T. Siebert (1991)

**105:** *American Poets Since World War II,* Second Series, edited by R. S. Gwynn (1991)

**106:** *British Literary Publishing Houses, 1820-1880,* edited by Patricia J. Anderson and Jonathan Rose (1991)

**107:** *British Romantic Prose Writers, 1789-1832,* First Series, edited by John R. Greenfield (1991)

**108:** *Twentieth-Century Spanish Poets,* First Series, edited by Michael L. Perna (1991)

**109:** *Eighteenth-Century British Poets,* Second Series, edited by John Sitter (1991)

**110:** *British Romantic Prose Writers, 1789-1832,* Second Series, edited by John R. Greenfield (1991)

## Documentary Series

**1:** *Sherwood Anderson, Willa Cather, John Dos Passos, Theodore Dreiser, F. Scott Fitzgerald, Ernest Hemingway, Sinclair Lewis,* edited by Margaret A. Van Antwerp (1982)

**2:** *James Gould Cozzens, James T. Farrell, William Faulkner, John O'Hara, John Steinbeck, Thomas Wolfe, Richard Wright,* edited by Margaret A. Van Antwerp (1982)

**3:** *Saul Bellow, Jack Kerouac, Norman Mailer, Vladimir Nabokov, John Updike, Kurt Vonnegut,* edited by Mary Bruccoli (1983)

**4:** *Tennessee Williams,* edited by Margaret A. Van Antwerp and Sally Johns (1984)

**5:** *American Transcendentalists,* edited by Joel Myerson (1988)